BRUTALIST
JAPAN

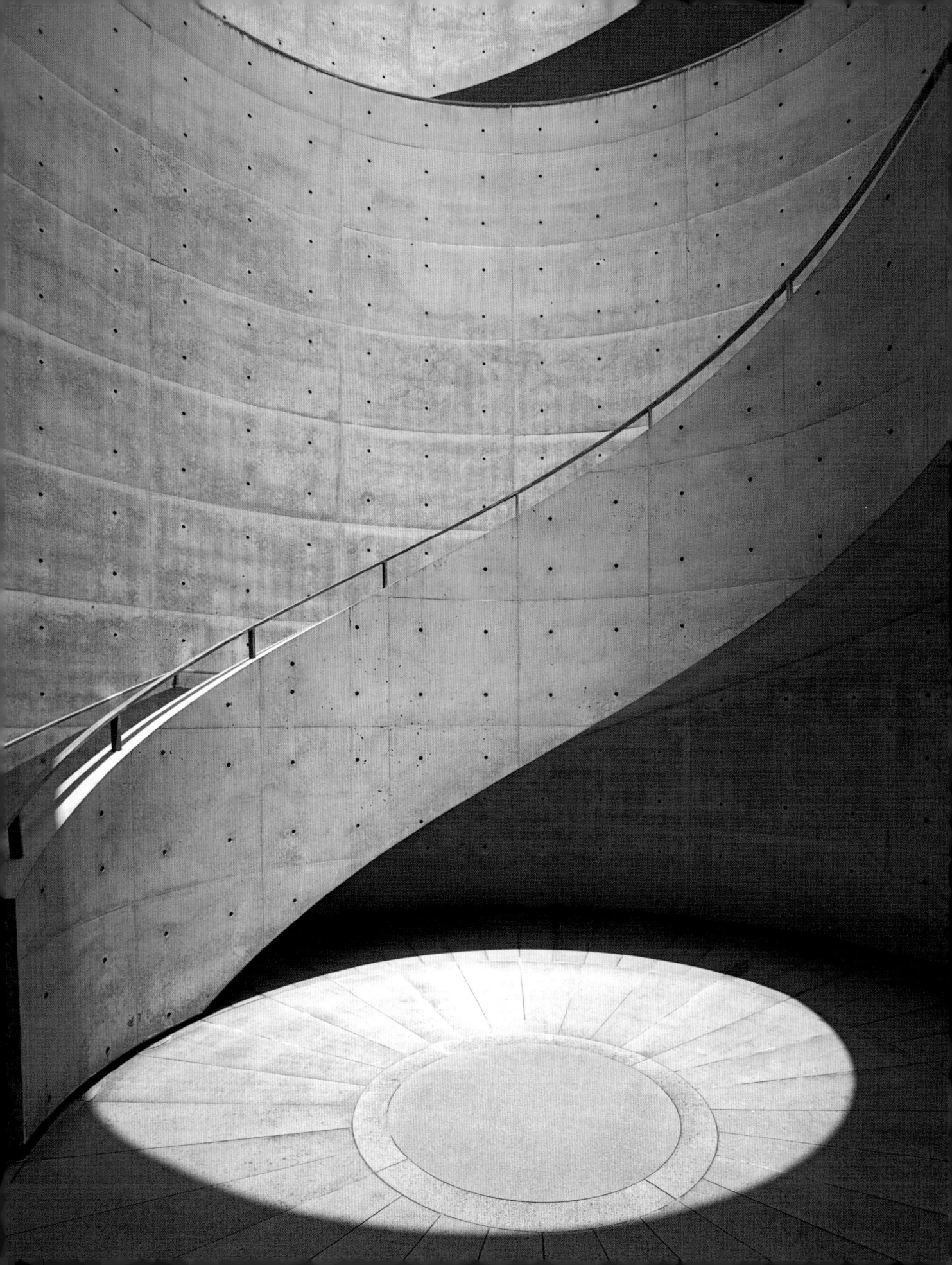

PAUL TULETT

BRUTALIST JAPAN

PRESTEL

Munich · London · New York

CONTENTS

BÉTON NÉCESSAIRE	7

Kihoku Astronomical Museum, Kanoya	12
Row House in Sumiyoshi, Osaka	18
Kobe Port Museum, Kobe	19
Tanimura Art Museum, Itoigawa	20
Breeze Apartments, Tokyo	24
Matsubara Civic Library, Matsubara	25
Itoman City Hall, Okinawa	26
Akiha Ward Cultural Center, Niigata Prefecture	30
Miyazaki Prefectural Comprehensive Youth Center, Miyazaki	34
Dr Minezaki House (Dragon Fort), Shizuoka Prefecture	38
Private Residence, Nagoya	40
Car Park Tower, Hiroshima	41
Hiroshima Peace Memorial Museum, Hiroshima	43
Konan Ward Cultural Center, Niigata Prefecture	44
Okinawan Cemeteries	48
Chichu Art Museum, Naoshima Island	49
Labor Welfare Office, Nago	50
Resort Complex, Sesoko Island	51
Memorial Cathedral of World Peace, Hiroshima	52
Private Residence, Okinawa	53
Kyoto International Conference Center, Kyoto	55
Nagano Olympic Stadium, Nagano	62
Mixed-Use Complex, Nago	66
Private Residence, Okinawa	67
Nanzan University, Nagoya	69
Divine Word Seminary Chapel, Nagoya	70
Naruto Cultural Hall, City Hall and Welfare Center, Tokushima Prefecture	72
Cube 21, Naruto	74
Nichinan Cultural Center, Miyazaki Prefecture	77
Sako House, Nagoya	81
Kagawa Prefectural Gymnasium, Takamatsu	82
Kagawa Prefectural Government Building, Takamatsu	86
Keihan Uji Station, Uji City	91
Villa Bianca, Tokyo	96
Naha Civic Hall, Okinawa	97
Book Café Okinawa Rail, Kunigami	98
Chiba University Inohana Memorial Hall, Chiba	100
Chiba University School of Medicine Inohana Alumni Hall, Chiba	104
Cosmo GI – Multi-Use Complex, Nago	106
Dam Utility Building, Kunigami	107
Gunma Music Center, Takasaki	108
Hoki Museum, Chiba	111
Inter-University Seminar House, Tokyo	114
Kadokawa Musashino Museum, Tokorozawa City	121
Japan Lutheran College, Tokyo	122
Makina Resort, Nakijin	124
Toilet Block, Nago	125
Nagaragawa Convention Center, Gifu Prefecture	126
Junior High School, Nago	130
Resort Apartment Block, Sesoko Island	134
Public Toilet, Urasoe	135
Nagasaki Peace Museum, Nagasaki	136
Nago City Hall, Nago	138
Baseball Stadium Scoreboard, Ginoza	144
Village Community Center, Nakijin	145
Seaside Gallery, Naoshima Island	146
Guesthouse and Restaurant, Nakijin	147

National Theatre, Tokyo	148
Oita Prefectural Government Building, Oita	150
Suntory Museum Toilet Block, Osaka	151
Oita Prefectural Library, Oita	152
Elementary School, Nago	155
Private Residence, Nago	158
National Theatre, Urasoe	159
Daichi Okinawa Villa M, Yagaji Island	160
Setagaya Ward Office, Tokyo	164
Okinawa Prefectural and Art Museum, Naha	166
Iwata Girls School, Oita	173
Komazawa Olympic Park Control Tower, Tokyo	176
Nakanoshima Children's Library, Osaka	178
International Ferry Terminal, Osaka	180
Environmental Office, Okinawa	181
Ceramics Park Mino, Tajimi	182
Metropolitan Festival Hall, Tokyo	185
Nago Civic Hall and Center, Nago	186
Warehouse C, Nagasaki	190
Aquaculture Farm, Motobu	193
Komazawa Olympic Park Athletic Stadium and Gymnasium, Tokyo	194
Supreme Court, Tokyo	196
Sunwell Muse, Tokyo	197
Kyoto International Conference Center New Hall, Kyoto	198
St Anselm's Meguro Church, Tokyo	201
National Museum of Western Art, Tokyo	202
Ichimura Memorial Gymnasium, Saga	204
Chikatsu Asuka Historical Museum, Osaka	208
Okuma Memorial Hall, Saga	210
Shibuya Extension, Tokyo	212
Sea Wall, Okinawa	213
Tama Art University Library (Hachioji Campus), Tokyo	214
Shime Coal Mine Tower, Fukuoka	215
Shizuoka Press and Broadcasting Tower, Tokyo	216
Saga Prefectural Museum, Saga	217
Shonan Church, Fujisawa	219
Sayamaike Historical Museum, Osakasayama	220
St Mary's Cathedral, Tokyo	222
Gunkanjima	228
Watarium, Tokyo	226
Tower House, Tokyo	227
Yoyogi National Gymnasium, Tokyo	229
Kumarajiva Memorial Meditation Hall, Tokyo	232
Hair Salon and Apartment Block, Okinawa	234
Toyonokuni Library, Oita	235
21st Century Forest Gymnasium, Nago	236
Miyagi House, Yomitan	238
Acknowledgements / Author Biography	240

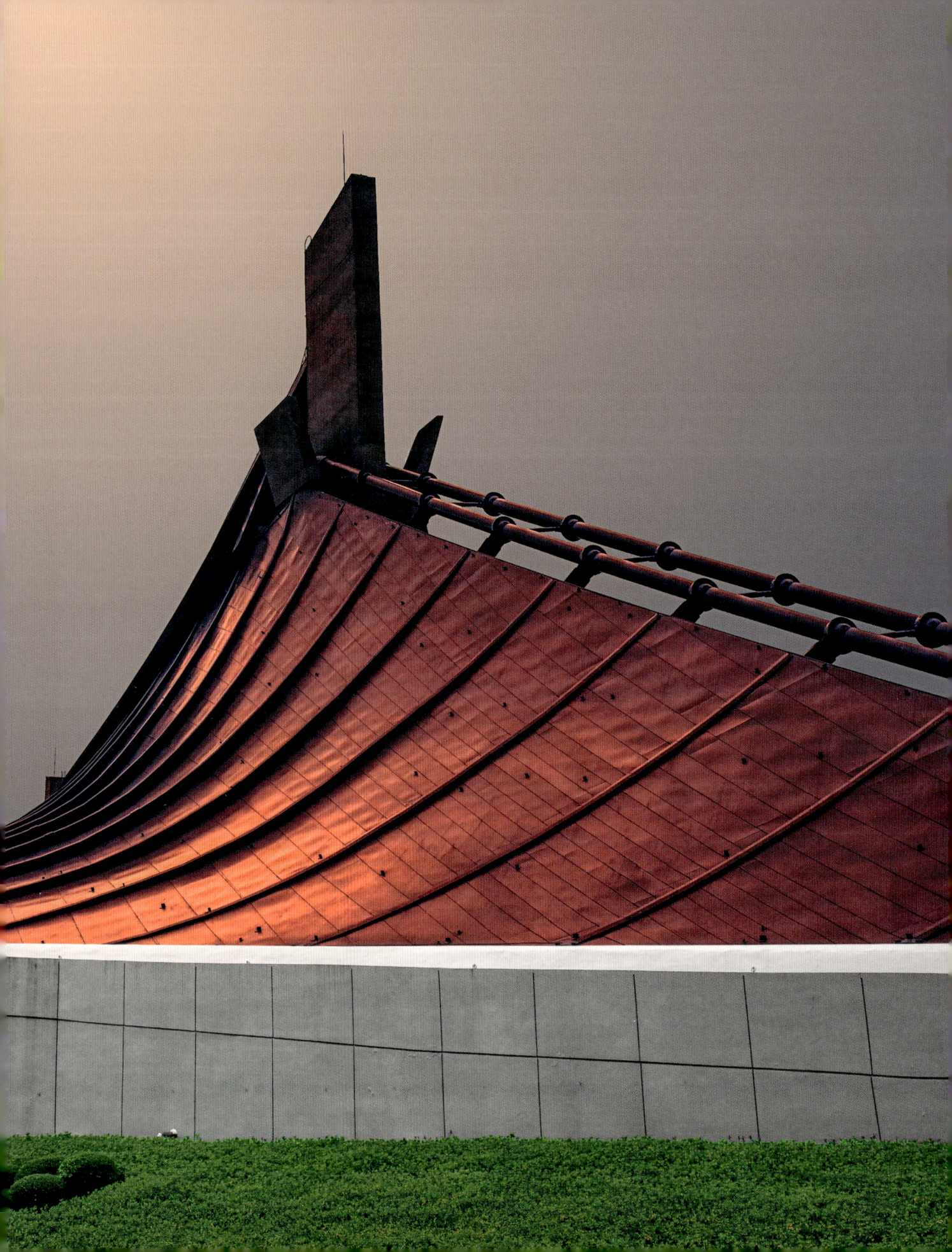

BÉTON NÉCESSAIRE

Brutalist architecture in Japan might not ruffle feathers locally but it's considered an aggro merchant elsewhere.

Its divisiveness stoked my interest whilst looking into built heritage. Should personal architectural taste shape preservation decisions? Clearly not. To what extent is such subjectivity shaped by fear and misunderstanding? Totally. Little did I know that this early exploration would lead to my current photographic niche.

Having failed to do the most basic research before moving to Okinawa, I was pleasantly surprised by the preponderance of Brutalism here and the absence of negative associations: no links to totalitarianism, or thoughts of piss-drenched stairwells in dodgy housing blocks.

Okinawa is famed as a "blue zone" of long life expectancy and for its importance in the closing chapters of the Second World War. This subtropical island prefecture of Japan should be equally well known among concrete connoisseurs for its plethora of Brutalist architecture. Housing anything from schools, museums and theatres to barber shops and aged-care centres, buildings often fit the Brutalist moniker. This architectural style is also widespread on mainland Japan.

Fully functional, fully utilized iterations of a style so controversial outside of Japan promised lessons in successful urban planning – my field of study. More specifically, could an understanding of Brutalist Japan lead to broader appreciation of Brutalism and stem its demolition both here and overseas? Seismic and maintenance concerns, not subjective hatred, threaten the flattening of concrete gems in a country that has hailed and embraced Brutalism.

The general line is that the Brutalism here is borne of necessity, for Okinawa is seasonally battered by typhoons. *Béton nécessaire* rather than *béton brut*.

Homes must be robust and 90 per cent of new dwellings are made of concrete. Swift adoption of the material was prompted by post-war reconstruction needs, as it was on the mainland. Building processes used to establish US military bases have been an ongoing influence.

We also need to factor in concrete's resistance to termites – pests greedy for the traditional material of wood. There is also a damp climate to combat.

A rather Eurocentric take is that the likes of Le Corbusier and Antonin Raymond simply showed the likes of Kenzo Tange what's what.

Those with a static, Disneyfied perception of Japan balk at Brutalist buildings existing in a land of pagodas and temples. Something like a tracksuit at a black tie event.

The fact is that Brutalism's progenitors, Alison and Peter Smithson, stated that the main influence upon their work was traditional Japanese architecture. Whilst the influence may have resulted from some naivety on their part, the overlap can be seen in material expression, reverence for materials used, emphasis on spatial relations, bold geometry and integration with nature.

Their aim was to encourage the Japanese conception of architecture as a "way of life" and reflection upon how a building is actually constructed – the importance of form and rationalism but also openness, inside-outside dialectics and versatility. For the Smithsons, traditional Japanese architecture provided lessons for British architecture at a time of post-war austerity. How to make do.

In 'How Other Peoples Dwell and Build', architectural historian E. A. Gutkind believed the traditional Japanese identification of form and function and standardization of all structural elements of a home did not lead to monotony but rather "good proportions, simplicity and plain form … clarity of construction and purposefulness of expression." Whatever the assumptions and misunderstandings surrounding Brutalism, these are attributes generally associated with it.

The Beef

Brutalism outside of Japan is like Marmite. Love it or hate it.

Some find it refreshingly raw – an honest counterpoint to contemporary glass-based disingenuous attempts at state transparency. Others are reminded of communism or when the UK nearly slid down the pan in the 1970s.

Brutalist buildings can be as welcoming as a slap in the face with a wet fish. The raw concrete and minimalist design of *béton brut* screams "Va te faire foutre!" to those craving *bucolia* within the urban fabric. Just the word "Brutalism" seems like a kick in the nuts.

Weathering and deterioration of concrete can lead to stains, cracks and crumble that upset some. Intended radical philosophical statements become eyesores.

With hindsight, I became a concrete-sniffing tragic at a young age. During a school trip to London, I envisaged a battalion of Stormtroopers pouring from Queen Elizabeth Hall, the Hayward Gallery and Lasdun's National Theatre. Since growing up, I've recognized that a sure gauge of whether something is Brutalist or not is this: Would it look good in a sci-fi movie?

To the haters, Brutalism reflects the increased intrusion of government and state power. It is no accident that Brutalist architectural forms often harboured state departments. Brutalist buildings afford sobering historic reflection – much like the preservation of communist statues in former Soviet states.

Fellow concrete sniffers bray at the misassumption the heathen hold about Brutalism. No, it wasn't cheap. Nor was it easy. Rather, Brutalism more often than not reflects the work of architects at the peak of their craft and a belief that technological progress should deliver social benefit.

Recognition of the misassumption surrounding Brutalism would better inform contemporary planning and architecture – particularly in relation to issues about heritage and preservation. Yet opinions on Brutalism remain based upon taste and fashion. It deserves better.

Urban Planning, Brutalism and the Public Realm

As I delved into Brutalism during urban planning studies, I could not foresee that living and working among the Japanese style would reveal that the urban academics and designers I admired seemed to have drawn lessons from it without ever admitting to being here.

What they decried for being missing in urban planning and design, Japan had in droves. Public participation in planning? Tick. Design that affords legibility, accessibility and permeability? Tick.

Built environment expert Anna Minton laments the overstatement of fear that has resulted in misanthropic design measures (Secured by Design) that prioritize security rather than the civic engagement that is required for successful twenty-first-century urbanism. Design driven by security has heightened perception of insecurity and increased suspicion amongst urbanites. Design measures that raise feelings of urban insecurity have been combined with the privatization and erosion of the public realm.

Security specialist Sophie Body-Gendrot advocated for design measures focused on civic engagement within the public realm. Minton promotes public space in pursuit of liveable, socially sustainable, dense cities. Such public space should facilitate "doing nothing" as opposed to unhindered consumerism. Her frustration is compounded by the fact that public space and civil liberty erosion through insensitive, exclusively private "regeneration" has happened without due consultation.

The neoliberal tactic of reducing the public realm must be combated if "the commons" are to be reclaimed.

Physically, the public realm must present robust variety, or rather a range of uses available to all; legibility, that is, an understanding of opportunities offered; visual appropriateness that makes people aware of the choices available; a rich choice of sensory experiences; and personalization, that is, the extent to which people can put their own stamp on a place.

Sociologist Lyn Lofland said it should be a rich learning environment that provides needed respite and refreshment, operates as a centre of communication, allows for the "practice" of politics, is the stage for the enactment of social arrangements and social conflicts, and assists in the creation of cosmopolitans.

She argued that such creation is assisted through promotion of cooperative motility, civil inattention when appropriate, audience role prominence, restrained helpfulness and civility towards diversity.

Political scientist Robert Axelrod argued more durable and more frequent interactions must be created: "Continuing interaction is what makes it possible for co-operation based on reciprocity to be stable." He called for a change of payoffs that tip scales towards cooperation, teaches people to care about each other through reciprocity, and improves people's ability to identify and analyse other players and their actions.

Adoption

Arriving in Japan, I quickly realized that the dons of my academic field echoed the task laid before the architects of post-war Japan. Astoundingly though, the desirable public realm and civic building features I had read so much of had been achieved through Brutalism.

Falling foul of the over-association with communism myself, I had expected to see plenty of Brutalism whilst living in China. However, a falling out with the Soviet Union in the 1950s cut off influence from Eastern Europe. Anything from the West on the other hand was "Capitalist Structuralism". A Chinese architect designing in the Brutalist style would have been as wise as wearing jeans in Pyongyang. Conversely, Japanese Brutalist architects became national heroes.

Like many countries after the Second World War, Japan was a picture of destruction and needed to rebuild physically. The difference was that replacement hardware needed to inculcate new software. Civic architecture needed to foster a civil society accepting of democracy, pacificity, decentralization and an openness to not just new technology but new ideas as well.

Brutalism became the method of choice for anything from civic halls, gymnasia, government offices, schools, libraries, theatres, museums and cultural centres.

In part, this is explained by the availability of aggregate and the general influence of the post-war need for rapid construction of buildings with fire, climatic and seismic resistance met by the characteristics of concrete.

Yes, there was the influence of Le Corbusier upon Kunio Maekawa and Maekawa's upon Kenzo Tange. What seems overlooked is the importance of "shuttering" in concrete construction. Also known as "formwork", this is moulding used to support and shape concrete before it hardens and becomes self-supporting. Whilst it can be steel or plastic, the use of wood brings in the importance of Japanese carpentry. This is a respected profession in Japan and carpenters here put your average chippy to shame. It might explain why Japanese Brutalism has a level of unparalleled refinement.

An architectural form commonly disliked for a perceived inaccessible and imposing coldness offers quaint warm humble hints as to the construction process. Concrete surfaces embossed with timber grain signify the use of wooden moulds in the construction of the most behemothic buildings.

The combination of concrete and steel with exquisite nail-less carpentry allowed for continuation of tradition whilst adopting new building technology. The likes of Maekawa could simultaneously and deftly present modernity and tradition in a way that placated the more patriotic. Hence a critical regionalism – the rooting of architecture in local tradition, culture, history, geography and environment – that predates uptake elsewhere by around thirty years.

This can be seen in the inflated eaves of Maekawa's Tokyo Metropolitan Festival Hall, the mimicry of timber by concrete beams in Tange's pagoda-like Kagawa Prefectural Government Building, and Hiroyuki Iwamoto's rendering of the National Theatre in eighth-century wooden storehouse style. Traditional post-and-beam replication can be seen in the supposedly "Internationalist" Hiroshima Peace Memorial Museum.

Brutalist architecture, with its use of concrete and steel, allowed for more expansive expressions of temporal and spatial transitions inherent in traditional Japanese architecture. Sculptor Antony Gormley talks of the counter-intuitive deployment of the density of mass to activate space – an attempt to put human biological time in relation to planetary time: "Movement, your space-time experience, is amplified." He speaks of the modern equivalent of standing stones, but ones that people live and breathe in.

I think of Raymond's Gunma Music Center (1961), Tange's Nichinan Cultural Center (1963) and the much later Okinawa Prefectural Museum (2007) by Niki and Ishimoto Architects. Vertically folded or horizontally cascading mass permitted by concrete is employed in the replication of ancient Japanese castles. Time travel.

Enabling the presentation of modern notions of form as function with nuanced nods to local tradition, the Brutalist style clearly lent itself to the lighting, auditory and seismic considerations of monumental public buildings such as civic halls, theatres and museums.

Acceptance and Appreciation

So much for the adoption of Brutalism here. What about the enduring appeal? Many old-school examples of Brutalist architecture still stand fully functional, well used and appreciated. Construction in the style continues to this very day – from grand public monumentality to the smaller-scale vernacular. You cannot speak of a Brutalist "revival" here. The fact is that it never went away.

Recent part-demolition of the only Tadao Ando building in the United Kingdom got me thinking. Whilst the stated reason only concerned a fragmentary six-metre-long wall blocking sight lines, it reminded me of the offence concrete can cause outside Japan. Why the lack of upset here? Why the acceptance?

It has been argued that concrete is the "natural choice" of construction material in Japan as it resonates with the half-a-millennium-old practice of *sukiya* – the considered composition of raw and rough natural materials. The material expression of concrete's rawness is deemed to chime with an almost genetic appreciation for an elemental, unrefined aesthetic. Apparently, the Japanese have a unique long experience with wood, pottery and stone, but for what people are these not traditional materials? I can only think of the Inuit.

To understand the continuing acceptance of concrete in Japan, we might need to get a bit *wabi-sabi*. This is the Japanese aesthetic that embraces the beauty of imperfection. Whilst the appearance of aged concrete bolsters its detractors, it's the very patina that comes with its aging that is appealing to others. Inspired by the cycles of nature, it is no surprise that Japanese architects saw in it an aesthetic, not just practical, strength.

Mono no aware is a Japanese term that describes the bittersweet awareness of the fleeting nature of beauty and the poignant transience of things. Despite its own subjection to ultimate decay, concrete provides a juxtaposed backdrop of seeming permanence to, say, the brief appearance of cherry blossom.

Ma refers to the concept of negative space, pause, or the interval between objects or events, often highlighting the importance of emptiness in design, art and life. Japanese architects saw in concrete and steel an opportunity to provide thought-provoking transitions between, and the blurring of, large areas of internal and external space. This overlaps with the centrality to Japanese architecture and urban planning of harmony – both that between built form and its environment and that generated among its users.

Acceptance of concrete architecture may well result from the importance of these concepts in the Japanese psyche and the thoughtful application of them by talented architects and consummate execution by skilful craftsmen.

On Photography

I was told twenty years ago by a war photographer at *The Guardian*, "You've got to find yourself a niche, son." Call me a slow learner but, armed with a genuine architectural and urban interest, I now have one.

Urbanist Charles R. Wolfe highlights the importance of the discerning photographic observation of the urban scholar. He encourages the use of photographic urban diaries to capture urban spaces that generate feelings of safety and identity, examples of successful urban space – particularly those that align with lessons gleaned from successful, pedestrianized, dense cities that respect human scale and prioritize the public realm.

It should be noted that photography has been previously deployed to promote architectural and urban planning policies and concepts. Urban advocate Jane Jacobs spoke of the photographic approach of city historian Lewis Mumford and urban planning educator Catherine Bauer. Bauer's photographic pursuit was aimed at proselytizing a decentrist approach to planning through the negative framing of the dense city. It was perhaps the success of her photography in denigrating the city that inspired the criticism of city processes by Jacobs.

Photographic urban explorations can catalyse and inform a discursive participatory approach to tackling architectural and urban issues and vice versa.

The photography of Ingrid Pollard transposes Black people into English rural locales – mocking their exclusion from traditionally accepted sites of "Englishness". It jeers at the idea that non-whites belong in degraded inner urban areas. As I mentioned earlier, some dislike the idea that Brutalism exists in a land of shrines and pagodas.

The Message

In the early throes of this brutal photographic journey, I wondered if I was just enjoying annoying the detractors. For them, I was documenting a mistransposition. This without the weight of Pollard's message. Was I presenting the punchy, supposedly out-of-place aesthetics of Japanese Brutalism just to wind people up? Definitely. The initial appeal of Brutalism to me was certainly the discord it sows. I needed some purpose beyond having a laugh. Especially when people started to like it.

The epiphany came with the awarding of the 2021 Pritzker Prize to Anne Lacaton and Jean-Phillipe Vassal and my reading their succinct philosophy: "Never demolish, always transform." Ding!

Brutalist architecture even here in Japan faces the prospect of demolition. This includes Tange's remarkable Kagawa Prefectural Gymnasium in Takamatsu, Iwamoto's impeccable National Theatre in Tokyo, and the historically significant Naha Civic Hall in Okinawa by Nobuyoshi Kinjo. In contrast to the inclusiveness of post-war Japanese urban planning, demolition has been slated without the once-vaunted public participation. The failing of seismic audits is often invoked to justify destruction. There are rumours that my local muse, Nago City Hall, will be condemned, and wilful neglect does not bode well for other examples in Okinawa.

Civic and public halls by architectural legends such as Takeo Sato, Junzo Sakakura and Kiyonori Kikutake are gone. So too Kisho Kurokawa's internationally

BÉTON NÉCESSAIRE

famous Metabolist Nakagin Capsule Tower. Land value trumps any humane architectural message. Japan is not immune.

By presenting the Japanese experience, I hope to challenge the stereotypical negative attacks levelled at Brutalism more broadly. The aim is to provoke thought about examples of Brutalism closer to you. With understanding comes appreciation. Appreciation may lead to more considered decisions regarding built heritage.

Environmental concerns are the very reason concrete architecture should not be demolished. Demolition releases huge amounts of carbon dioxide. The environmental argument for preservation is stronger than the one for razing. Environmentally sensitive repurposing of Brutalism that honours the original architectural message is increasingly and rightly seen as key. Demands for demolition are undermined by the concept of embedded energy and the fact that concrete proves to be an on-going carbon sequestration sink. Any self-proclaimed environmentalist calling for the destruction of a concrete building needs to wind their neck in. All should question feigned pseudo-environmental concerns that cloak personal aesthetic distaste.

So *kanpai* and let's get amongst it …

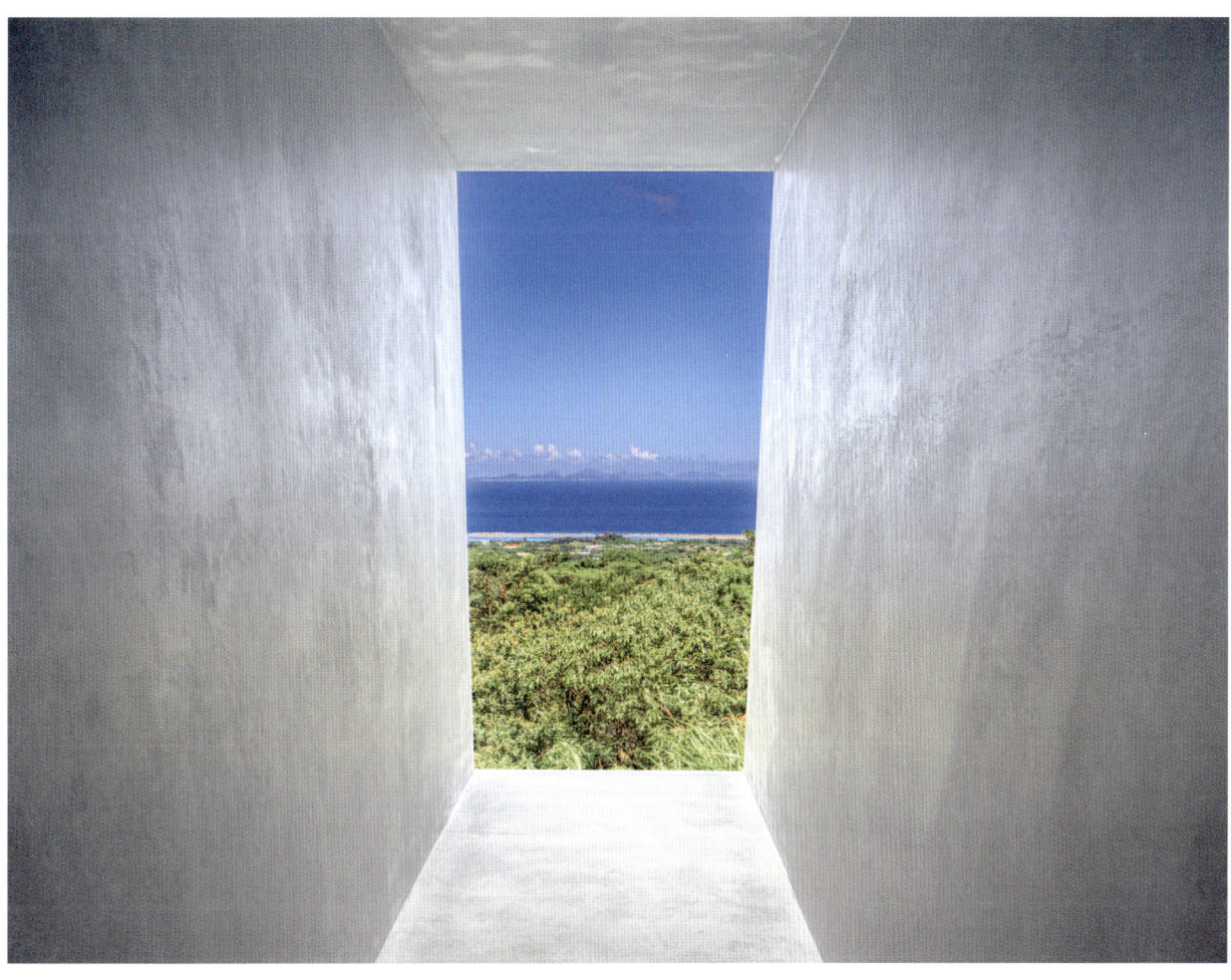

KIHOKU ASTRONOMICAL MUSEUM

KANOYA, KAGOSHIMA PREFECTURE · Architect: MASAHARU Takasaki · Completed 1995

Clearly in the throes of his 'Smack My Bitch Up' phase, architect Takasaki Masaharu took appropriate inspiration from the moon crab on The Prodigy's *The Fat of the Land* album cover. From certain angles, this Cancerian creature seems to be either embracing the stars in rave-like rapture or wondering where it left its whistle and helium balloon.

Actually, the design slightly predates The Prodigy's third album. More cerebral appraisals cover Masaharu attempting a cosmic connection between Earth and the universe.

The observatory affords views of the active Sakurajima volcano, Kinko and Shibushi Bays, Miyakonojo Basin, the Kirishima Mountains and stunning night skies, but locating it 550 metres above sea level without public transport access seems inconsiderate.

The site selection resulted from it winning night sky visibility awards over four consecutive years. Fair enough. A participatory approach by Masaharu allowed for the ageing local community to showcase the potency of the region's mushrooms. Architectural bloggers tend to focus on more interesting aspects such as floor area and staff and visitor numbers.

Intended to attract visitors to a depopulated area with an average age astronomical itself, this brutal oddity is increasingly less visited. Local authorities might do well to tout its spiritual aspects. Indeed, the build is designed to constantly interact with land energy and provide a sanctuary for contemplation of nothingness – the universe's origin.

What is basically a four-storey reinforced concrete building comes equipped with a Cassegrain telescope and houses a cocoon incubating a blood-thirsty alien. Studio Ghibli might have borrowed a bit of its architectural magic for the flying fortress in *Howl's Moving Castle*.

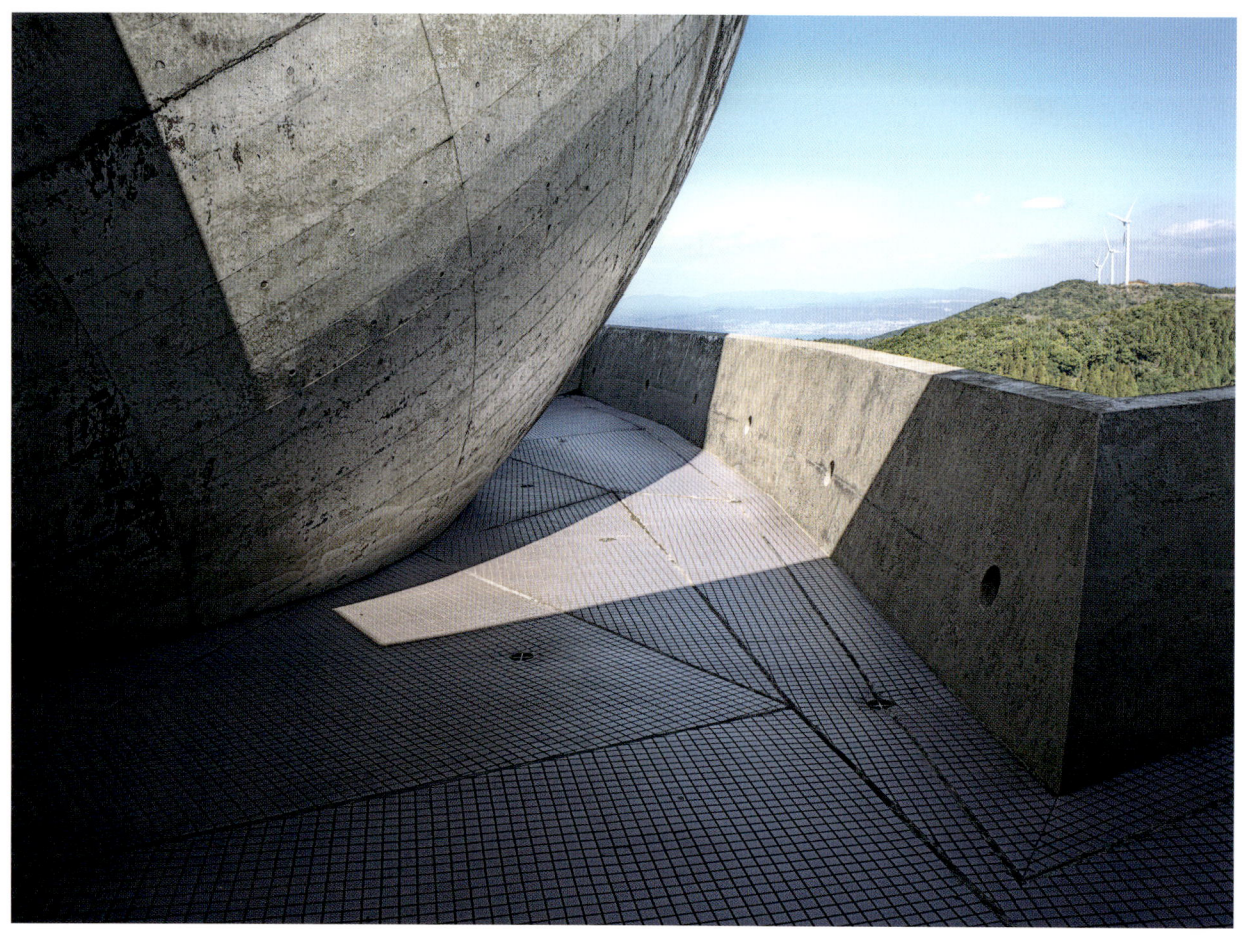

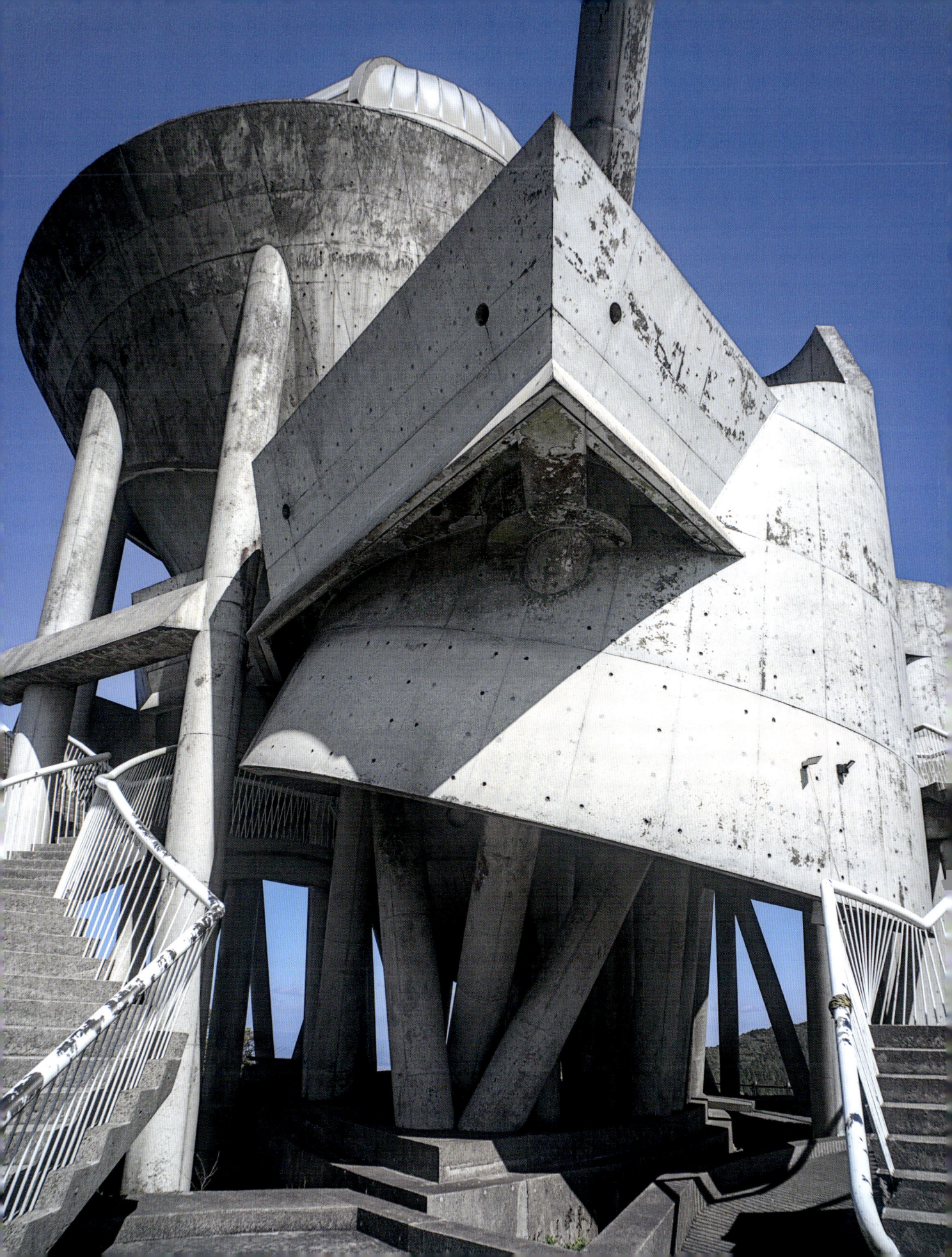

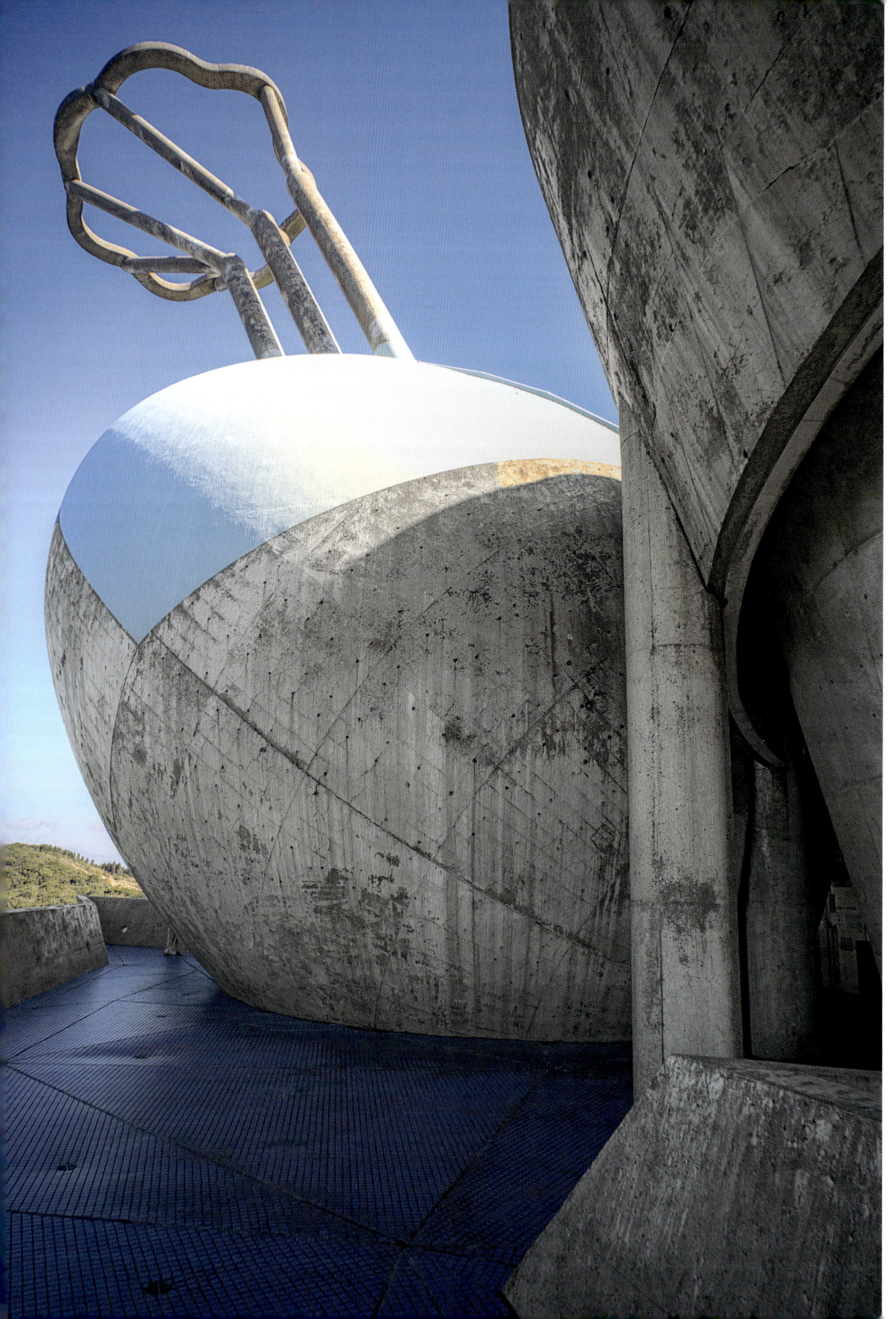

KIHOKU ASTRONOMICAL MUSEUM

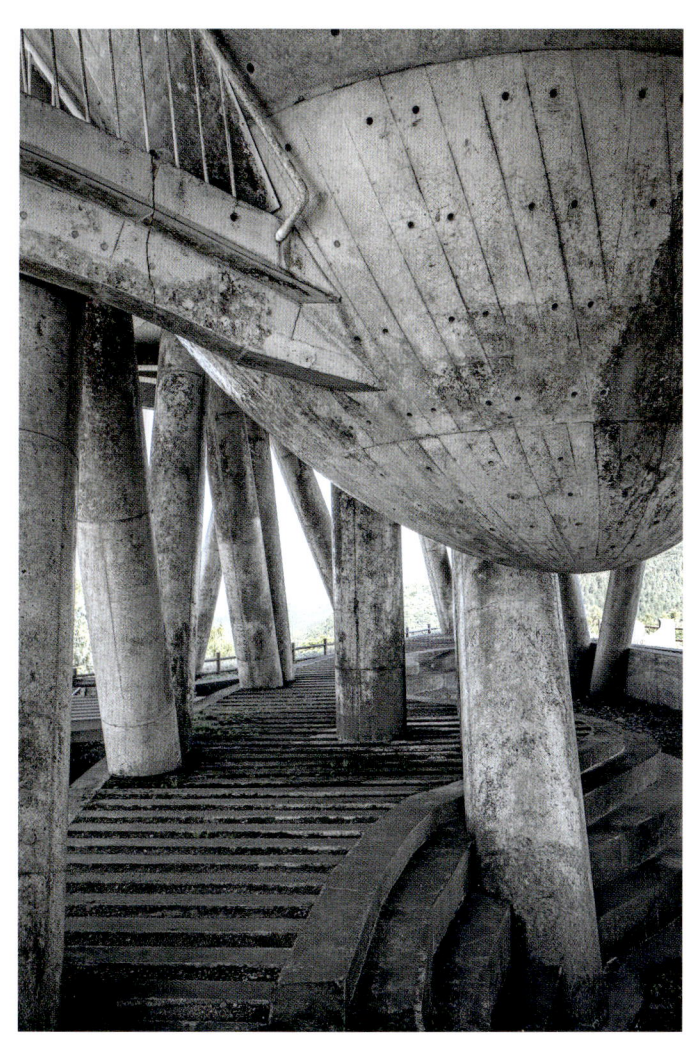
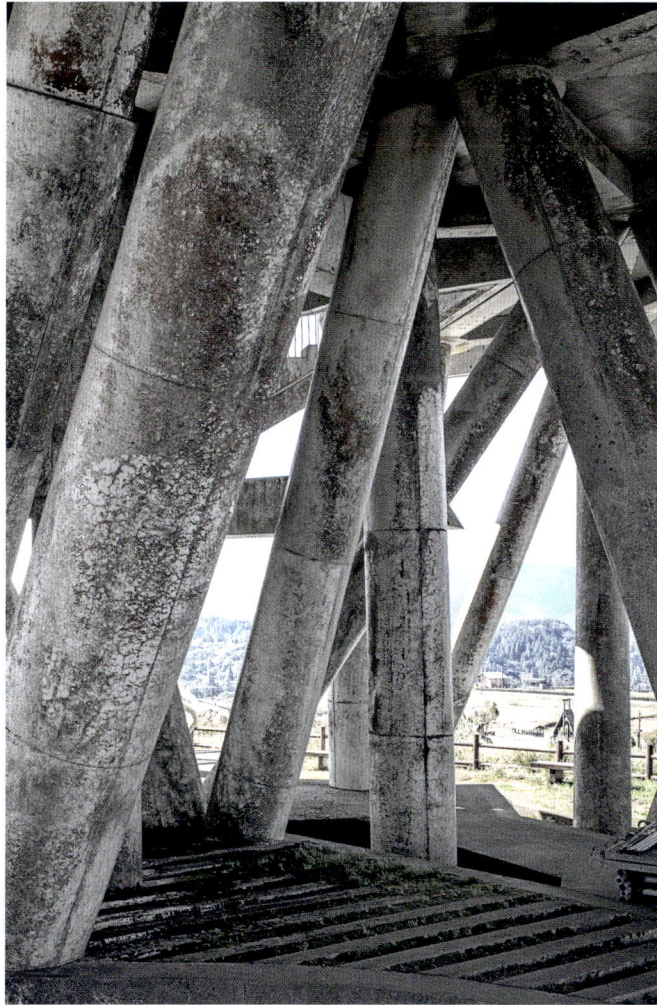

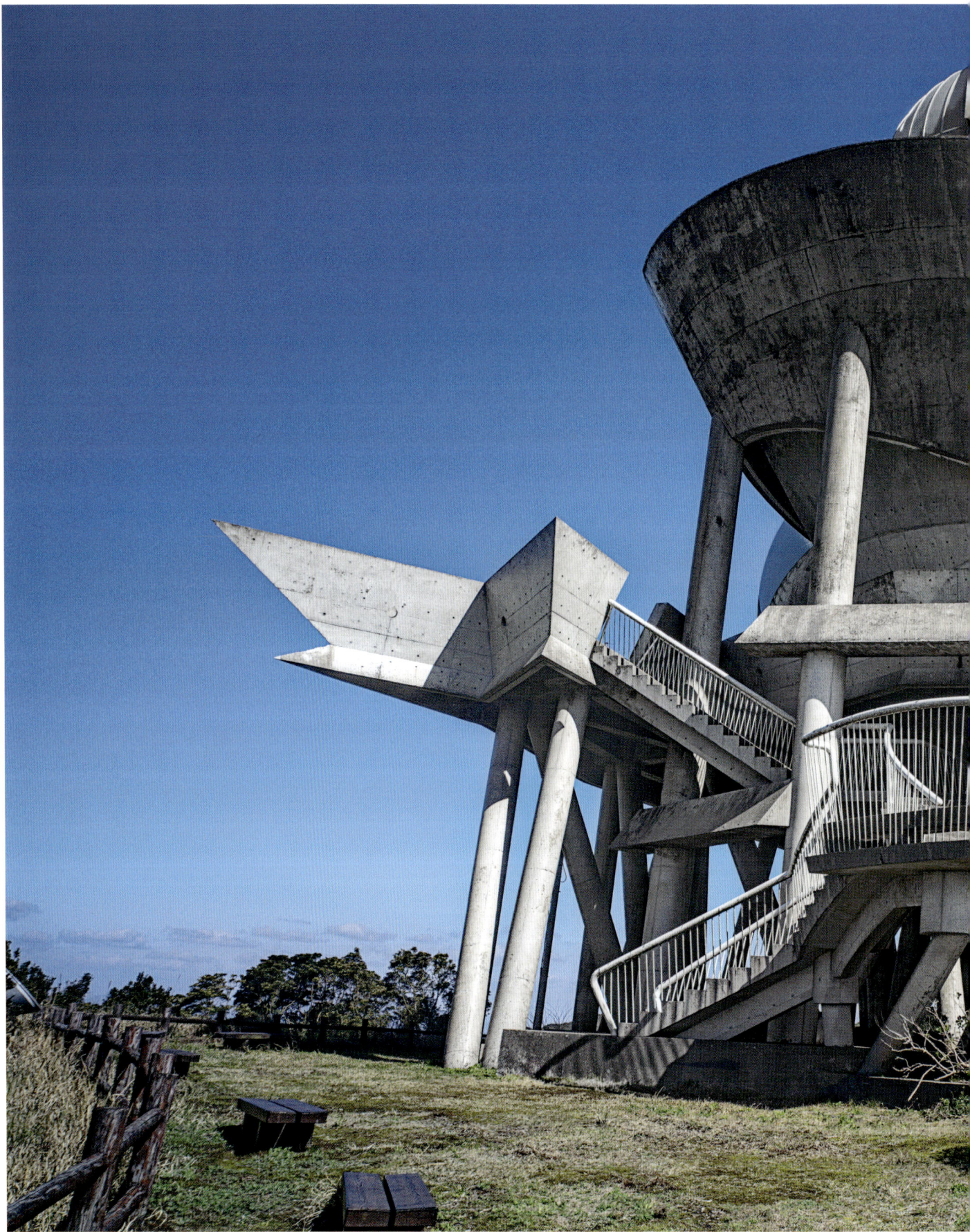

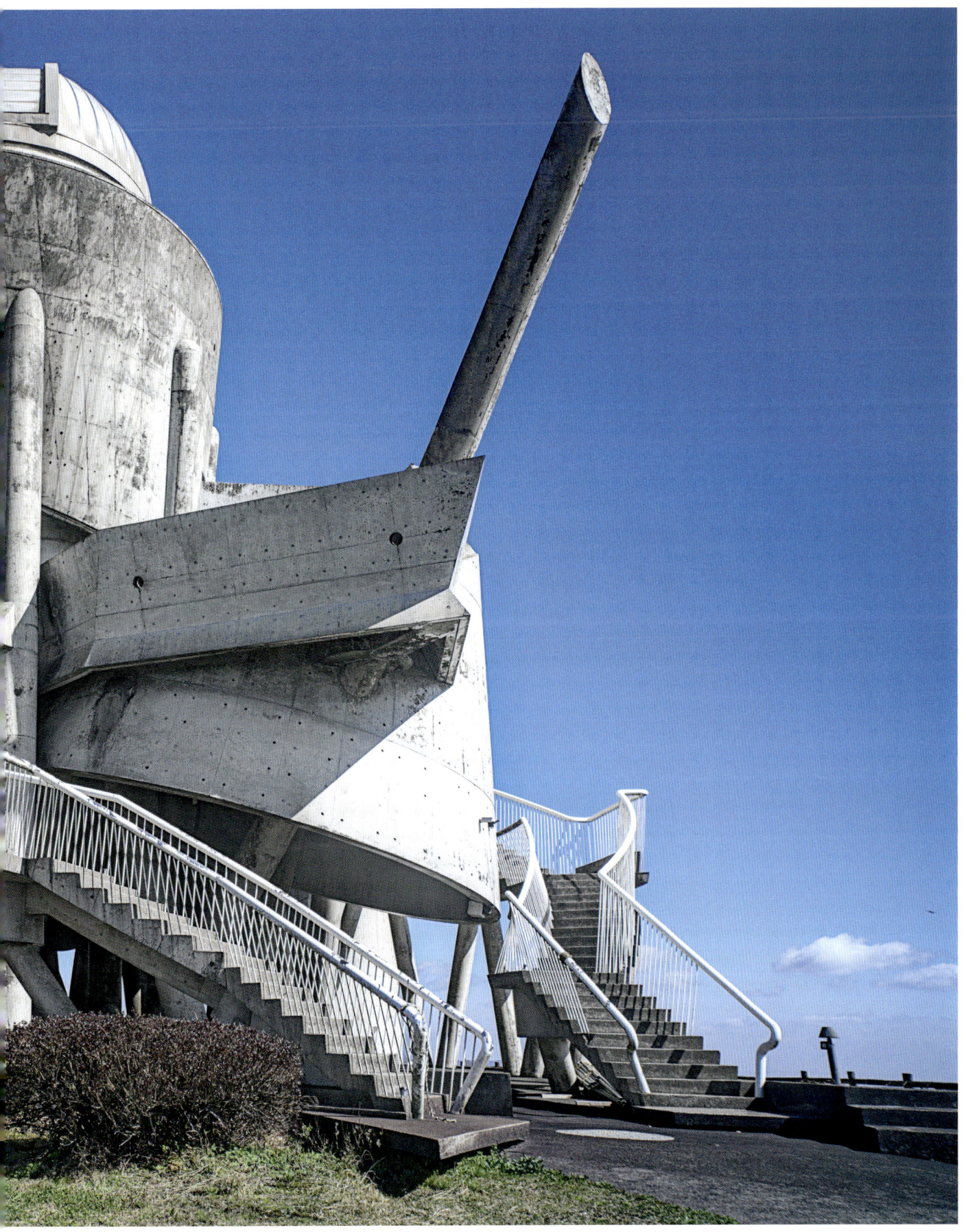

ROW HOUSE IN SUMIYOSHI

OSAKA · Architect: ANDO Tadao · Completed 1976

This is an awkward early inclusion for a book about Brutalist architecture in Japan. Ando, the master of modern concrete architecture, has annoyingly claimed his work is not Brutalist. Come on!

Although his work unrelentingly features assertive geometry through exposed concrete, he constantly prioritizes and strives for an ethereal experience of light and space. Material expression of concrete, a sure sign of Brutalism, is demoted in favour of this. That said, polishing concrete doesn't help this ex-pugilist box himself out of a corner. No apologies, sensei, for including your work in this book.

Holes left over from concrete ties, which are used to hold formwork together, smack of the honesty of Brutalism. So too the simple palette of standardized ingredients seen in Ando's resume.

Covering a land area of just sixty-six square metres and concerned with the concept of a microcosmic living space within broader urbanity, this was a humble start to Ando's career which still inspires Japanese architects less inclined to deny the Brutalist label.

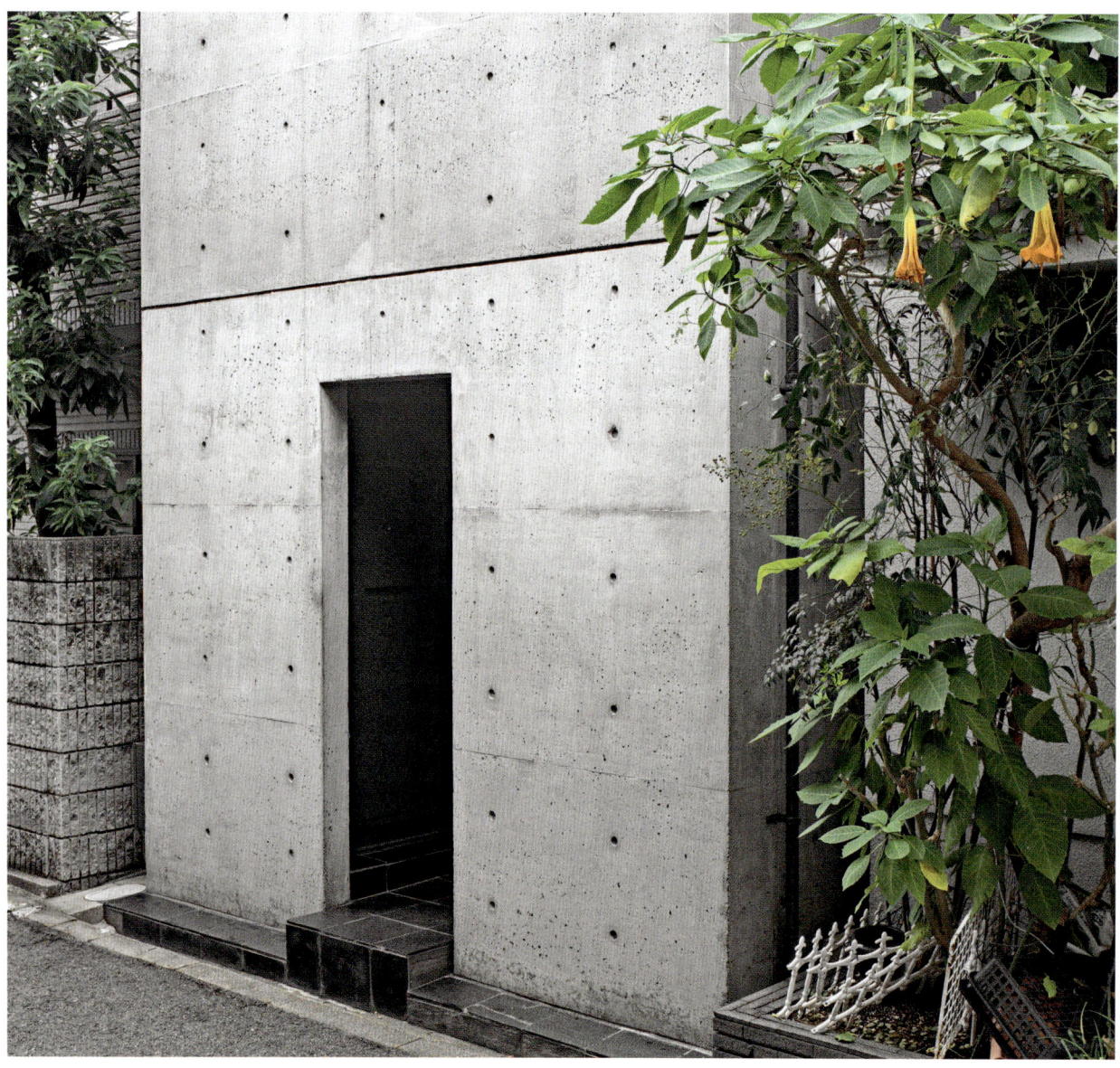

KOBE PORT MUSEUM

KOBE, HYOGO PREFECTURE · Architect: Taisei Corporation · Completed 2001

Rising like a geological protrusion, the KPM complex is where architecture meets sea, reflecting the theme of "Rising Earth and Eroding Water" according to the promoters. Inclusion of aggregates from Mount Rokko and the Seto Inland Sea mirror the deep terrestrial layers of the area. Thanks to its robust, quake-ready framework and a cleverly engineered pile foundation, the museum is built to stand firm against seismic shock. Bear in mind Kobe was hit by an earthquake that killed 6,434 people in 1995.

Flow and functionality are enhanced by an oval blueprint. Internally, a spherical aquarium boasts pre-stressed beams that eliminate columns, offering unobstructed views of the imprisoned sea life that no one here really cares about.

Watching that deep dark shadow progress across the textured façade is enhanced by a couple of stouts from the ground-floor bar and restaurant.

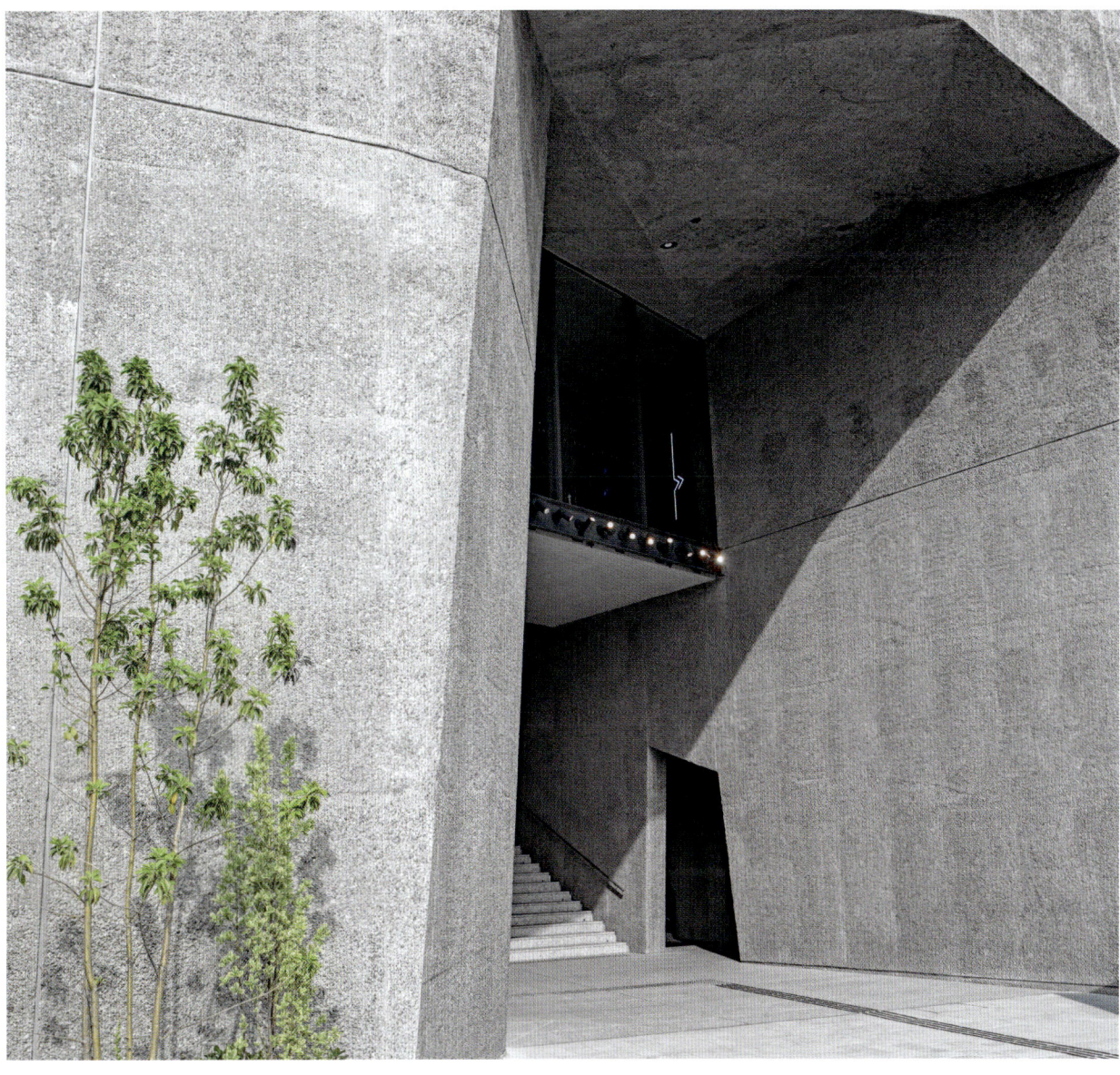

TANIMURA ART MUSEUM

ITOIGAWA, NIIGATA PREFECTURE · Architect: MURANO Togo · Completed 1983

Opened in the same year *Return of the Jedi* was released, this Murano masterpiece smacks of a Tatooine abode. Its primeval appearance suggests it was handcrafted by a giant, gifted rancour. You can picture C-3PO berating R2-D2 for getting stuck in the pebbly Zen forecourt.

There are dubious claims it is not built in the image of Tatooine but rather the Dunhuang Caves on the Silk Road. Either way, Murano's use of concrete reminds us of the fact that it is an ancient material used in Roman times despite its association with modernity.

The interior is home to wood carvings of Bodhisattvas by renowned sculptor Masahiro Sawada. These meditate in curved, cave-like atria that permit a nuanced changing light through recessed slits and skylights.

Murano's vision for the museum results from a minimalist ethos. Sleek lines, unembellished forms and fidelity to functionality ensure that the sculptures are the focal point within a tranquil, organic interior. Externally, the minimal approach results in a refined, timeless architectural expression. Rawness and elegance coexist.

Exiting the museum permits a closer look at the exterior if you haven't already ignored signs and walked over the Zen garden. Lap up the combination of block forms and curvature.

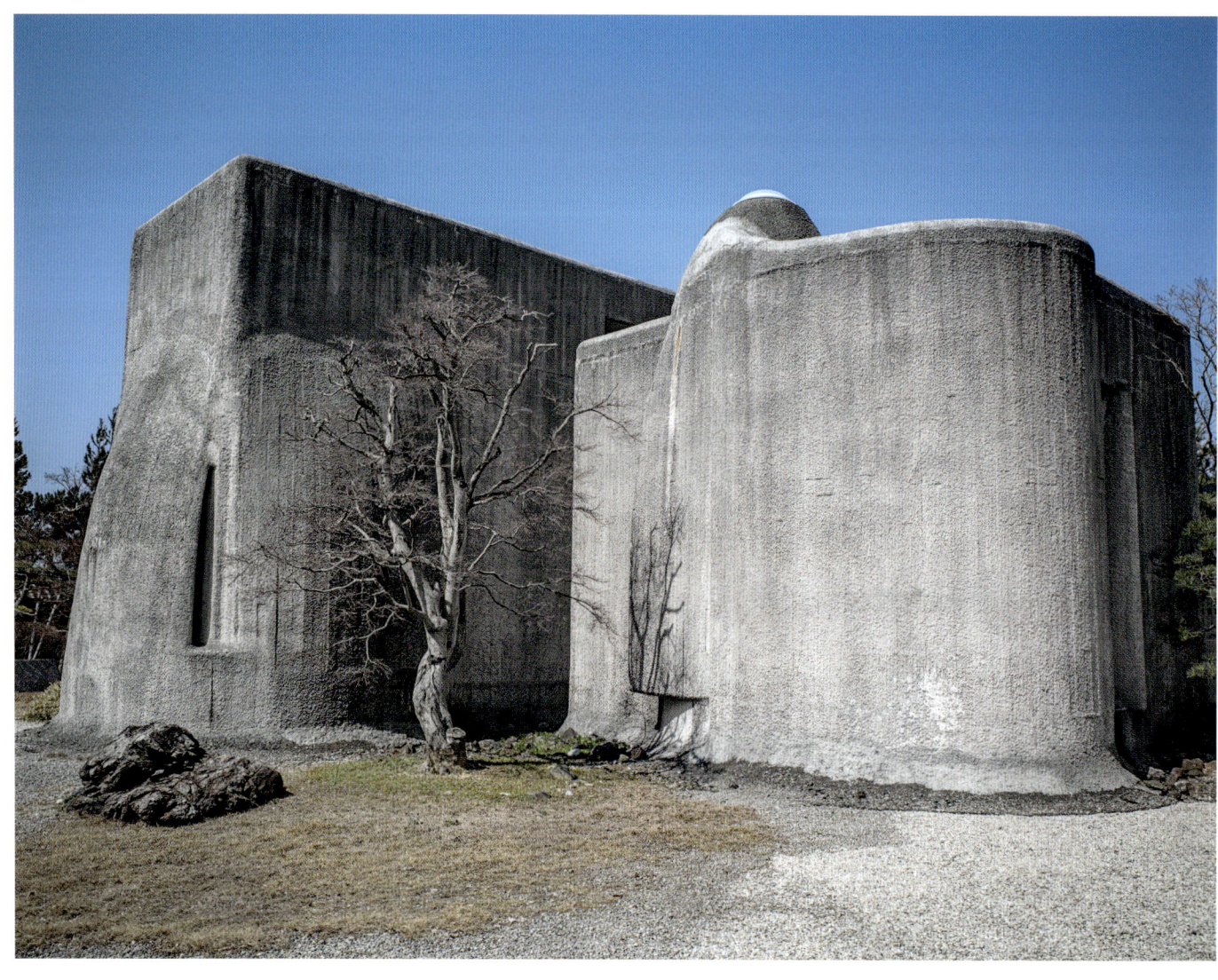

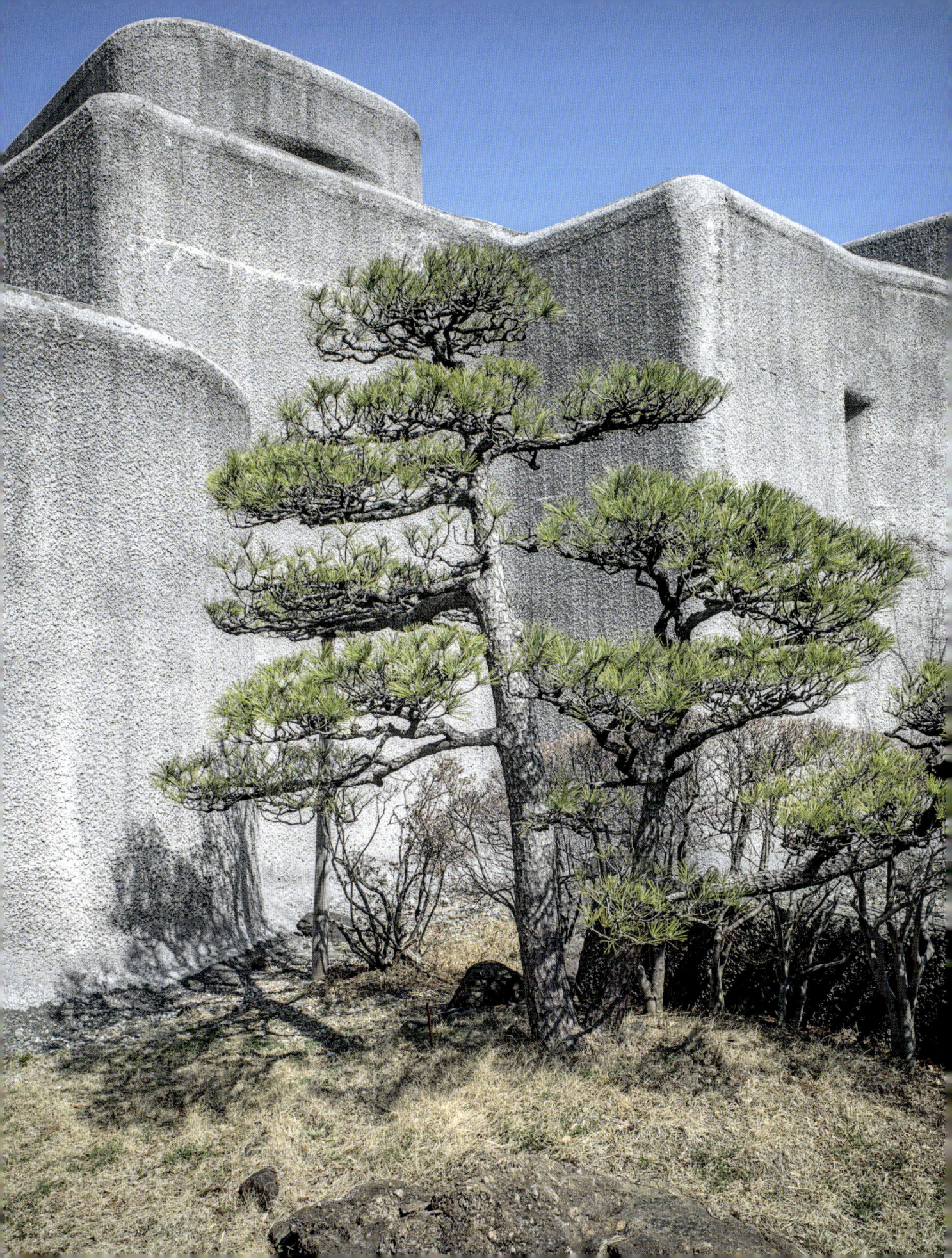

TANIMURA ART MUSEUM

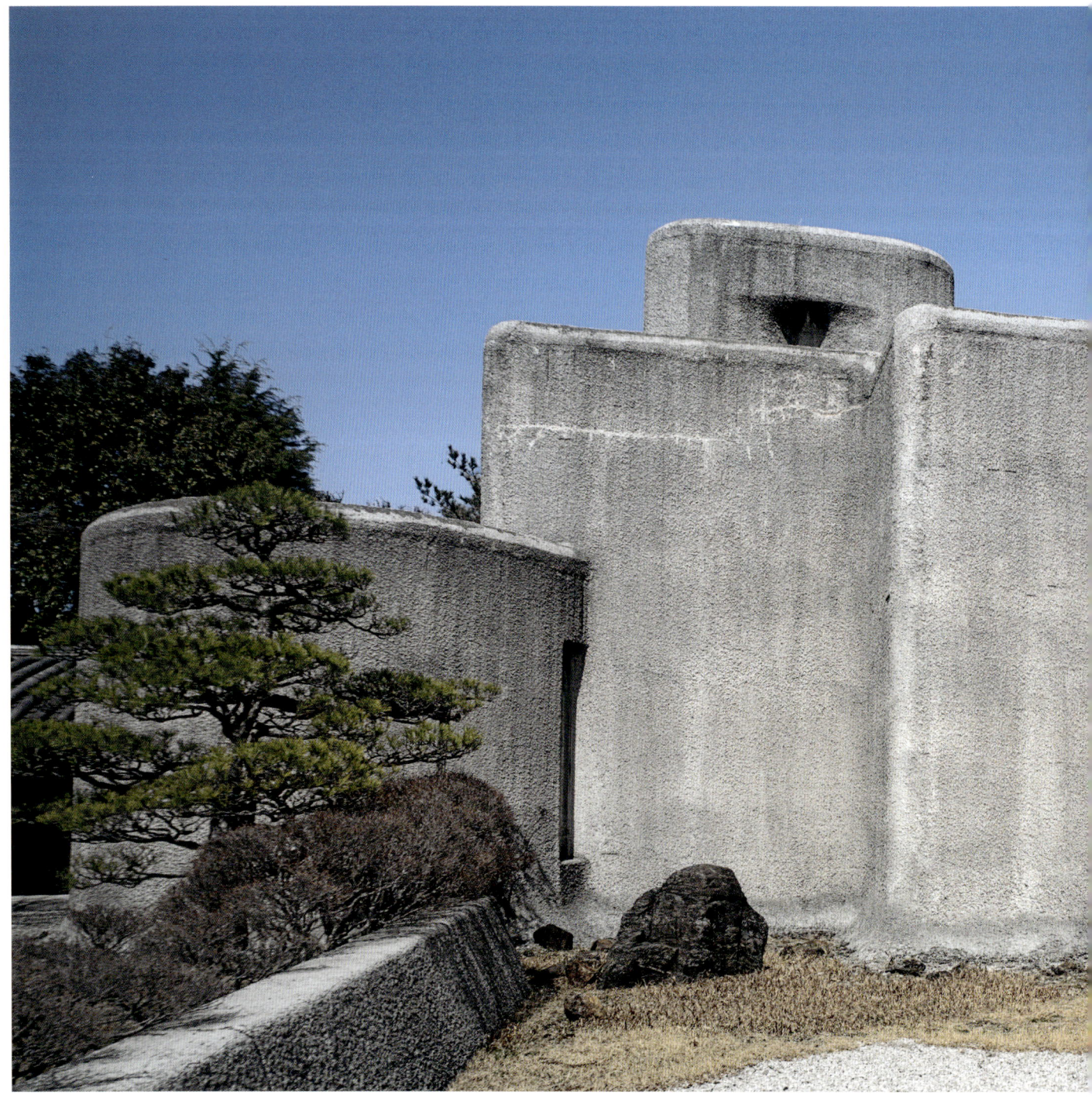

TANIMURA ART MUSEUM

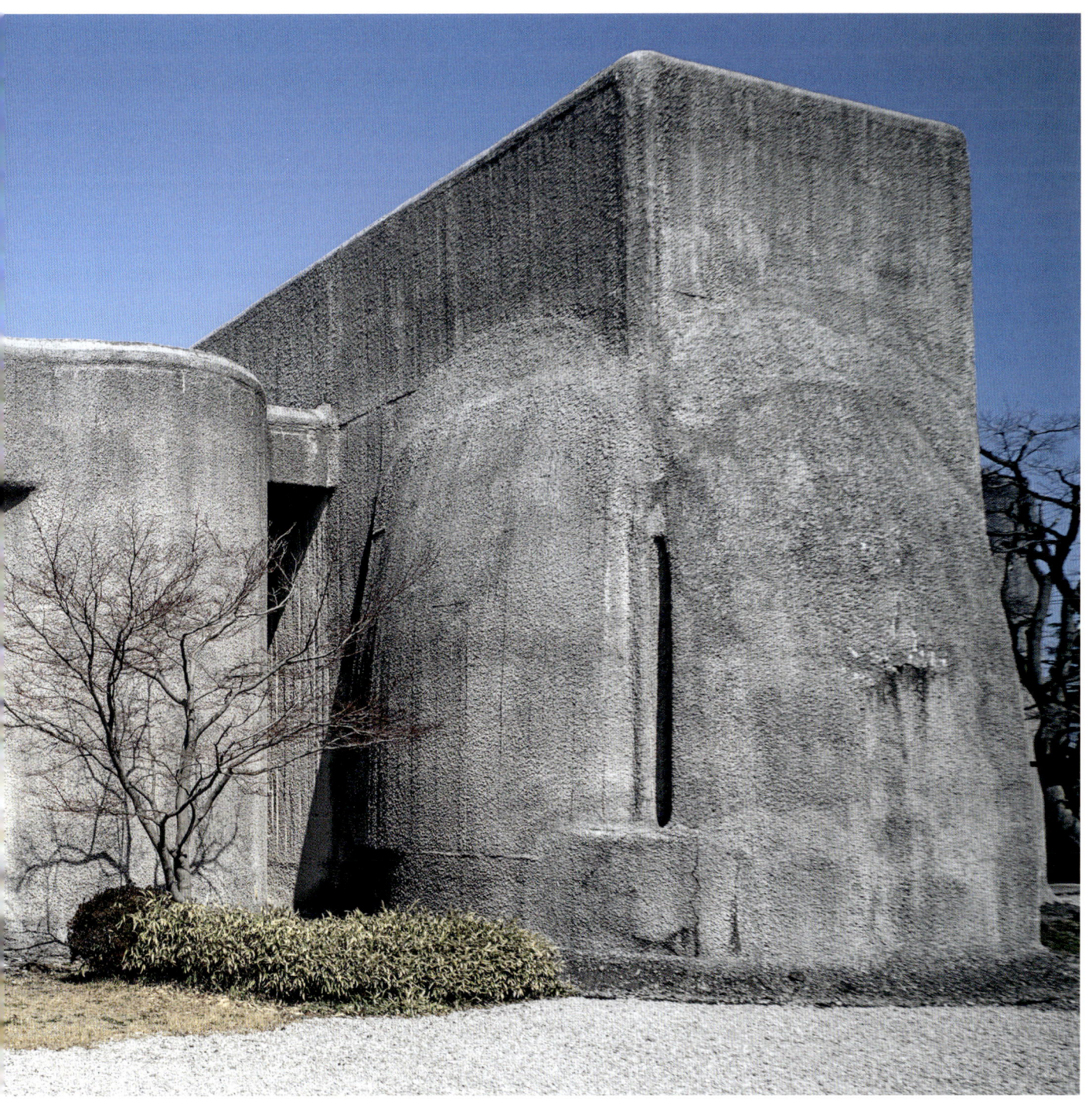

BREEZE APARTMENTS

TOKYO · Architect: IDE Kotaro (ARTechnic Architects) · Completed 2012

This is neo-Brutalism designed by Kotaro Ide whom I had the pleasure of meeting whilst shooting the building. The friendly bloke invited me into his cool office which is part of the apartment complex. Surprisingly, he bemoaned the calibre of young Japanese architects and their uptake of architectural software in relation to international counterparts.

Admitting the poor insulation performance of concrete, Ide, who takes environmental performance seriously, explained that the concrete exterior is simply an embracing shell. It is not structurally integral to the inner building which has foam insulation. Nevertheless, it is aesthetically integral. Brutal aesthetics are maintained internally with exposed concrete walls.

Kotaro Ide had a coup with his more recent residential design, PATH, featuring in *Architectural Record*. Armed with a copy he kindly gave me, I marched to this to find a totally different presentation of concrete – dark, almost imposing when compared to the elegant refinement of BREEZE.

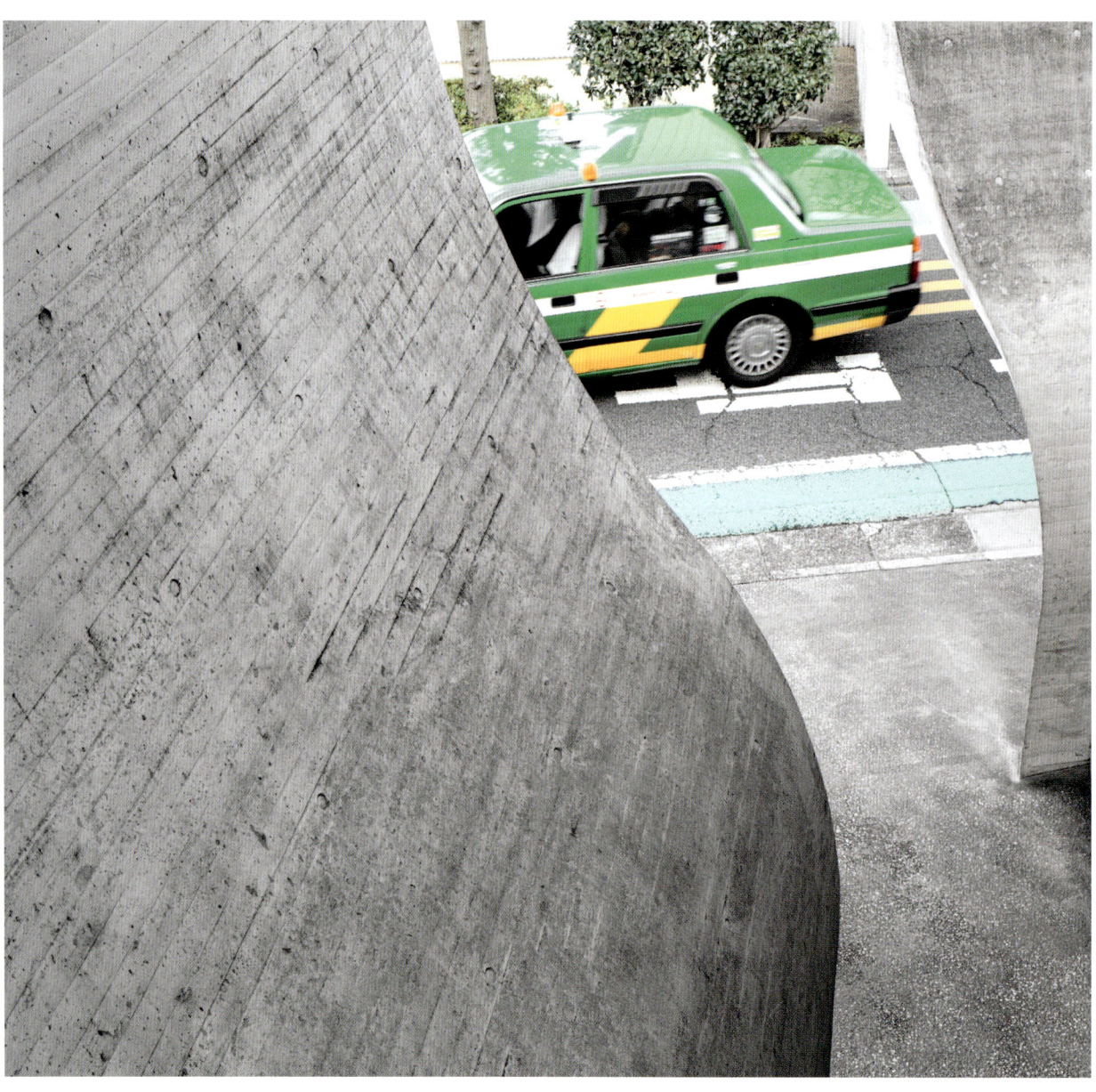

MATSUBARA CIVIC LIBRARY

MATSUBARA, OSAKA PREFECTURE · Architect: MARU · Completed 2019

Beside a tranquil pond, the Matsubara Civic Library rises like a tome from the annals of time, its spine crafted from 600-millimetre-thick concrete. The architects, in a stroke of narrative genius, penned a story of integration rather than erasure, allowing the library to float out into the water like a literary ark. Inside, the seismic-resilient walls have inscribed freedom into the library's chapters, with split levels that unfold storeys upon storeys, where readers perch like characters in a plot, poised between lines of text and water. The design, borrowing a leaf from civil engineering's grand volumes, breathes through windows that draw in the pond's cool whispers. Over time, the library's façade has come to narrate its own tale, with textures ageing like the pages of a well-loved book. A building not just to be read, but to be experienced as well, it stands as a testament to a community's chronicle, forever bookmarked in the annals of Matsubara.

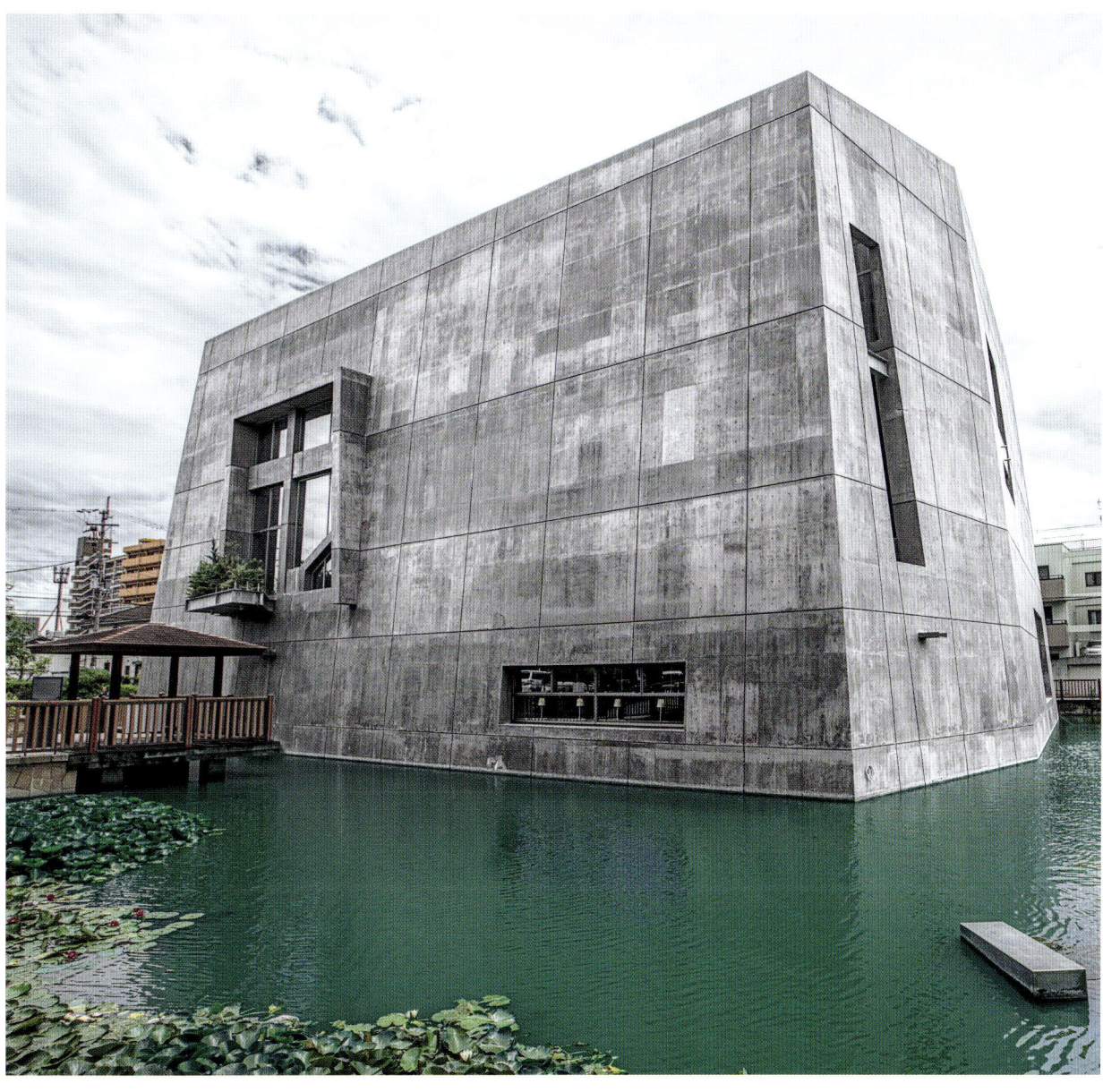

ITOMAN CITY HALL

OKINAWA · Architect: Nihon Sekkei · Completed 2002

Itoman City, situated at the southernmost tip of Okinawa's main island, is home to a remarkable city hall with a dynamic exterior. East and west sides are adorned with breeze-blocks. Vertical louvres on the north façade are nicely complemented by glass. However, most striking is the south side with its continuous horizontal louvre screen arranged diagonally.

Inspired by the traditional Okinawan architectural style of *amahaji*, meaning "under the eaves", the design incorporates precise millimetre adjustments to ensure each louvre avoided casting shadows on solar panels now removed . This clever arrangement blocks intense tropical sunlight while maintaining clear interior views.

Standing alone, the building seamlessly integrates with its surroundings. The south-facing louvre screen aligns with the civic plaza presided over by the government building, creating a gentle transition between indoor and outdoor spaces through the *amahaji* area. Similarly, the west side's bridge and grand staircase connect the interior to a terrace with views of the Kerama Islands.

Hinges at the base of the southern louvre screen are part of a structural system designed to enhance the resilience of buildings in Okinawa. This hinge mechanism allows for controlled movement and flexibility, which is crucial in an area prone to earthquakes and typhoons. By incorporating such hinges, the structure can absorb and dissipate seismic energy, reducing the risk of structural damage during an earthquake. Additionally, the hinge allows the building to sway and adjust during strong winds, common in Okinawa's tropical climate, thereby maintaining its stability. This innovative approach to building design ensures both safety and longevity, adapting traditional architectural concepts to modern engineering solutions that address the unique environmental challenges of the region.

By blending traditional semi-outdoor spaces with modern technology, this city hall beautifully honours Okinawan architectural heritage.

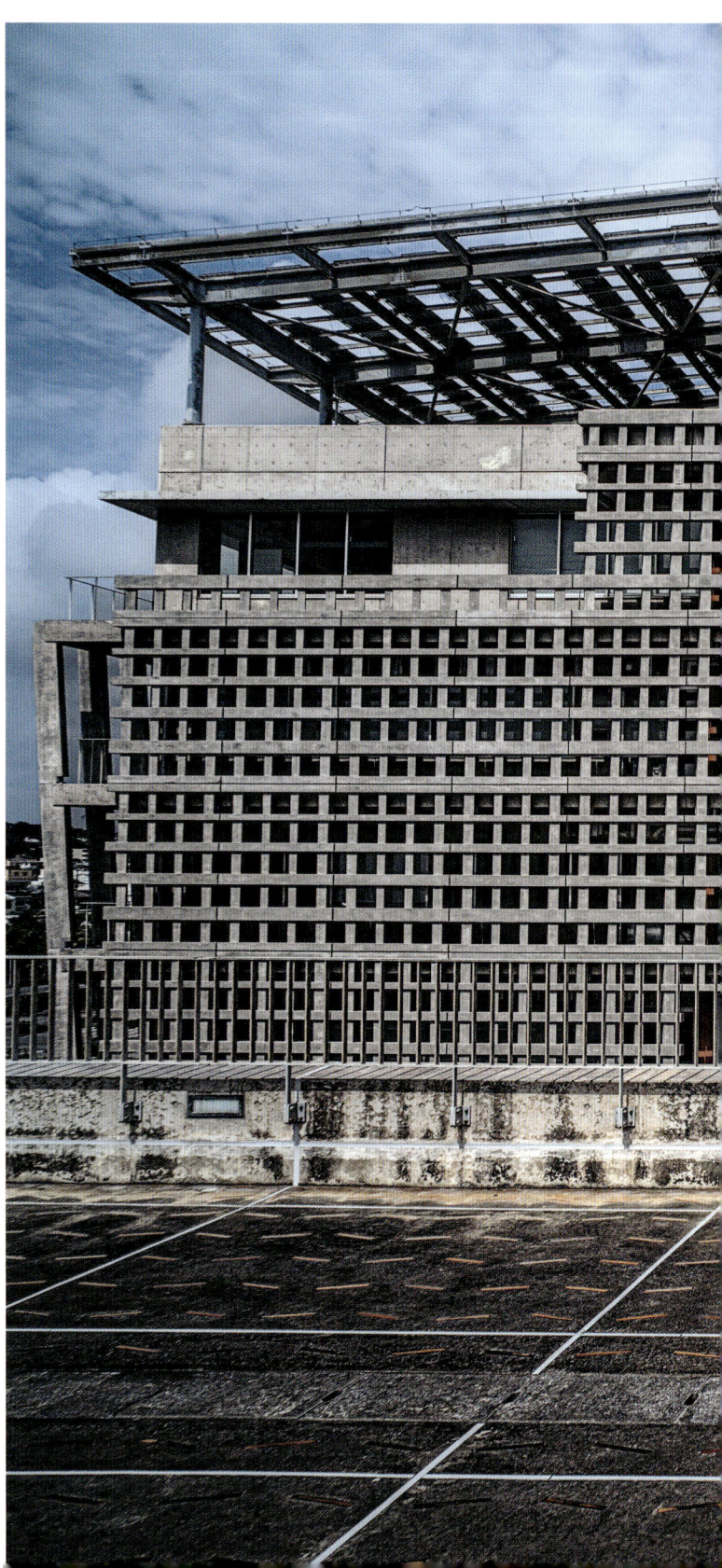

ITOMAN CITY HALL

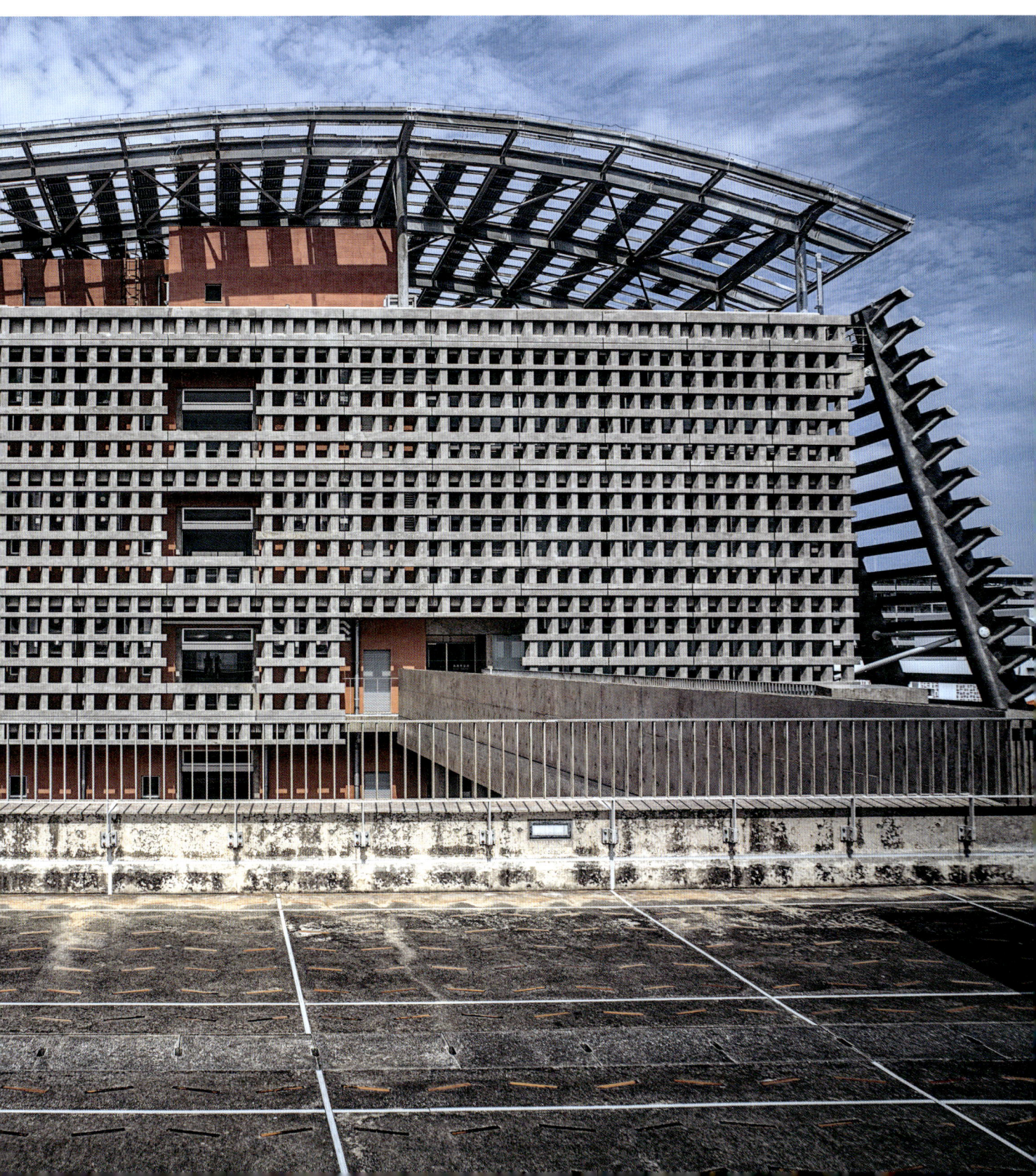

ITOMAN CITY HALL

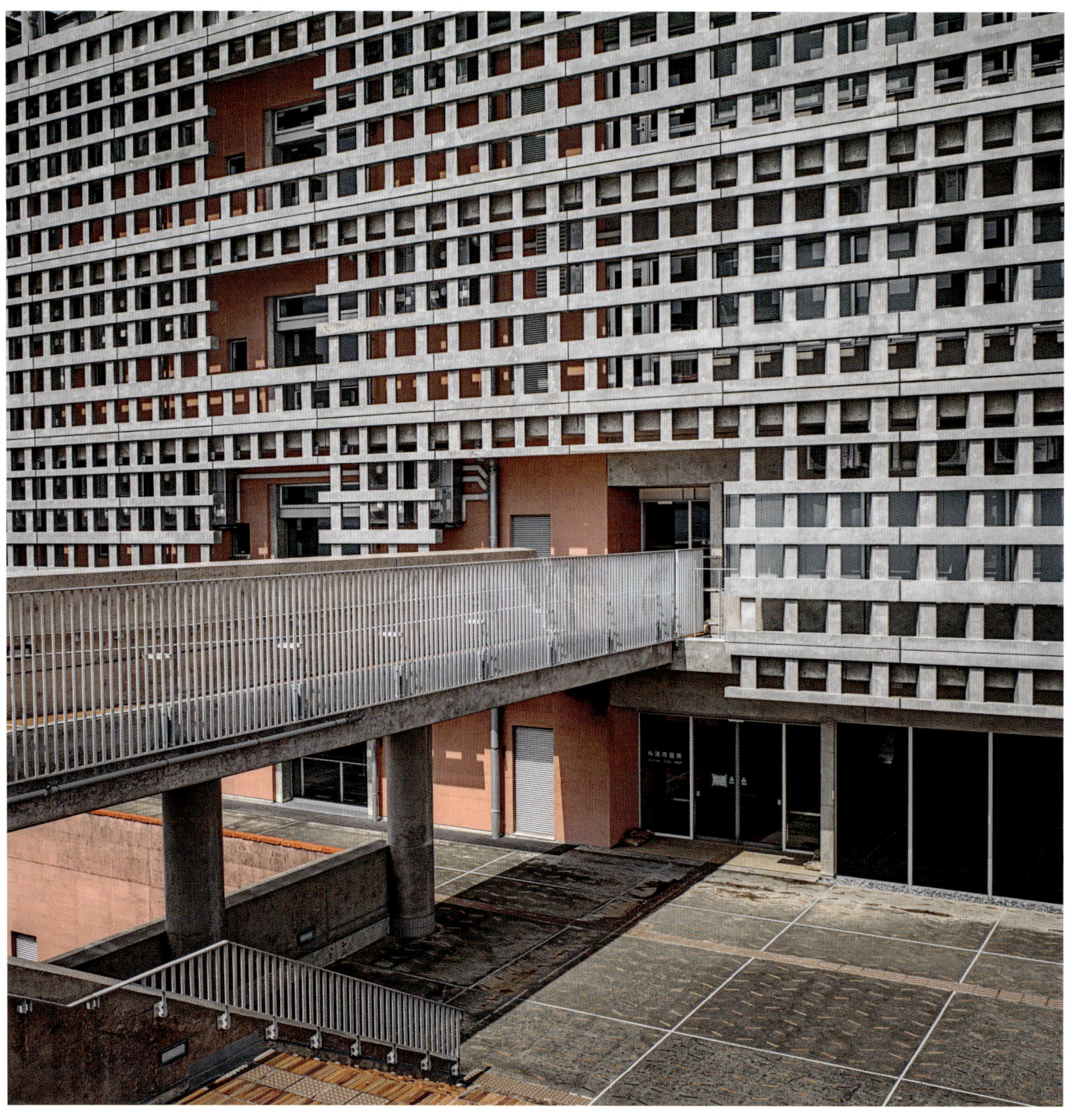

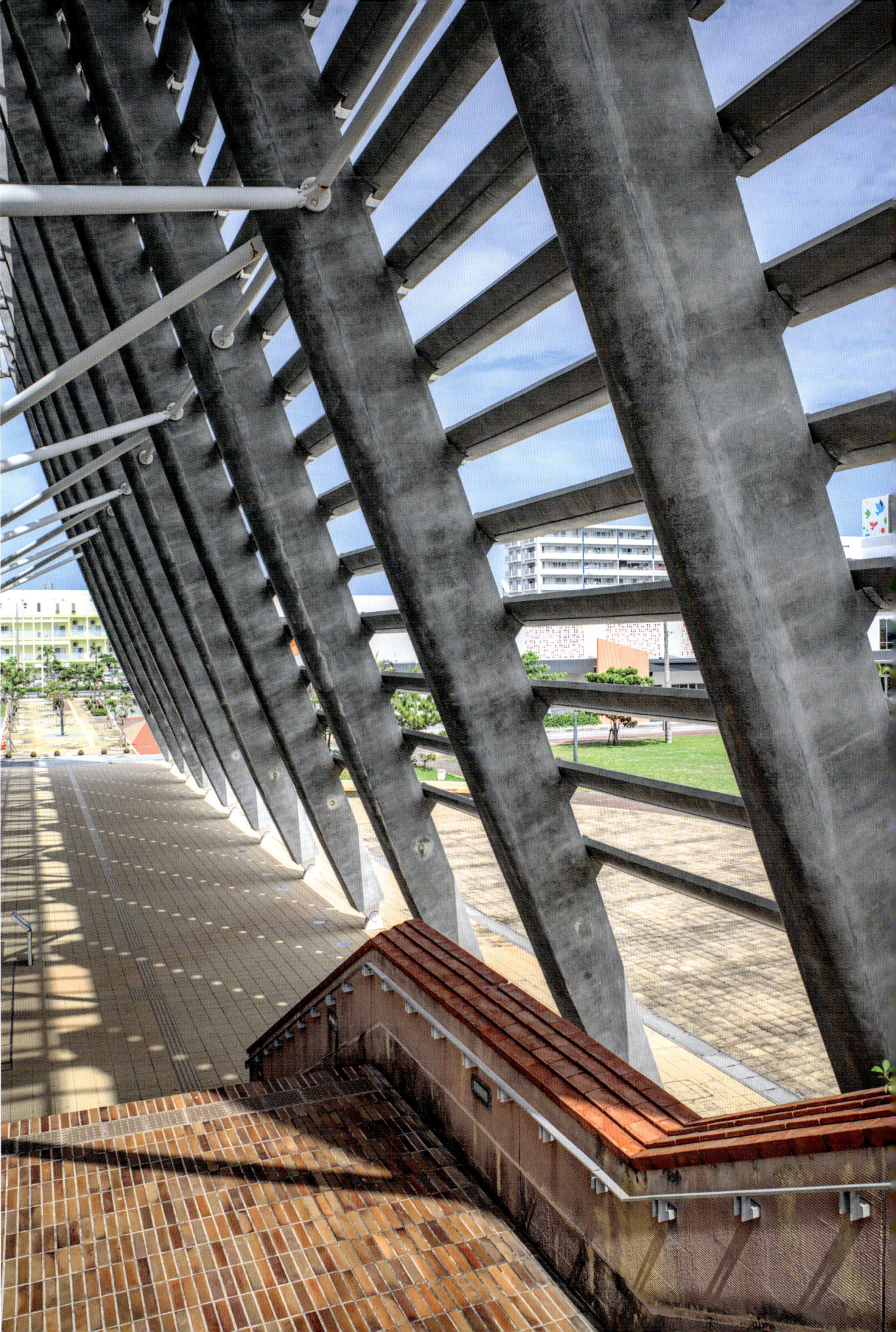

AKIHA WARD CULTURAL CENTER

NIIGATA PREFECTURE · Architect: Chiaki Arai Urban and Architecture Design · Completed 2014

The Akiha Ward Cultural Center unfolds like a modern-day *bunka no satoyama*, a cultural landscape nurturing communal life. Born from citizen workshops, its architectural narrative pivoted from a perfect circle to a dynamic tangent arc, spanning a radius of forty-six metres. The building, twisting to reconcile its stepped silhouette with a flat plan, is a sure stroke in the city's skyline, like an exclamation mark punctuating the end of a thought-provoking passage.

The interior whispers tales of a wooded village cave, where lightly beaten concrete walls echo with the wisdom of the forest. This material does more than charm the eye; it orchestrates a chorus of sounds that dance off acoustically reflective surfaces. Aluminium plates, set within the concrete, act as librarians, quietly moderating the acoustics while allowing shafts of light to leaf through, page by page, into the space.

This hall is not a mere building; it is a living organism designed to foster discovery even in stillness, echoing the satoyama landscape's ethos, where life thrives in diversity. The building's very essence encourages exploration, from its park-like surroundings to the top of its hill-like structure that affords panoramic views. The design elements beckon casual passers-by to dip their toes into the local cultural waters.

Strategic windows act like eyes, connecting the beating heart of cultural activities to those wandering through the lobby, sparking encounters with the arts. Rooms within the facility serve multiple purposes, from rehearsals to conferences, mirroring a bookshelf laden with genres aplenty. The lobby itself is a prologue, setting the stage for community engagement with its welcoming array of tables and chairs.

The stage is grand, an open canvas for the theatrical, musical and everything in between, equipped with curtains and acoustic reflectors, all in service of the cultural narrative. The Akiha Ward Cultural Center spirals as an architectural tome, its pages filled with the stories of those it serves.

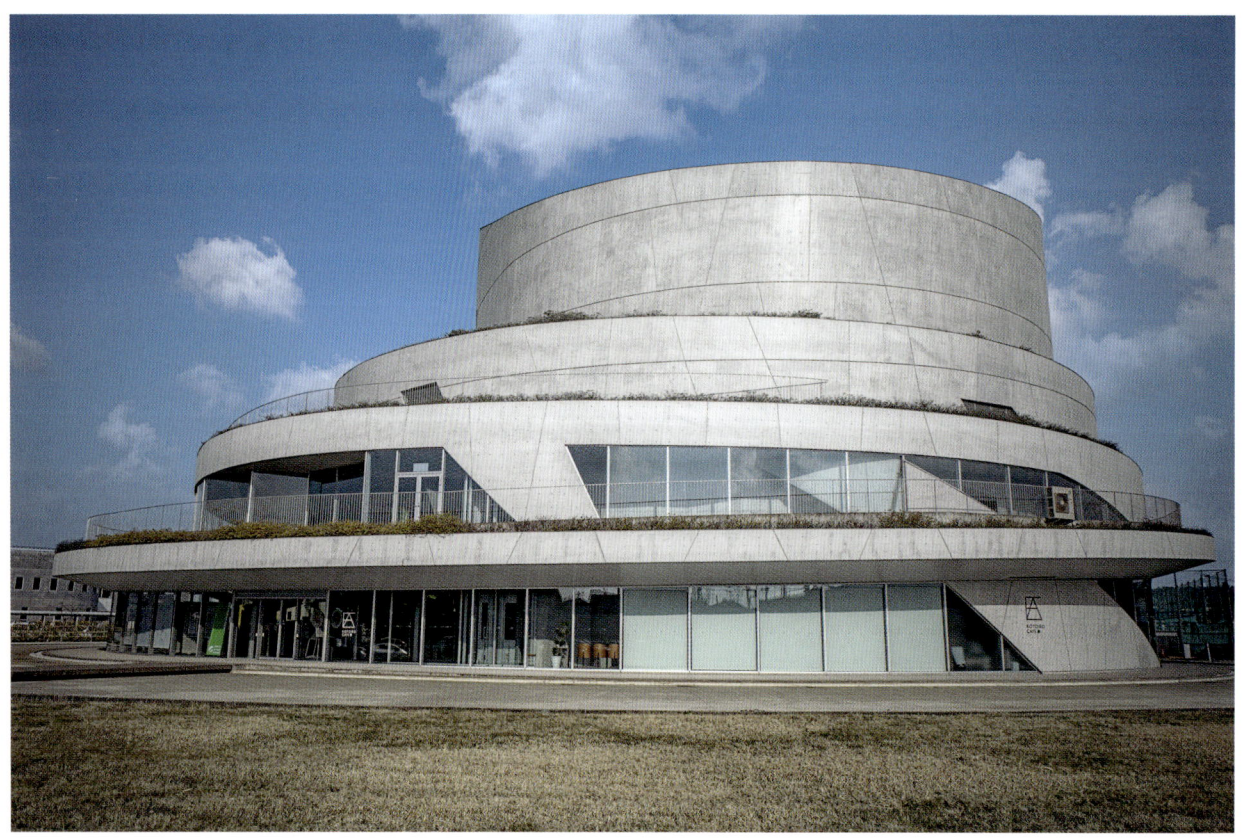

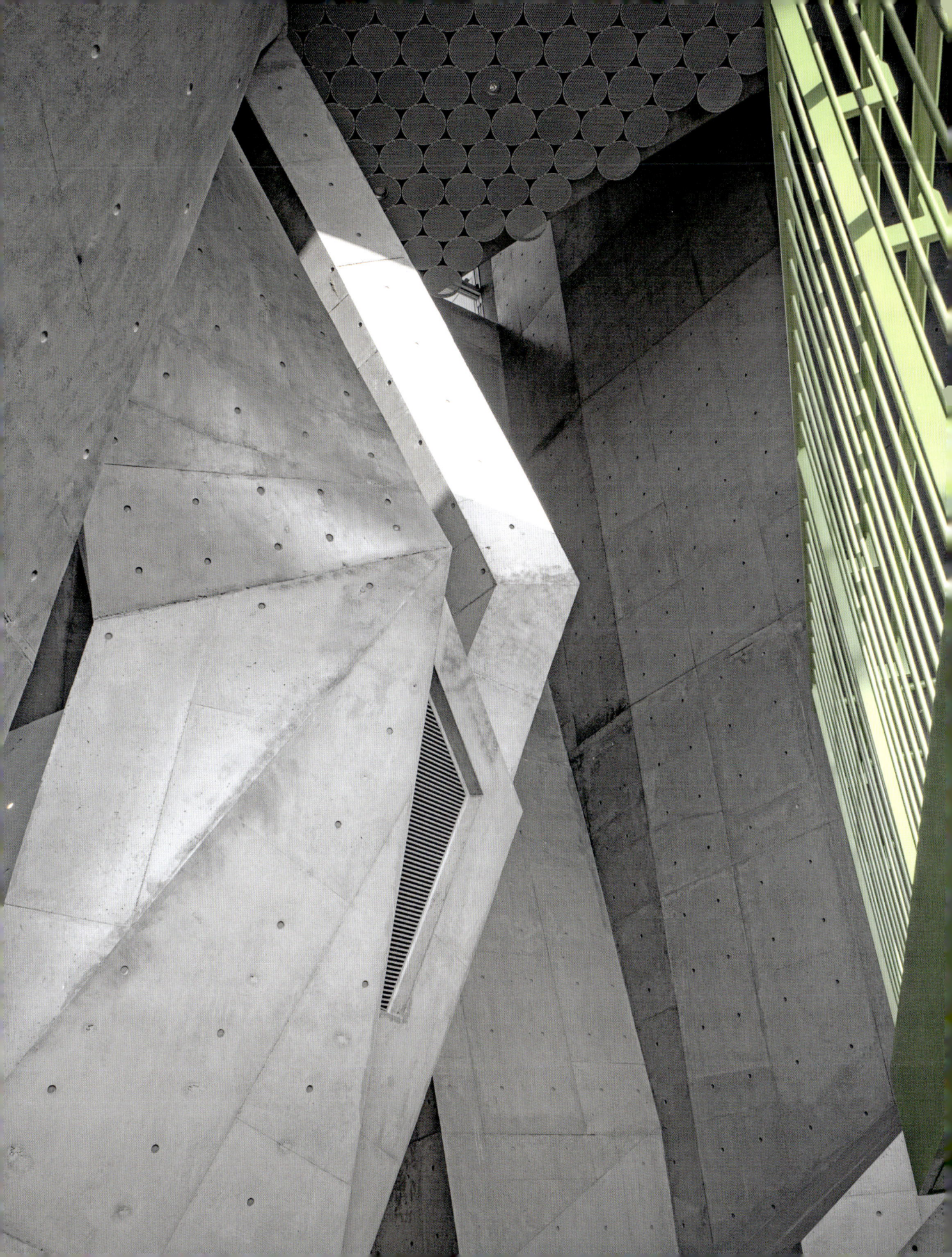

AKIHA WARD CULTURAL CENTER

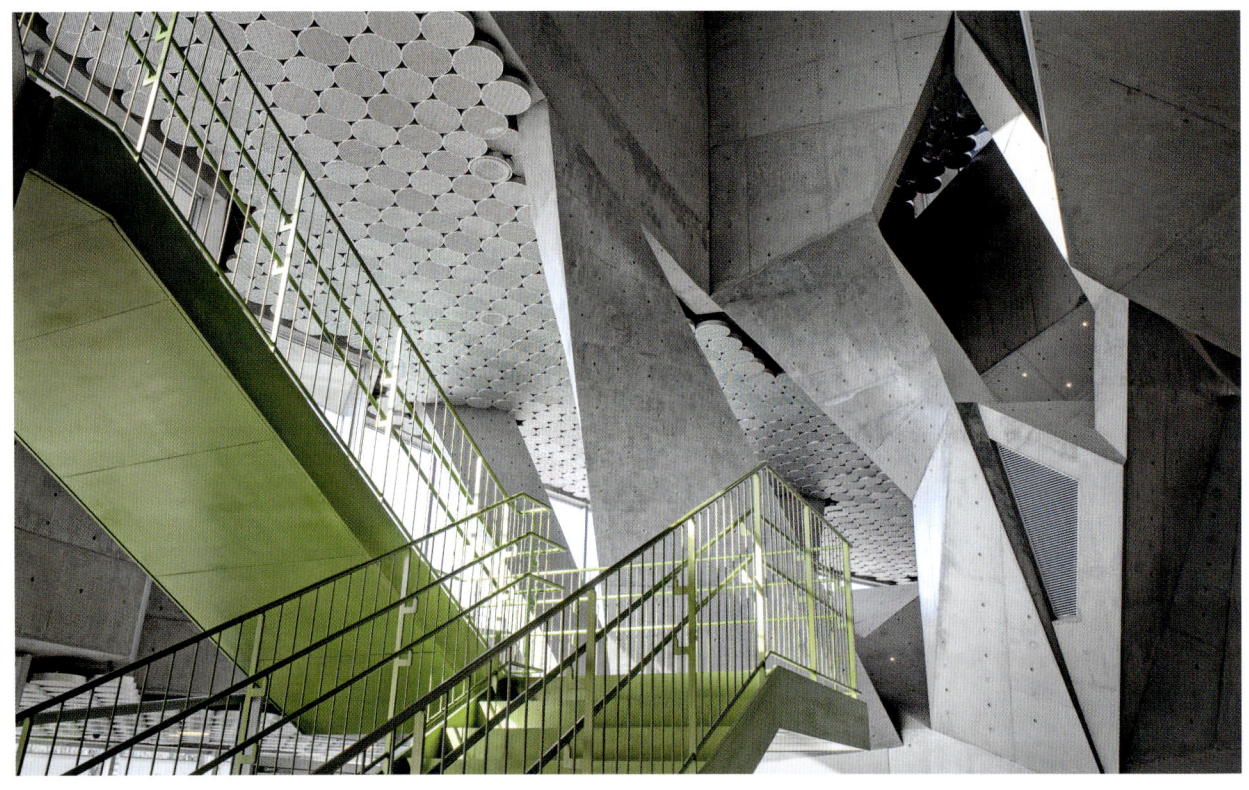

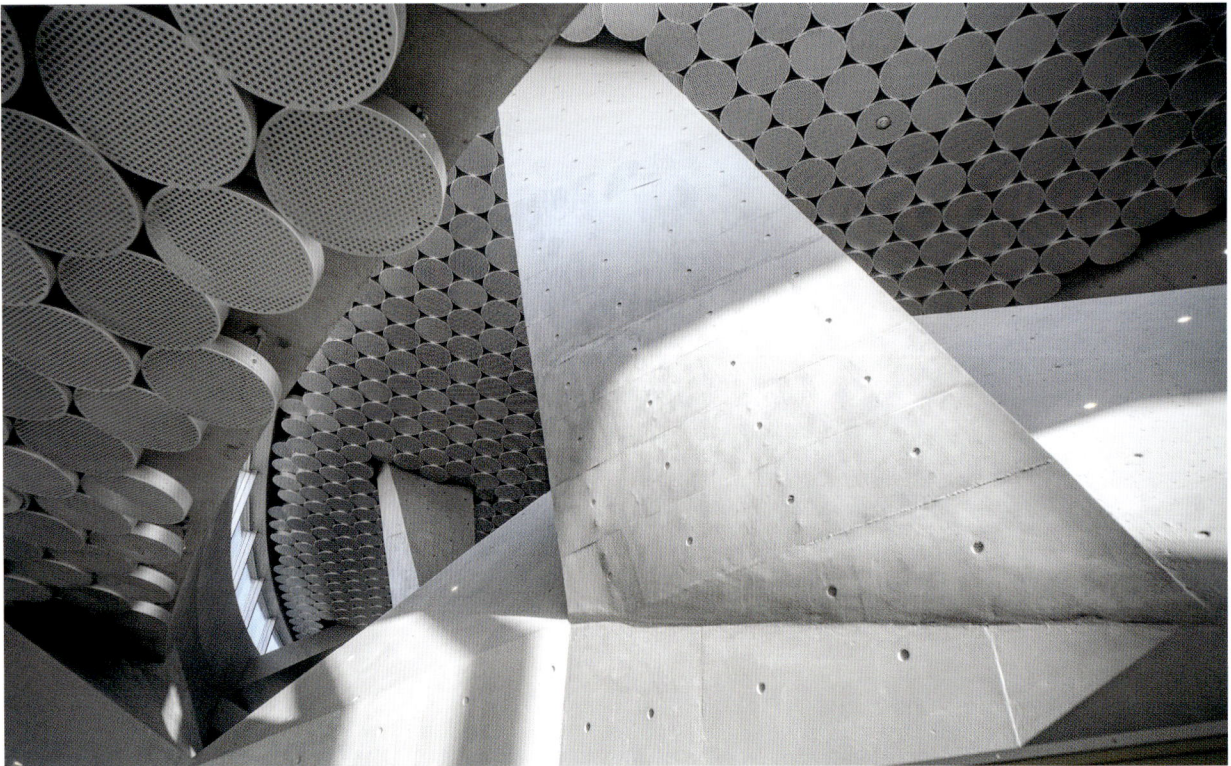

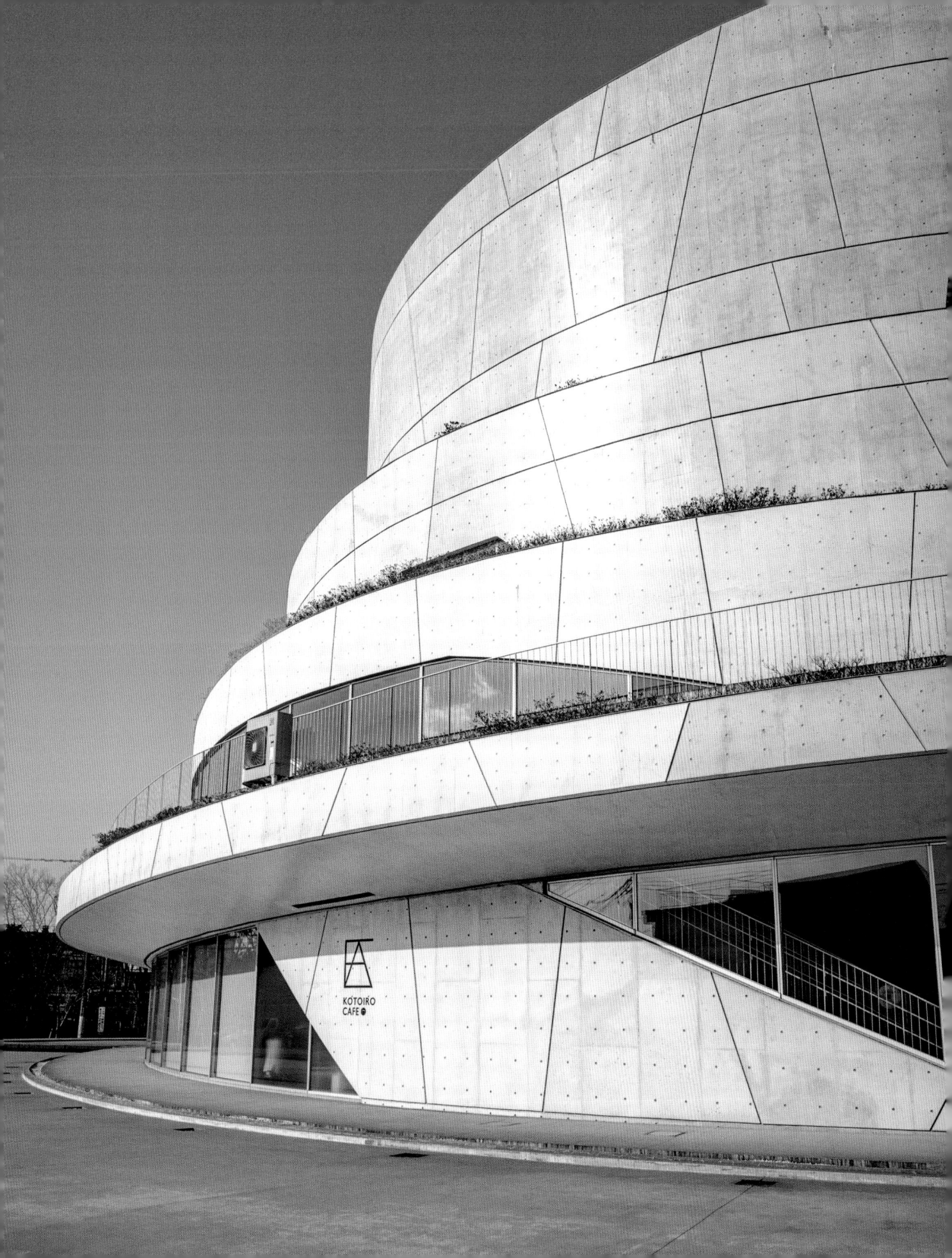

MIYAZAKI PREFECTURAL COMPREHENSIVE YOUTH CENTER
Architect: SAKAKURA Junzo · Completed 1975

Also known as Aoshima Youth Center, this is a notable example of Sakakura's architectural style, blending modernist principles with a strong connection to the surrounding landscape.

Located in Miyazaki, near the coast, the design of the Aoshima Youth Center is characterized by its linear, Brutalist forms that contrast with and yet respect the natural environment. The use of raw concrete and geometric shapes common in Sakakura's designs is evident, providing the building with a monumental presence while maintaining human scale through its interaction with natural light and landscape elements.

The building's L-shaped layout orients it towards the artificial lake from two angles, creating the visual effect of a spaceship hovering above the water. The design challenge was integrating the architectural structure with Miyazaki Prefecture's tropical climate and the region's intense subtropical sunlight. The solution employed is the use of pilotis, elevating the living spaces well above the ground or water level. These pilotis also function as a ventilation mechanism, channelling the southerly breezes throughout various sections of the building.

The Youth Center serves as a multi-purpose facility, providing educational and recreational spaces for young people. Its design emphasizes openness and accessibility, with large windows and terraces that offer views of the nearby ocean, integrating the building with its coastal setting. Sakakura's work here demonstrates his ability to create functional spaces that also act as cultural landmarks, enhancing the community's interaction with architecture and nature.

Junzo Sakakura, a leading figure in Japanese modernism, was pivotal in bringing Brutalist architecture to Japan. A disciple of Le Corbusier, he infused Brutalism's bold concrete forms with Japanese minimalism, creating striking, functional structures that underscored raw textures and structural integrity. His influential designs significantly sculpted Japan's mid-twentieth-century architectural identity.

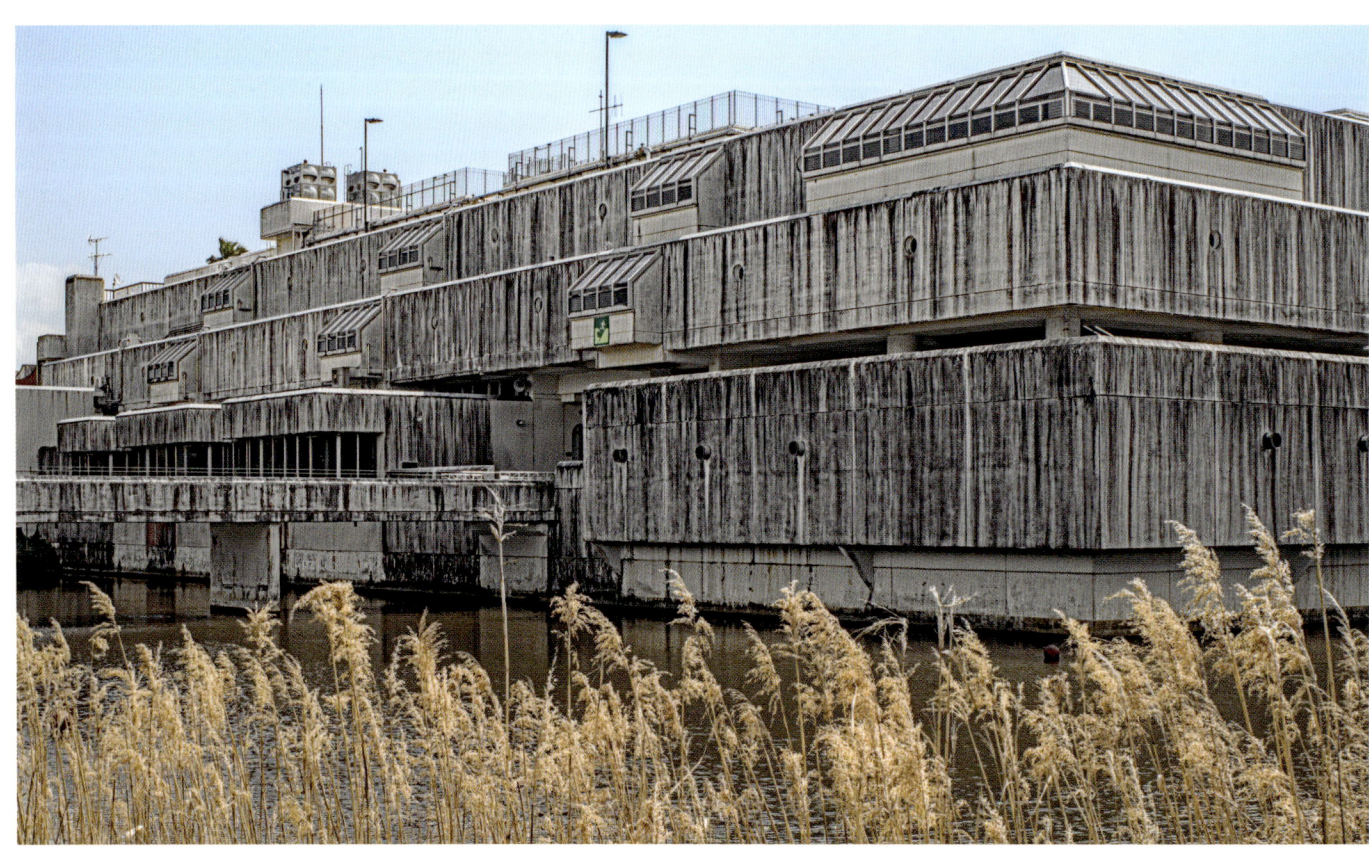

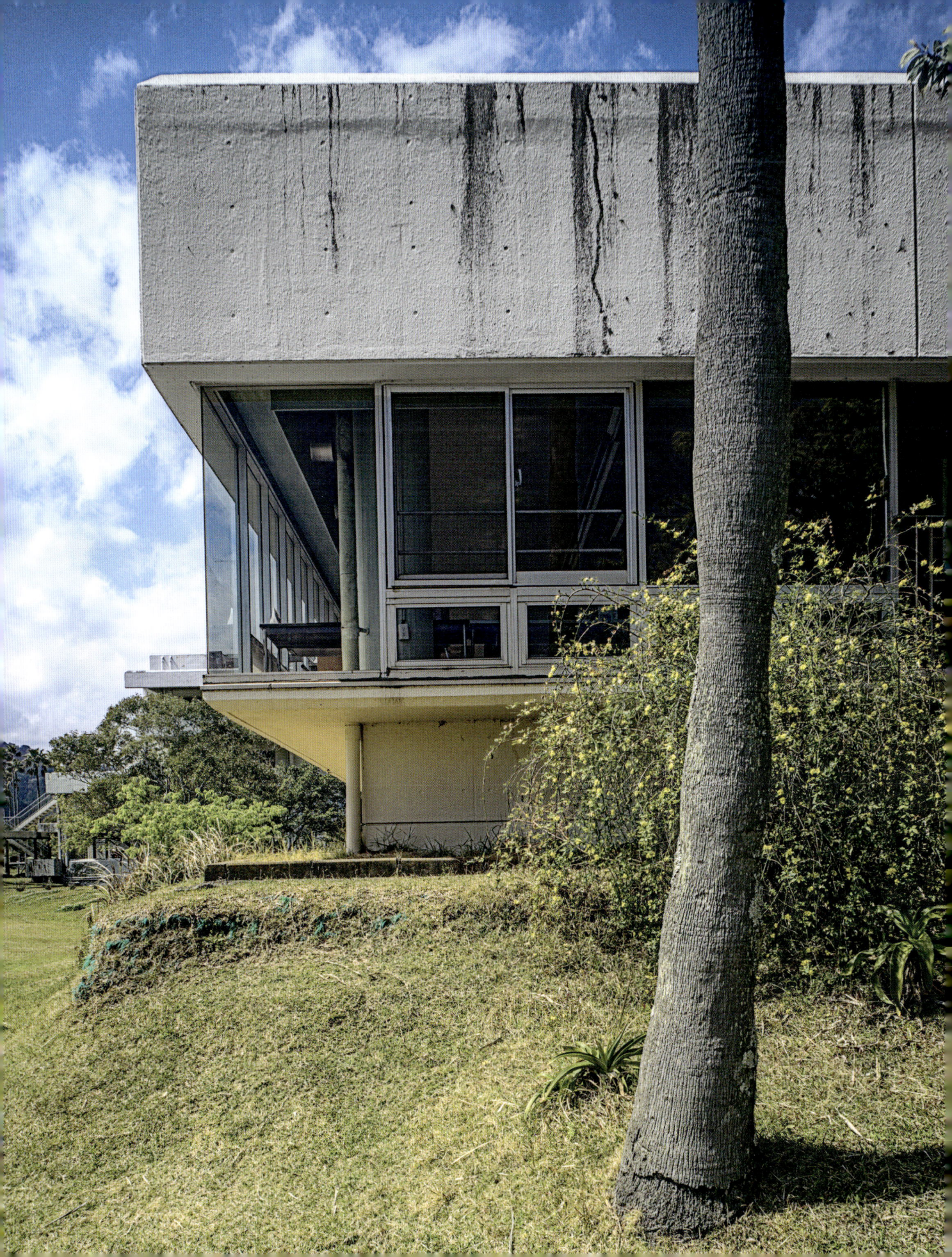

MIYAZAKI PREFECTURAL COMPREHENSIVE YOUTH CENTER 36

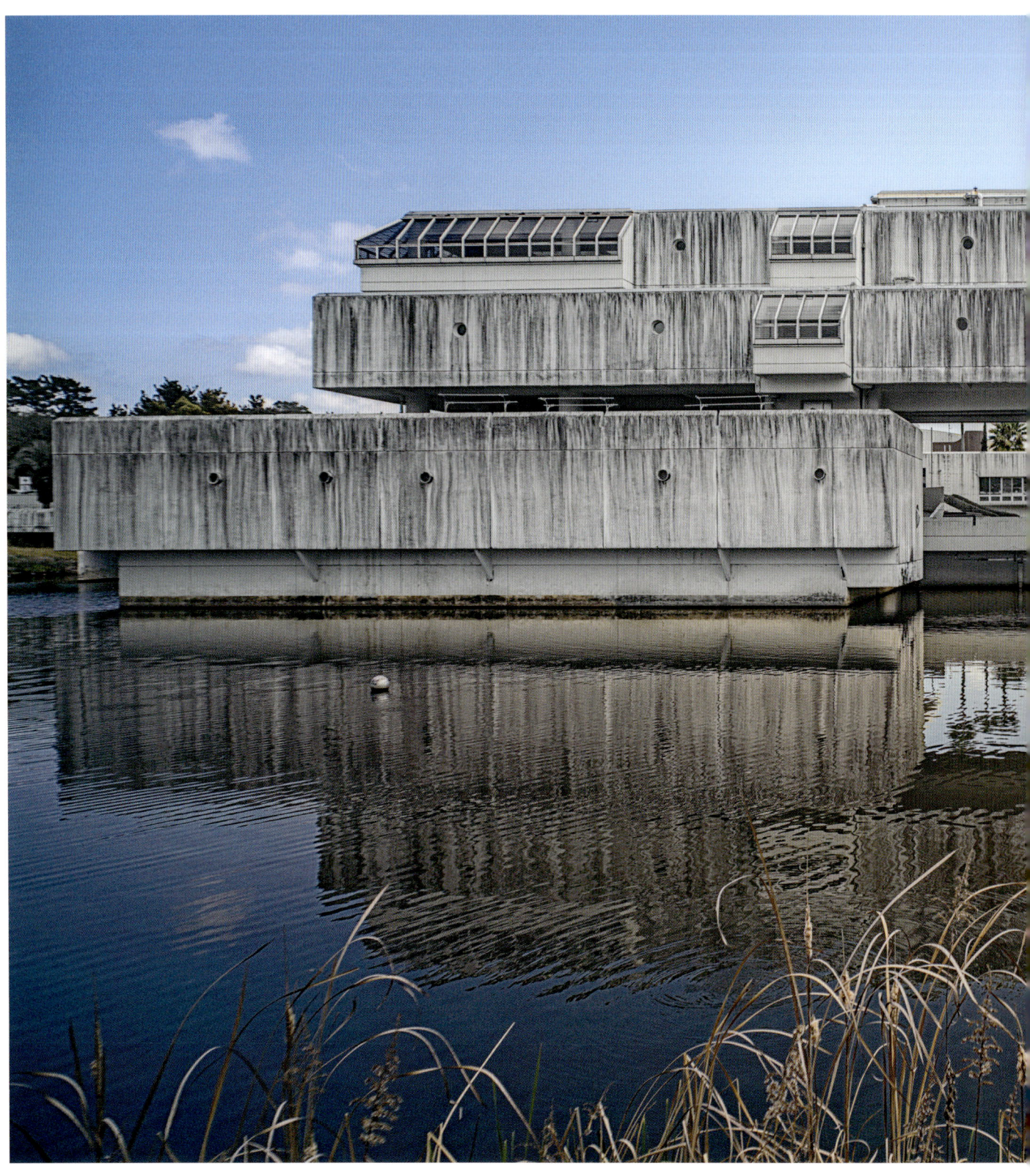

MIYAZAKI PREFECTURAL COMPREHENSIVE YOUTH CENTER

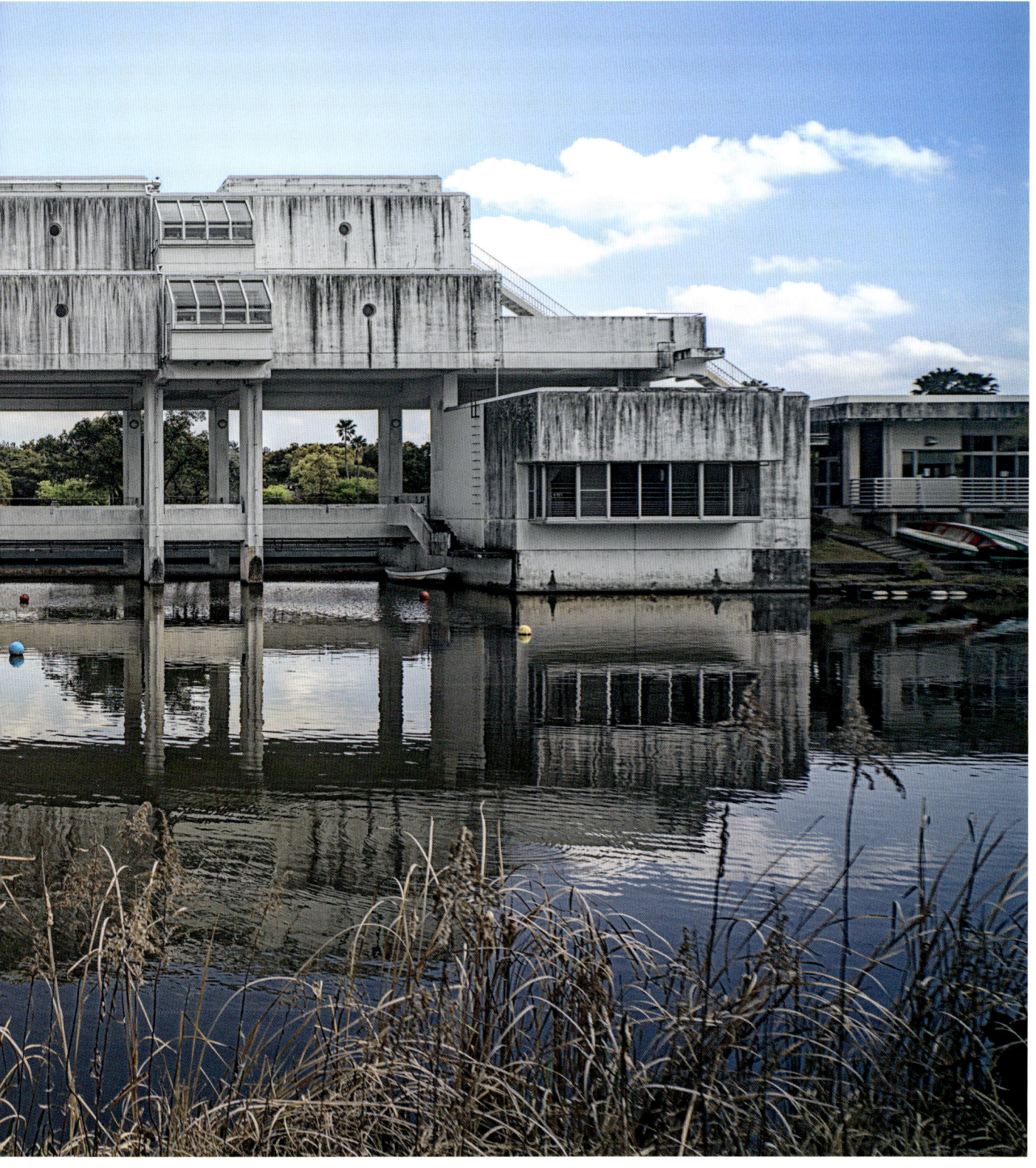

DR MINEZAKI HOUSE (DRAGON FORT)

SHIZUOKA PREFECTURE · Architect: WATANABE Youji · Completed 1968

In a land where castles stand tall and dragons are more than just myth, the Dragon Fort slumbers like a fantastical beast on the Izu Peninsula. Crafted by the whimsical Youji Watanabe, known for defying architectural norms, this building coils with the splendour of a dragon guarding its lair. Originally a den for medical practitioners, the fort was lovingly restored by Katai Yamazaki, a retired property manager with a penchant for archery and a respect for history. A Second World War II-era Rising Sun flag has been removed from the roof.

While Tadao Ando played with concrete for its thriftiness and the Metabolists envisioned futuristic habitats, Watanabe's sturdy dragon scales – concrete on wood – prioritise durability over economics. His designs, although dismissed by some for their simplicity, were the stuff of legends, from a temple cruising on land to the battleship-esque New Sky Building No. 3.

The Monster Hospital, as the locals dubbed it, held a two-bedroom home and a doctor's office within its belly until 2014. When Yamazaki stumbled upon it, it was destined to be razed. Instead, armed with historical photos and his own hands, he breathed new life into its interiors, crafting a stronghold of memories where visitors are now welcome by appointment.

Yamazaki's labour of love remains unsullied by municipal funds, yet he champions the fort as an architectural dragon worthy of recognition.

A friendly old woman living opposite told me the owner's idea is simple: "He cherishes this building and preserved it for others' pleasure. Let the future decide its fate."

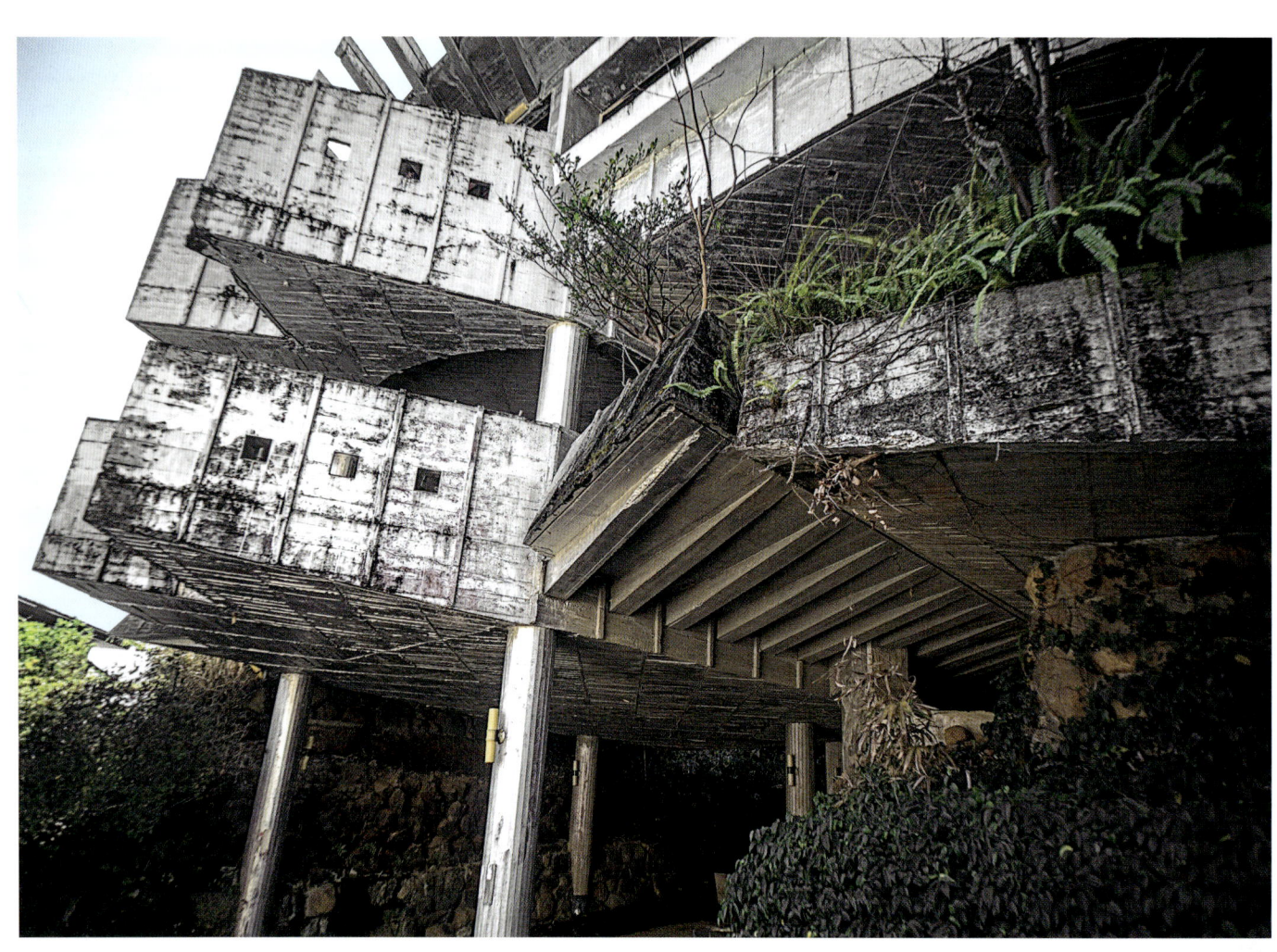

DR MINEZAKI HOUSE (DRAGON FORT)

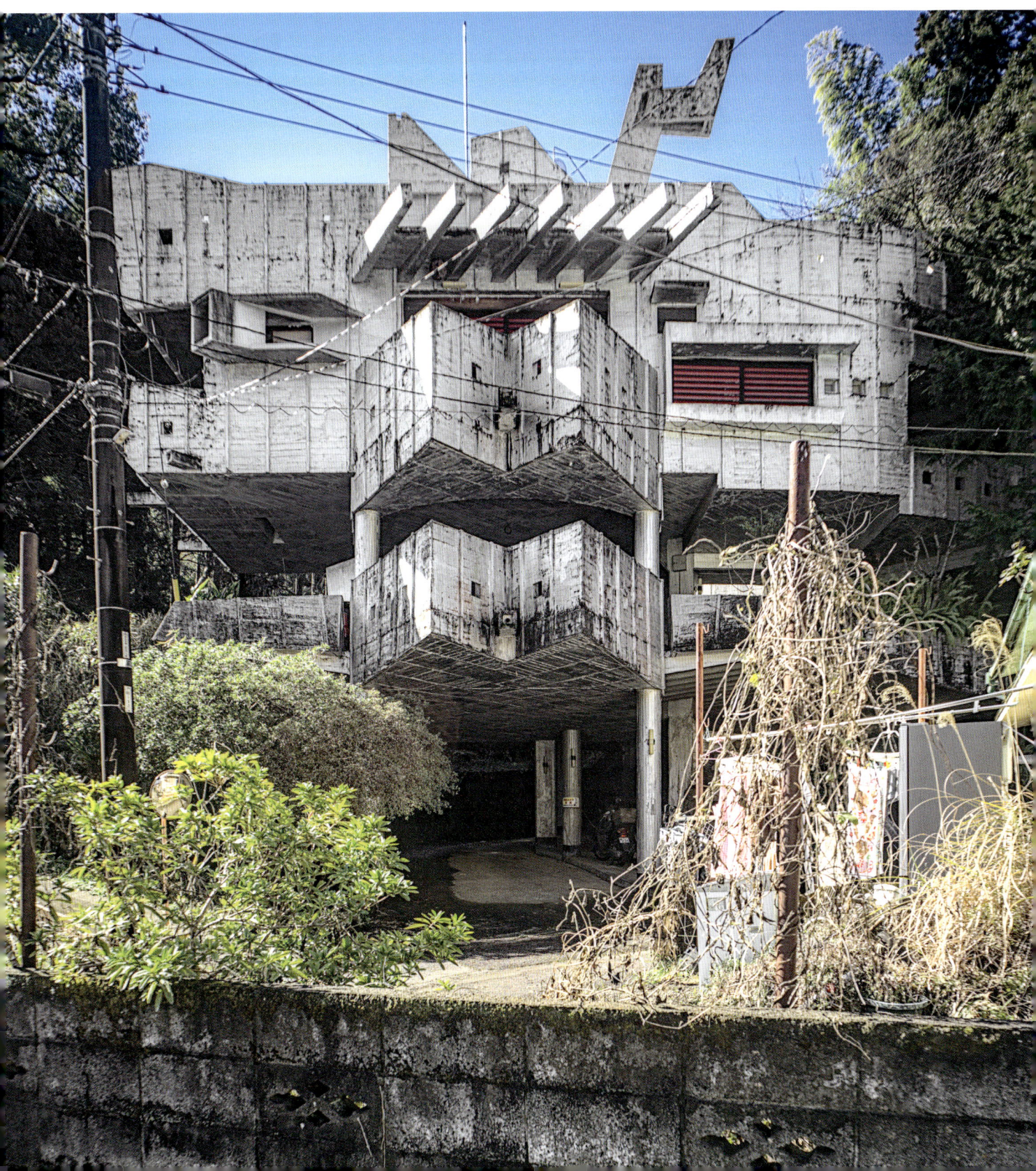

PRIVATE RESIDENCE

NAGOYA

40

This image perfectly encapsulates the neo-Brutalist movement in contemporary Japanese architecture, merging minimalist aesthetics with elements that echo traditional Japanese philosophy. The clean lines and the use of raw concrete in the structure reflect a minimalist approach that emphasizes simplicity and functional beauty – key tenets of traditional Japanese design. The incorporation of balcony plants adds a soft, organic touch that contrasts with the hard concrete, suggesting a philosophical balance between man-made structures and nature. It's not just greenwashing. This thoughtful integration of greenery hints at the Japanese concept of *wabi-sabi*, the appreciation of the imperfect and transient aspects of nature, effectively softening the often harsh perception of Brutalist architecture. This blending of old and new invites global viewers to reconsider any preconceived biases against concrete structures, recognizing them as canvases for profound aesthetic and philosophical expression.

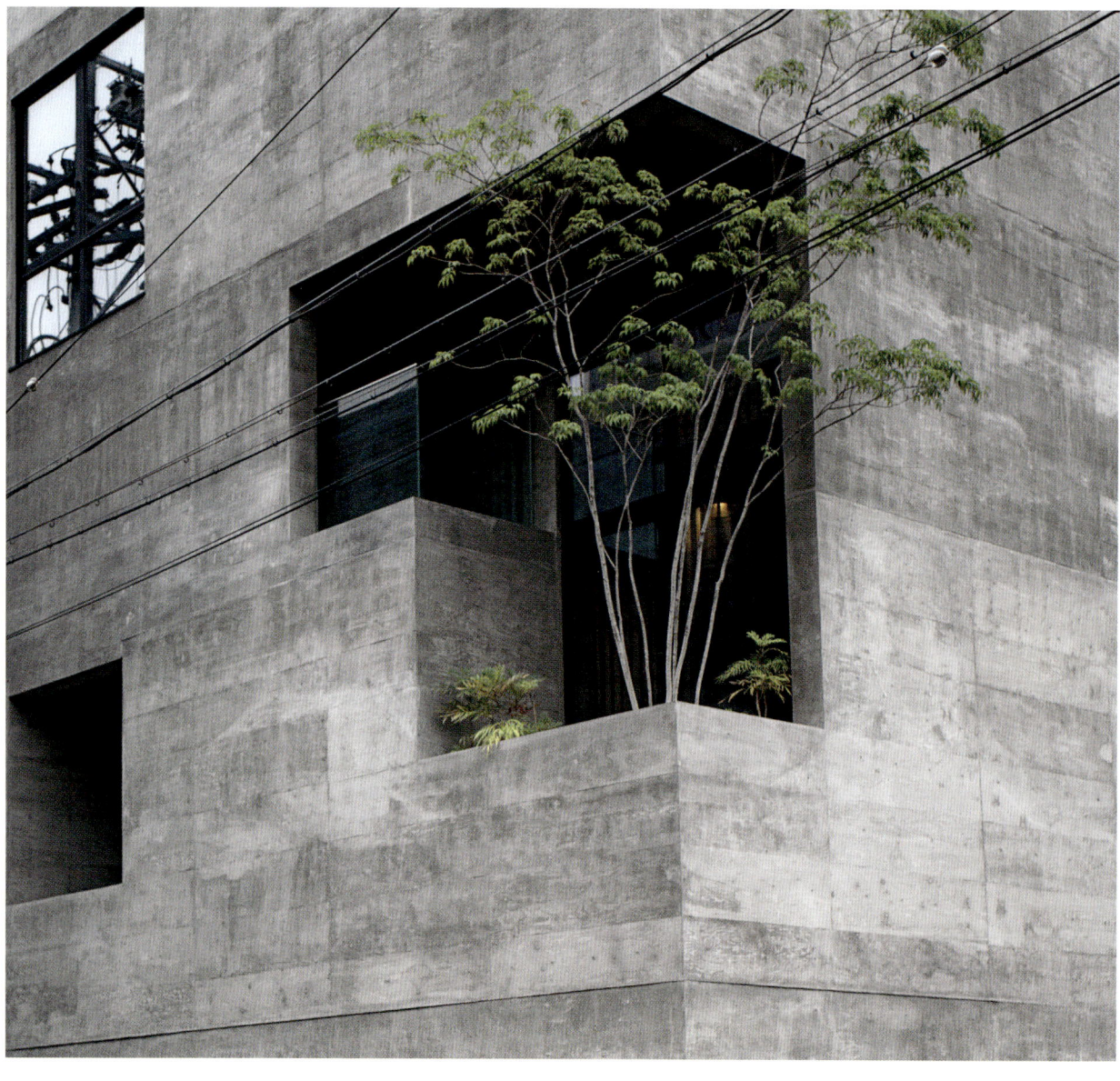

CAR PARK TOWER
HIROSHIMA

A car park tower in Hiroshima showcases an aesthetic appeal grounded in the functional yet dramatic use of curved concrete ramps, exuding a robust elegance rare in utilitarian structures. Concrete, ideal for such buildings in Japan, offers substantial benefits including durability, fire resistance and the capacity to withstand Japan's seismic activity. This structural choice not only meets strict safety standards but also adheres to a minimalist aesthetic that complements urban settings.

The now demolished Welbeck Street car park in London, despite its iconic diamond-patterned façade, suffered from the UK's less rigorous approach to concrete preservation and differing priorities in urban planning and development. London's rapid development pressures and the high value of inner-city land often lead to the replacement of older buildings, regardless of their architectural value. Hiroshima's car park, built with longevity in mind within a different urban and environmental context, faces fewer such threats, ensuring its continued use and preservation in the face of urban evolution.

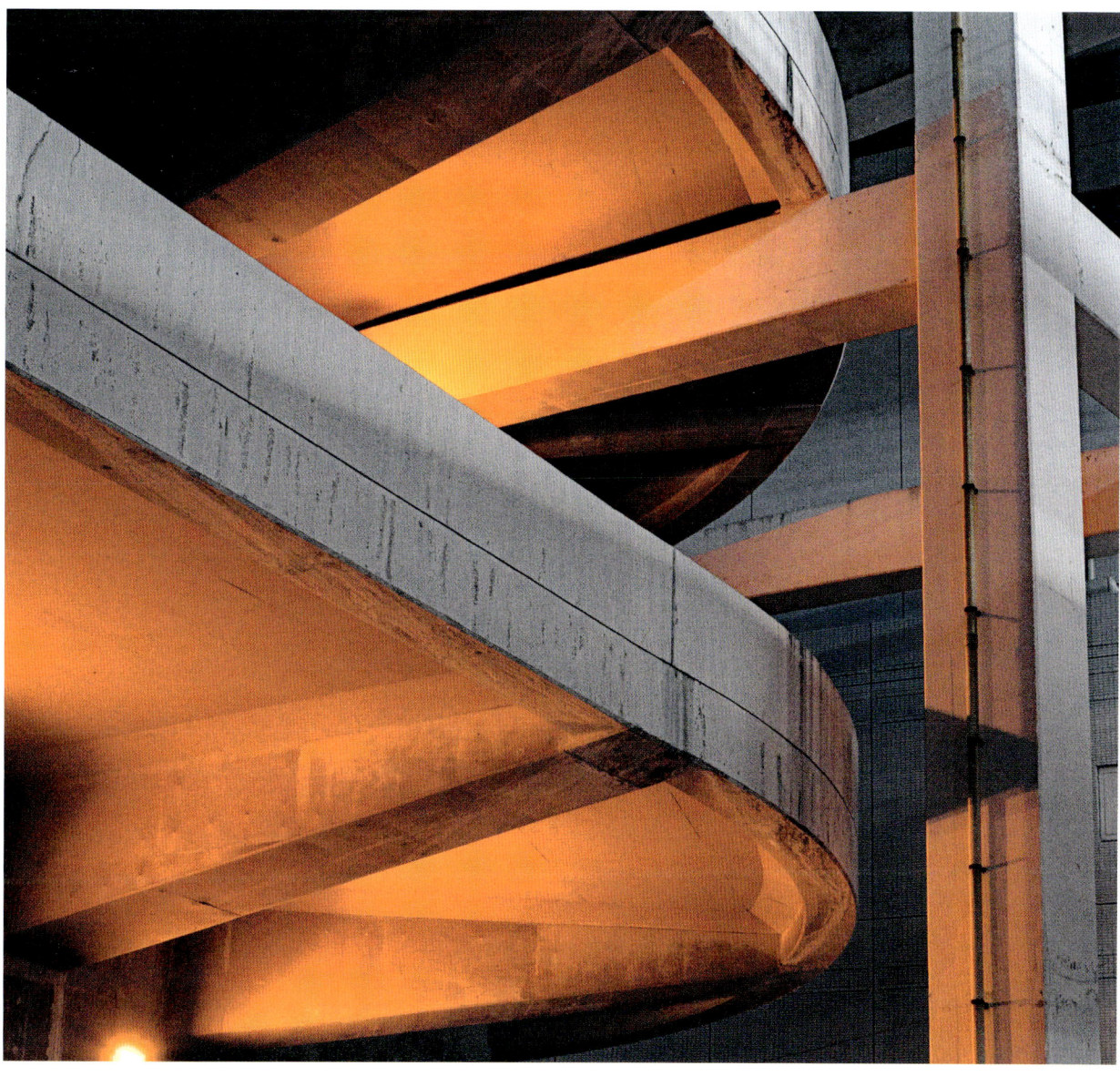

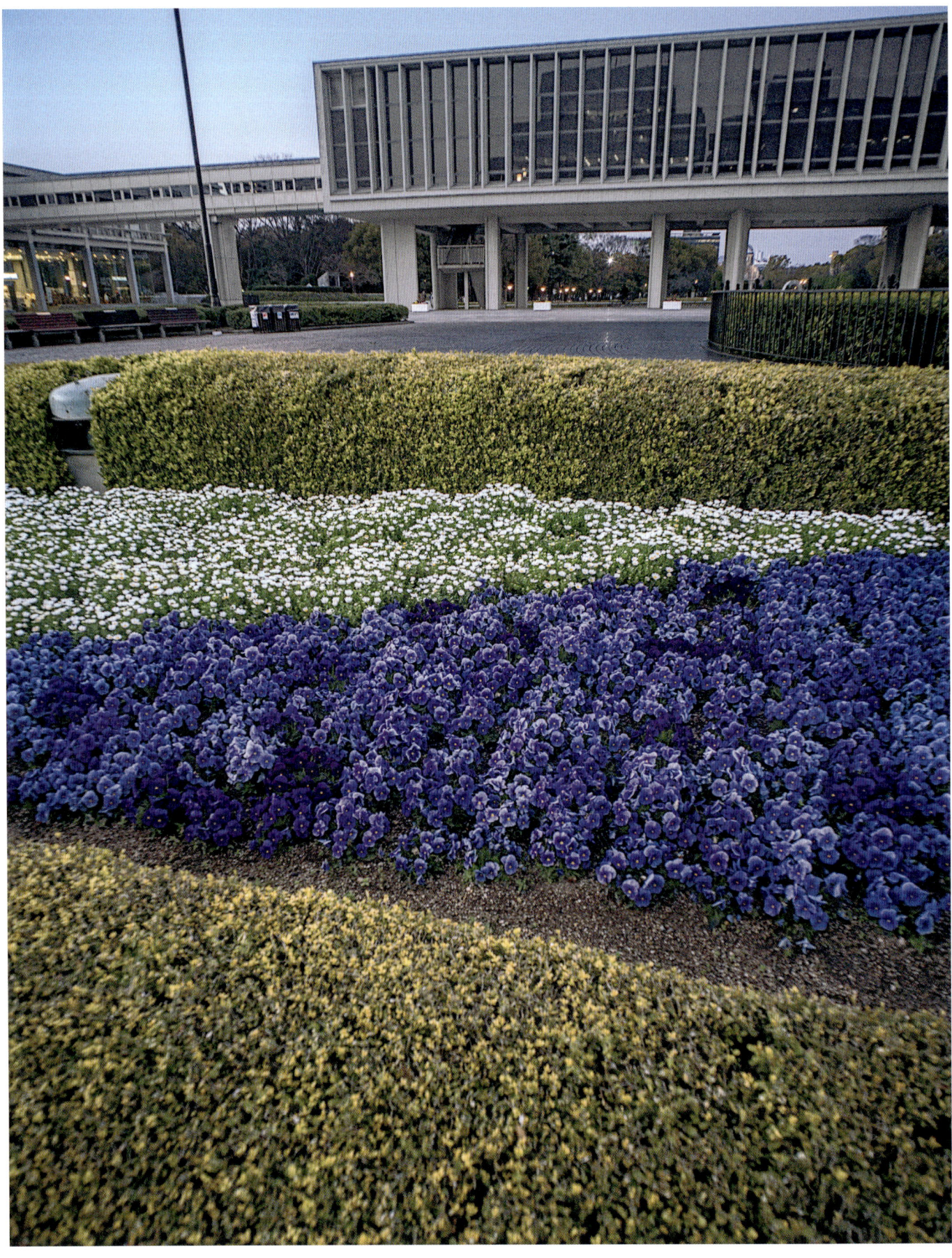

HIROSHIMA PEACE MEMORIAL MUSEUM

HIROSHIMA · Architect: TANGE Kenzo · Completed 1955

In the atomic aftermath, the Peace Museum emerged as Japan's architectural phoenix, a symbol of rebirth and resilience. Tange's winning blueprint wove a narrative of renewal, enfolding Le Corbusier's five points of new architecture into a museum that would anchor a cenotaph and an eternal flame. This sanctuary of remembrance was meticulously choreographed along an axis that stretched from the A-Bomb Dome's skeletal crown, a haunting silhouette against the Hiroshima sky, to the museum's heart.

Tange, in his architectural diplomacy, embraced Western methodologies to paint a portrait of Japan's renaissance, a country poised to step back into the global fold. This was a marked pivot from his war-era ethos, which had venerated Japan's sovereign icons and eschewed Western influences for a formidable and austere Japanese aesthetic.

Yet beneath the surface of this modernist veneer, Tange's design whispered of nationalism, encoded with the DNA of Japan's own architectural lineage. The blueprint resonated with echoes of the Byōdō-in's Amida-do and the mathematical grace of the Katsura Imperial Villa's columns. As noted by architect Arata Isozaki, Tange's fusion of modernist form and nationalist spirit was executed with a cunning subtlety, a veiled homage in concrete and flame to a nation standing at the crossroads of its past and future.

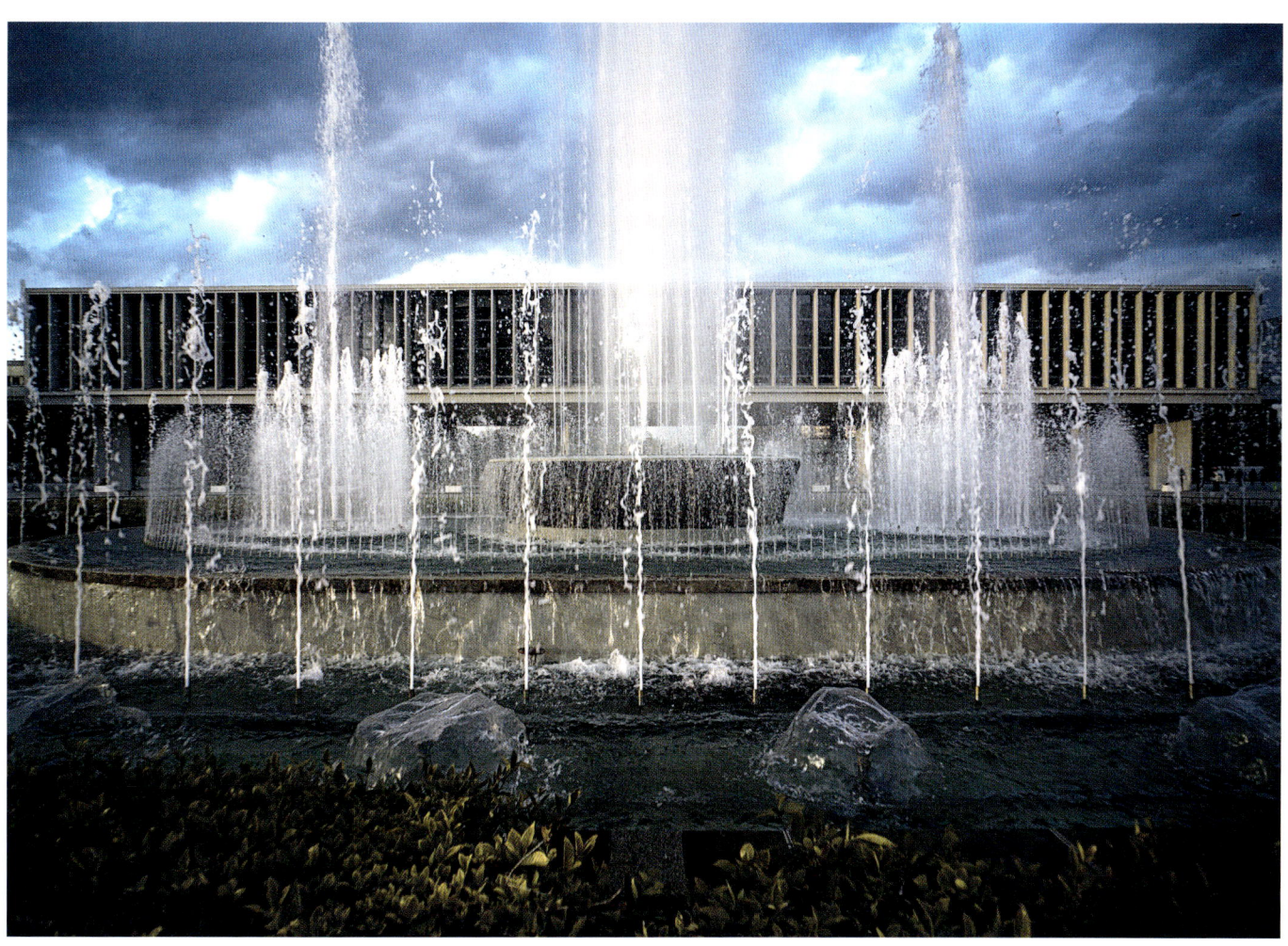

KONAN WARD CULTURAL CENTER

NIIGATA PREFECTURE · Architect: Chiaki Arai Urban and Architecture Design · Completed 2012

Despite its futuristic façade that might make one think it is better suited for a sci-fi blockbuster than a community hub, the Konan Ward Cultural Center is deeply rooted in a participatory design approach that involves its local community as much as it embraces its avant-garde aesthetics. This cultural nexus, designed by Chiaki Arai, serves as a striking example of how innovative architecture can effectively incorporate public input to reflect and enhance the cultural and social fabric of its locality.

The design process of the Konan Ward Cultural Center was characterized by a series of workshops and meetings where residents could voice their opinions and influence the outcome. This democratic approach ensured that the building was not only a reflection of the architect's vision but also a canvas of the community's collective imagination and needs. It's a place where locals can see their input moulded into concrete, steel and glass, making it a living testament to the area's collaborative spirit.

This method of incorporating public opinion into architectural design is particularly poignant in a region known for its rice wine and rice crackers – products that are themselves the result of careful cultivation and community effort. Just as the fermentation process enhances the flavours of sake, so too does the infusion of local voices enhance the relevance and functionality of the cultural centre. The building, with its futuristic forms and sweeping curves, might look like it's ready to blast off into space, yet it remains firmly grounded in the community's heritage and aspirations.

It's a place where tradition meets modernity, not just in its design but in its daily function – hosting events that range from local rice wine tastings to avant-garde theatre productions. The Konan Ward Cultural Center symbolises the spirit of communal identity and architectural daring, proving that even the most forward-thinking design can have its roots deeply embedded in traditional *mochi* fields.

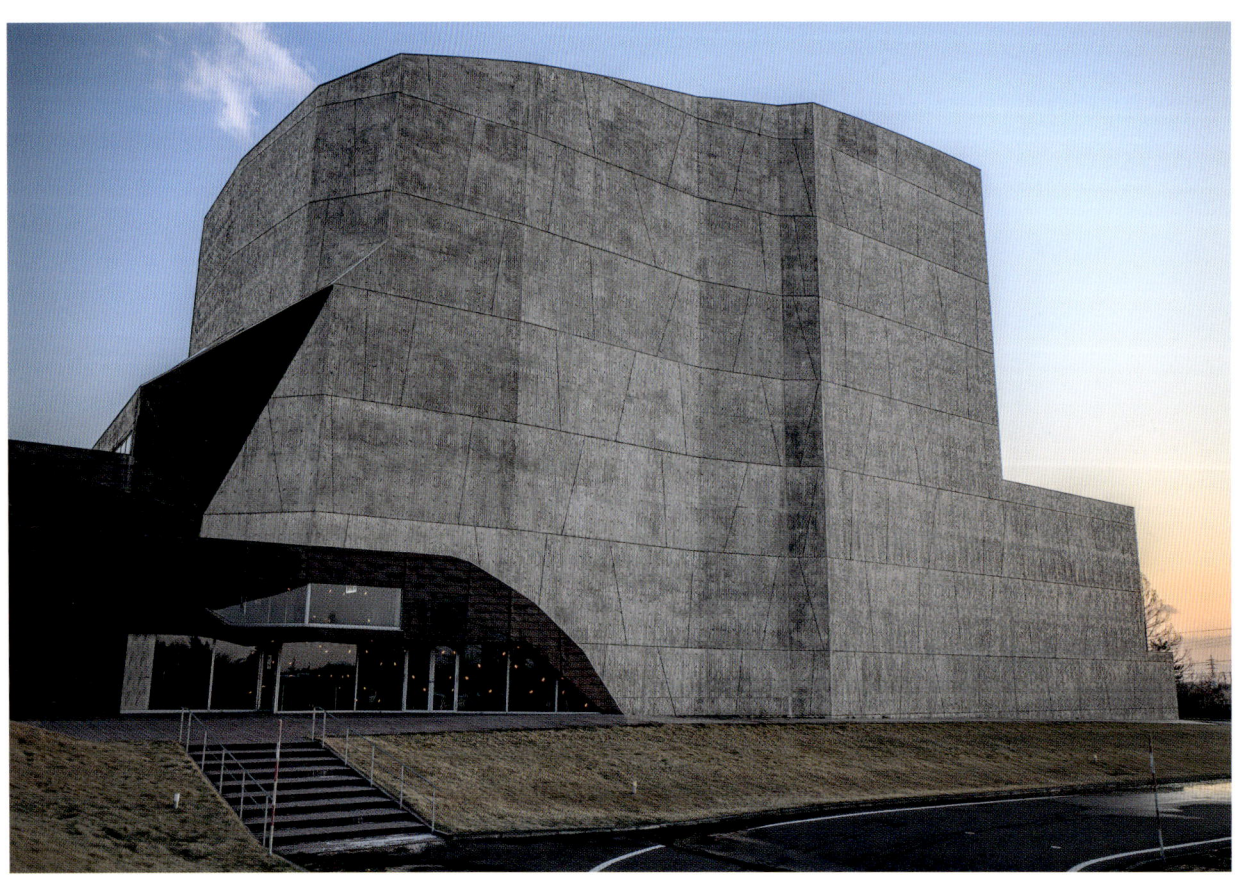

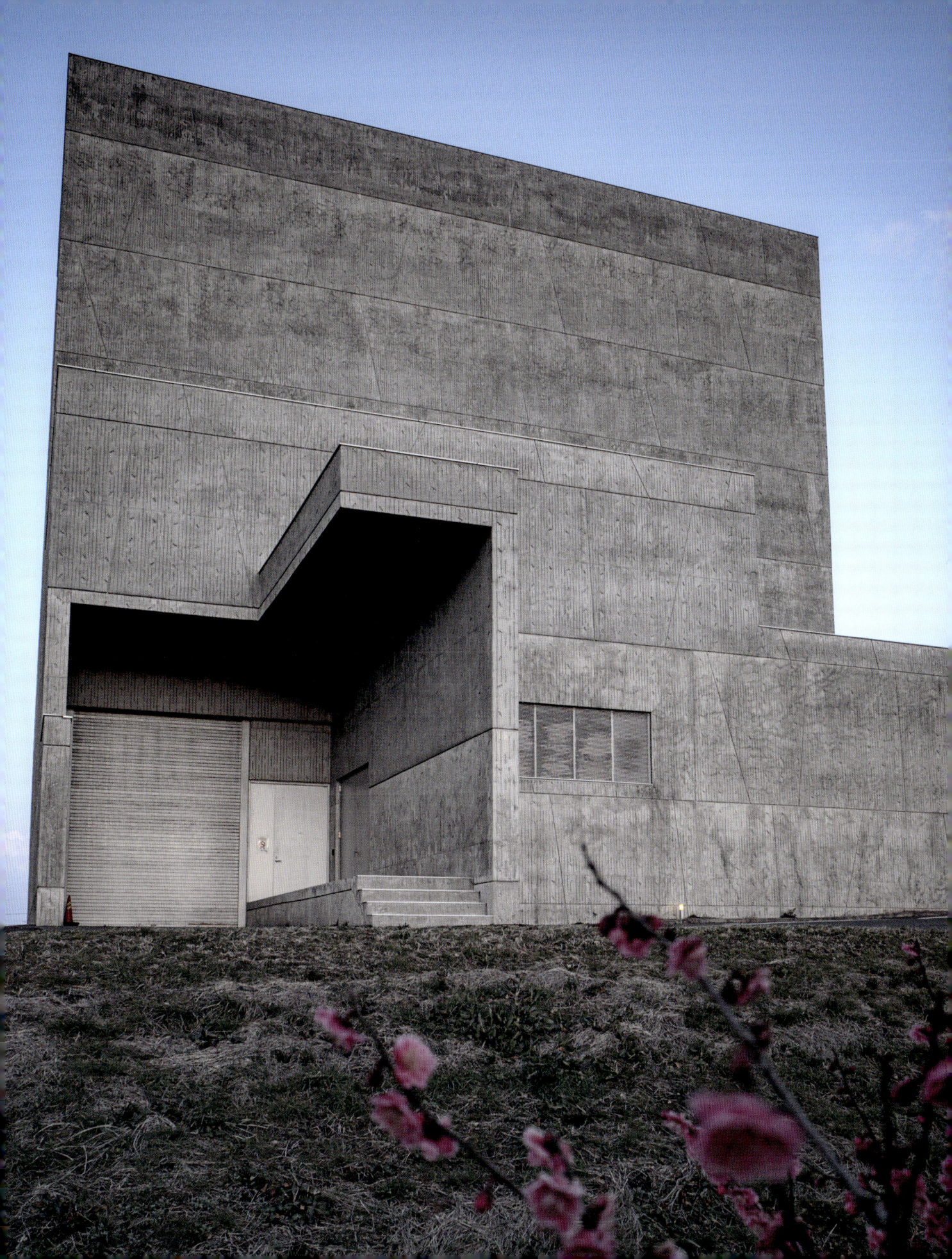

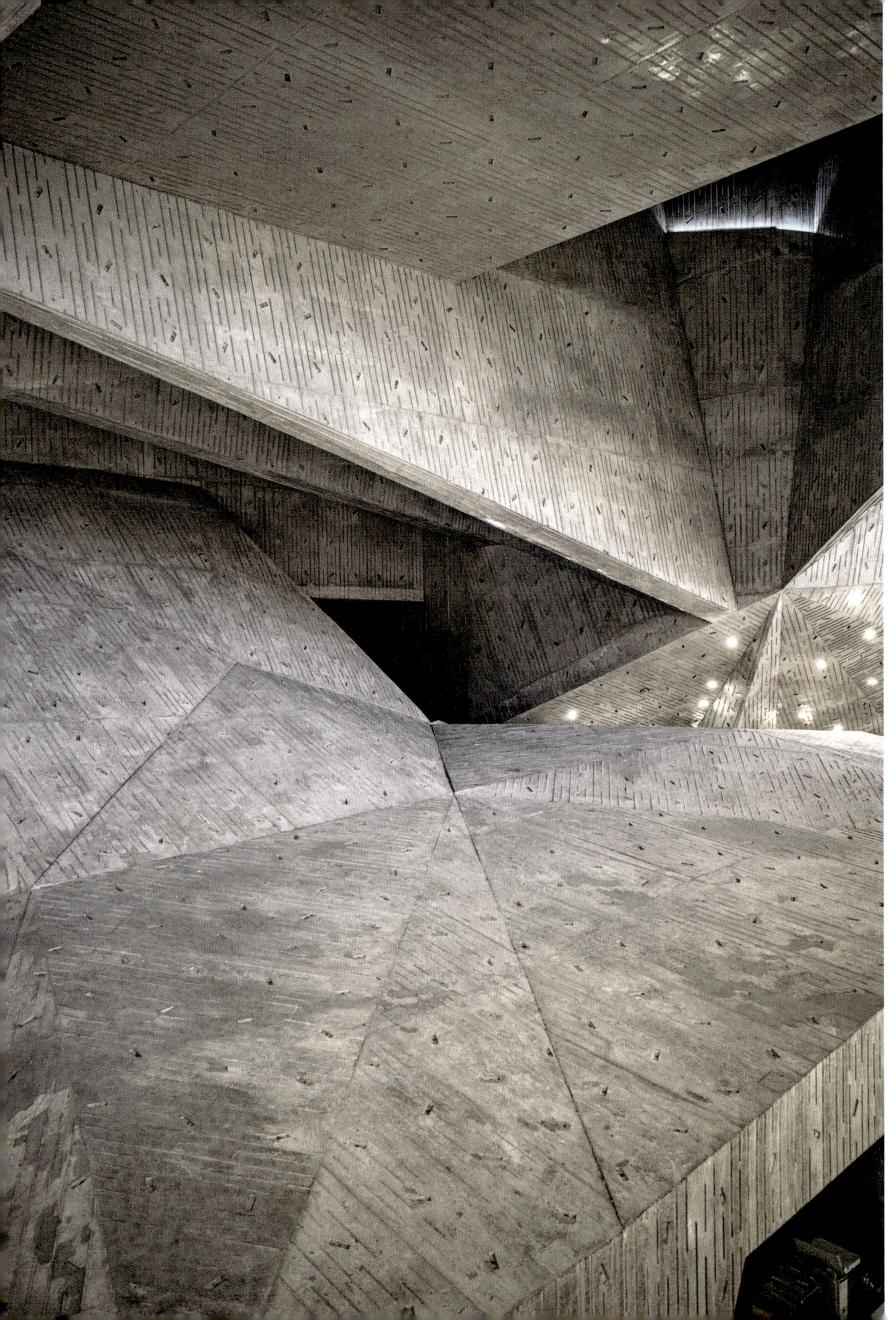

KONAN WARD CULTURAL CENTER

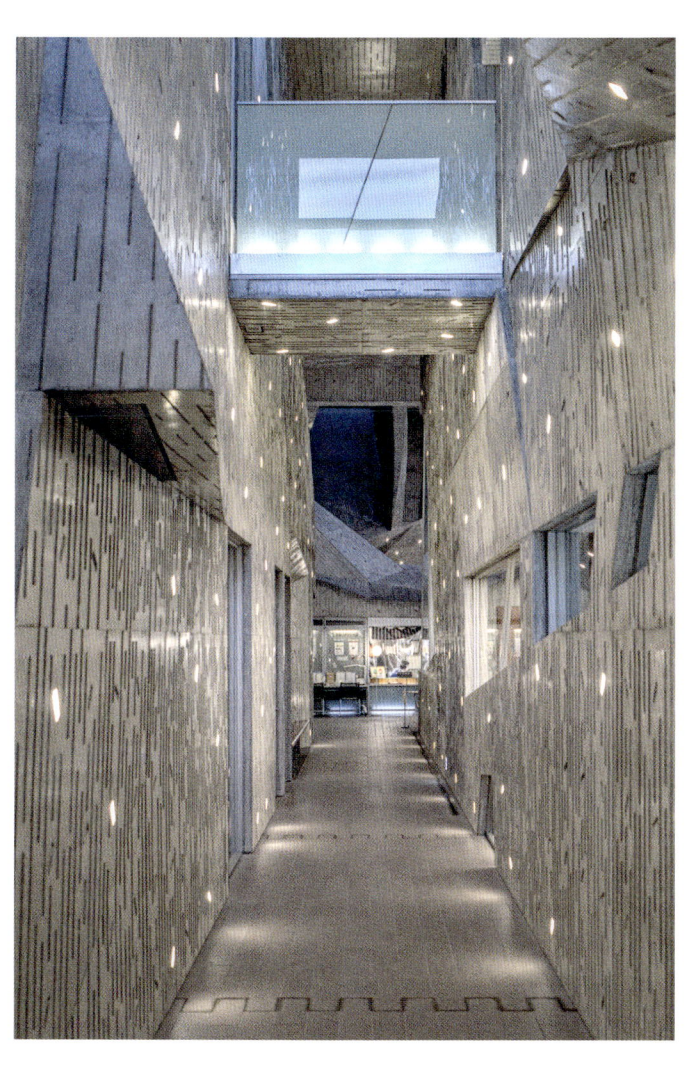
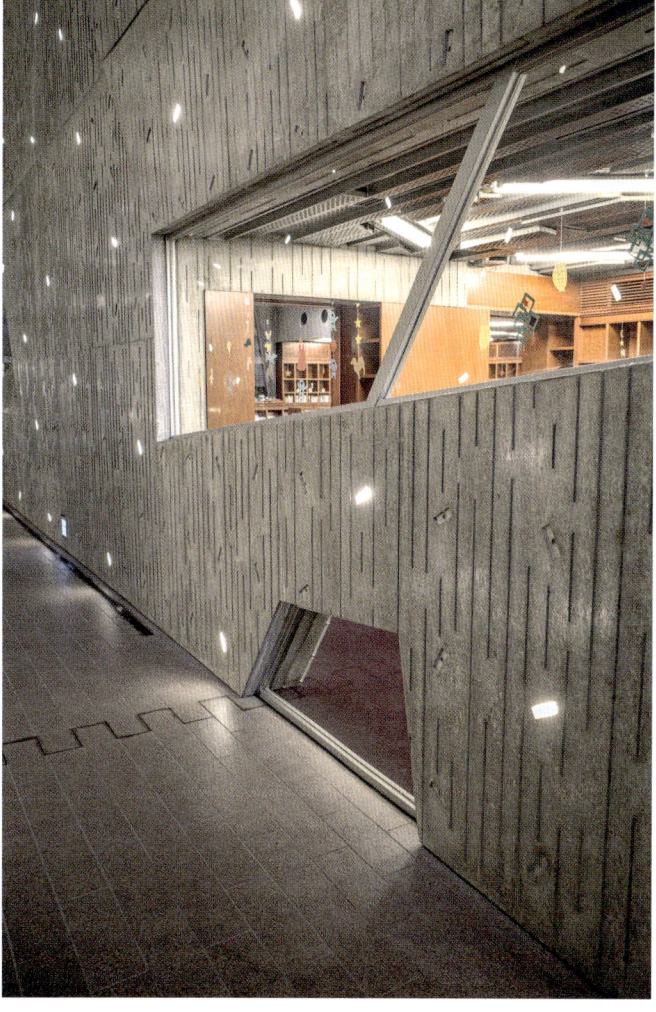

OKINAWAN CEMETERIES

Teenage Mutant Ninja Turtles. Heroes in a half-shell. Turtle power.

Okinawan cemetery homages often mimic turtle backs and the wave-like forms of the sea. Concrete, a durable and readily available material, has been used extensively in these structures long before the advent of Brutalism. It symbolizes strength and permanence.

Turtles here are revered as a symbol of longevity and protection.

Does this design choice reflect a belief that ancestors are like turtles – watching over and protecting their descendants? Maybe not.

In addition to their resemblance to turtle-backs, Okinawan cemeteries can also be seen to mimic the shape of the womb – symbolizing the cycle of life, death, and rebirth in Okinawan spirituality and belief systems. The womb-like structures can be seen as a place of transition, where the souls of the deceased prepare for their journey to the afterlife or their next reincarnation.

The use of concrete in these structures further enhances their symbolism, as concrete is a material that can be moulded and shaped, much like the womb is seen as a vessel for new life. Overall, the mimicry of the womb in Okinawan cemeteries adds a profound layer of meaning to these sacred spaces, emphasizing the spiritual connections between the living and the dead.

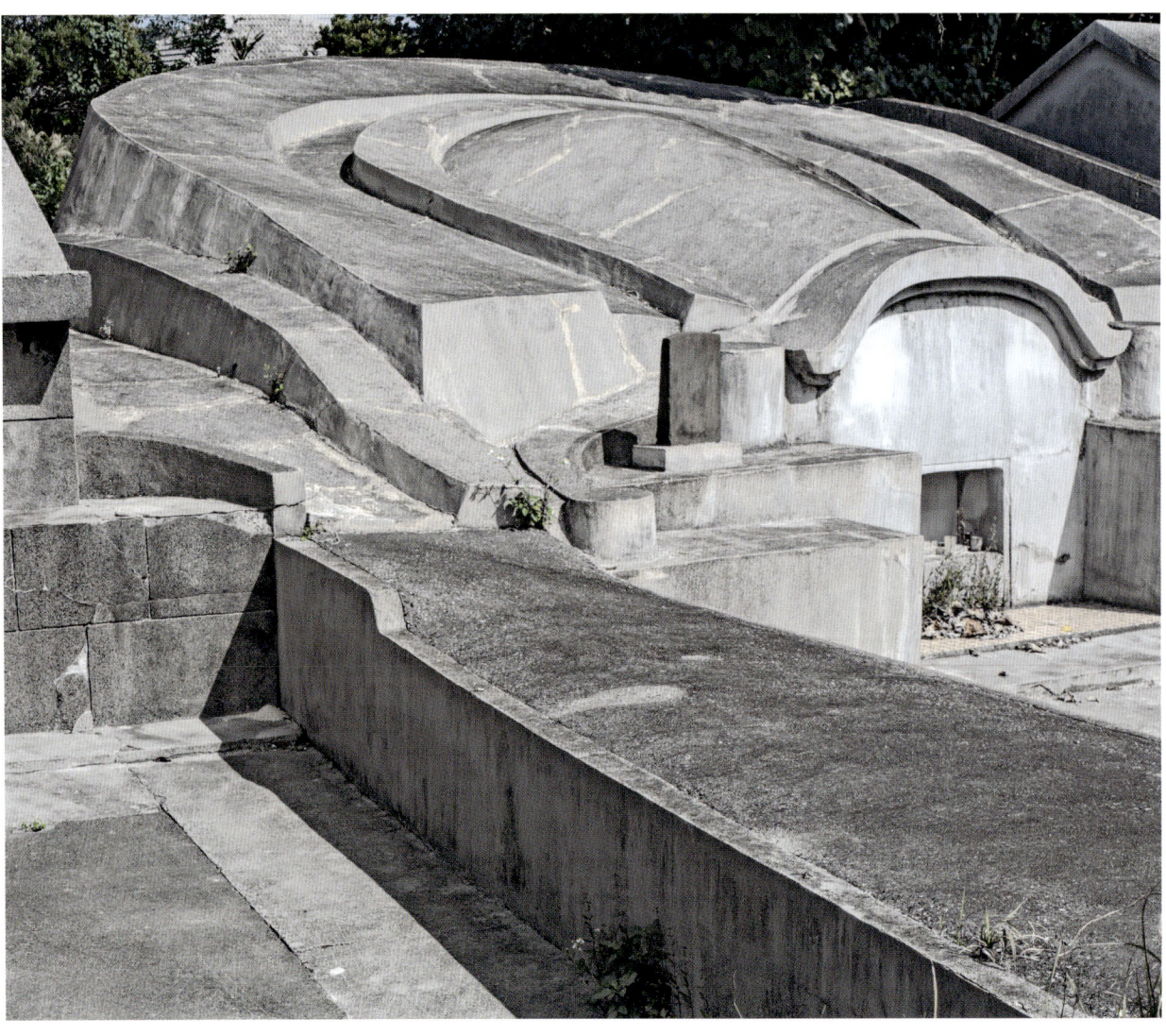

CHICHU ART MUSEUM

NAOSHIMA ISLAND, KAGAWA PREFECTURE · Architect: ANDO Tadao · Completed 2004

The Chichu Art Museum, designed by Tadao Ando, emerges subtly from its location on Naoshima Island, entwining with the landscape in a physical manifestation of Ando's philosophy of "architecture merged into the landscape". An art sanctuary hidden underground, it hosts a permanent collection featuring the distinct works of Claude Monet, Walter de Maria, and James Turrell. The museum's unique approach to exhibition space is embedded in its structure, which delves into the hillside where a salt pan once existed. Ando's design is a deliberate contrast between nature and human intervention, a dialogue between the art within and the natural world outside. The museum's architecture is marked by its use of natural light, which interacts with the artworks and the concrete surfaces to create an ever-changing experience, blurring the boundaries between the art, architecture and the surrounding environment. Visitors to the Chichu Art Museum find themselves on a contemplative journey, not just through art, but also through the essence of space and light, all masterfully orchestrated by Ando's architectural prowess.

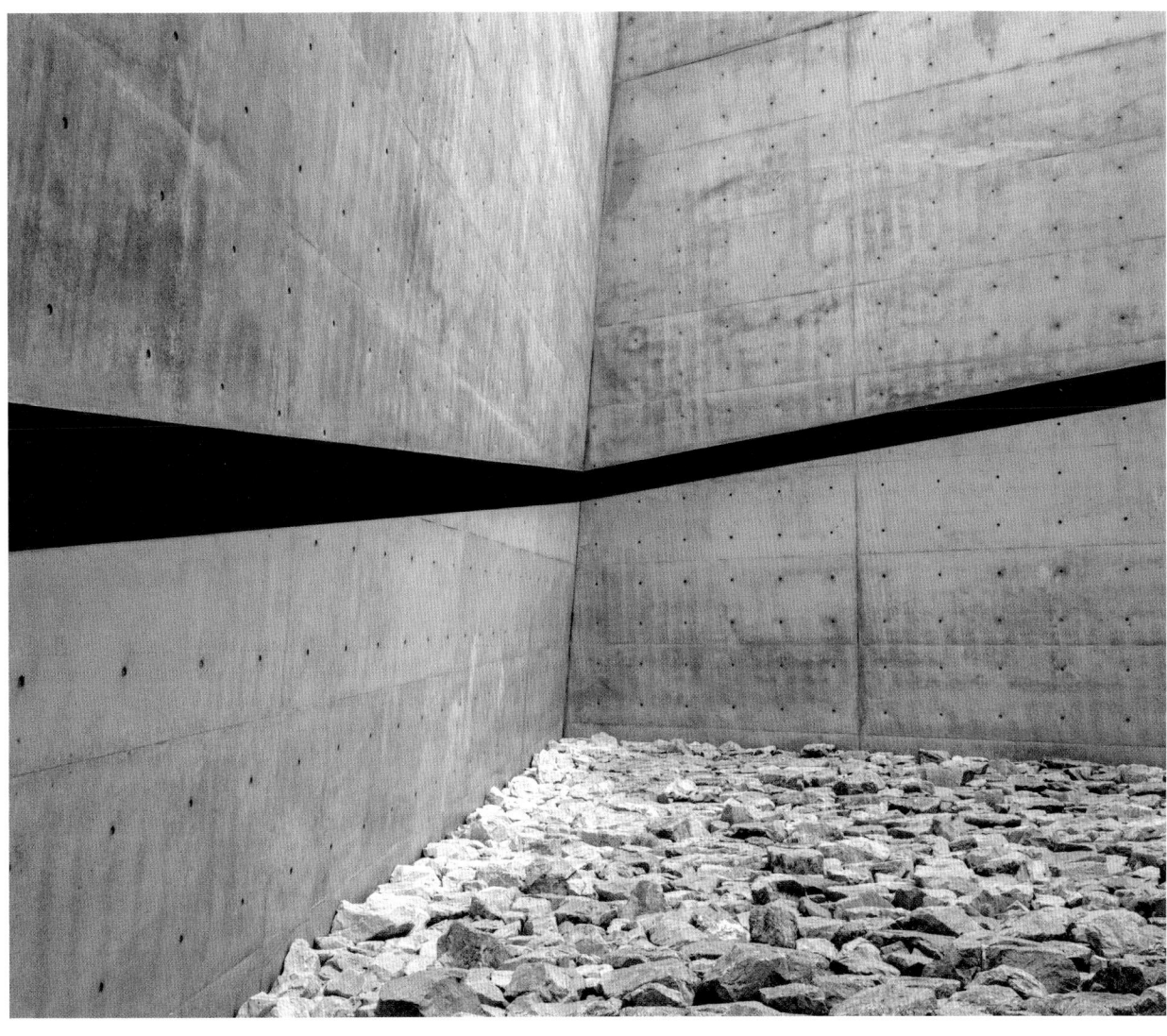

LABOR WELFARE OFFICE

NAGO, OKINAWA · Architect: Chinen Architectural Design Office · Completed 1994

Here presented is a unique fusion of Art Deco elegance and Brutalist strength, encapsulating a design that mirrors the industrious spirit of an insect. This architectural amalgamation brings together curved concrete shells and expansive glass, much like the exoskeleton of a hardworking beetle, symbolizing the centre's dedication to labour welfare. While its style diverges from the typical angular Brutalism seen in other local structures, suggesting a softer, more organic approach, it doesn't stray from the essence of resilience and utility. The building's design cleverly nods to the notion of "hard labour" – both through its robust materiality reminiscent of Brutalist endurance and the flowing curves that echo the agility of an insect. This blend ensures the centre remains a distinctive yet harmonious part of Okinawa's architectural landscape, proving that even in the realm of concrete jungles, there's room for inspired reinterpretation of form and function.

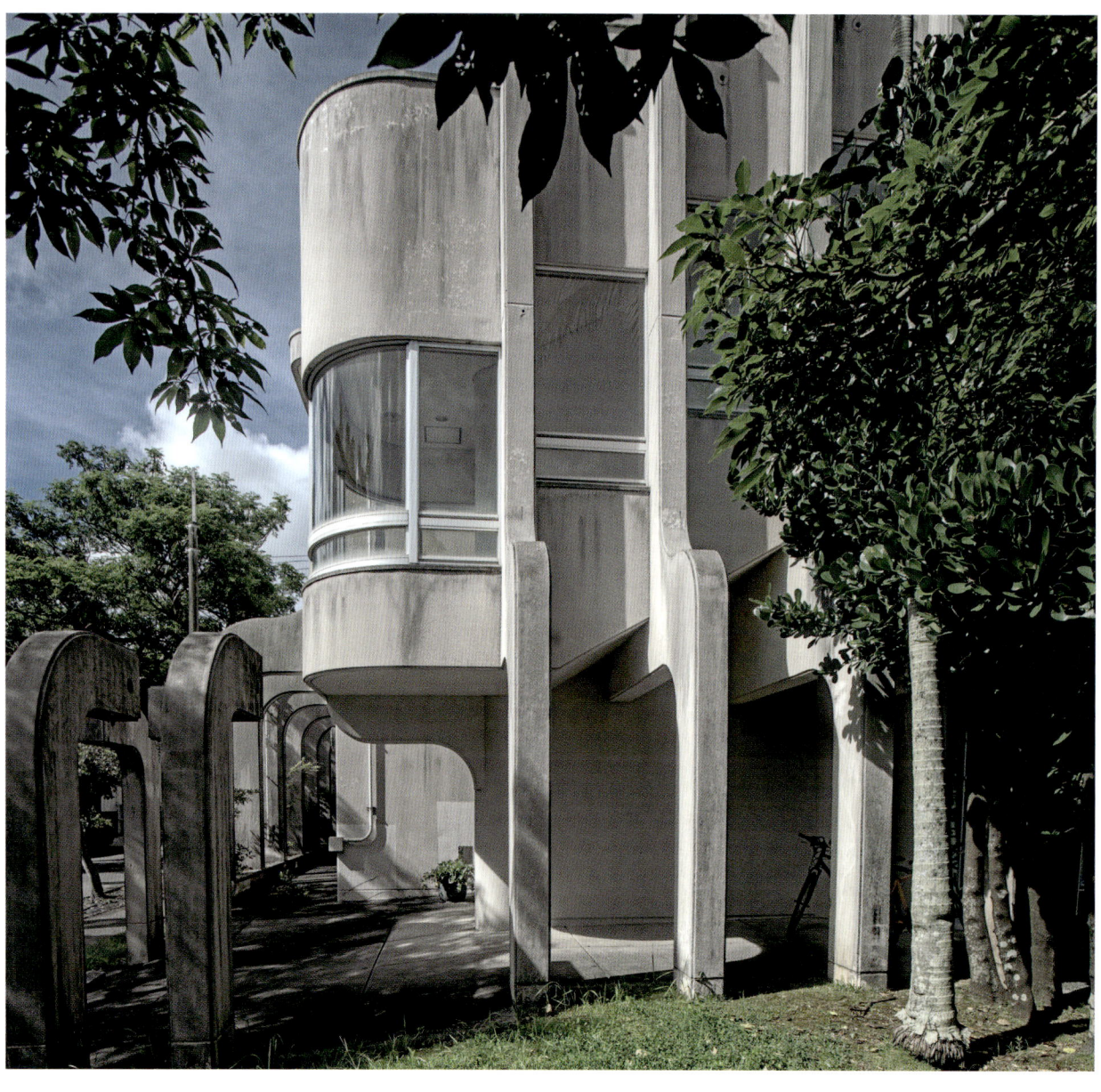

RESORT COMPLEX

SESOKO ISLAND, OKINAWA · Architect: SHIKAUCHI Takeshi · Completed 2020

In this Okinawan resort, the integration of contemporary design with elements of traditional Japanese architecture is suavely achieved through the use of expansive concrete walls. These walls are not just structural; they embody the Japanese aesthetic of *shakkei*, or borrowed scenery, by framing and enhancing a tranquil pool area, thus creating an enclosed, peaceful oasis reminiscent of serene Zen gardens. Concrete is especially suited for this purpose in Okinawa, providing resilience against the humid, tropical climate while maintaining a minimalistic elegance that is a hallmark of Japanese design. This blend of functionality and form makes the resort a modern-day sanctuary, offering guests a secluded retreat that mirrors the isolated tranquillity of historic Japanese estates. This architectural approach transforms a simple holiday into an immersive experience, where the barriers between the bustling outside world and peaceful inner sanctum encourage relaxation and reflection, akin to a verdant escape within ancient walled compounds.

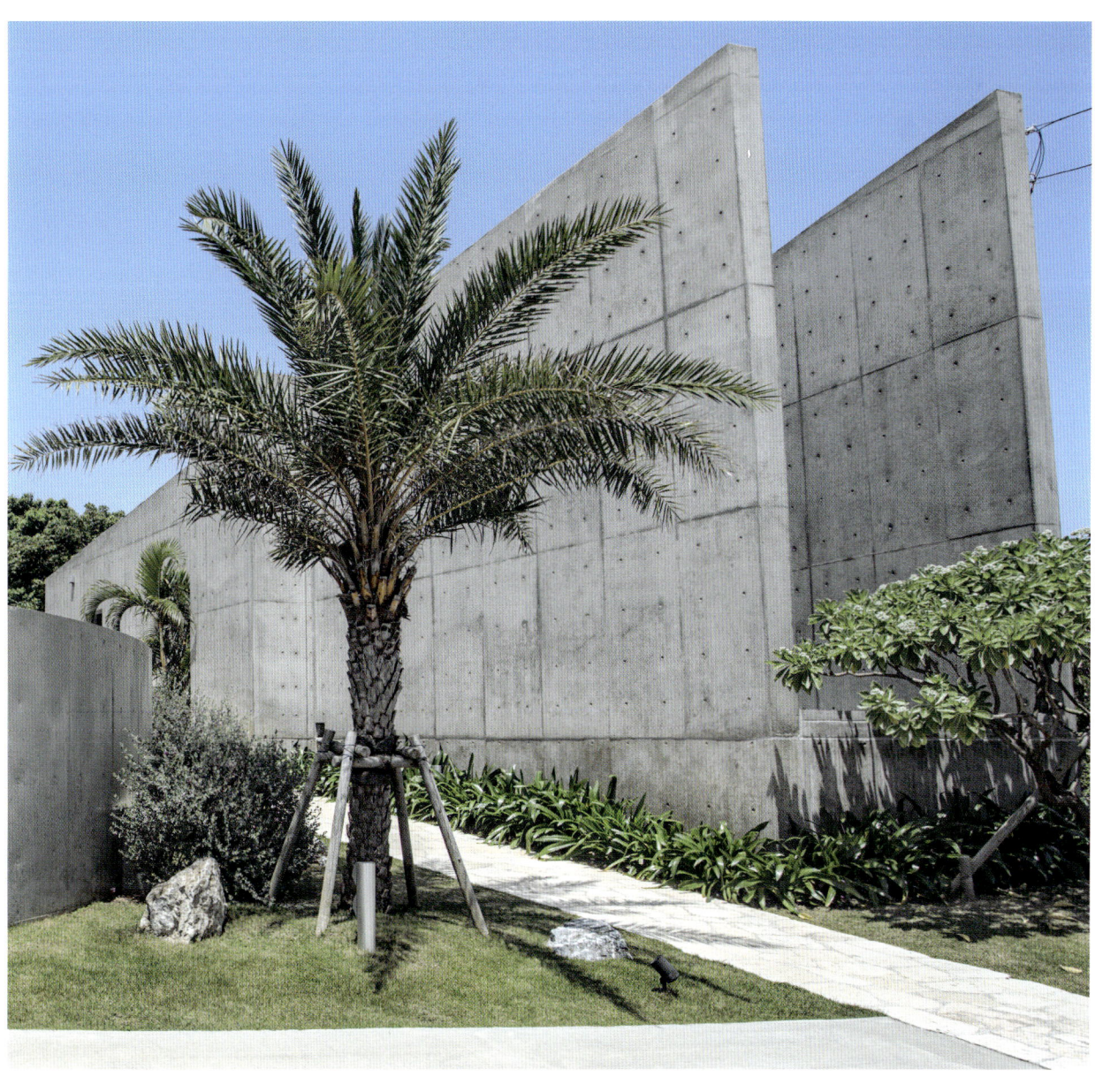

MEMORIAL CATHEDRAL OF WORLD PEACE

HIROSHIMA · Architect: MURANO Togo · Completed 1954

Rising from the devastating aftermath of the atomic bombing on 6 August 1945, which obliterated the original Noboricho parish church, the Memorial Cathedral of World Peace in Hiroshima represents resilience and reconciliation. Launched through a design competition that attracted 177 entries from prominent Japanese architects like Kenzo Tange and Kunio Maekawa, the project found its architect in an unexpected twist – Togo Murano, a jury member, took the helm of the design. Influenced by Auguste Perret, a pioneer in using reinforced concrete, Murano embraced a robust post-and-beam concrete framework complemented by internal panels that echo traditional Japanese architectural sensibilities. The cathedral's brick infills, incorporating ashes from the destructive impact of the atomic bomb, lend a textured depth to its façade. Murano, an early disciple of Brutalism who later embraced Catholicism, thus crafted a profound synthesis of his architectural and spiritual journeys within this monumental edifice.

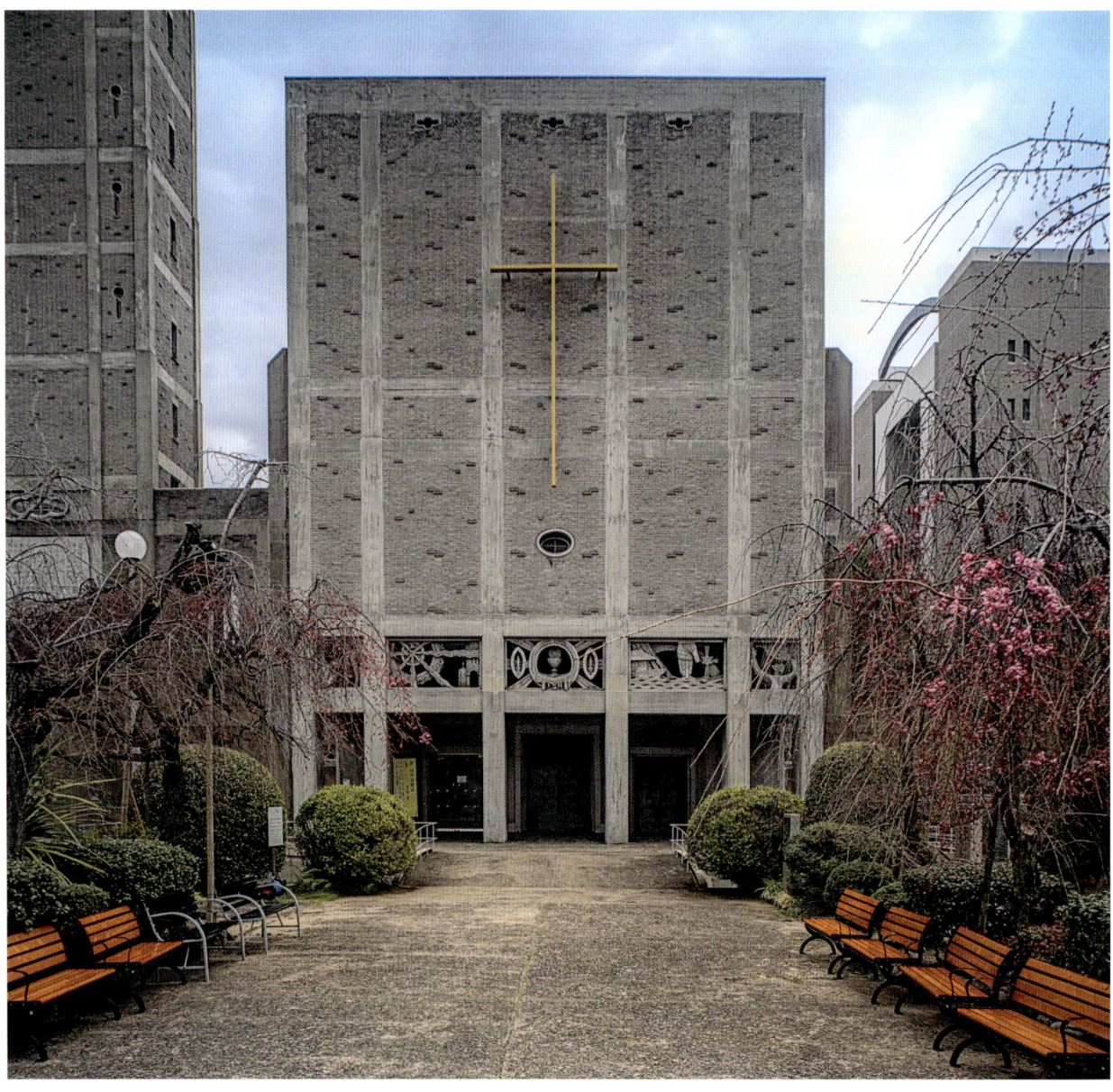

PRIVATE RESIDENCE

OKINAWA

This private residence flaunts a harmonious blend of modern and traditional Japanese architectural elements. The use of exposed concrete is a nod to modernist materials, while the wooden door and trim introduce a traditional material known for its importance in Japanese architecture, suggesting a respect for nature and simplicity. The concrete's raw texture contrasts with the warm tones of the wood, which may also be reflecting the Japanese aesthetic principle of *wabi-sabi*, embracing the beauty of imperfection and transience.

The asymmetry of the window placement aligns with the Japanese design philosophy, where asymmetry and balance rather than symmetry are often more aesthetically valued. The stepping stones leading to the entrance echo the *engawa* concept in traditional Japanese homes – a transitional space between the outside and inside.

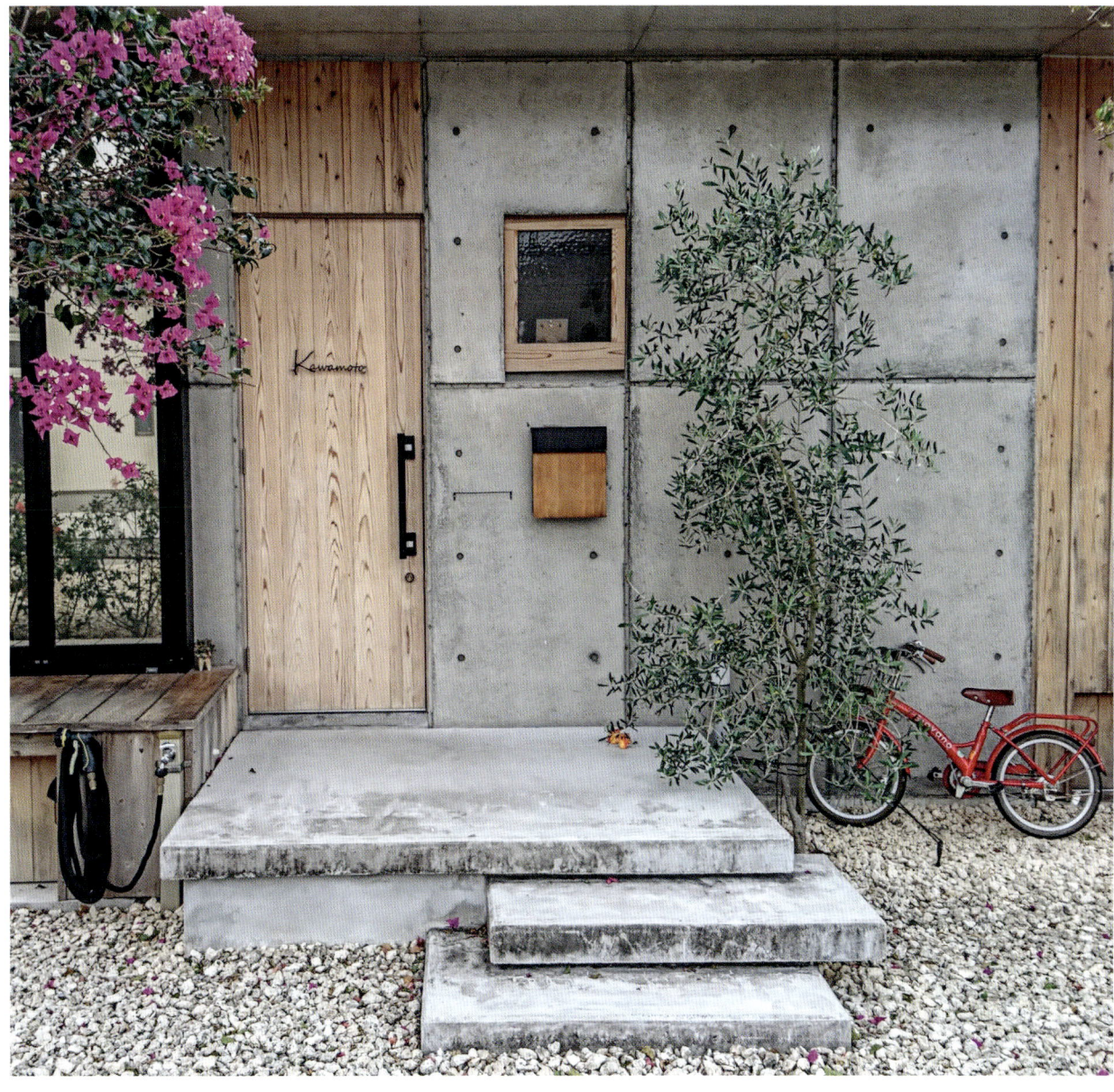

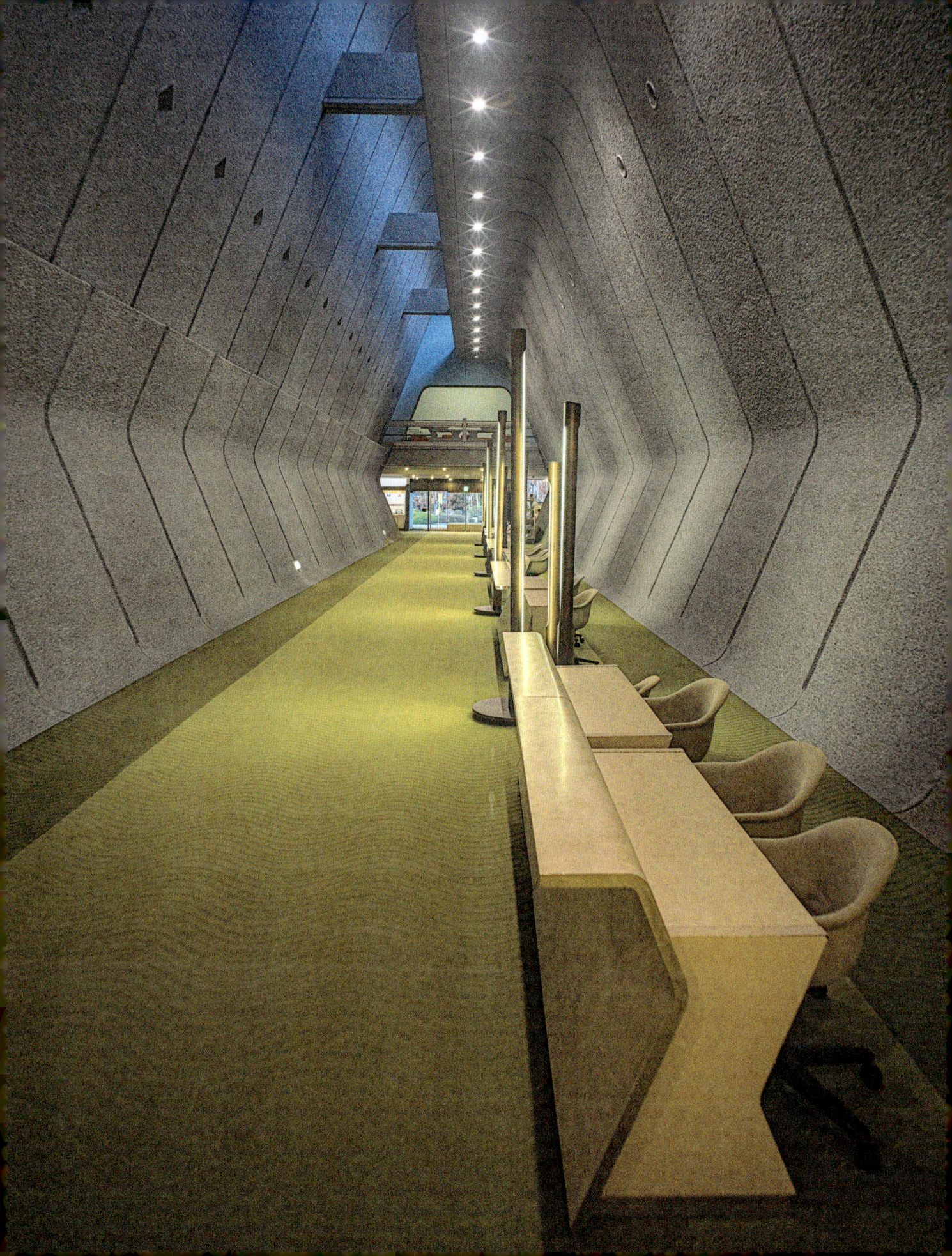

KYOTO INTERNATIONAL CONFERENCE CENTER

KYOTO · Architect: OTANI Sachio · Completed 1966

Enshrined amidst Kyoto's venerable aura, the Kyoto International Conference Center, completed in 1966 by Sachio Otani, straddles the architectural zeitgeist of its time. This edifice stirs a lively discourse: Does it belong to the Brutalist canon, or does it bear the hallmark of Metabolist architecture?

The centre's silhouette, a composition of bold geometric lines and the stark honesty of exposed concrete, channels the Brutalist ethos. Its colossal, forthright forms stand in sharp relief to Kyoto's delicate tapestry, an assertion of Brutalism's unapologetic gravitas.

Yet, within its robust frame, the structure nurtures the flexible, organic essence of Metabolism – a Japanese architectural vanguard of the 1960s. The centre's design, a tessellation of modular units and transformable spaces, breathes the Metabolist vision of perpetual evolution.

Influenced by youthful memories of the grandeur of Frank Lloyd Wright's Imperial Hotel lobby in Tokyo, Otani infused the Kyoto International Conference Center with an assortment of spaces designed to encourage casual dialogue and exchange. He envisioned lobbies, foyers and staircases complete with nooks for conversation, recognizing these as vital for the informal interactions that are the lifeblood of any conference hub. Remarkably, such communal areas constitute 70 per cent of the building's total space.

The duality of the Kyoto International Conference Center – its Brutalist skin married to a Metabolist soul – fuels an ongoing architectural debate. Otani's narrative, honed under Kenzo Tange, crafts a symbiosis of Western modernism and Japanese storytelling. Echoes of Ise Jingu's sanctity, the Gassho-style farmhouses' pragmatism, and even the poetic functionality of rice-drying racks, permeate his design.

It is in this synthesis of global and local dialects that Otani's interpretation diverges from Tange's. While Tange interlaced Western motifs with Japanese symbolism, Otani's vernacular is distinctively more Nipponese, his Brutalist vocabulary narrating a uniquely Japanese tale. This multifaceted approach to design renders the Kyoto International Conference Center not just a site of international discourse but also a monument of architectural introspection – a confluence of two potent forces in modern architecture.

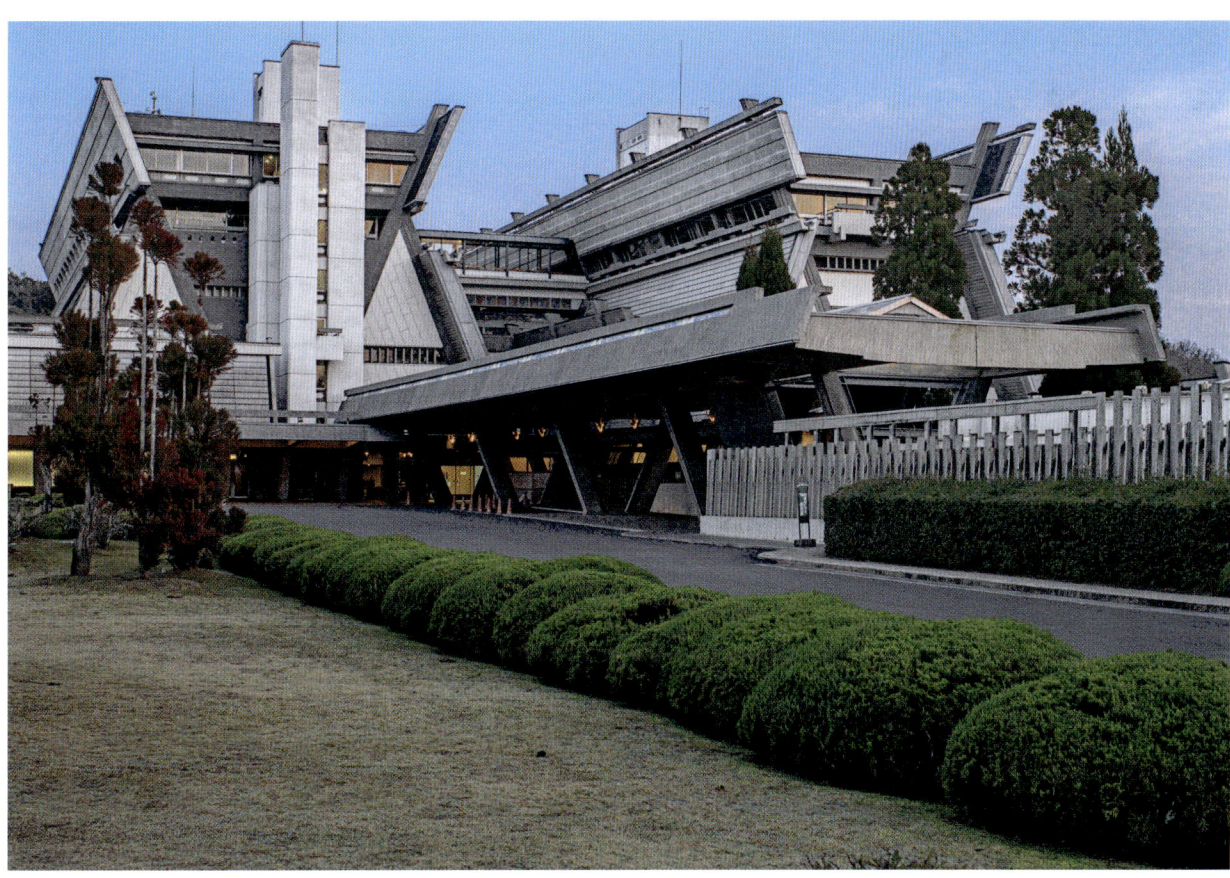

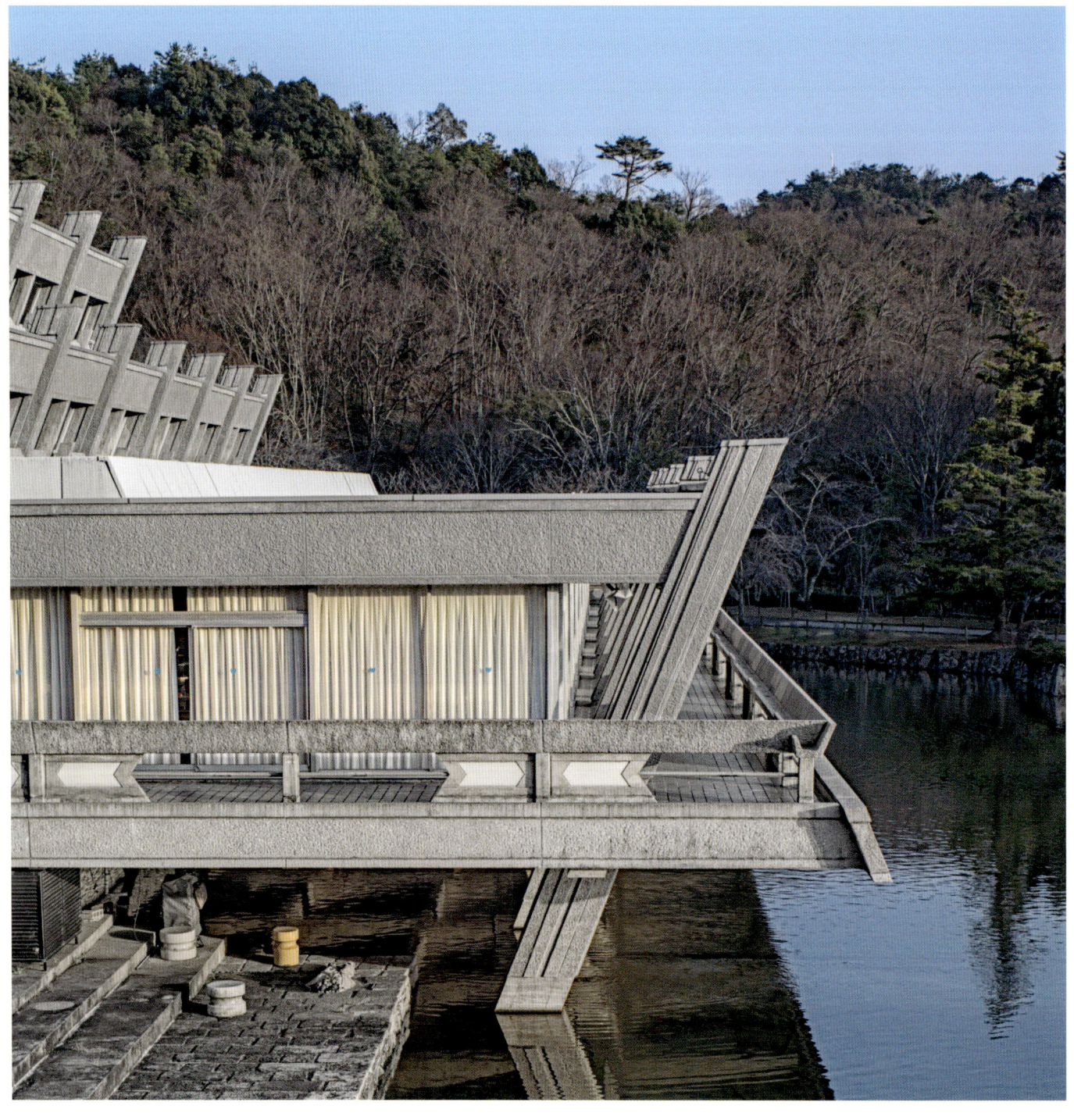

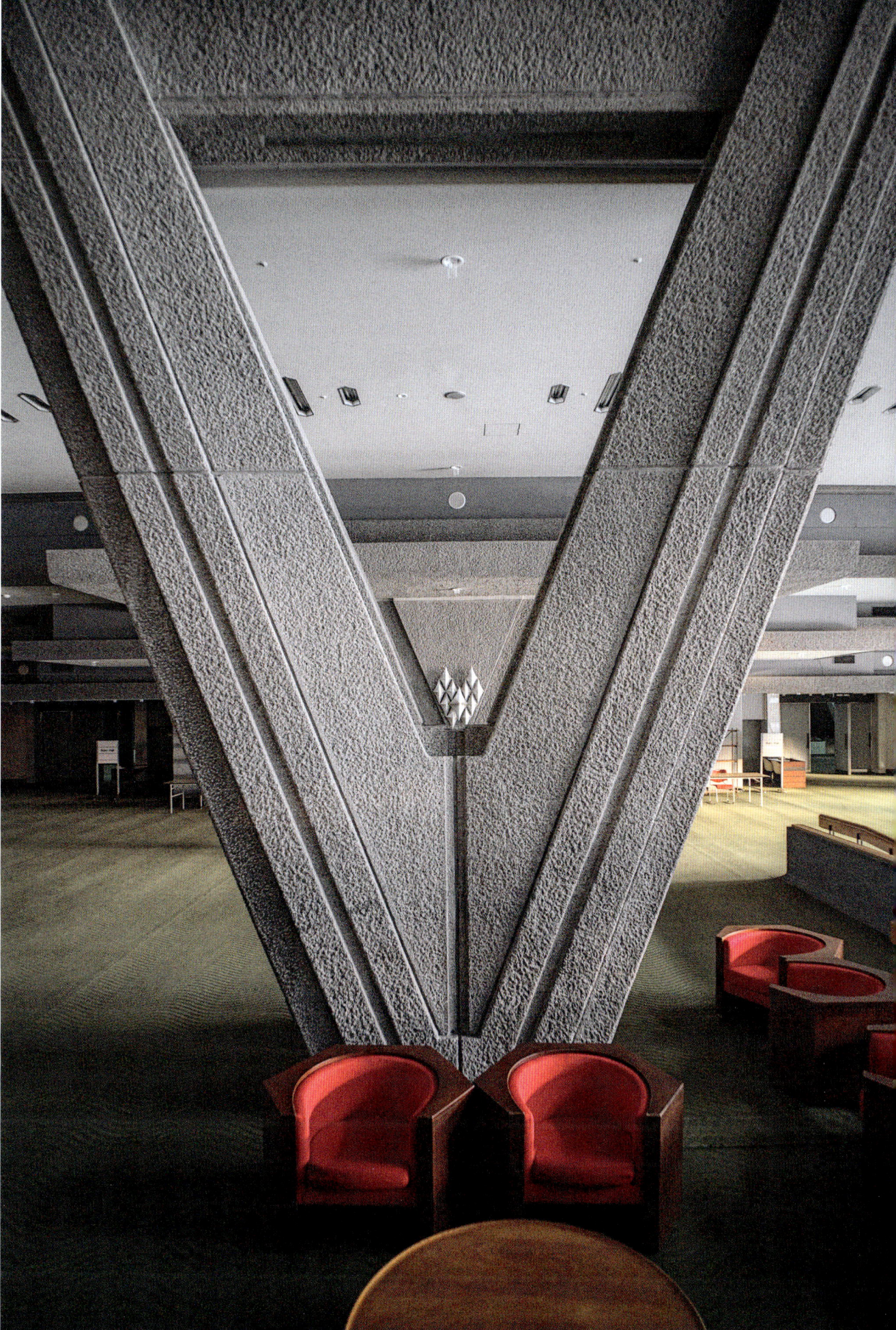

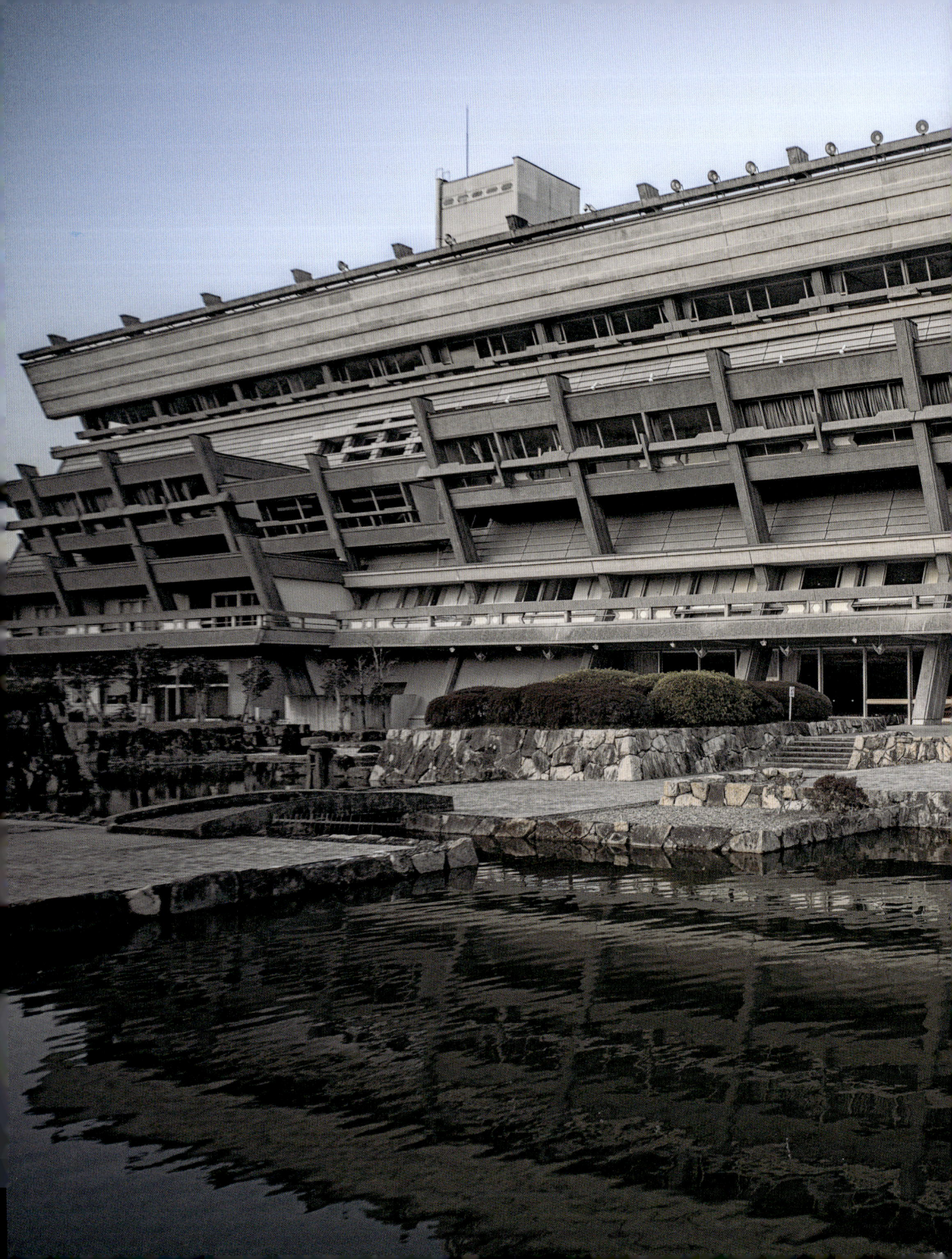

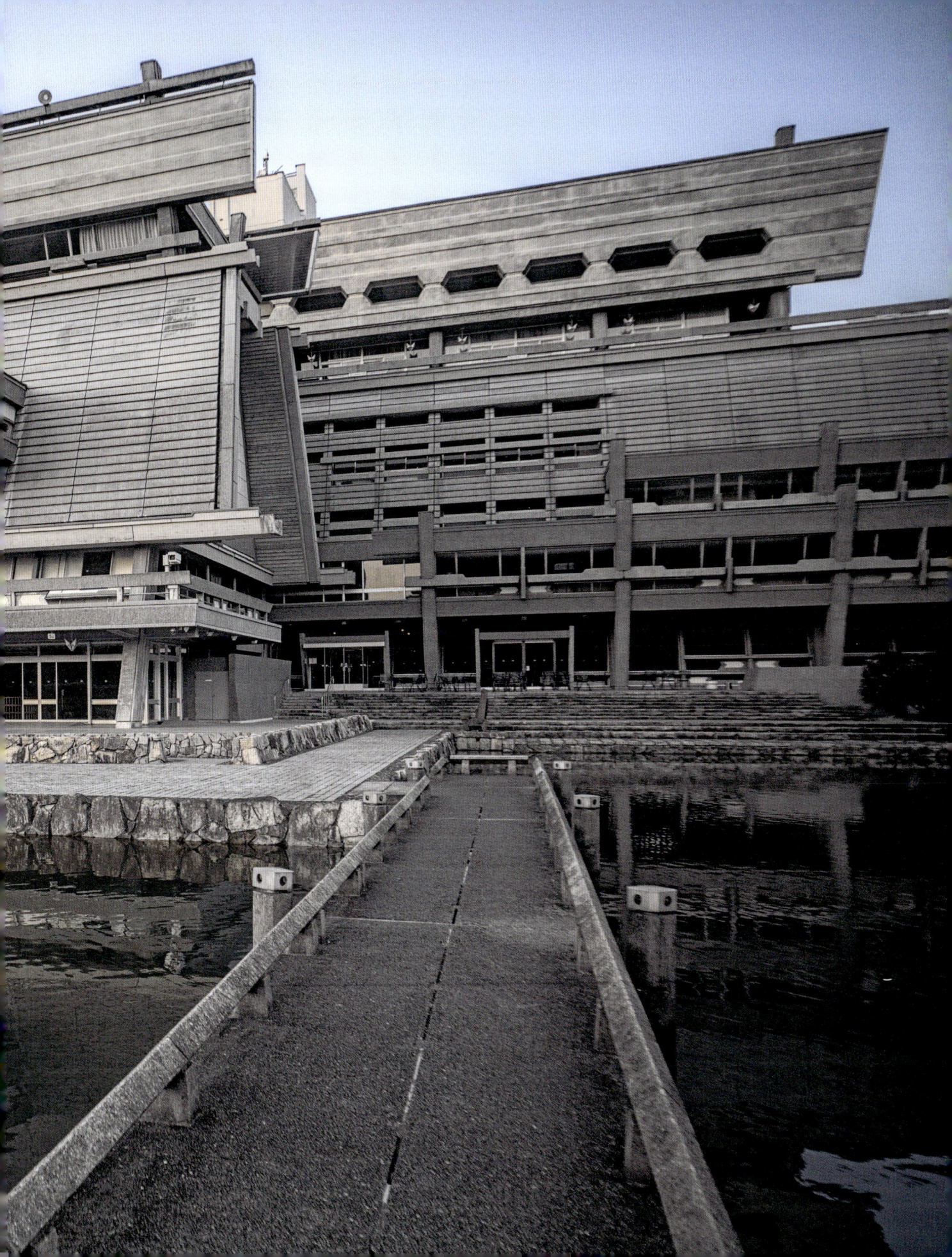

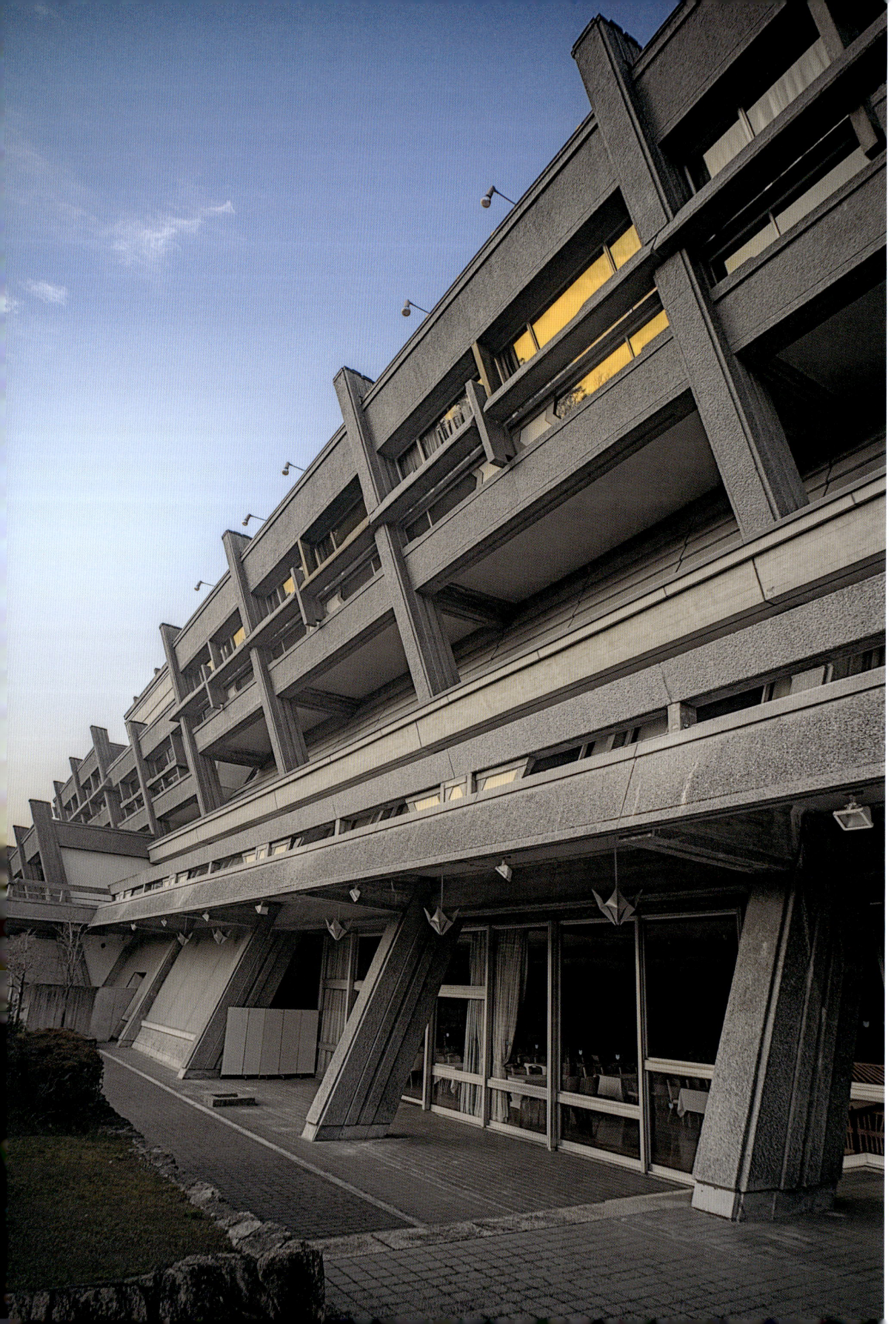

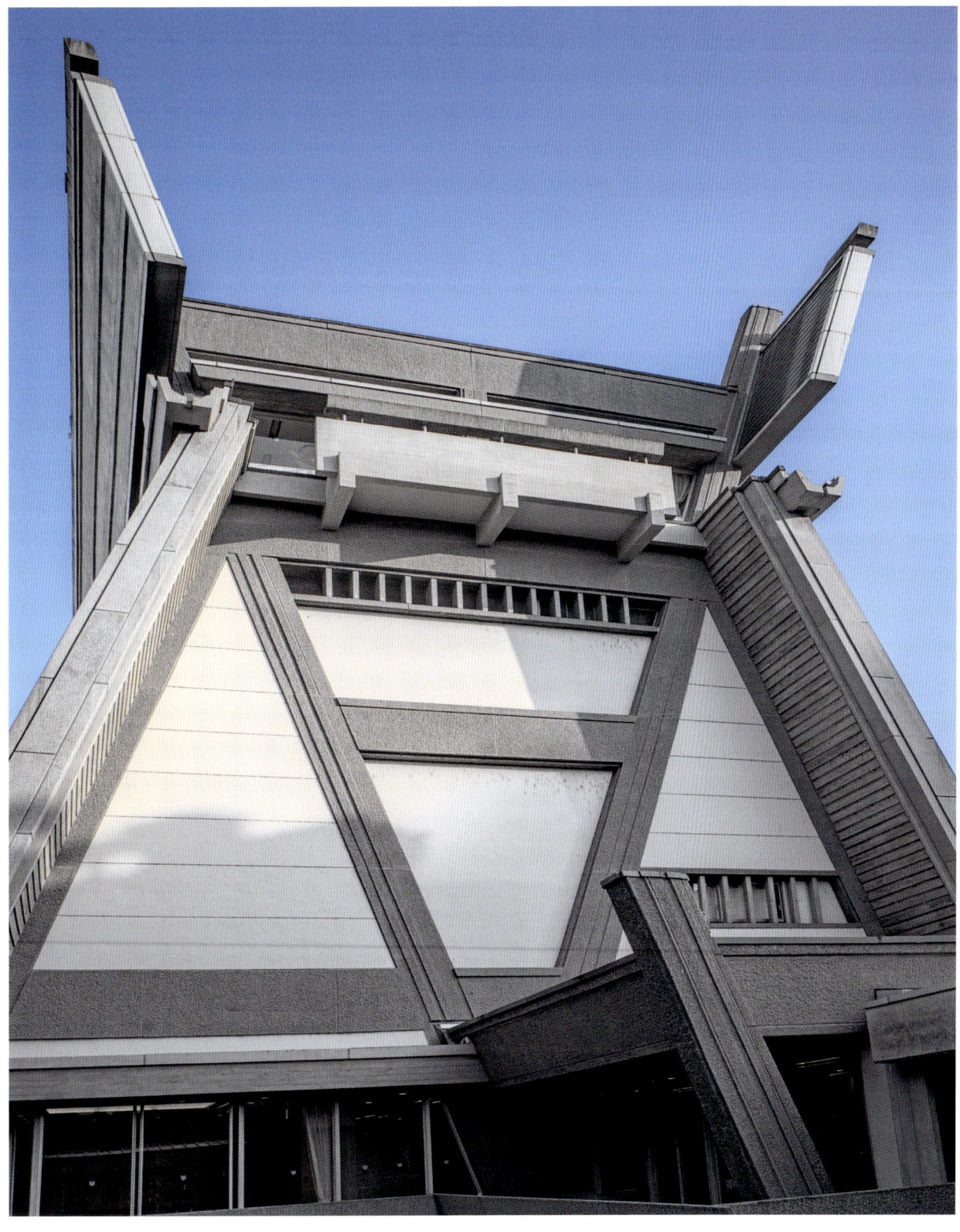

NAGANO OLYMPIC STADIUM

NAGANO · Architect: Rui Design Office · Completed 1998

This venue is a perfect fusion of Brutalist architecture and traditional Japanese aesthetics, drawing heavily from the Jomon period, which revered nature and its ephemeral beauty epitomized by the cherry blossom.

The stadium's structure is thoughtfully designed to mirror natural elements, with each third-storey block crafted to resemble a cherry blossom petal, and towers evoking the image of a flower's stem. This organic motif extends even to the functional aspects of the building, such as the air vents and bathrooms, which are shaped like budding flowers, symbolizing growth and renewal.

Architects incorporated key elements from Japanese culture including flame earthenware, sacred trees and *torii* gates, using materials like plain finished PCa, concrete and stone to seamlessly blend ancient cultural symbols with modern design principles. The meticulous design process involved extensive sketching and modelling, culminating in a decisive concept meeting with 60 participants who ensured that each architectural element – from staircases to elevator shafts – harmonized with the overall organic theme.

The stadium pays homage to the Jomon culture's harmonious existence with nature, revered in numerous ceremonies and festivals celebrating the cherry blossom. These design choices not only are reflective of Japan's aesthetic values but are also a message of unity and respect for nature to the global community.

Throughout the design and construction phases, the team faced challenges such as adapting the designs to cost constraints and technical limitations, which required abandoning some initial ideas like three-dimensional curved surfaces. Nevertheless, through persistence and creativity, they achieved a design that mimics the softness of flower petals, demonstrating Japan's dedication to blending tradition with modernity and showcasing its architectural prowess on the world stage. The stadium's design, particularly the curved "PCa petals" supported by robust concrete pillars, ensures clarity in layout and safety in evacuation, proving that functional design can also be an artistic expression of cultural pride and technological achievement.

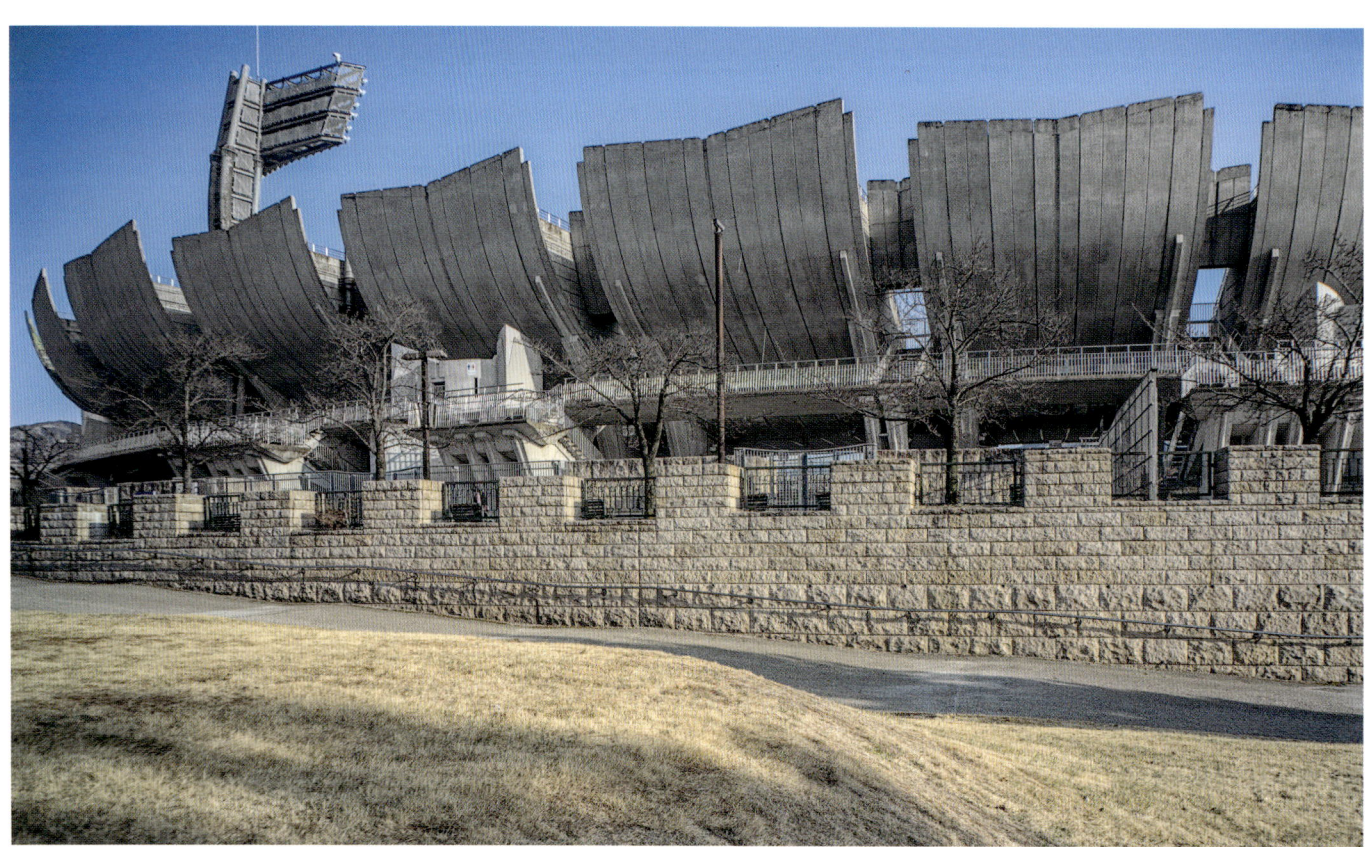

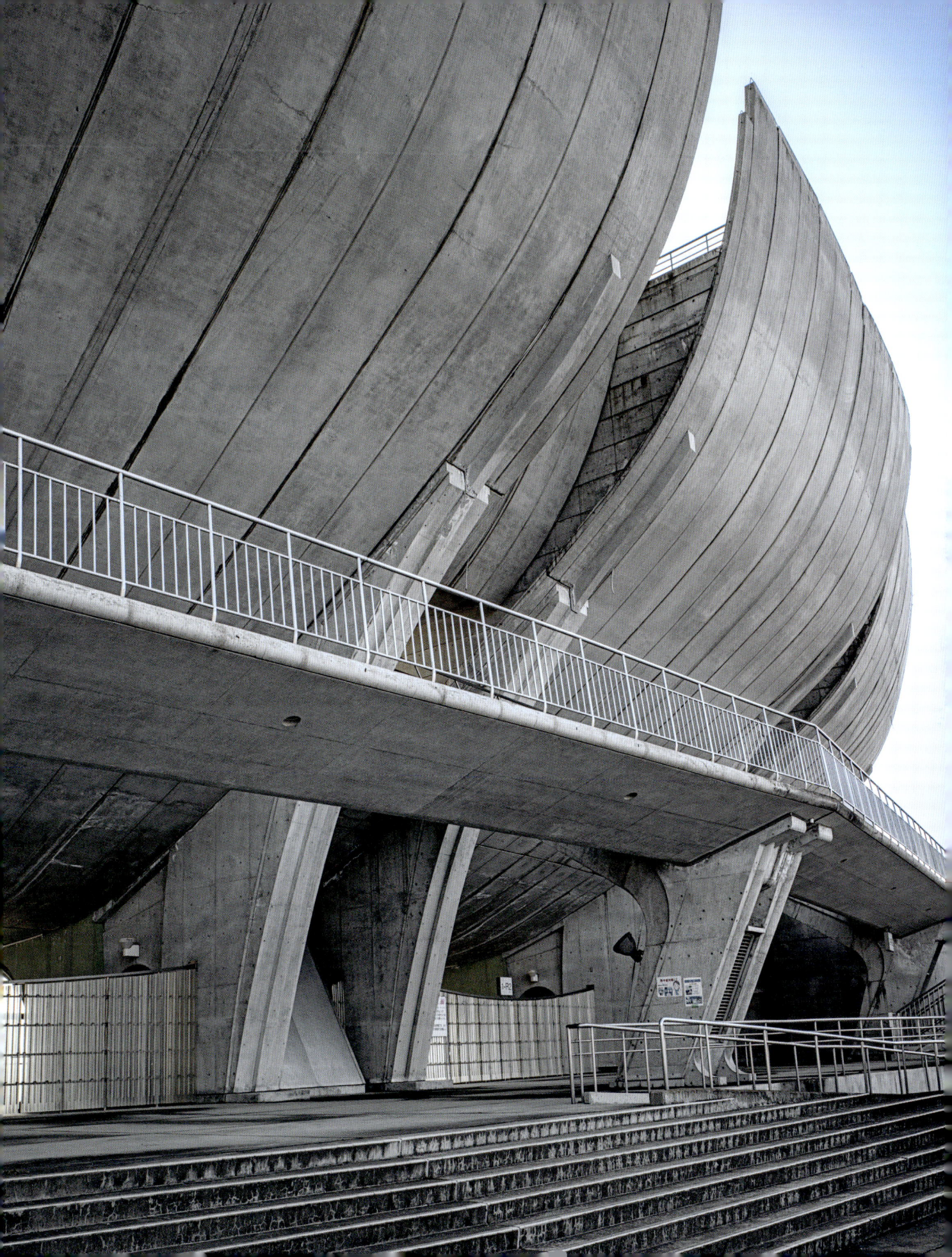

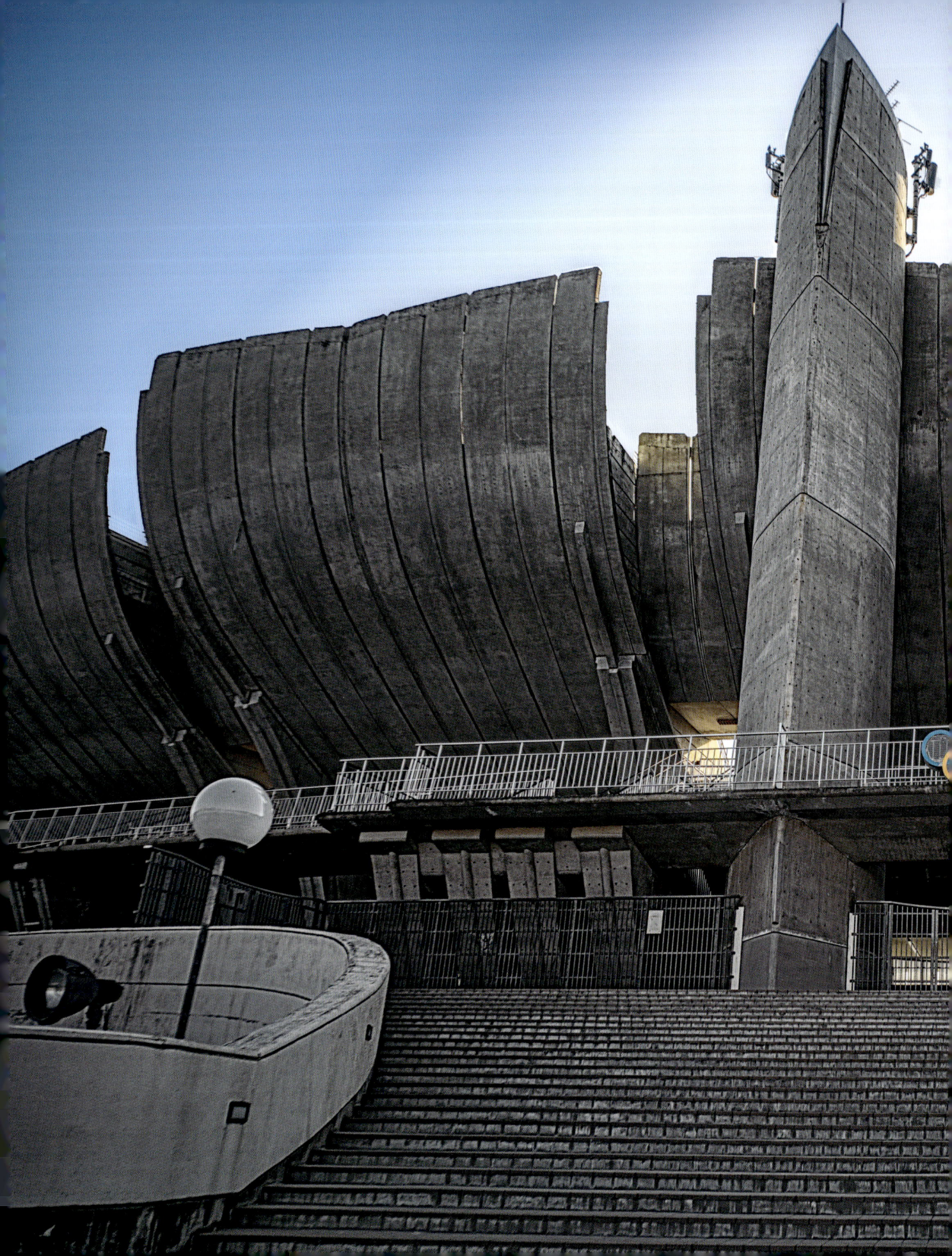

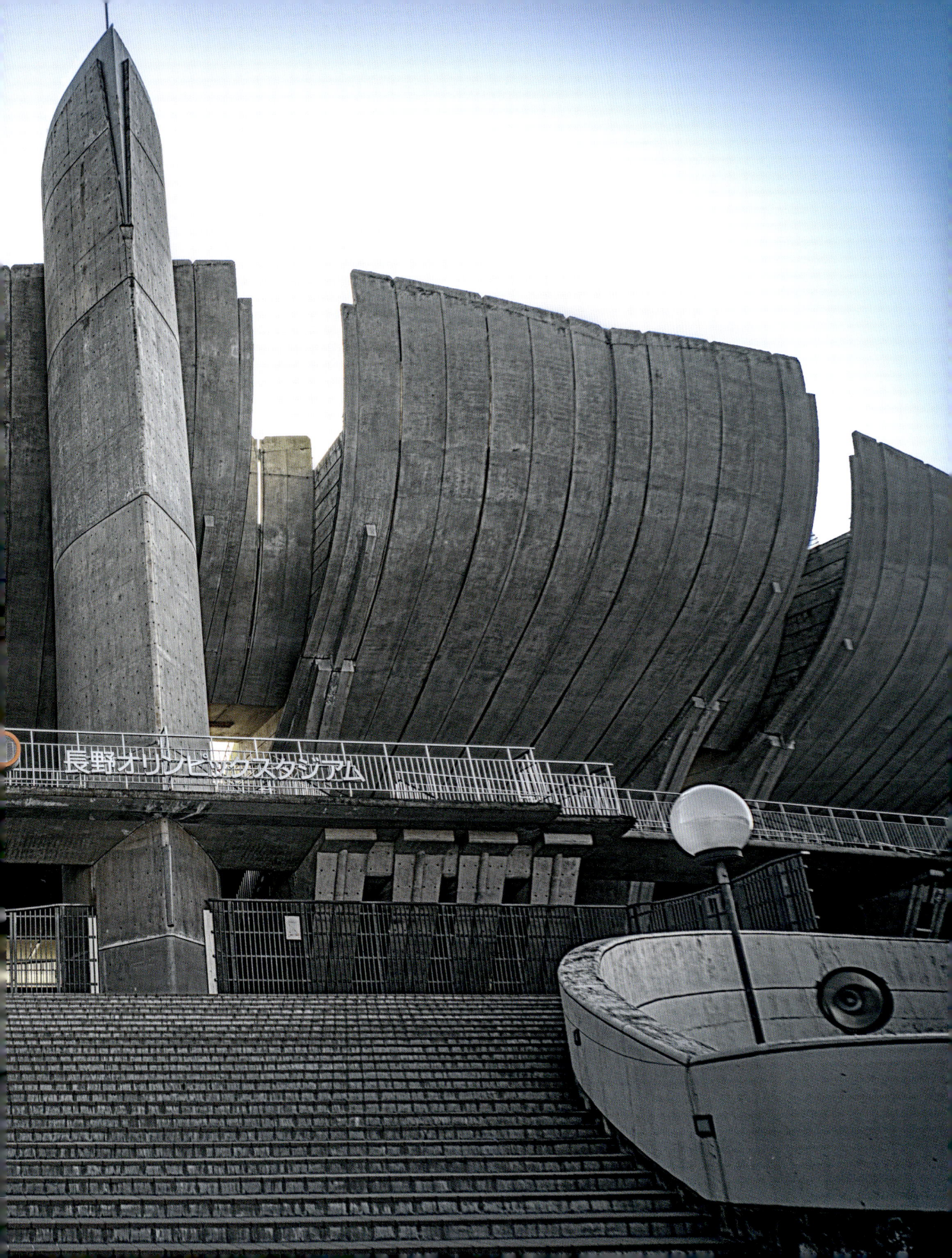

MIXED-USE COMPLEX

NAGO, OKINAWA · Architect: Kuniyoshi Design · Completed 1994

Darth Vader's holiday home? Nah. This striking complex features affordable housing stacked above a ground-floor elderly day care centre. It models Okinawa's social aspect of planning, more characterized elsewhere by the interests of private developers.

The "reverse inequality theory", foundational to Nago City's 1973 "Comprehensive Plan/Basic Concept", challenges development strategies focused solely on income growth. It underscores the significance of community-centred urban planning. In Okinawa, where communal ties and collective wellbeing are highly valued, such approaches are essential. The region emphasizes sustainable development that respects local cultures and environments, promoting a balance between economic growth and community wellbeing. This planning philosophy seeks to create urban spaces that nurture community bonds and ensure equitable access to resources.

That said, a friend of mine had the opportunity to move into one of the apartments but his wife declined, arguing it wasn't close enough to a convenience store. Definitely grounds for divorce.

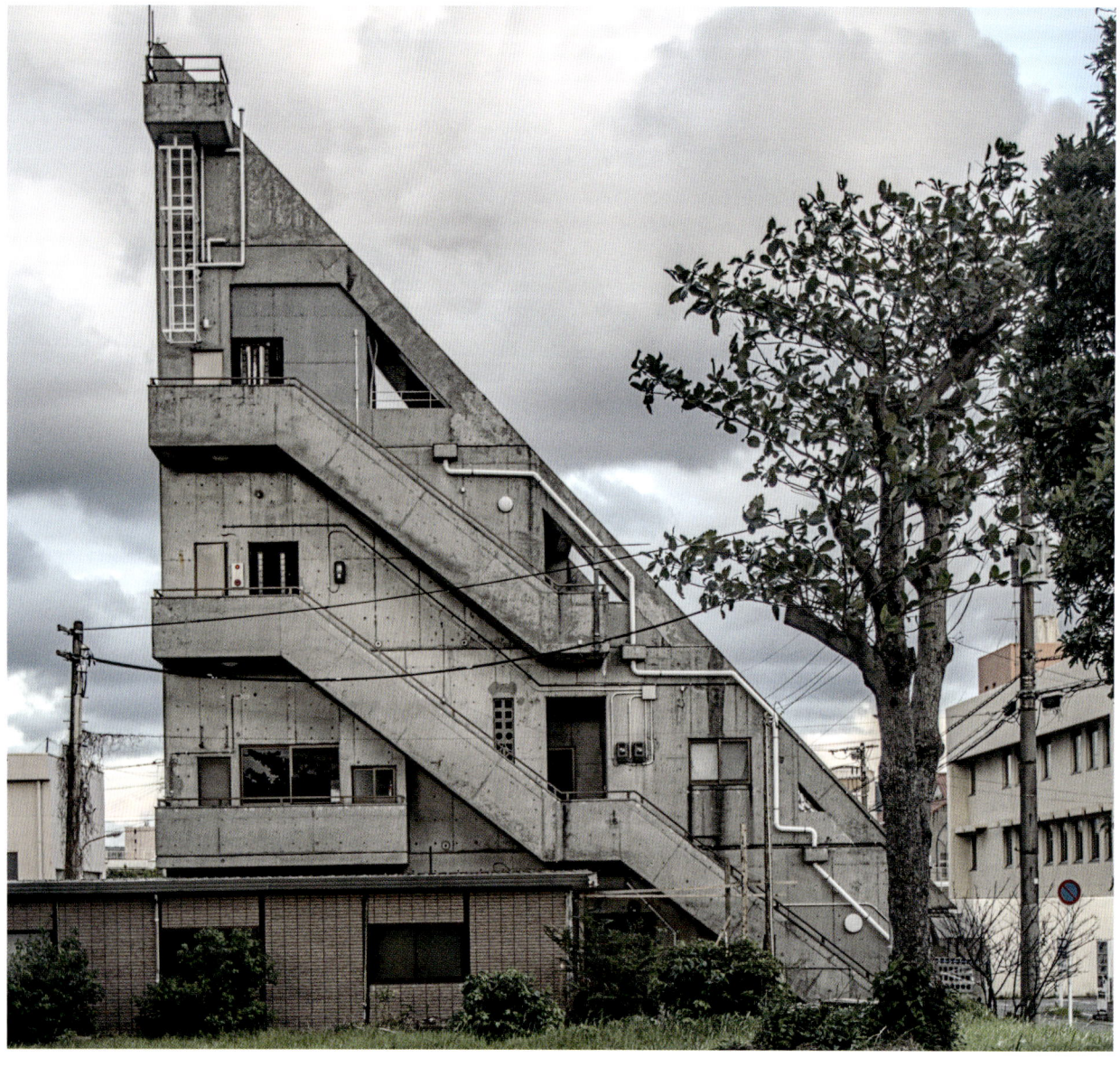

PRIVATE RESIDENCE

OKINAWA

Here in northern Okinawa, where tradition whispers through the winds and modernity echoes in the concrete, exists a residence that achieves the fusion of past and present. The *hinpun*, a quintessential element of traditional Okinawan architecture designed to shield homes from nature's whims and life's uncertainties, finds new expression here. This contemporary interpretation of the *hinpun* serves not just as a bulwark against the gusts, embers and enigmas, but also as a testament to cultural endurance.

Crafted minimally in concrete, the modern *hinpun* acts as guard, a sentry at the threshold that marries the utility of ancient wisdom with the austerity of modern design. Its presence is a dialogue between eras, offering seclusion from the public eye and a serene refuge within. Here, the spirit of Okinawa's architectural heritage lives on, thoughtfully integrated into the fabric of a home that speaks of both legacy and innovation, guarding against the elements as much as it does against the erosion of time-honoured customs.

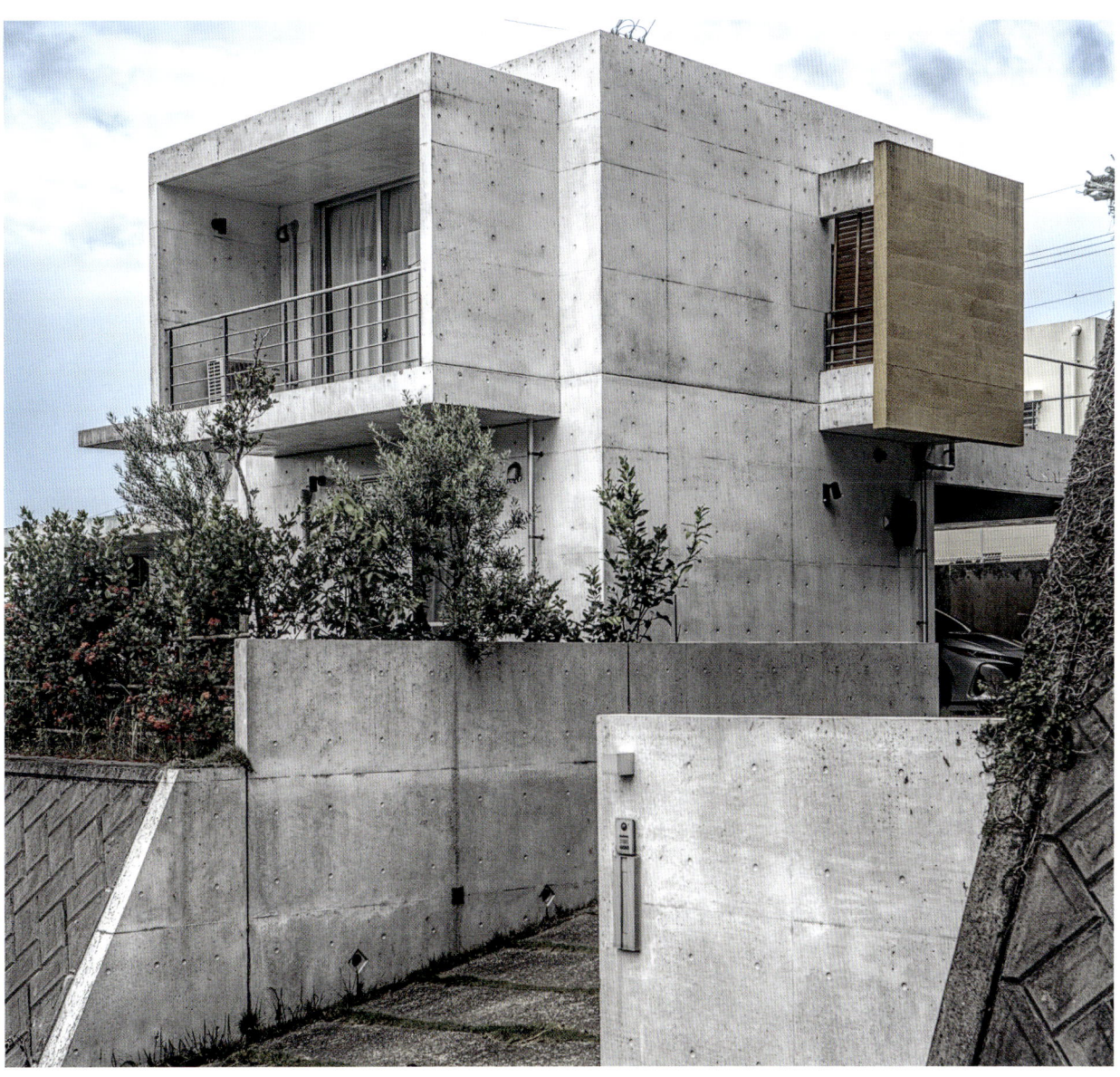

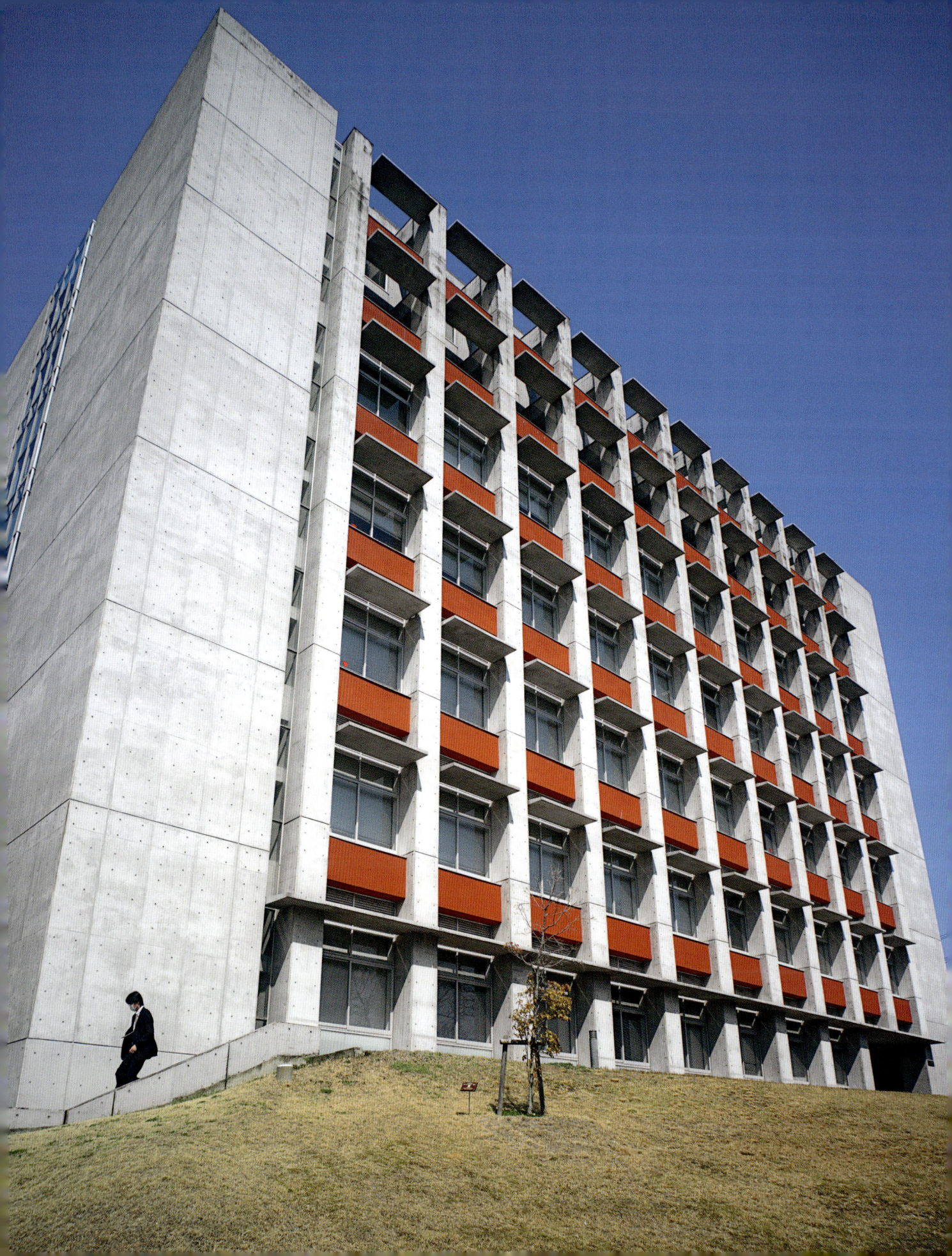

NANZAN UNIVERSITY

NAGOYA · Architect: Antonin and Noémi Raymond · Completed 1964

Although Antonin Raymond was a protégé of Frank Lloyd Wright, his architectural style drew more significantly from Le Corbusier, marking a shift seen across many early modernist architects in Japan. Initially, German architectural movements like the Bauhaus and German Expressionism dominated. However, post-Second World War, a new wave led by architects like Kunio Maekawa, Takamasa Yoshizaka and Junzo Sakakura – who had worked in Le Corbusier's Paris office – brought Le Corbusier's principles to the forefront of Japanese modern architecture.

These architects were inspired by Le Corbusier's evolution from pre-war frame structures to his post-war style characterized by massive, sculpturally expressive forms. This shift influenced many in Japan, although the Raymonds critiqued this move, attributing the "brutalities" in post-war Japanese architecture to Le Corbusier's robust use of concrete in projects like Ronchamp and Chandigarh.

The Raymonds, adhering to a modernist ethos, emphasized internationalism, modern technology and traditional Japanese values of simplicity, lightness and material economy. These principles are clearly reflected in their design of the Nanzan University Campus. The campus features several buildings, predominantly employing a rational post-and-beam construction, with some featuring thin-shell, barrel-vaulted concrete roofs.

As one of the Raymonds' most extensive projects, the campus is composed of eight building groups that cascade down the sides of a central axis, mirroring the natural undulations of the site and minimally altering the existing topography. The campus architecture demonstrates a harmonious blend of varied functional needs and structural forms – ranging from beam and slab to thin-shell vaults – unified by consistent use of materials, colour schemes and façade treatments that include concrete frames and vertical concrete louvres.

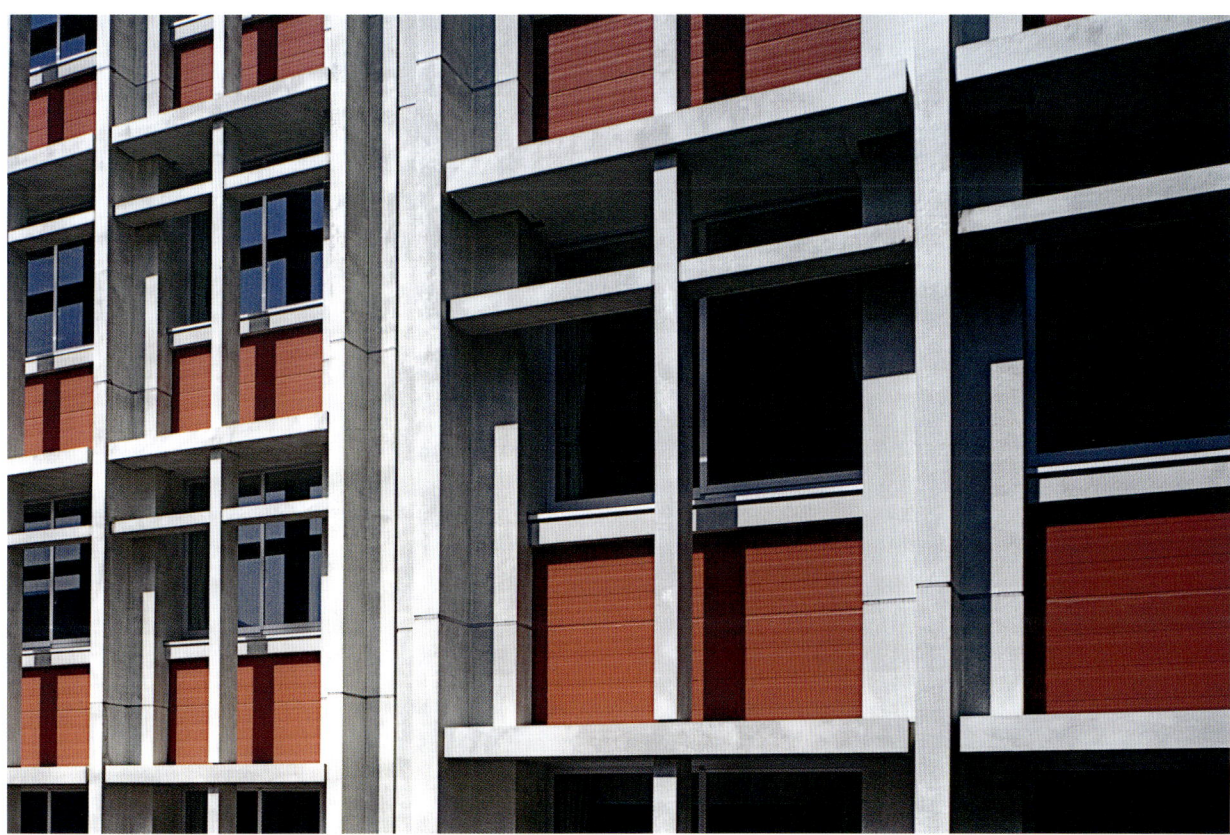

DIVINE WORD SEMINARY CHAPEL

NANZAN UNIVERSITY, NAGOYA · Architect: Antonin and Noémi Raymond · Completed 1960

The heavenly exception to the Raymonds' somewhat standardized, formulaic approach to the Nanzan campus is the Divine Word Seminary Chapel, which uses heavy, sculptural, load-bearing concrete in a manner reminiscent of Le Corbusier's church at Ronchamp – despite the slagging off the French architect received from Antonin. Indeed, the Raymonds were not immune to the movement towards more mannerist, sculptural forms.

In a delightful twist of architectural intertextuality, the chapel's design could be seen as a "citation" of Le Corbusier's work, albeit without the formal acknowledgement often found in scholarly papers. This building integrates a formidable nested spire and stairway walls painted in the red hues of eastern Nagoya's clay, suggesting a localized adaptation of global architectural ideas. The roof comprises five shell-like structures, reminiscent of seashells, which add to the chapel's distinctive profile.

In 2012, the chapel underwent significant renovation to restore its original aesthetics and enhance its functionality, reaffirming its structural integrity and earthquake resilience. This durability underlines the Raymonds' thoughtful consideration of longevity and adaptability in their designs.

While the Raymonds are celebrated for their architectural prowess, pinning down a distinct "Raymond style" is as challenging as defining the precise source of an academic idea that has been paraphrased multiple times across various papers. Their work in Japan, extensive and influential, often blurs the lines between borrowed inspiration and original creation, reflecting a broader practice in Japanese architecture of adapting and assimilating diverse influences.

Thus, the Chapel to the Divine Word serves as a place of spiritual gathering and as an example of the complex interplay of innovation, cultural synthesis and subtle homage that characterizes the Raymonds' architectural legacy. What is clear is that they had a deep understanding of Japanese culture and aesthetics.

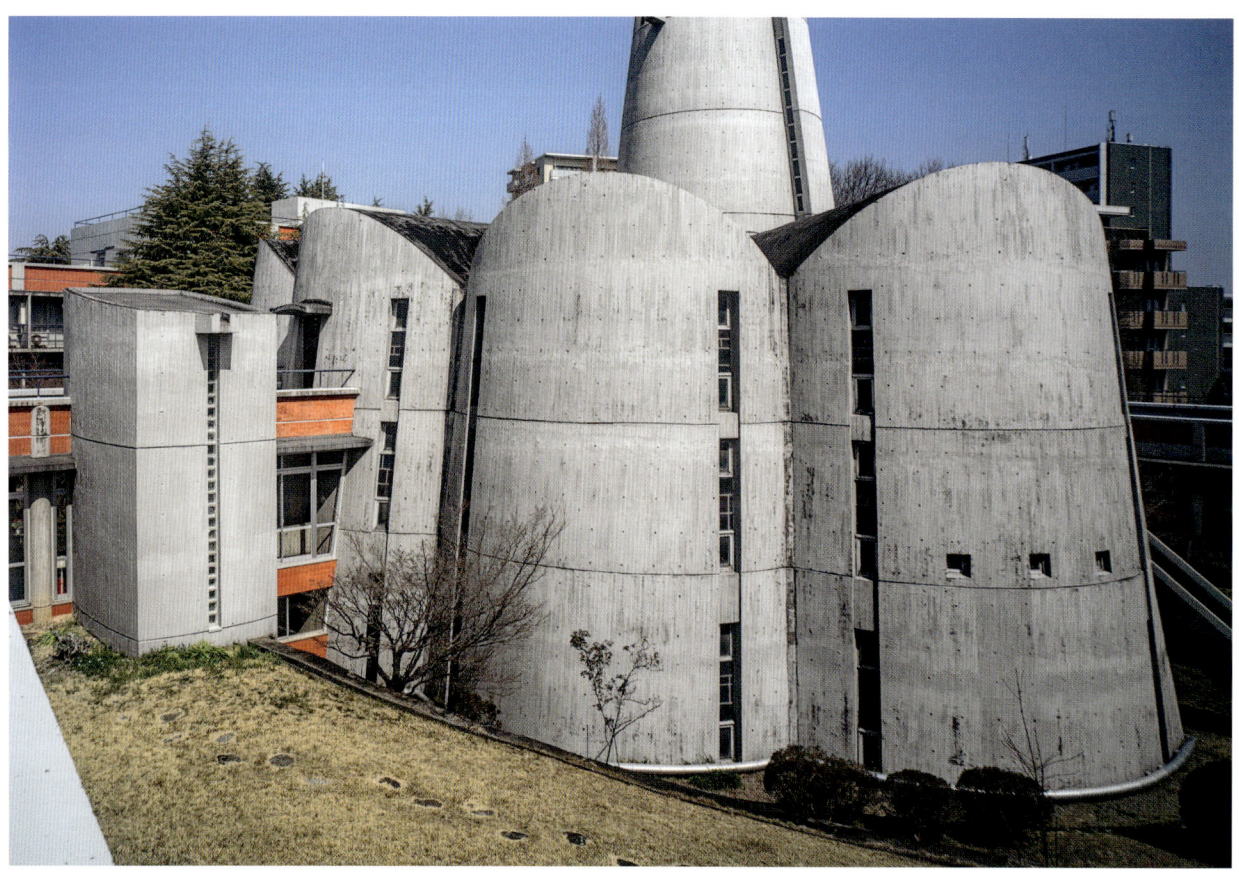

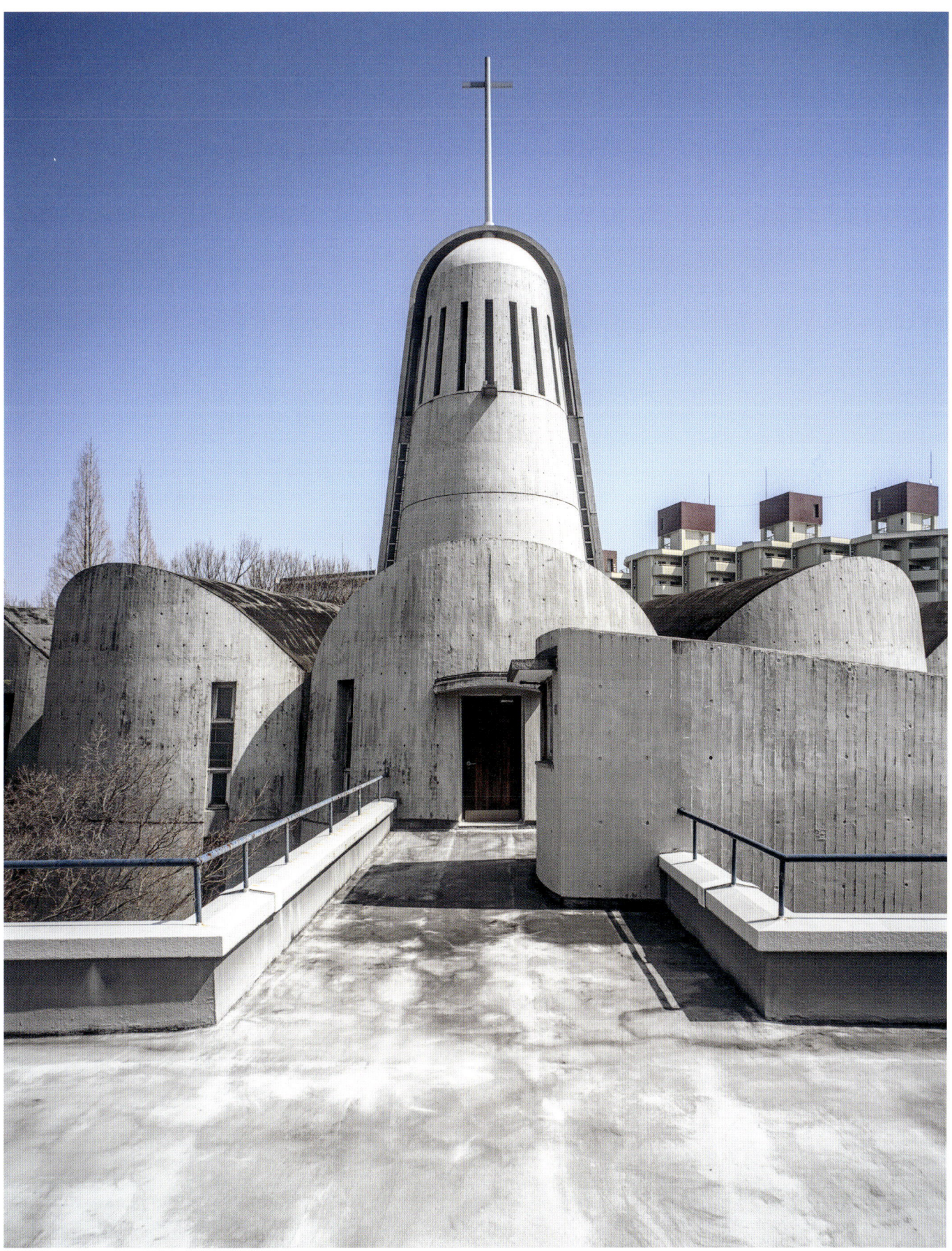

NARUTO CULTURAL HALL, CITY HALL AND WELFARE CENTER
TOKUSHIMA PREFECTURE · Architect: MASUDA Tomoya · Completed 1975

In the transformative landscape of public architecture, the Naruto Cultural Hall attests to the modern movement's revolutionary ethos, reshaping regional perceptions of civic spaces.

Tomoya Masuda, throughout his prolific career, brought his creative fervour to approximately 140 projects, yet he poured his soul into only six exceptional designs. These designs, perfected to his exacting standards, are celebrated as his masterpieces. Among them, the Naruto Cultural Center, commemorating the 35th anniversary of Naruto City's establishment, marks a pivotal achievement. Constructed on a former salt field, this cultural container took shape over nine years, capturing nearly half of Masuda's two-decade tenure in Naruto and culminating as his final work.

This ensemble of three facilities, strategically facing the Fuyo River, harmonizes through uniform eave heights and a series of louvres positioned at the second-floor slab. These elements impose an urban rhythm and integrate the spaces between the buildings to function as a communal square. The eastern terminus of this plaza gracefully transitions into the Fuyo River Water Park, extending its reach to the river itself.

The meticulously aligned louvres, reminiscent of a stately colonnade, cast their reflections on the river, creating a serene visual dialogue between architecture and nature. Within the cultural centre, various functions are seamlessly accommodated within the wedge-shaped interstices of a dominant 7.2-metre grid and an adjoining hall that slightly deviates from this framework. Moreover, the interior spaces thrive on a dynamic tension inherent in the structure, subtly complemented by the finesse of Japanese aesthetics.

In this civic ensemble, the bridging of spaces serves a functional purpose but also symbolizes the bridging of community ties, engendering a confluence of civic pride and collective identity.

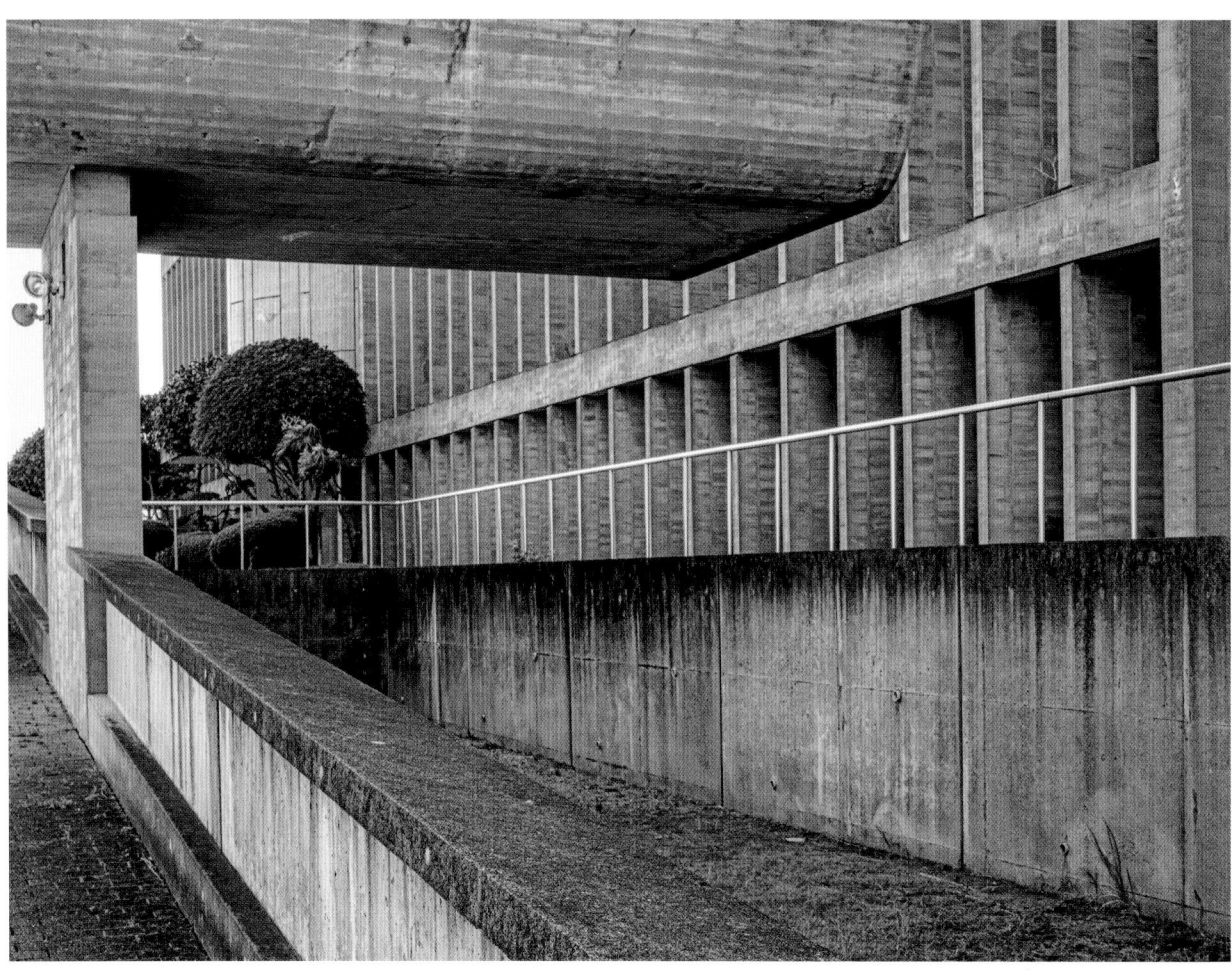

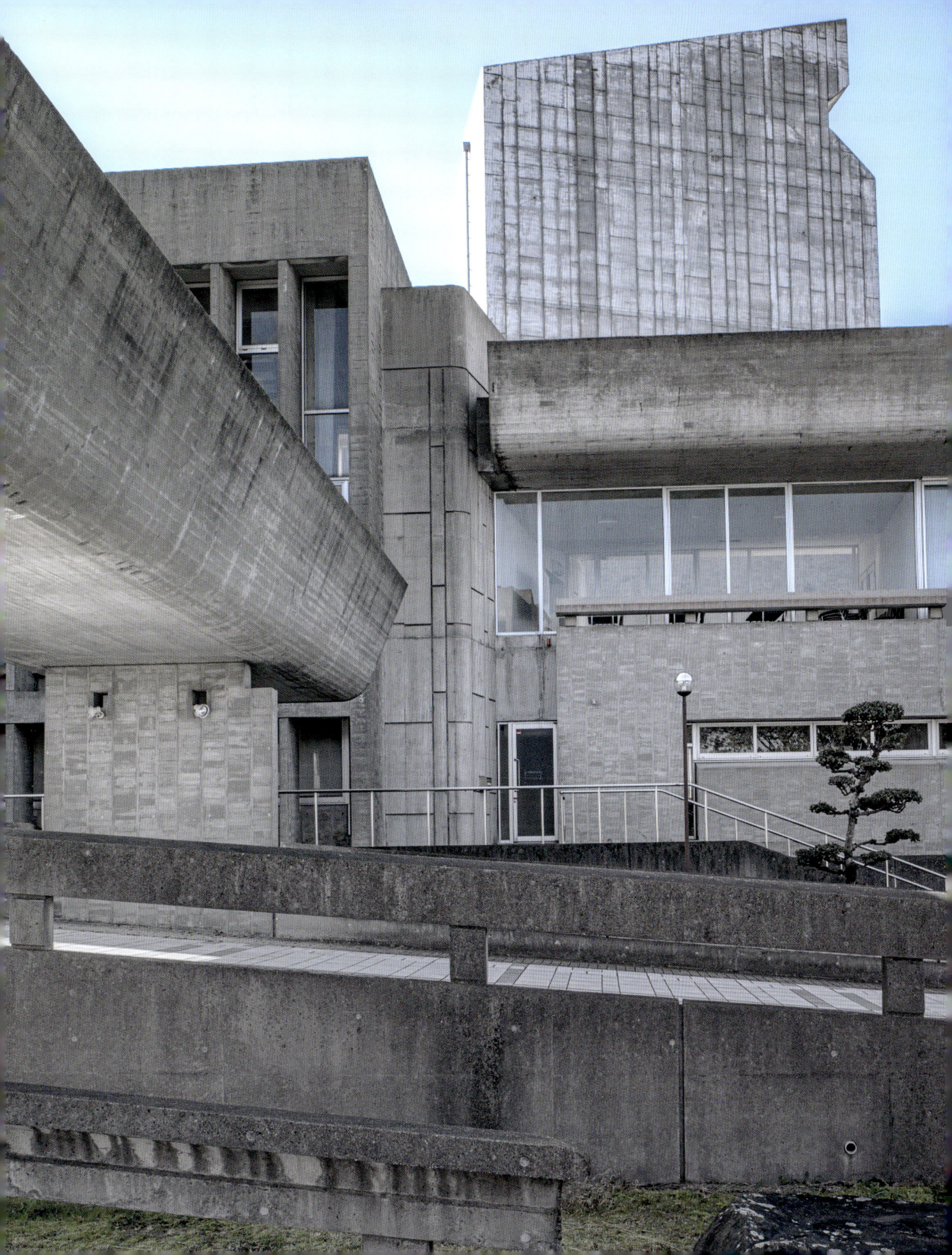

CUBE 21

NARUTO, TOKUSHIMA PREFECTURE · Architect: Unknown · Completed 1985

The architectural prowess of Japan is demonstrated by this six-storey apartment block which employs a *ramen* (frame) structure, offering a harmonious blend of practical design and cultural aesthetics. This approach to architecture, prominently featuring a network of horizontal beams and vertical columns, is well-adapted to the unique challenges and philosophical considerations of Japanese construction.

Practically, the *ramen* structure is incredibly suited to the seismic context of Japan. The interlocking grid of beams and columns is designed to flexibly absorb and redistribute the stresses caused by earthquakes, much like the traditional wooden constructions of ancient Japan, which were similarly adept at withstanding seismic forces. The modularity of the *ramen* structure also allows for efficient use of space within dense urban environments, another practical necessity in Japan's often crowded cities.

Culturally, there is a deep-seated respect for the materials used in construction, which stems from a traditional appreciation for the natural world. The raw concrete seen in these structures can age and evolve over time, echoing the Japanese aesthetic value of *wabi-sabi*, which finds beauty in the natural cycle of ageing and impermanence. This philosophy celebrates the textures and imperfections that emerge as the building weathers, lending a unique character and a sense of continuity with the past.

The repetition of forms and the raw, unadorned surfaces of concrete in the *ramen* structure connect to another Japanese concept, that of *ma*, referring to the spatial relationships between elements. The voids and solids of the building create a rhythm, with the openness of the structure allowing for light and air to permeate, connecting inhabitants to the external environment, and ensuring that the building itself is a living element in concert with nature.

Therefore, the *ramen* structure, particularly when executed in concrete, is a manifestation of Japan's innovative approach to building in a seismically active region, while also reflecting the everlasting cultural principles that inform its architectural traditions. These buildings stand as enduring examples of Japan's capacity to integrate the pragmatic demands of architecture with its philosophical engagement with natural beauty and materiality.

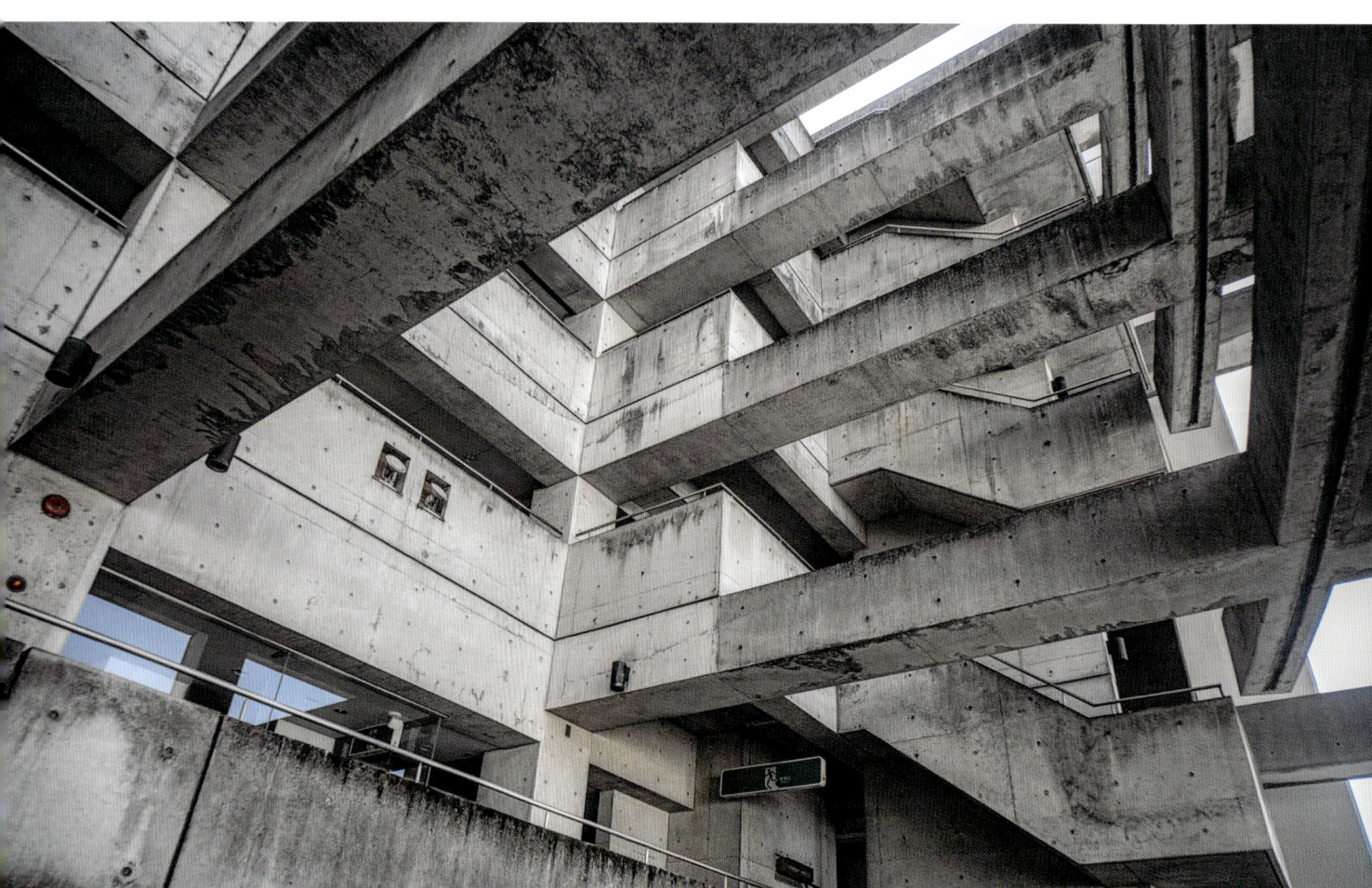

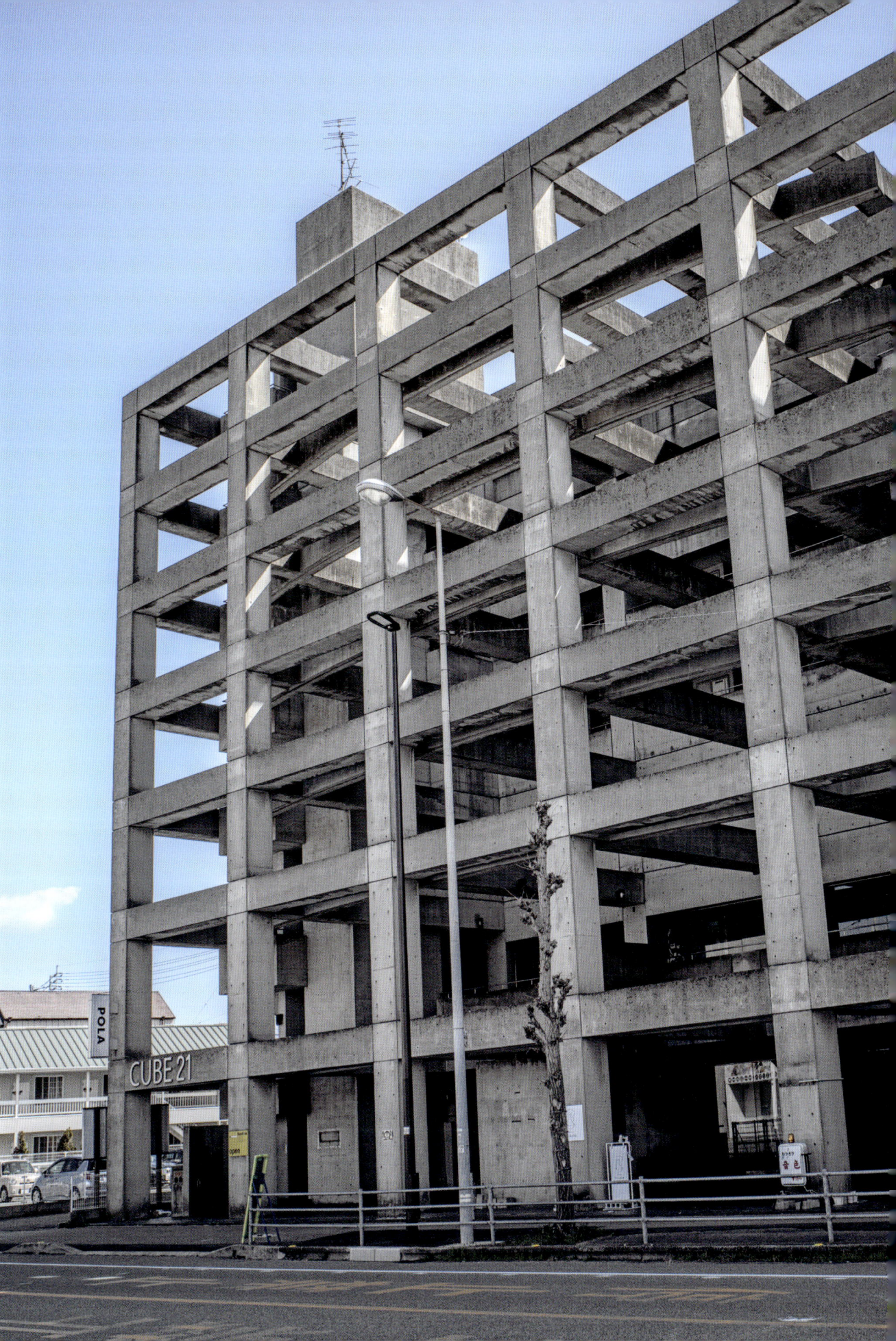

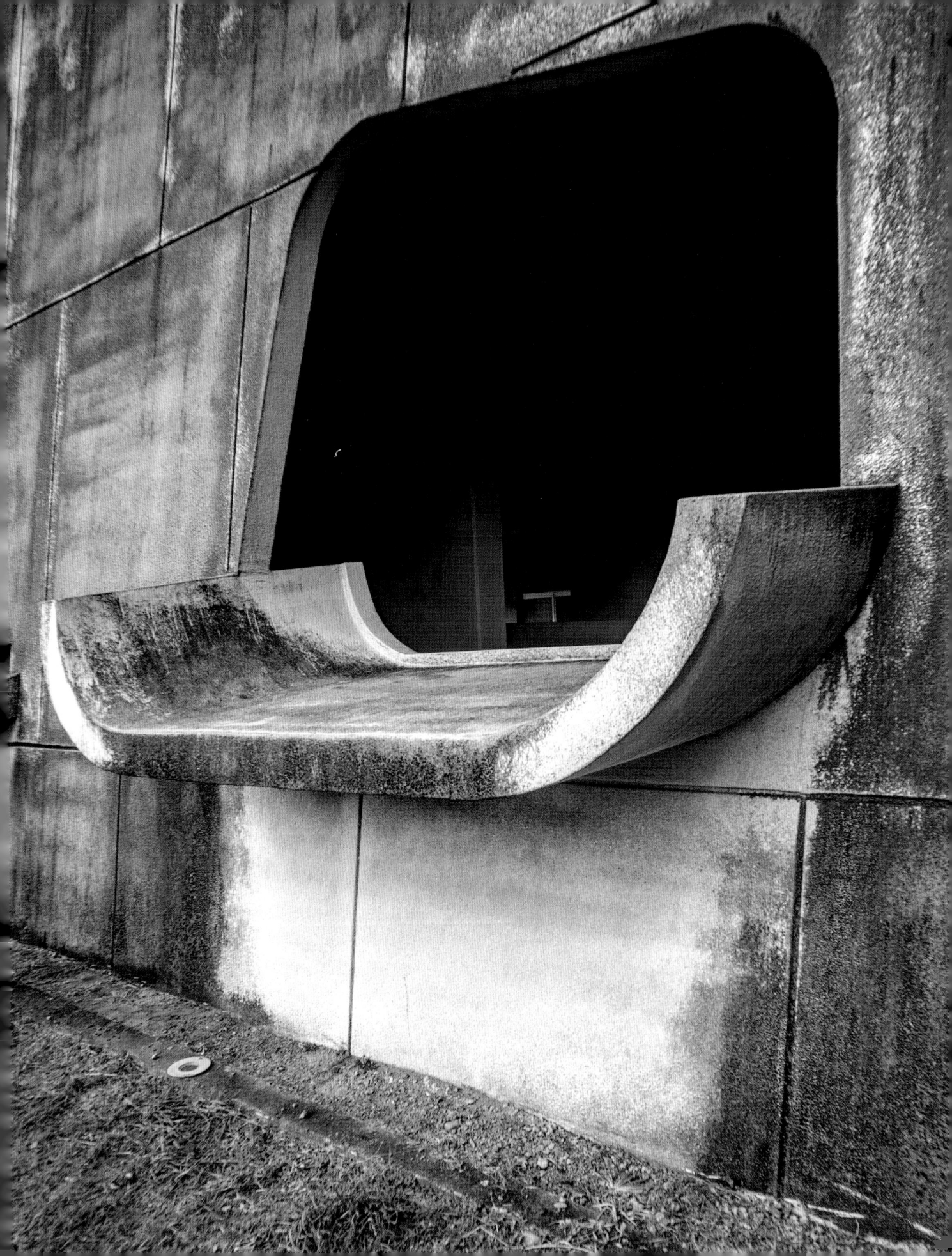

NICHINAN CULTURAL CENTER

MIYAZAKI PREFECTURE · Architect: TANGE Kenzo · Completed 1962

The Nichinan Cultural Center, a monumental work by architect Kenzo Tange, represents a significant chapter in the narrative of Brutalist architecture. This singular work in Kyushu, erected to celebrate Nichinan City's establishment, displays a fortress-like grandeur that pays tribute to the rugged cliffs of the region. The centre conveys a certain imperviousness and sculptural power, characteristics often sought in Brutalist design.

Tange's use of cast-in-place concrete for the centre gave it a sculptural and rhythmic façade, complementing the building's powerful volume and creating an interior space that almost seems crystallized. The distinctive shape of the large hall, formed by three intersecting triangles, and the placement of a multi-purpose hall as another triangle facing them, give rise to a beautifully complex exterior. The overlapping triangular forms create a semi-outdoor space, adding to the structure's sculptural quality.

The design's interaction with light and shadow across its sloped surfaces is as dramatic as it is intentional, highlighting the building's unique profile. Tange's design, which features openings and overhangs on the gently sloping exterior walls, creates an engaging rhythm, an homage to the dynamism of Brutalist architecture.

The Nichinan Cultural Center is more than a facility composed of an auditorium, a multi-purpose hall and a conference room; it is a statement of architectural intent. The building, firmly rooted in its landscape, has weathered the decades with character, symbolizing the resilient nature of Brutalism and its capacity to evoke the past while resisting the passage of time, much like a fortress against the elements.

As a landmark in Brutalist architecture, the Nichinan Cultural Center is significant for its austere yet expressive use of concrete and for capturing Tange's visionary approach that both respects tradition and innovates, reflecting a unique point in history when architecture was not only a shelter but a bold declaration of identity and permanence.

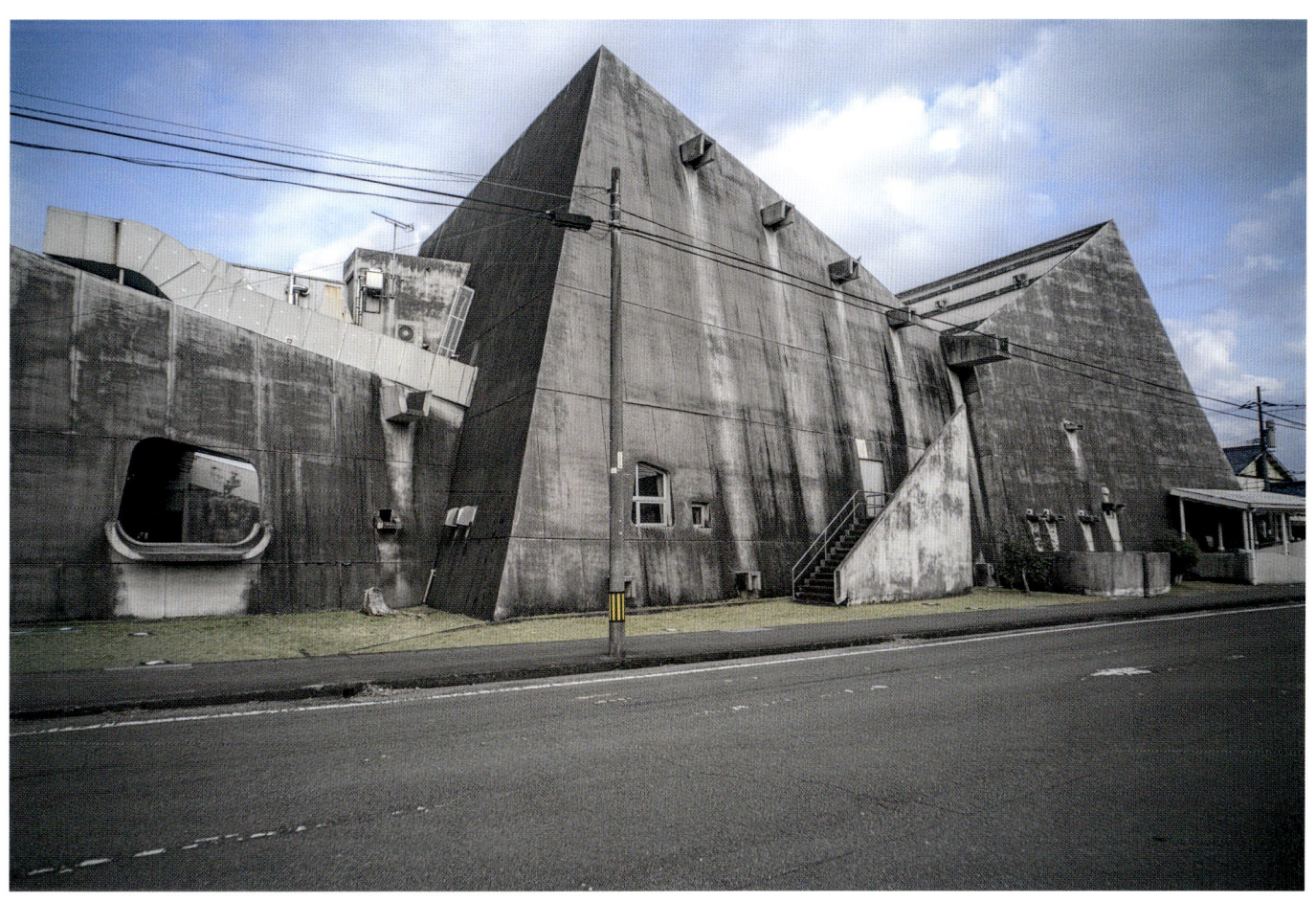

NICHINAN CULTURAL CENTER

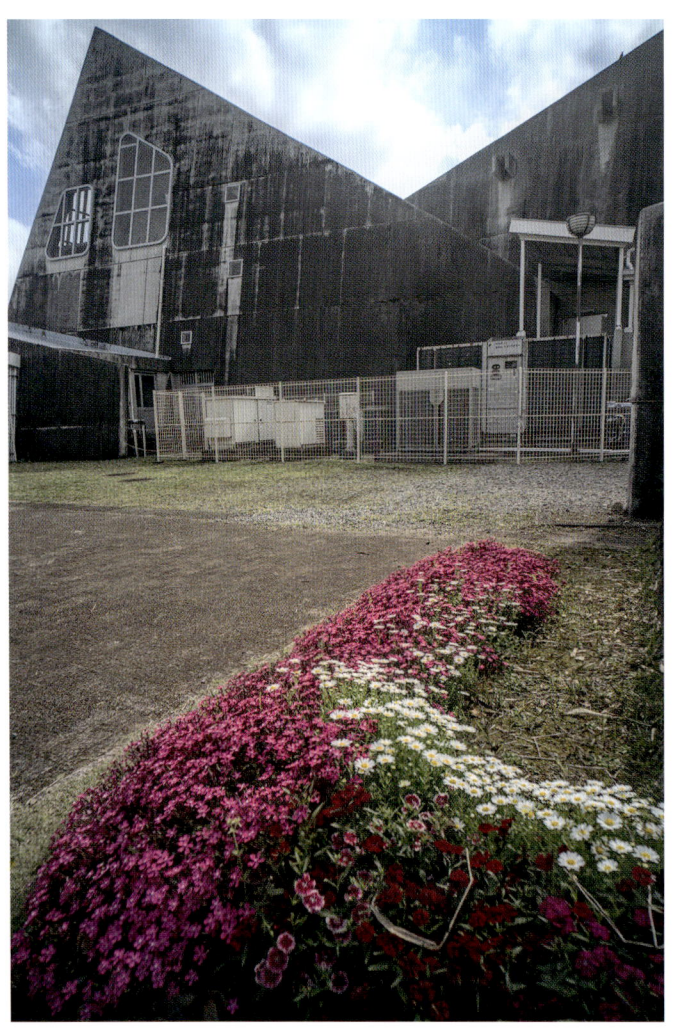
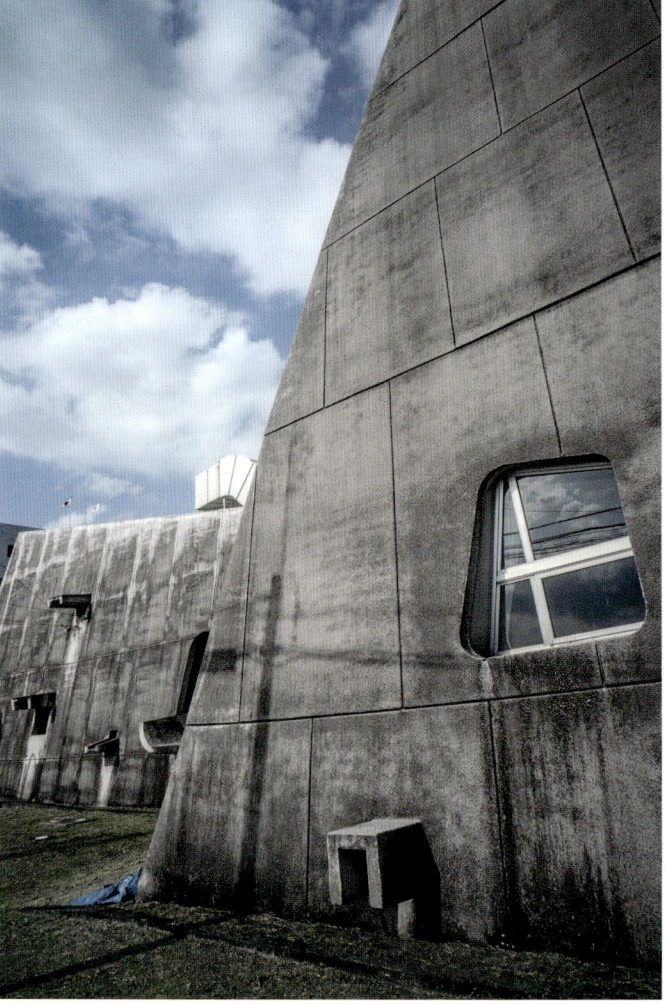

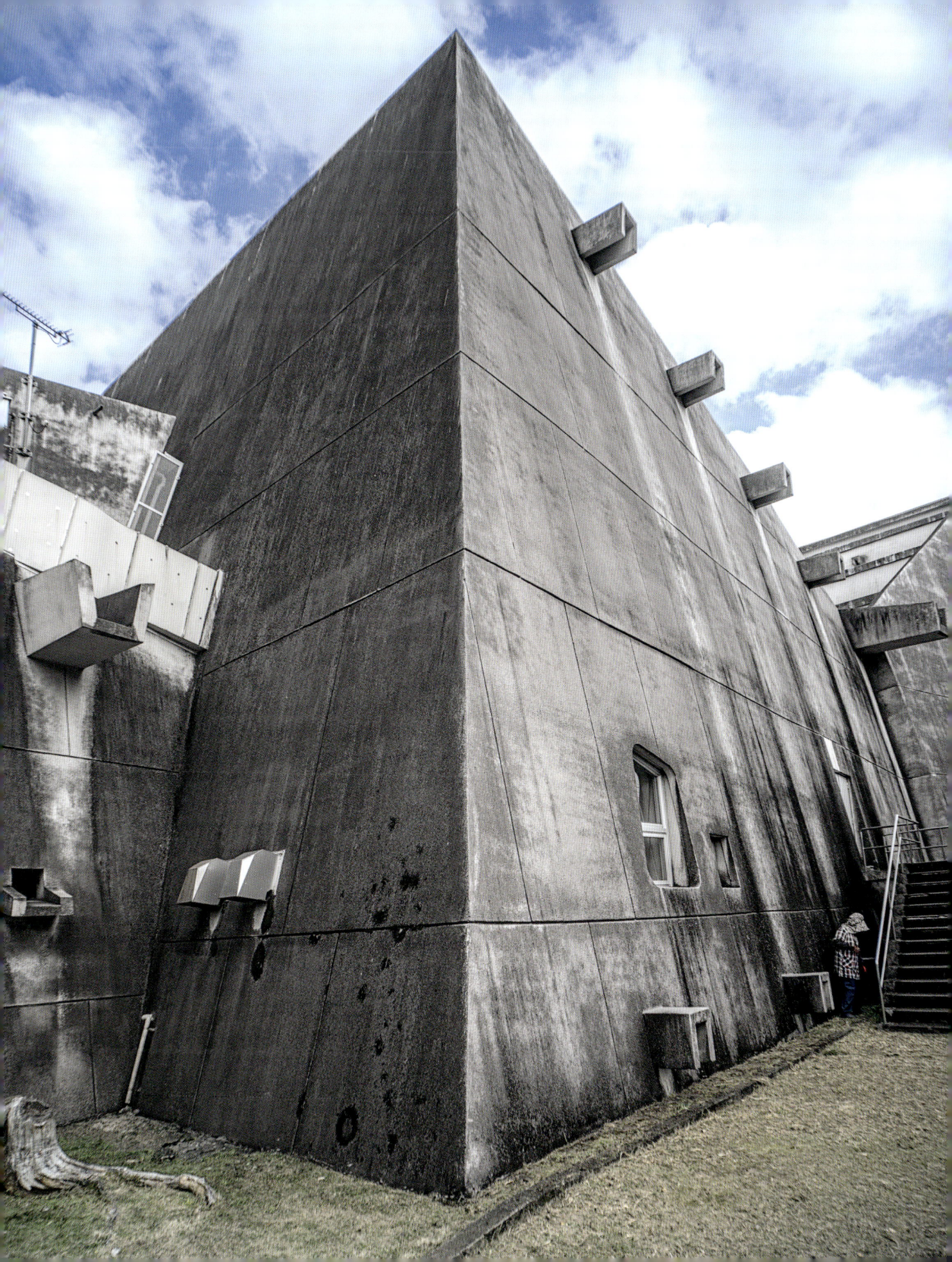

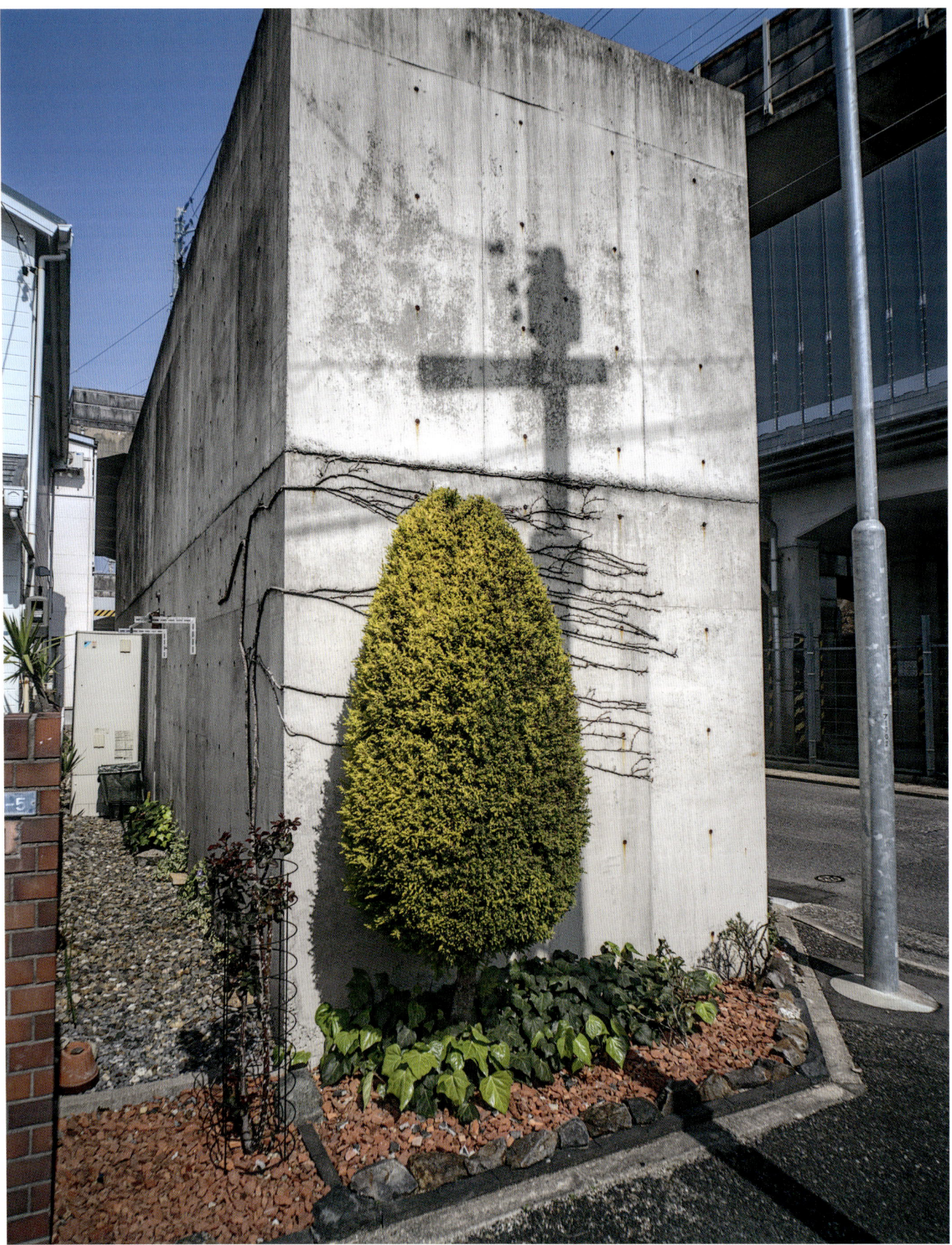

SAKO HOUSE

NAGOYA · Architect: Tomoaki Uno Architects · Completed 2017

In the heart of a neighbourhood where houses chatter like a conference of overcaffeinated academics, sits this concrete hermitage – a paradoxical monolith that's as much a fortress as it is a library. Commissioned by a design professor who has had more homes than he's had sabbaticals, this concrete citadel is his latest and last abode, designed to offer the kind of solitude that only a middle-aged scholar could fantasize about.

The façade is a Brutalist sonnet, with walls unadorned save for a door that looks like it could withstand a campus riot. It's the architectural equivalent of "Do Not Disturb" in 60-point font, quite possibly designed for a professor who'd rather debate Le Corbusier than attend a faculty mixer.

As one ventures inside – preferably with a stack of unread journals – the spiral staircase folds like a DNA helix, a spatial narrative unwinding with each scholarly step. It's an ascent into an ivory tower of one's own making, where getting lost is not a bug, it's a feature. Amidst this labyrinth of learning, one might ponder whether they've stumbled into a maze or the physical manifestation of a footnote gone rogue.

Skywards, the skylights perform an illuminating ballet, a dance of light and shadow that changes with the academic calendar. Each skylight is like a professor's query, shifting and challenging with the time of day, the season's whim. And those concrete walls? They're packed with enough insulation to mute the cheeriest of carollers, ensuring that the only chill one feels is from the spine-tingling thrill of a well-crafted thesis.

In summation, this house is less a domicile and more a sanctum of solitude. It's where thoughts are free to roam without the shackles of small talk, and where every room whispers, "Quiet, please – genius at work."

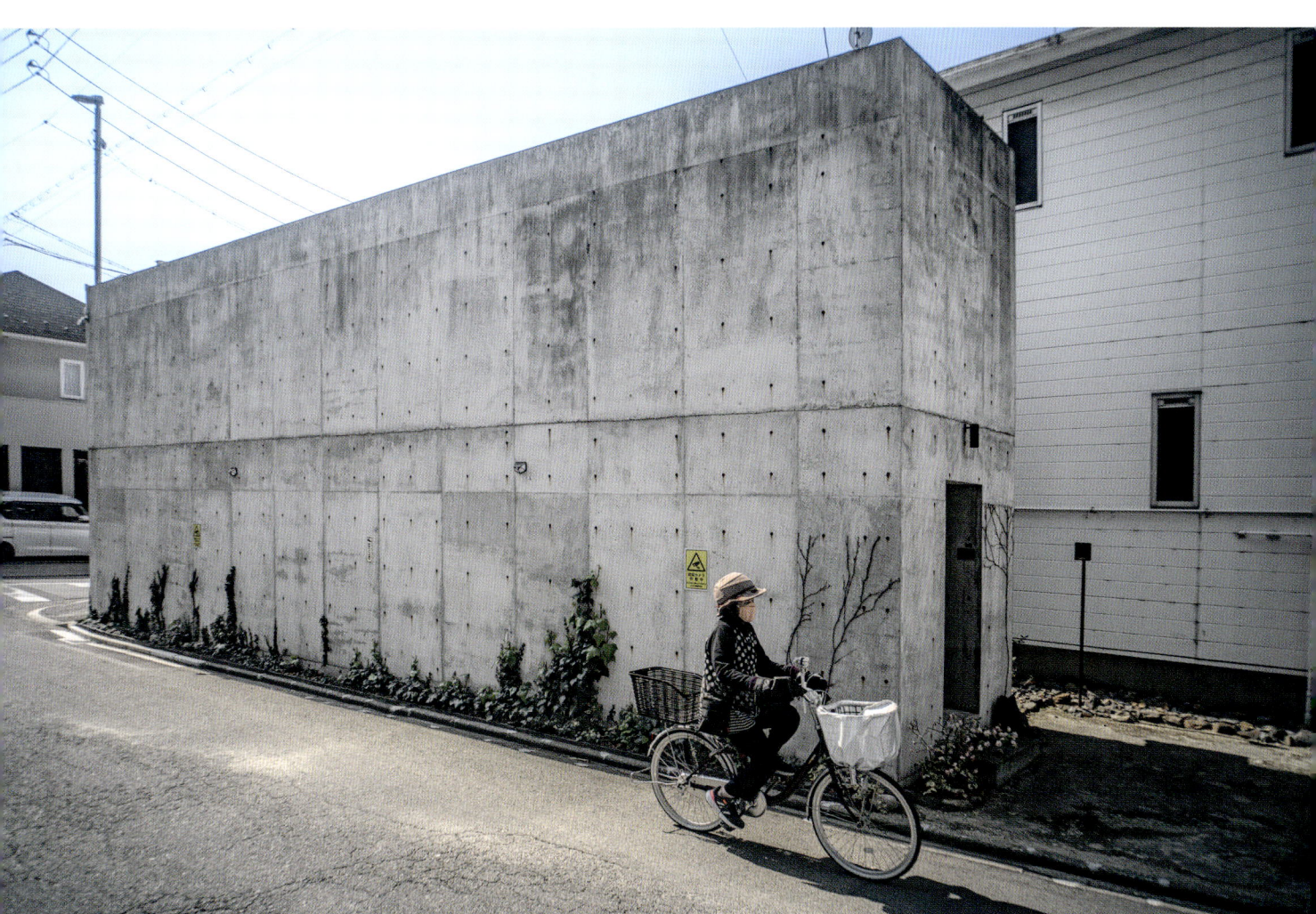

KAGAWA PREFECTURAL GYMNASIUM

TAKAMATSU · Architect: TANGE Kenzo · Completed 1964

Concurrent with Kenzo Tange's creation of Tokyo's mammoth Olympic structure for the 1964 Summer Games, a humbler athletic vessel was birthed further west. Between 1962 and 1964, the Kagawa Prefectural Gymnasium arose in Takamatsu, with a Brutalist silhouette strong enough to renounce any kinship with its neighbours.

An oval hull is hoisted by four titanic columns, extending its form in a defiant cantilever that bestows upon it the visage of a seafaring leviathan, mirroring both the formidable might and grace of an Olympian. The colossal interior, a twenty-metre-high cavernous expanse, is crowned by a roof sculpted into a hyperbolic paraboloid, akin to the poised sail of a vessel challenging the high seas.

This canopy, a mere five centimetres thick, is a hanging of precast concrete slabs, strung together by a network of cables, inducing a sense of ponderous permanence. Here, concrete reigns supreme, shaping not just the structure but the very aura of gravitas that envelops it.

After half a century of anchorage, serving as a site for local sporting endeavours, this proud ship of Takamatsu found itself adrift when a breach in its rooftop – brought on by the corrosion of its very sinews, the suspension cables – forced its closure in 2014. This once stalwart structure now faces the tempest of obsolescence, its survival hanging in the balance, its cables as vital and vulnerable as the rigging of a ship braving stormy seas.

To rescue this sinking ship of Brutalist lineage would be no small feat – requiring not only a technical overhaul to its cable system but also a bolstering against the tremors of the earth. And with the rise of a new sports complex in Takamatsu, the future of Tange's mid-century titan wades in uncertain waters, perhaps soon to be swallowed by the tide of progress and forgotten beneath the waves of time.

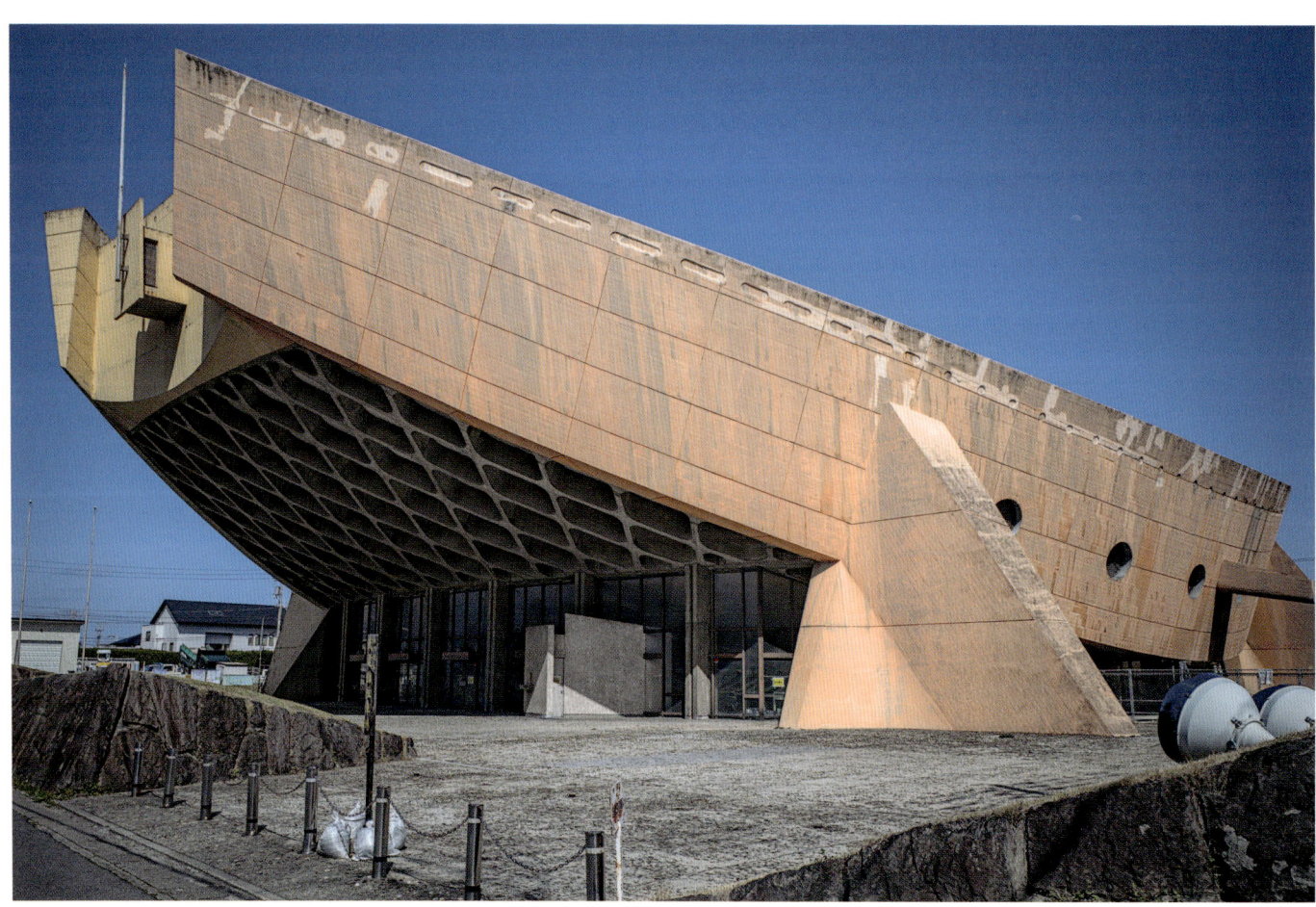

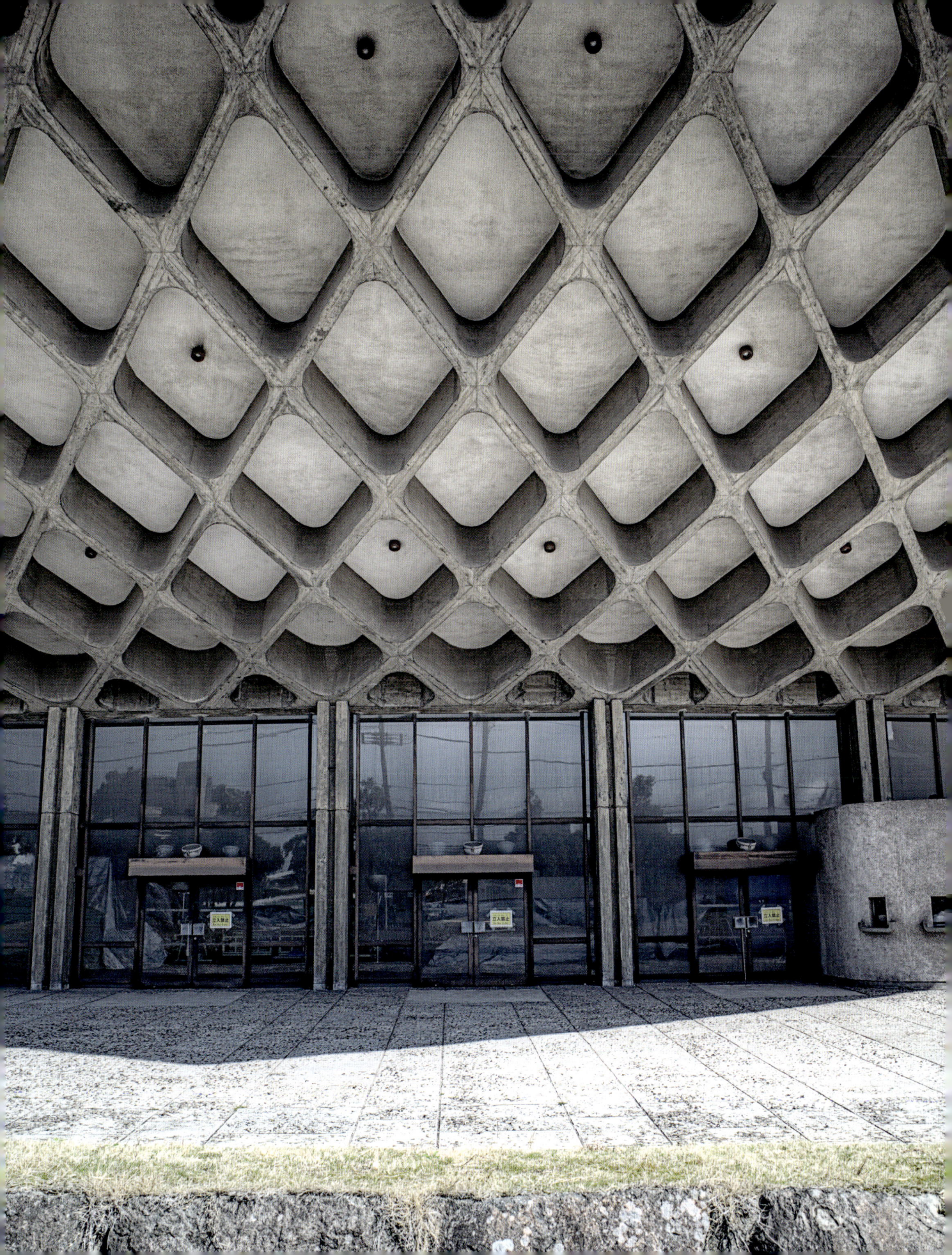

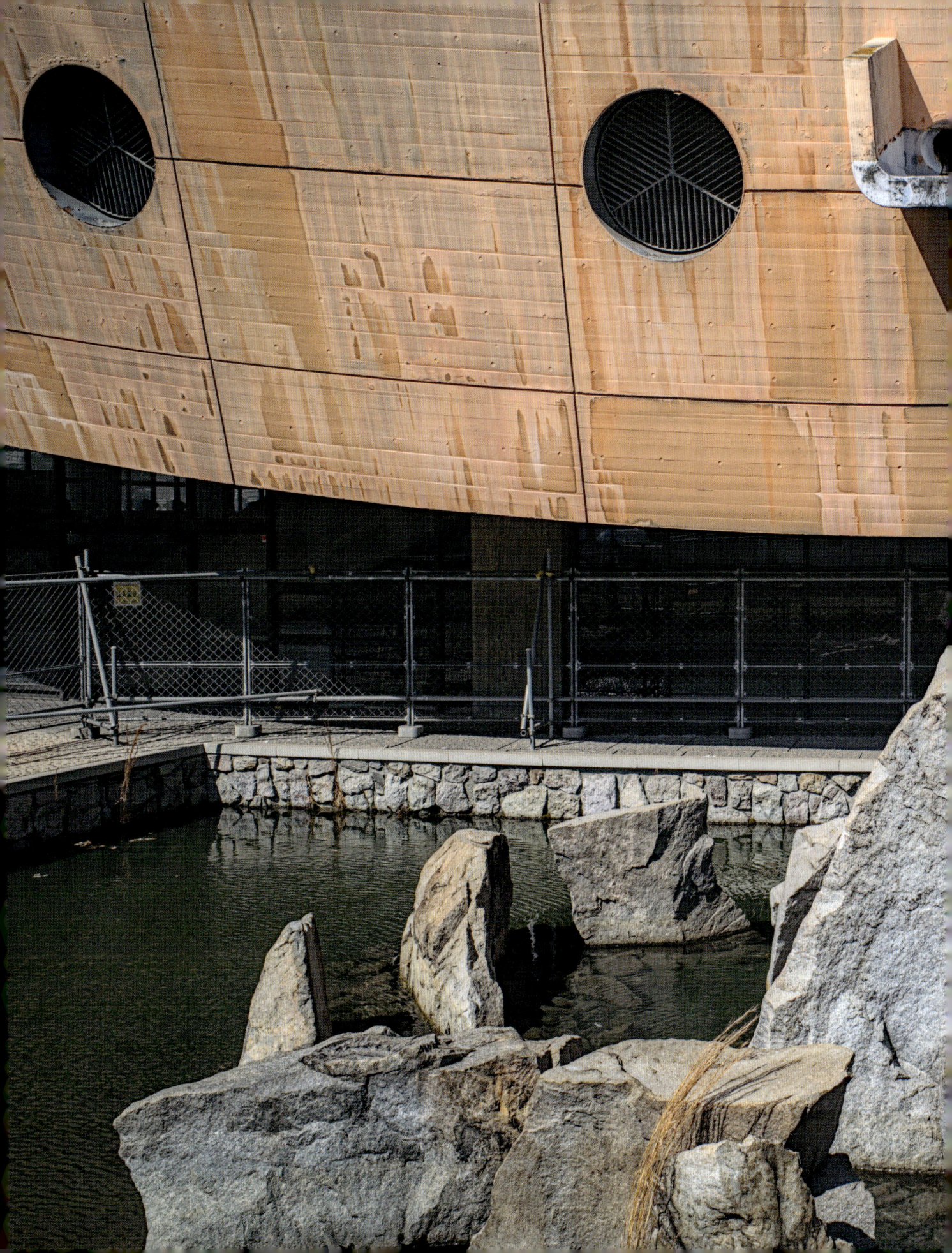

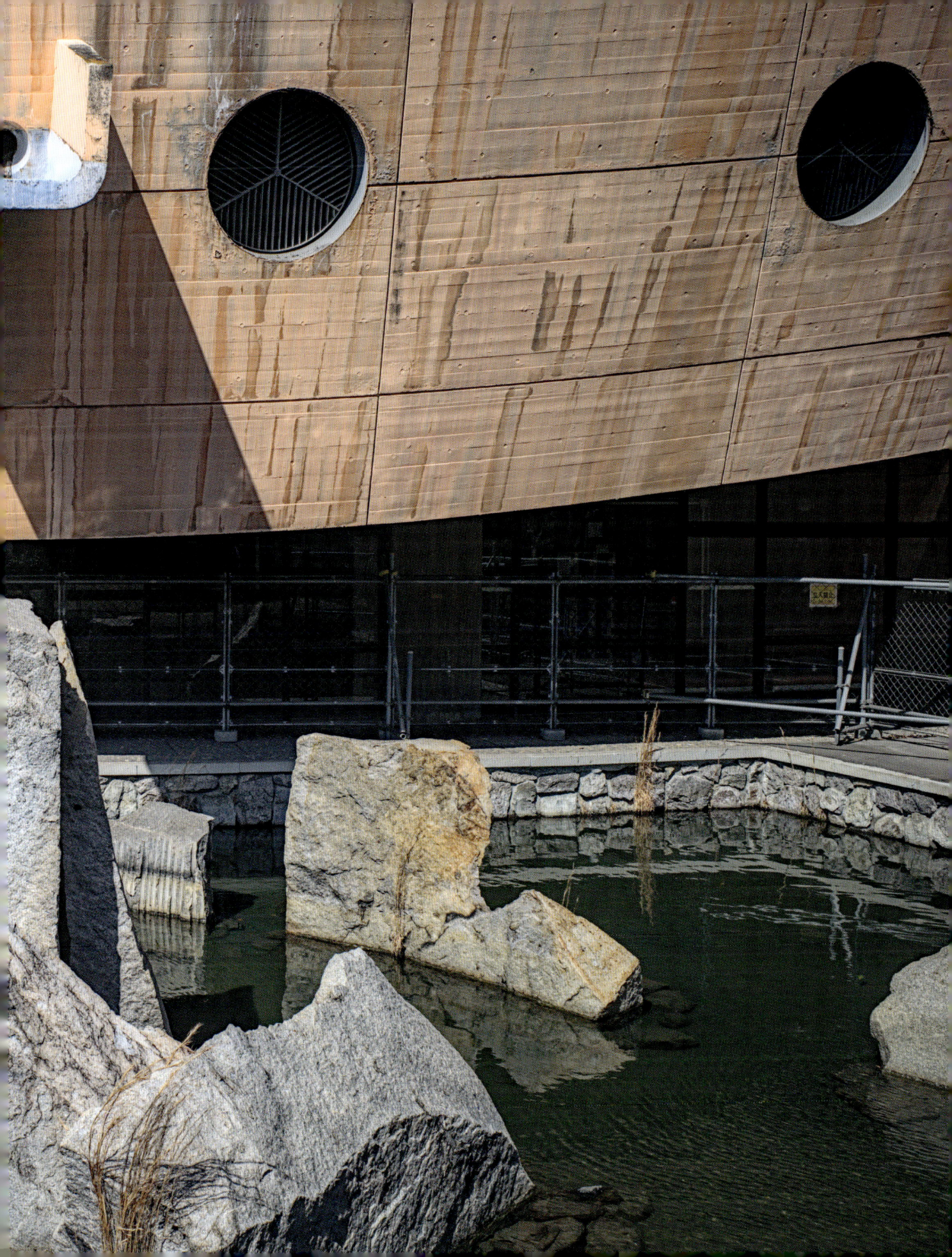

KAGAWA PREFECTURAL GOVERNMENT BUILDING TAKAMATSU · Architect: TANGE Kenzo · Completed 1958

Kenzo Tange's architectural magnum opus, the Kagawa Prefectural Government Building, strikes a chord as his grandest overture in the heated "tradition vs. modernity" jam session that was 1950s Japan. This tradition debate was known as *dento ronso*. Amidst the clash of architectural opinions, Tange's creation was a composition that married the nostalgia of Japan's venerable structures with the upbeat tempo of post-war progress.

The building struts the stage with a tower wing that's a dramatic backdrop, flaunting motifs of Japan's celebrated temples while rocking the latest in structural engineering. Teaming up with Yoshikatsu Tsuboi, Tange orchestrated a *ramen* rigid-frame that's as much a nod to Japan's storied pagodas as it is a high five to modern democracy.

This wasn't just about building up; it was about shaping spaces for Japan's new era. Imagine a garden that isn't just greenery but a social stage for the public's performance, where the choreography of community life plays out among classical nods and democratic strides. Tange wasn't just drafting blueprints; he was penning an invitation to the people, an open house where every square, garden and lobby was a call to mingle.

Like a triptych of public spaces, the garden was the public's playground, the assembly wing's pilotis were the community's living room – and the glassy lobby? The grand entrance to Japan's embrace of the future. Here, the lines between traditional and modern allure dance away, making room for people to not just see history but be a part of its making.

In the heart of Kagawa, Tange didn't just build; he sparked a dialogue with concrete and soil, inviting everyone to weigh in. It's more than architecture; it's the crossroads of a nation's past and its pulse-quickening leap forwards, with the doors wide open for debate.

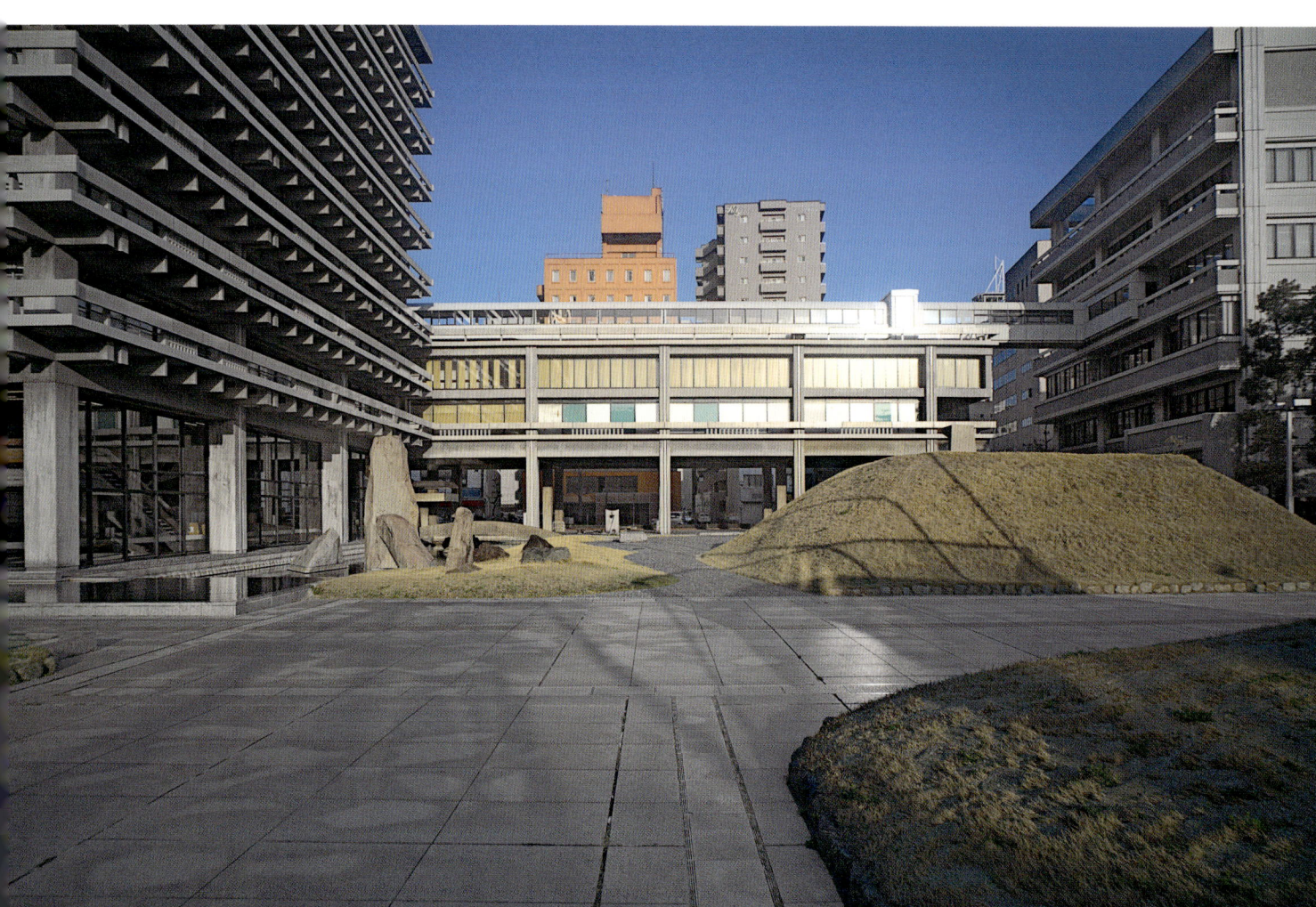

KAGAWA PREFECTURAL GOVERNMENT BUILDING

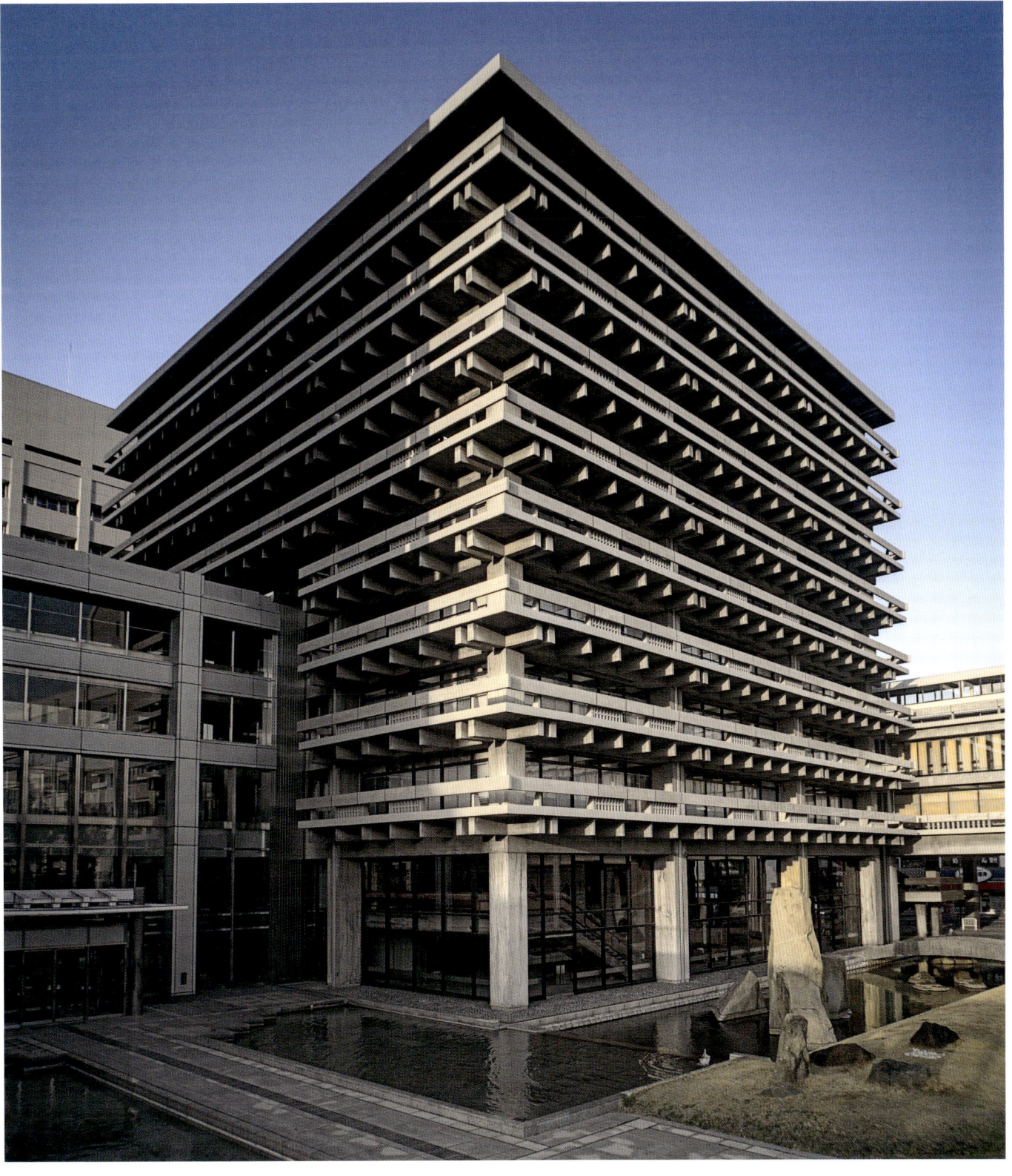

KAGAWA PREFECTURAL GOVERNMENT BUILDING

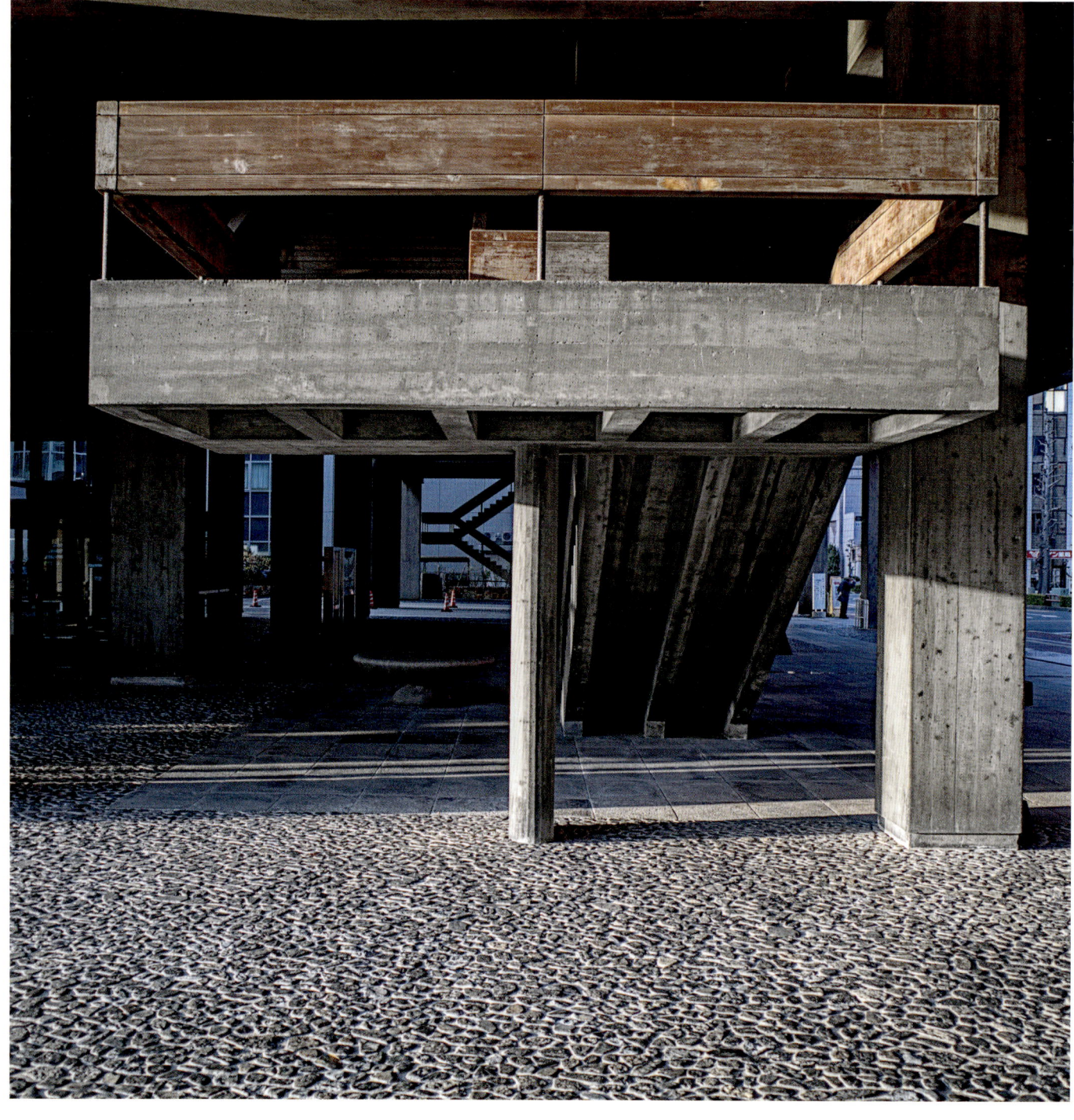

KAGAWA PREFECTURAL GOVERNMENT BUILDING

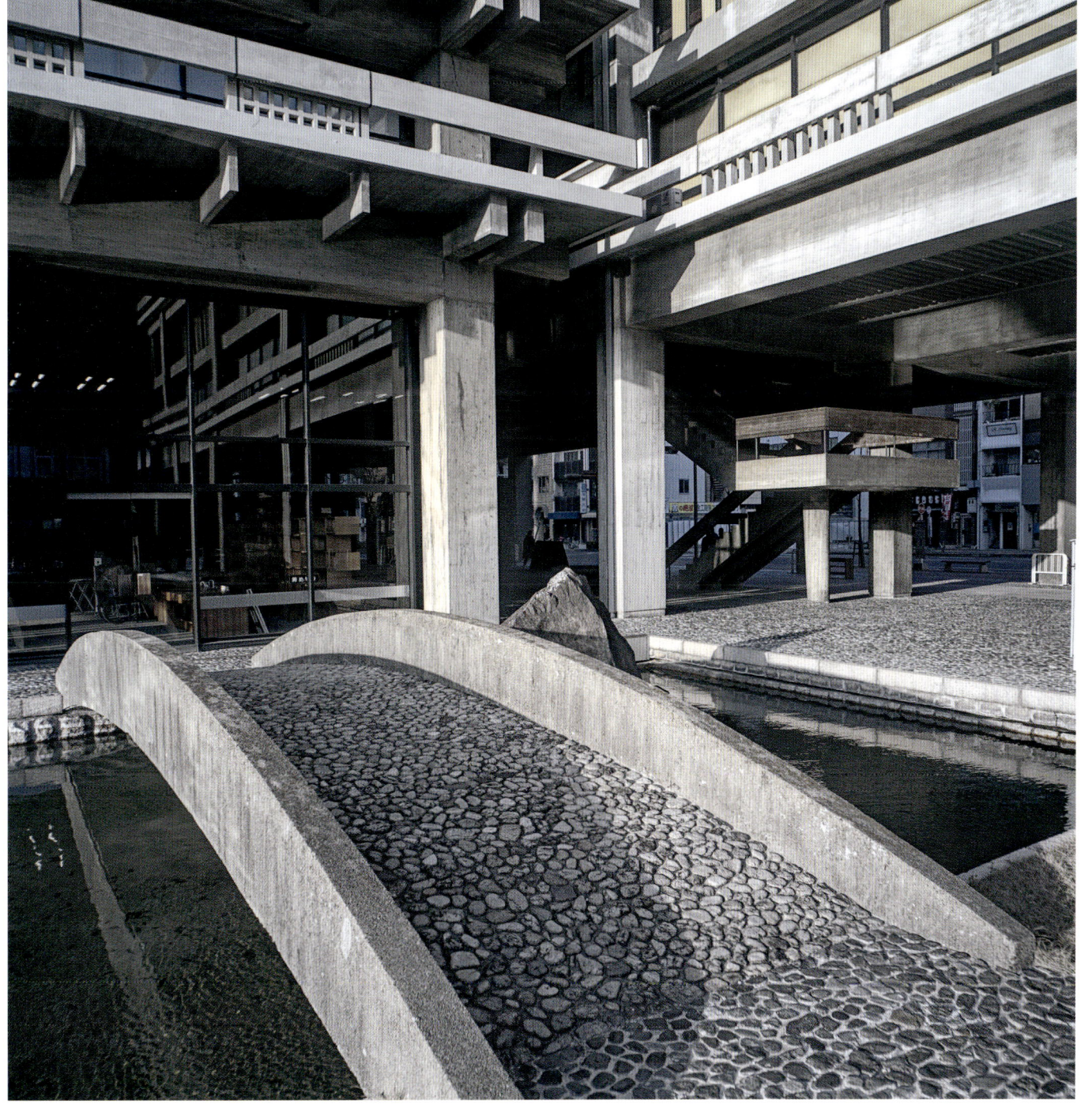

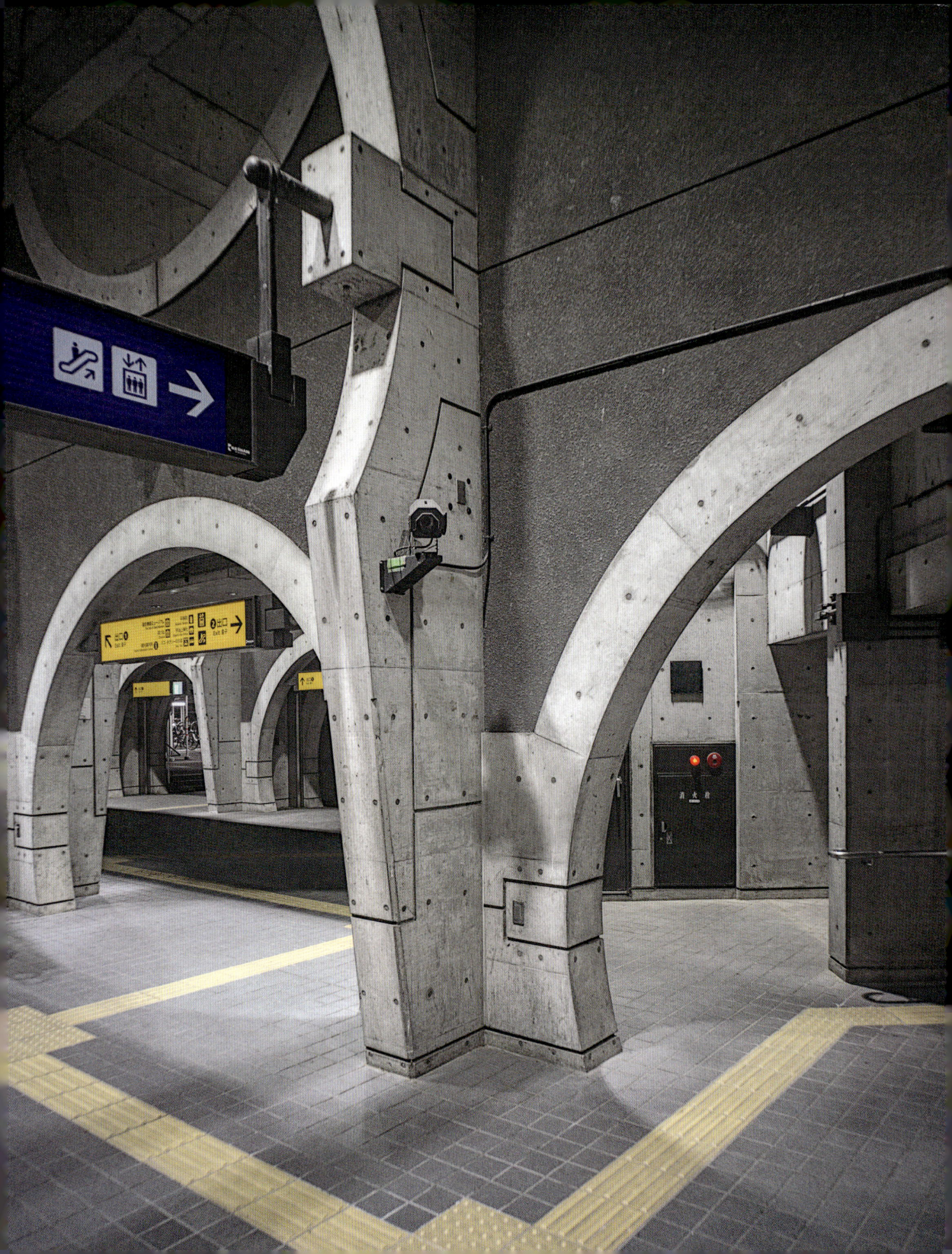

KEIHAN UJI STATION

UJI CITY, KYOTO PREFECTURE · Architect: WAKABAYASHI Hiroyuki · Completed 1995

In the shadow of tradition, where the air hums with tales of ancient temples and the crackle of fireworks over the Uji River, Keihan Uji Station emerges like a scene from a sci-fi odyssey. This architectural spaceship, helmed by visionary captain Hiroyuki Wakabayashi and launched in 1995, defies its historic backdrop with a daring leap into futurism.

The station, a stargate to the storied city of Uji, greets travellers not with wooden *torii* gates, but with a concrete vault that arcs like the heavens above a distant planet. The design is audacious, a semicircular cocoon that dares to embrace both the circle's Zen-like simplicity and the boundless possibilities of the cosmos. Within its grasp lies a portal where past and future converge, inviting pilgrims of progress into its hallowed, echoing dome.

Step inside this mothership and you're enveloped in an otherworldly realm where the curved lines of the vault replicate the infinite orbit of electrons, while block glass panels in the ceiling sprinkle daylight like stars across a galaxy. It's a celestial theatre where the outside world's cacophony fades, replaced by the hush of cosmic awe. This is a station that doesn't just serve passengers; it transports them.

Yet, in a dance as delicate as a tea ceremony, this futuristic vessel pays its respects to the old masters. The landscape's dual nature is mirrored within – here, the traditional and the avant-garde intertwine, much like the intertwining paths of a samurai's garden. Wakabayashi's alchemy melds the concrete and the ephemeral, the local and the extraterrestrial, into a fusion of space and time.

Winner of the Good Design Award, Keihan Uji Station is no mere transit point. It conveys the idea that history need not be a tether but can be a launch pad for new voyages. It is an invitation to travellers from all walks and worlds: step aboard, and let your journey transcend the here and now.

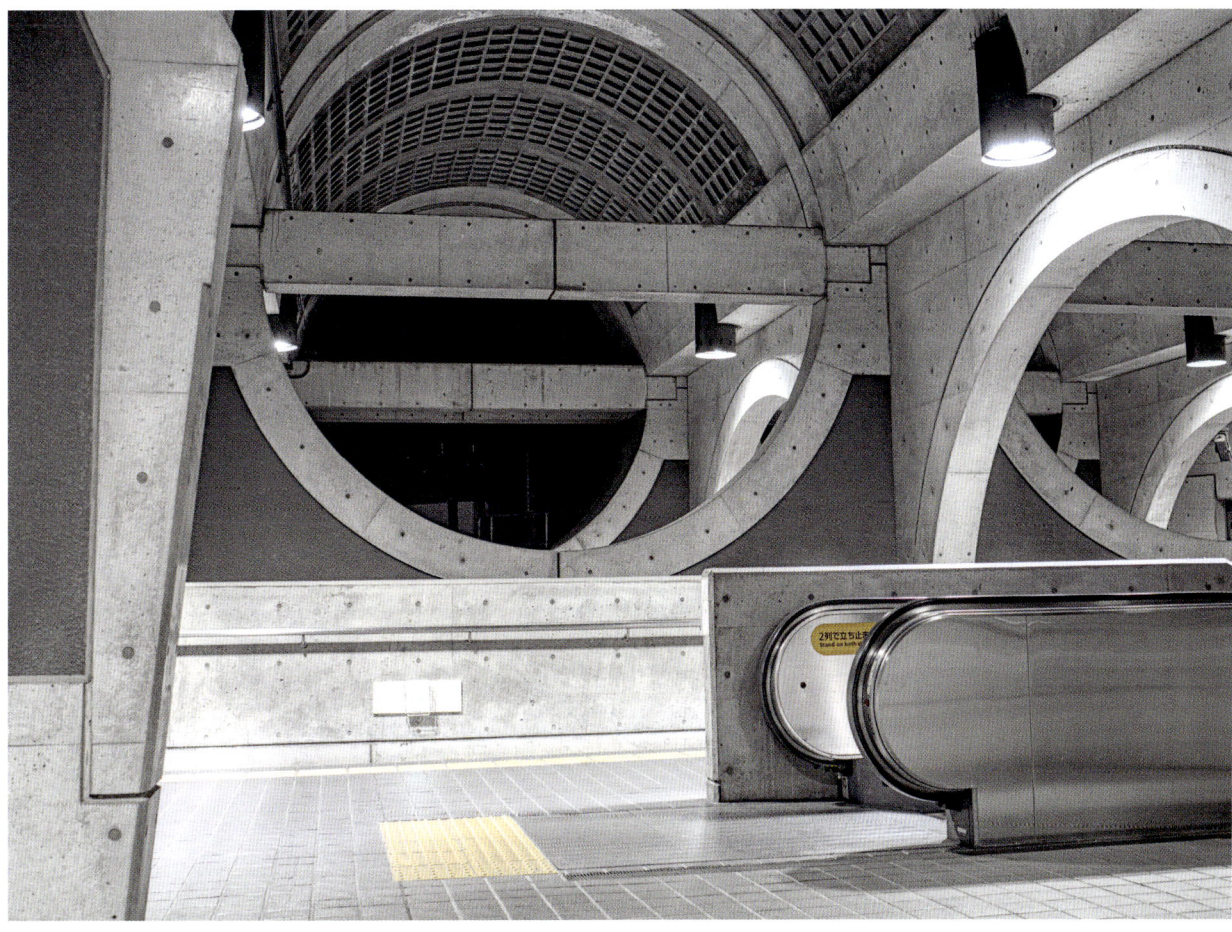

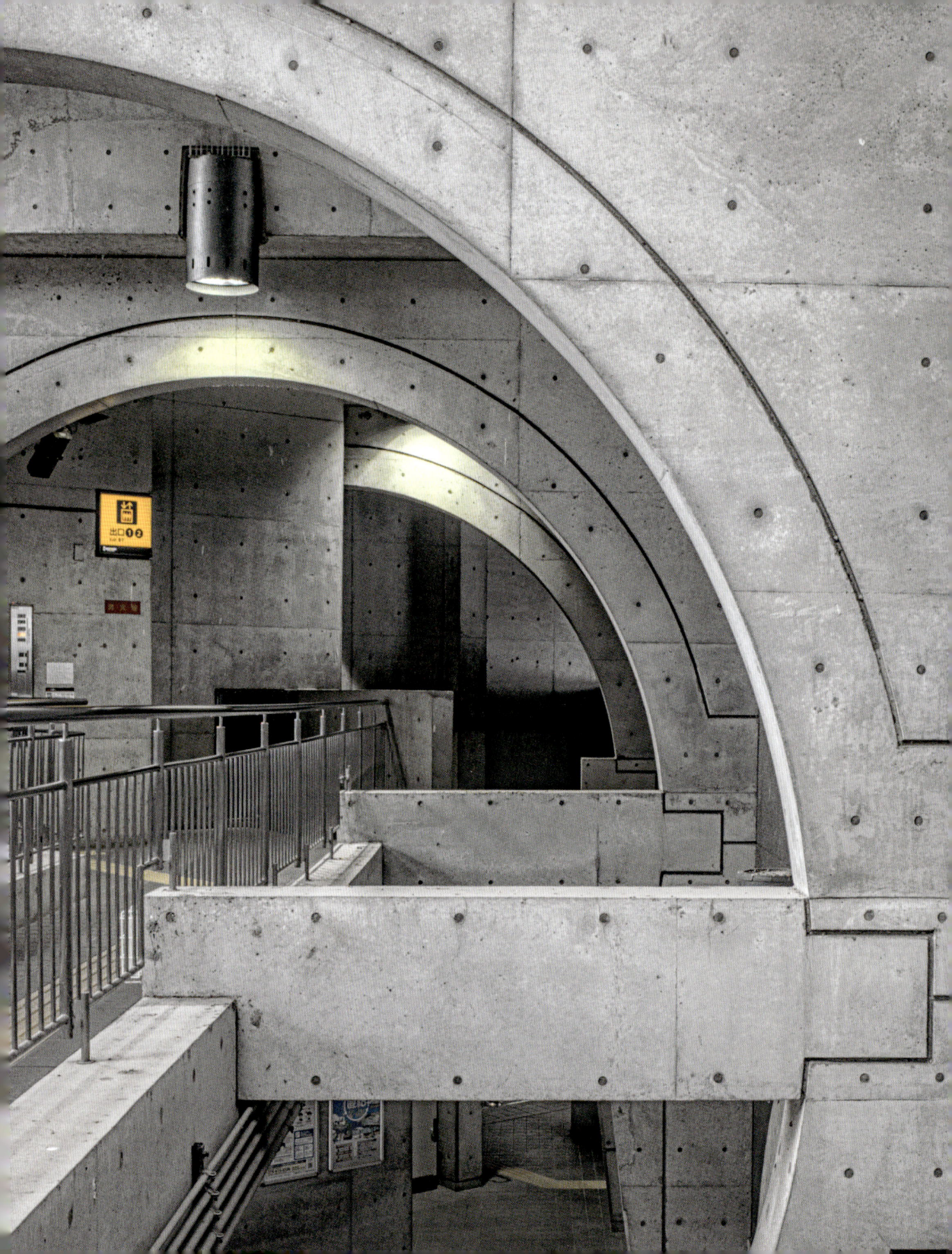

KEIHAN UJI STATION

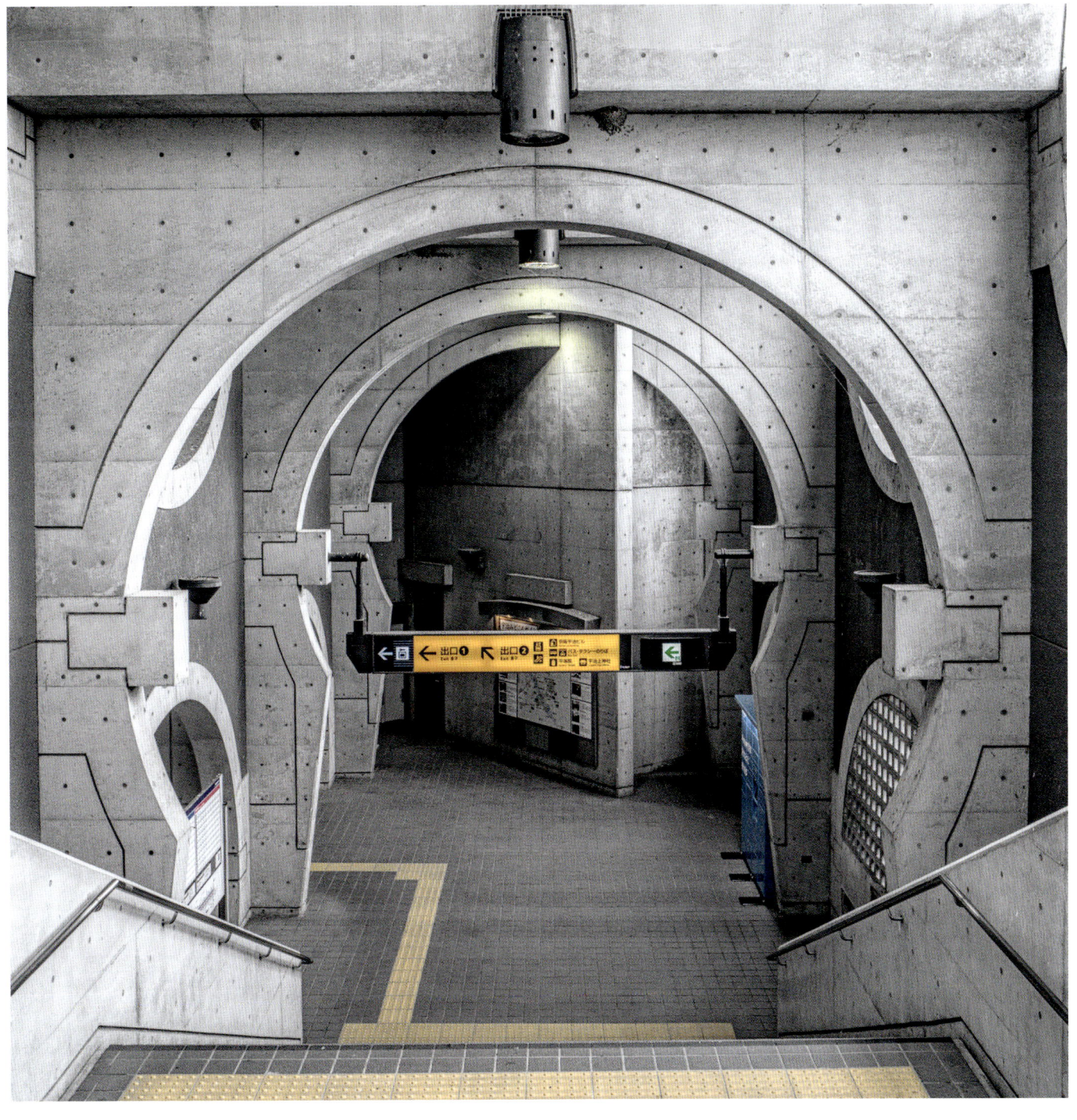

KEIHAN UJI STATION

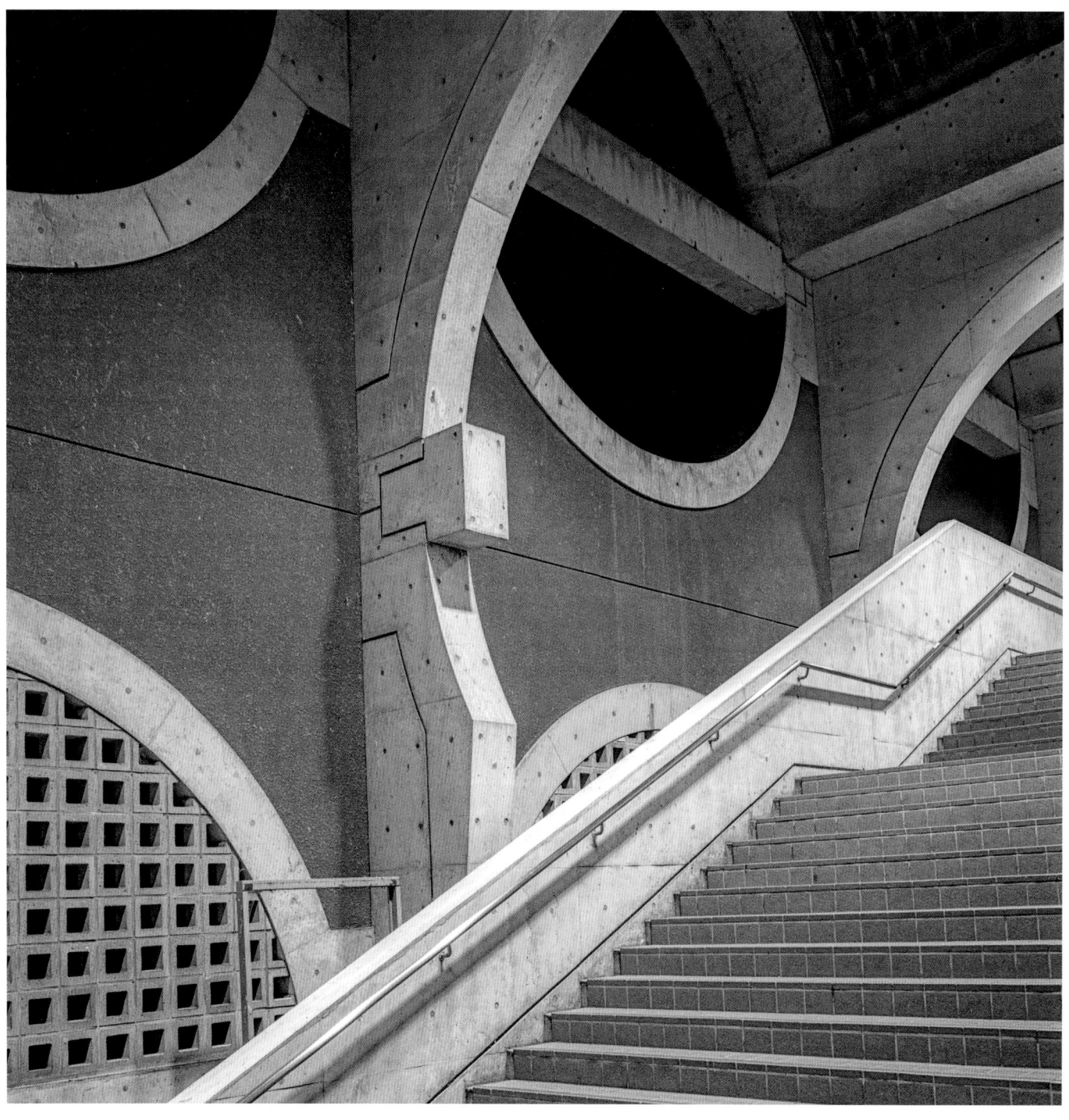

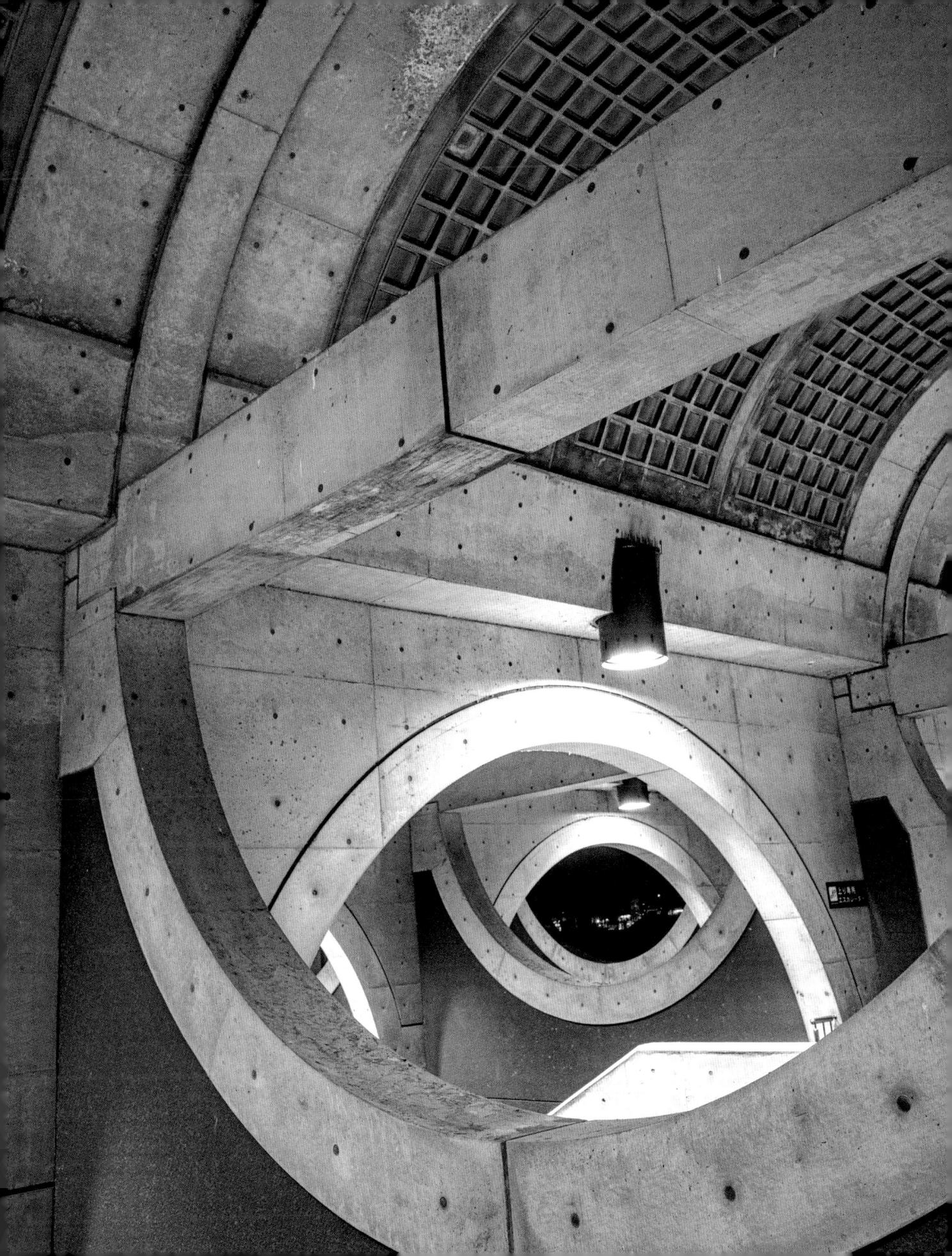

VILLA BIANCA

TOKYO · Architect: HOTTA Eiji · Completed 1966

As Tokyo basked in its Olympic glory in 1964, Villa Bianca ascended as an exemplar of futuristic living – the pioneer of designer condominiums in Japan. A confident vision carved from concrete cubes, this architectural gem marked the dawn of urban sophistication, catching the eye of global tastemakers and gracing the glossy pages of *LIFE* magazine.

Villa Bianca was a prophecy in concrete and steel. Determined to defy the status quo, Hotta embarked on a quest to craft a home for the future – two decades ahead of his time.

Infusing contemporary chic with Japanese soul, Villa Bianca's hand-carved wooden doors and cobblestone-clad halls offer a warm embrace amidst the strong lines of its avant-garde exterior. More than half a century later, it continues to stand resolute – proof of the visionary belief that design can indeed shape destiny.

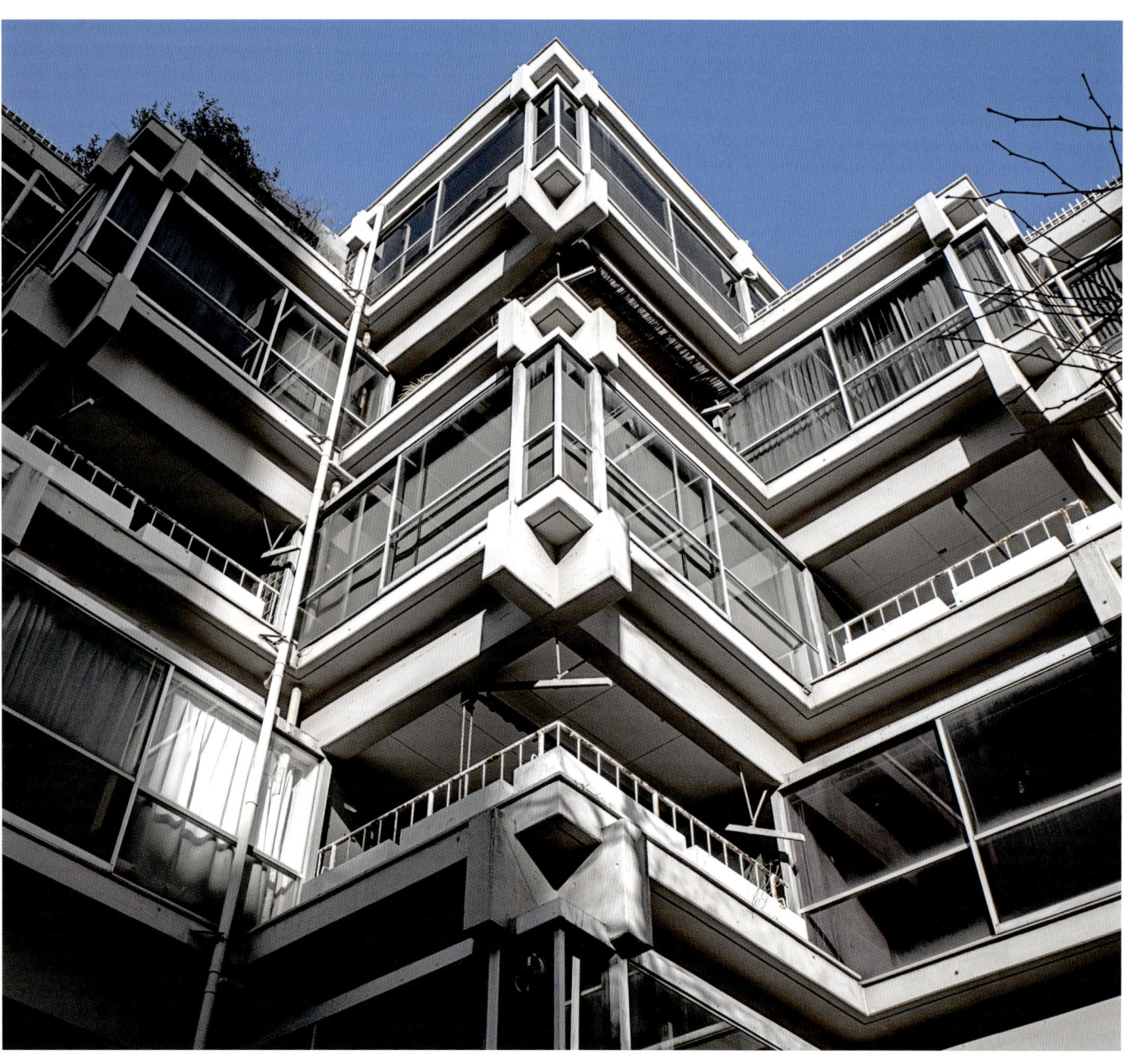

NAHA CIVIC HALL

OKINAWA · Architect: KINJO Nobuyoshi · Completed 1972

This wonderful building was slated for demolition due to failing a seismic audit some time ago. It was the host site for the official return of Okinawa to Japanese sovereignty on 15 May 1972. Perhaps emotion has saved it – until now. Plans to make 3D renders were recently announced. This doesn't bode well.

Nobuyoshi Kinjo played a major role in the development of Okinawan architecture. Here, he placed a red tiled roof on a reinforced concrete building to express Okinawan architectural identity. Along with large diagonally projecting eaves, this mimics the technique of *amahaji* found in old houses in Okinawa and denotes the critical regionalism of the period. 3D renders will be small consolation.

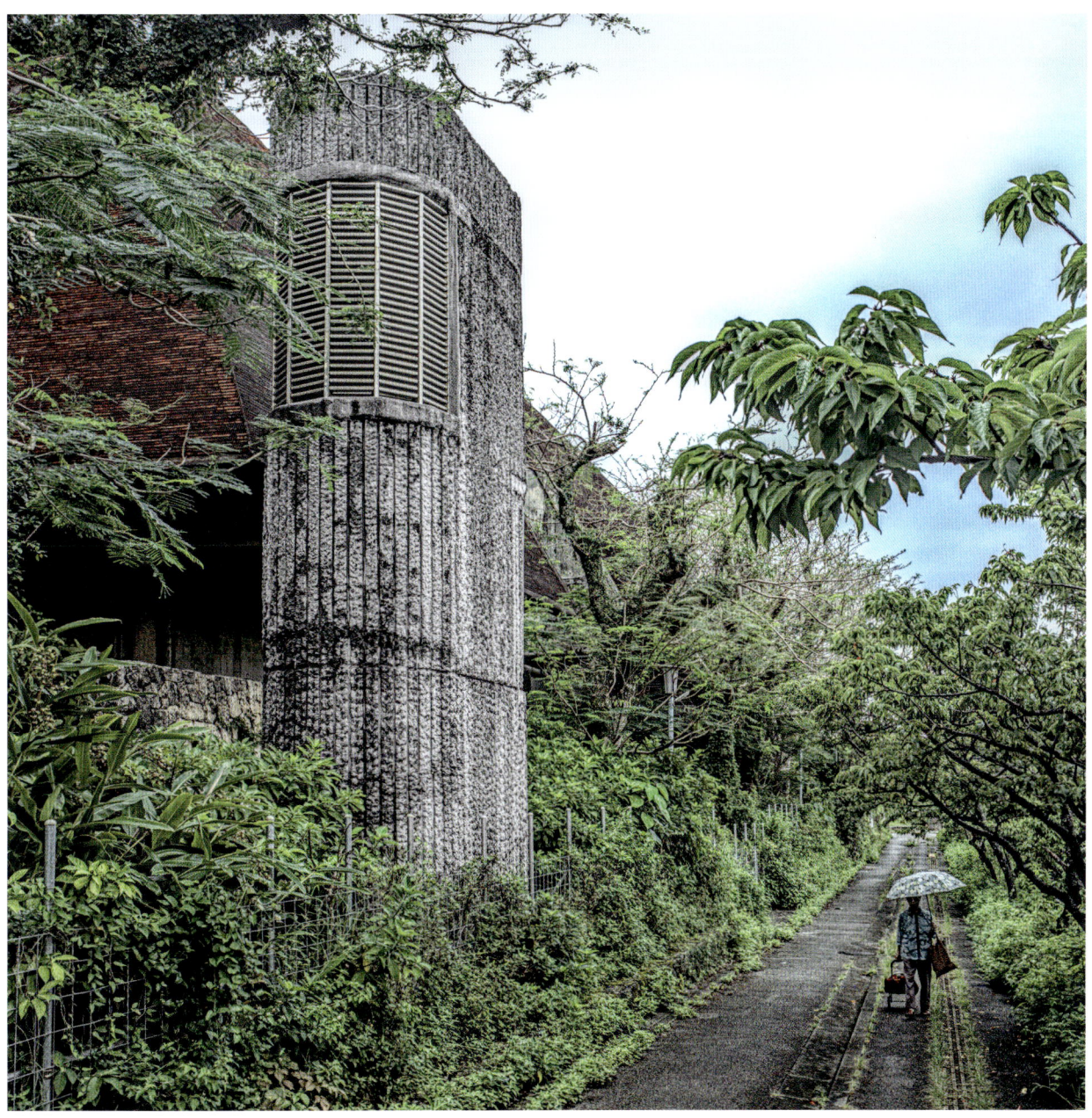

BOOK CAFÉ OKINAWA RAIL

KUNIGAMI, OKINAWA · Architect: TOMORI Tadashi · Completed 2016

Amidst a copse of whispering leaves, this third place settles as a solemn tribute to Japanese architecture's profound dialogue with the land – a tale as layered as any literary classic. Here, concrete is crafted with the eloquence of prose and positioned with the precision of punctuation, creating a narrative that honours the environment as the protagonist of the plot.

This book café, a silent sentinel among the trees, speaks volumes of an architectural language where structures are inscribed into the landscape, not as forceful declarations, but as footnotes that accentuate the earth's natural poetry. It's as though the architect has leafed through the pages of Japanese aesthetic principles, penning a structure that is a *haiku* in form, succinct in its expression yet deep with meaning.

Taking a leaf from the annals of traditional Japanese design, the building is reminiscent of *engawa* – a space that blurs the lines between inside and out, inviting the reader to dwell not just within the walls of literature but within the embrace of nature itself. The window is a bookmark placed carefully along the façade, a reminder to pause and reflect, not only on the written word but on the ever-present narrative of the changing seasons outside.

Within this book café, one can imagine patrons leafing through tomes of Japanese poetry, the verses echoing the symbiosis outside, or delving into novels that explore the human condition, as the boundary between humanity and nature quietly dissolves around them. Like the best of literature, the design speaks to the reader, telling a story of integration, balance and respect.

In this secluded nook, a chapter of architectural lore is written with the landscape as its canvas, inviting bibliophiles to immerse themselves in a storybook setting where the lines of man-made and natural beauty are blurred – a perfect place for a reader to turn the page under the canopy of the living, breathing world.

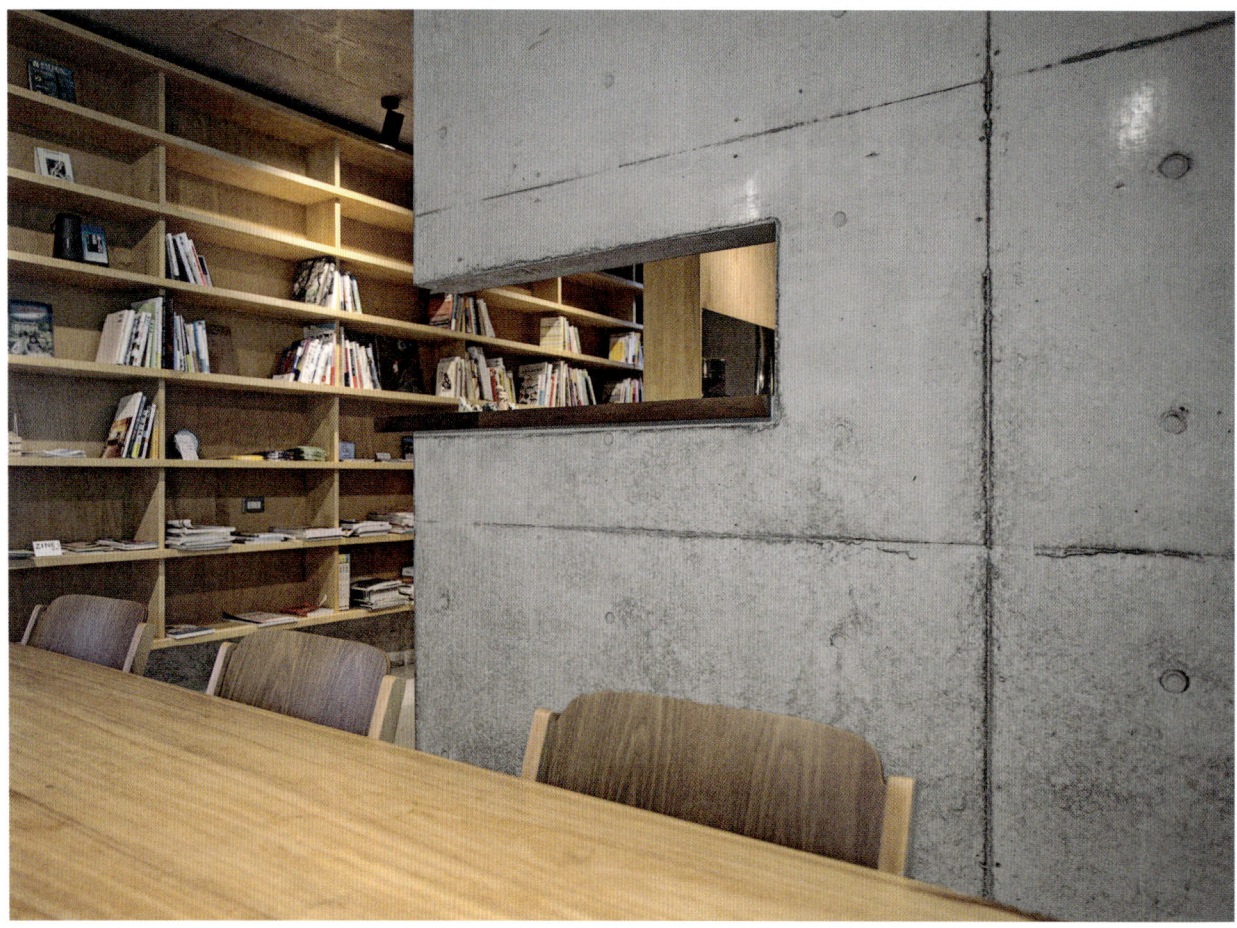

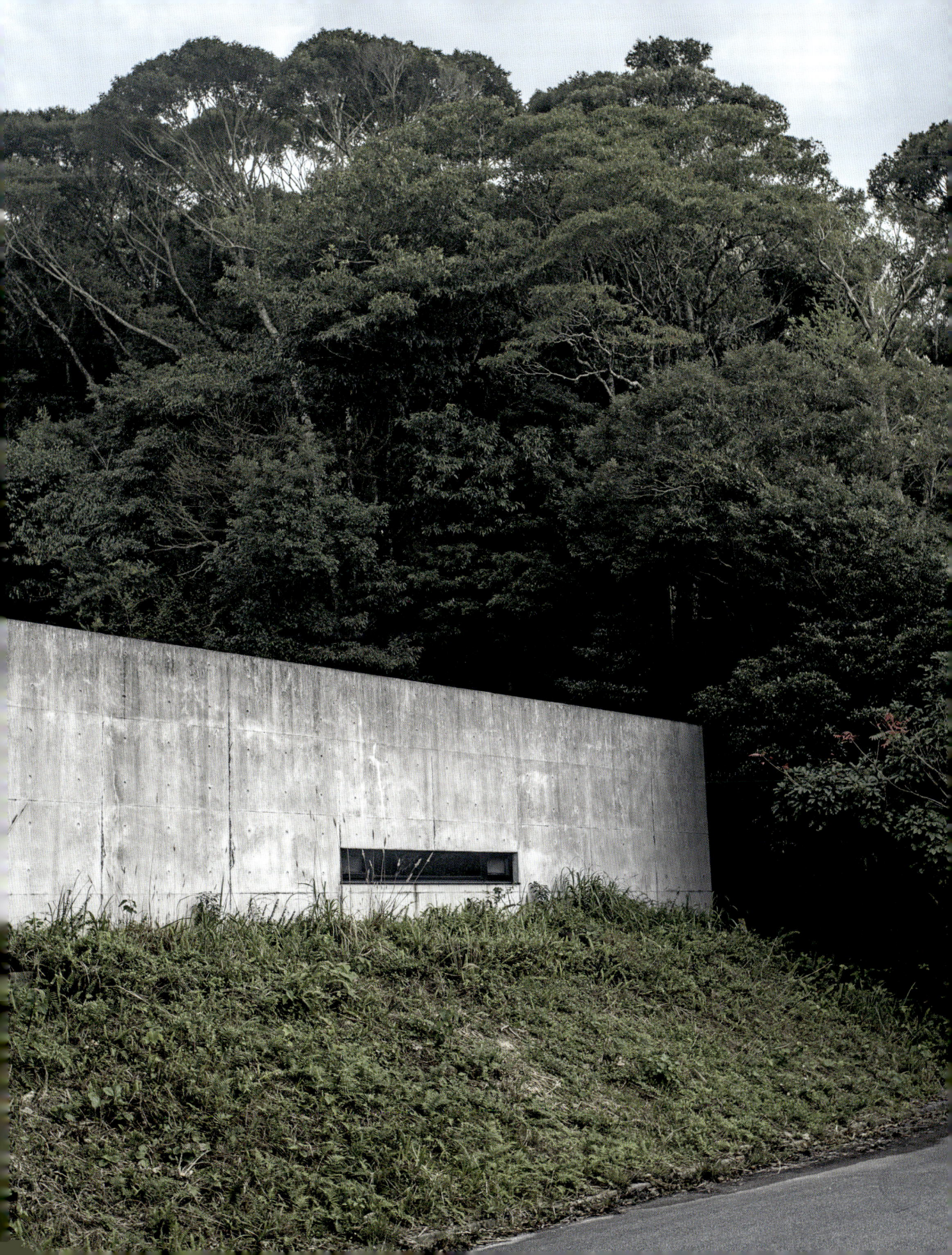

CHIBA UNIVERSITY INOHANA MEMORIAL HALL

CHIBA · Architect: MAKI Fumihiko · Completed 1963

The Memorial Hall at Chiba University's Inohana Campus, completed in 1963 and designed by the visionary Fumihiko Maki, performs as a grand symphony of architectural elements, beautifully orchestrating a blend of tradition and modernity. This iconic auditorium, with its distinctive trapezoidal framework, projects a symbolic silhouette that harmonizes with the campus square, akin to a shrine in a sacred forest, dedicated to the local deity.

Originally constructed to enrich the cultural and educational experiences of its students, the auditorium faced significant structural challenges after the 2011 Great East Japan Earthquake. This prompted a comprehensive renovation in 2013 that meticulously preserved the building's historical essence while enhancing its functionality and safety. The renovation involved reinforcing the main structure, repairing the unique cedar-board cement concrete walls that display the wood's natural grain, and partially reinstalling the glass curtain wall. Additionally, asbestos was carefully removed, and acoustic and lighting improvements were made to accommodate modern performances.

The redesign of the seating area was particularly thoughtful, reducing the total number of seats from 720 to 526 on the first floor, thereby increasing space per seat and integrating small desks. This adjustment not only improved comfort but also refined the hall's utility for its audience, akin to fine-tuning a musical instrument for superior acoustical performance. Above the entrance, a large gong sculpture sets a dramatic prelude, while the foyer atrium is transformed by a glass wall that allows natural light to stream in, dynamically changing the space's ambiance throughout the day.

Sixty years post-construction, the Memorial Hall remains one of Japan's most precious modernist buildings. Fumihiko Maki's design, a blend of robust concrete structures and subtle wooden aesthetics topped with a copper shingle roof, continues to serve as a rhythmic core of cultural vitality at Chiba University. It results from the power of thoughtful architectural design to host a harmony of educational and cultural events that resonate well into the future.

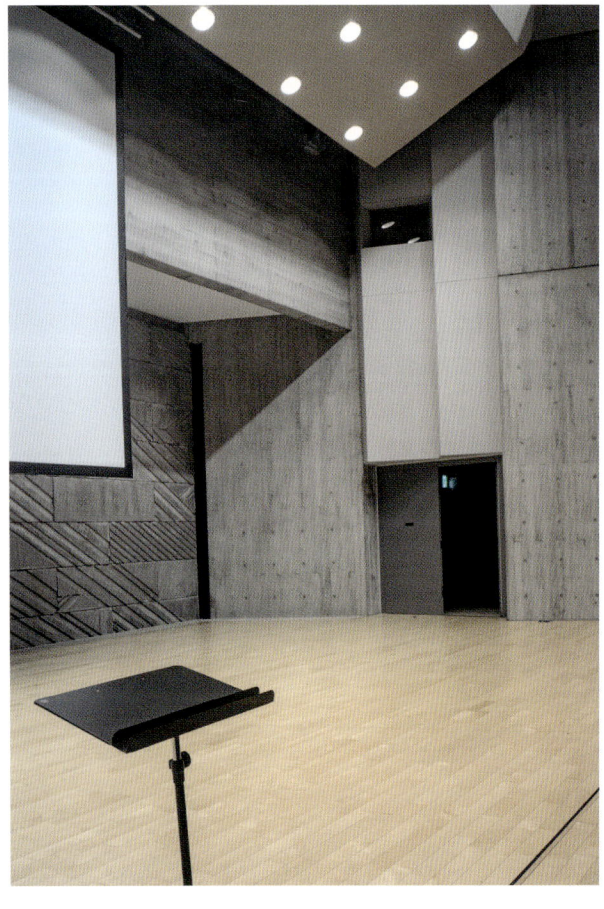
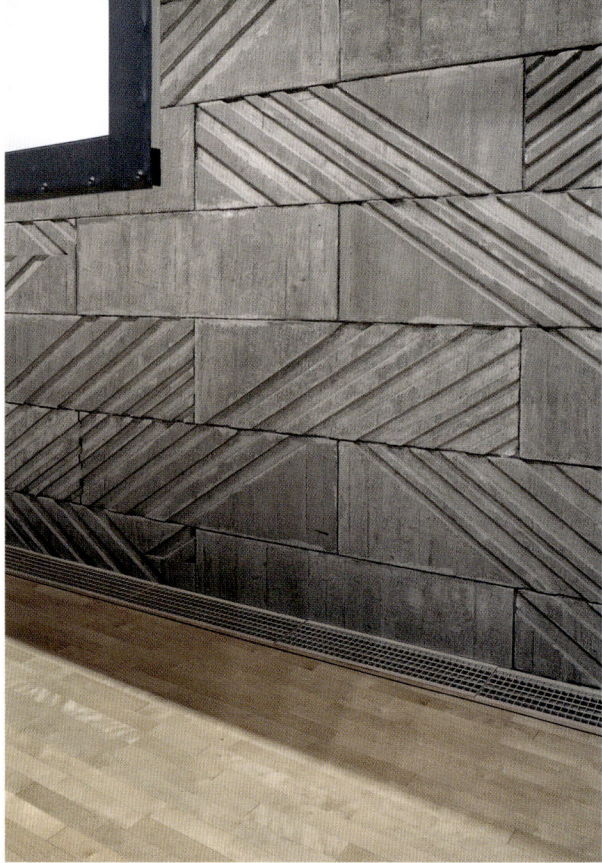

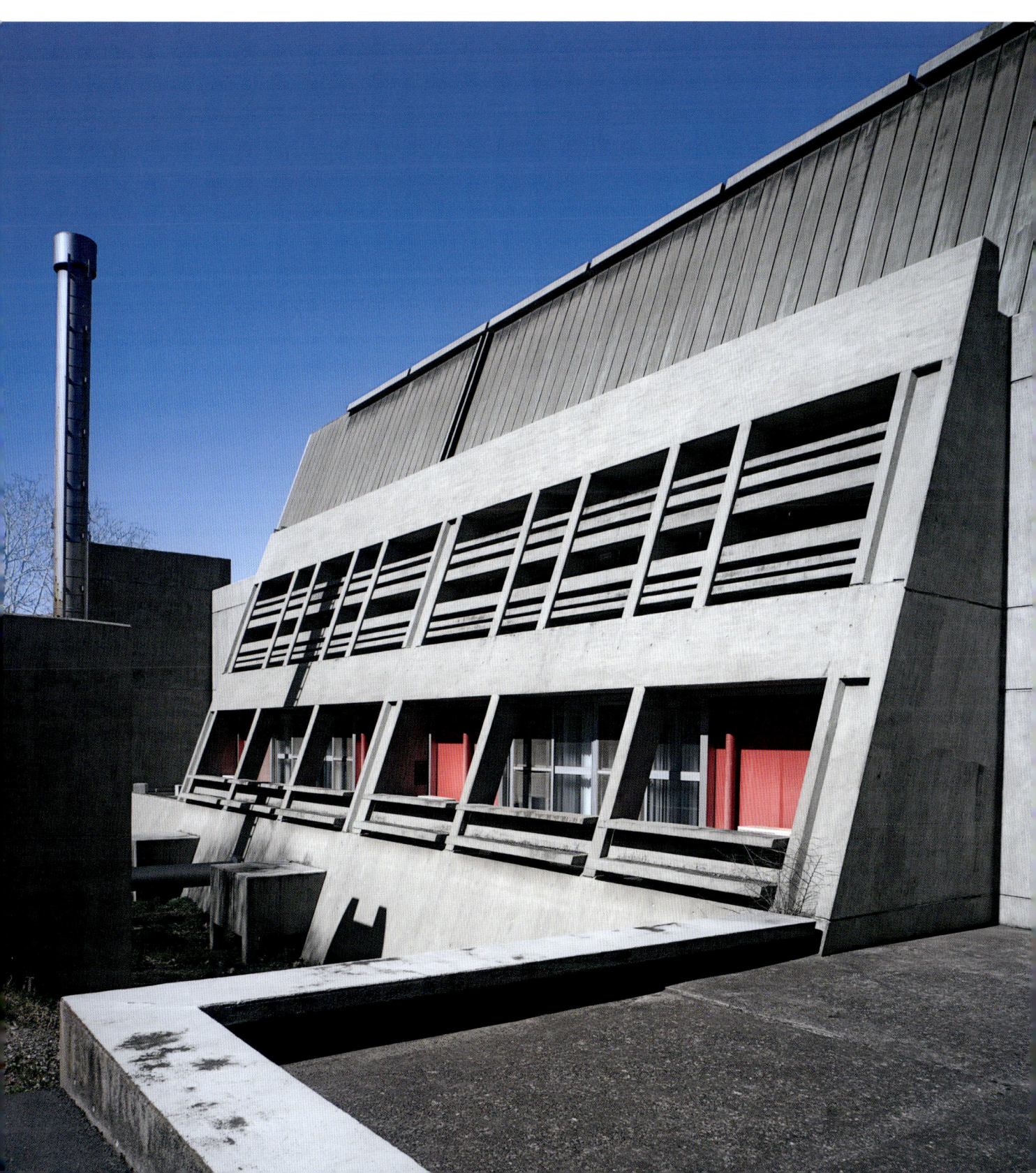

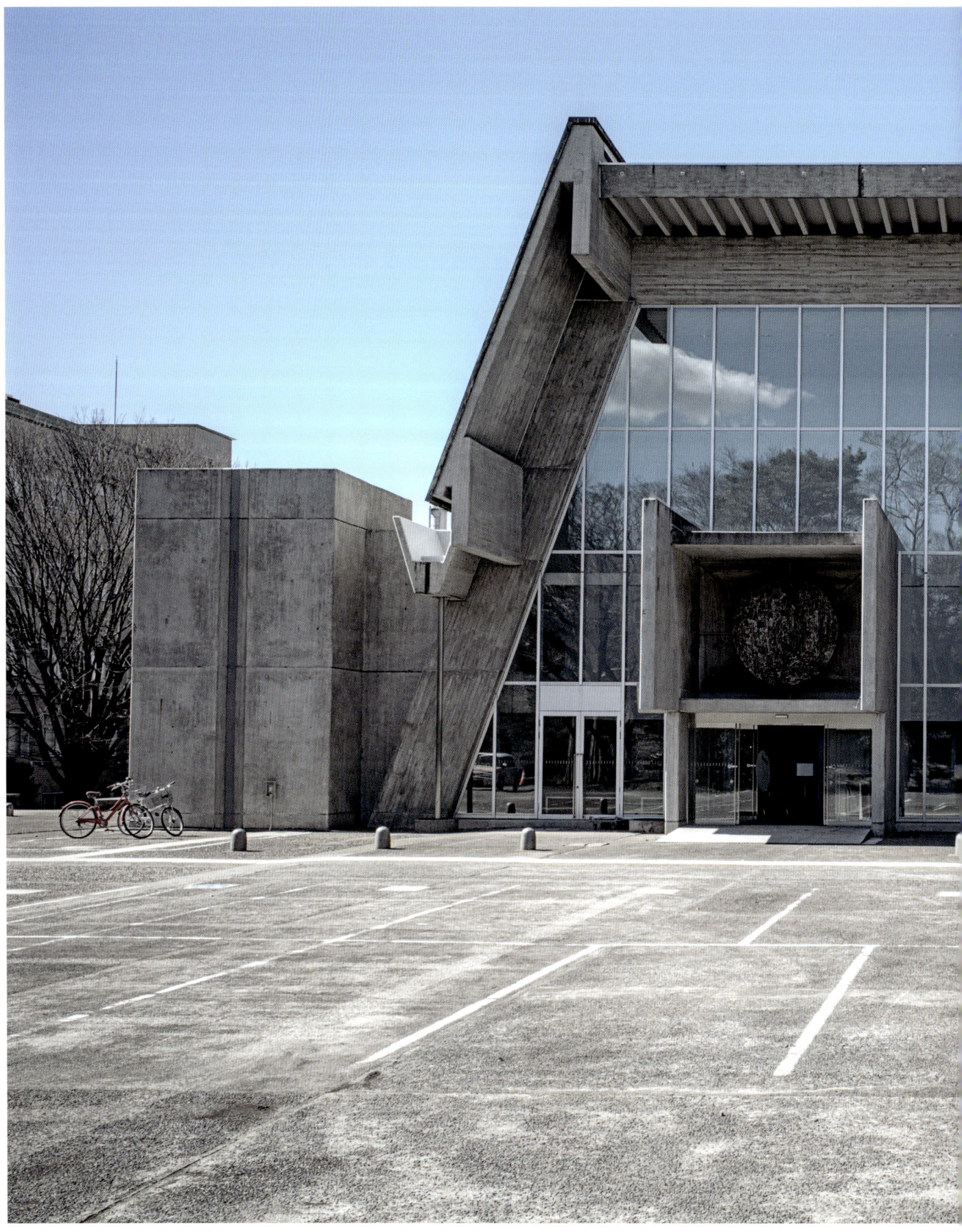

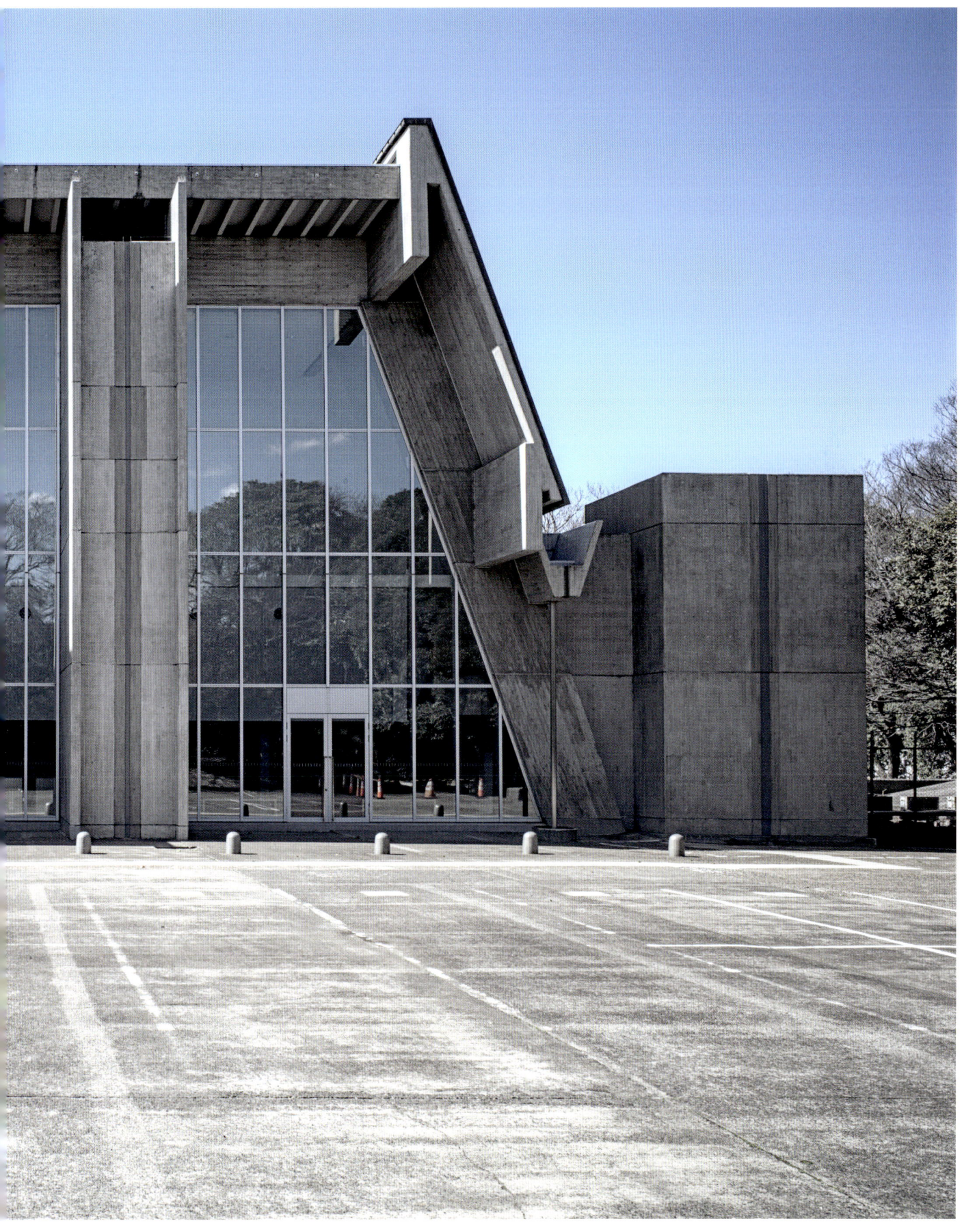

CHIBA UNIVERSITY SCHOOL OF MEDICINE INOHANA ALUMNI HALL

CHIBA · Architects: SUZUKI Hiroki and TANAKA Tomohisa · Completed 2013

This neo-Brutalist combination of concrete and glass serves as a gathering place for the alumni of a university's medical faculty. Its architectural design cleverly incorporates elements that resonate with both cultural heritage and the medical profession. Structurally, the centrepiece is a multi-purpose hall designed in the distinct style of a pagoda, utilizing cascading white eaves that are reminiscent of traditional Buddhist architecture. This design choice gives the building a serene and elevated appearance and cleverly mimics a rib cage, symbolically reflecting the medical theme.

The use of a singular colour theme, primarily white, further enhances its thematic alignment with the medical profession, echoing the purity and simplicity of a doctor's white coat. This monochromatic scheme also helps to unify the structure's various components, which include a Japanese-style room, a conference room and office spaces.

The building, positioned centrally on the campus, gains a monumental presence through these architectural choices.

The overlapping eaves create an optical illusion that suggests more levels than are actually present, thus amplifying its stature and significance within the university grounds. Internally, the design remains minimalist, using the surrounding campus greenery as a natural backdrop, which adds a refreshing contrast to the bare interior.

The construction of this facility was a collaborative effort led by an architect who is also a professor at the university. This collaborative aspect ensures ongoing maintenance and involvement by the students, who use the building for their academic pursuits and engage in the practical study of its architecture. The building is a functional space and a living lab where architecture and medicine intersect, offering a continuous learning environment for the students.

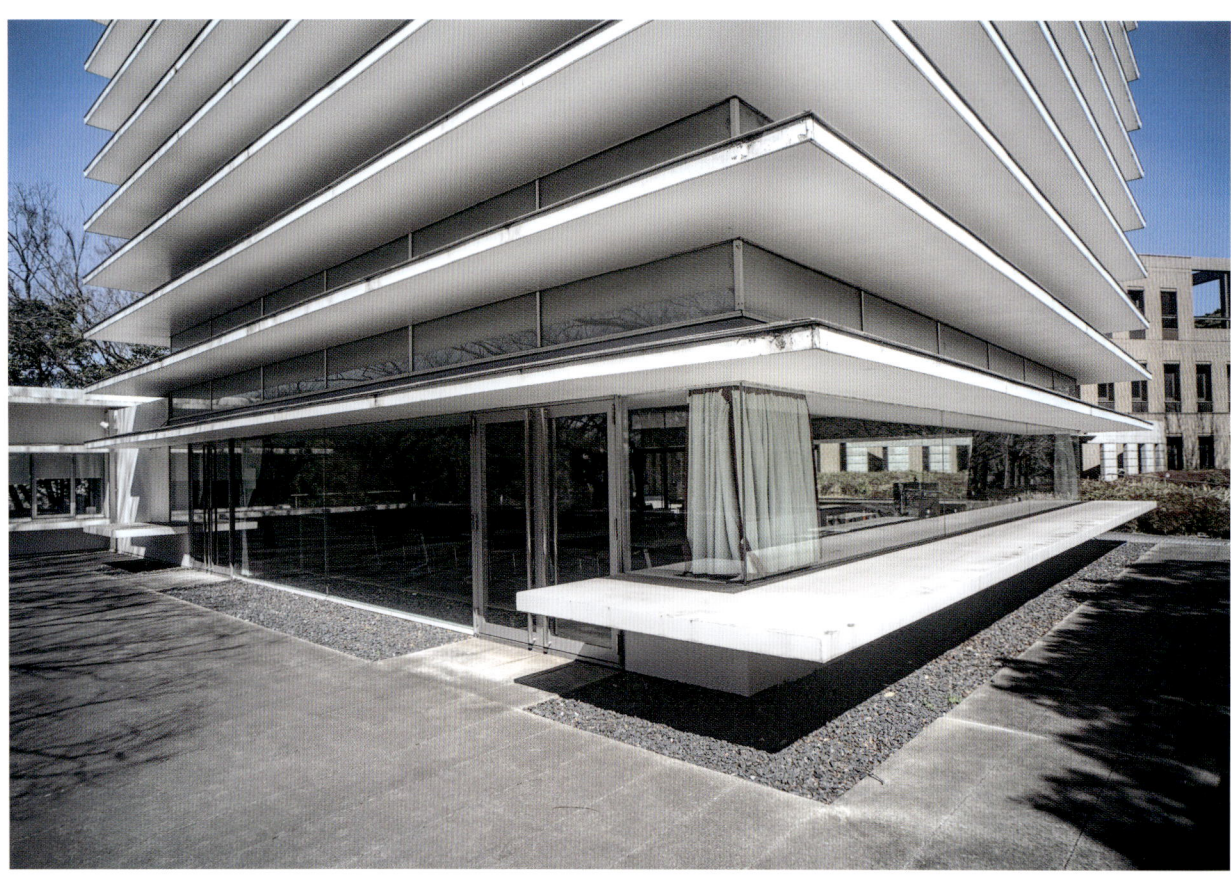

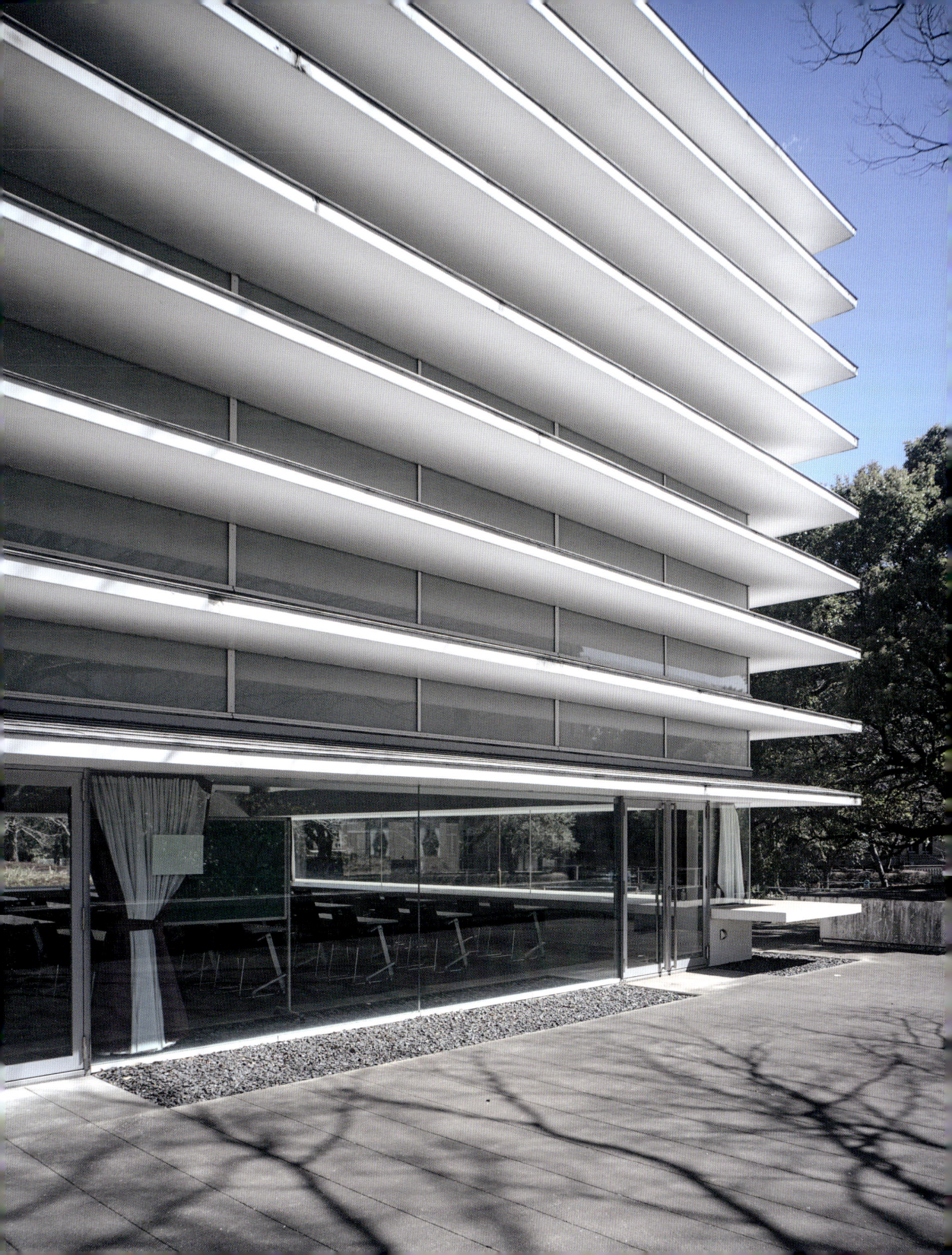

COSMO GI – MULTI-USE COMPLEX

NAGO, OKINAWA

In the cosmic ballet of architecture, this complex pirouettes with a dual identity, fusing the universality of nightlife with the tactical precision of a soldier's hideout. Its façade – a concrete atlas – bears a crevice that strikingly resembles Argentina doing the tango with Idaho, a geographical caprice etched into its very skin.

This structural cosmos, weathered like a seasoned GI's uniform, shelters a galaxy of dodgy bars, each a star in the firmament of after-hours escapades. Here, the universe contracts into dimly lit corners where stories unfold, alliances form, and the night marches on with the strategic intent of a covert operation.

Like a metaphorical mess hall for the starry-eyed and the earthbound foot soldier alike, Cosmo GI stands at ease, its martial façade opening up into a realm of escapism – where the revelry is as boundless as space and as grounded as the grit of military boots.

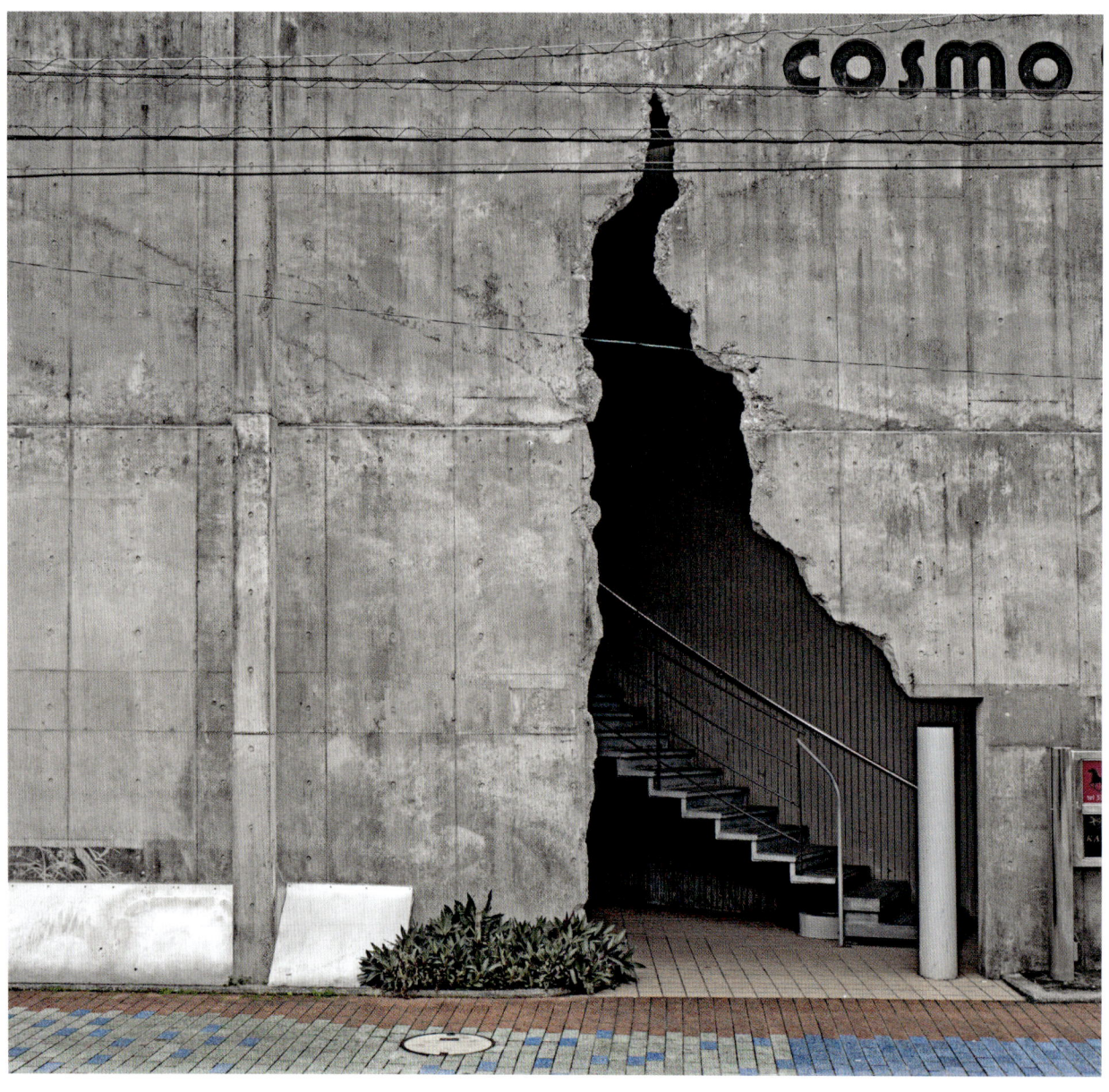

DAM UTILITY BUILDING

KUNIGAMI, OKINAWA

This image captures a mesmerizing game of hide-and-seek between man-made structure and wild nature in Kunigami, Okinawa – a place where the shadows of militarization have receded, leaving behind a landscape where serenity and security embrace. In the verdant embrace of this demilitarized zone, the building emerges like both a forgotten relic and a silent symbol of a newfound peace.

The appeal lies in the contrast – the stern, grey geometry of the structure set against the unruly, lush green weave of nature. It's a visual rhapsody of resilience, where the rigid lines of human endeavour are softened by the forgiving growth of the forest. The sight is a balm, knowing that in Kunigami, once subject to military prowess, it is now safe to discover such hidden jewels without the echo of a troubled past.

Hopefully, this composition accurately reflects a tune of reprieve and reclamation, where what was once under strict military control is now gently embraced by nature itself, symbolizing a harmonious coexistence and a future where the only invasions are those of foliage against concrete.

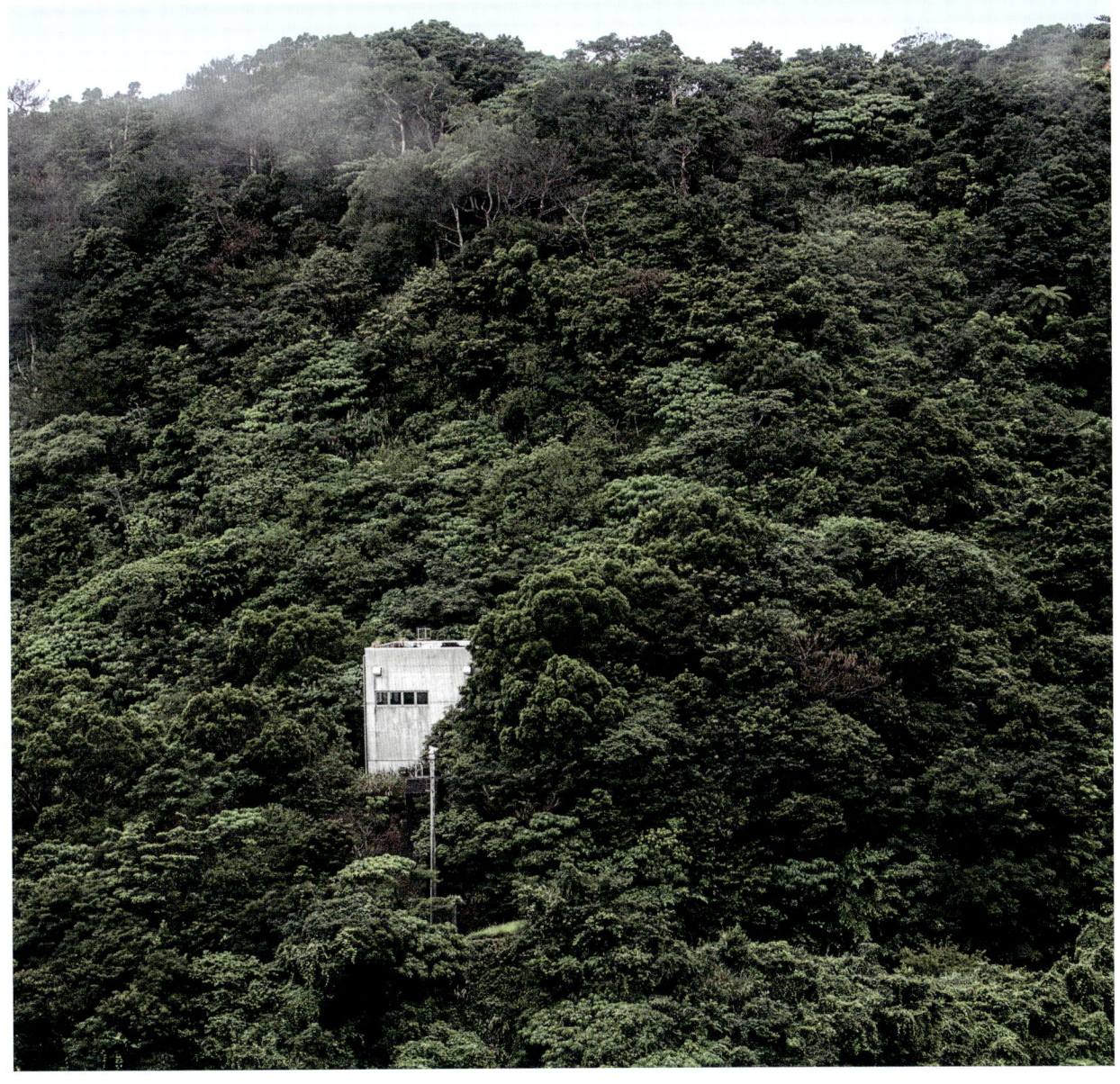

GUNMA MUSIC CENTER

TAKASAKI , GUNMA PREFECTURE · Architect: Antonin and Noémi Raymond · Completed 1961

In a grand ensemble of frugality and foresight, the site of an erstwhile feudal stronghold was transformed by harmonized local funds and public generosity into an architectural concert hall. Dual maestros, the Raymonds, conducting with a concrete baton, orchestrated a trifecta of aims: to craft a venue as lasting as a classic vinyl, to compose a democratic chamber where every seat resounded with the clarity of a high-fidelity speaker, and to create a profile as respectful to history as a ballad to bygone eras.

With walls and a roof as slender as the staves on a sheet of music yet strong enough to resist the tremors of the earth's deepest bass notes, this folded concrete pavilion hits a high note in structural ingenuity. Its design, debatable in cost but not in quality, has proven to be a timeless hit.

This building became Takasaki's visual anthem – a prelude to the "Bilbao Effect" – striking a chord as an emblem of the city, even if the Raymonds might have preferred a more understated melody.

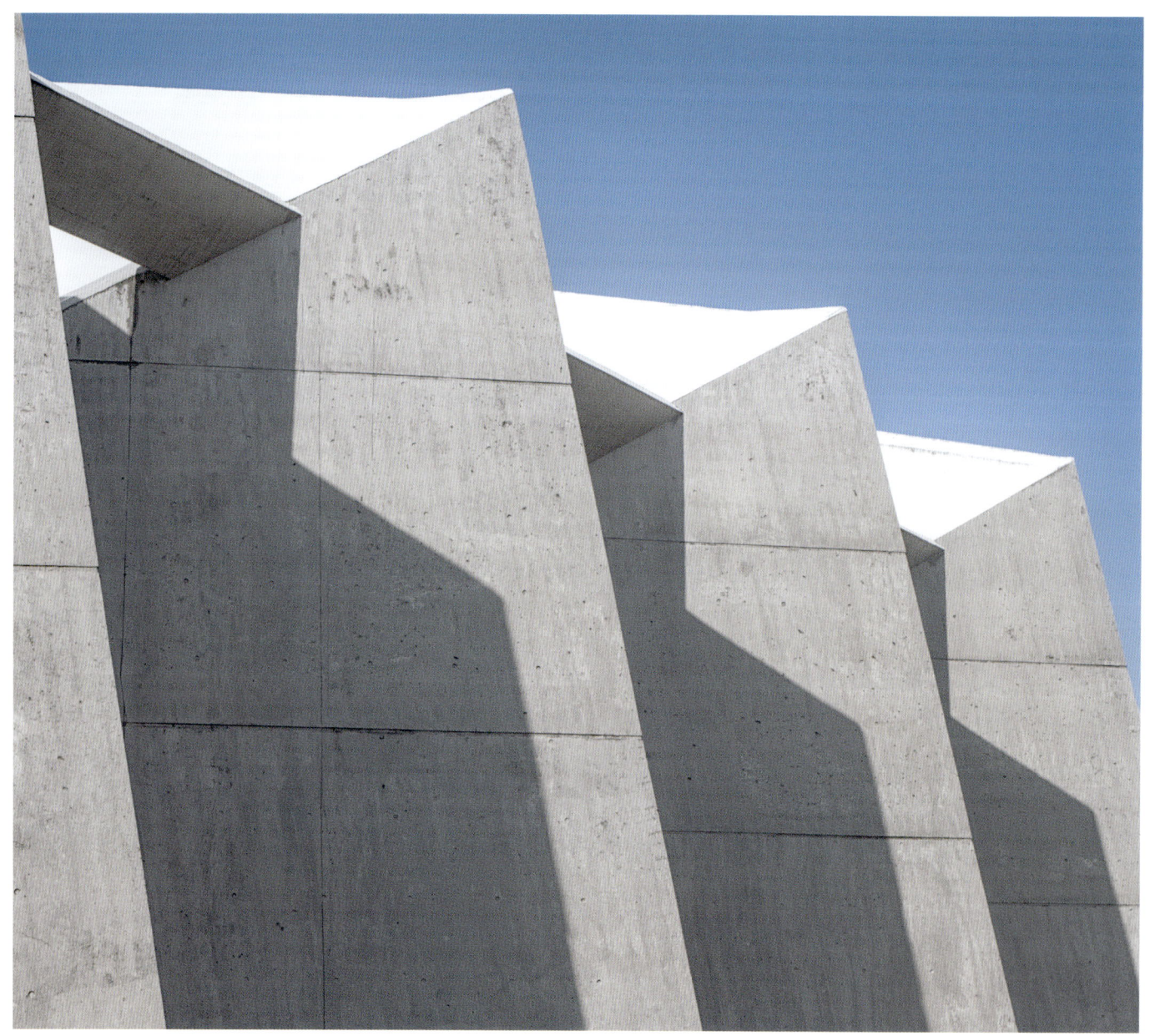

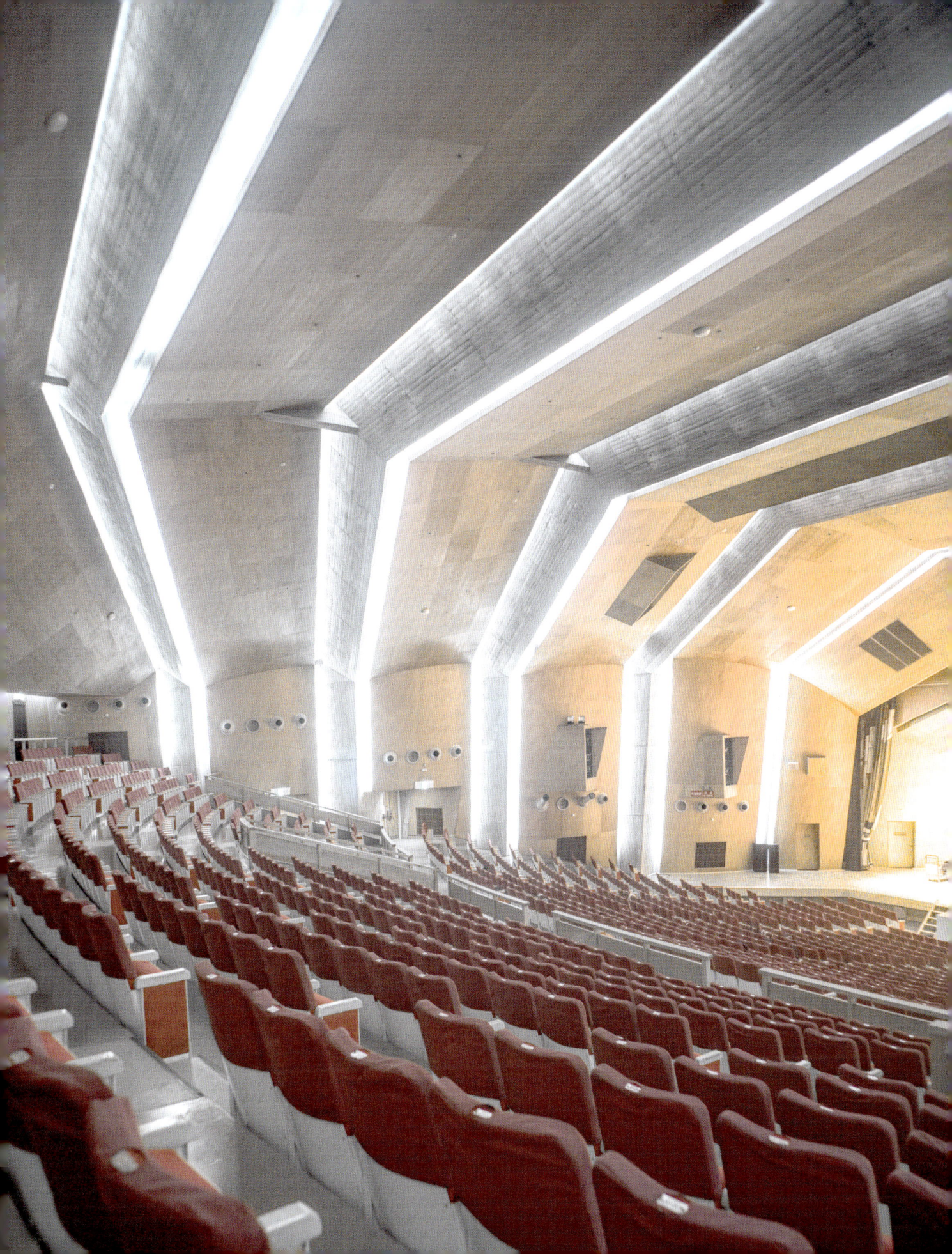

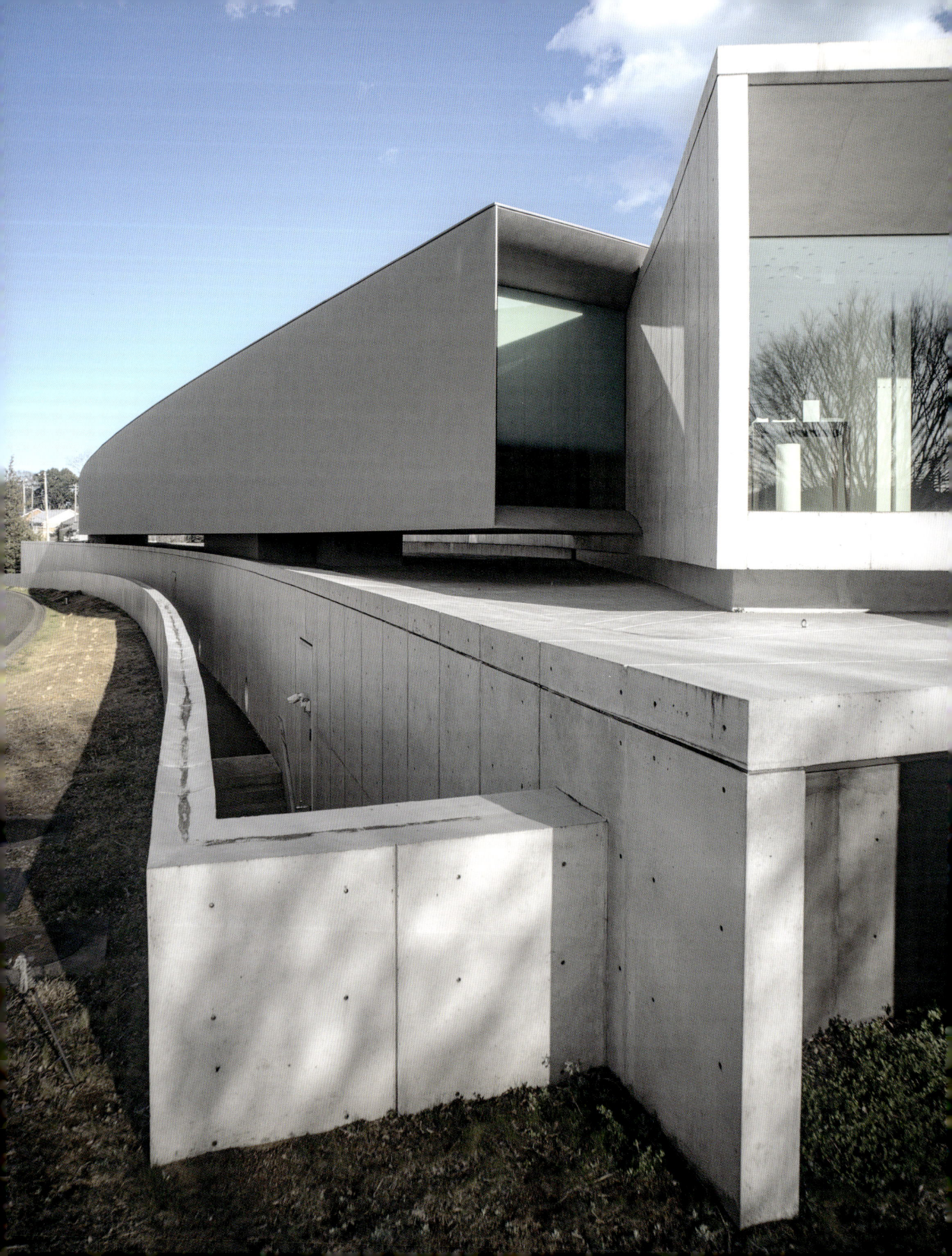

HOKI MUSEUM

CHIBA · Architect: Nikken Sekkei Ltd. · Reopened 2020

This neo-Brutalist design aptly marries the resilience of concrete with the clarity of glass, creating an environment where the depth of realist art is vividly illuminated. Reopened in 2020 after rehabilitation from flood damage, the museum features impressive thirty-metre cantilevers that arc gracefully, mirroring the delicate yet definite strokes of the realist paintings it houses. This architectural choice enhances the museum's aesthetic and subtly nods to the curves of a wine glass, an elegant allusion to the founder Mr Masao Hoki's passion for wine collecting.

Inside, the museum's layout facilitates an encounter with art that is both sequential and random-access, thanks to the slight curvature of the galleries. This design enables visitors to appreciate each artwork in isolation or in a collective sweep, akin to a wine tasting where each sip can be savoured individually or as part of a broader palette. The interior, free from the clutter of wall-finish and flooring joints, focuses solely on the artworks, much like how a finely aged wine stands out in a crystal-clear glass.

Externally, the museum's stacked galleries balance harmoniously with the surrounding residential area on the west, while on the forest-facing sides, the galleries are arranged to reveal the museum's function through their discrete composition. The cantilevered upper gallery stretches towards the forest like a vine reaching for sunlight, integrating nature with architecture. The horizontal slits between the galleries not only architecturally accentuate the structure but also channel breezes that animate the courtyard's trees, reminiscent of the lively dance of leaves in a vineyard.

This strategic use of concrete and expansive glass in the Hoki Museum fortifies the structure against natural elements and creates a refined sanctuary for art-lovers, echoing the complexities and subtleties of a well-curated wine collection. The museum embodies the idea that, like a good wine, great architecture hits a high note when offering layers of discovery and enjoyment.

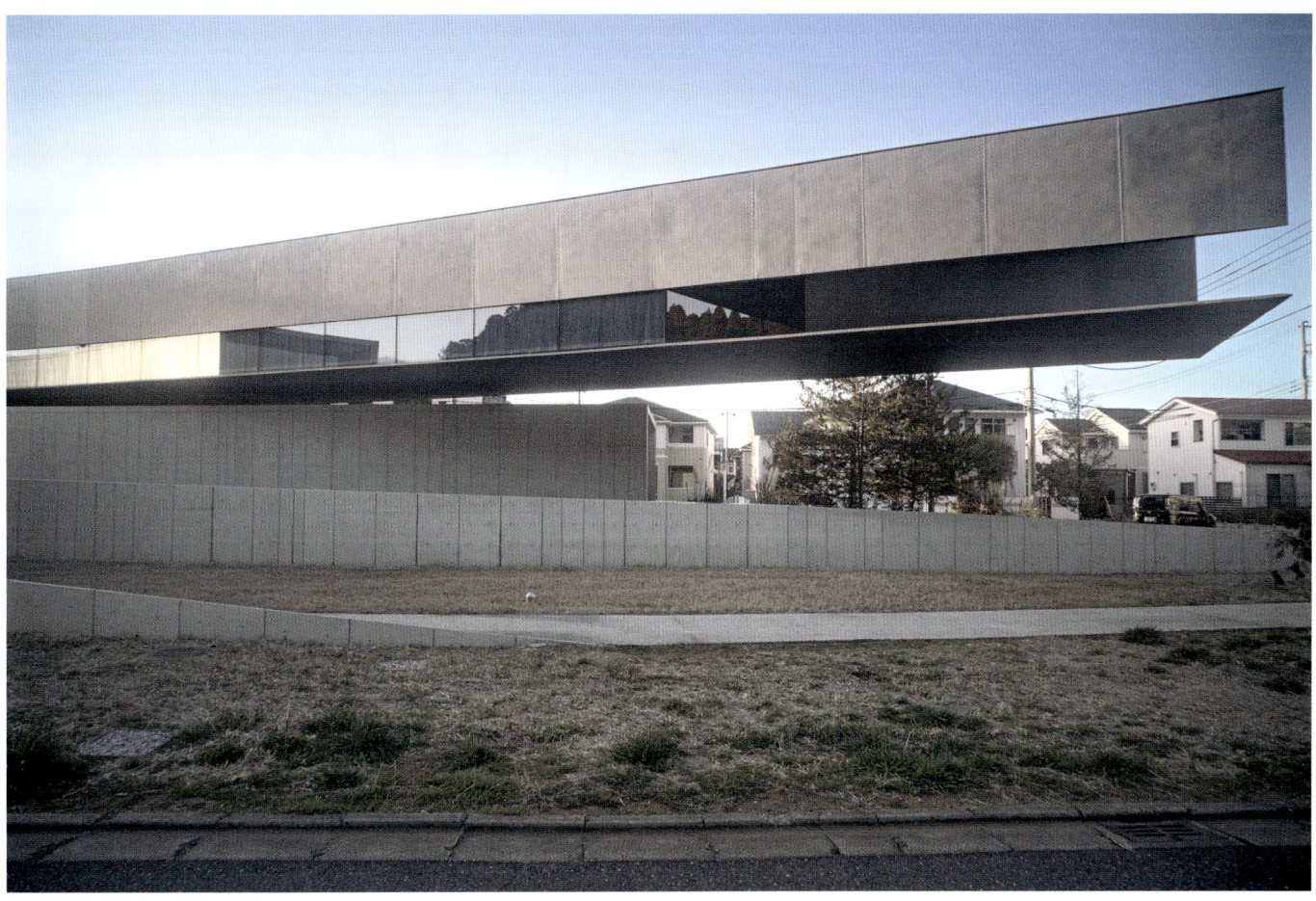

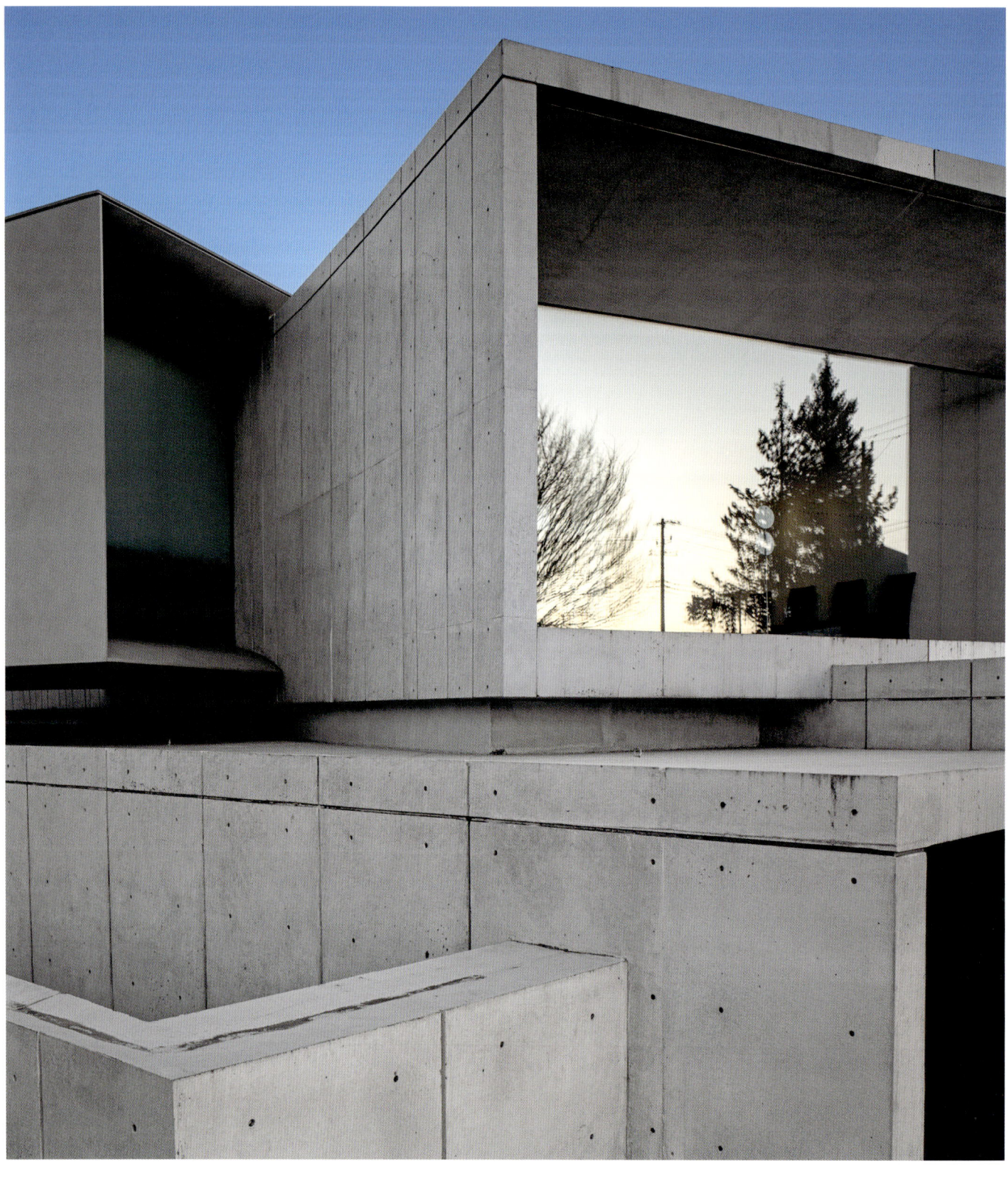

HOKI MUSEUM

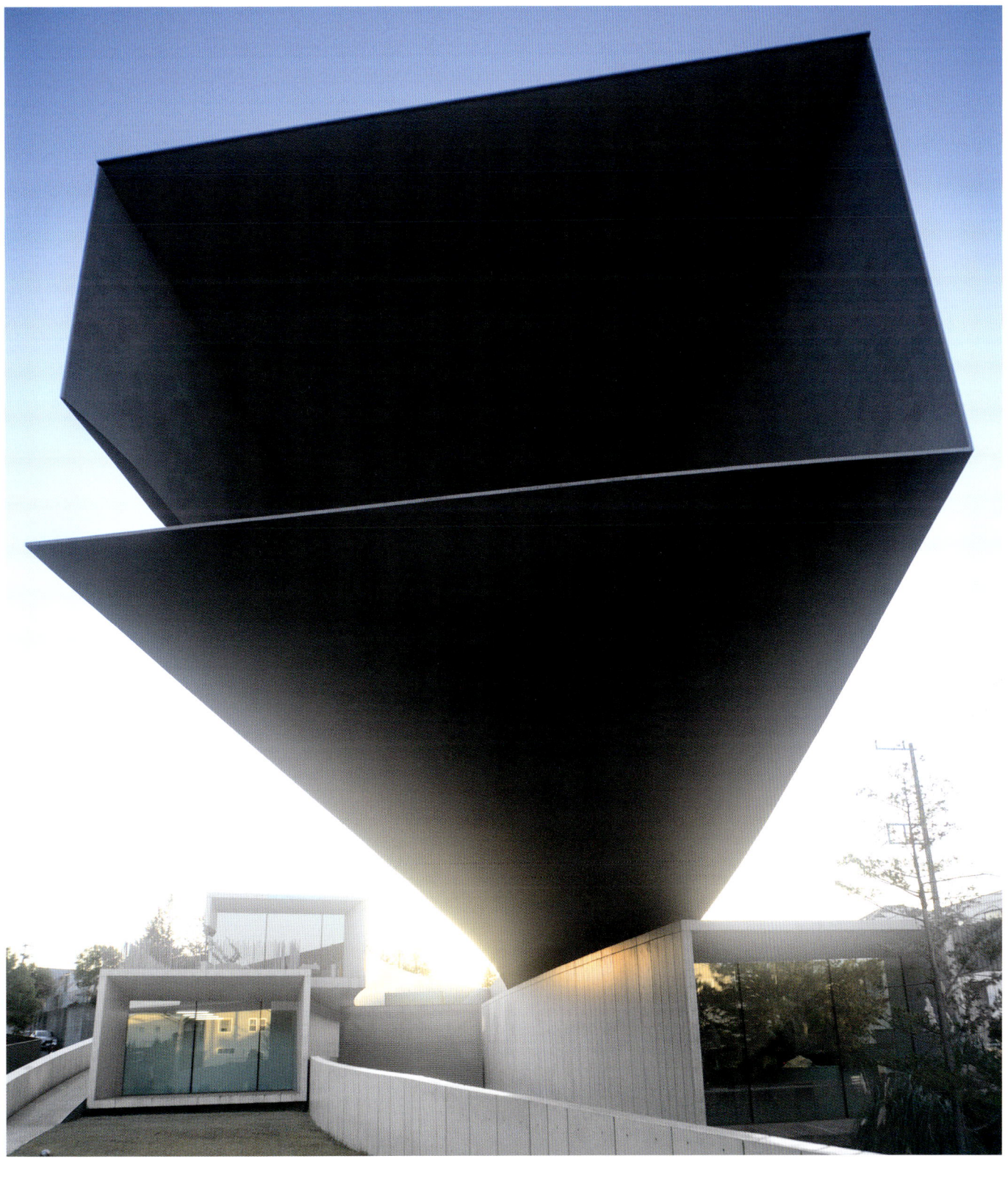

INTER-UNIVERSITY SEMINAR HOUSE

TOKYO · Architect: YOSHIZAKA Takamasa · Completed 1965

The Inter-University Seminar House is a creation of Takamasa Yoshizaka, whose design prowess blossomed under the tutelage of Le Corbusier in Paris. The building reflects a fusion of international modernist ideals with a distinctly Japanese sensibility. Its Brutalist concrete walls reach skywards, ending in a precisely cut roof that marks Yoshizaka's inventive approach to design.

The structure's inverted-pyramid silhouette is both visually arresting and functionally astute. More than an aesthetic spectacle, it strategically orientates towards the verdant vistas behind, framing them through a puzzle-like arrangement of windows – a signature of Yoshizaka's ethos to blend architecture with the environment.

The Seminar House was designed as a collaborative venue for a myriad of universities, corporations and research bodies from the Kanto region, built on the foundation of sharing knowledge. Its design, characterized by repetitive forms and a tessellation of windows cutting through its concrete façade, exhibits Yoshizaka's flair for crafting spaces that captivate the eye and serve the occupant.

The architectural significance of the Seminar House has been lauded over time. Selected by DOCOMOMO Japan in 1999 as one of the country's pre-eminent modern buildings, it garnered further acclaim in 2017 when the Tokyo Metropolitan Government bestowed upon it the title of historic building, cementing its role in Japan's rich tableau of architectural milestones.

Change has touched the Seminar House; the turn of the millennium saw the cessation of joint university seminars. Yet, its essence remains untainted as a nexus for intellectual and innovative collaborations. The legacy of Yoshizaka's creation continues to inspire given the ongoing impact of thoughtfully designed architectural spaces.

In every aspect, from its defiant geometry to its symbiotic relationship with the landscape and surrounding campus buildings, the Seminar House typifies the spirit of its era and the quest for spaces that foster communal learning and advancement.

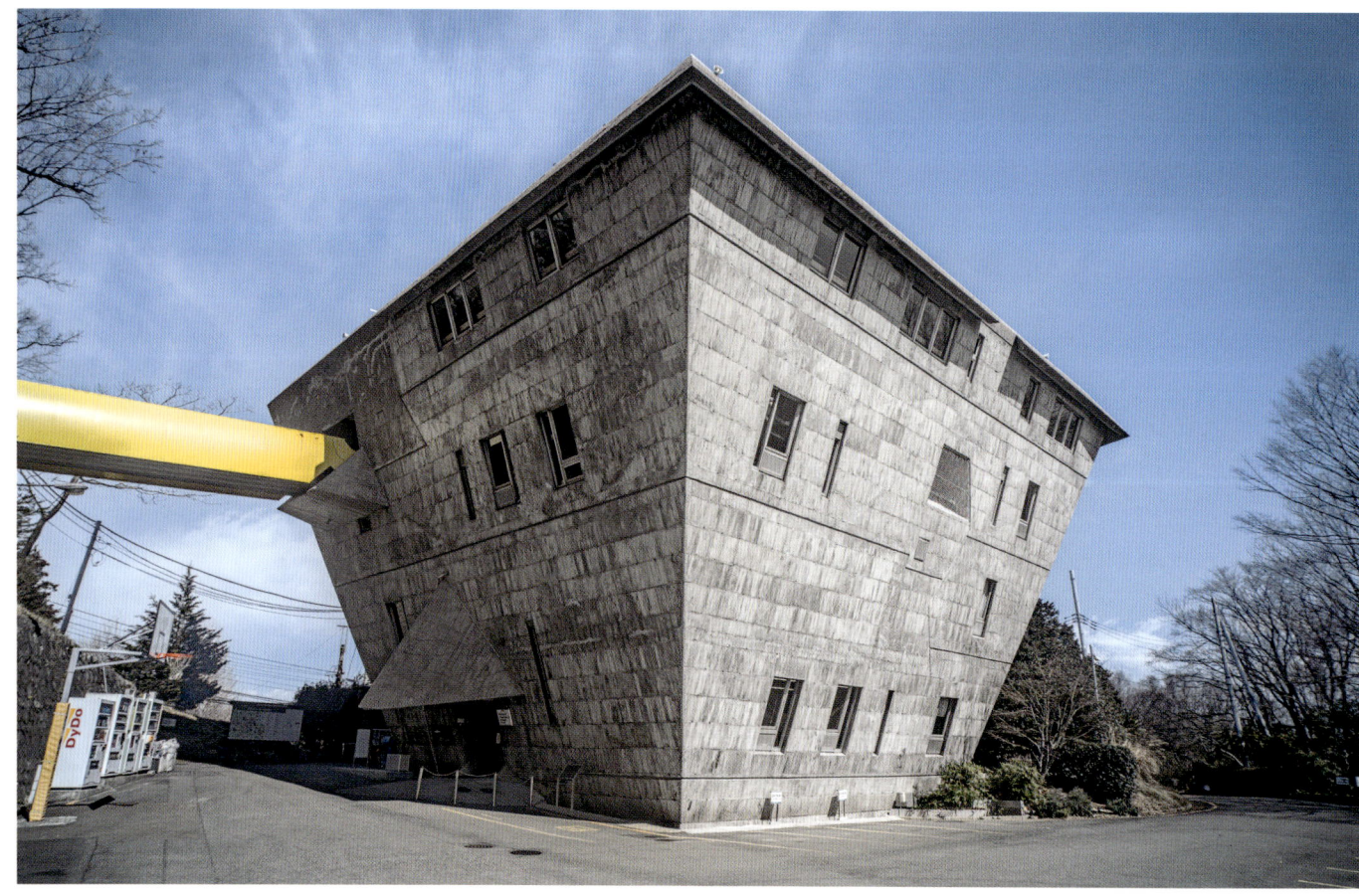

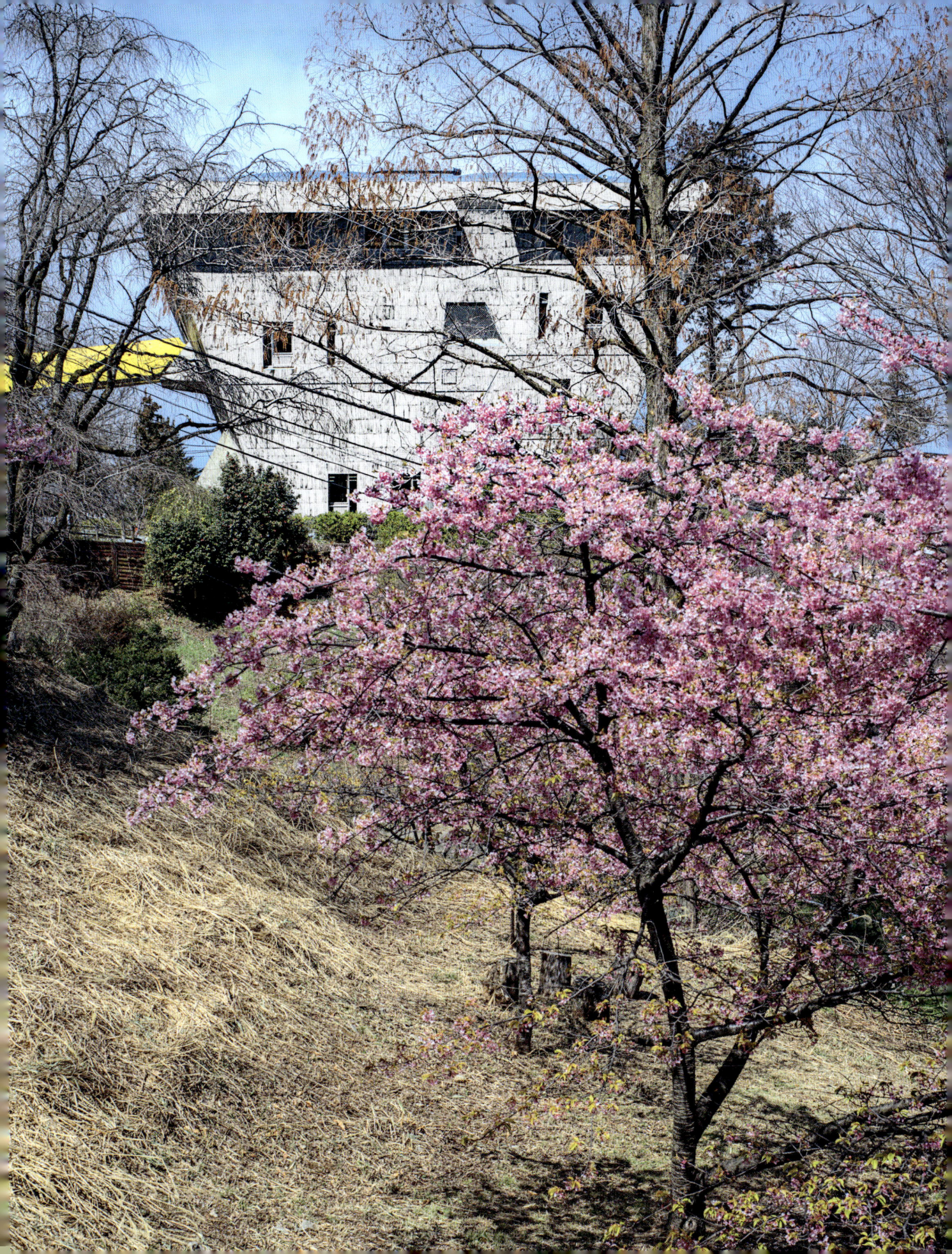

INTER-UNIVERSITY SEMINAR HOUSE

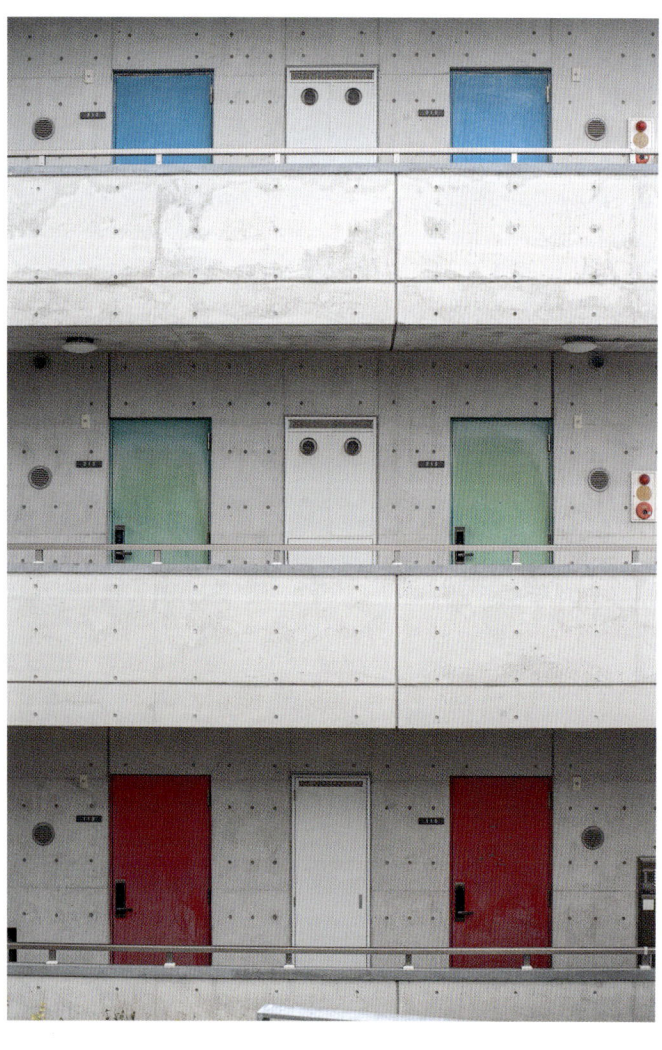
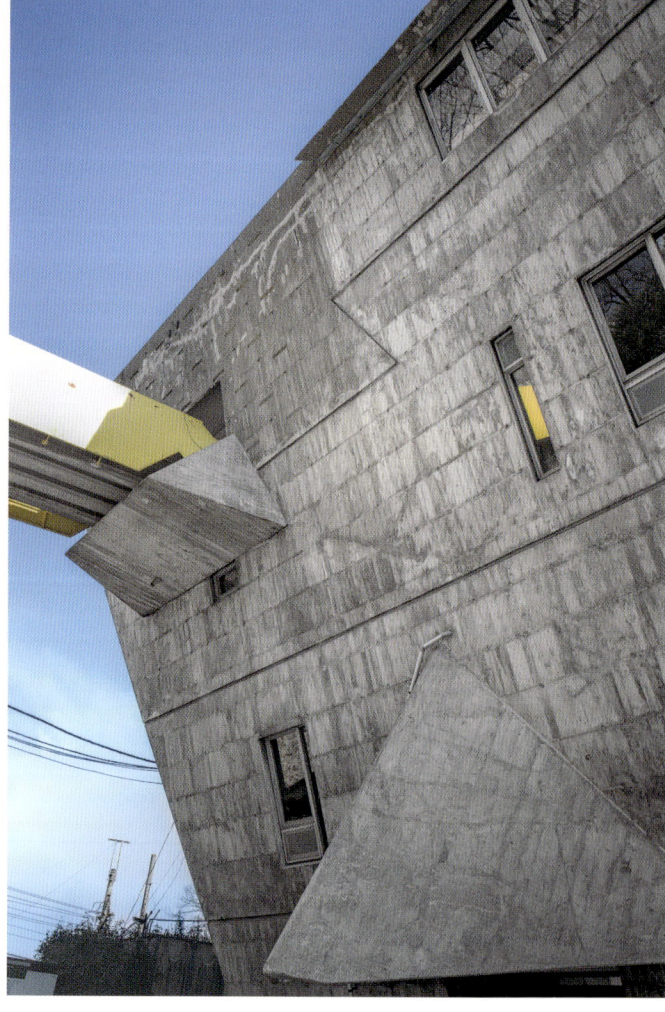

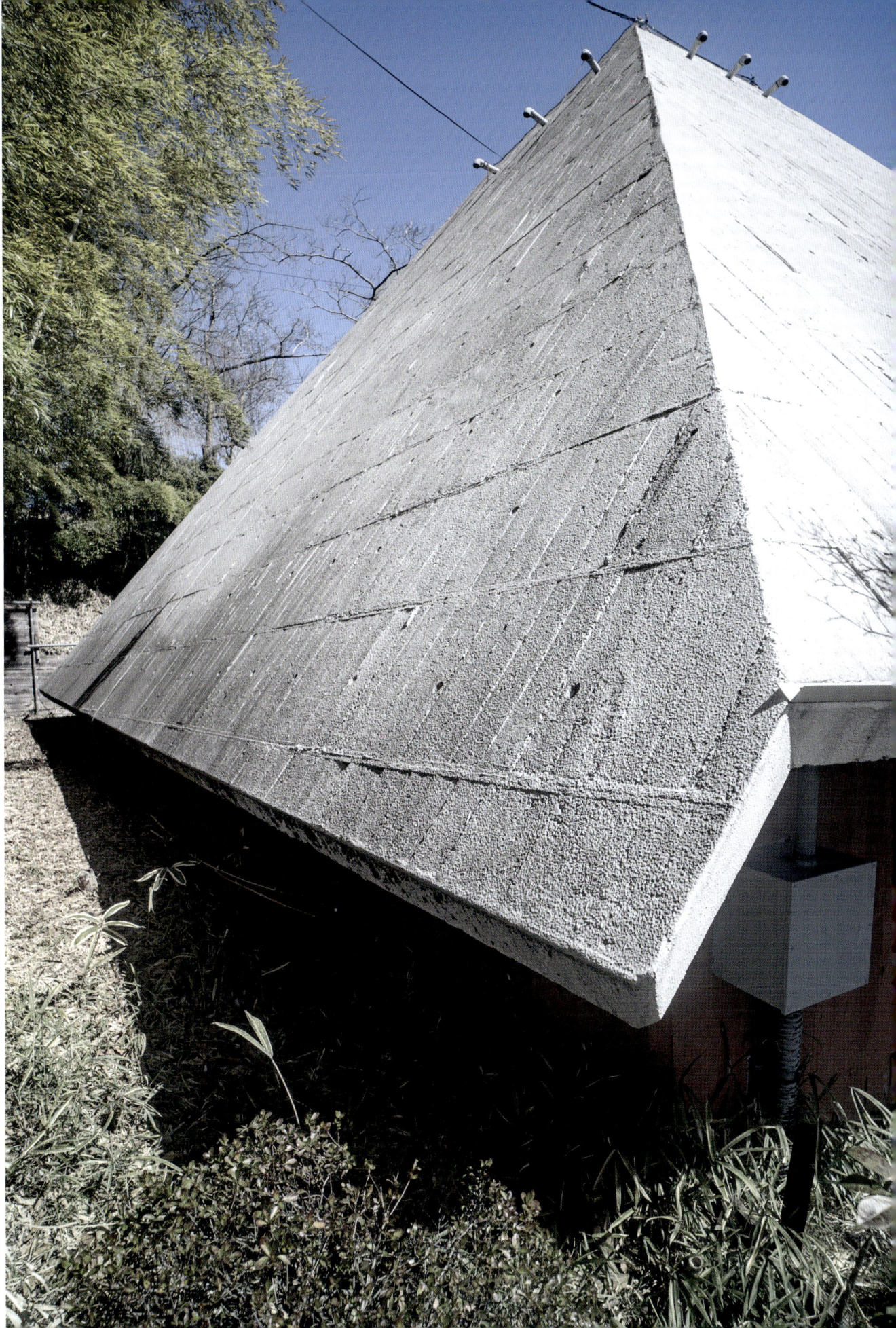

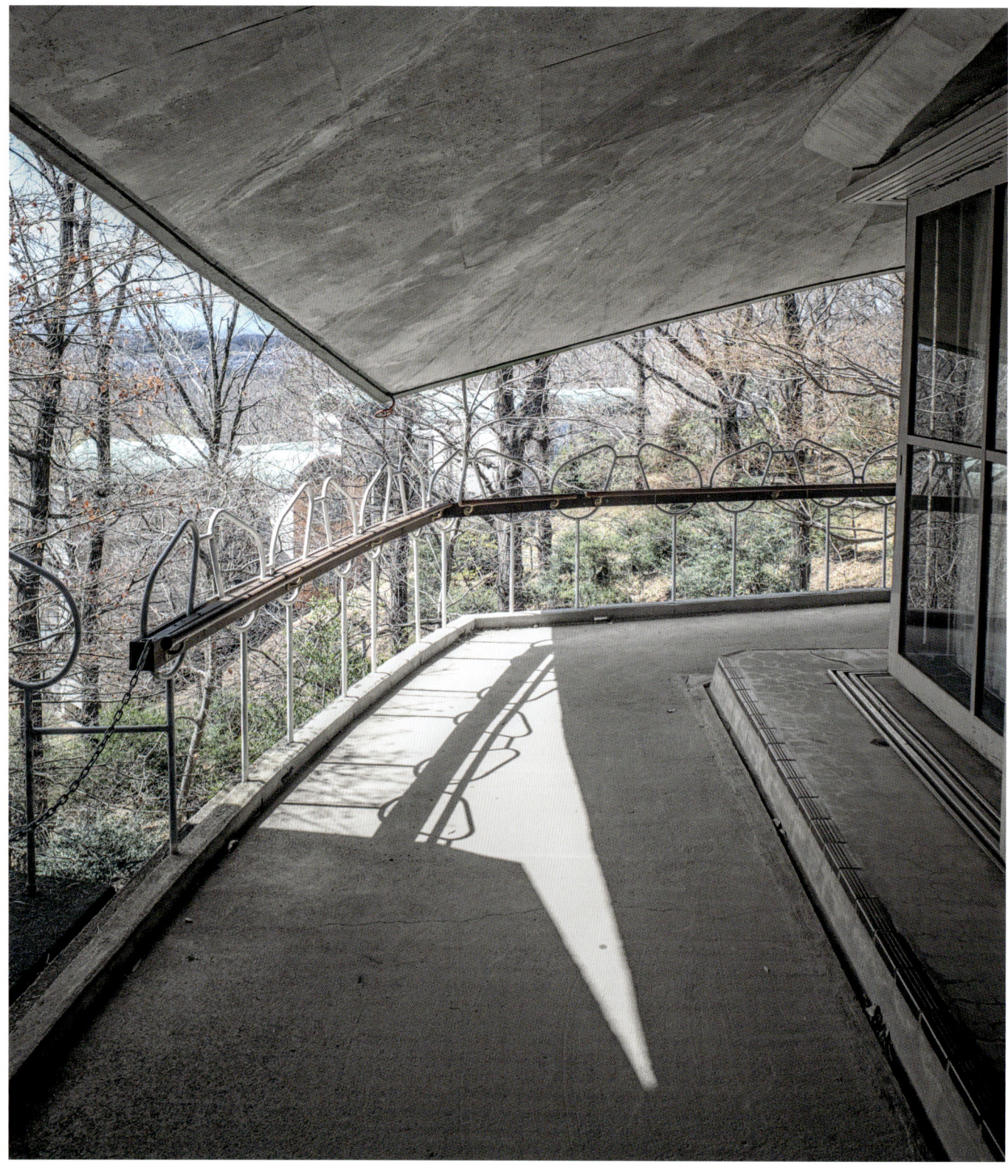

INTER-UNIVERSITY SEMINAR HOUSE

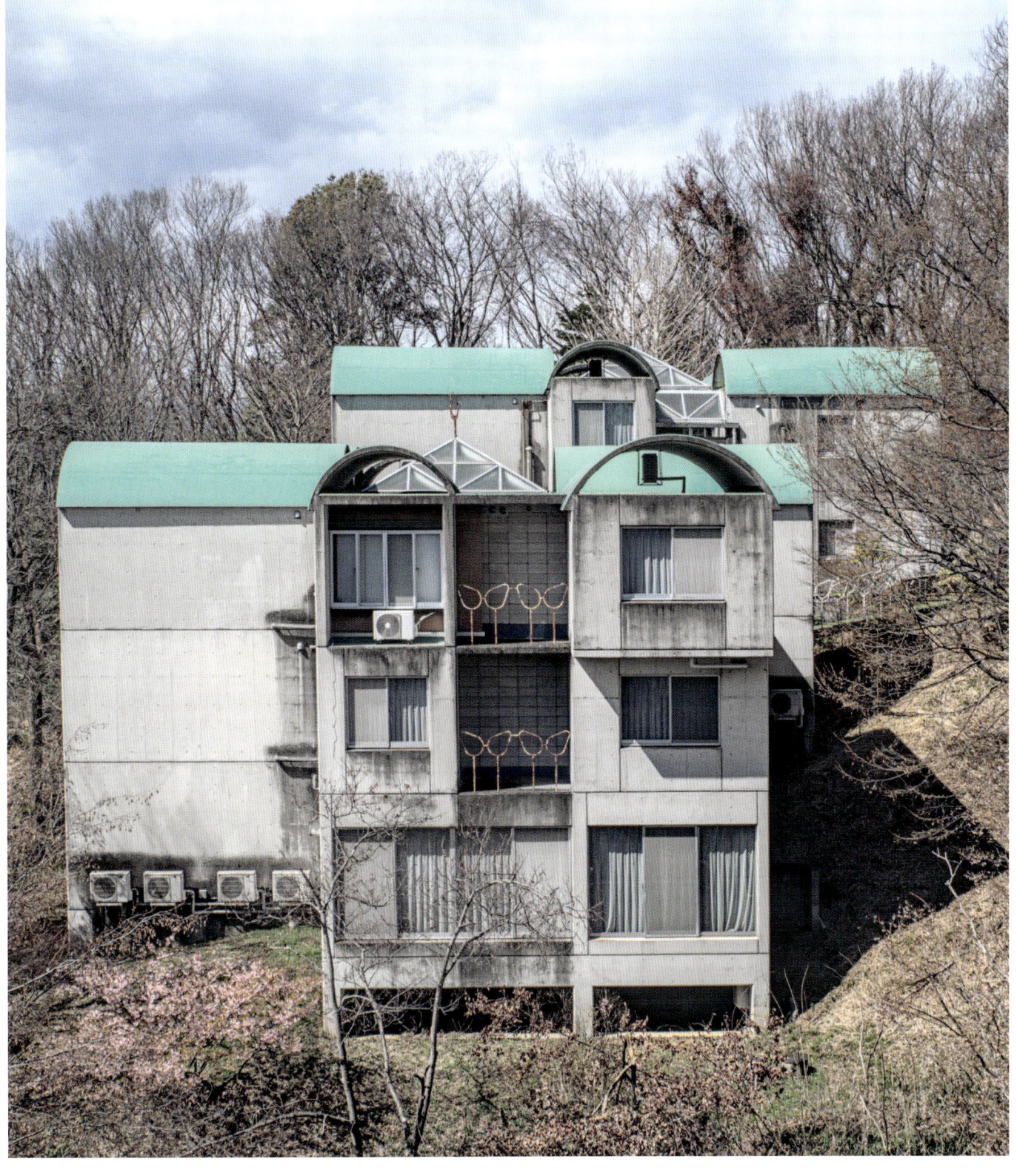

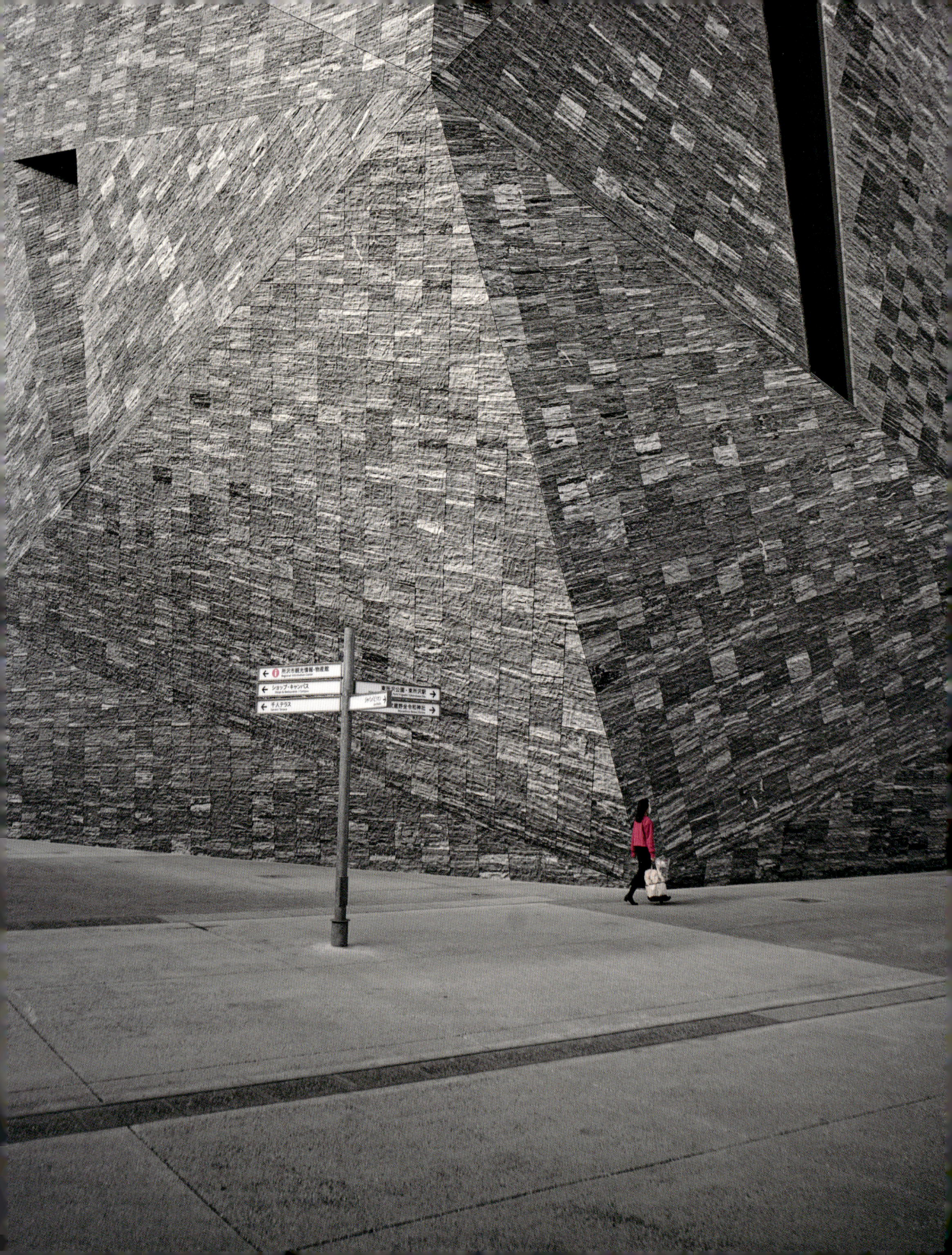

KADOKAWA MUSASHINO MUSEUM

TOKOROZAWA CITY, SAITAMA PREFECTURE · Architect: KUMA Kengo · Completed 2020

The Kadokawa Culture Museum, arising from the distinctive Musashino plateau – a geological marvel borne from the collision of four tectonic plates – emanates as an example of neo-Brutalism and an ode to the synthesis of culture and technology. Encased in twenty thousand seventy-millimetre-thick black and white granite slabs, the building's façade emerges from the ground with an ethereal lightness, despite its monumental scale. Each slab, intentionally misaligned, contributes to the illusion that the structure has pierced through the earth's crust independently, creating a stunning contrast of shadows and highlights that impart a sense of motion, as if the building itself is in a state of becoming.

This multi-purpose complex is a seismic statement and a crucible of cultural amalgamation where high-brow art and pop culture intersect in a futuristic labyrinth. It melds a digital printing factory, a sophisticated computer-controlled distribution warehouse, offices and creative spaces such as an art gallery, library, museum and an anime-themed hotel. This interweaving of diverse functions epitomizes a cross-sectoral approach to modern design, where boundaries are blurred and the flow of creativity is unimpeded.

Within, the vast interior spaces evoke the cerebral corridors of the mind, with bookshelves resembling misty clouds suspended in the sky, composed of structural plywood to form a cellular matrix. This unique design fosters a three-dimensional blend of ideas and genres, where visitors can navigate through a physical manifestation of collective human knowledge and imagination.

Amidst the industrial textures, large stone seats echo the ruggedness of the granite façade, while an expansive metal fence encircles the sacred precincts of the Musashino Reiwa Jinja Shrine, where wave motifs and traditional gables harmonize in a tranquil embrace. Architectural elements within the shrine subtly personify the male and female divine, inviting a reflective contemplation on duality and unity.

The Kadokawa Culture Museum transcends its function as a regional cultural centre, crafting a sanctuary that exhibits resilience, adaptation and the ever-evolving narrative of human expression. It is a tangible chronicle of our times, rooted in heritage yet soaring towards the future.

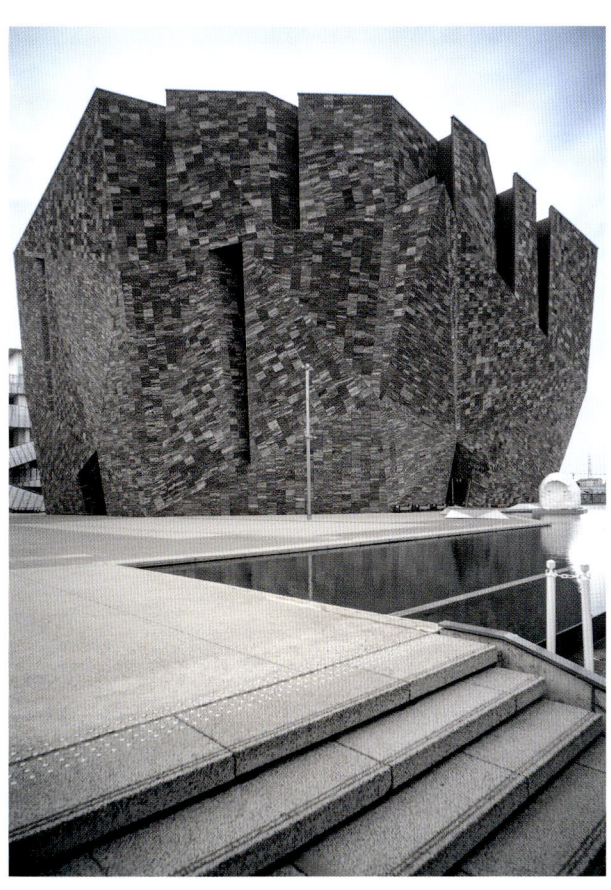
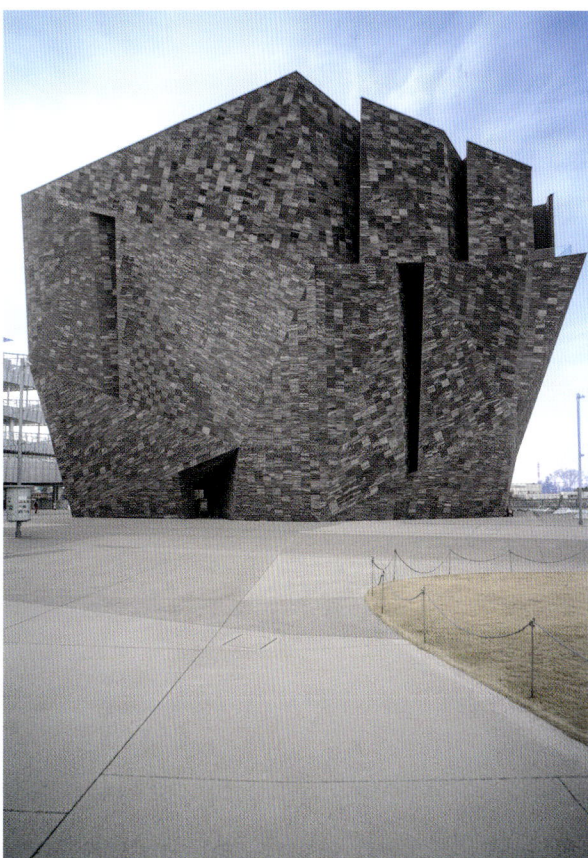

JAPAN LUTHERAN COLLEGE

TOKYO · Architect: MURANO Togo · Completed 1969

Set in the calm suburb of Mitaka, Tokyo, the Lutheran College evidences Togo Murano's architectural acumen, blending fervent spirituality with the rhythm of academic life. This educational haven, adjacent to the Japan Theological Center, was conceived as a sequential ensemble of functional structures amidst a sanctuary of mature trees, fostering communal exchange and quiet reflection.

Murano, in his ambitious endeavour, replaced earlier wooden structures with a cohesive campus that breathes with the vitality of its inhabitants. Each building – be it residence, classroom or chapel – represents a chapter in a story of continuous growth and unity, completed in stages yet narrating a single compelling tale. This balance of seclusion and collective effervescence is Murano's homage to the sacred and the scholarly.

Drawing from E. A. Sövik's insightful lectures on the architecture of religious buildings, Murano crafted spaces that encapsulate the serenity of faith. His design echoes the sculptural romanticism found in Eero Saarinen's works at Yale University, fusing it with a contextual sensitivity to the Japanese setting. The result is a series of structures where function and symbolism hold an intimate dance.

The southern tip of the campus holds residences and a guest house that face faculty apartments across a lush carpet of greenery, floral arrangements guiding the way. Considered placements and orientations of windows and structures preserve privacy while acknowledging the communal milieu of campus life. The modulation of the buildings' massing, alongside tactile spray-stucco walls, plays with light and shadow to echo the natural splendour surrounding them.

It is within the intimate embrace of the chapel where Murano's vision finds its zenith. Light filters through, creating a sanctuary aglow with quietude and reverence, inviting a reflective pause. The architectural language throughout the college, marked by its serene shadows and profound stillness, captures the essence of a spiritual journey enfolded within the academic experience. Here, within these walls, the future leaders in theology find a place to kindle the flame of insight and wisdom, nurtured by the landscape's embrace and the structures' guiding presence.

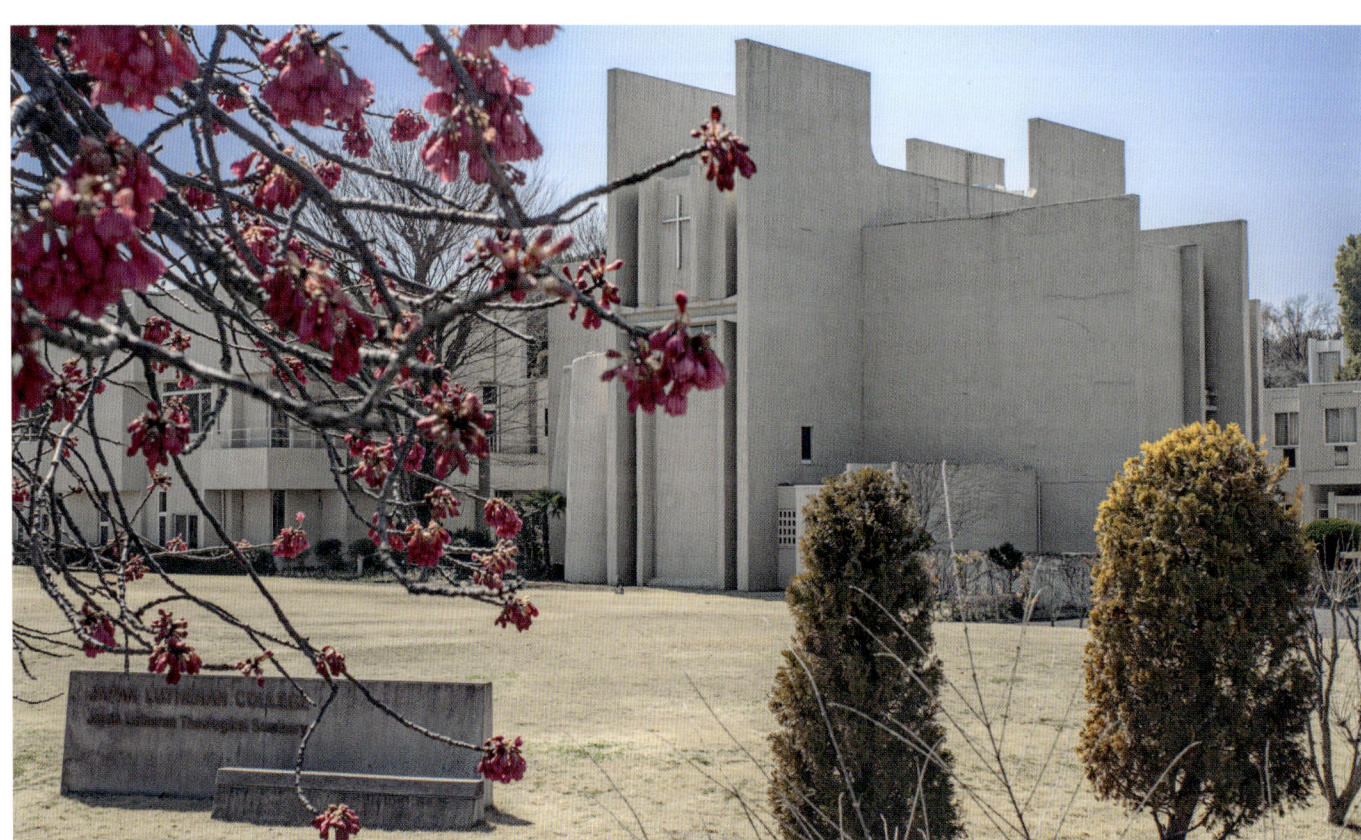

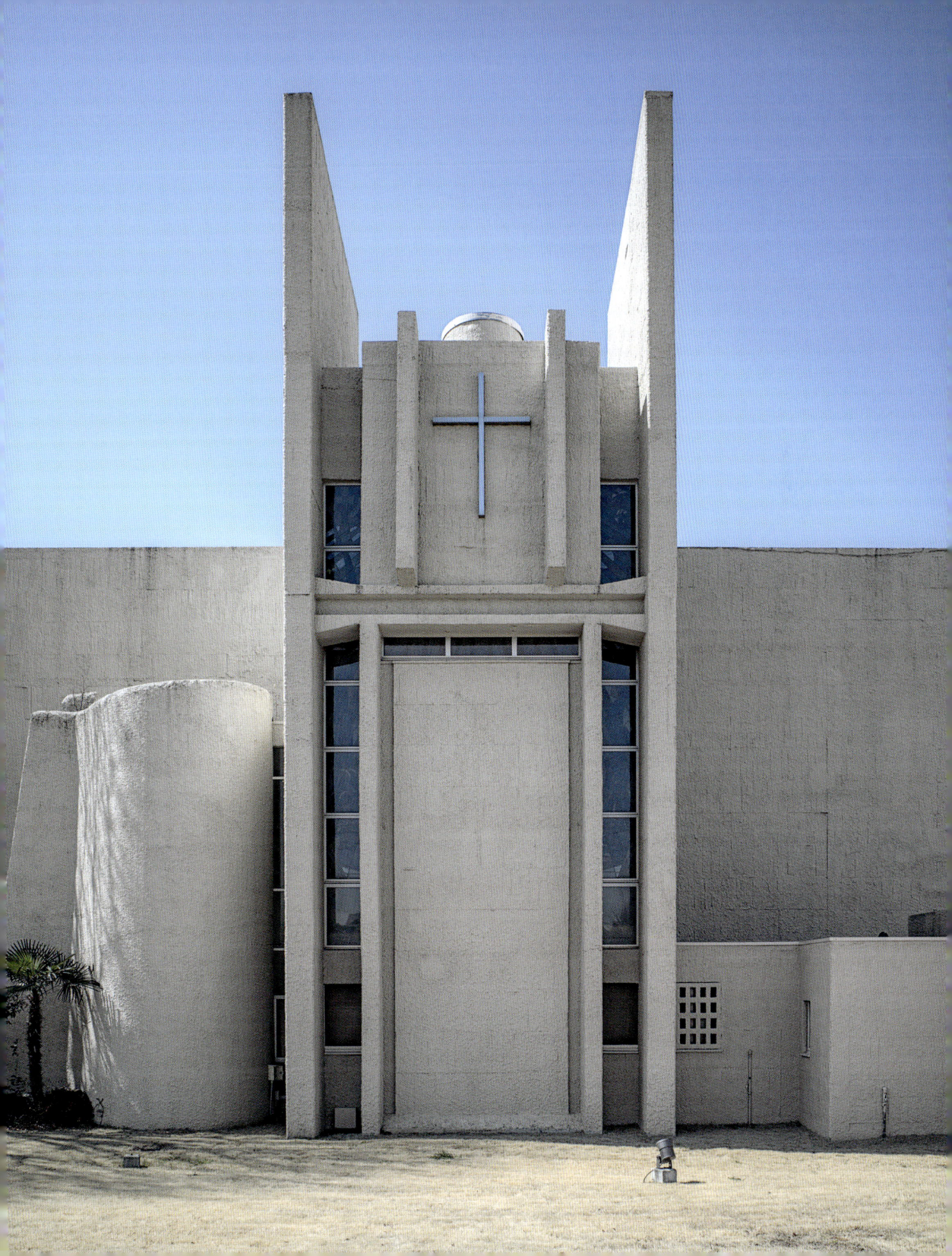

MAKINA RESORT

NAKIJIN, OKINAWA · Architect: Studio Cochi · Completed 2021

A great example of neo-Brutalism, this raw resort exudes strength and permanence despite being a recent addition to the landscape. Its plain, minimalist façade, unadorned with superfluous ornamentation, captures Brutalism's unflinching honesty of structure and texture. The exposed ascending concrete steps to the sky offer a sculptural aesthetic, reminiscent of the massive geometric shapes that characterize Brutalist architecture.

The building integrates traditional Okinawan and Japanese architectural elements through its harmonious coexistence with nature. Its tiered design parallels East Asian step-paddy fields, while the fronds of greenery breaking through the concrete evoke the Japanese principle of *shakkei* or borrowed scenery, where the external landscape becomes part of the building's aesthetic. This blurring of lines between the man-made and natural realms is deeply entrenched in traditional Japanese philosophy, creating a serene dialogue between the structure and its environment.

It's also next door to the best restaurant in Japan: Cafe Kokuu. Enough said.

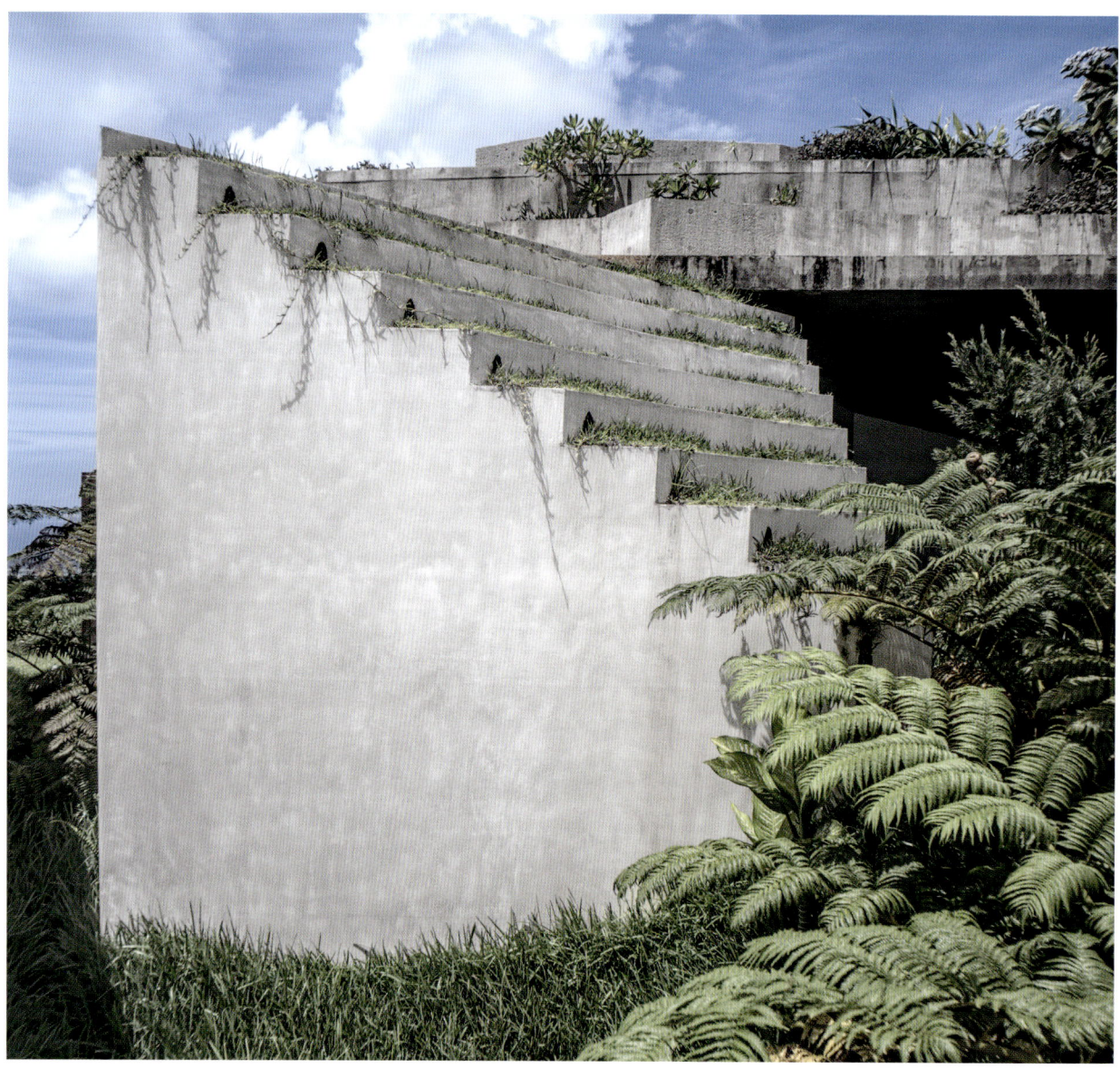

TOILET BLOCK

NAGO, OKINAWA

This public toilet block, a modest cubicle of modernist design, is an honest homage to the continuing influence of traditional Japanese and Okinawan architecture. Cast in raw concrete, its vertical fluting mirrors the wooden grooves found in classic Japanese structures, while the narrow, slightly recessed entrance recalls the *genkan* – an elemental space in Japanese homes separating the inside from the outside. Even the basic functionality of the design speaks of the minimalist efficiency that is a hallmark of traditional Japanese spaces. On a subtler level, the surrounding grass hints at the integration with nature characteristic of Ryukyuan (Okinawan) and Japanese architecture, where boundaries between man-made and natural environments are often deliberately blurred, fostering a sense of harmony even in the most utilitarian of structures.

I left here sooner than I wanted – not for fear of getting a reputation for hanging around public toilets with camera in hand, but because I was harassed by an incredibly territorial crow.

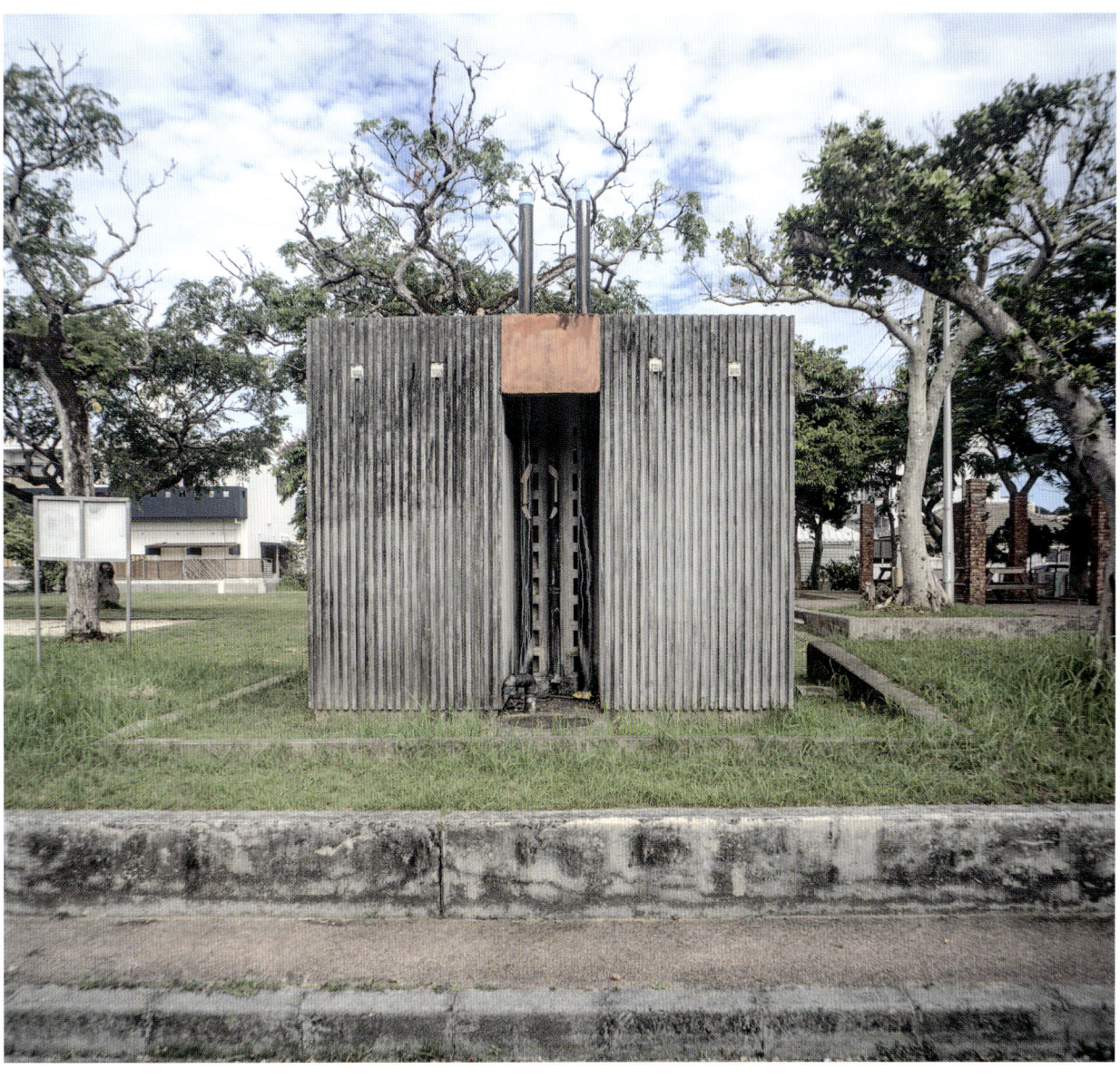

NAGARAGAWA CONVENTION CENTER

GIFU PREFECTURE · Architect: ANDO Tadao · Completed 1995

A bold contender in the architectural ring, this centre shows Brutalist brawn and Ando's penchant for bare concrete elegance. From the outside, it looks as if a colossal concrete egg was meticulously sliced to nestle in the urban landscape of Gifu. Its exterior is as robust as a sumo wrestler, yet the interior floats like a butterfly, with light and shadow dancing through the space in a delicate ballet orchestrated by Ando's masterful hand.

Visitors stepping inside might half expect to find a giant yolk at the centre, given the building's ovoid façade, but instead they are greeted by an airy, serene atrium that could easily serve as a *dojo* for meditative thought. While Ando shies away from being tagged as a Brutalist, the Nagaragawa Convention Center sizzles as a solid "eggs-ample" of his ability to scramble expectations, offering a space that is both imposing and inspiring – cracking the shell of conventional design to reveal an architectural pearl within.

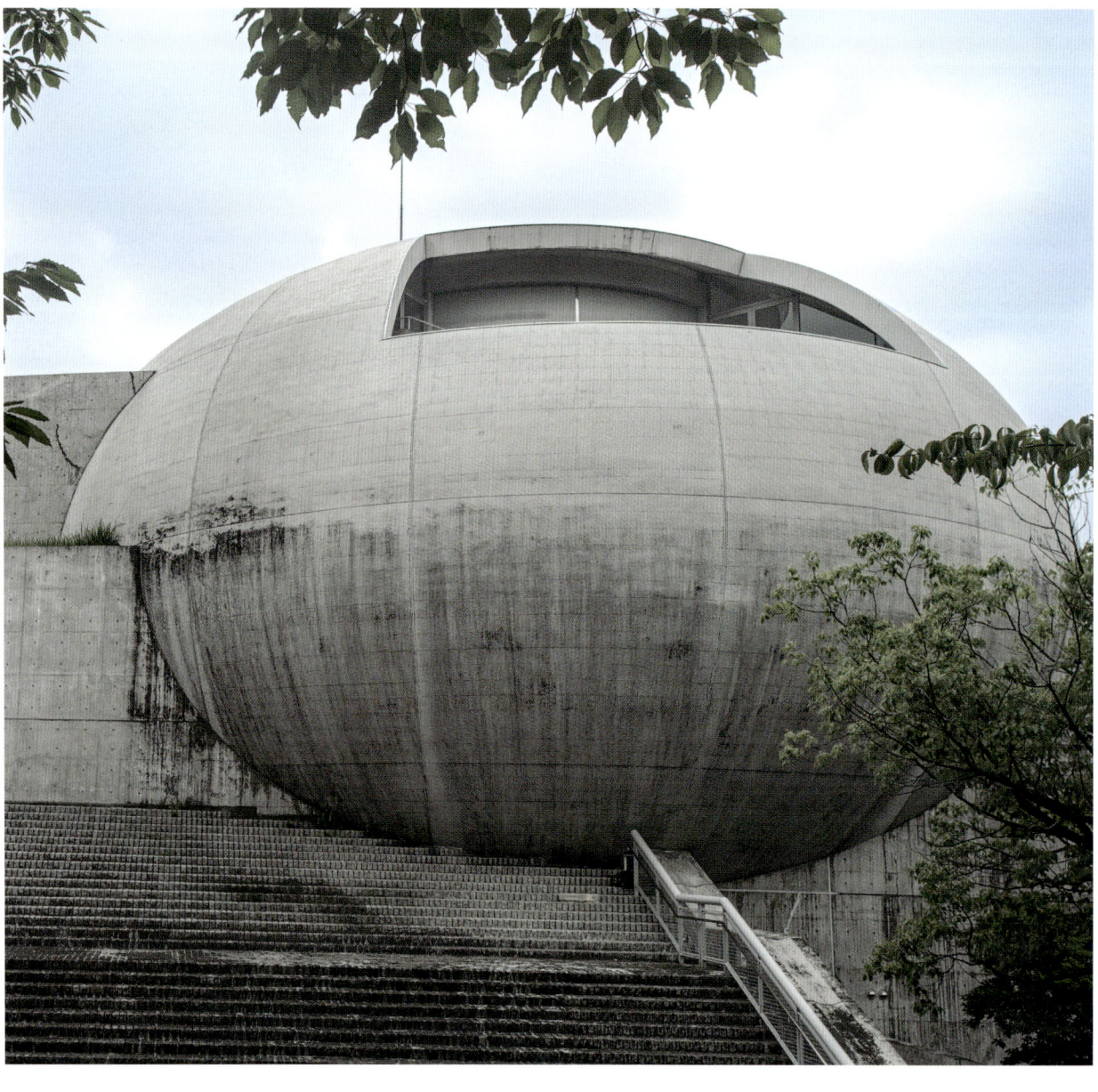

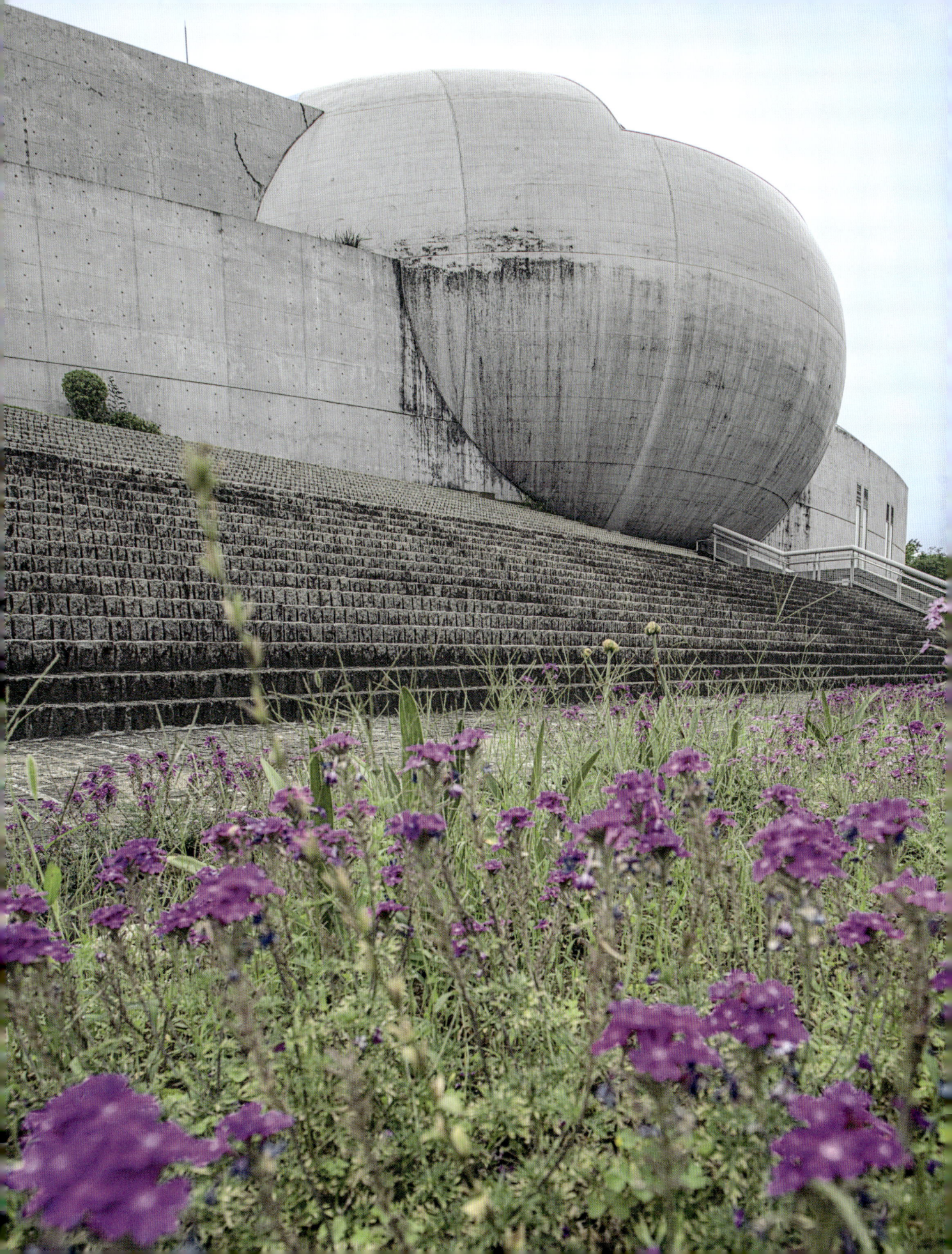

NAGARAGAWA CONVENTION CENTER

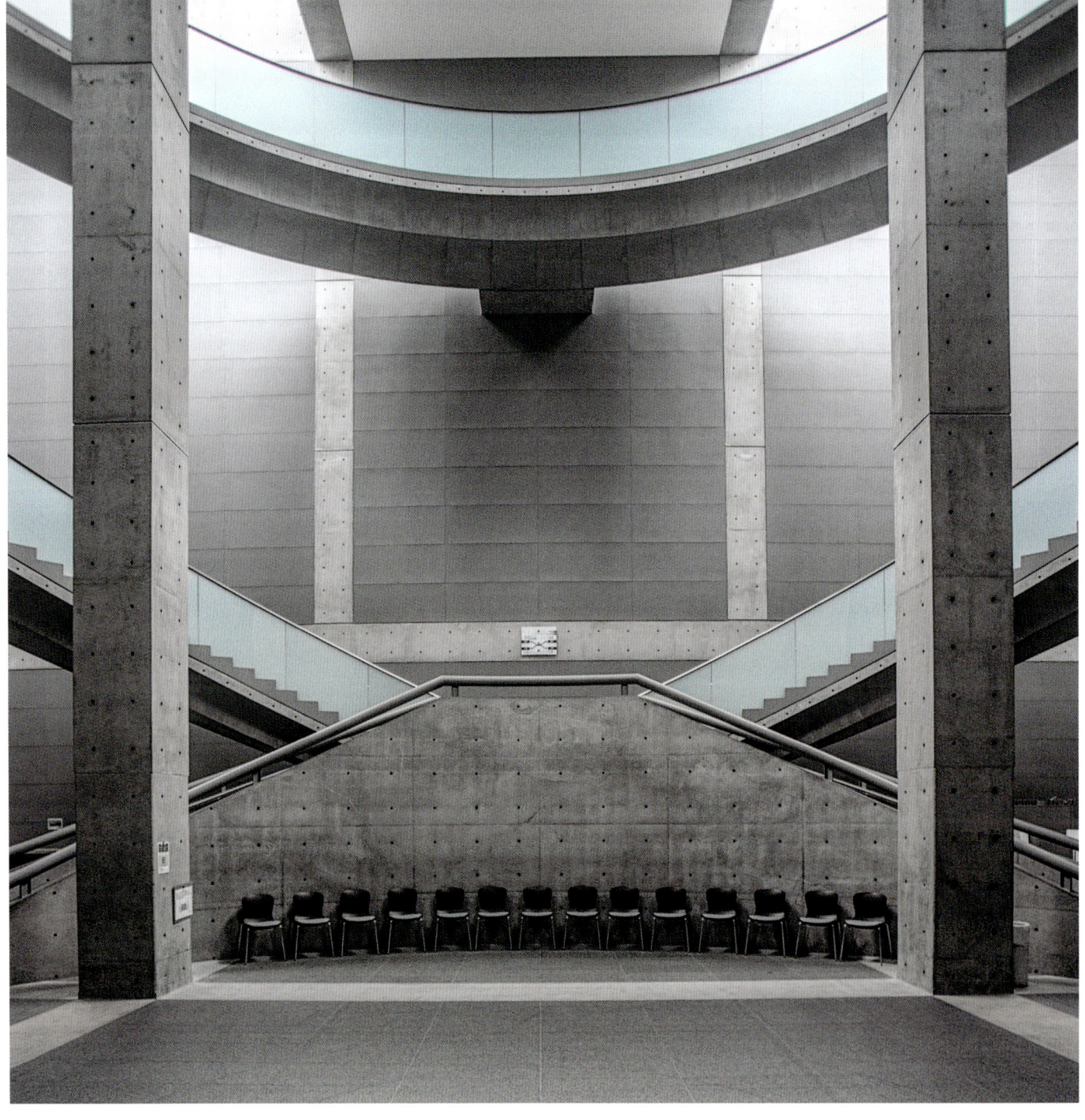

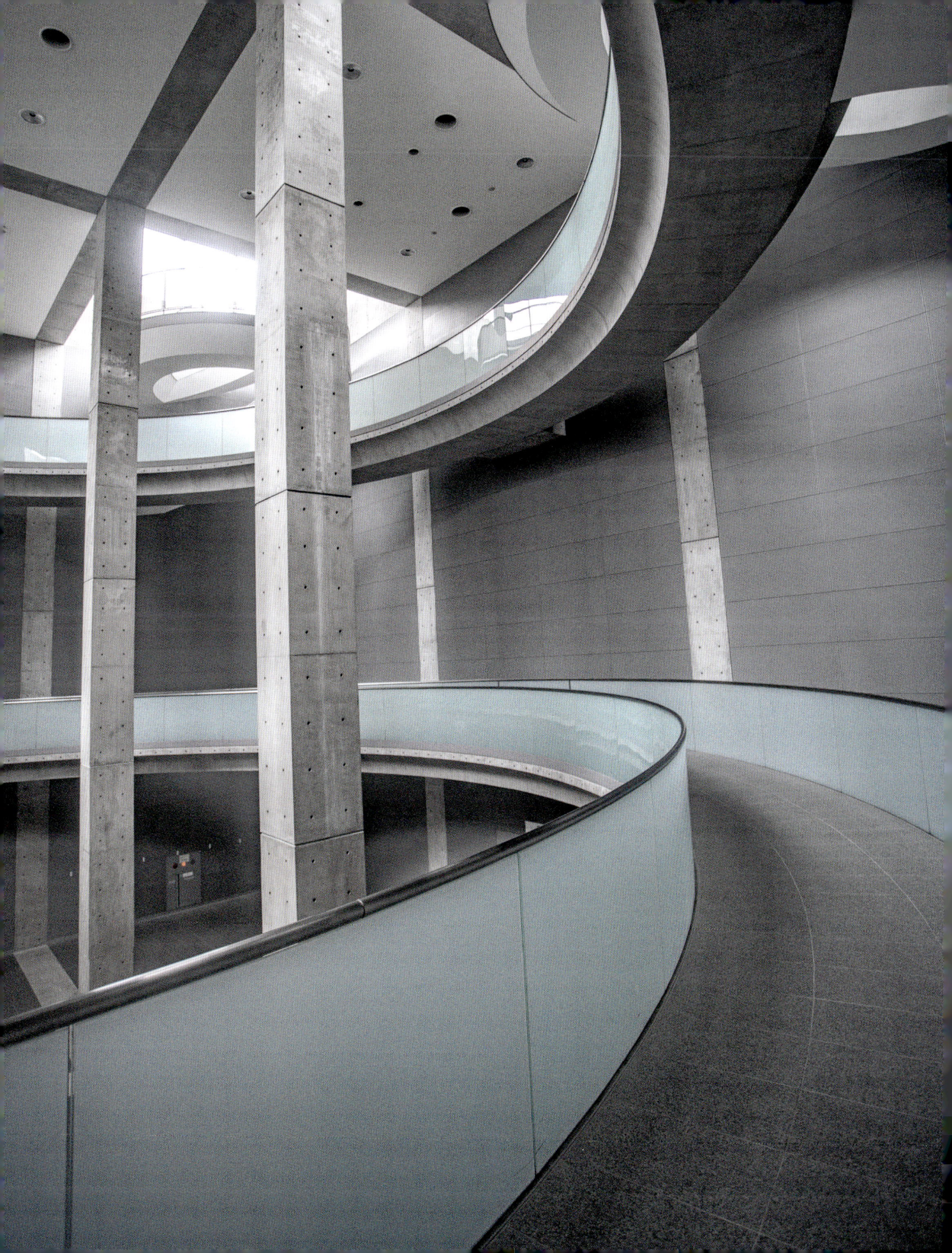

JUNIOR HIGH SCHOOL

NAGO, OKINAWA · Architect: Kou Design · Completed 1987

Whereas Western and Soviet Brutalism can often be deemed to reflect the intrusion of government power, this school building engenders a different feel. It delivers more accessibility than either old-school Brutalism or the glass and steel nonsense of contemporary public buildings elsewhere. This is achieved through a construction material commonly associated with an inaccessible, impersonal coldness and despite the fact that this school would not look out of place in the Soviet Union.

Its broad open exterior corridors smack of a successful application of the Smithsons' "streets in the sky" concept – lazily mocked by architectural critics in the West with their blinkered class-based interpretations of things that happened in their mind. These allow for unhindered views of the practice of the "software" I speak of in this book's introduction.

Okinawa is disrespectfully regarded as the poor brother within broader Japan. Post-war builds allowed for a rebuilding of not just infrastructure but also pride in local culture. Note that stairwells incorporate breeze-blocks – a quintessentially Okinawan feature addressed later.

Practice and learning of the local Eisa culture makes up a large part of school life. The dance, music, costumes and community customs of Eisa reflect a connection between agriculture, the sacredness of nature, seasonality and the belief that ancestral spirits reside in natural elements.

Despite the cultural connection with farming, my students stubbornly refused that tomatoes are not vegetables. I constantly had to berate them for referring to football as "soccer".

National school exams suggest that such Okinawan schools are failing. Whatever. The fact is that they foster a sense of community unseen anywhere I have lived. Their success might be more accurately gauged by the fact that Okinawa outbreeds the mainland.

The kids do not seem to be particularly keen to get home. Although karate originated here in Okinawa, the extra-curricular martial activity of choice is kendo.

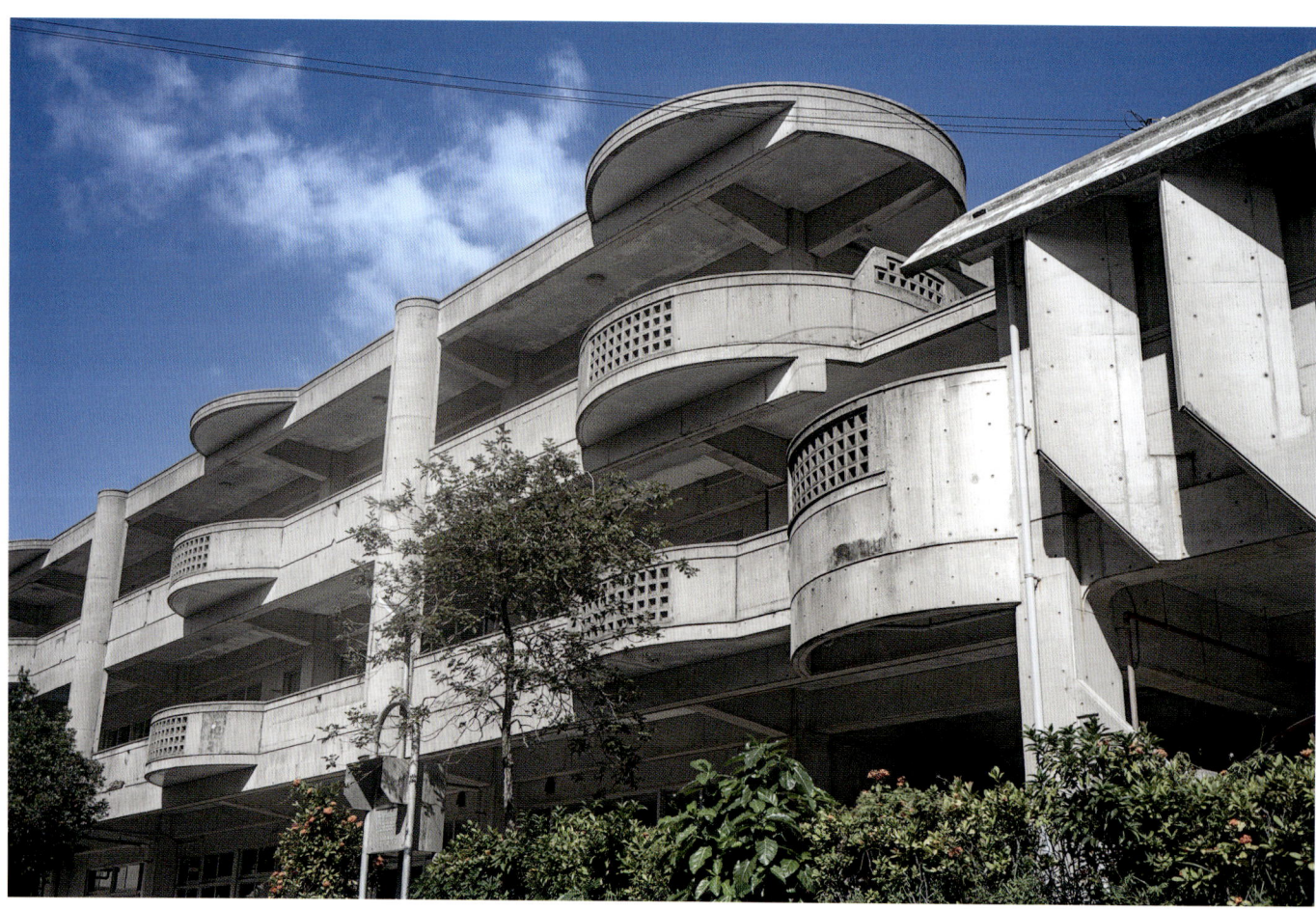

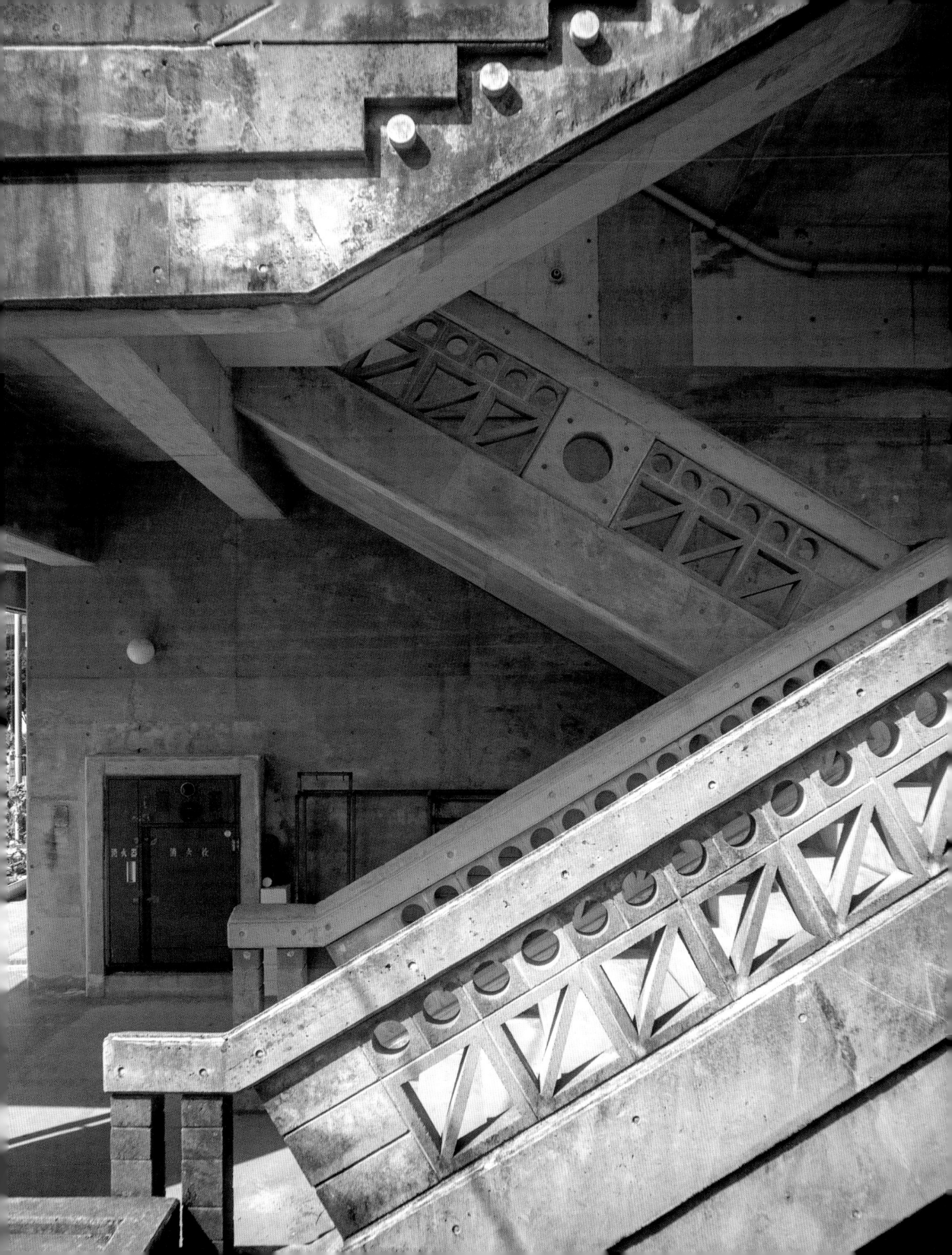

JUNIOR HIGH SCHOOL 132

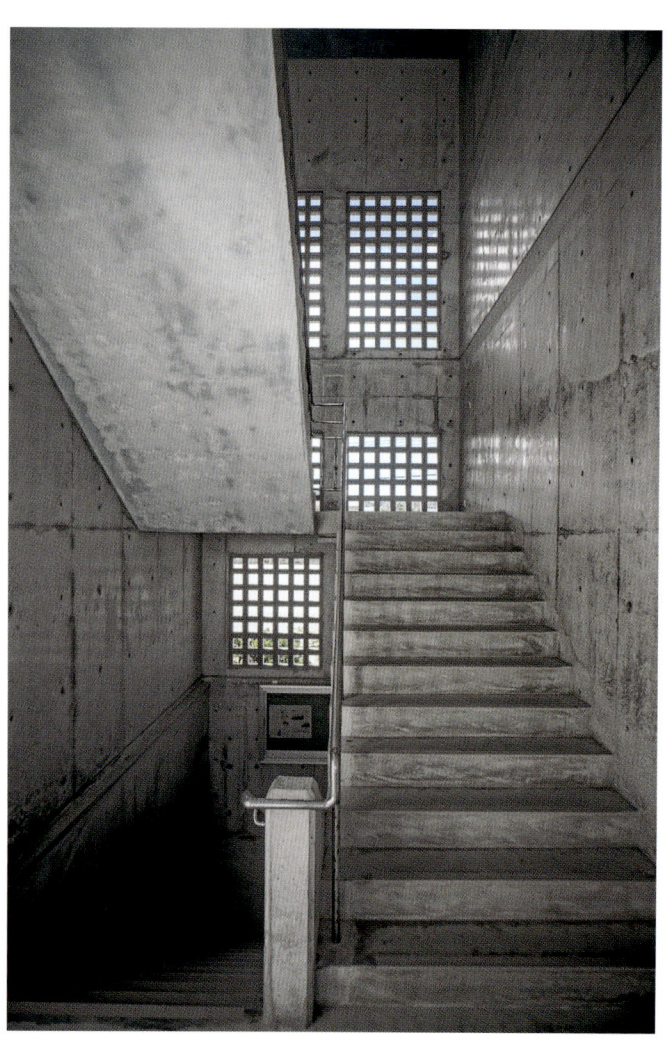
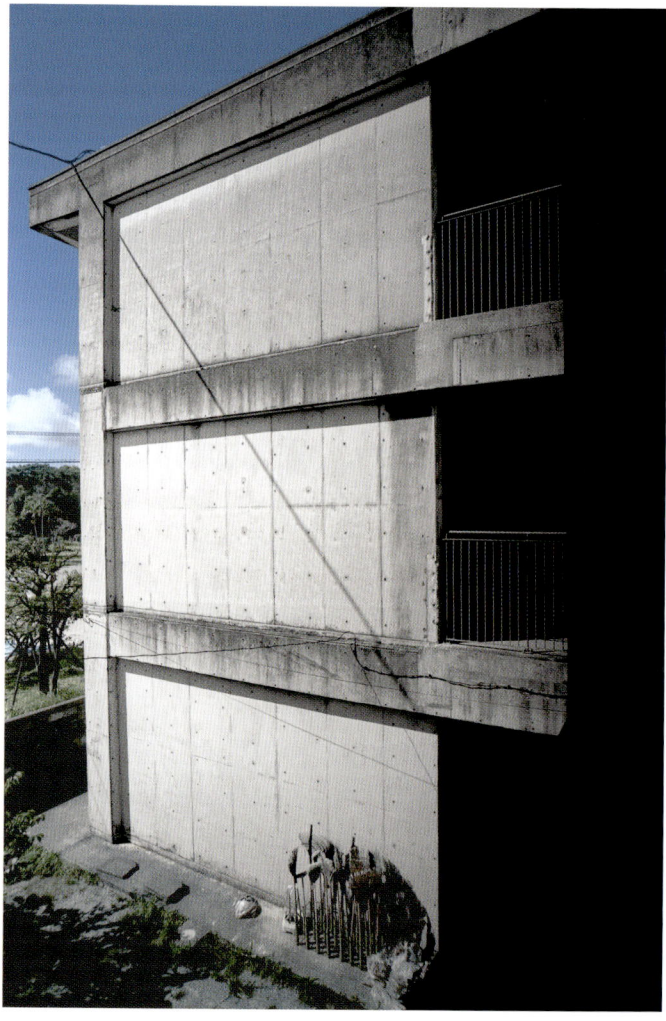

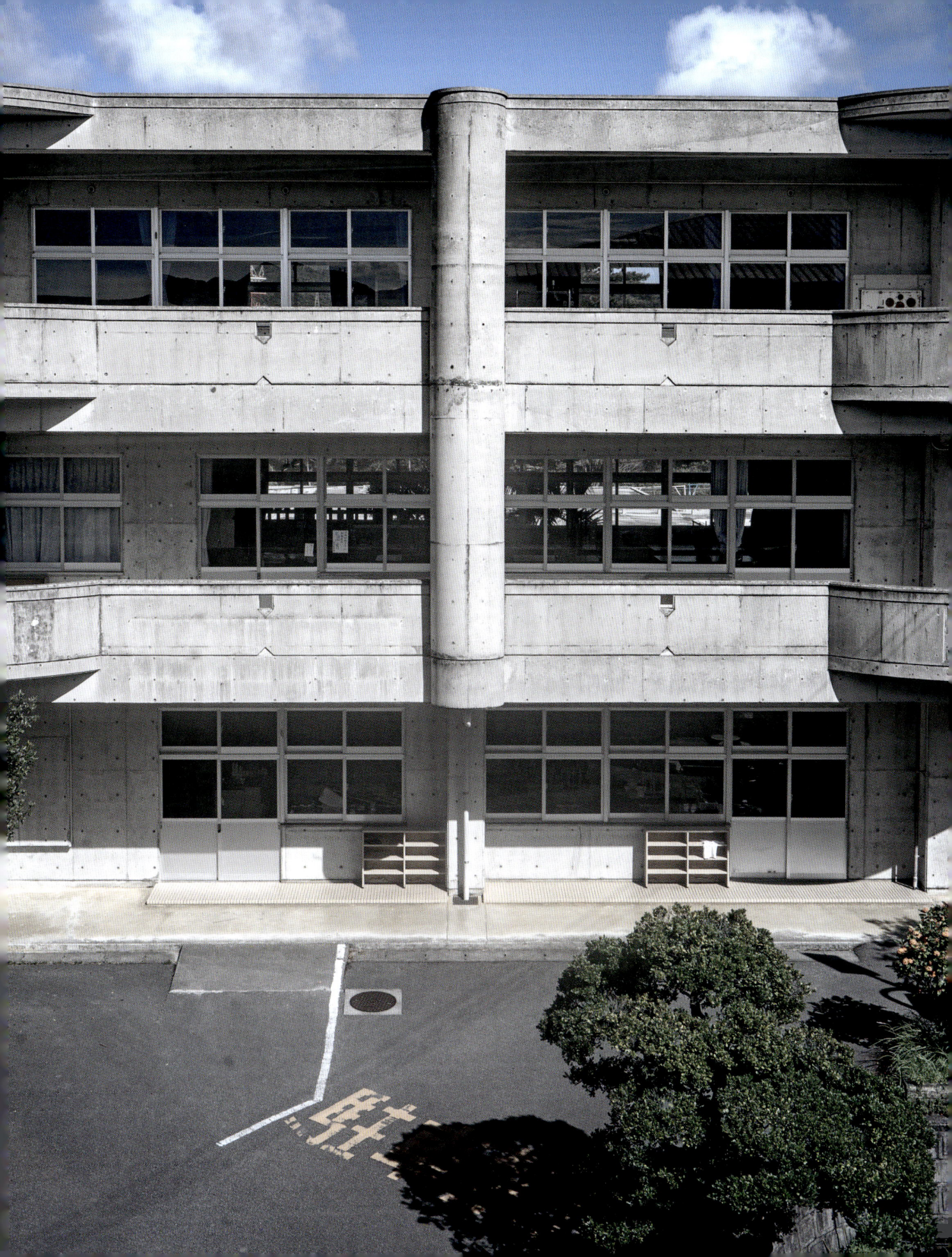

RESORT APARTMENT BLOCK

SESOKO ISLAND, OKINAWA

The allure of Brutalism, a style once divisive, finds renewed appreciation in a world where unapologetic concrete forms are celebrated for their solitary grandeur. Their newfound charm resonates with a generation unburdened by historical biases, drawing influences from the realms of gaming and science fiction, where concrete's cool, clean lines signify futurism, not oppression.

Amidst this shift, I hope that Brutalism's embrace is not just aesthetic but rooted in an enlightened understanding of past misapprehensions and, crucially, in the recognition of its environmental merit. The argument for preserving over demolishing grows compelling as eco-conscious repurposing becomes the vanguard of architectural conservation.

This image, in which rugged concrete is complemented by lush greenery, is an example of a genre I label "Brutal Botanics", where the hard and the organic coexist, challenging preconceptions and sowing seeds for a future where Brutalist structures are not only preserved but treasured within our urban landscapes.

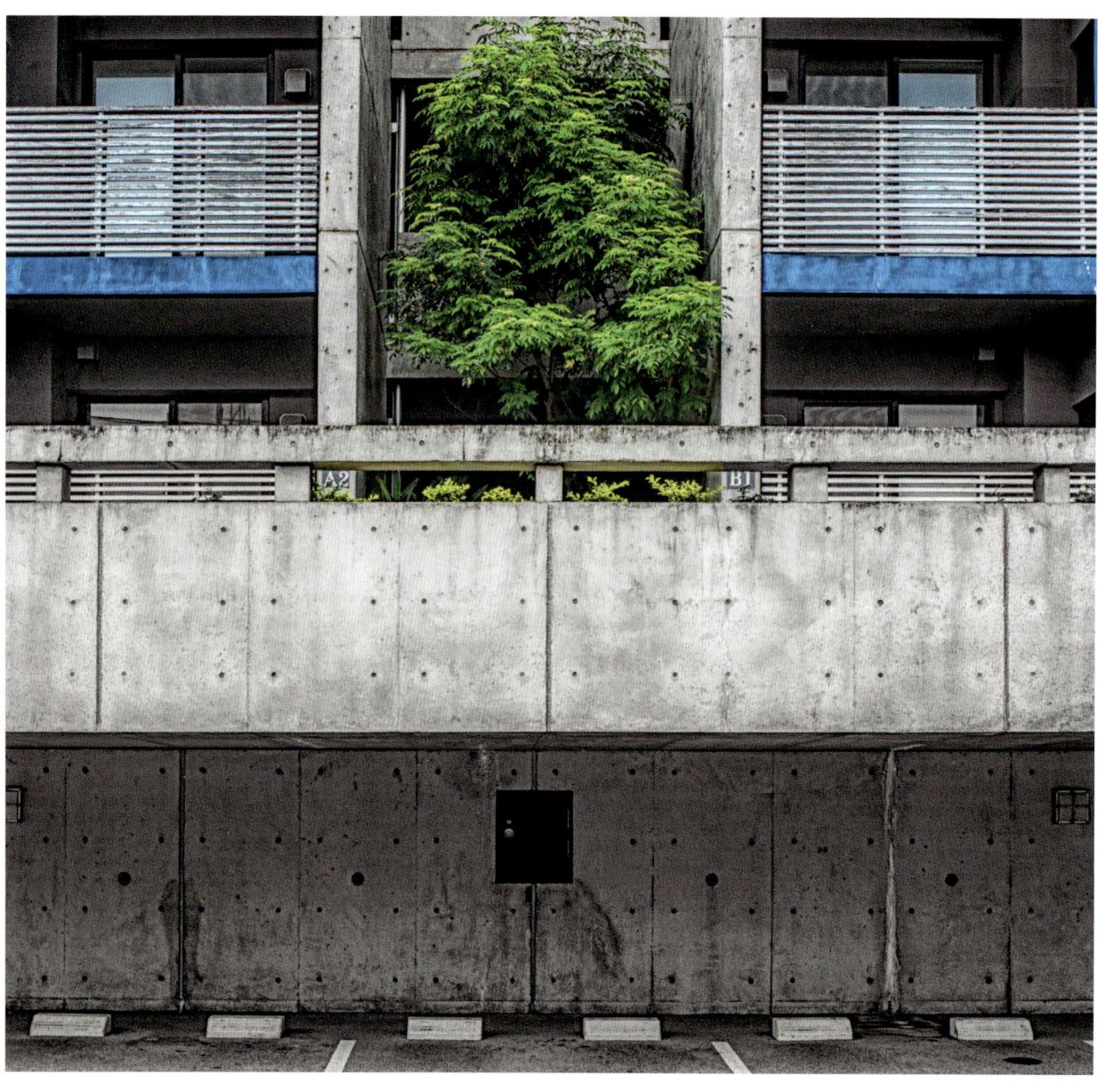

PUBLIC TOILET

URASOE, OKINAWA

Sporting my *Star Wars* goggles again, I saw a rebel base camp on Endor rather than an honest public toilet. Prior to spotting it, I had just visited a Banksy exhibition. Picturing this in the UK, it would be covered in graffiti by those less talented.

Remaining unvandalized here, the gritty geometry of raw, unadorned concrete is allowed to develop its patina and build character. Angularity and the weighty presence of the concrete convey a sense of robustness and functionality, hallmarks of Brutalist design.

Public toilets in Okinawa prioritize durability and practicality, often reflecting a blend of utilitarian purpose and distinct local aesthetics. In the humidity and lushness they appear as modernist sculptures contrasted against the natural environment.

Remarkably, every public toilet here, despite often adopting the Brutalist style, remains truly unique.

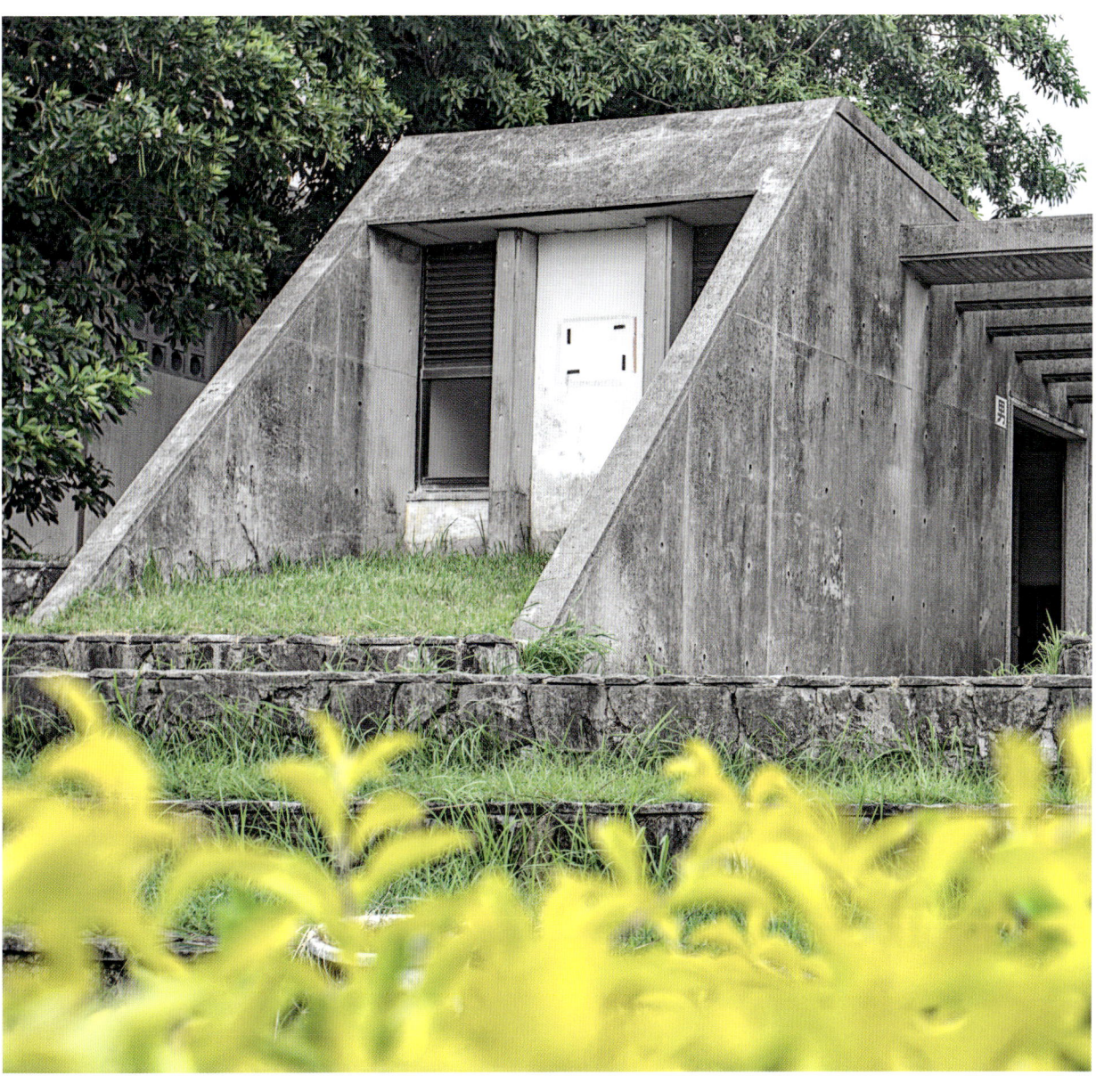

NAGASAKI PEACE MUSEUM

NAGASAKI · Architect: Furuichi and Associates · Completed 2004

Furuichi and Associates' Nagasaki Peace Museum, a minimalist structure by Nagasaki Bay, beckons visitors towards peace. Rising near the atomic blast's heart, it juxtaposes the city's hum with contemplative calm. The museum's path, a zigzagging journey reflecting the complex path to harmony, leads from a bustling highway to a serene space. Transitioning from the urban to the introspective, visitors are greeted by a triangular expanse, where light filters through concrete, crafting a hushed ambiance. Within its modest bounds, water flows, its soft sound a soothing overture to peace. In this haven, each visitor's passage echoes Nagasaki's resilient spirit, channelling a silent pledge to transform sorrow into a steadfast commitment to a peaceful tomorrow. It is a narrative that provides hope – a space dedicated to the silent reflection on a world without war.

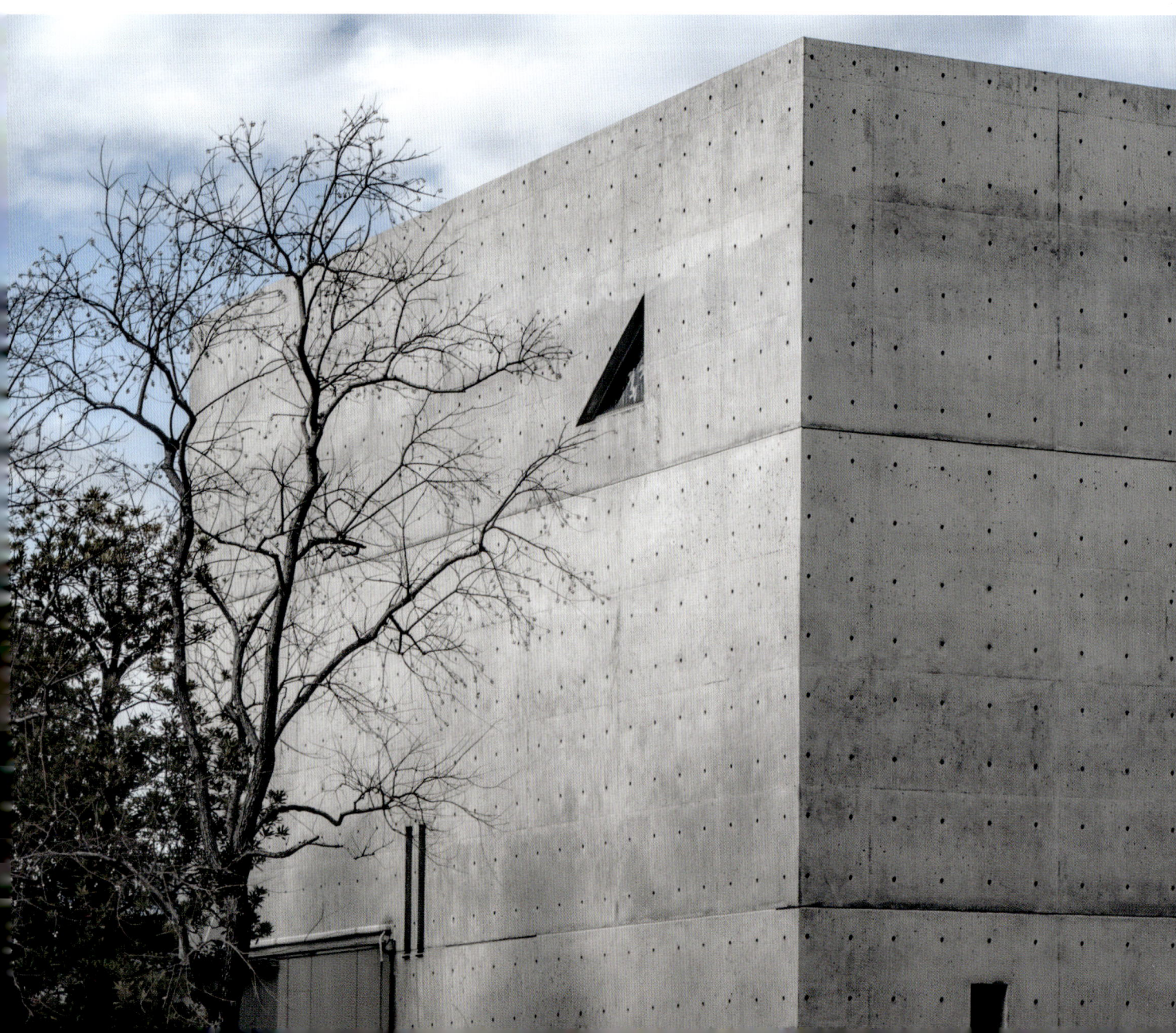

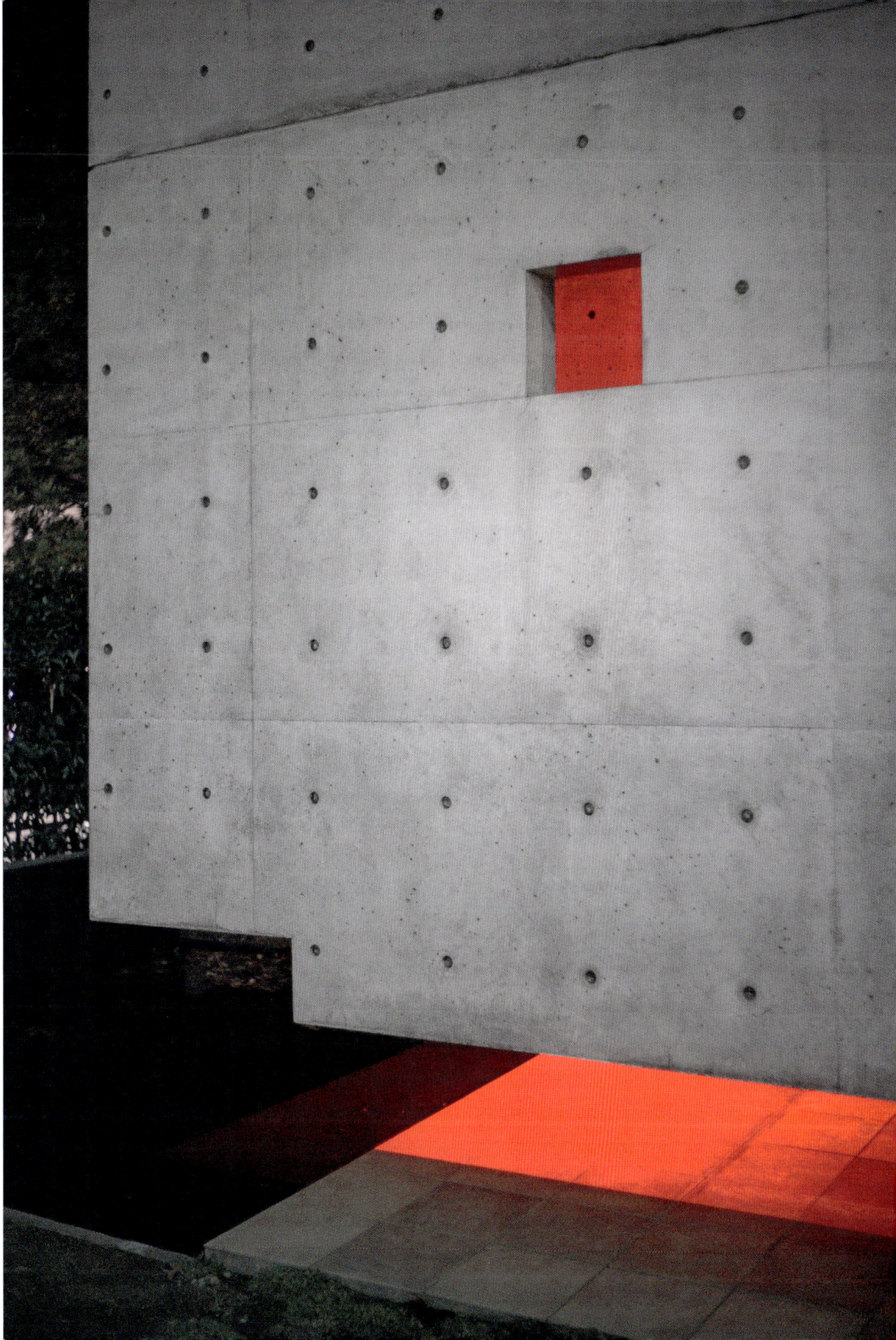

NAGO CITY HALL

NAGO, OKINAWA · Architect: Team Zo (Elephant Design Group) · Completed 1981

The 1979 design brief for Nago City Hall was an undiluted demand for critical regionalism, egalitarianism and a tangible homage to local culture – a true, inclusive expression of Okinawa at a time of renewed hope for autonomy from Tokyo. An architectural call to arms met by a load of loony elephants.

For some, commissioning the contrarian Zo with an idealistic design brief has made for an onanistic eyesore. From its main southern flank, the City Hall presents as an incongruous and lackadaisically constructed wall of concrete breeze-blocks. To boot, the façade's incomplete blandness has been exacerbated by the recent removal of individually, locally crafted gargoyles (*shishas*) due to salt erosion and the risk they would fall on someone's head during a typhoon. Why, then, was it awarded an Architectural Institute of Japan Award?

Appreciated from its northern flank, Zo's didacticism bears fruit with a tumbling agglomeration of colonnades, pergolas and terraces set upon a floor plan that resembles the outline of a B-2 stealth bomber. The colonnades are formed of porous vermillion and grey concrete blocks. Tilted concrete screening slats set within the pergola roofs absorb ambient moisture and provide a breeding ground for moss. The whole structure exudes an earthy pungency that is tempered by the fragrance of weaving bougainvillea. Drinks vending machines aside, the place smacks of an undiscovered jungle ruin. Welcome relief from intense heat and humidity is found within its shaded interior.

Critical regionalism is represented visually by pergola roofs matching the angles drawn by eaves (*amahaji*) on traditional homes and functionally through deployment of "banyan tree architecture". This local approach to building seeks to mimic the sun-shading and ventilation functions of the plant's aerial root system. Hence, a labyrinthine wind path affords complex yet open vistas from terraced levels.

Nago City Hall represents a watershed moment in not only Okinawan but Japanese architecture as well.

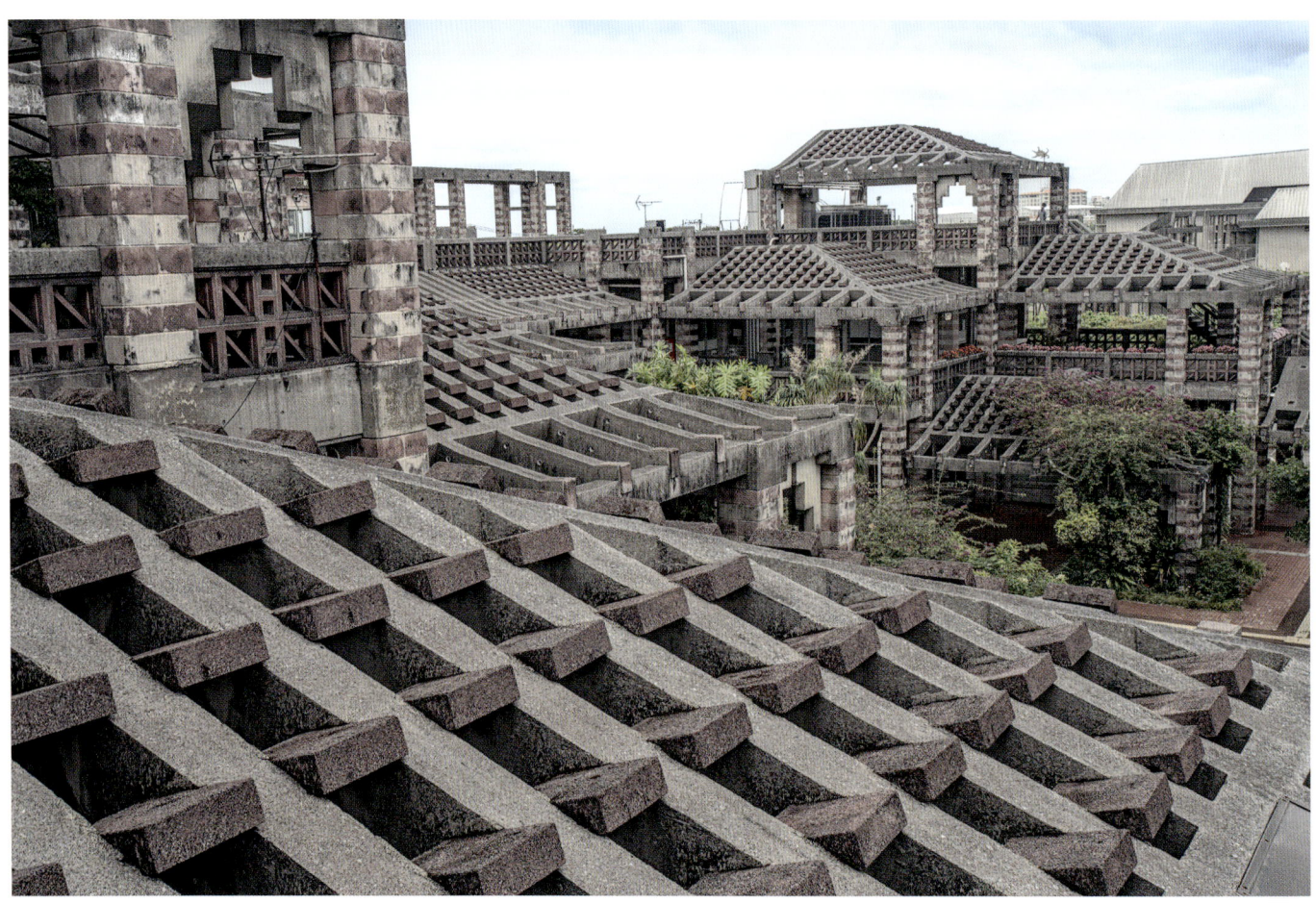

NAGO CITY HALL

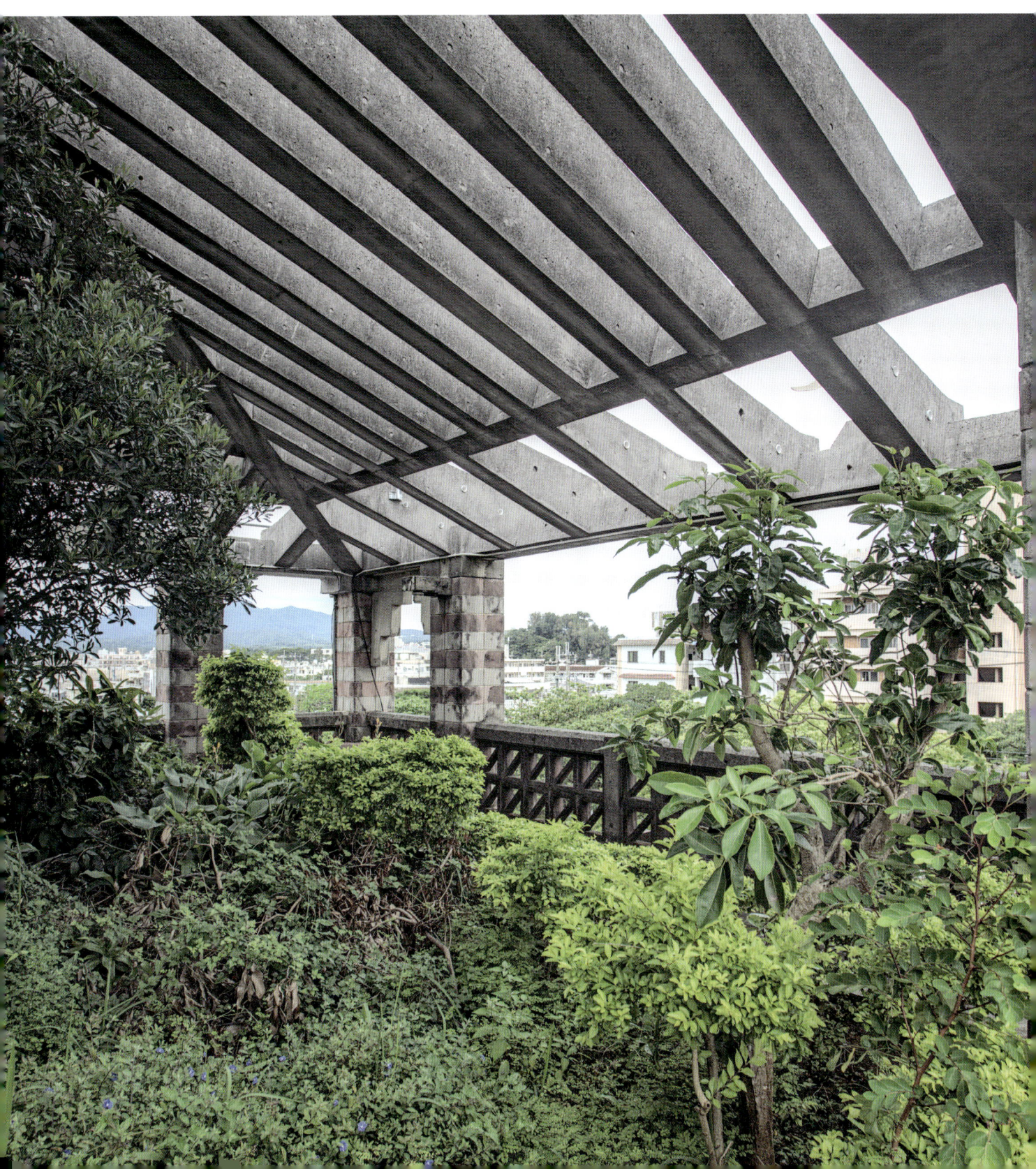

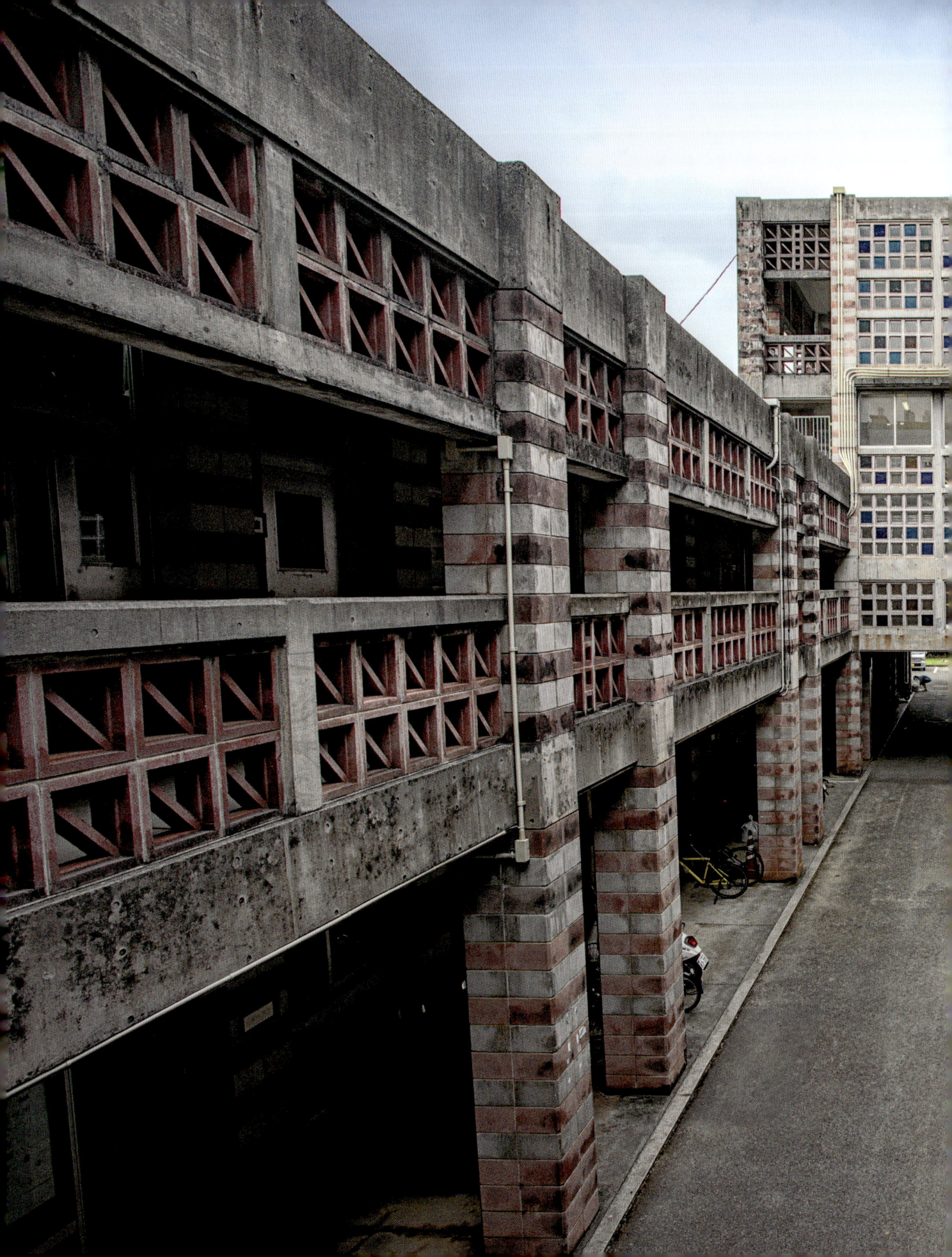

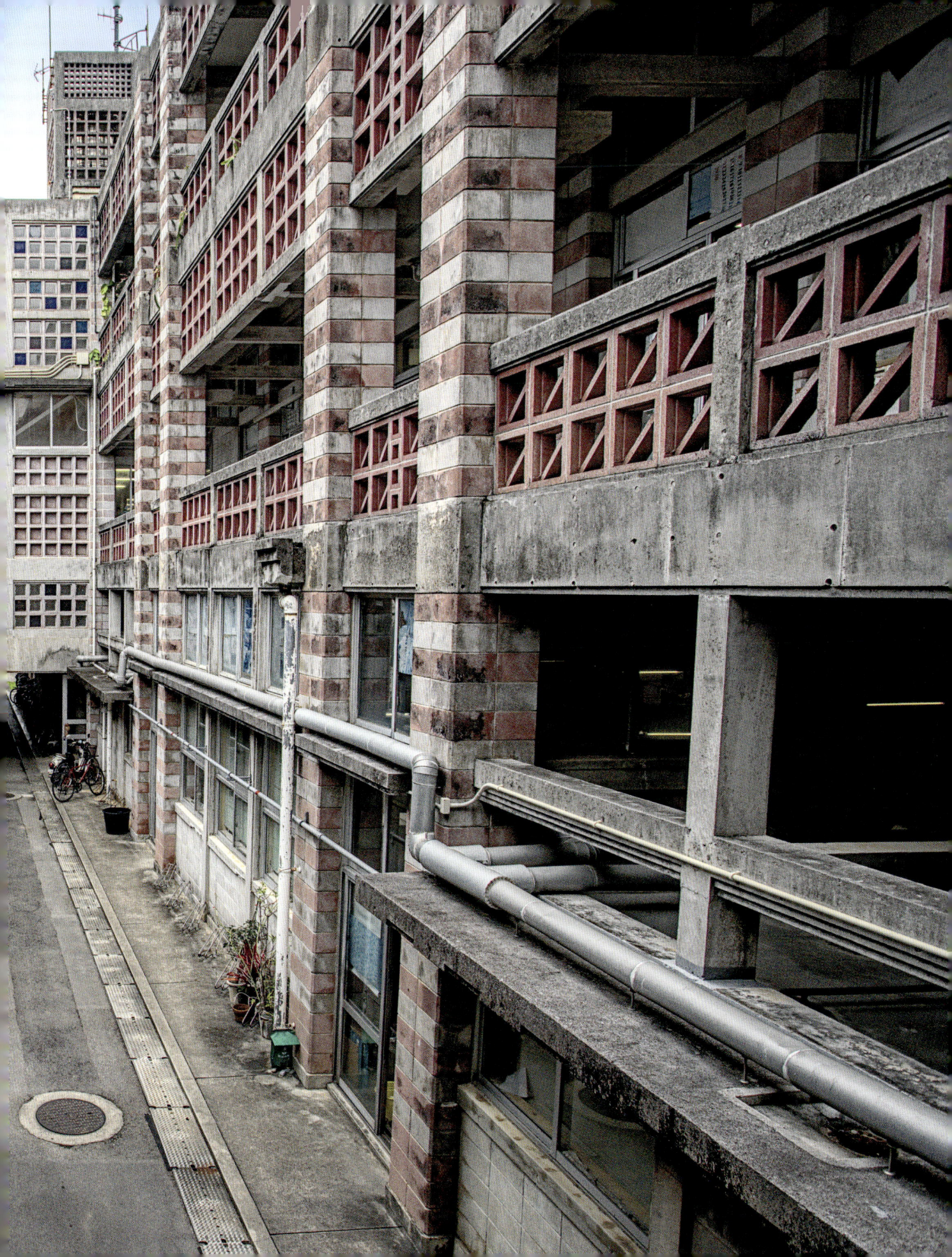

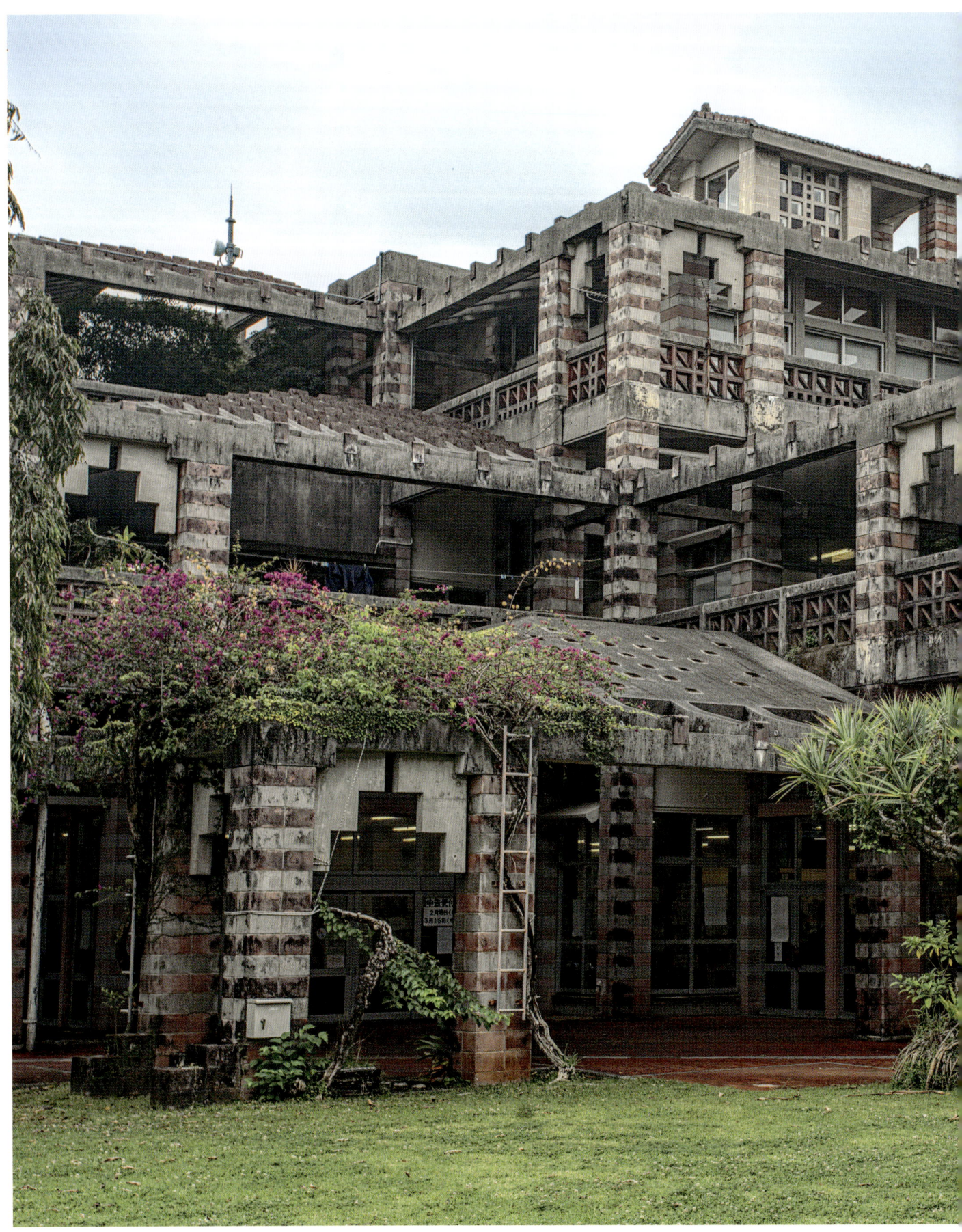

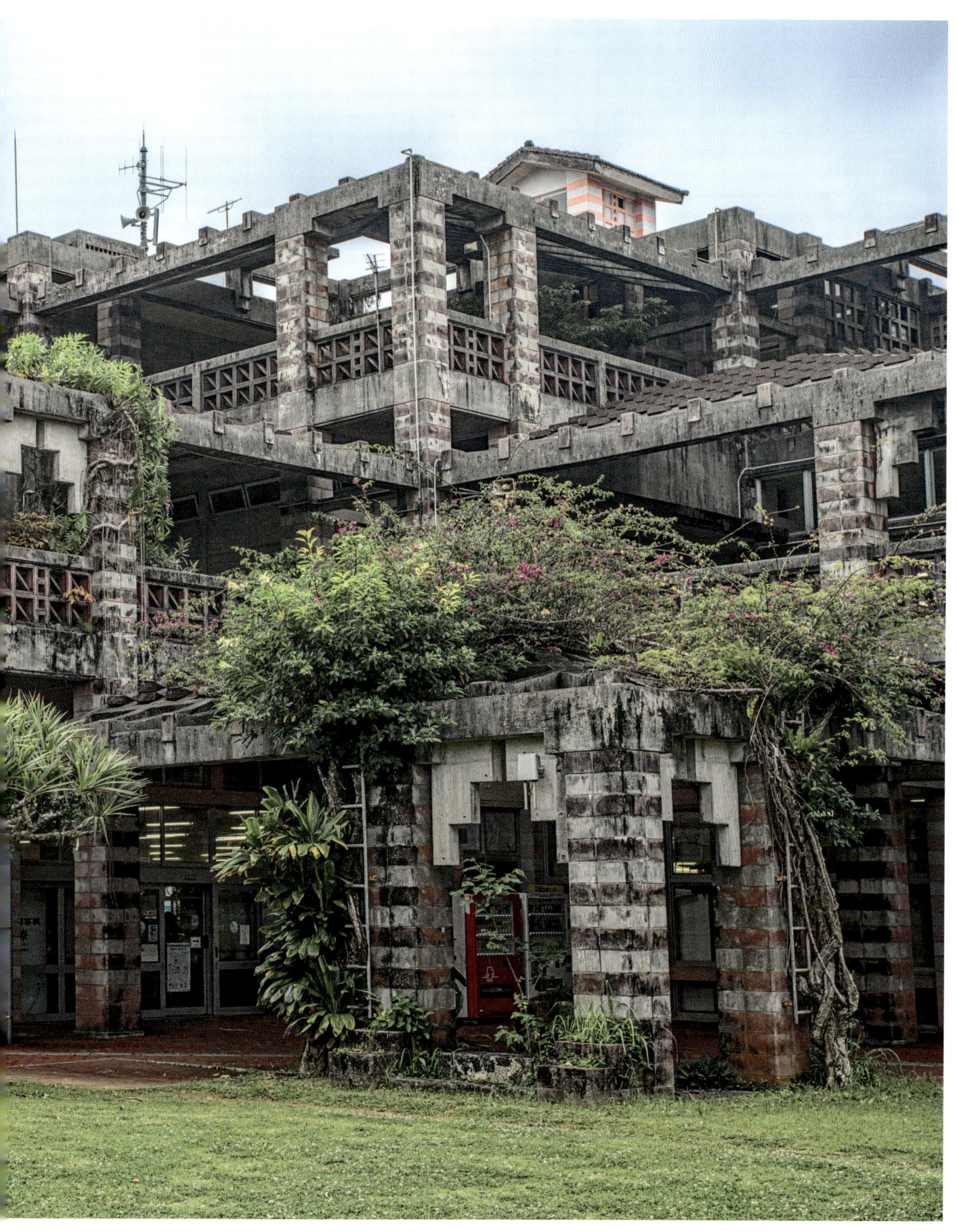

BASEBALL STADIUM SCOREBOARD

GINOZA, OKINAWA

To be fair, the painting of the cantilevered section of this scoreboard is not the most annoying example of a worrying trend I have noted in Okinawa.

A heathen may consider the painting of concrete as akin to putting lipstick on a gorilla. To the Brutalist Puritan it is sacrilege – utterly preposterous and missing the point entirely. Brutalism, a movement synonymous with raw, unadorned honesty, celebrates the rugged beauty of naked material. To a purist, painting concrete is a betrayal of the very ethos that makes Brutalism, well, brutal.

Nago's scoreboard didn't get such a subtle paint job. Instead it has been smothered in paint and rendered characterless. Nearby, a once monumental apartment block goes unnoticed now that it has been given a brown coating. A local school has made the textbook error of allowing students to paint over its concrete walls and breeze-blocks.

Unpainted concrete provides a compelling narrative. Every weathered crack and mottled patch speaks of time, use and resilience. Painting it is like varnishing the Mona Lisa, thinking it needs more shine. This act disrespects the material's integrity and the creator's vision.

Furthermore, painting concrete isn't just a cosmetic crime; it's a functional faux pas. Concrete's porous nature requires it to breathe. Coating it with paint is akin to wrapping your face in cling film. It may appear smooth at first, but regret will soon arise. The paint traps moisture, causing bubbling, peeling and ultimately a disastrous architectural makeover.

Then there is the environmental argument against painterly crimes on concrete. High-pressure washing is far more ecologically friendly than bucketloads of toxic paint that needs endless coating in a semi-tropical environment prone to heavy rain and strong wind.

Misplaced municipal vanity should not compromise Okinawa's unique Brutalist built heritage.

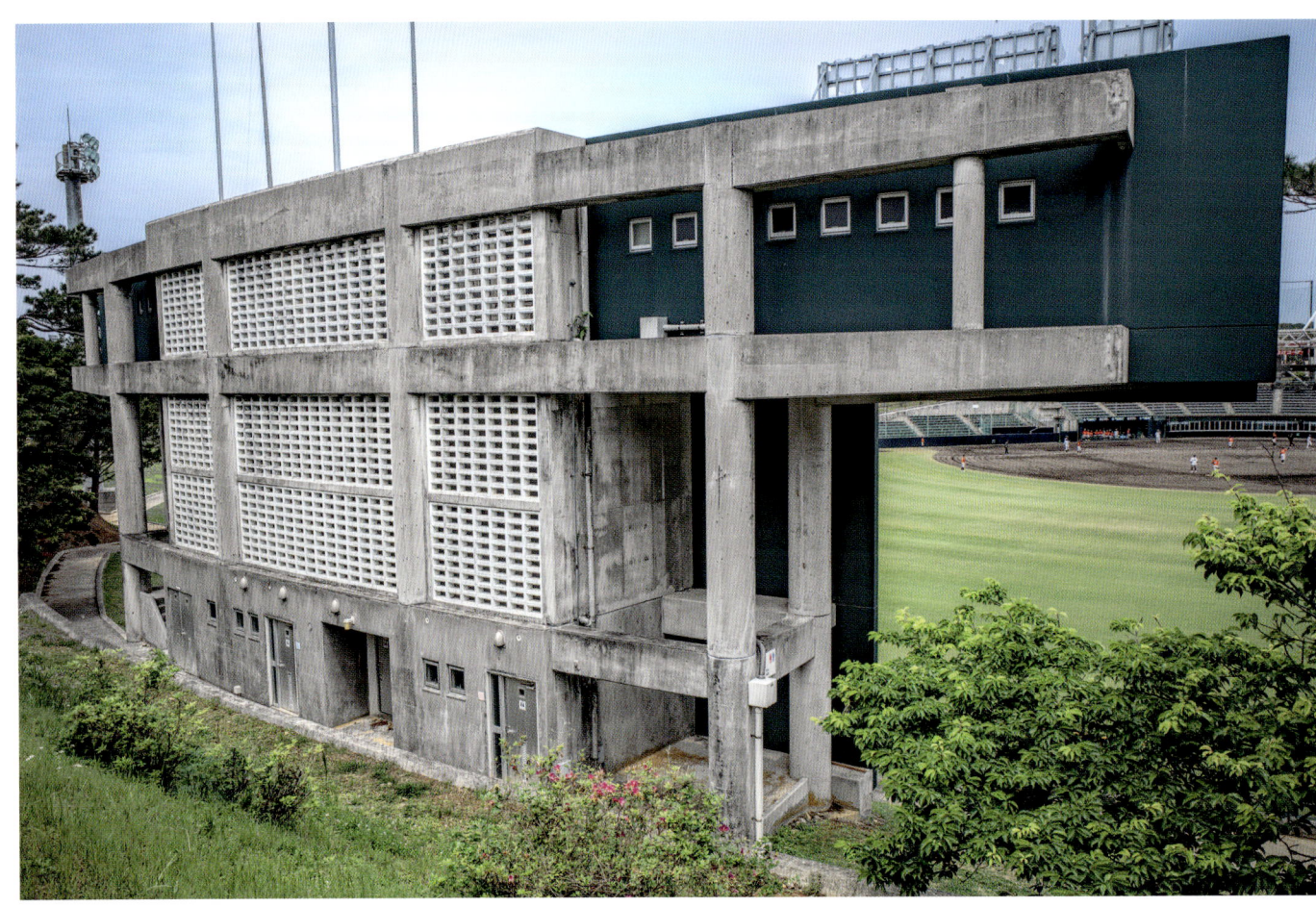

VILLAGE COMMUNITY CENTER

NAKIJIN, OKINAWA · Architect: Team Zo (Elephant Design Group) · Completed 1975

See those palm trees that perfectly complement the horizontality of the building? Gone. Chopped down. Shells embedded in the floor? Gone. Deliberate vandalism and wilful neglect suggest this one is a goner.

Like the preceding Nago City Hall, this was designed by Team Zo, armed with their seven principles: expressing place, understanding building use, diversity, sensory and emotional experience, enhancing and enjoying nature, *aimaimoko* (something limited and ambiguous) and "exertiveness". Still operating nearly fifty years later, Zo architects "favour: a bunch of people rather than machines; human wisdom rather than knowledge; continuity rather than speed; passion and zeal rather than reason; excessiveness rather than adequacy; extra-norm rather than the norm; endless questions rather than a conclusion."

Led by Takamasa Yoshizaka, a disciple of Le Corbusier, the group advocates for principles like "expressing place" and "ambiguous space", focusing on adapting to regional climates and lifestyles. These principles are vividly illustrated in their design of the Nakijin Village Community Center. Bright red pillars and semi-outdoor spaces leading to a courtyard create something of an outdoor theatre feel. It encourages community interaction while reflecting Okinawa's unique climate and culture. Awarded the Minister of Education's Art Encouragement Prize in 1977, it is also listed among Japan's 197 Best Modern Movement Architectures.

Currently, the large reinforced concrete roof is exposed, but once it was intended to be covered with bougainvillea. The design's original integration of nature and architecture aimed to echo the local landscape and lifestyle but is now compromised by neglect and damage. Let's hope this one survives.

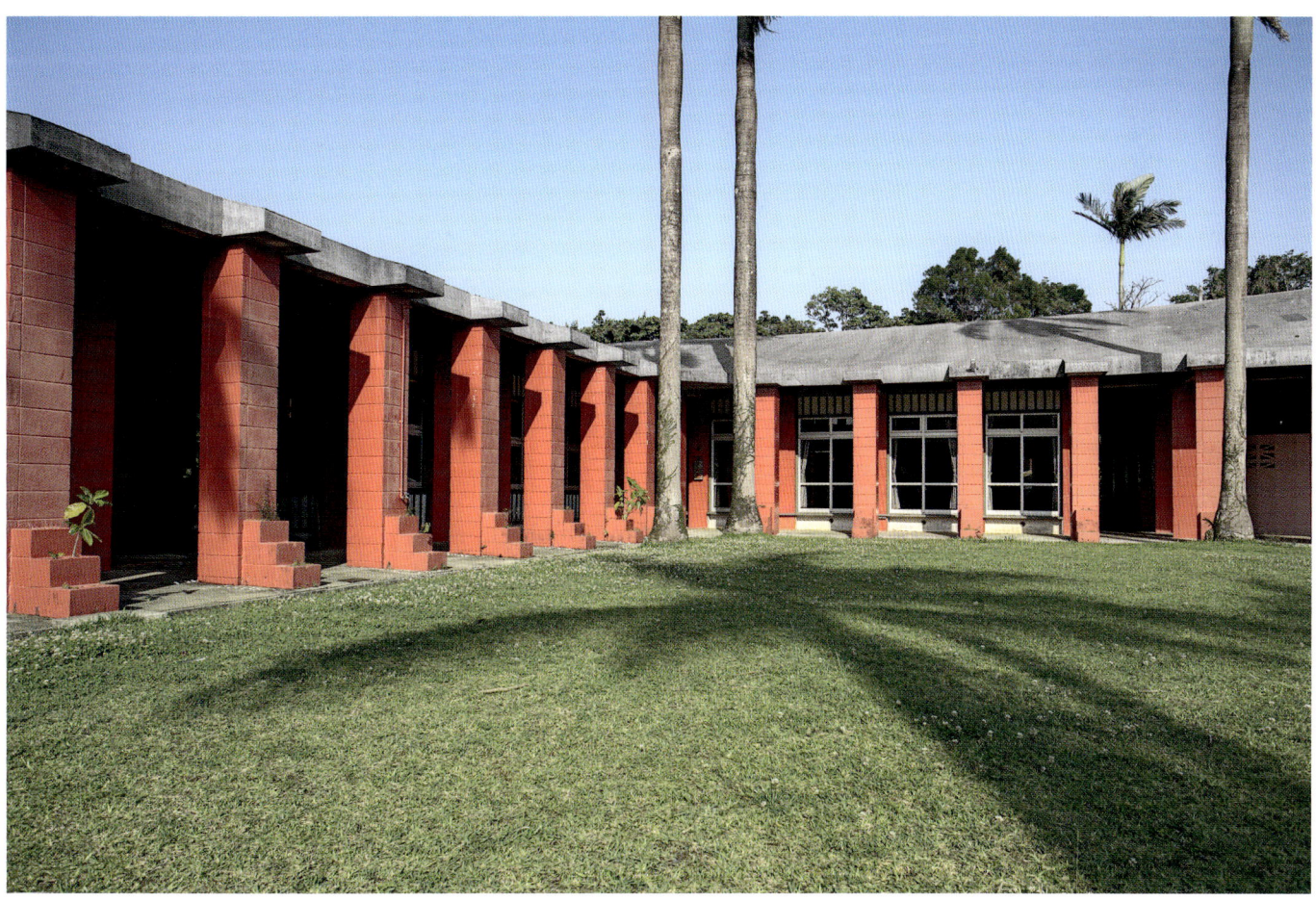

SEASIDE GALLERY

NAOSHIMA ISLAND · Architect: ANDO Tadao · Completed 1999

This gallery, conceived by Tadao Ando and perched on a terraced plaza adjacent to the Benesse House Museum, gazes upon the sea. Its elongated form stretches from north to south, harmonizing with the landscape while eastern light floods in through a vast aperture.

Ando's architectural lexicon is sparse, yet powerful, often confined to elemental shapes and a palette of select materials, resulting in a signature style. His approach is deeply rooted in Japanese tradition, balanced with influences from Western modernists like Le Corbusier, the Bauhaus and Louis Kahn. His favoured material, concrete, evolves with time, its surface capturing the subtleties of light. This concrete, though appearing untouched, is meticulously crafted to a smoothness that rivals finished surfaces.

The architecture is an oasis, a serene reprieve from the bustle of urban life. Ando designs spaces that serve as sanctuaries, isolating the inner sanctum from the public domain, offering solace within its minimalist refuge.

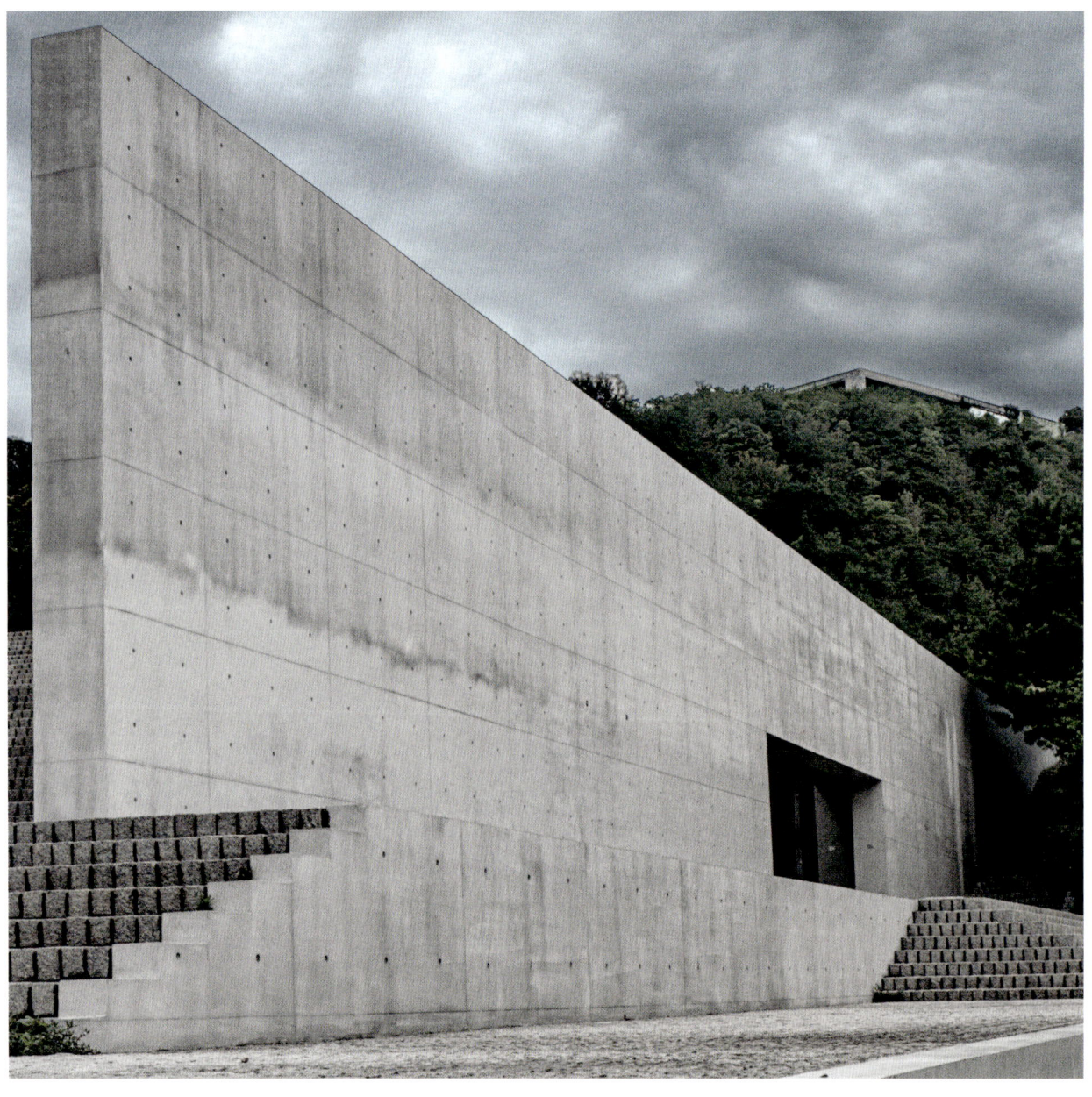

GUESTHOUSE AND RESTAURANT

NAKIJIN, OKINAWA

In a world where the youth scale pixelated towers and concrete citadels with the tap of a key, Brutalist architecture strikes a resonant chord. It's as if the genre was forged from the same digital anvils that birth colossal realms in their favourite games. A simple guesthouse and restaurant becomes a solid Brutalist bastion – not just a structure, but a level waiting to be conquered, a challenge etched in concrete. That pipe is certainly "climbable"!

This younger generation, joystick warriors and mouse masters alike, find an odd kinship with these concrete leviathans. Here, in these geometric jungles, lies a dystopian playground, a tangible mirror to the virtual worlds they dominate. The tactile becomes interactive, the climbable not just an idea but an invitation. In the rigid lines and raw surfaces, they see not just buildings, but the landscapes of their digital escapades made real – Brutalism not as a style, but as an avatar of their virtual conquests.

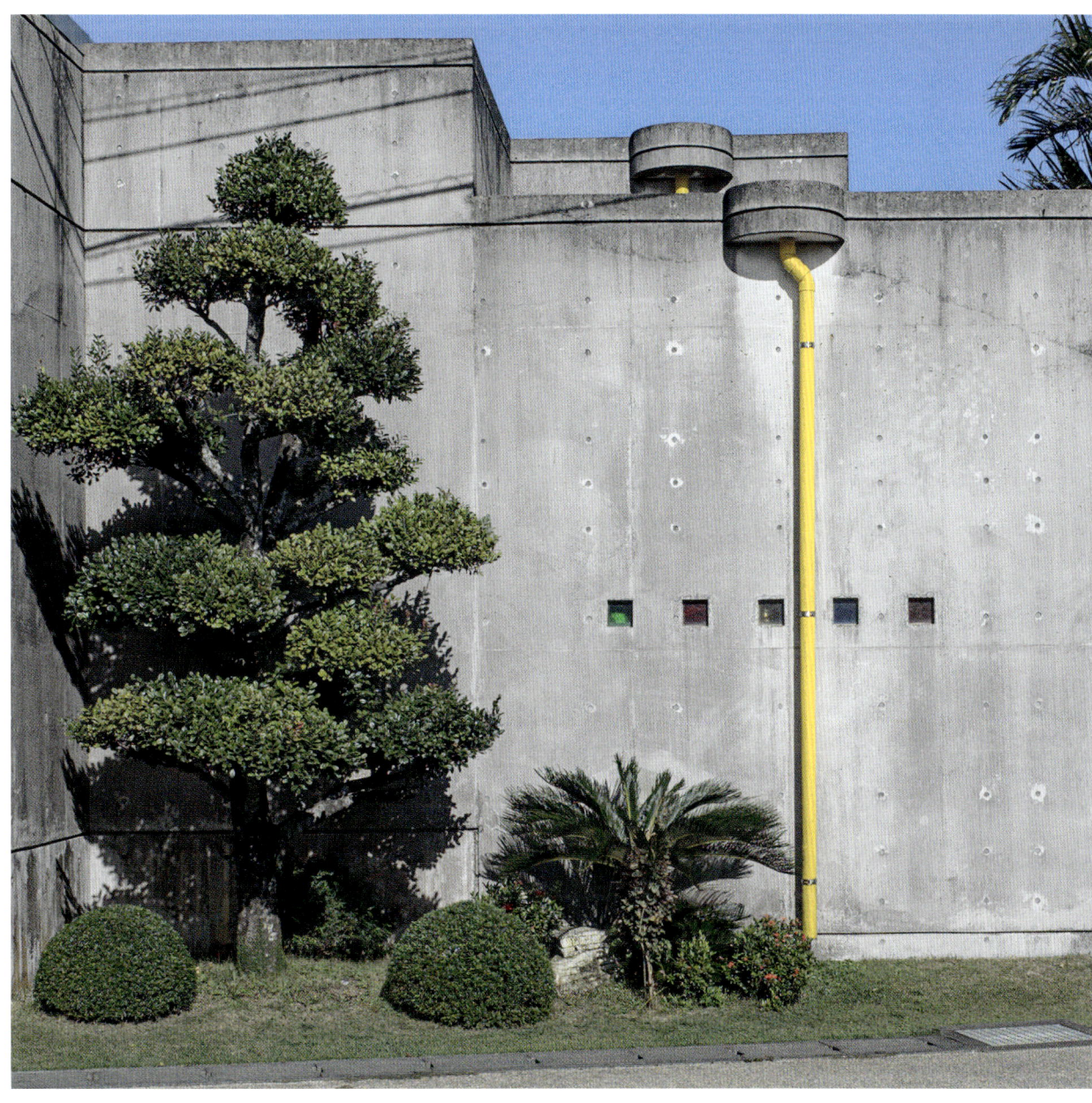

NATIONAL THEATRE

TOKYO · Architect: IWAMOTO Hiroyuki · Completed 1967

As is often the case, seismic concerns have been used to justify demolition of what appeared to me just recently as immaculate.

Designed by Hiroyuki Iwamoto of the Takenaka Corporation, this architectural gem draws its inspiration from the Shōsō-in repository of the twelfth century – a storied structure originally serving the Tōdai-ji temple in Nara before coming under the Imperial Household Agency's care. The theatre, much like the Shōsō-in, was conceived as an elegant "black box", a custodian of cultural treasures. Iwamoto's design skilfully adapted the *azekura-zukuri*, an ancient interlocking log construction technique, into the modern medium of precast concrete. This choice, while symbolically rich, was not without its critics.

The concrete was tinted an earthy brown and sand-blasted to soften its appearance, mimicking the texture of traditional Japanese log buildings and evoking a subdued elegance that resisted the harsh glare of light. This architectural decision was meant to blend tradition with modernity, but it also sparked debates on authenticity and adaptation. It has been argued that replicating timber details in concrete was not only functionally meaningless but reduced the technique to mere decoration.

The theatre's design highlighted the prowess of Takenaka Corporation's in-house team, known for producing well-detailed, timeless buildings characterized by their understated elegance and meticulous attention to material and proportion. However, the choice to prioritize aesthetic mimicry over functional integrity upsets some.

As the National Theatre of Japan faces its final curtain, the architectural community reflects on the delicate balance between innovation and tradition, pondering the legacy of a building that stood as a bridge between the past and the present, yet is now poised to become a memory.

Interestingly, though, demolition and rebuilding plans are turning into a national debacle amid escalating controversies over government expenditure and efficiency. How fitting that such drama may save a theatre.

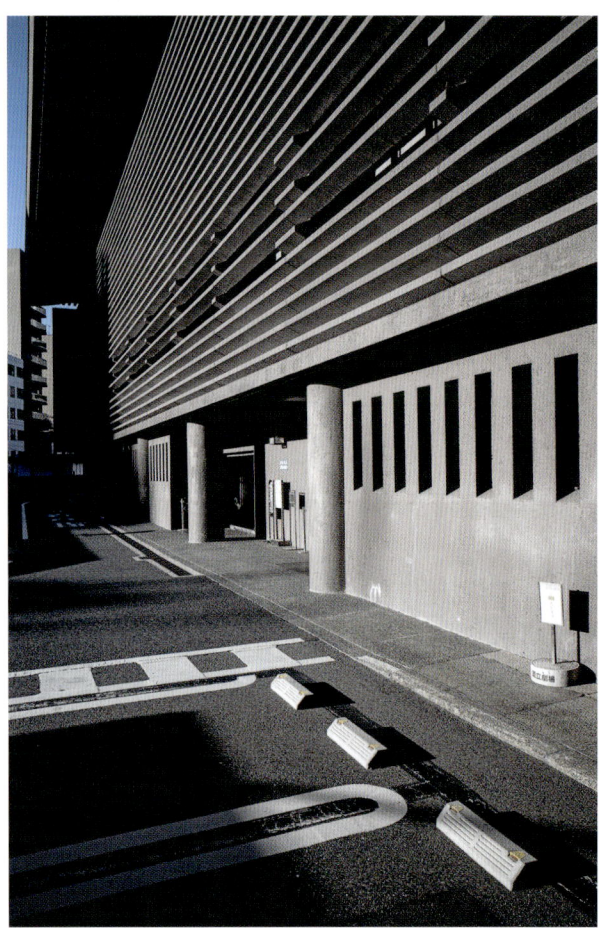
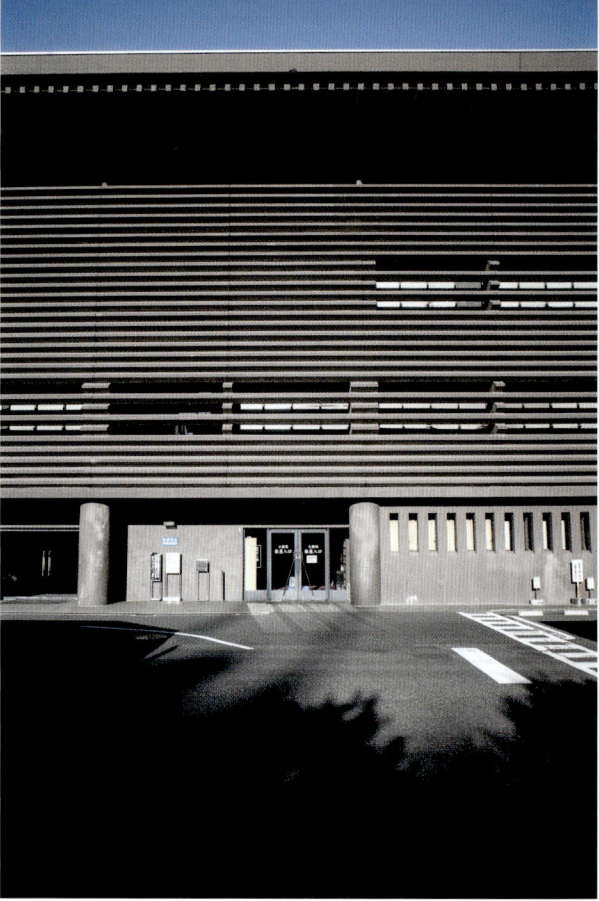

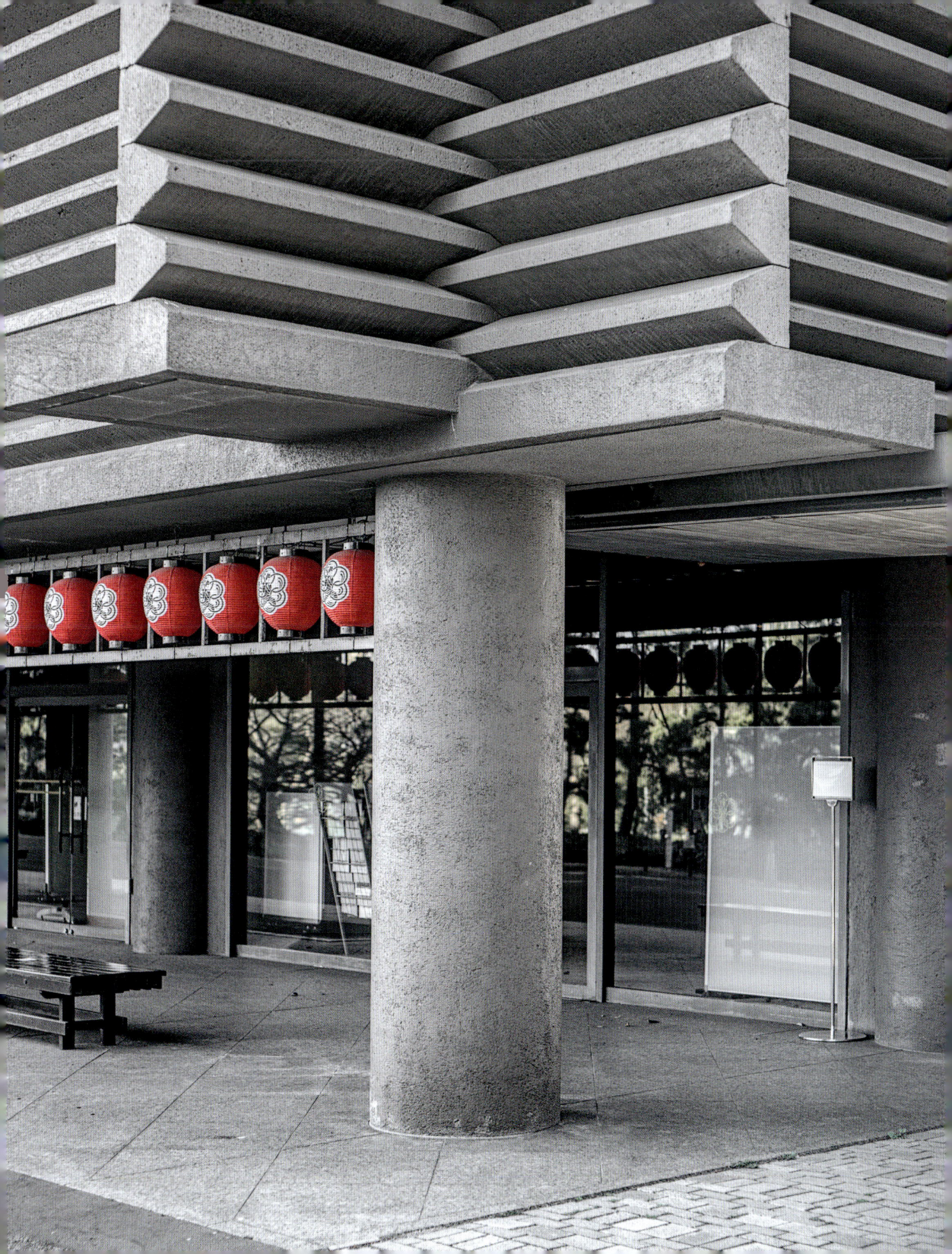

OITA PREFECTURAL GOVERNMENT BUILDING

OITA · Architect: YASUDA Katashi · Completed 1962

The Oita Prefectural Government Building is a classy piece of modernist design, presenting a fascinating contrast between its low-rise base and an elevated high-rise section, supported by pilotis. The building is a hallmark achievement of the architect, whose previous role as head of the Construction Ministry's Repair Bureau informed his career.

This marvel earned the Architectural Institute of Japan Award in 1962, a distinction not shared by any other prefectural government building since.

The lower part of the administrative building is opened up by way of the pilotis and, together with the "Festival Garden" built in front of the welfare building, it was planned as a place of relaxation for the citizens of the prefecture. Such combination of pilotis and garden echoes the Kagawa Prefectural Office Building (designed by Kenzo Tange, 1958), and trends of the time can be seen throughout, such as the use of exposed concrete and the adoption of a folded-plate structure for the roof of the assembly hall.

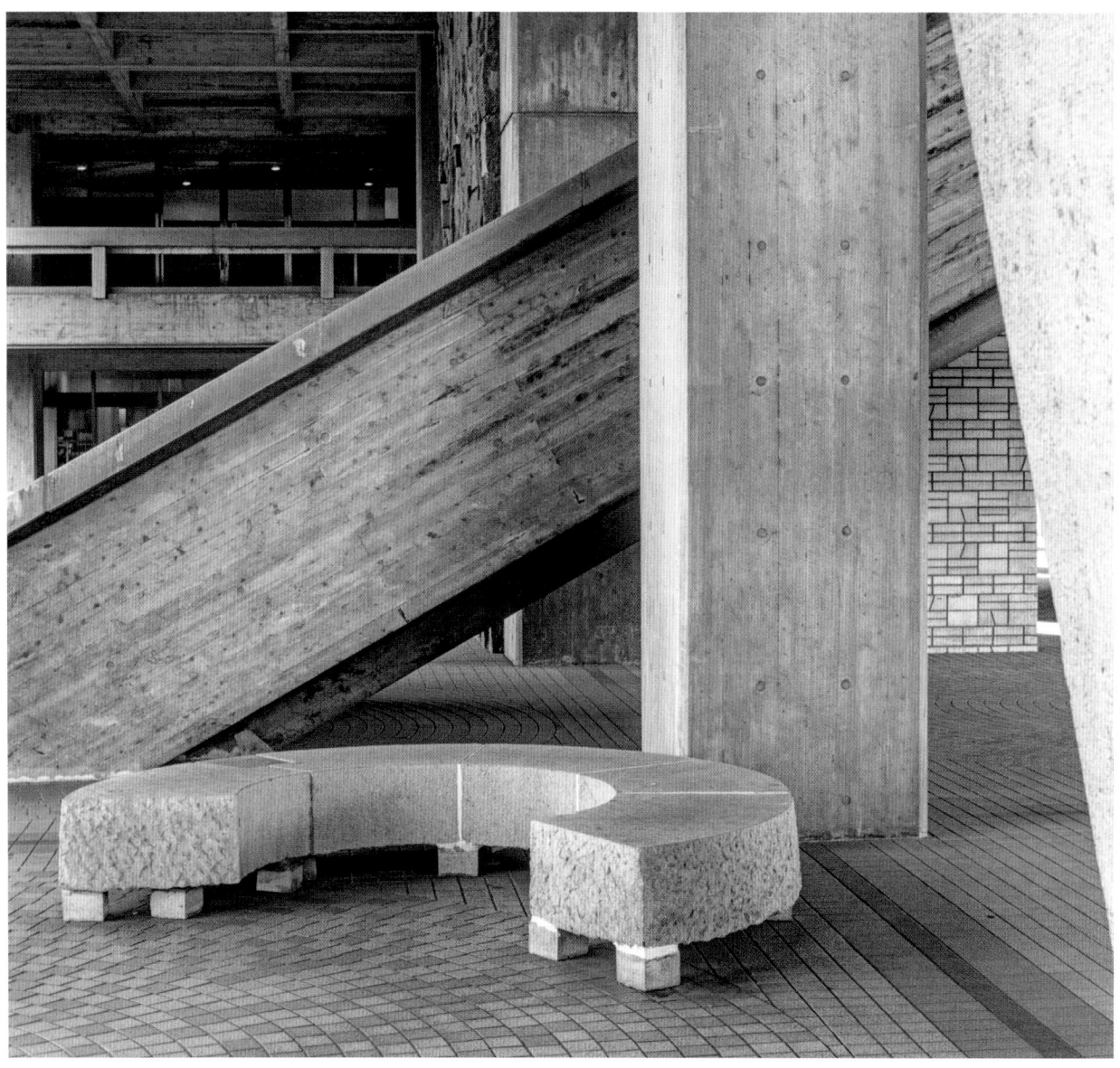

SUNTORY MUSEUM TOILET BLOCK

OSAKA · Architect: ANDO Tadao · Completed 1994

Suntory Museum forms part of the most important interventions in Osaka's waterfront. Designed by the maven, Ando, why you might ask was the Brutal Zen lens focused on a toilet yet again and not the grander elements of the broader design? Issues?

I hail from a land where public toilets are less "chamber of reflection" and more "portal of despair". The UK's public bogs are a frightful affair, offering less a call of nature and more a cry for help.

But Ando's toilet? It is a sanctum of sanitary ware, a form of concrete potty poetry (*haiku!*) – a silent ode to the most human of acts. To me, it's not just a toilet – it's a keep of hope, a place where one can contemplate life's great mysteries while having a leak.

Even the most basic of needs is elevated to an art form. And so, with a chuckle and a click, I captured this thronely treasure. Each flush resonates with the echo of architectural brilliance.

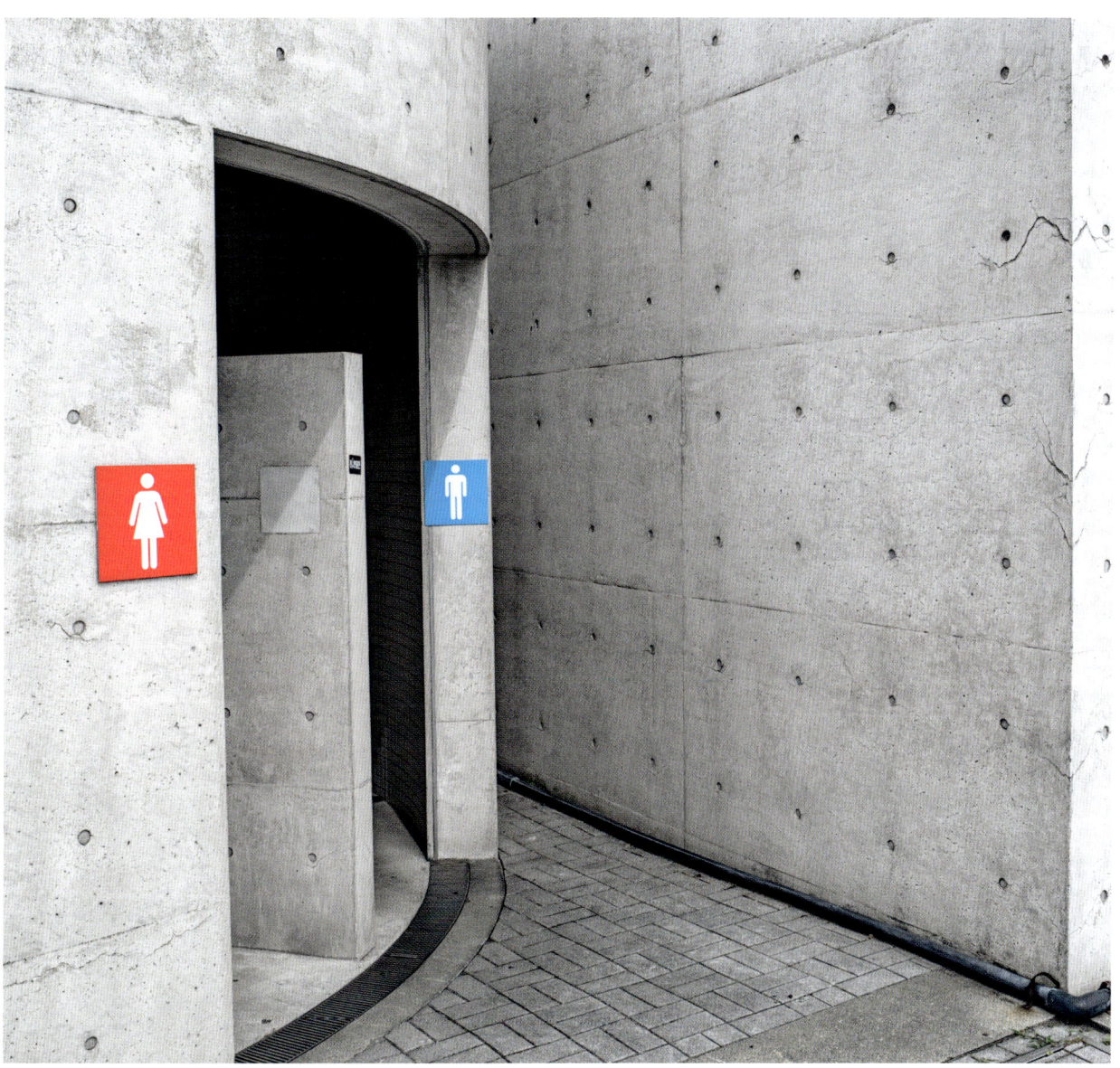

OITA PREFECTURAL LIBRARY

OITA · Architect: ISOZAKI Arata · Completed 1966

Isozaki's library design reflects his concept of "growing architecture", rooted in "process planning theory", which eschews the notion of completed structures in favour of adaptable, evolving forms. This approach directly addresses the Brutalism versus Metabolism debate by merging Brutalist permanence with Metabolist flexibility. The library combines late Corbusian modernism and Brutalism while challenging Metabolist dynamics by illustrating "frozen stasis" and hypothesizing growth cut-off. Stark exposed concrete tubes are poised for future adaptation.

The library's design, inspired by the human skeletal system, uses a concrete framework of suspended tubular beams that integrate spatial, structural and mechanical elements, allowing for potential future expansions. Unlike the typical 1950s Japanese concrete architectures that imitated wooden constructions, Isozaki's design draws on masonry styles, particularly Roman ruins – a result of his international influences. The interior features a play of darkness and light, moderated by carefully designed skylights. Despite plans for expansion, the structure remains unchanged despite now being an art plaza.

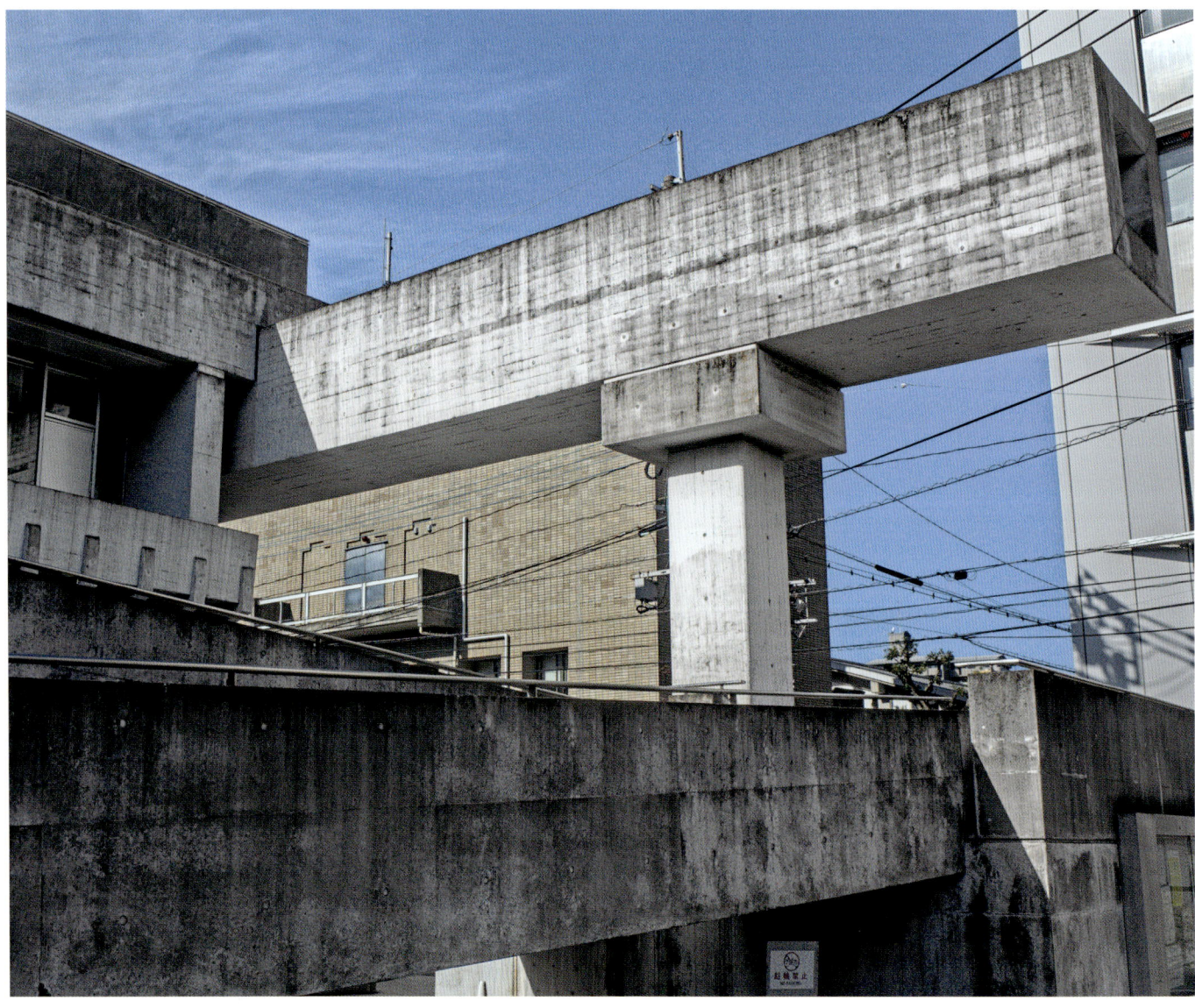

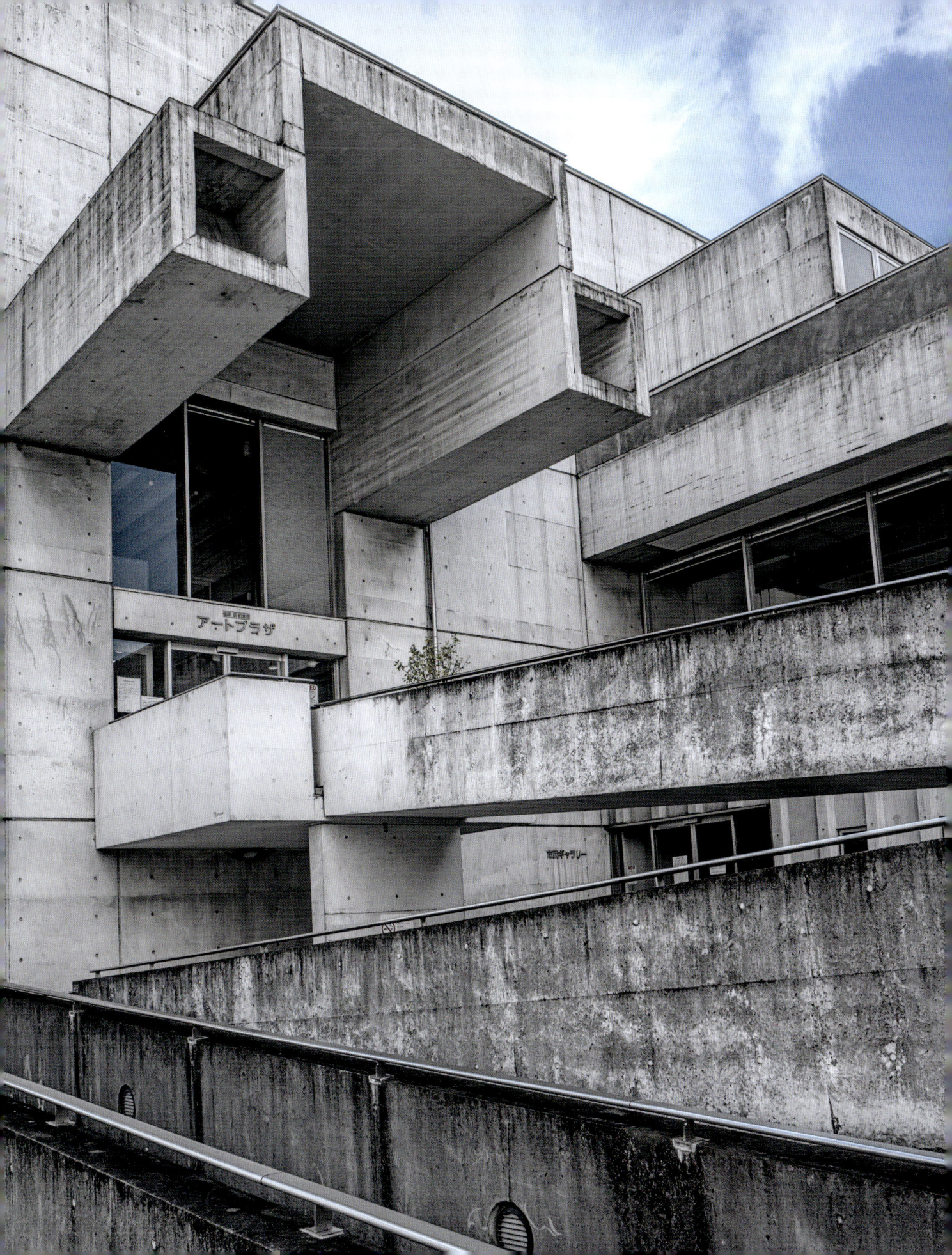

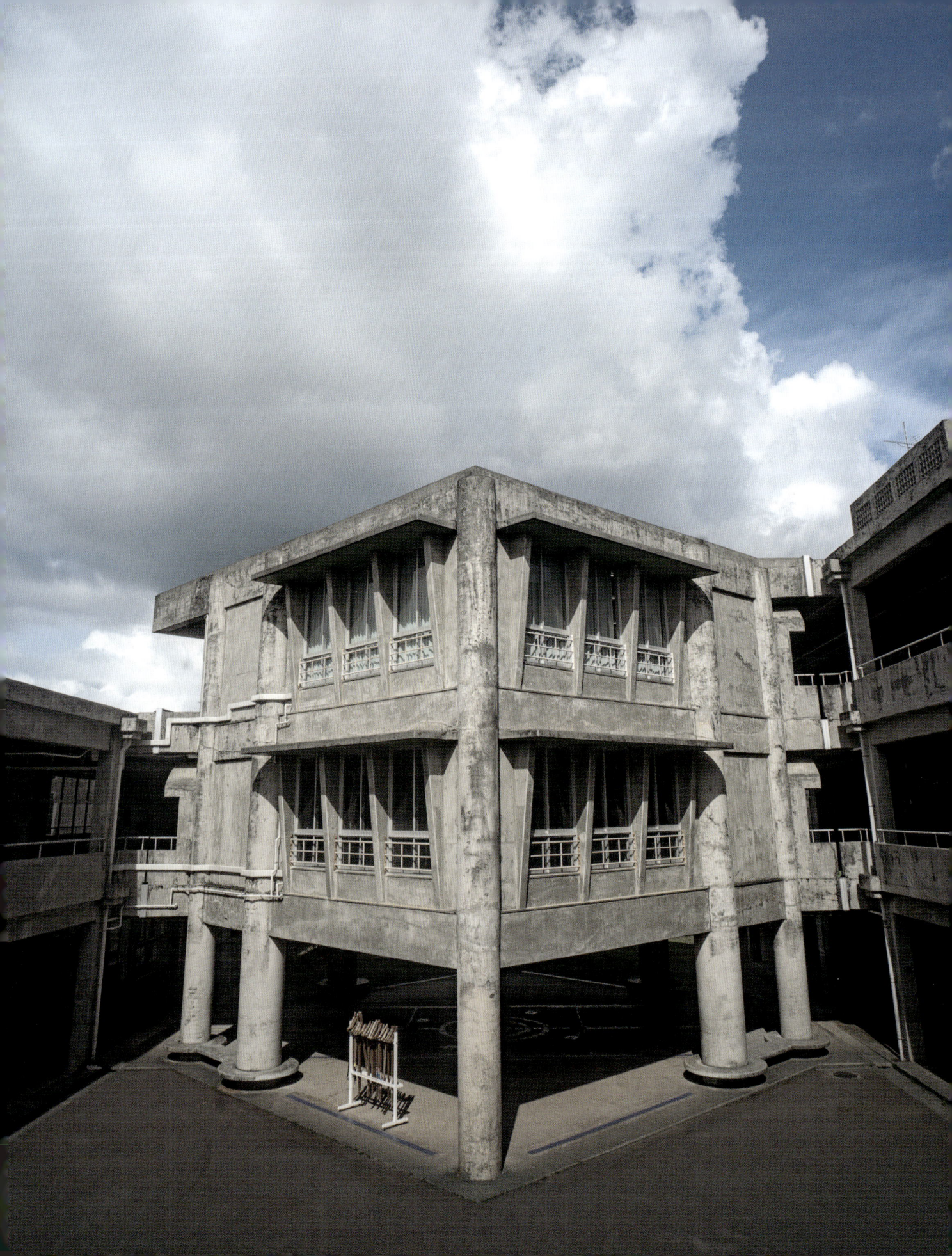

ELEMENTARY SCHOOL

NAGO, OKINAWA · Architect: Kuniyoshi Design · Completed 1985

I have been told that Okinawan schools have been designed to double as hospitals in times of crisis. This multi-functionality stems mainly from the island prefecture's unique historical and geographical context. Being a strategic location in the Pacific used as a buffer for mainland Japan, it went through the trauma of the Battle of Okinawa. This resulted in massive destruction and a high civilian casualty rate. Some estimates state one-third of the population.

This experience explains school designs that prioritize swift adaptation to emergency needs and the building of resilience into broader community infrastructure.

To boot, schools are designed to be robust and versatile so that they can provide shelter and emergency services during typhoons and the aftermath of earthquakes. This design philosophy reflects a pragmatic approach to dealing with the realities of living in a geopolitically sensitive area prone to natural disasters.

Schools are strategically positioned throughout communities to ensure accessibility for all residents. They frequently feature open areas, like gymnasia and playgrounds, which can be converted into temporary holding areas or treatment centres in times of crisis.

I have also heard that the multifunctional design of schools is intended to allow for adaptation to prisons and mental asylums – the latter in consideration of the less documented realities of war.

Having worked at this particular school, I can testify as to its observational aspects which are reminiscent of panopticon prisons. Now banned, these were designed for centralized surveillance whereby a single guard could watch all inmates without being seen.

The lovely kids I taught here needed no such surveillance. Despite the dark features I have covered, the schools I have experienced in Okinawa, and wider Japan, exude an openness and warmth. I have visited many with camera in hand and been welcomed to take shots. Can you imagine that where you come from? Cue a phone call to the police.

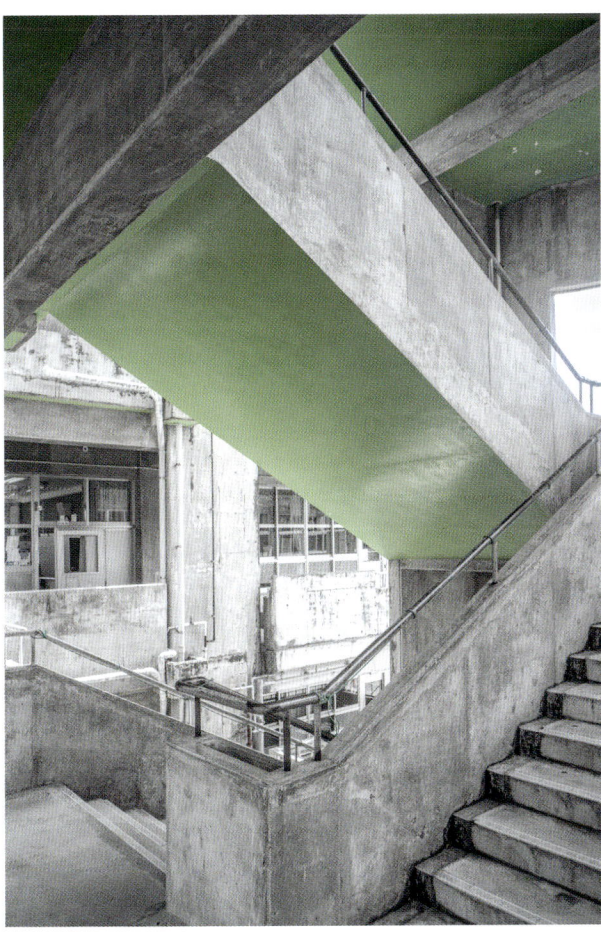
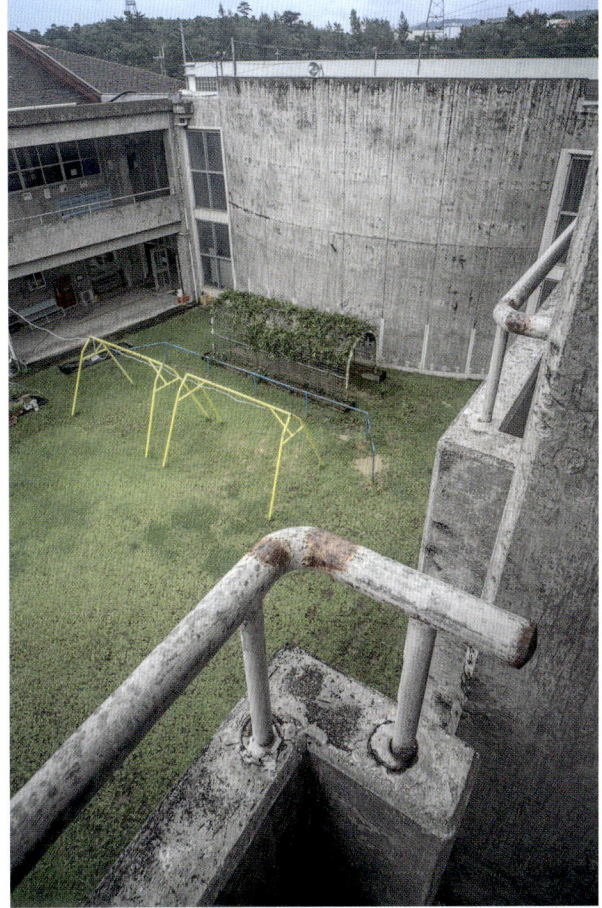

ELEMENTARY SCHOOL

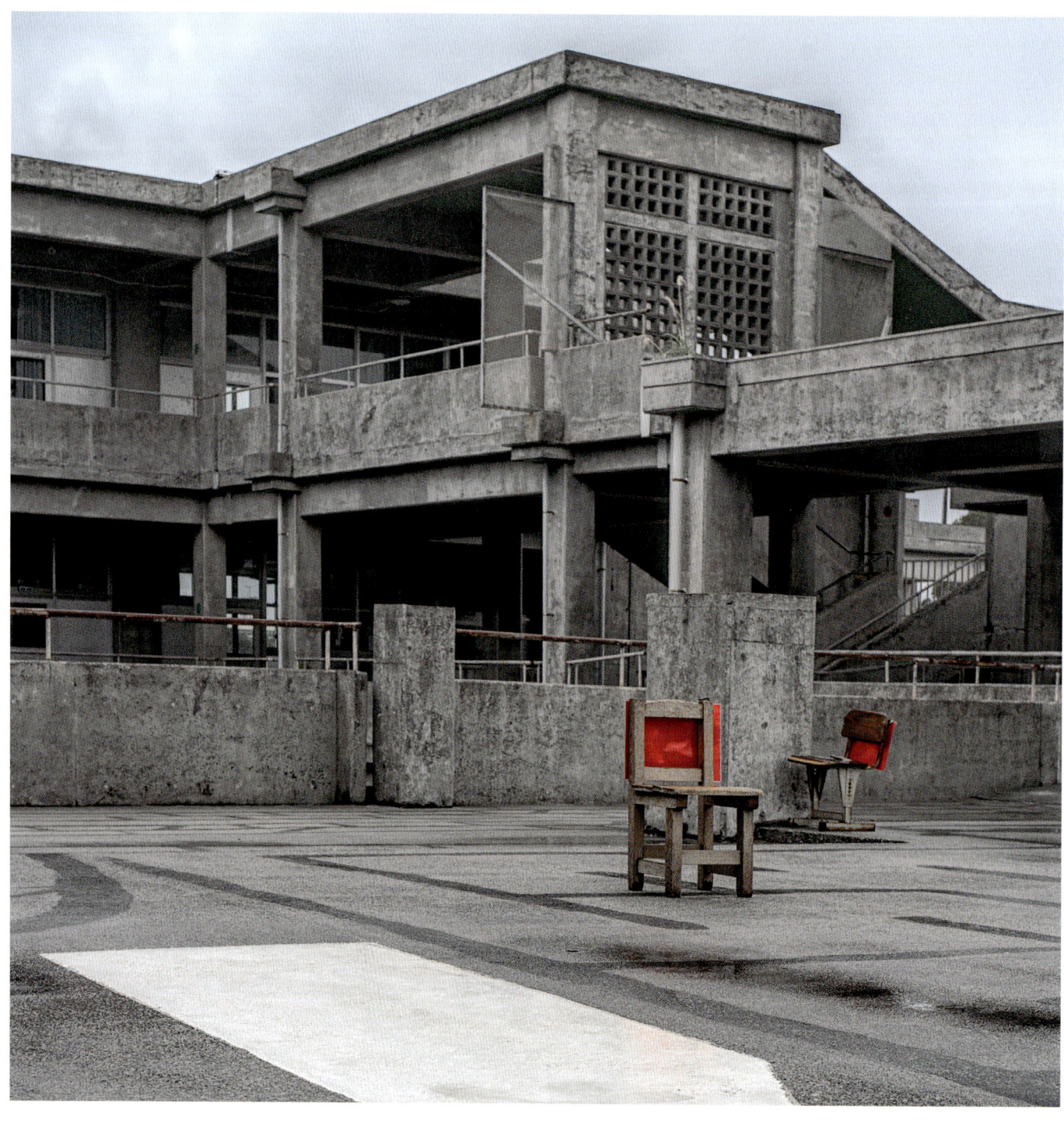

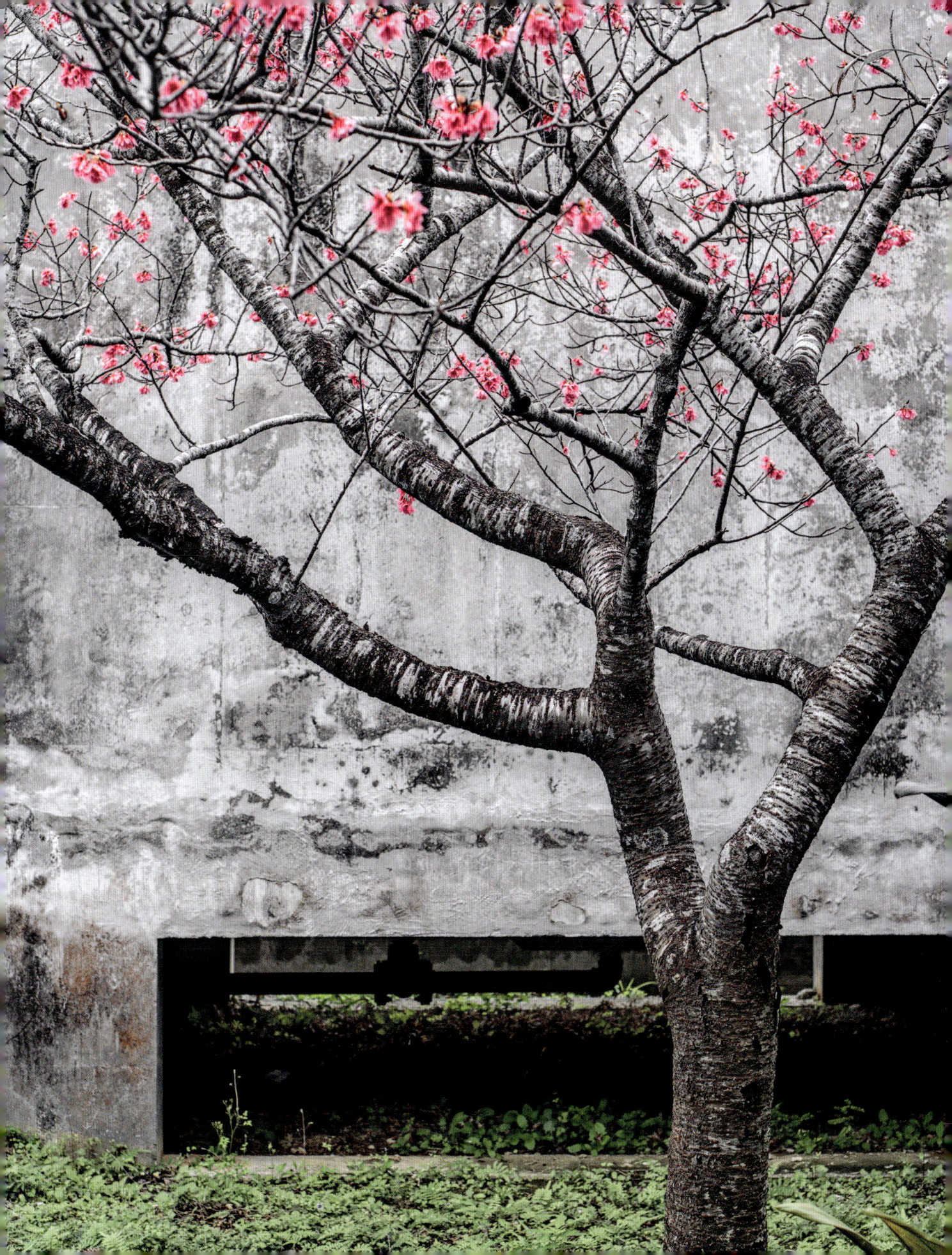

PRIVATE RESIDENCE

NAGO, OKINAWA · Architect: UEHARA Ken · Completed 1980

This architectural piece presents an intriguing amalgamation of traditional Okinawan and Japanese aesthetics with contemporary materials. The use of *hana* blocks, a form of breeze-blocks, creates patterns that are both decorative and functional, providing ventilation while alluding to the Okinawan penchant for airflow in architecture, a necessity in their warm climate. Glass blocks are interspersed, contributing to the building's luminosity and privacy, a modern interpretation of the translucent *shoji* screens found in traditional Japanese architecture. Timber sliding doors offer a natural warmth that contrasts with the starkness of the concrete. This concrete, formed and left unfinished, reveals in parts the wood grain imprint from its forming, a gentle hint at the wooden constructs of classic Japanese design. Together, these materials – *hana* blocks for cultural relevance, glass blocks for light, timber for natural warmth, concrete for solidity – create a tapestry that honours tradition while embracing modernity.

Blending architectural themes incorporated into grander public schemes seen elsewhere throughout Nago, this private residence proves to be something of a microcosm that reflects broad trends of the time.

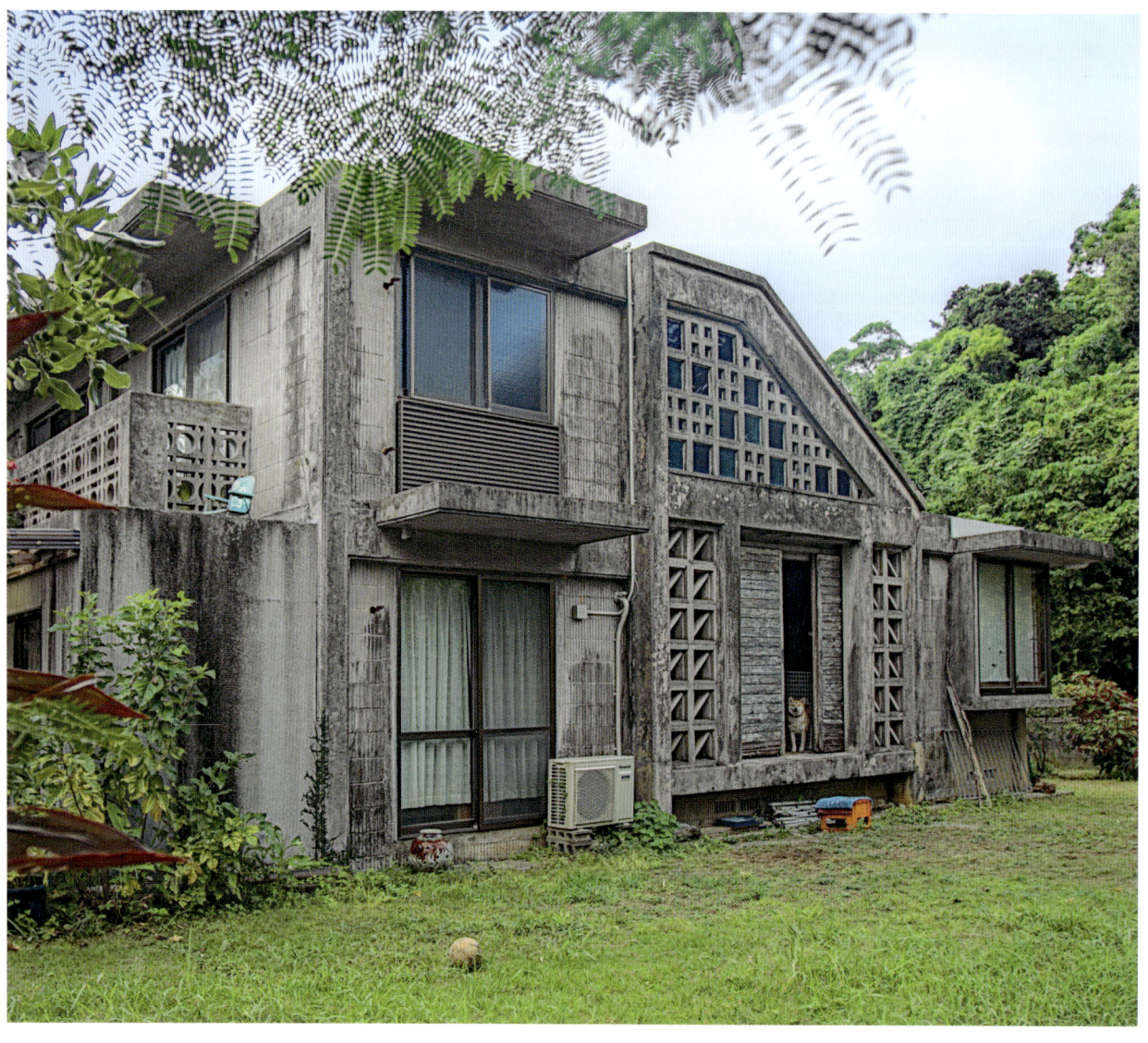

NATIONAL THEATRE

URASOE, OKINAWA · Architect: TAKAMATSU Shin · Completed 2003

The four sides of this building soar as one integral latticed curved rhomboid. Some see it as mimicking the local Deigo flower in full bloom.

Actually, Shin Takamatsu employs critical regionalism by deploying an aesthetic that mimics the traditional Okinawan perforated wall known as *chinibu*.

The *chinibu*, referring to traditional bamboo walls in Okinawan homes, is a unique architectural element deeply rooted in the region's cultural and environmental context. These walls are crafted from locally sourced bamboo, skilfully woven together to create structures that are both functional and aesthetically pleasing. *Chinibu* walls offer excellent ventilation and temperature regulation, vital in Okinawa's humid climate, while also providing flexibility and resilience against frequent typhoons. Modern architects integrate *chinibu* into contemporary designs to evoke a sense of heritage and to harness its natural properties. This fusion simultaneously pays homage to traditional craftsmanship and promotes sustainability by utilizing renewable resources, making *chinibu* a symbol of cultural continuity and ecological awareness in modern architecture.

I had the pleasure of meeting a student of Shin Takamatsu. He said he is personally investigating boosting the sustainability of modern concrete architecture by incorporating black volcanic ash. The results will be fascinating.

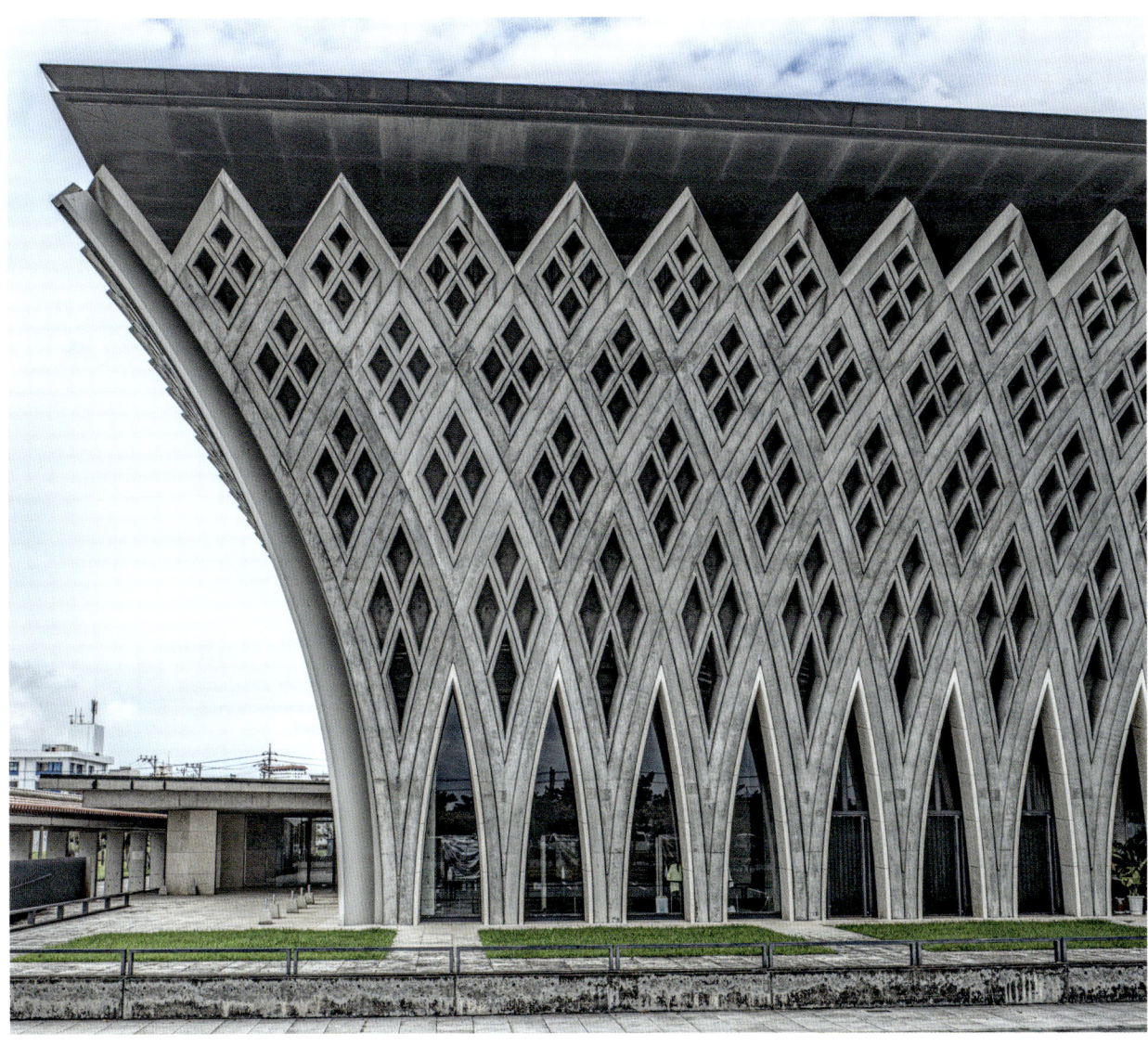

DAICHI OKINAWA VILLA M

YAGAJI ISLAND, OKINAWA · Architect: Suppose Design Office · Completed 2023

Here is a remarkable architectural synthesis, blending elements of modernism, critical regionalism, Brutalism and traditional Okinawan and Japanese architecture.

In its essence, the structure is deeply rooted in modernism, characterized by its clean lines, functional form and lack of ornamentation. The open floor plans and expansive glass walls echo the modernist ethos of form following function, promoting transparency and a seamless indoor-outdoor flow. The assured use of concrete and geometric shapes points to a modernist approach to materials and form.

Critical regionalism is evidenced by the building's sensitive response to its location. Okinawa's subtropical climate, natural landscape and cultural context are reflected in the structure's orientation, use of overhangs for shade and the strategic positioning to capture natural ventilation. The incorporation of these elements demonstrates a conscious effort to create a building that belongs to its place.

The Brutalist aesthetic is unmistakable in the building's raw concrete façades and substantial massing. Its monumental scale and weight anchor the building to its site, while the textural qualities of the concrete surfaces reveal the marks of their making, a characteristic of Brutalist architecture that invites a tactile and visceral reaction.

Meanwhile, echoes of traditional Okinawan and Japanese architecture resonate in the deep eaves, which resemble the protective overhangs of traditional Okinawan homes designed to offer shelter from the tropical sun and rain. The structure's cantilevered volumes create a sense of suspension and lightness reminiscent of traditional Japanese architecture's interplay with nature and the surrounding environment.

Overall, the building displays an ability to reconcile the demands of a contemporary space with respect for the cultural and environmental specificity of its location. It is both a tribute to and a reinterpretation of the diverse architectural influences that inform its design.

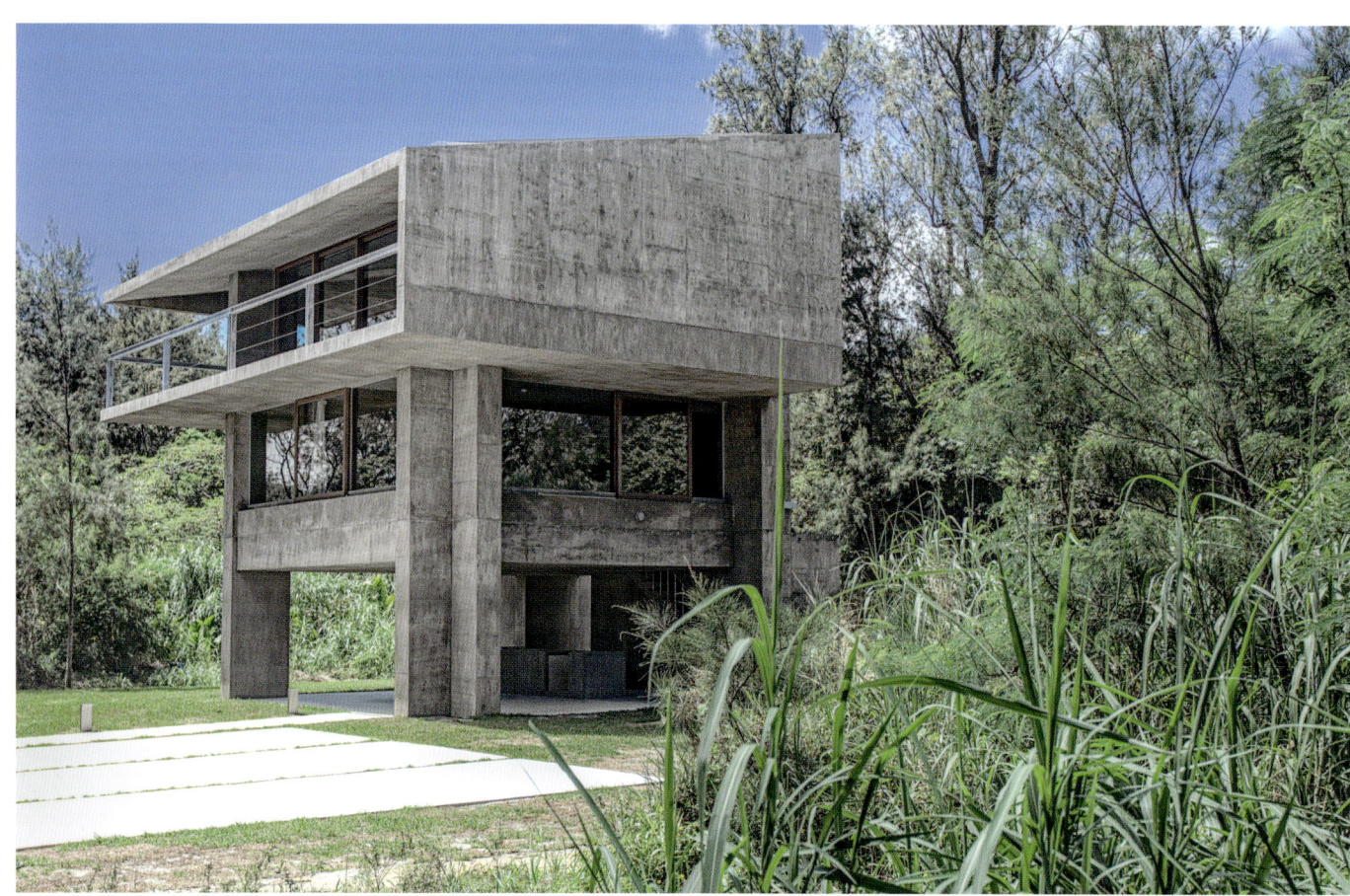

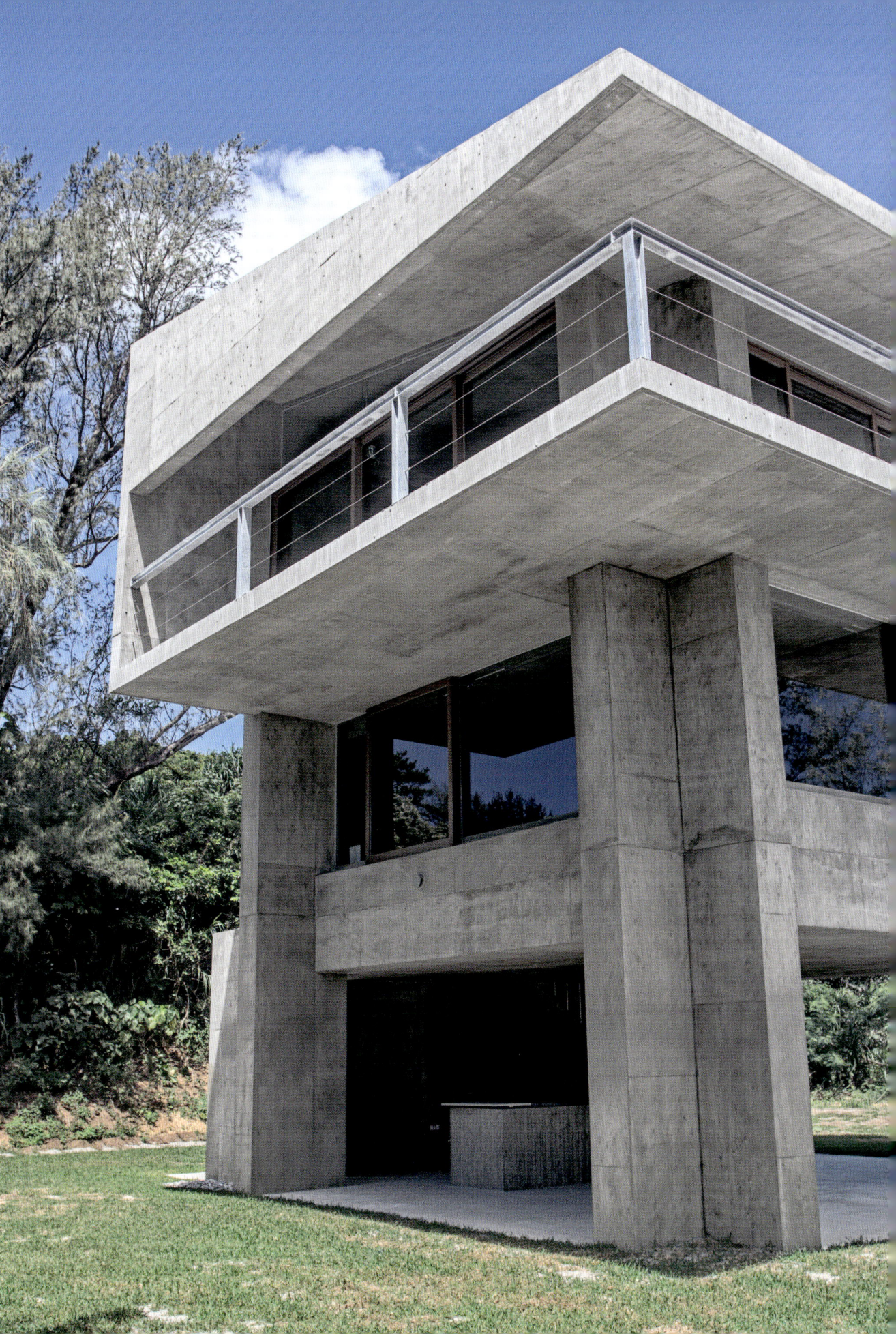

DAICHI OKINAWA VILLA M

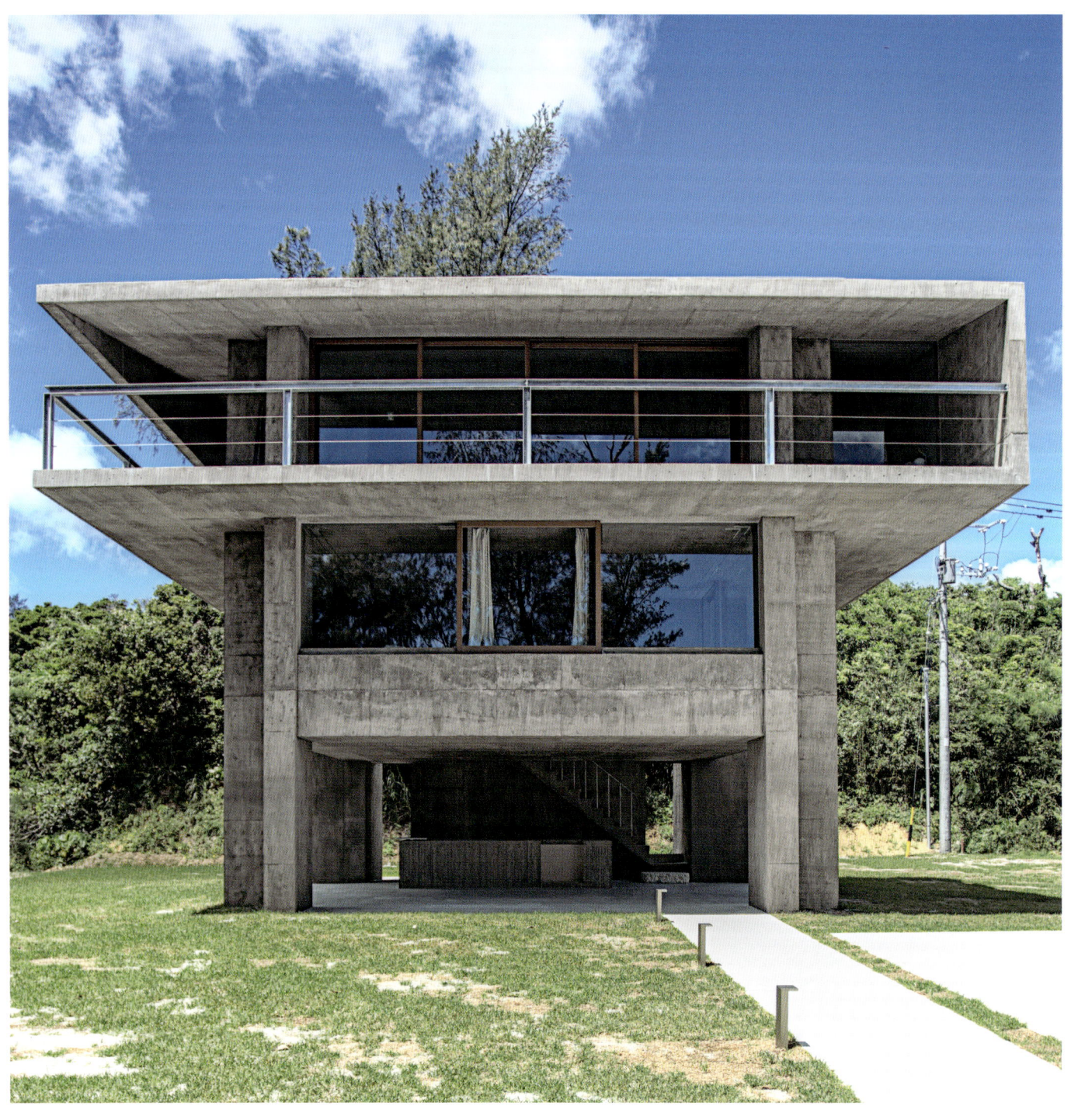

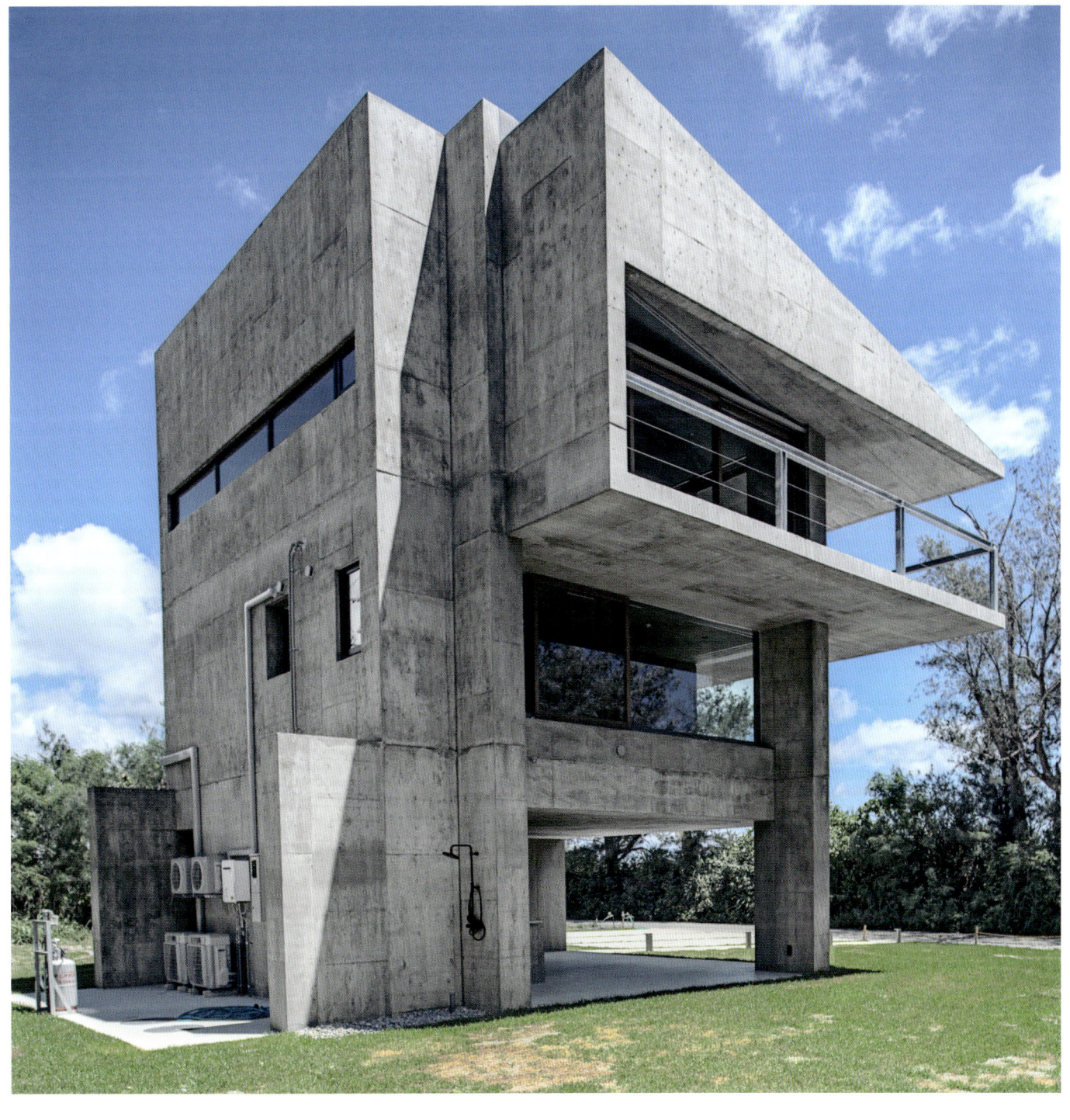

SETAGAYA WARD OFFICE

TOKYO · Architect: MAEKAWA Kunio · Completed 1959

This administrative office is a striking example of post-war Japanese modernism. Kunio Maekawa, who was mentored by Le Corbusier, brought to life the expressiveness of concrete in his architectural works. This particular building incorporates a dynamic folded-plate structure in the auditorium, which exhibits a dramatic sculptural quality. Maekawa's affinity for modernist, especially Le Corbusier's proto-Brutalist, concrete designs, shines through in this project, as well as in his concurrent work for UNESCO in Paris. These designs reflect the freedom that Maekawa and his contemporaries experienced in the post-war period when modernist ideas were no longer perceived as a threat to the state. This was a time marked by innovation in traditional building methods aligned with modernist design philosophies.

Unfortunately, on 25 June 2016 Setagaya Ward announced considerations for demolishing and reconstructing the ward office buildings. The existing structures do not comply with contemporary earthquake standards and are at risk of collapse in the event of a major seismic event. As part of the ongoing redevelopment, there is an emphasis on how to preserve and evolve Maekawa's architectural legacy. The plan proposes a consolidation of scattered facilities and a new government office building designed to improve operational efficiency. The new building will feature a gate-shaped structure, constructed in two phases: initially, a fire-resistant timber structure followed by a precast concrete (PC) frame that echoes the concrete grid frame of the original building. Additionally, the design includes an indoor promenade and the civic hall will retain its original shape by transitioning from a concrete to a timber folded-plate structure.

The project reflects a deep respect for Maekawa's architectural contributions, aiming to maintain the essence of his design while upgrading the infrastructure to meet modern needs and safety standards. The redevelopment of Setagaya Ward Office not only addresses practical concerns but also represents a thoughtful approach to preserving architectural heritage in the face of urban renewal.

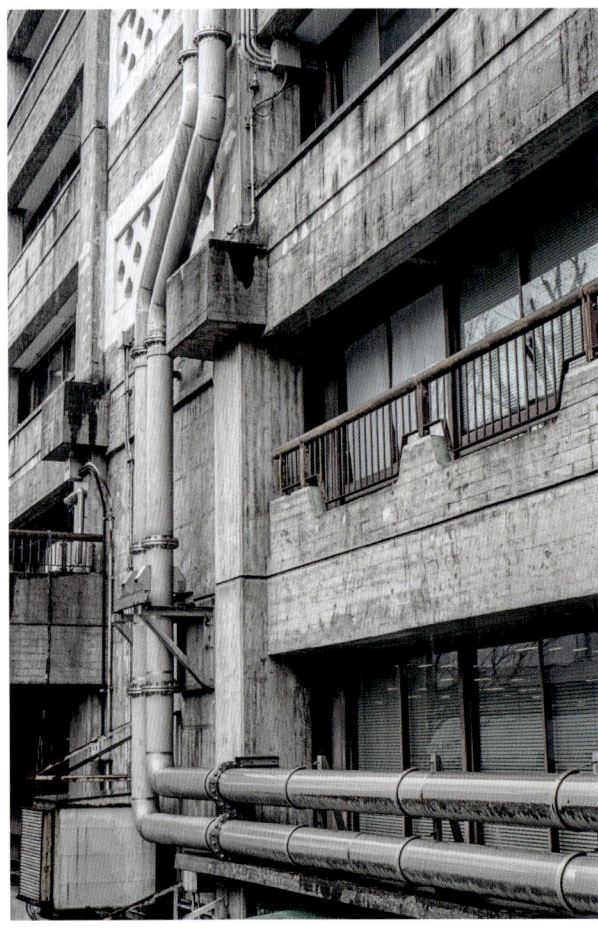
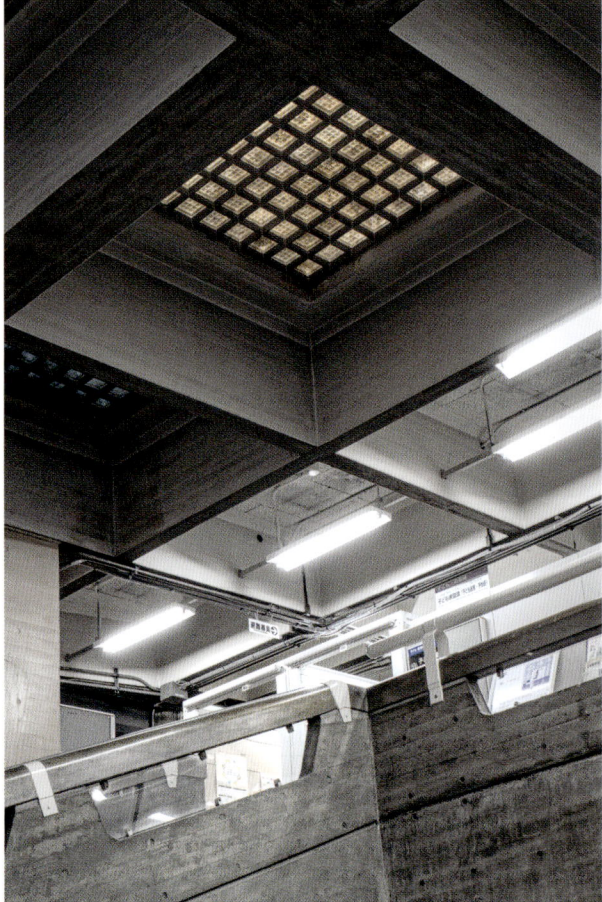

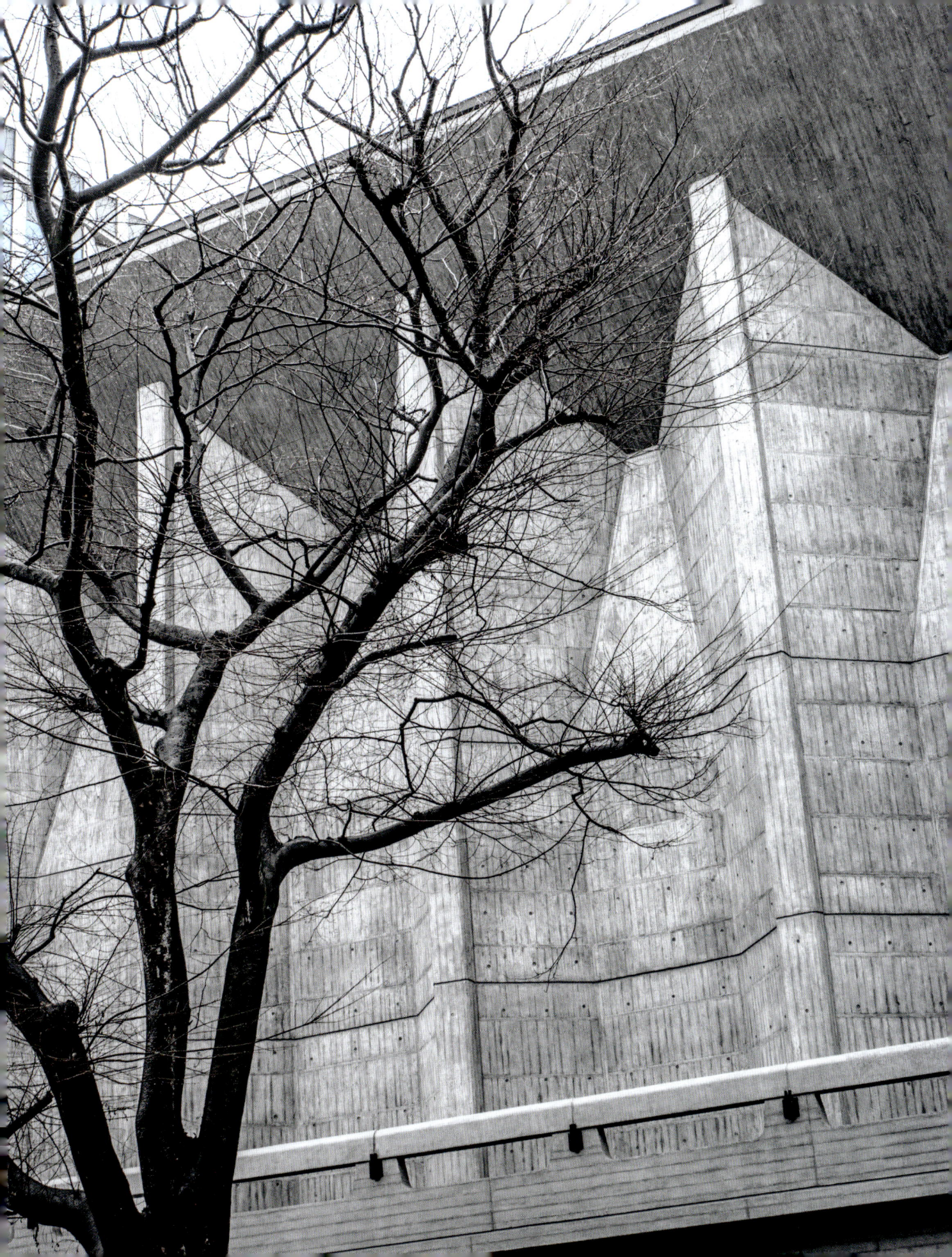

OKINAWA PREFECTURAL AND ART MUSEUM

NAHA, OKINAWA · Architect: Ishimoto and Niki Associates · Completed 2007

A joint venture between Ishimoto and Niki design houses, the Naha Prefectural Museum appears as both a cascading, multi-tiered limestone waterfall and immovable monolith – the result of a geological phenomenon eons ago. A large footprint coupled with steeply slanted precast sides render it strangely squat yet soaring. Its appearance borrows from ancient Okinawan fortresses (*gusuku*) yet is simultaneously futuristic with gentle curves, rectilinear geometry and stacked forms.

Despite the sci-fi feel, gridded wall patterns and the resulting chiaroscuro actually represent deference to the humble and ubiquitous breeze-block – widely used for screening, ventilation and decoration. Further winks at the local are made with the inclusion of a red-tile-roofed traditional home and thatched dwelling within its grounds.

The museum is adapted to the climate by virtue of a double skin that protects against intense sunlight and typhoons. A precast wall envelops a reinforced outer wall structure and the gap serves as a space for guttering and ventilation chambers. A look of natural stone is achieved through the use of white cement – local limestone as the coarse aggregate and coral sand as the fine aggregate. Surfaces have been shaved to provide texture.

Opened only in 2007, this concrete beauty is a rare example of big stage neo-Brutalism. *Doctor Who* fans might see a Dalek and the more domesticated an upturned laundry basket.

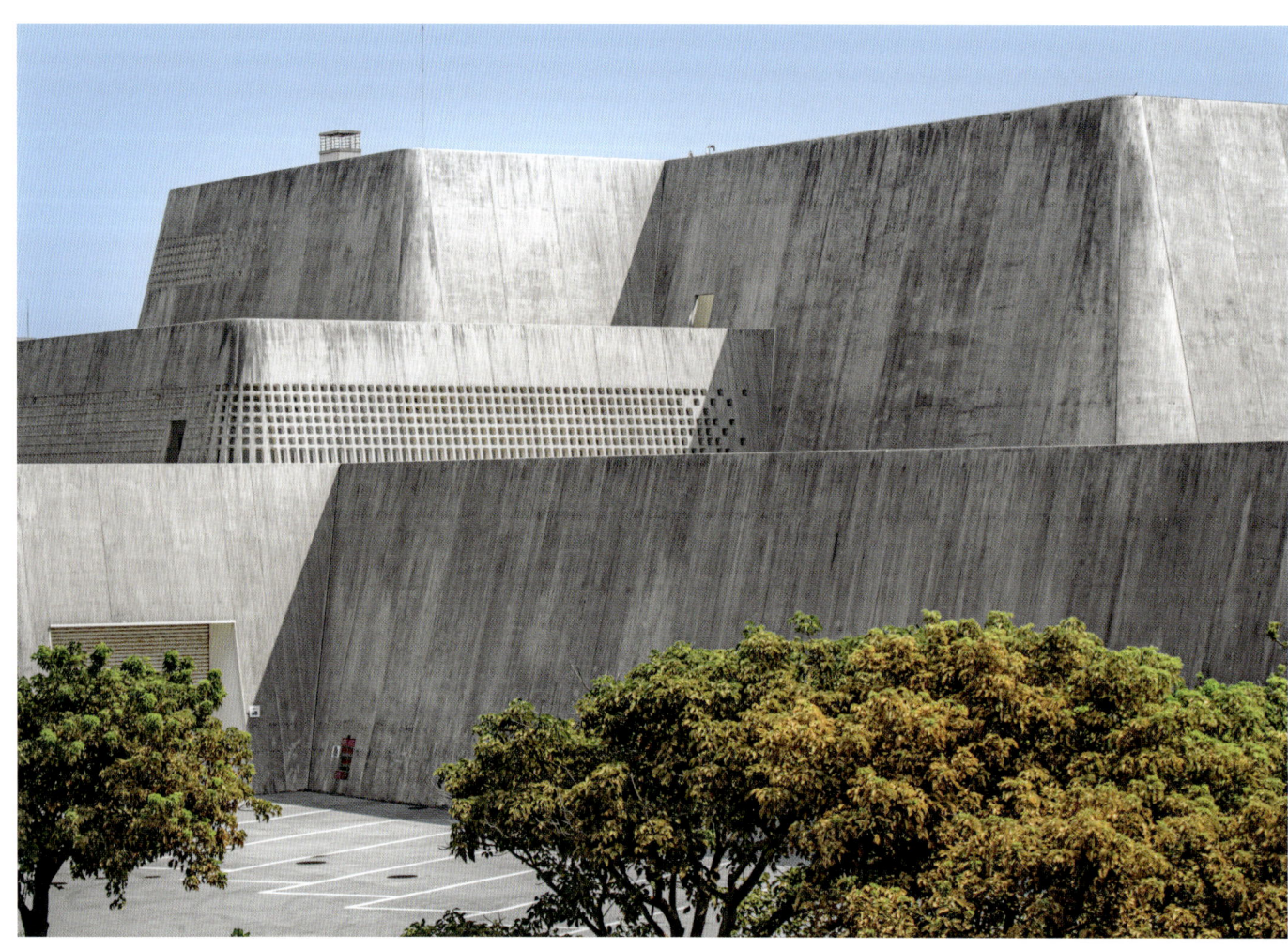

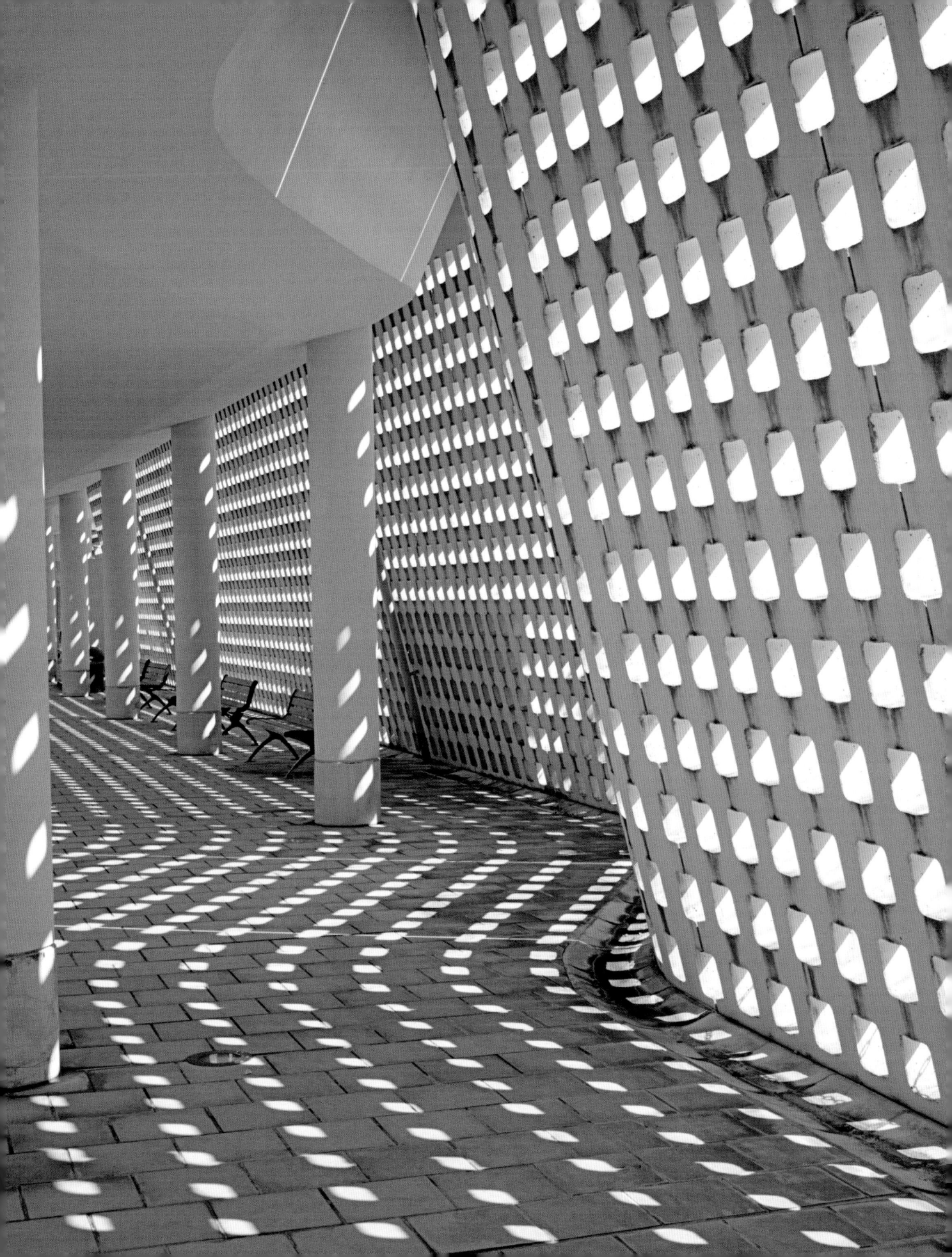

OKINAWA PREFECTURAL AND ART MUSEUM

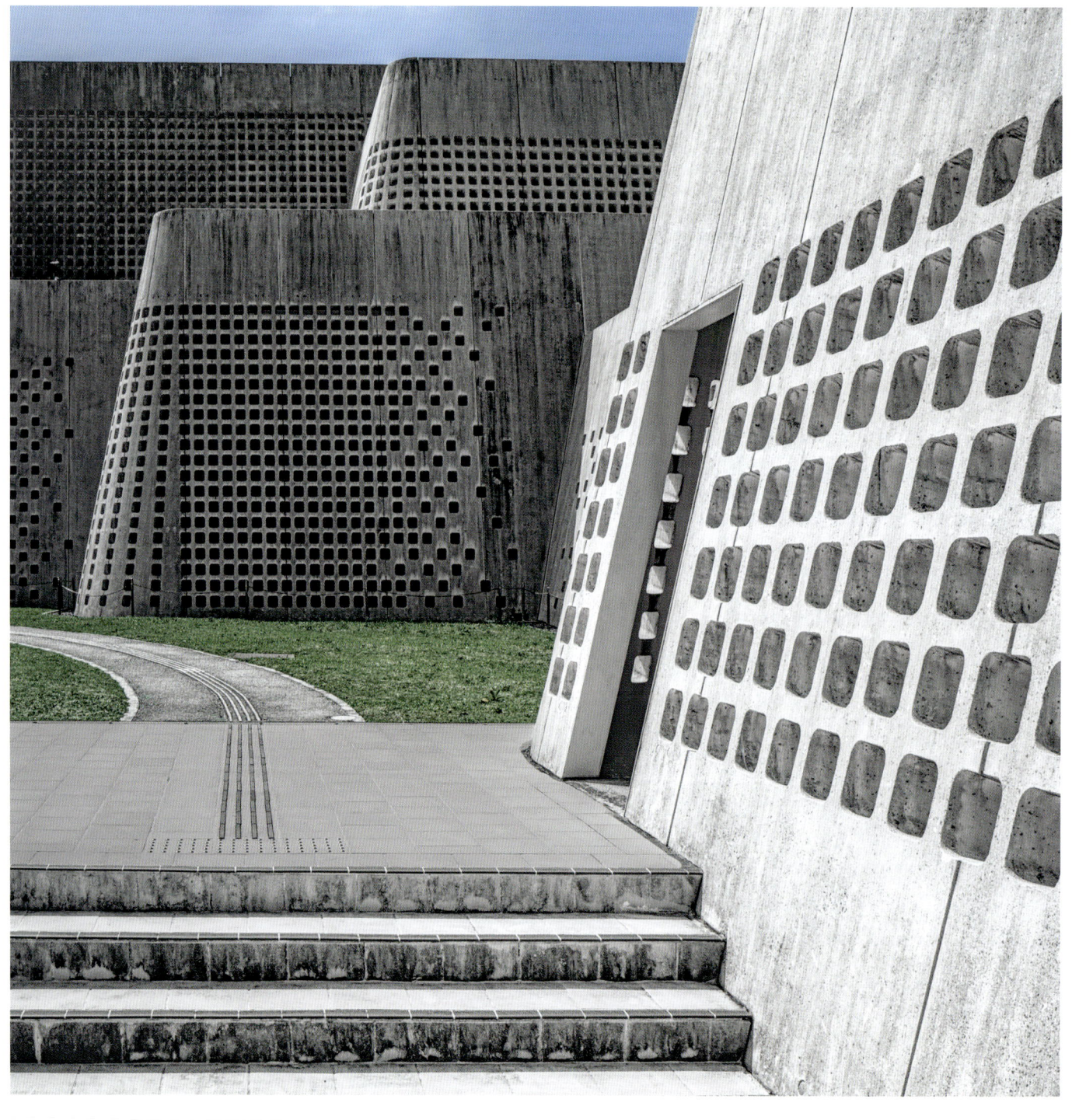

OKINAWA PREFECTURAL AND ART MUSEUM

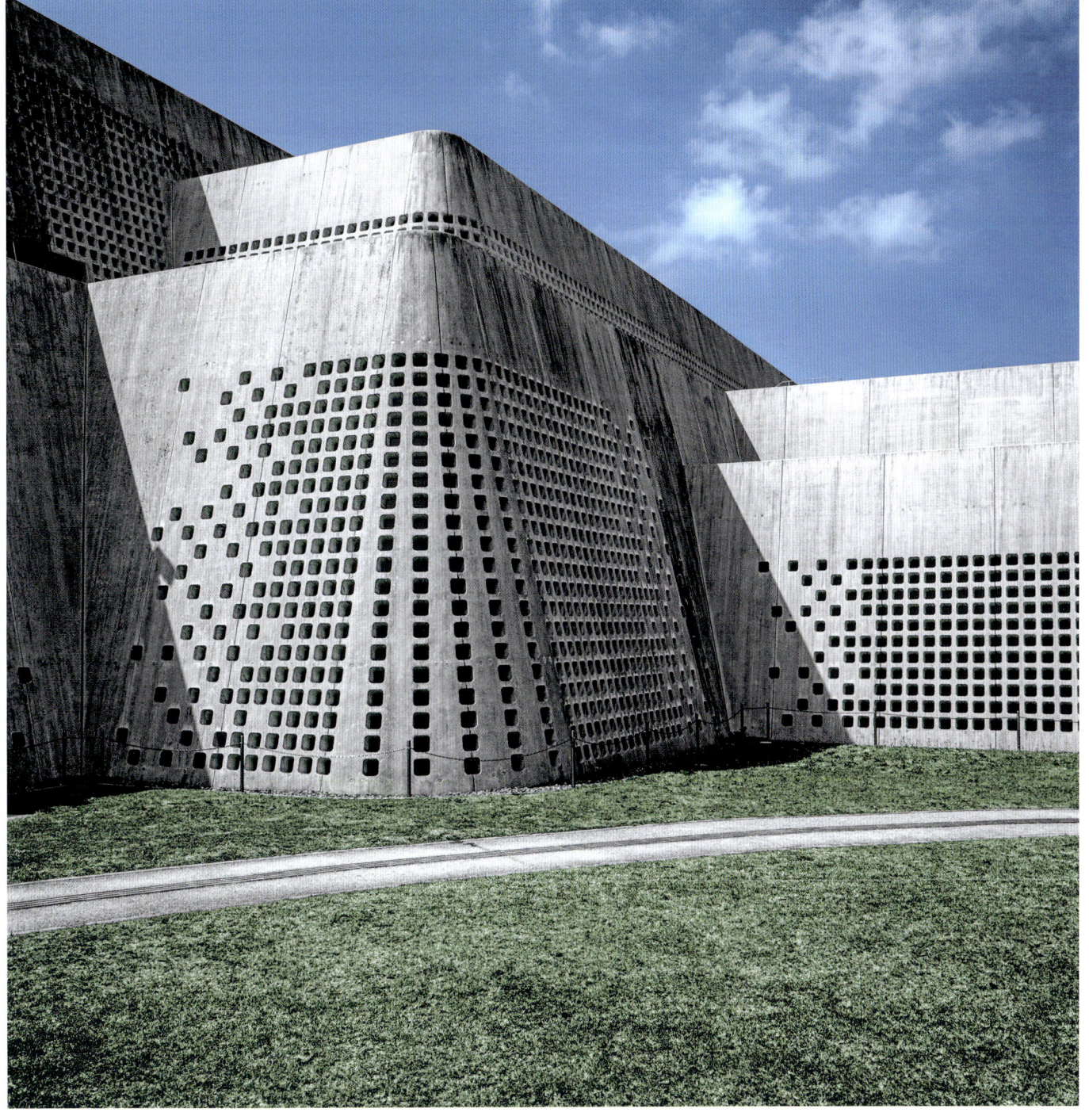

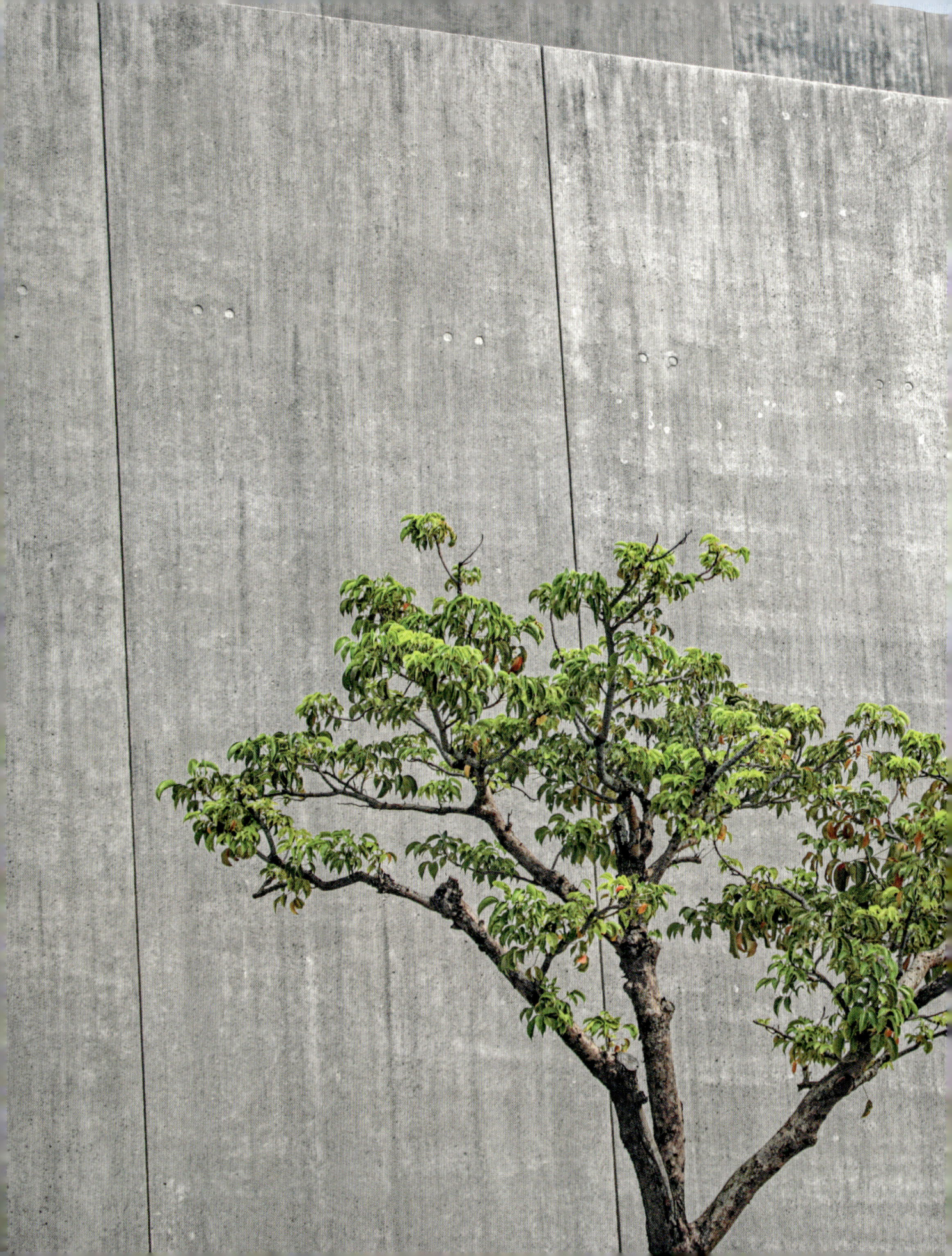

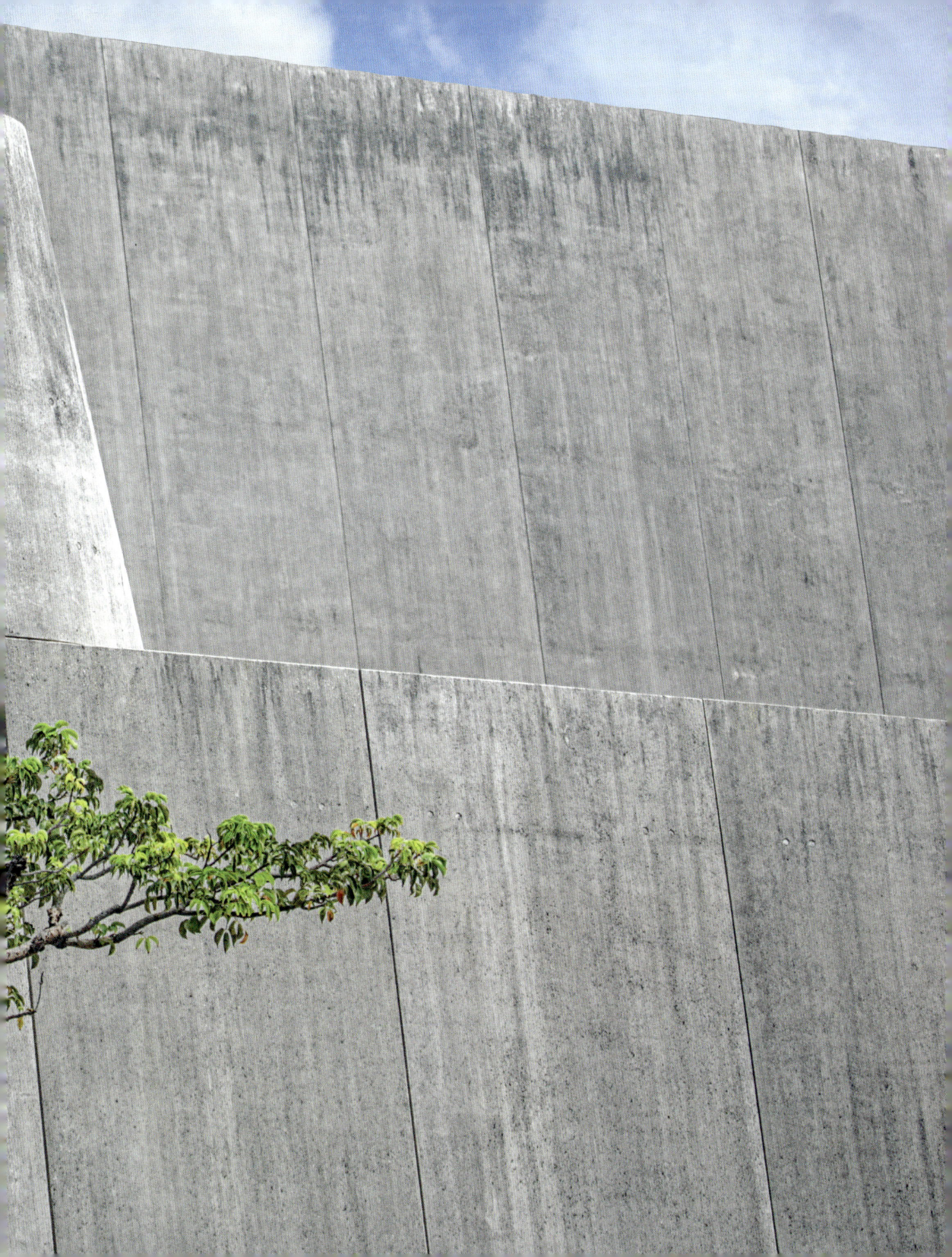

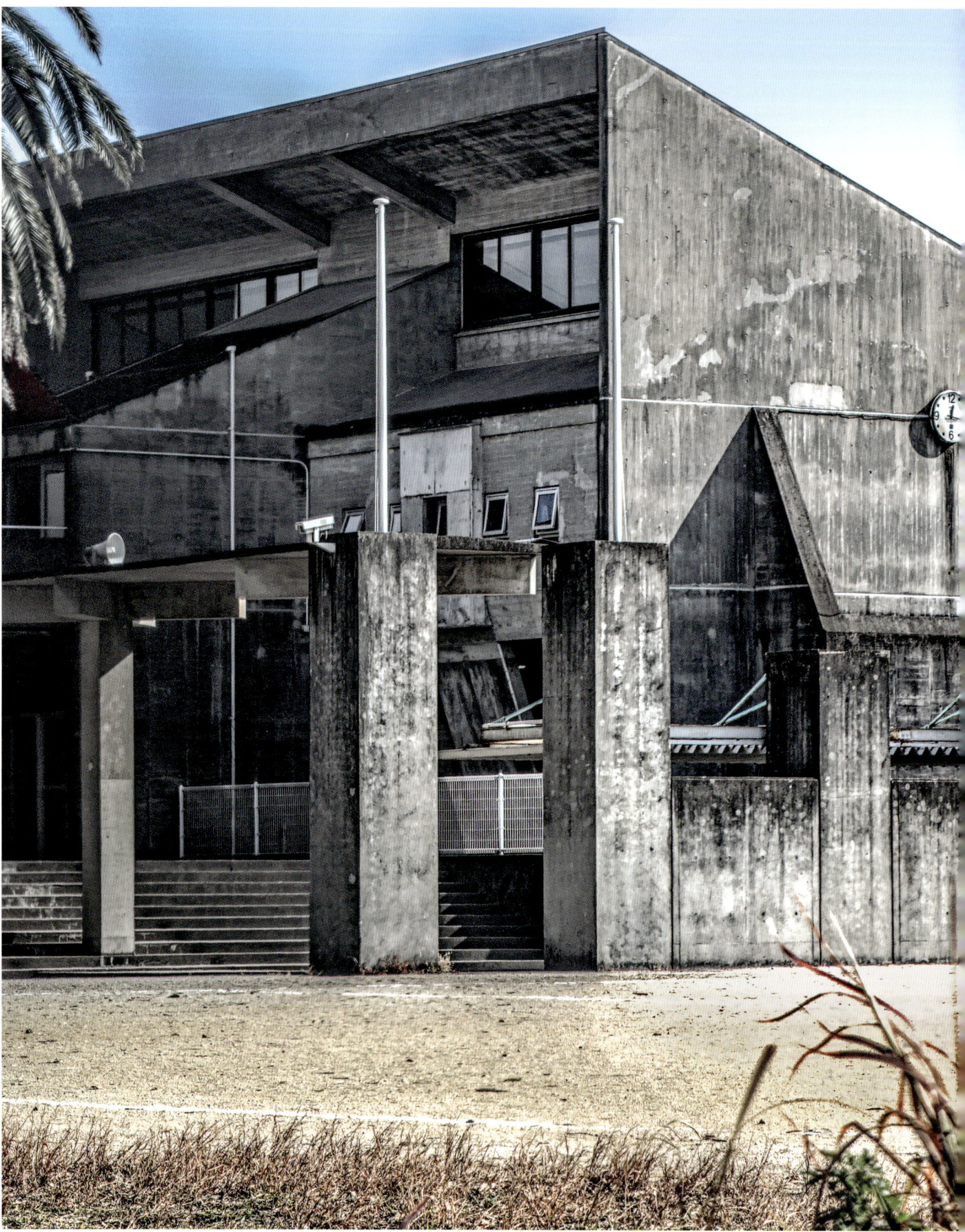

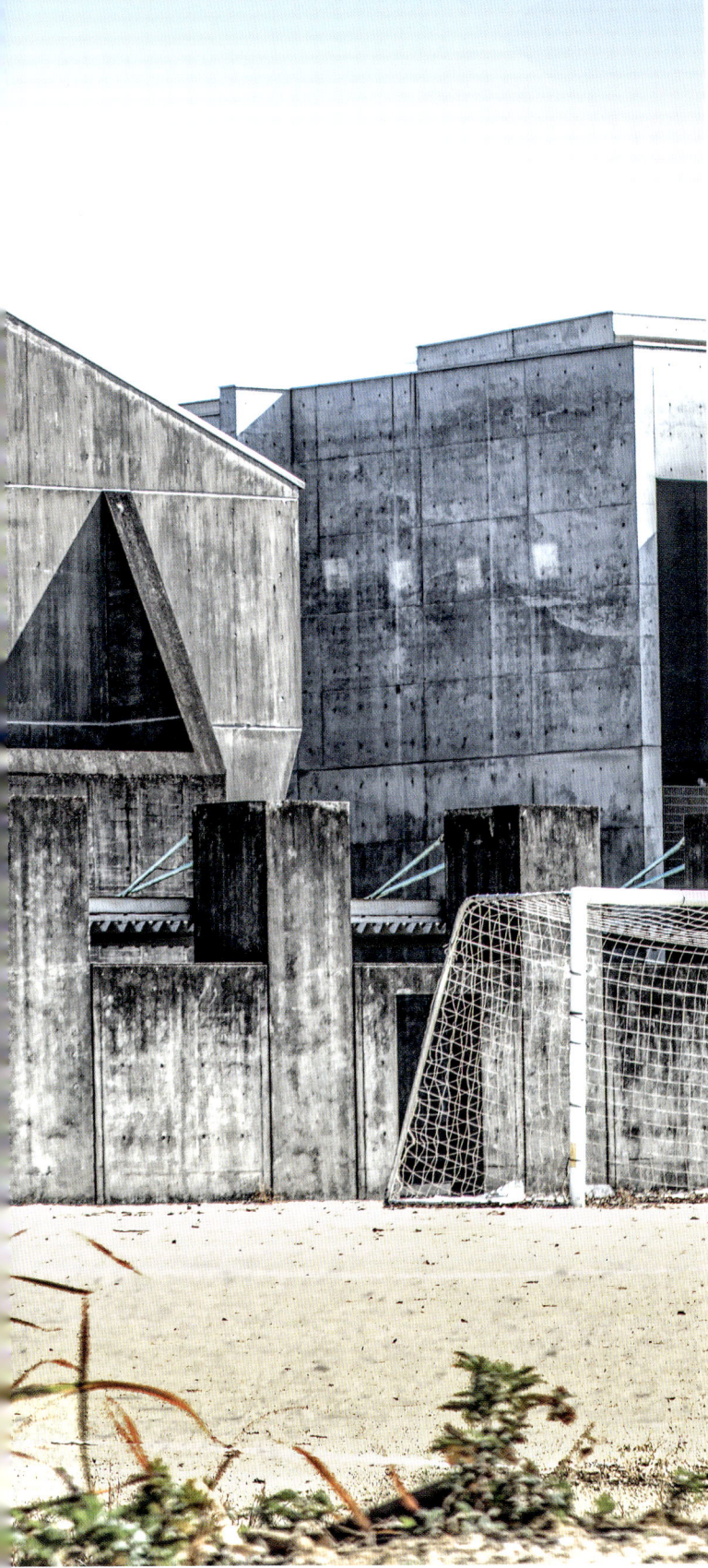

IWATA GIRLS SCHOOL

173

OITA · Architect: ISOZAKI Arata · Completed 1985

The Iwata Girls School, designed by the acclaimed Arata Isozaki, is a proud addition to his portfolio of works in his hometown. Erected in a local architectural era of metamorphosis and experimentation, it is a proud paragon of Brutalism. Isozaki's approach encapsulates the movement's honest, raw aesthetic, with the school's asymmetrical massing and the rhythmic placement of windows creating a visual play of light and shadow.

Commanding concrete planes define the structure's façades, giving it a fortress-like presence that may well match a somewhat military approach to education. The interior is characterized by functional spaces designed to lend adaptability. Each classroom, hall and common area within is a robust frame for the bustling activity of intellectual growth.

Isozaki's Iwata Girls School dictates the landscape with its monumental form, reflective of the architect's belief that buildings are culturally crucial entities – chronicles of their time and space in history.

IWATA GIRLS SCHOOL

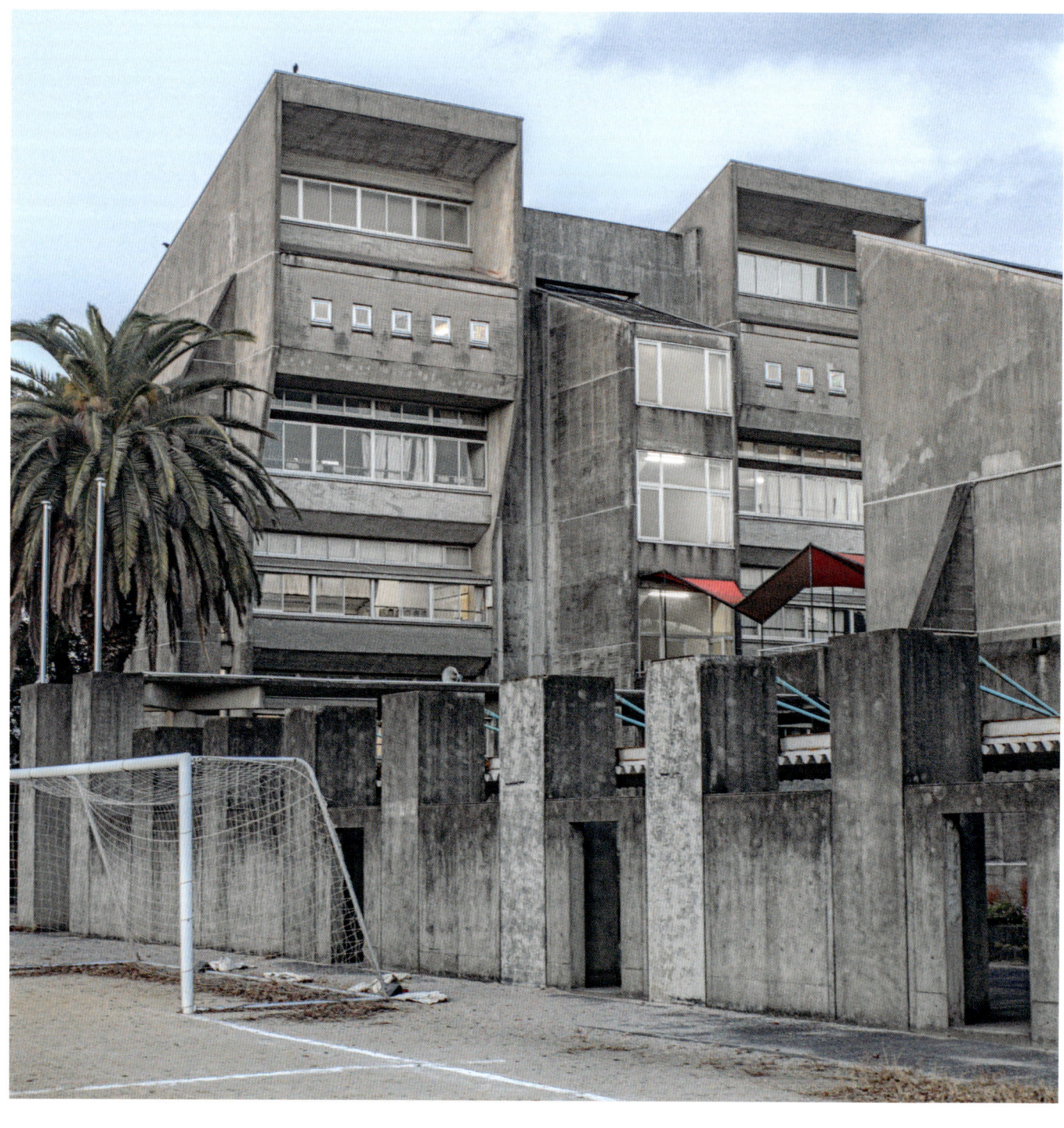

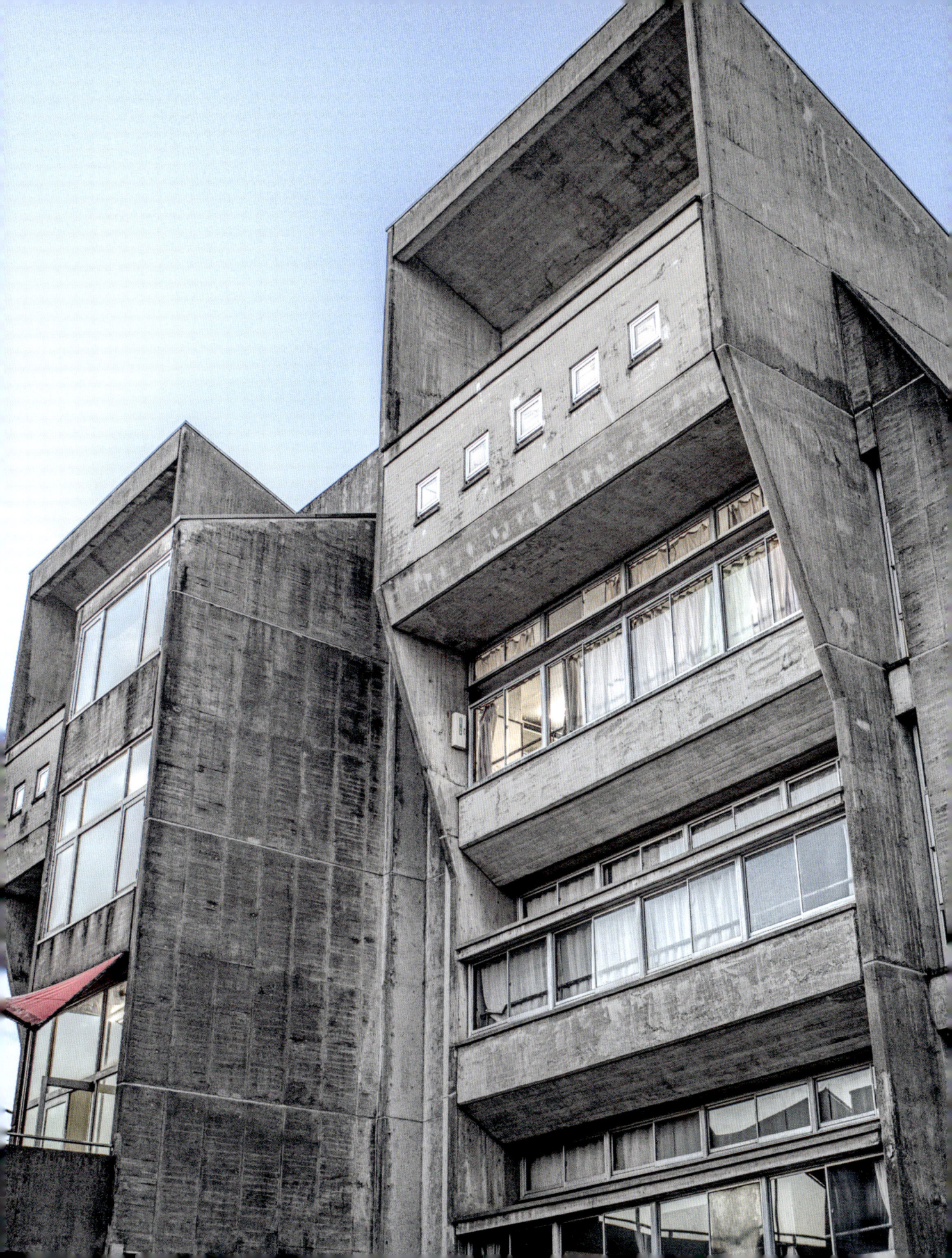

KOMAZAWA OLYMPIC PARK CONTROL TOWER

TOKYO · Architect: ASHIHARA Yoshinobu · Completed 1964

While the design of the Olympic Control Tower in Tokyo may evoke the traditional form of a pagoda, the architect Yoshinobu Ashihara prioritized functionality in its conception.

Situated within Komazawa Park, the tower had to support a substantial thirty-three-ton water tank above ground, which was essential for supplying water throughout the park. Additionally, it accommodated an antenna for television broadcasts. Below ground, the structure housed a general electric room, machine room, broadcast room and telephone exchange. It also played a pivotal role in controlling traffic within the park and served as a commemorative landmark. Ashihara opted for a post-and-beam construction that efficiently organized the floors according to the dimensions of the water tank and elevator shaft. The architectural design of the tower emerged not from an aesthetic desire to mimic historical structures, but from a rigorous focus on functional needs, affirming that its resemblance to a pagoda was coincidental rather than intentional.

Originally rendered in raw concrete, the tower is now painted. This is an unfortunate trend that is increasingly seen.

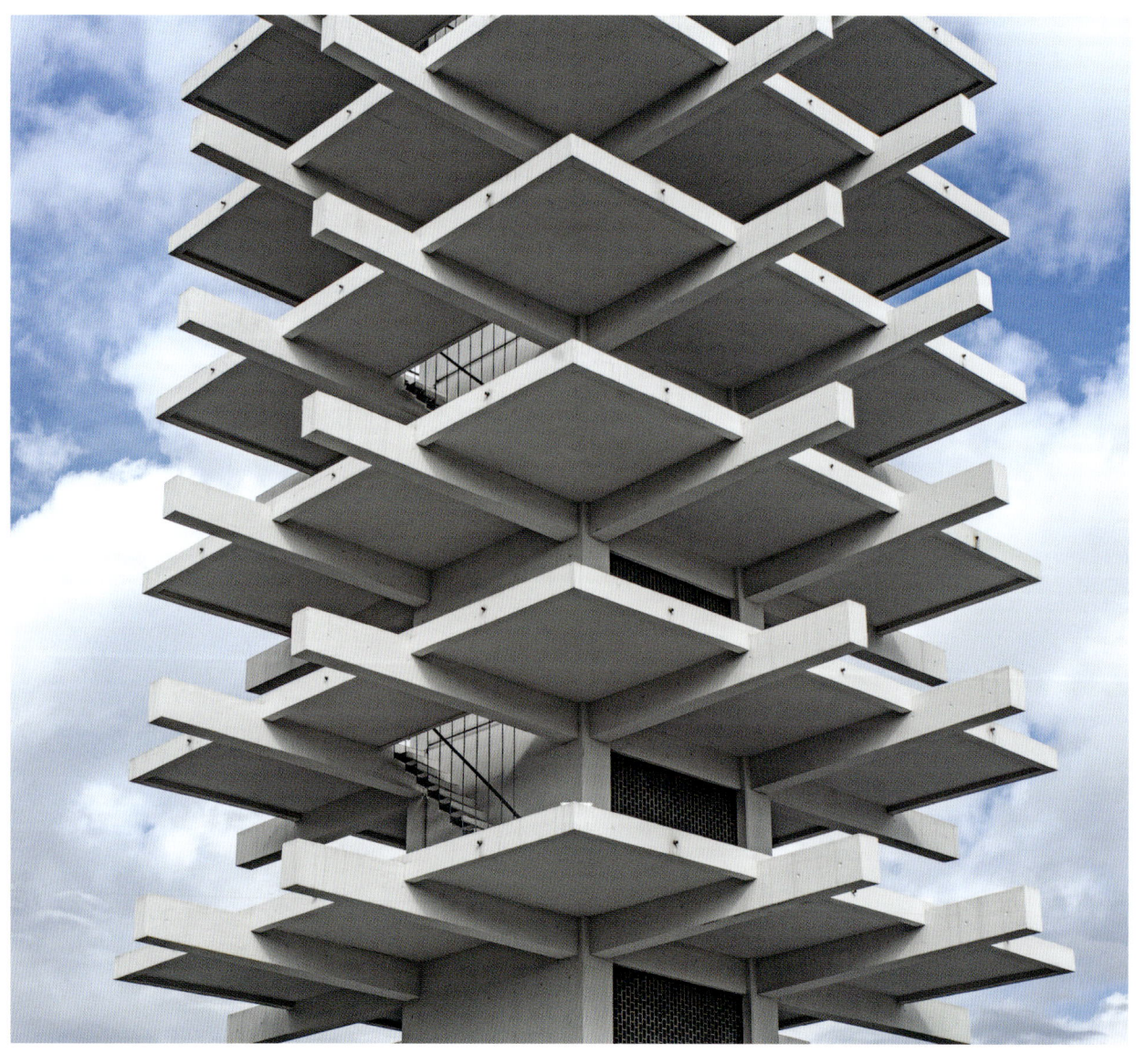

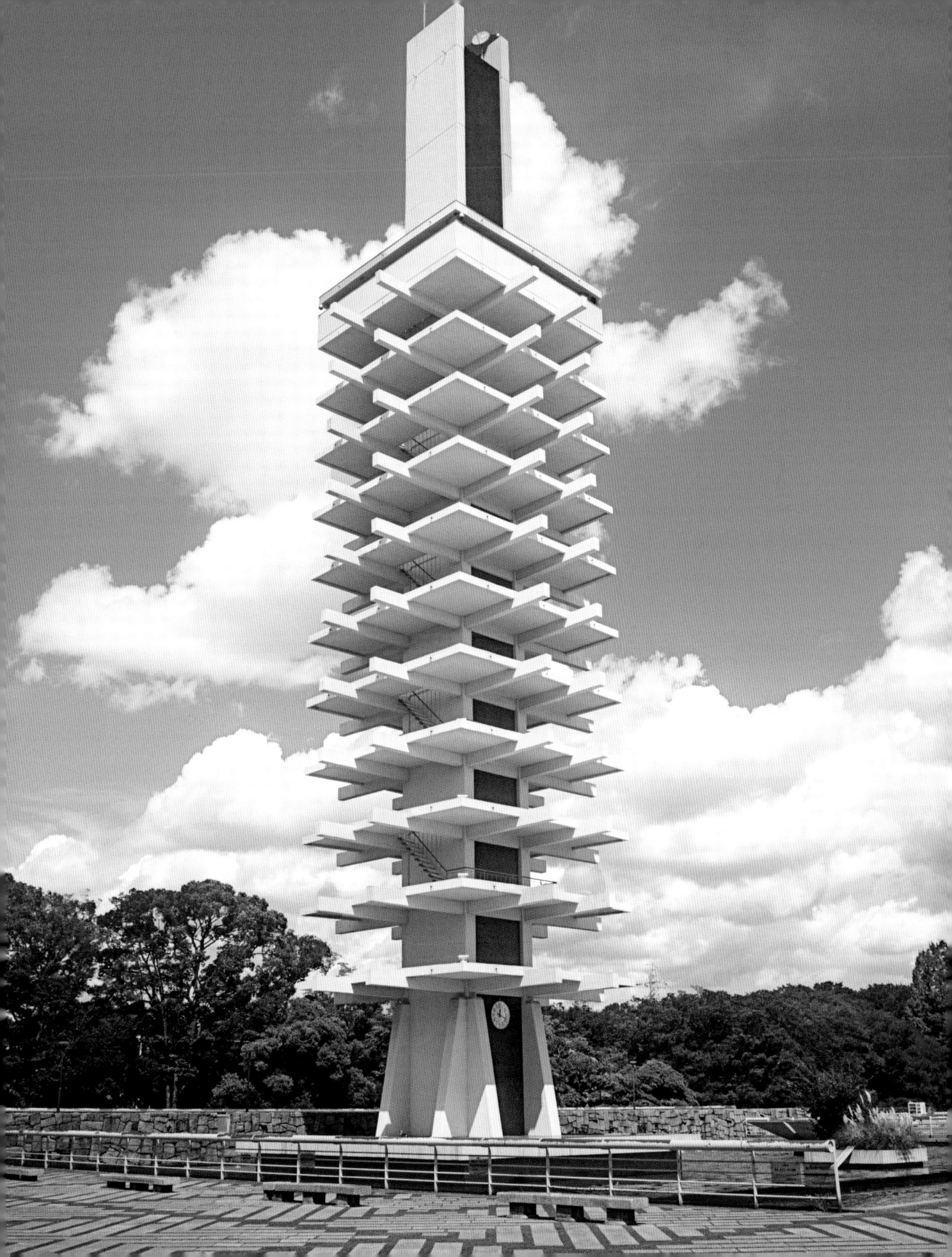

NAKANOSHIMA CHILDREN'S LIBRARY

OSAKA · Architect: ANDO Tadao · Completed 2019

Tadao Ando's Children's Book Forest in Osaka is a lyrical composition of concrete and culture, designed as a haven for the young minds of tomorrow. Placed against the backdrop of Nakanoshima Park, this architectural marvel curves gracefully, echoing the flow of the adjacent Dojima River. Its three-storey arc forms an inviting gateway to a world of literature, uniting the urban landscape with the tranquillity of nature. Within, the library's heart beats around a cavernous atrium, where walls transform into towering bookshelves brimming with knowledge. Ando's design transcends the mere function of a building; it becomes a concrete "forest" where storeys and stories grow wild and free. The structure itself is a narrative of discovery, with stairways and passageways that weave like plot twists, leading young explorers through a labyrinthine world akin to an M. C. Escher drawing. This project indicates Ando's commitment to fostering growth and imagination through the nurturing power of architecture and literature. Here he got altruistic.

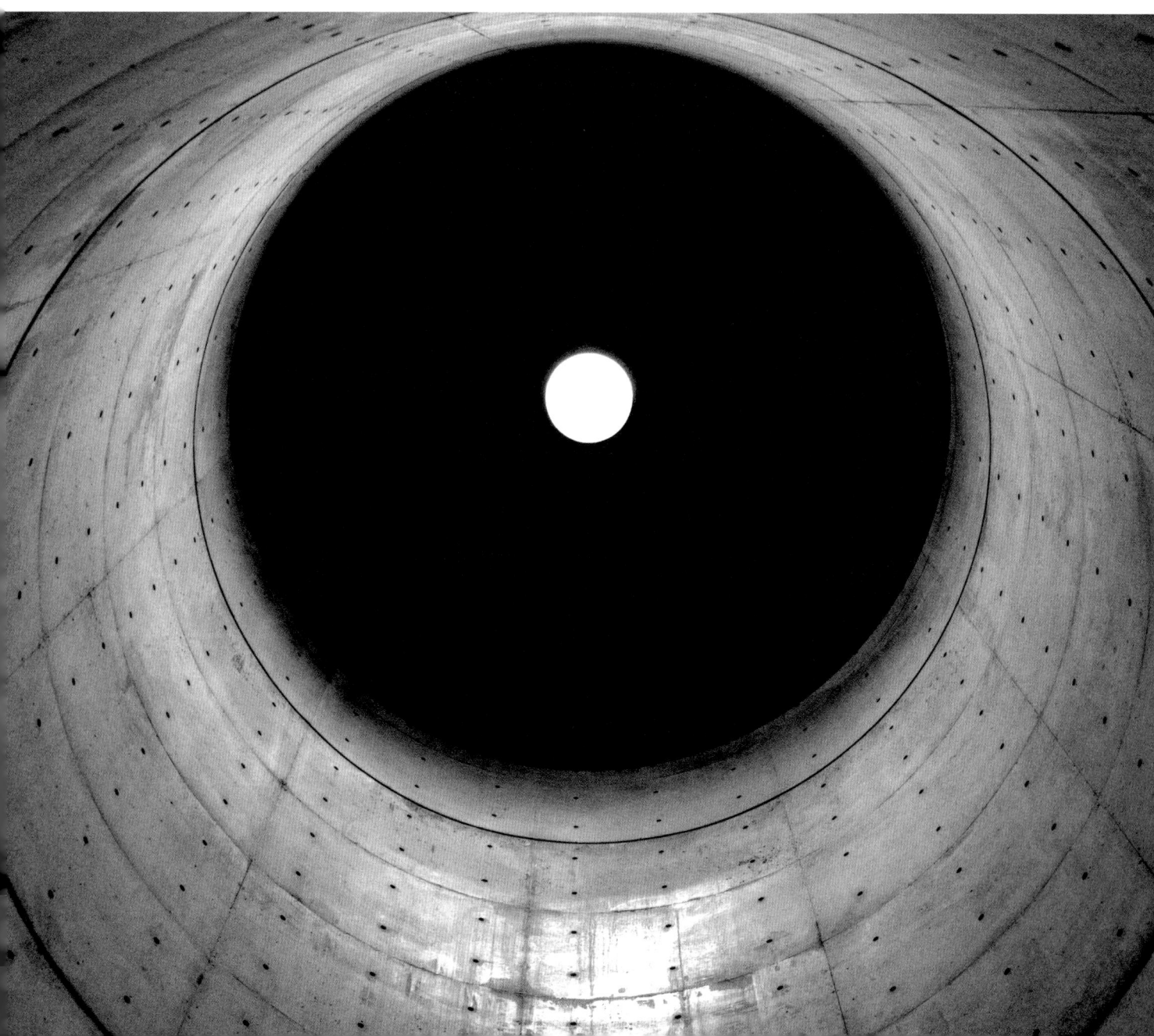

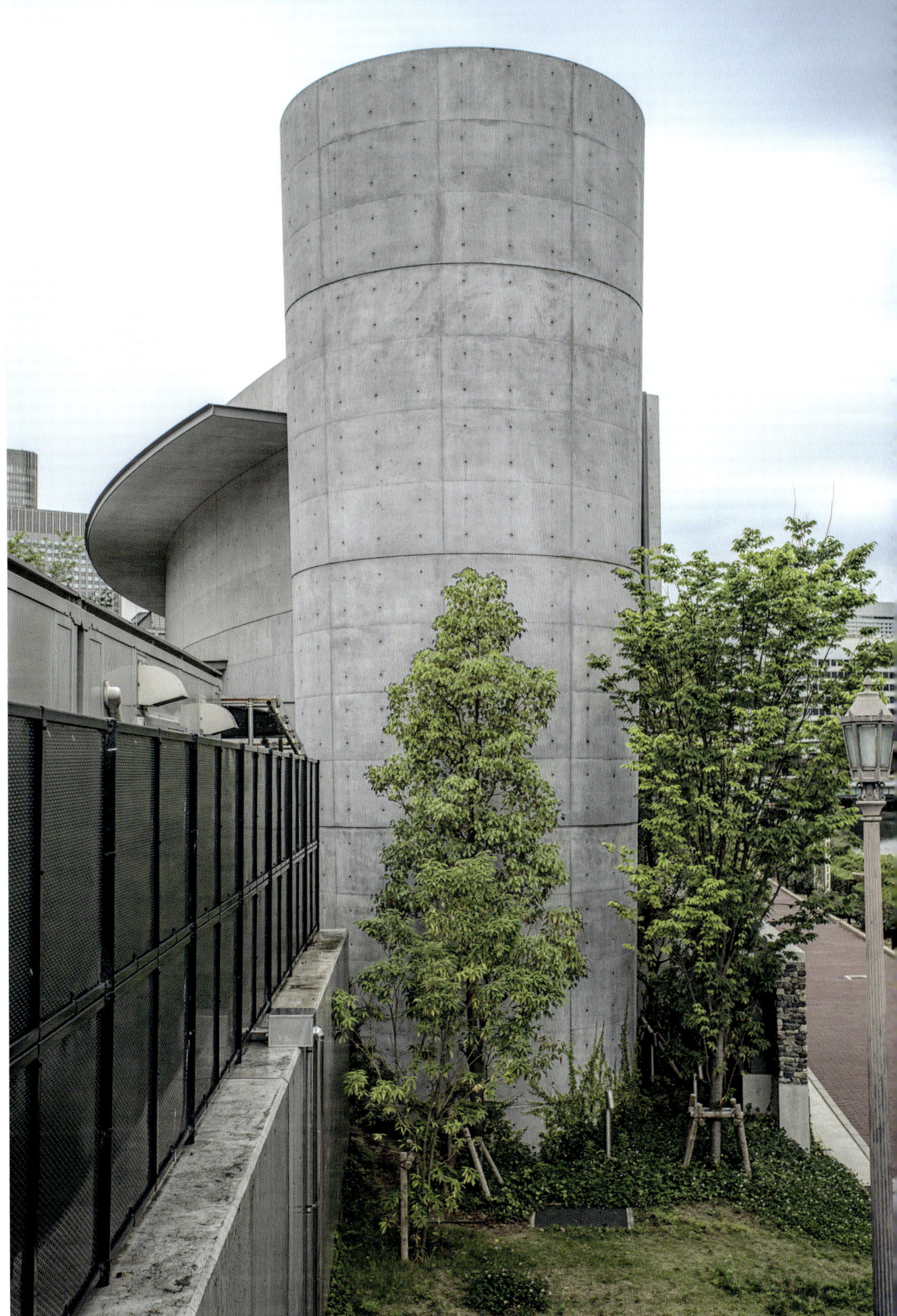

INTERNATIONAL FERRY TERMINAL

OSAKA · Architect: ANDO Tadao · Completed 1996

Tadao Ando's Osaka International Ferry Terminal is a maritime megastructure that melds modernism with the organic ebb and flow of its waterfront setting. Opened in 1996, this minimalist launchpad uses exposed concrete and sweeping glass to create a signpost to the shores of South Korea and China. Interestingly, both countries have seen a recent upsurge in Brutalist design – in no small way due to the influence of Ando. The building's undulating form and expansive windows embrace movement and light, serving as metaphors for the journey ahead. This concrete capstan invites travellers to navigate through the fluid transparency of Ando's design, onto the vast ocean, towards new horizons where the language of architecture transcends borders. It is both a point of departure and a departure from the ordinary, marking the unwavering course of Brutalism's voyage into the future.

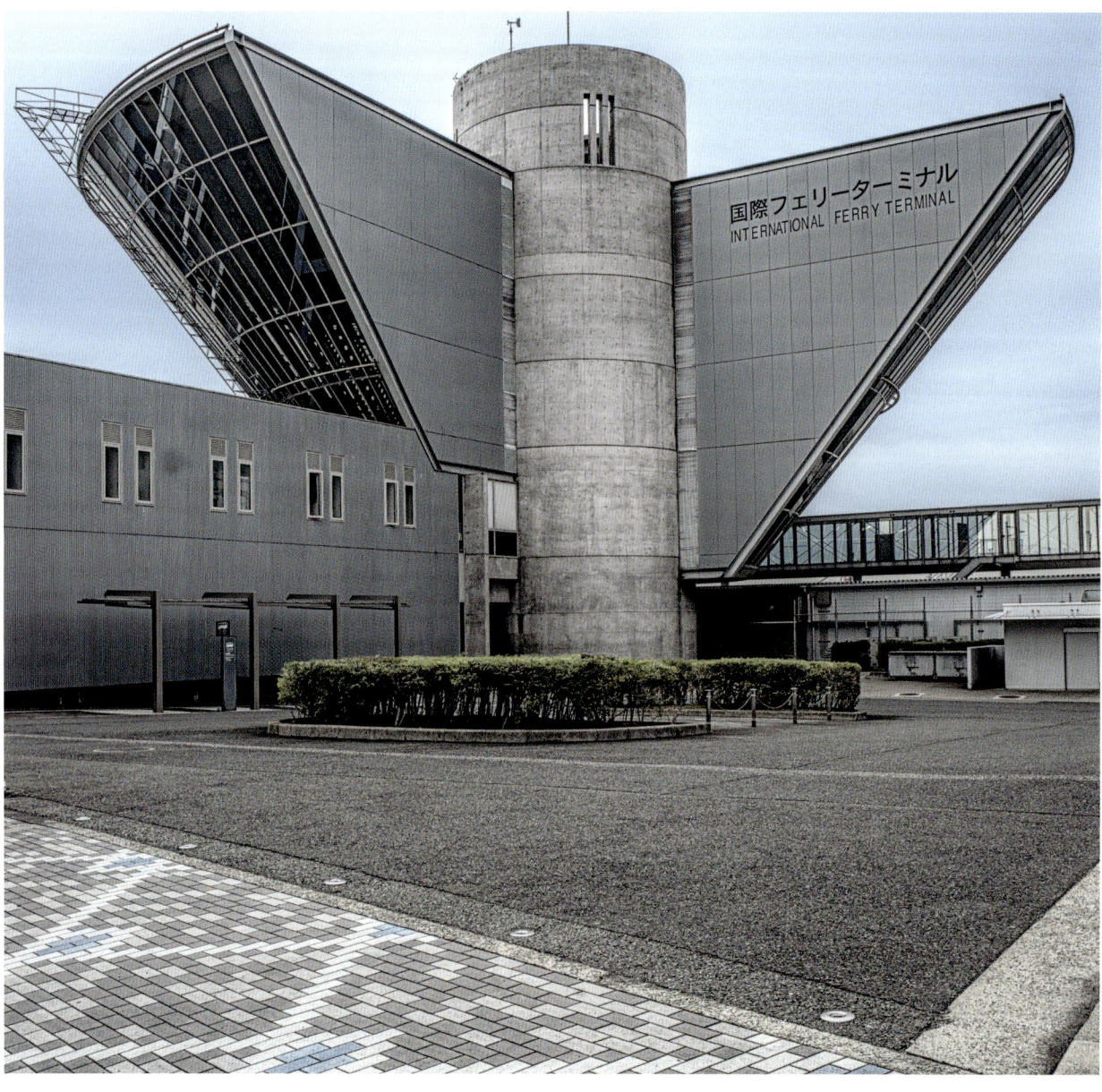

ENVIRONMENTAL OFFICE

OKINAWA

Using concrete for an environmental office might seem counterintuitive due to its high initial carbon emissions. However, concrete's suitability in subtropical climates like Okinawa's offers sustainable advantages. Its high thermal mass helps stabilize indoor temperatures, reducing reliance on air conditioning by absorbing heat during the day and releasing it slowly at night. This is particularly beneficial in Okinawa's warm climate. Moreover, concrete's durability makes it ideal for withstanding the region's frequent storms and humidity, enhancing building longevity and reducing the need for frequent repairs.

When sourced locally, the environmental impact of concrete is further mitigated, as reduced transport distances significantly lower carbon emissions. These factors make concrete a practical, sustainable choice for building in Okinawa, aligning with environmental goals when considering its lifecycle and maintenance efficiencies.

Environmentalists hating on concrete might need to get on that bike.

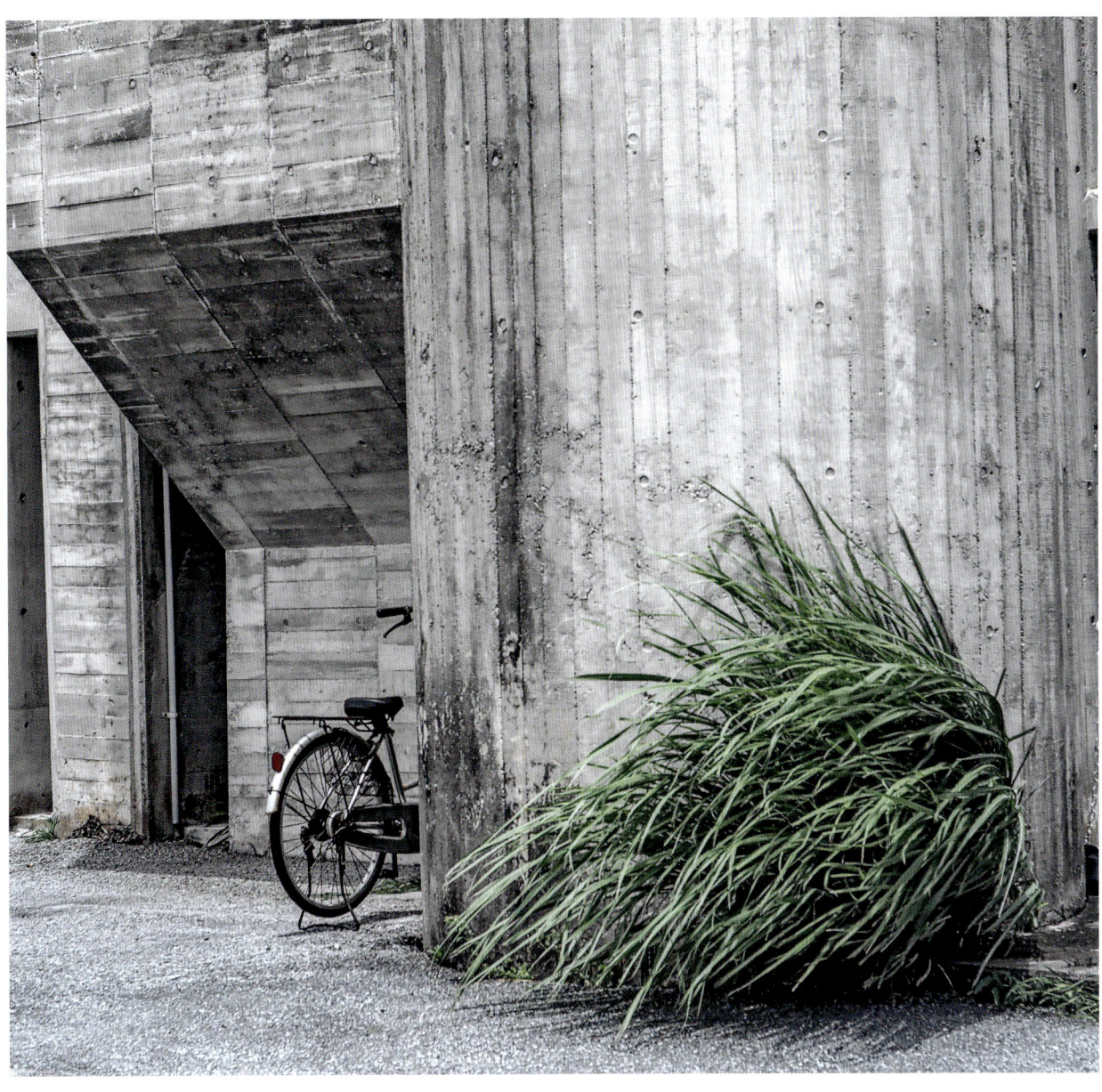

CERAMICS PARK MINO

TAJIMI, GIFU PREFECTURE · Architect: ISOZAKI Arata · Completed 2002

Pritzker Prize-winning Isozaki's hometown Ōita works feature elsewhere in this book. Over his six-decade-long career, Isozaki designed more than 100 buildings. From the 1960s, he demonstrated exceptional innovation in his designs, shaping the perspectives of Eastern professionals with his forward-thinking approach rooted in Japanese tradition. He passed away at the age of 91 at his home in Okinawa.

Situated in the hills of Tajimi in Gifu Prefecture, this Ceramics Park is another major project of his. Created to be a centre for promoting industry and culture in the Mino region, renowned for its ceramics, this building encompasses an art museum, event hall, international conference hall and other facilities. The design prioritizes integration with the natural landscape and extensively incorporates ceramic elements throughout its structure.

Mino's rich culture and history are symbolized in the concrete ceiling of the covered footbridge leading to the museum entrance; it is adorned with hundreds of embedded and suspended ceramic shards, adding a unique touch that honours the area's heritage.

A flat, open entrance plaza affords stunning views of a cascading, multi-tiered core that descends to ground level. Reflecting the diverse clays of the region, various coloured stone slabs were carefully chosen for the base of shallow ponds that trickle infinity pool-style over dark supporting bevelled façades. These are balanced by light-coloured concrete walls that bounce southern light. The pond tiers are presided over by a timber and glass tea house that appears to float elegantly on the top water level. External promenades also provide intriguing views of this water wonder. Breeze-block assemblages are probably in deference to Isozaki's adoptive home of Okinawa.

Although the versatile Isozaki cannot be associated with one architectural style, the expressive use of a combination of raw materials – wood, glass, clay, stone, timber and concrete – ticks an important defining box of Brutalism. It should be noted here that concrete is not required to fit the Brutalist mantle. Indeed, one of the first examples of Brutalism, the Smithsons' Hunstanton School in England, is predominantly comprised of brick and glass.

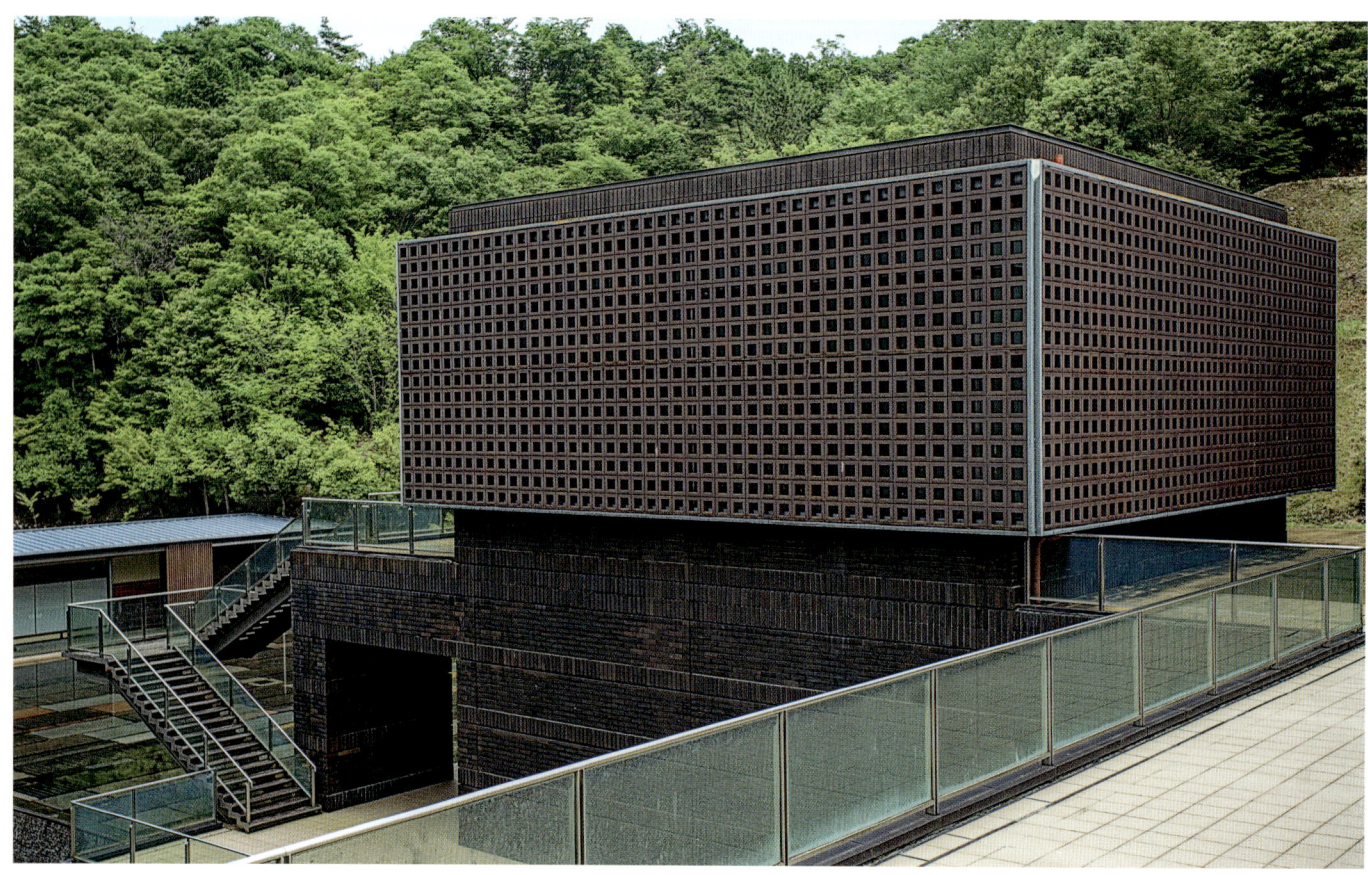

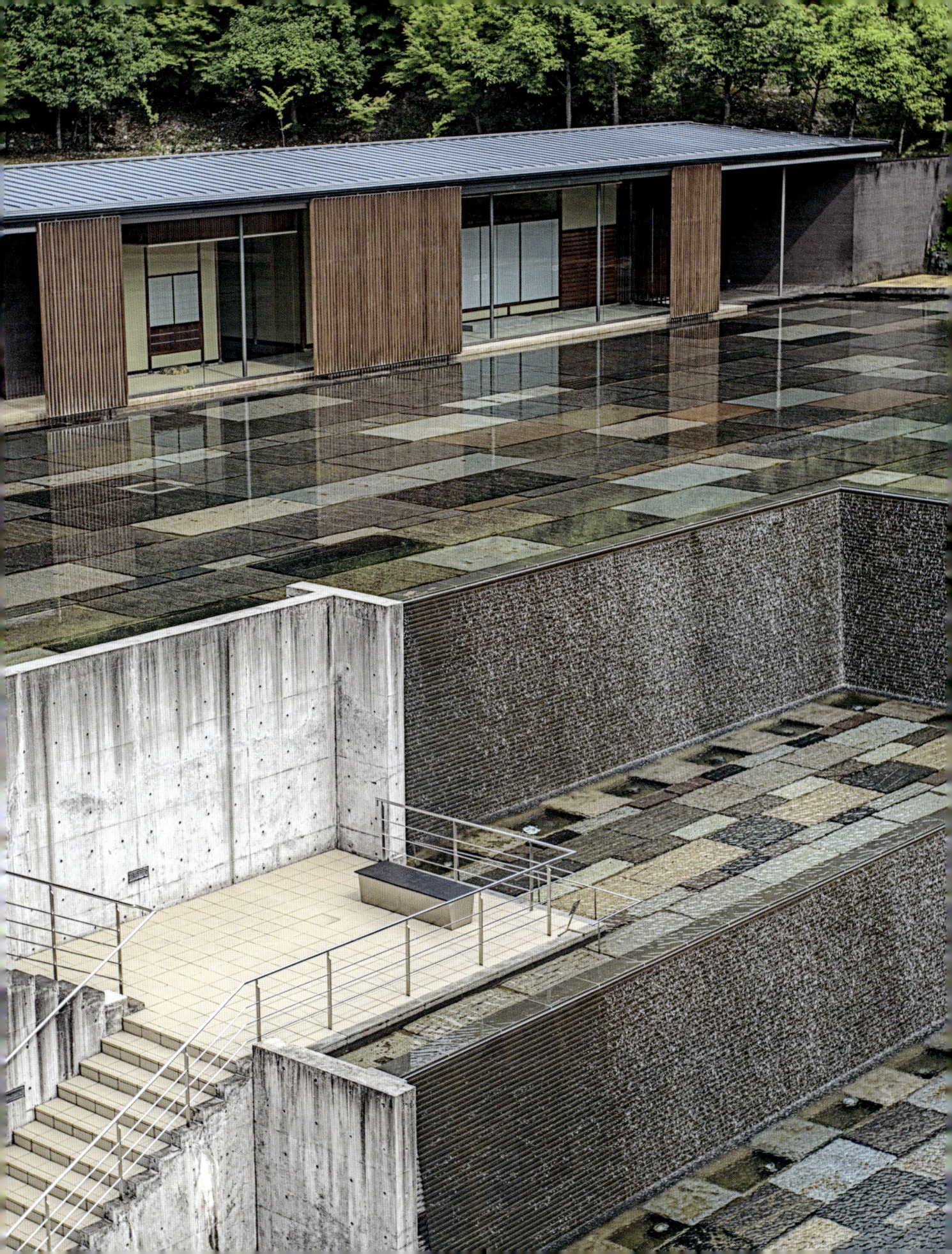

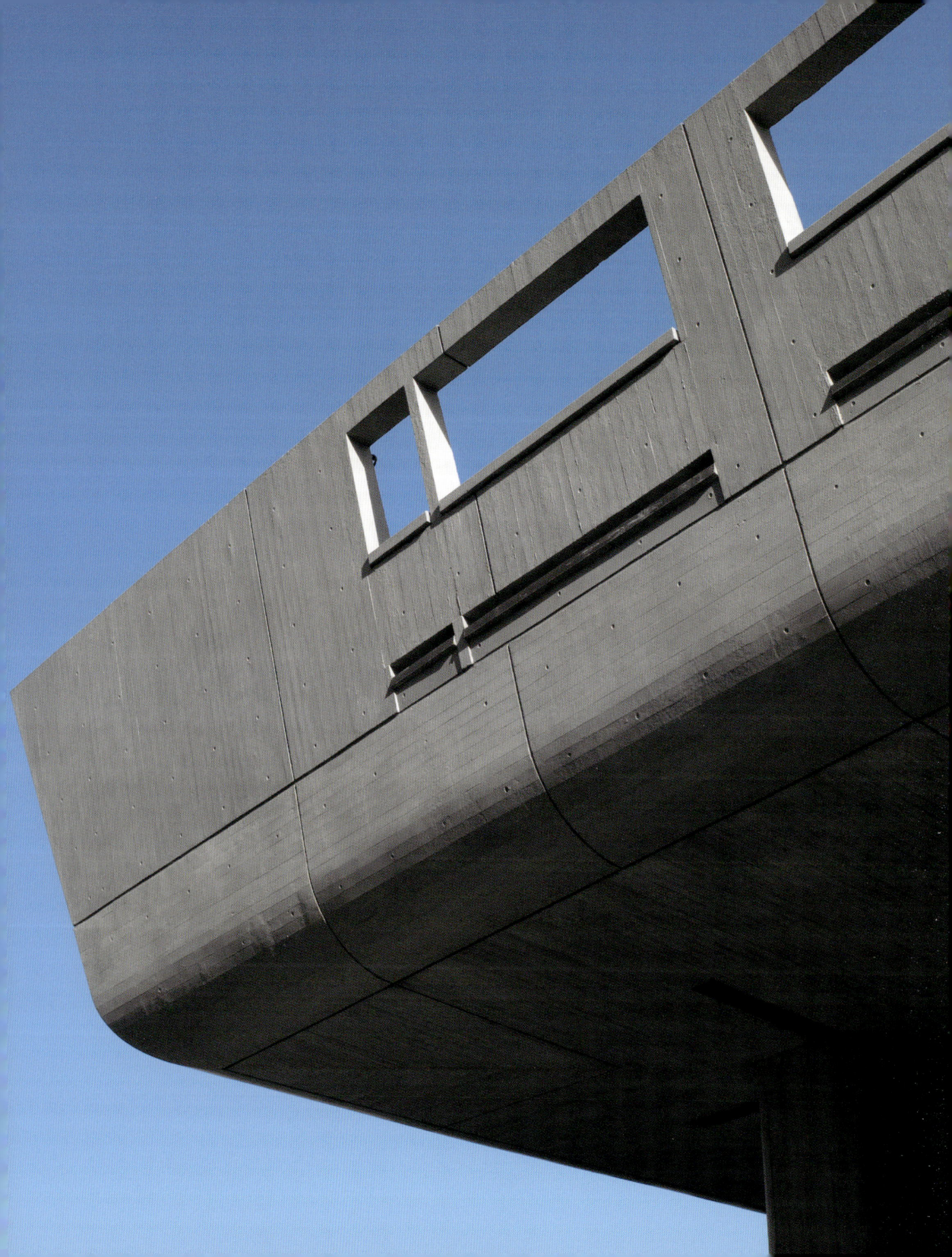

METROPOLITAN FESTIVAL HALL

TOKYO · Architect: MAEKAWA Kunio · Completed 1961

This Festival Hall is a medley of Japan's post-war modernist architecture, capturing the festive spirit of performance arts with its cadenced approach. It is an early and prominent example of a multi-purpose performance centre that harmoniously blends functionality with artistic flair.

Maekawa's architectural opus features massive concrete frames and expansive eaves, creating a visually striking structure. The prominent upturned eave, perched on sturdy concrete columns, frames a recessed glass façade, adding to the building's architectural melody. Inside, the hall's raw concrete walls and commissioned sculptures compose an artistic experience that chimes with visitors.

A key movement in this architectural concerto is the extensive public space, akin to festival grounds where people gather to celebrate and enjoy performances. The spacious lobby and foyer areas serve as communal spaces, echoing Maekawa's belief in creating environments that foster social interaction. This design ensures the hall is a lively social hub.

Maekawa's meticulous attention to detail is evident in the hall's harmonious integration with its surroundings. The roof height aligns with the nearby National Museum of Western Art, designed by his mentor Le Corbusier, creating a unified architectural dialogue. This thoughtful consideration underscores Maekawa's commitment to architecture that respects and enhances its environment.

The hall's exceptional acoustic design is another critical feature, making it a renowned venue for performances. Elements such as a unique ascending folding screen ensure superior sound quality, earning accolades from performers and audiences alike. This focus on acoustics guarantees that every performance is a memorable event, much like a grand festival, providing an unparalleled auditory experience.

Thus, Maekawa's Tokyo Metropolitan Festival Hall is a celebration of architecture and performance. It symbolizes post-war resilience and creativity, designed to bring people together and enrich Tokyo's cultural landscape.

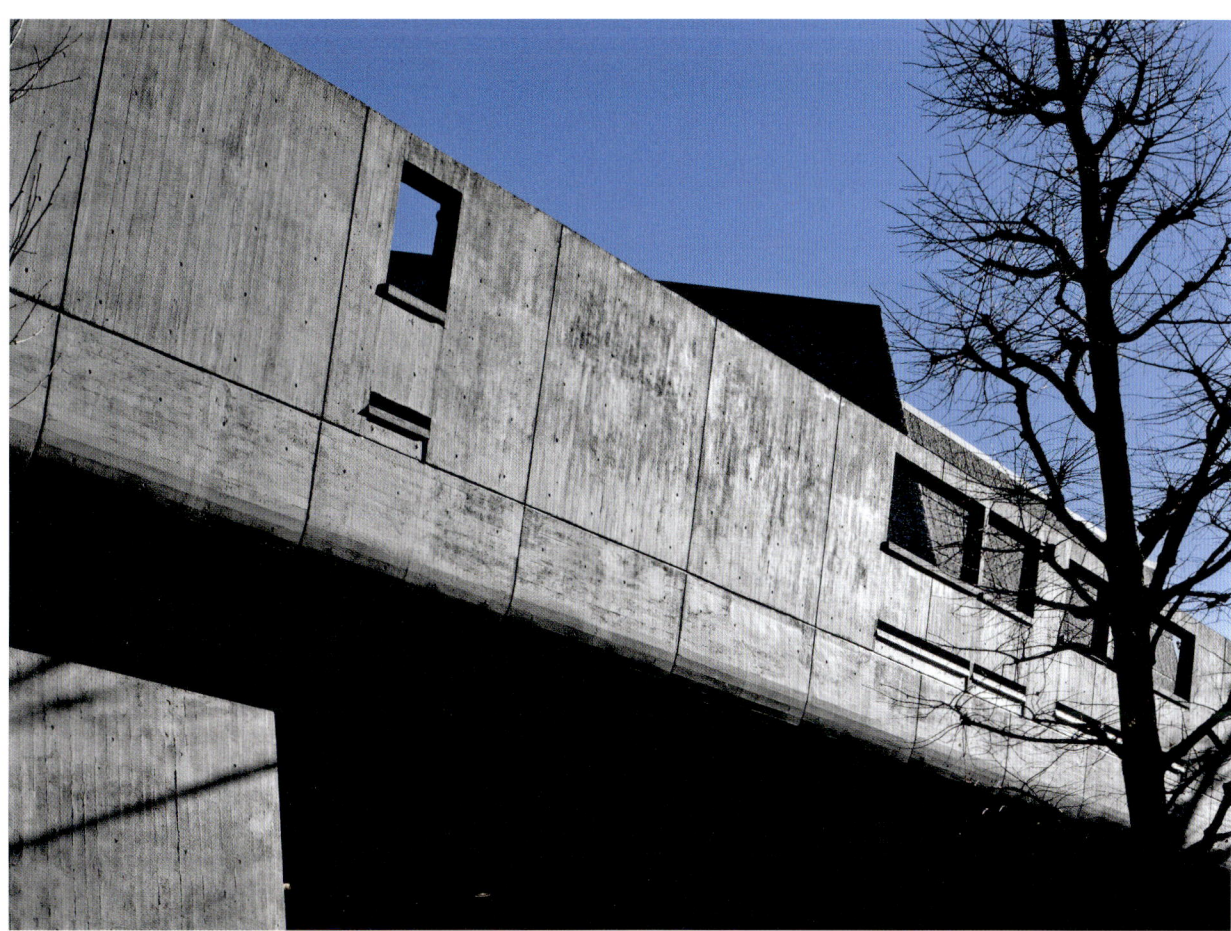

NAGO CIVIC HALL AND CENTER

NAGO, OKINAWA · Architect: OCHI Shiro · Completed 1985

Across the road from the City Hall, by Nago Bay, sits a U-shaped complex of civic centre, public halls and general welfare centre. Recognizable modernist features contrast with the mad tree-hugging neighbour and evoke a Corbusian rationality triumphing over nature.

The eastern flanks of the public halls display no-nonsense Brutalist aesthetics with right-angled flying buttresses supporting the smaller 500-seat hall. The larger 1,075-seater's eastern aspect presents a sheer impenetrable wall of concrete visible fifteen minutes' drive away. Reminiscent of Mayan architecture, a sharply terraced escarpment is carved down to the northern and western flanks of what would otherwise be a trapezoidal behemoth. The exterior austerity, punctuated with broad tracks of white paint, is juxtaposed by intricate interior precast trusses and sublime modulated concrete slabs either side of the stage. These emanate a peachy hue which compliments the velvety seating.

The exterior of the civic and welfare centres emanates an elegant mix of classicism and modernist Brutalism; the upper portion of the gap between equally spaced, tall, slim colonnades is bridged by four rows of white-painted horizontal concrete louvres hung over set-back windows bordered by breeze-block parapets. Corbusian influences upon the architect, Shiro Ochi, are evident in the main entrance's cylindrical stairwell and a secondary entrance by way of a sloping ramp. This permits access to equally Corbusian exposed corridors, open-planned interiors and upper terrace.

The inner sweep of the U-shaped complex forms an open grassed plaza oriented towards the sea. This is a postmodernist exercise as it reflects the centrality of the courtyard to traditional Okinawan life. Purely ornamental concrete columns have angular protrusions that match the angle of vernacular courtyard eaves. A local architectural historian believes the result would have been a touch too kitsch if not made from concrete. Indeed, criticism of mainland architects operating in Okinawa focuses on their perceived overzealous effort to represent locality – a misplaced, if not condescending, sense of exoticism.

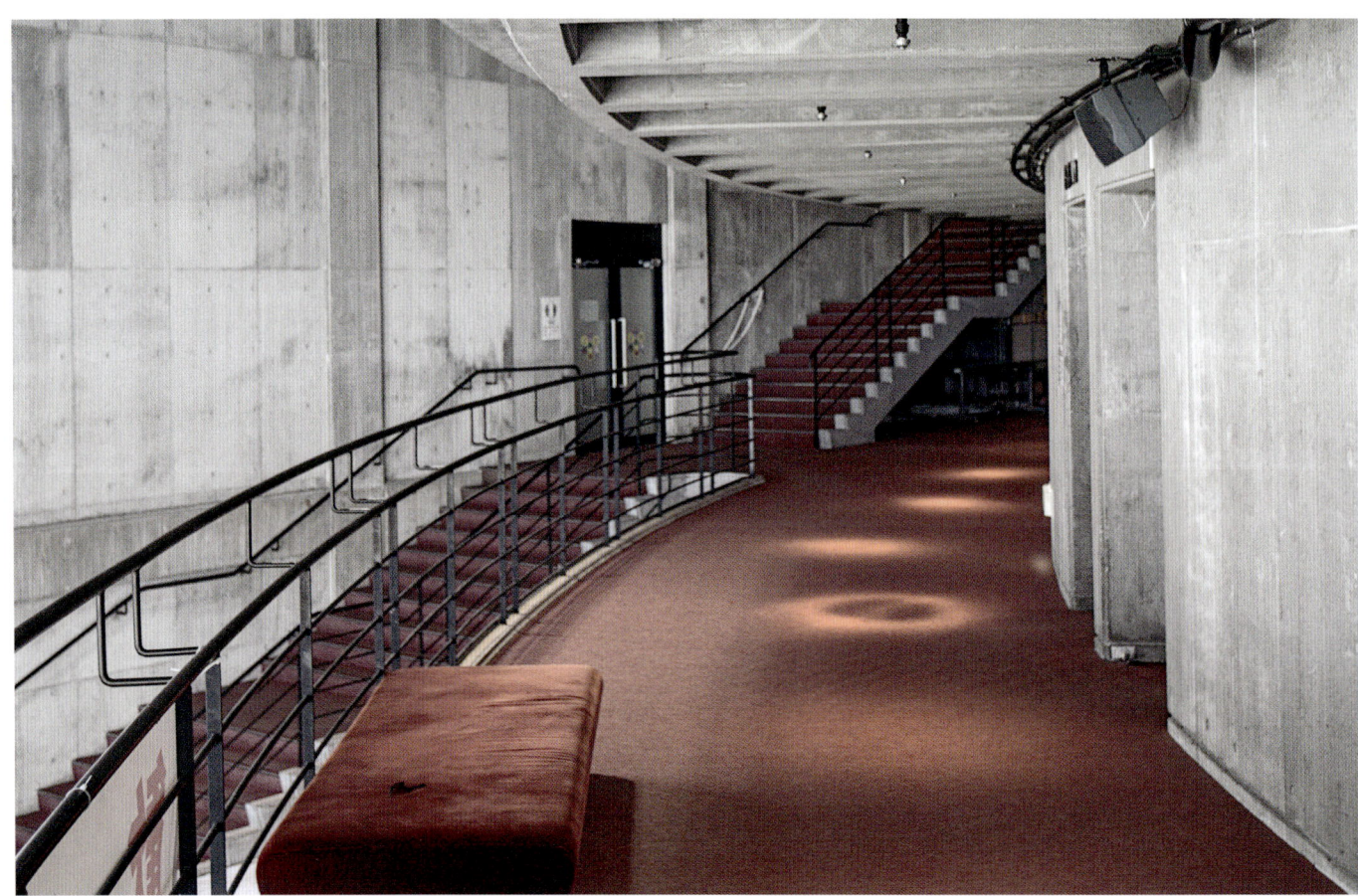

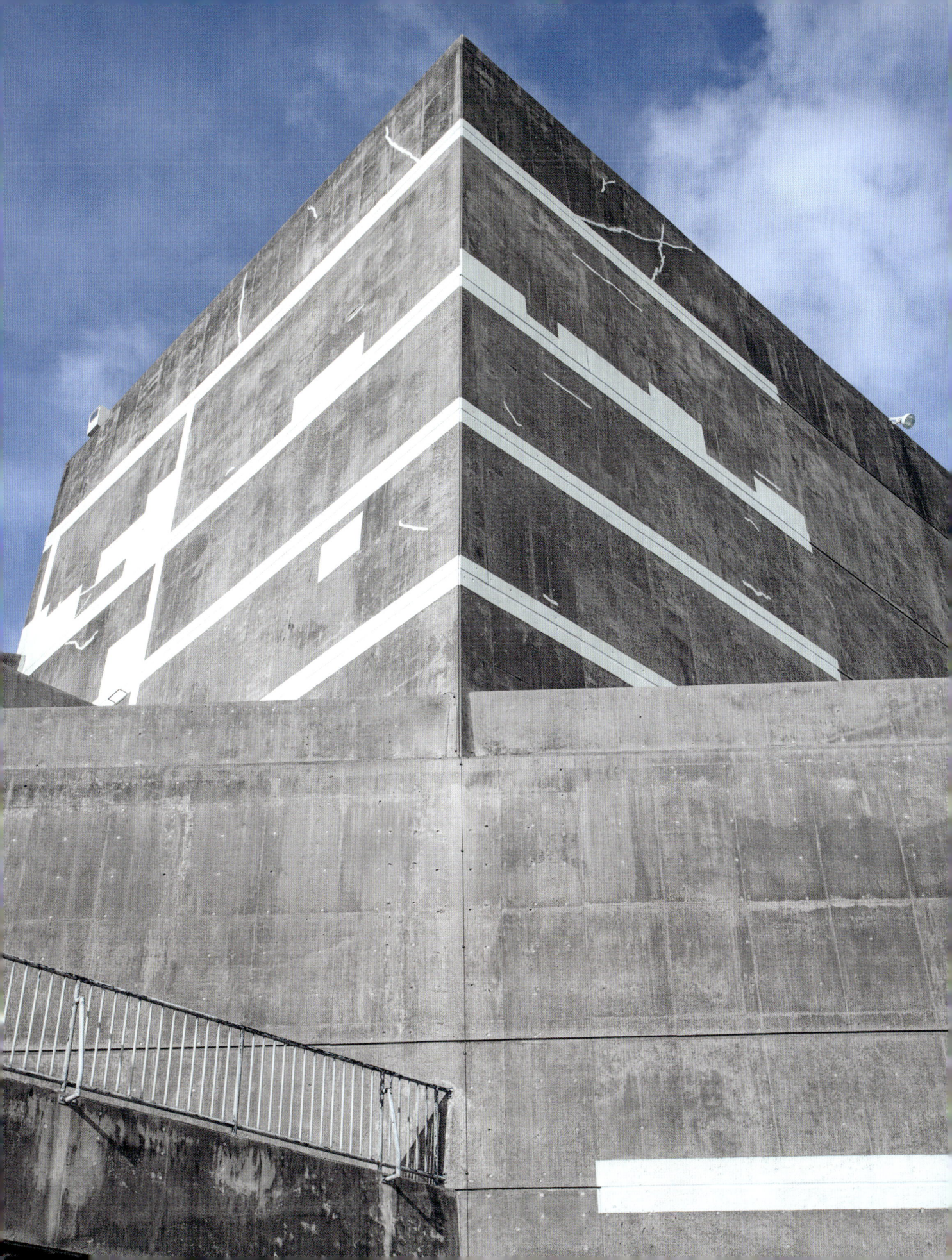

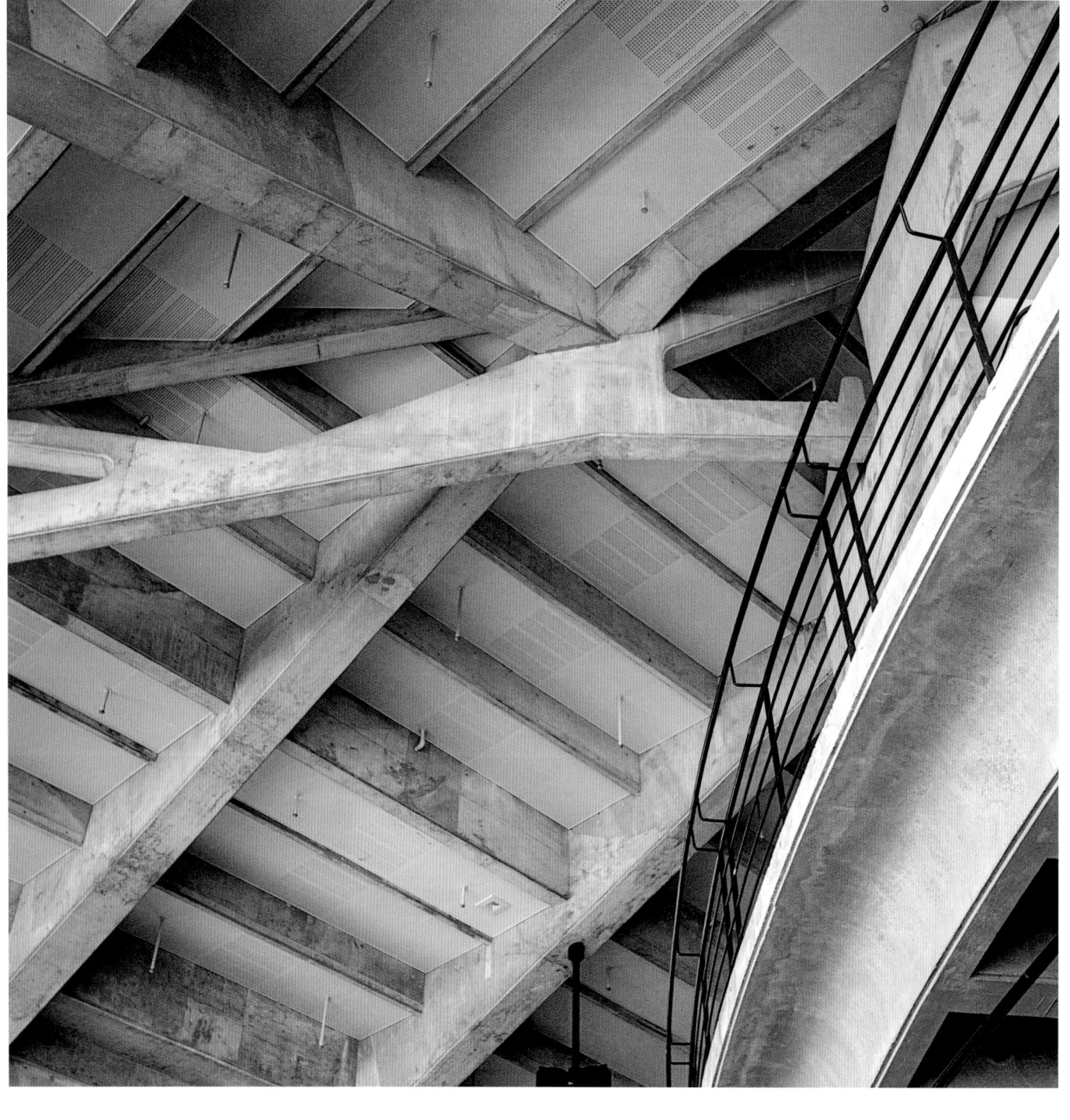

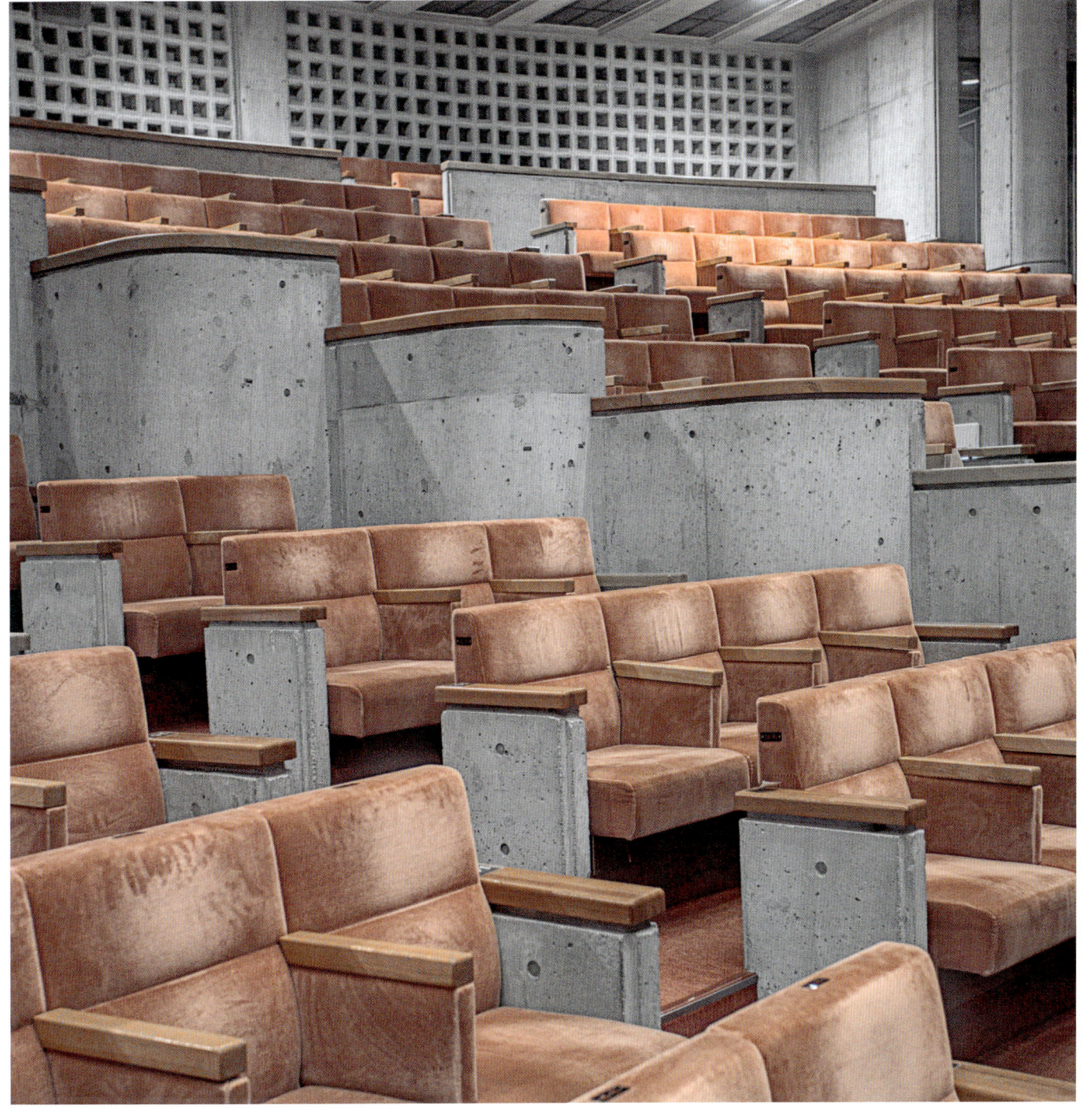

WAREHOUSE C

NAGASAKI · Architect: RoTo Architects · Completed 1997

Warehouse C shows the adaptive spirit of Brutalism, presenting itself as a storage facility, monumental matrix of industrial strength and public realm all at once. Along the Nagasaki waterfront, this behemoth extends 200 metres, its silhouette reminiscent of the formidable presence of a supertanker, yet its essence is intertwined deeply with the communal fabric of the city. Housing dry goods, the warehouse surpasses mere functionality by offering a rooftop retreat that resonates with the Zen tranquillity of Tokyo's rock gardens – a verdant intermission in the orchestra of urbanity.

Perched twenty-two metres high, Warehouse C unveils a twenty-metre-diameter spherical exhibition space, an orb of inspiration positioned among the rigid lines of storage and distribution. This globe is a hall that stimulates thought, encapsulating dreams within its curved embrace. The public garden atop, a juxtaposition to the industrial landscape below, offers a sanctuary where city dwellers can contemplate the fluid dynamics between urban growth and serene nature.

The colour palette speaks a visual language steeped in Japanese symbolism, articulating a narrative that weaves together the past and the present. It mirrors the resilience of the nation, with earthy undertones anchoring the structure to its roots and vivid accents that symbolize the vibrant future. The metallic sheen of Warehouse C shows the flexibility of Brutalism as an architectural style, an expression that isn't confined to the rawness of concrete alone. It echoes the Smithsons' Hunstanton School's innovative use of brick and glass, verifying Brutalism's capacity for a broader vocabulary of materials.

Warehouse C is a playful yet profound reminder that in the realm of Brutalism it is not the material but the intent that defines the movement. It's a structure where the practicalities of storage are harmoniously stored with the aesthetics of cultural symbolism, and where the warehouse becomes more than a place for keeping – it's a space for thinking, reflecting and engaging. This is Brutalism with a twist, not just in materials but in purpose – a structural metaphor for the storied layers and aspirations of the society it serves.

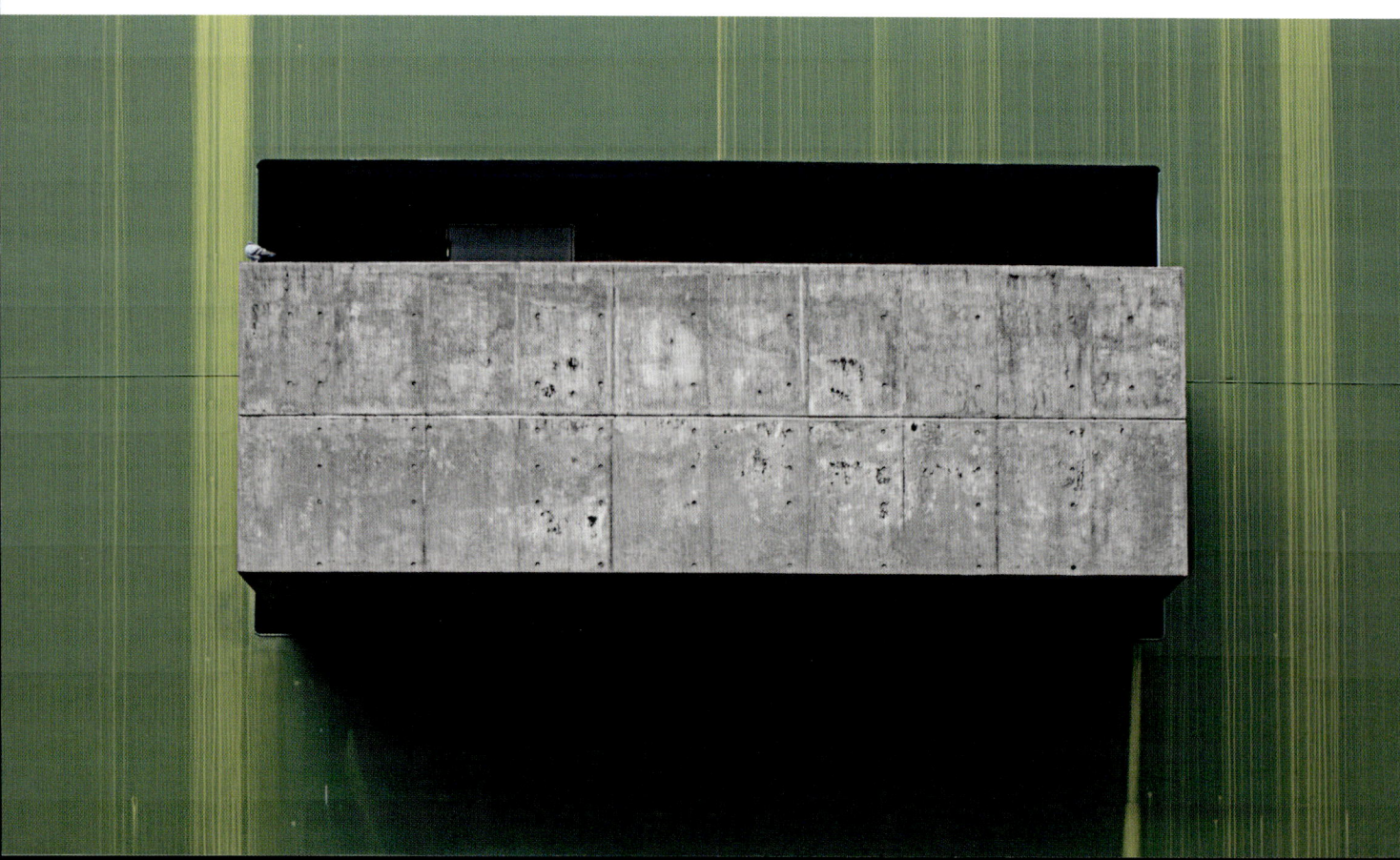

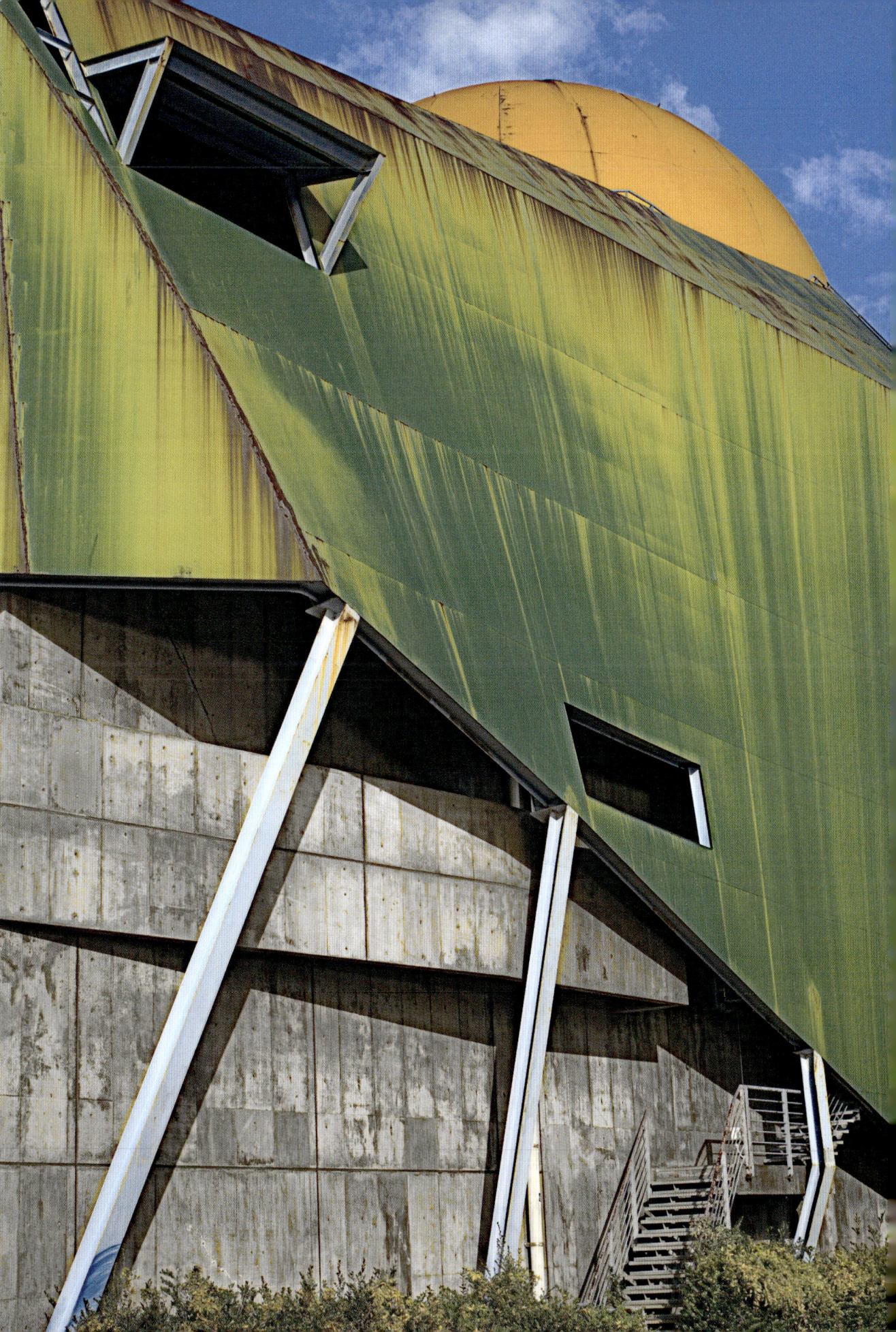

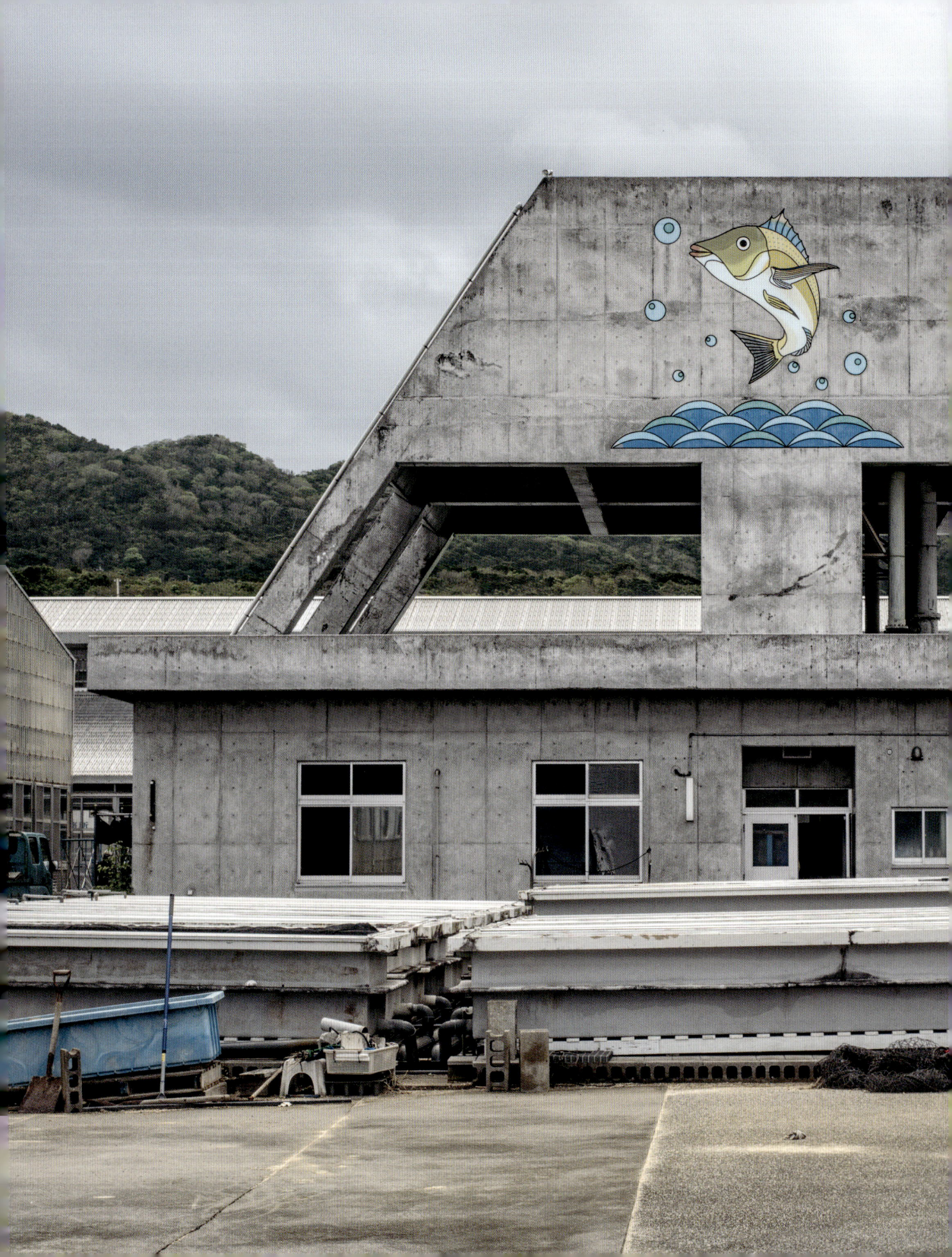

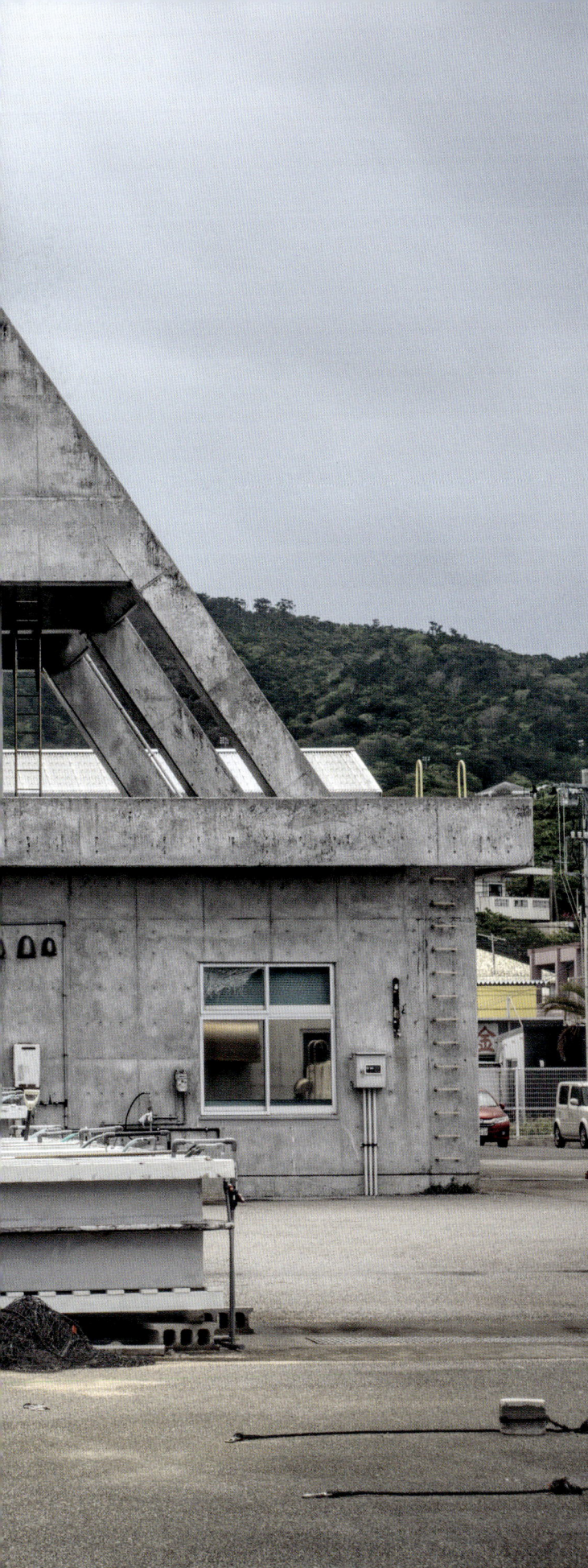

AQUACULTURE FARM

MOTOBU, OKINAWA

Surfacing amidst the modernist wave with its robust concrete form, this edifice playfully winks at traditional Japanese architecture while embracing the festive spirit of *Kodomo no hi* (Children's Day). Imagine this structure as an architectural *koinobori*, unfurled and anchoring its presence firmly against the urban stream. With a design that seemingly leaps through the air, the building becomes a metaphorical carp, its strong, purposeful lines evoking the creature's legendary ascent to dragonhood.

While its material palette speaks the language of modernism with an unadorned grey concrete canvas, the structure's apex is crowned with a whimsical mural of a carp. This artistic gesture nods to the traditions of what was formerly called Boy's Day, where colourful *koinobori* flutter above the landscape, symbolizing aspirations for youthful vigour and resilience. The building can be viewed as a structural metaphor for the dynamism and vigour needed in the carp's journey through cascading waters.

The geometric clarity of the building's façade harmonizes with the orderly chaos found in nature, akin to the balance sought in a traditional Japanese garden. Just as the *koinobori* is designed to swim against the wind, this structure is a solid insistence against the tides of architectural conformity, daring to combine utility with symbolic playfulness.

Its steadfast silhouette against the skyline becomes a public canvas celebrating growth, echoing the strength and determination of the children honoured in *Kodomo no hi*. As families hoist their vibrant carps into the sky, reflecting their hopes and dreams for their children, this building stands as a permanent fixture in the landscape, a constant reminder of the eternal values of strength, courage and the pursuit of higher heights.

In this way, the building transcends its primary function, symbolizing the collective cultural memory and community identity through its architectural form. It is a place where the currents of tradition and modernity meet – a crafted concrete cradle that honours the past while serving the present, much like the storied carps that soar through water, inspiring all who gaze upon them.

KOMAZAWA OLYMPIC PARK ATHLETIC STADIUM AND GYMNASIUM

TOKYO · Architects: MURATA Masachika and ASHIHARA Yoshinobu · Completed 1964

The Komazawa Olympic Park Athletic Stadium, a brainchild of architect Masachika Murata, is a sculptural monument of the 1964 Tokyo Olympics, symbolizing the event's high-flying aspirations. Its iconic concrete canopies, reminiscent of wings poised for flight, capture the Olympic spirit of striving for excellence. Yoshinobu Ashihara's adjacent gymnasium, with its striking hyperbolic paraboloid shells, echoes traditional Japanese architectural shadow play, hinting at movement and dynamism akin to the Olympic wrestlers it once hosted.

Incorporating functional elegance within its framework, the stadium's design gracefully melds with the park's natural elements, presenting a formidable fusion of raw industrial materials. This creates a versatile space that commemorates athletic feats and enriches community life. Preserving its Olympic heritage, the stadium continues to be a vibrant centre for sport and social interaction, reflecting the principles of unity and progress emblematic of the Games.

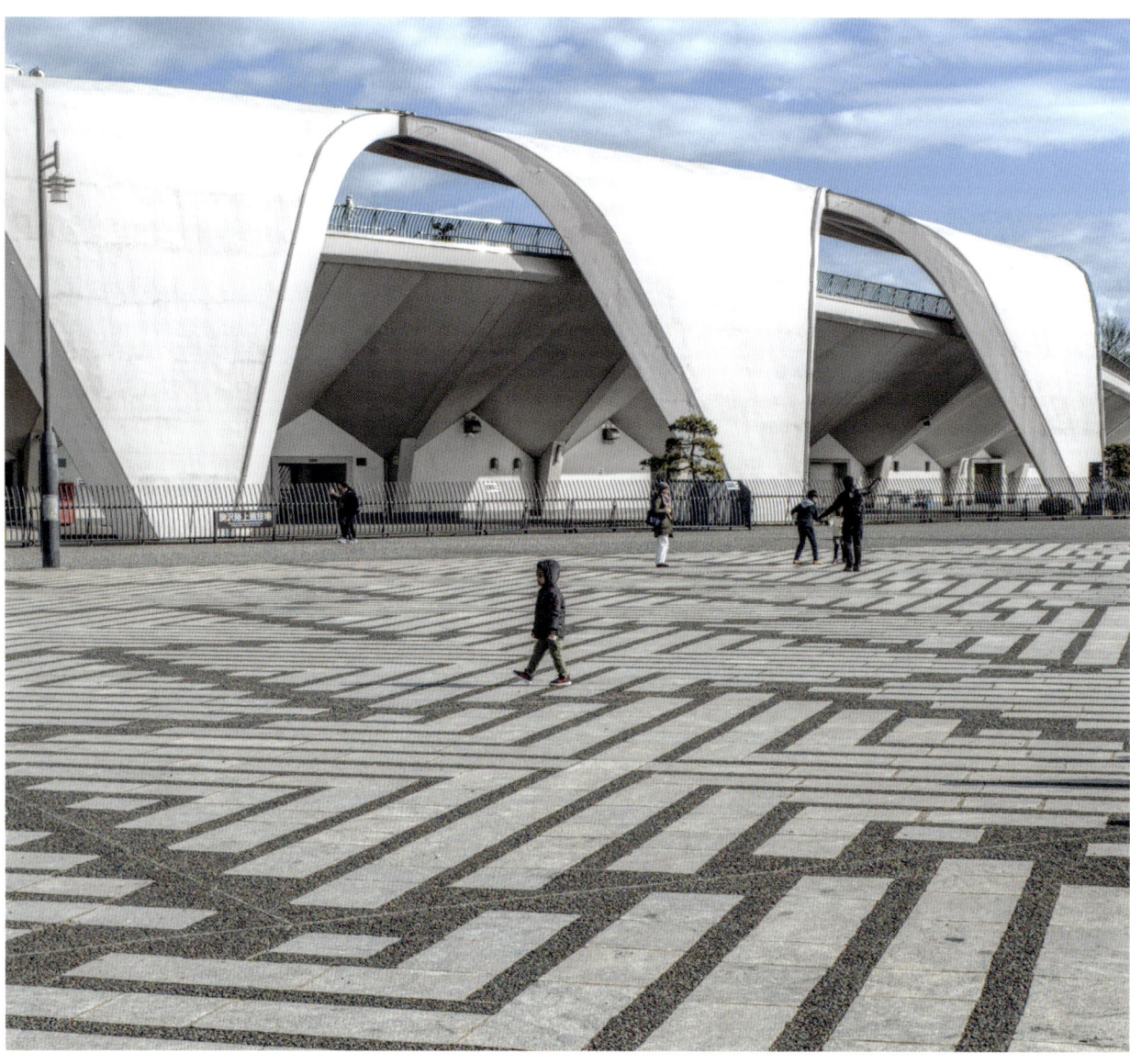

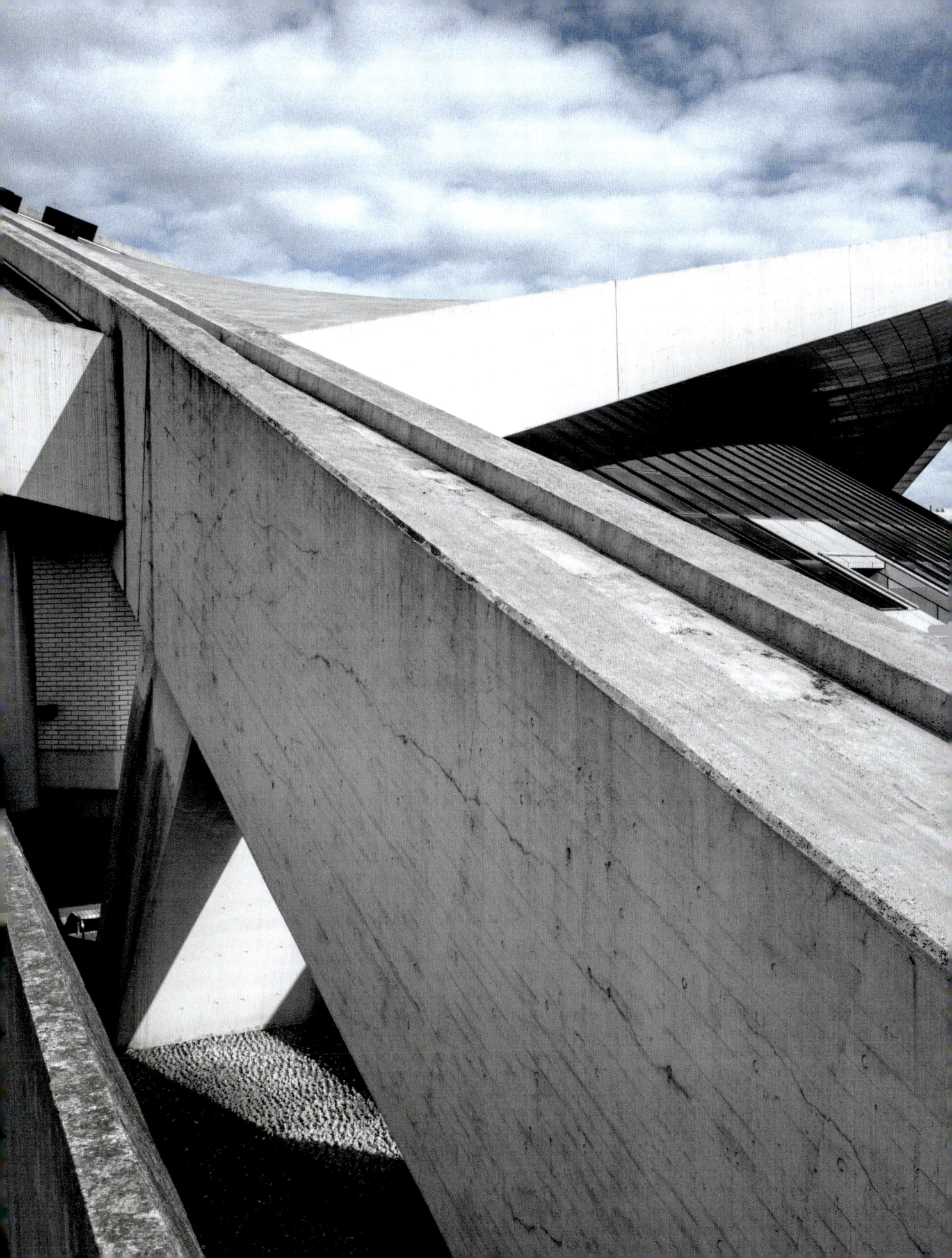

SUPREME COURT

TOKYO · Architect: SHINICHI Okada · Completed 1974

The architecture of Tokyo's Supreme Court, a concrete and granite monolith, manifests the gravity and permanence of justice. Constructed from June 1971 and completed in March 1974, the building's design – featuring seven interlinked structures within a grand total of 53,923 square metres – stresses structural ingenuity. It pioneers in its use of vibration analysis, ensuring its steadfast stance amidst Tokyo's urban rhythm.

Its façade, a courtly quilt of granite, was meticulously selected for its purity, primarily employing Inada stone from Ibaraki Prefecture. This meticulous process, where entire layers of inferior stone were discarded, reflects the court's dedication to upholding the highest standards. Indeed, stone work constitutes a significant 20 per cent of the construction cost.

Below the grand hall lies a bedrock pledge: "Here we lay down an everlasting foundation, striving for the establishment of our rule and the unwavering fortunes of our nation." It's a promise of immutable justice, mirrored by the robustness and dignity of the materials chosen. The Tokyo Supreme Court is a bastion of order, its very walls echoing the solidity of the law. It does speak: "Behave yourself!"

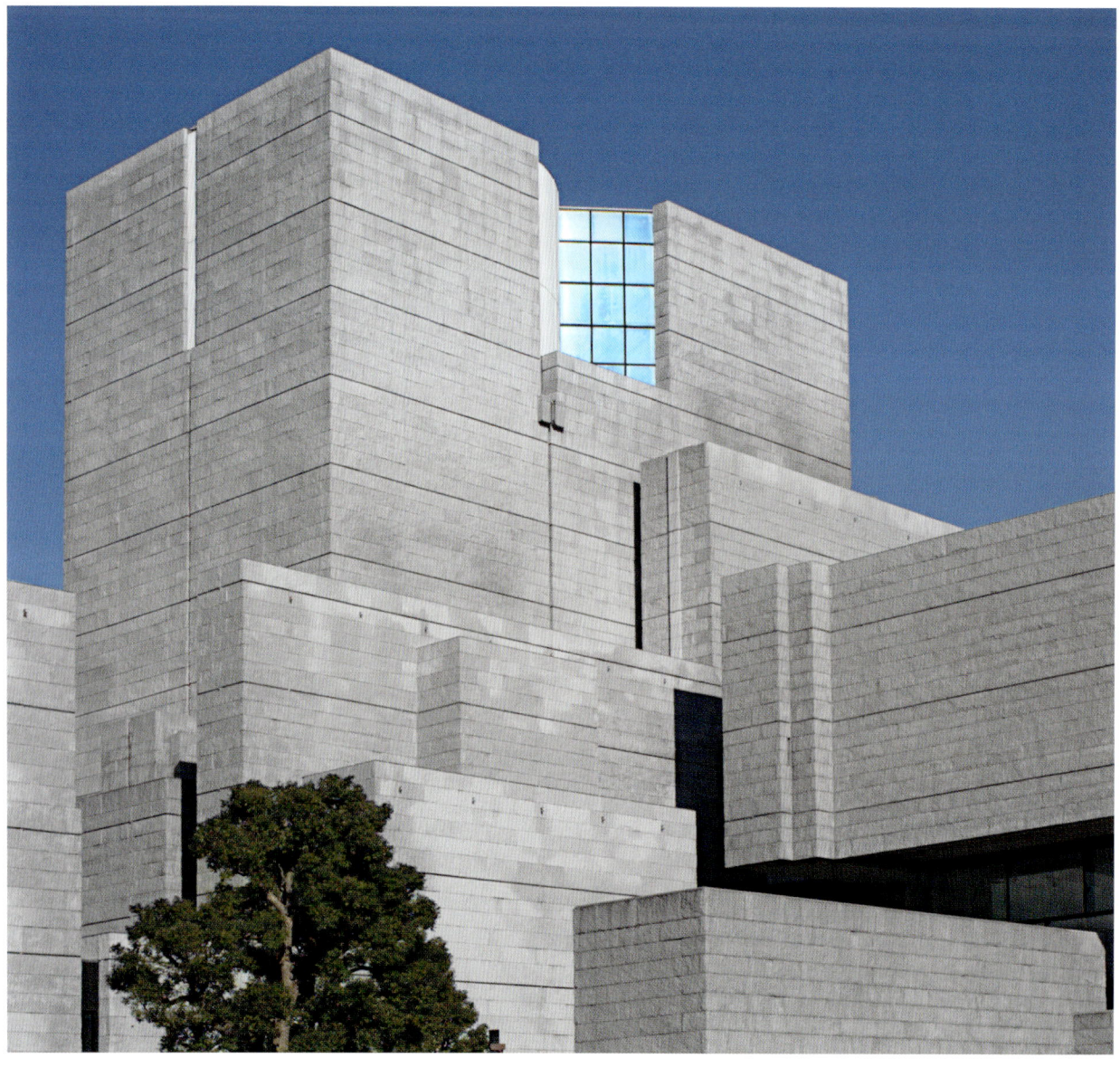

SUNWELL MUSE

TOKYO · Architect: TAMAGAMI Takato and Be-Fun Design · Completed 2008

The building, poised at a bustling Harajuku corner, unfurls like a sculptural tribute to the feminine form. It belongs to a textile planning and trading company, a fitting inhabitant for a structure that mirrors the elegance and fluidity of fabric. This five-storey curvature, dedicated to female apparel, uses its architecture to echo the company's focus on beauty and grace.

Two dominating curved walls draw in the passer-by, forming a sinuous passage that cuts through the block like a chasm. This path, reminiscent of a secluded alley or the quiet depth of a ravine, funnels visitors to an event hall below and showrooms above. These curves, a metaphor for the contours of a woman's silhouette, marry straight lines to create a graceful façade that speaks to the identity of its inhabitants. Within, this motif continues, a constant throughout the floors, reaffirming the building as the epitome of feminine elegance cast in concrete.

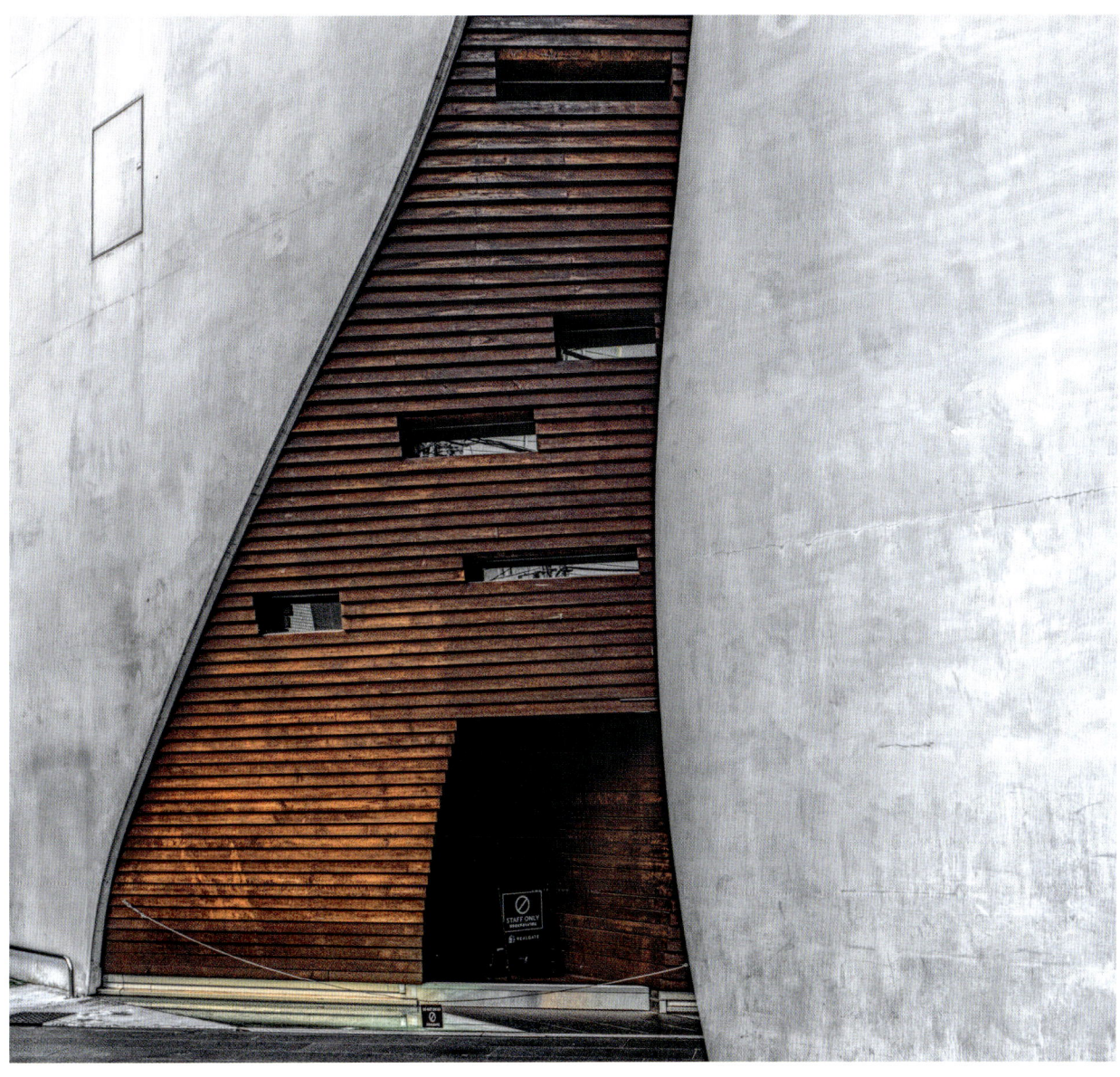

KYOTO INTERNATIONAL CONFERENCE CENTER NEW HALL
KYOTO · Architect: KOMATSU Toshiro · Completed 2018

The Kyoto International Conference Center's expansion, designed by Toshiro Komatsu of Nikken Sekkei Ltd., is a choreographed ensemble of four gardens, each offering a tranquil and meditative experience that mirrors the serenity of Zen. The front garden welcomes visitors with a Zen-like austerity, juxtaposed with the lushness of seasonal foliage that brings to mind a mountain hamlet in bloom. The folding screen garden, a reception area, charms with an earth jar's melodious drips, evoking a naturalistic soundscape.

The concrete components blend effortlessly with the dry landscape gardens of the courtyard, where Kyoto's iconic black Kurama stones lay in thoughtful placement, adding to the Zen narrative. The exclusive suite garden showcases the gardener's artistry with a Kyoto stone pathway reminiscent of scattered hailstones, encouraging a moment of pause and reflection.

Each space, connected yet distinct, crafts a sequence of Zen vignettes, inviting a journey through tranquillity and nature, emblematic of Komatsu's ability to infuse modernity with traditional Japanese aesthetics. This addition is an extension of physical space that manifests Zen principles, where architecture and landscape coalesce to foster introspection and harmony.

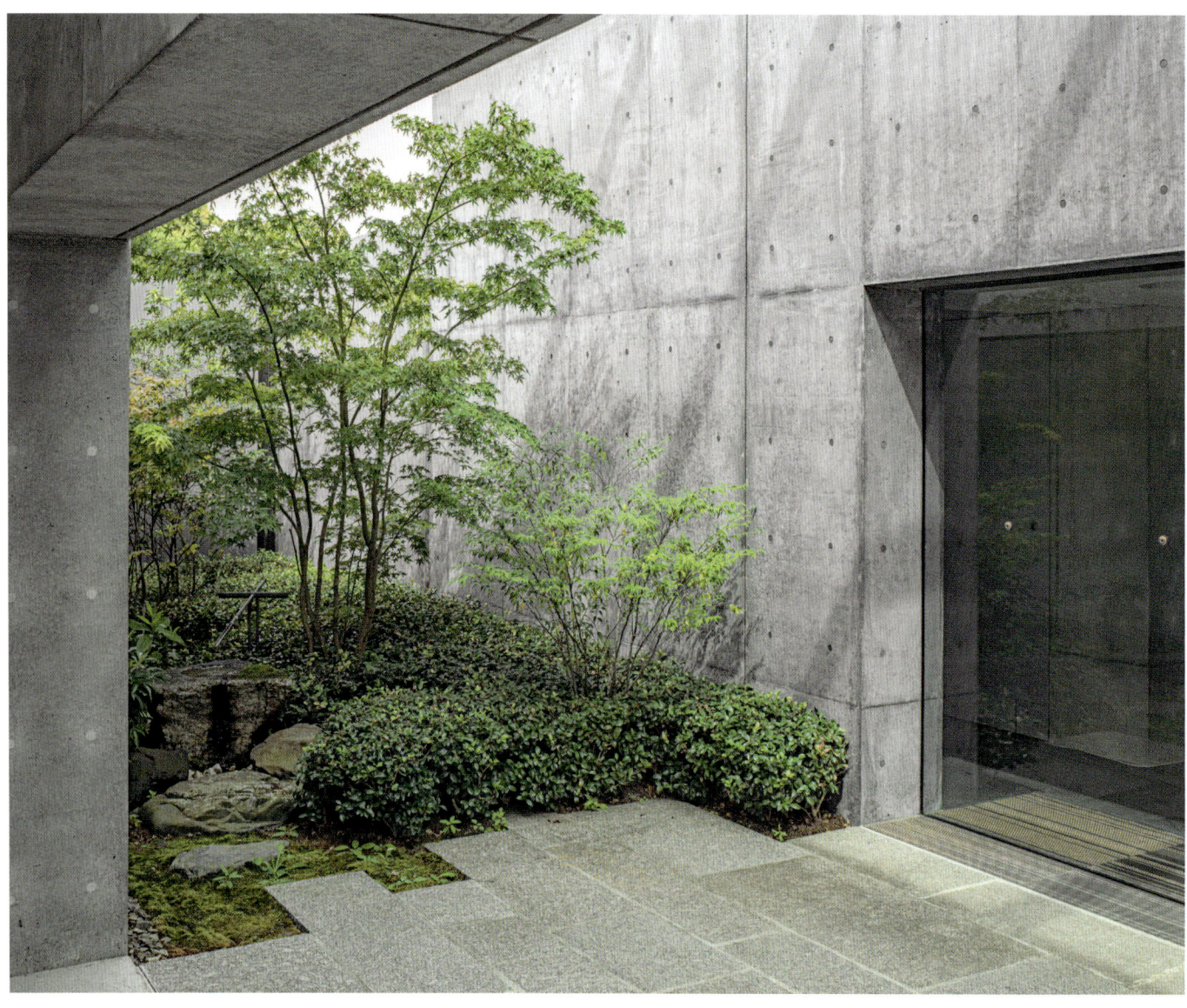

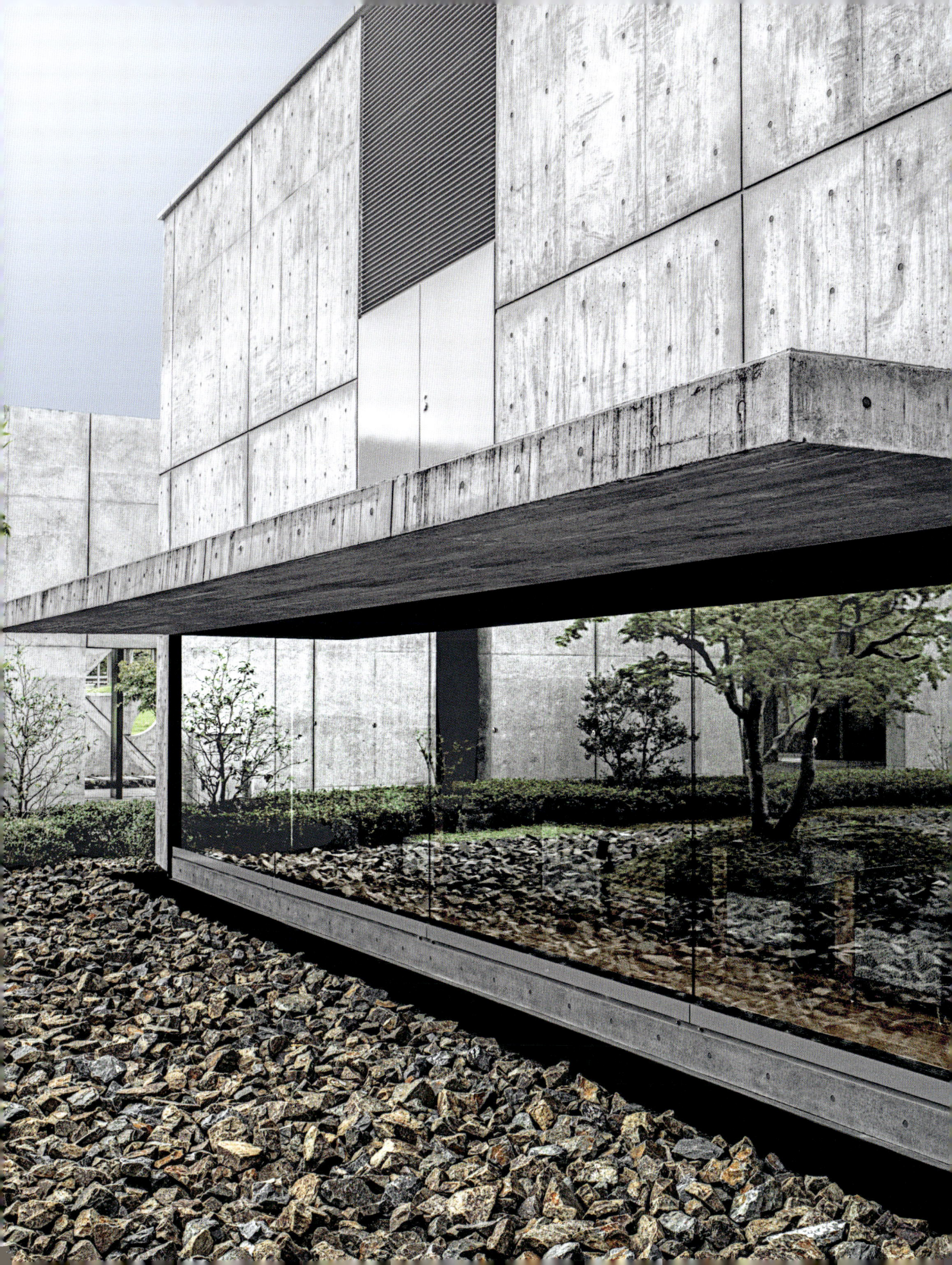

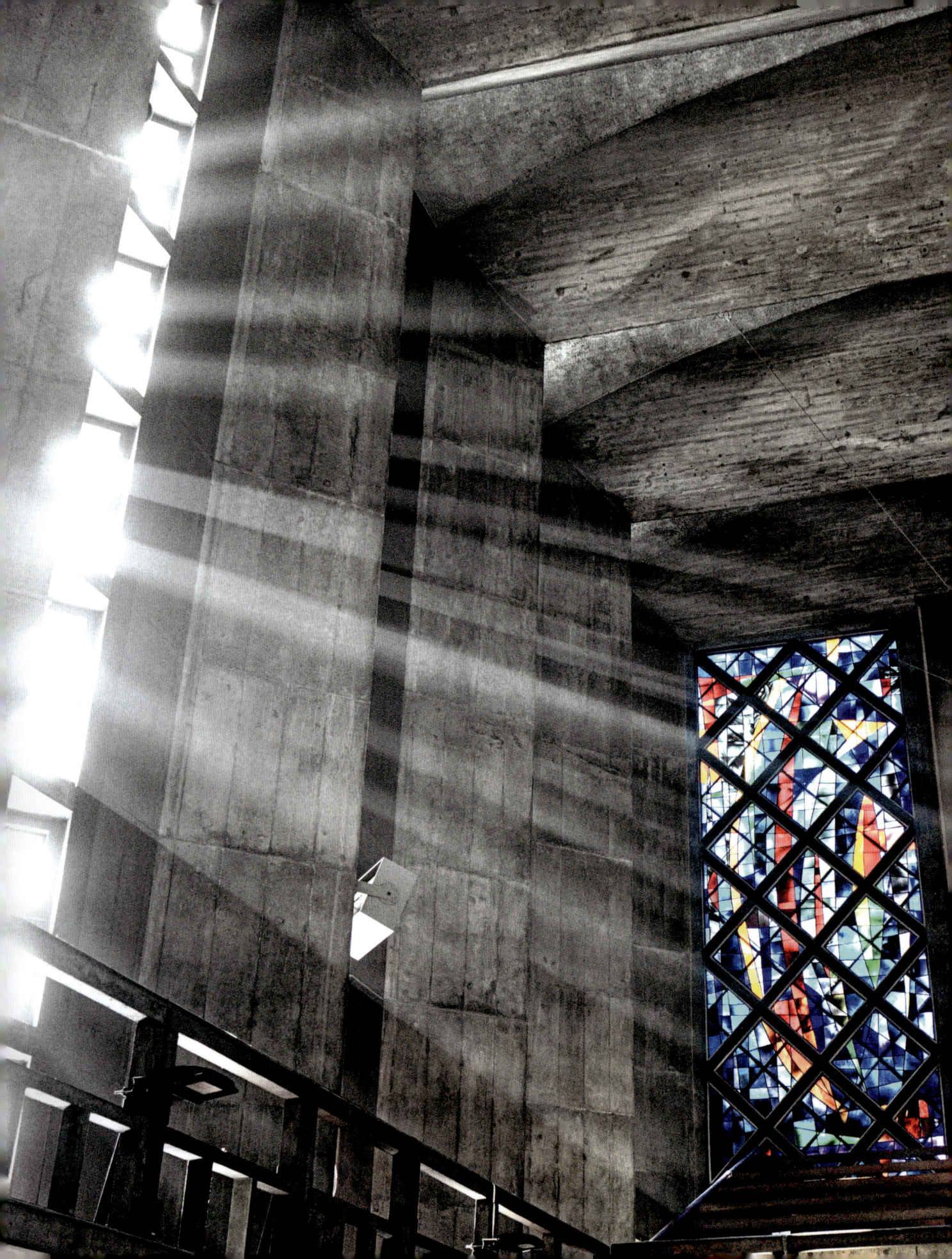

ST ANSELM'S MEGURO CHURCH

TOKYO · Architects: Antonin and Noémi Raymond · Completed 1954

East meets vestment – a divine blend of Japanese minimalism with a modernist twist. No sliding *shoji* doors. In comes a sanctified simplicity that marries the church's Catholic roots with a Zen-like calm. Gothic heights reach the heavens with the humility of *tatami*.

The Raymonds played matchmakers between European ecclesiastical grandeur and the understated elegance of Japanese craft. The church's design confesses a modernist creed but recites Japanese poetry, balancing clean lines with an intimate understanding of Japan's architectural soul. St Anselm's is an architectural hymn, praising tradition with one verse and humming the new with the next.

Here, you'll find no flying buttresses, just the grounded serenity of the East – holy witness to Japan's uptake of global influences while keeping its cultural compass pointed squarely at home. The Raymonds' creation is a spiritual space that knows its catechism but converses fluently in Japanese.

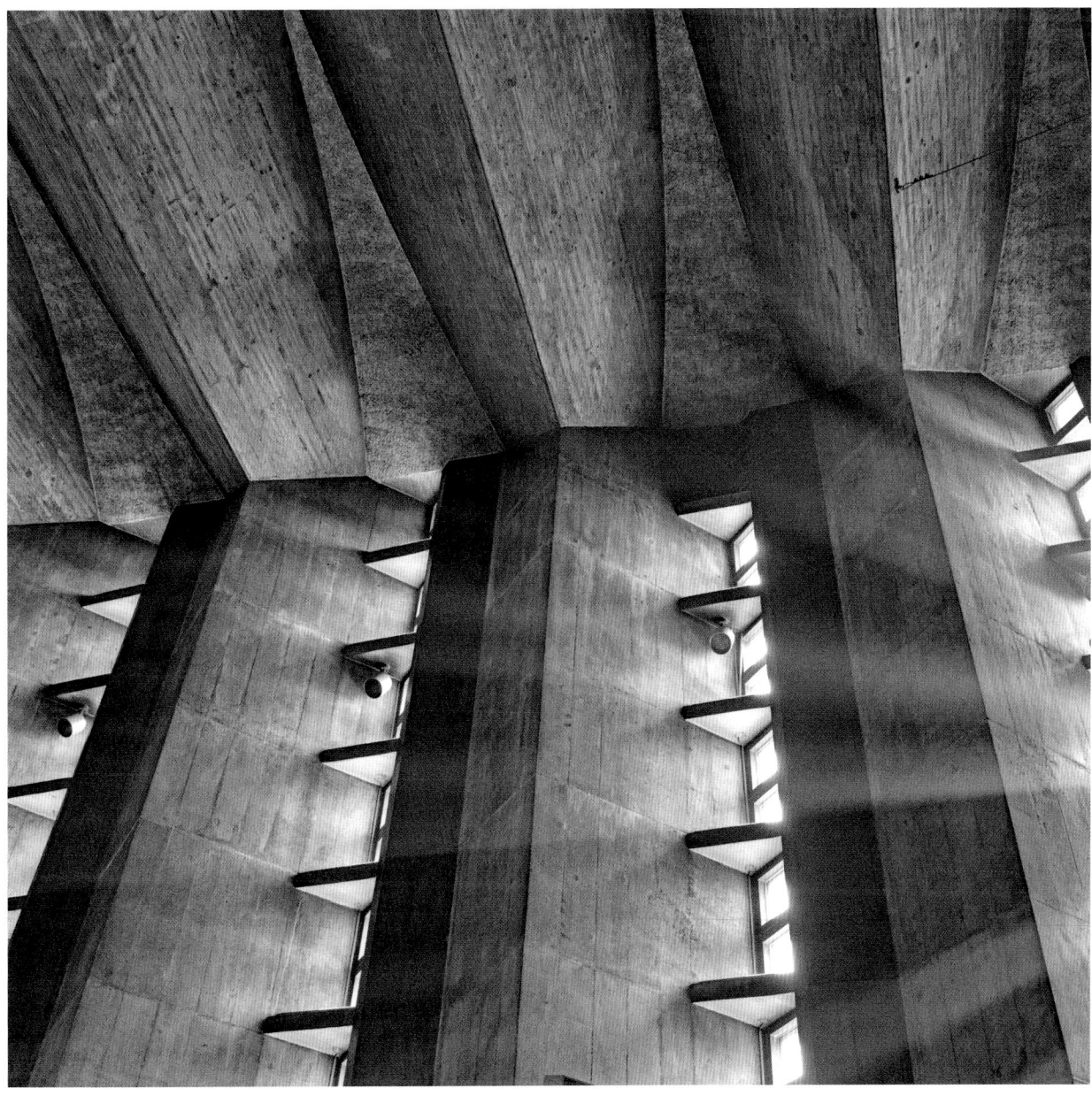

NATIONAL MUSEUM OF WESTERN ART

TOKYO · Architect: Le Corbusier · Completed 1959

This harbinger is a cornerstone of Japan's Brutalist story. Completed in 1959, the museum exhibits the interplay between Le Corbusier's modernist vision and Japan's evolving architectural identity. Its raw concrete surfaces and geometric, functional forms encapsulate the essence of Brutalism's textural aesthetics and structural candour.

The use of pilotis – reinforced concrete stilts – lifts the museum, creating an open, flowing ground space, exemplifying Le Corbusier's innovative approach to design that would resonate deeply with Brutalist philosophies. There are many examples of this throughout the book. Some exterior surfaces and the interior's suspended galleries have the textural imprint of wooden formwork, a hallmark of *béton brut* that underscores the raw beauty inherent in Brutalist architecture. To be honest, I am not a big fan of the pebble dashing. It reminds me of drab UK council estates. This is where I succumb myself to the negative associations mentioned in the introduction.

Le Corbusier's tour de force, the sole example of his work in the Far East, introduced Japan to the "Museum of Unlimited Growth", a modular concept that heralded Brutalism's adaptability. It featured open-plan floors enabled by pilotis, freeing interior spaces from supporting walls and allowing a functional flexibility celebrated in Brutalism.

The museum's influence extended beyond its concrete walls, seeding a generation of Japanese architects with the principles of structural expressionism. Disciples like Kenzo Tange and Kunio Maekawa, who apprenticed with Le Corbusier, infused his philosophies with local cultural intricacies to forge a distinct Japanese Brutalism.

Today, The National Museum of Western Art survives as a pivotal example of cultural synthesis and architectural innovation, marking the fusion of Le Corbusier's modernism with Japanese aesthetic sensibilities. It remains a foundational piece in the narrative of Japan's Brutalist architecture, affirming the perpetual influence of Le Corbusier's principles and the transformative power of international architectural discourse.

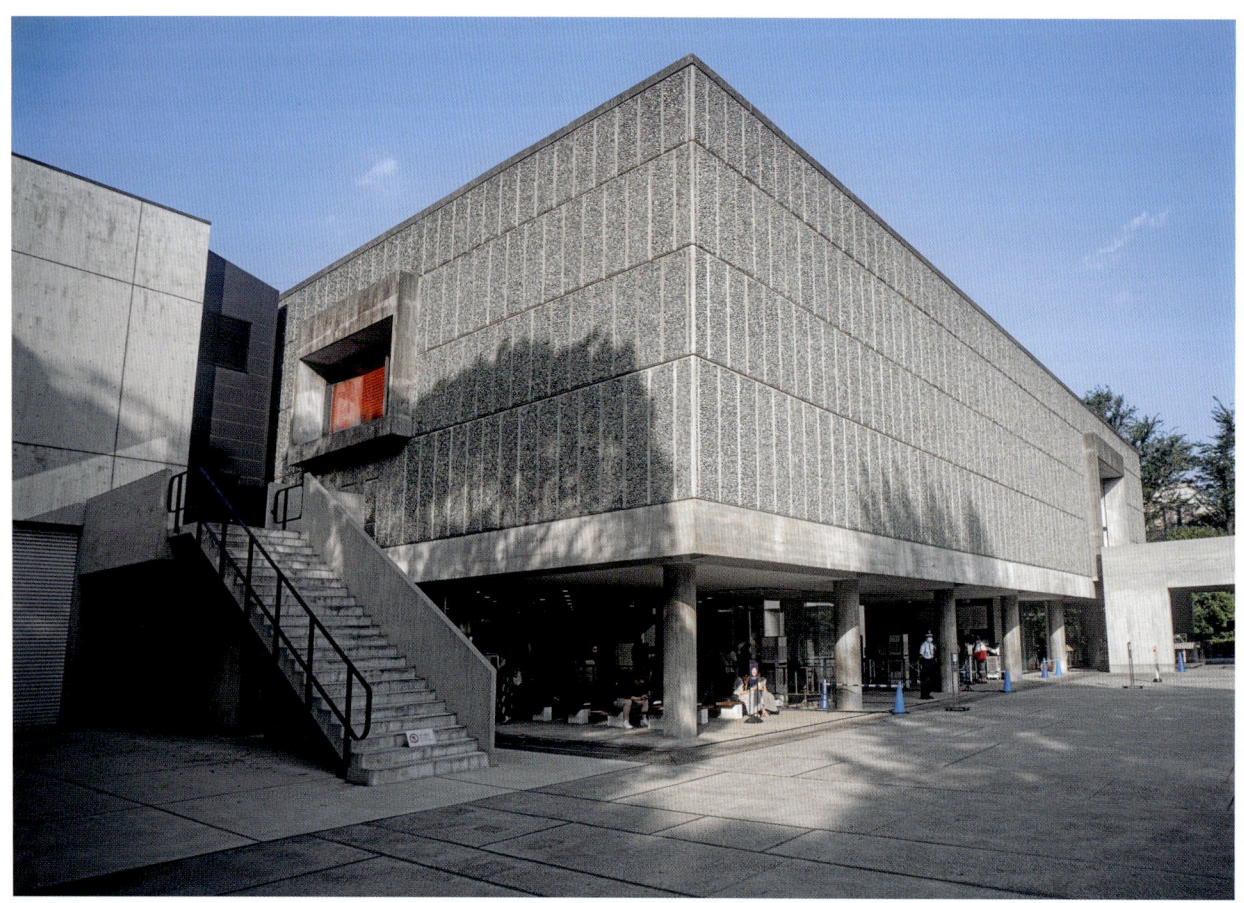

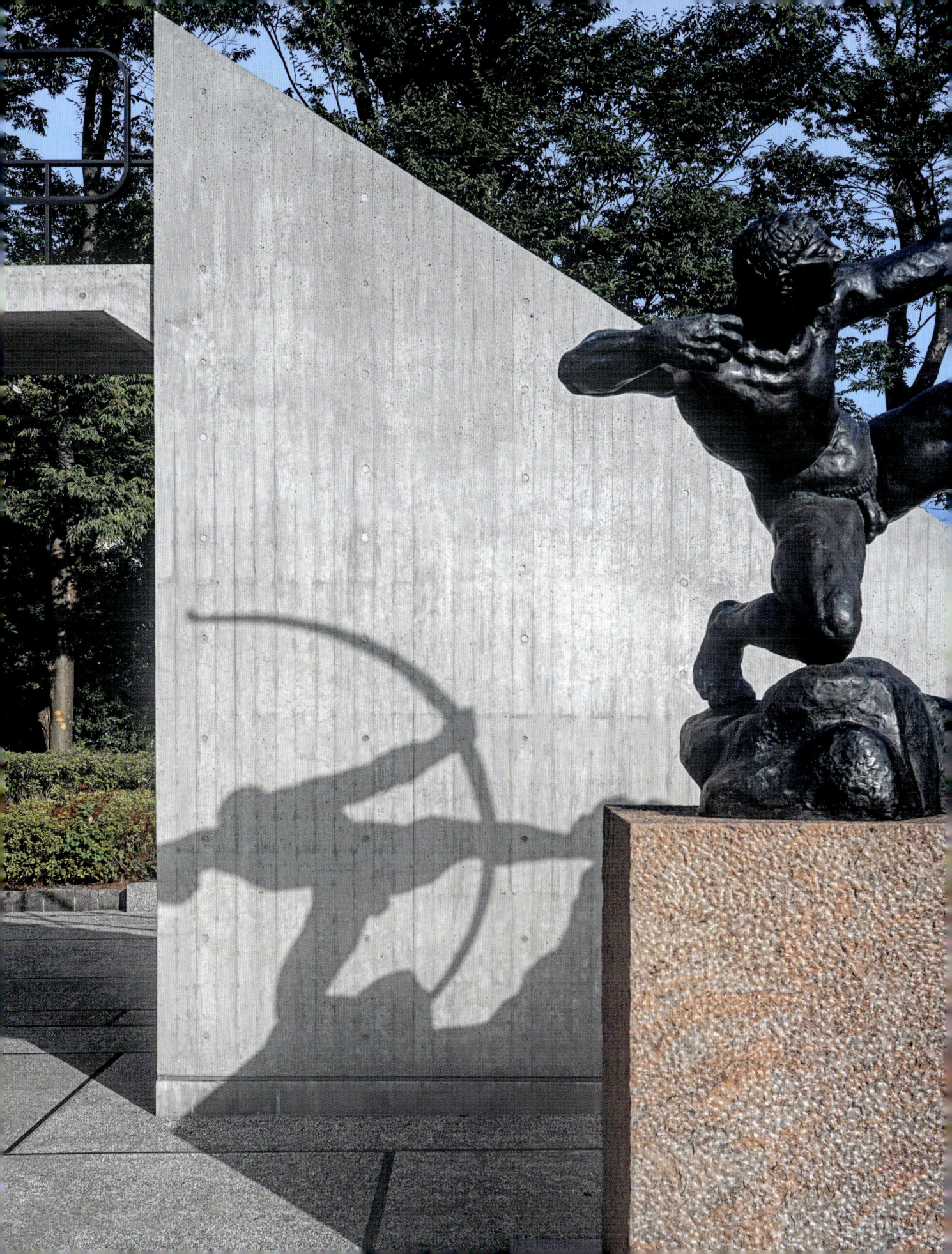

ICHIMURA MEMORIAL GYMNASIUM

SAGA · Architect: SAKAKURA Junzo · Completed 1963

Saga Prefecture cherishes the iconic Ichimura Memorial Gymnasium, recognizable by its distinctive, serrated silhouette reminiscent of a crown. Its unique structure is articulated through V-shaped walls that double as supporting pillars, crowned with a hyperbolic paraboloid shell roof draped over a circular beam.

Crafted by the modernist muscularity of Junzo Sakakura, an apprentice of Le Corbusier, the gymnasium was commissioned by Saga's own Kiyoshi Ichimura, the entrepreneurial spirit behind Ricoh – aptly documented here through the lens of my trusty Ricoh.

When seismic evaluations challenged its structural integrity, a committed preservation effort ensued. The original PC board roof was supplanted with trussed beams, lightening the load yet retaining the gymnasium's grandiose stance. This intervention assured the building's seismic compliance and conserved its striking aesthetic, allowing it to continue pleasing with its visionary design and communal memory.

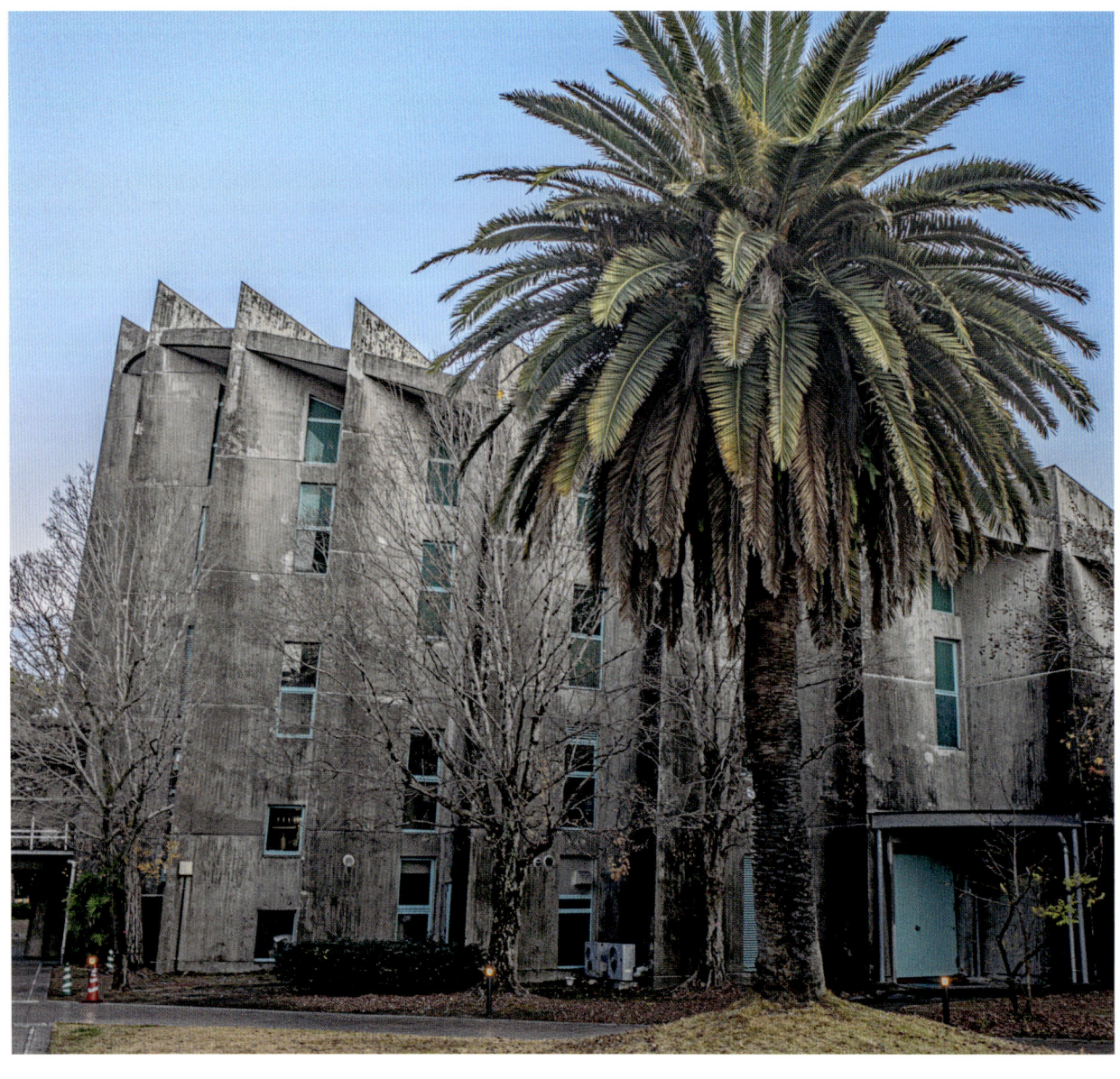

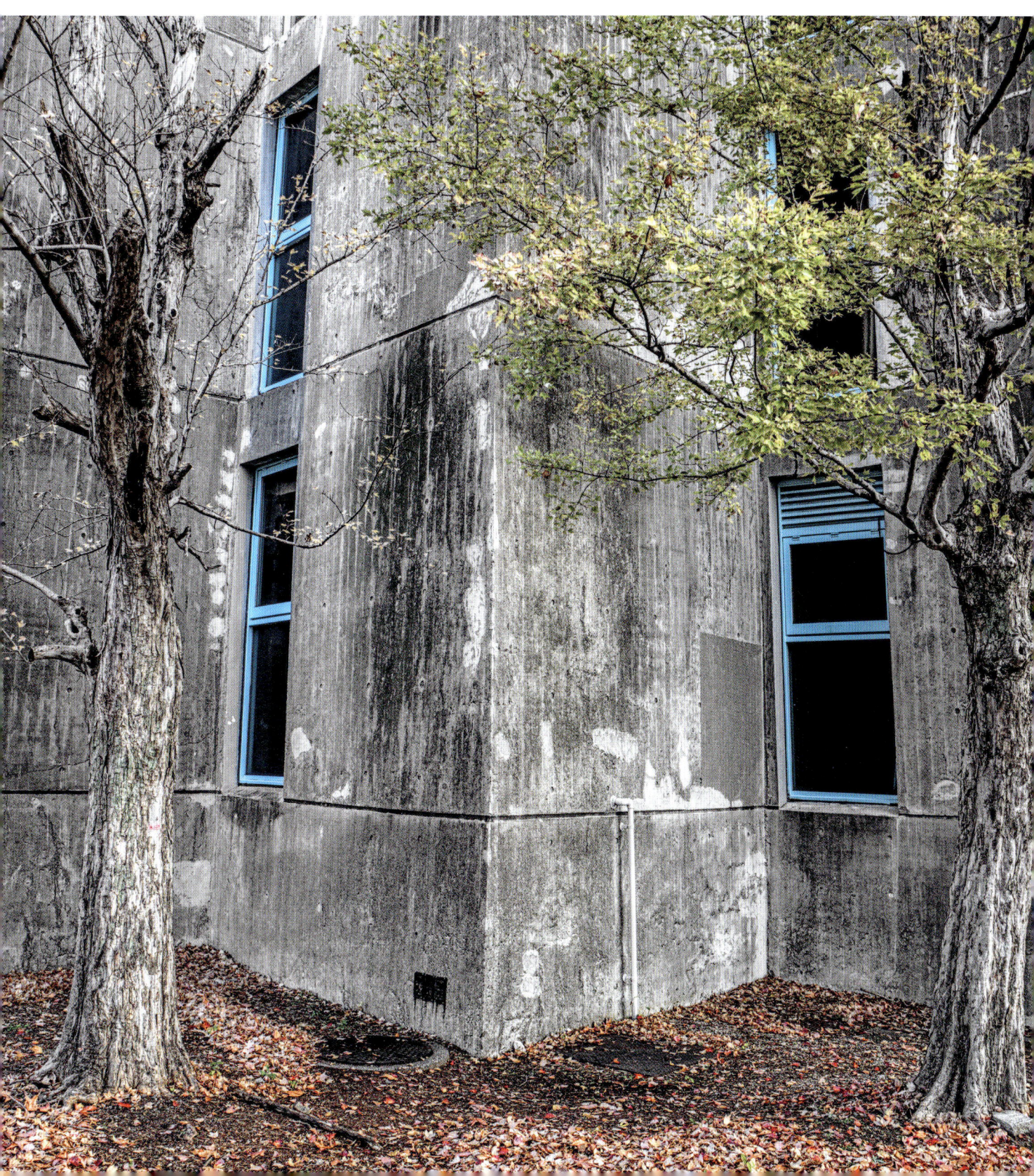

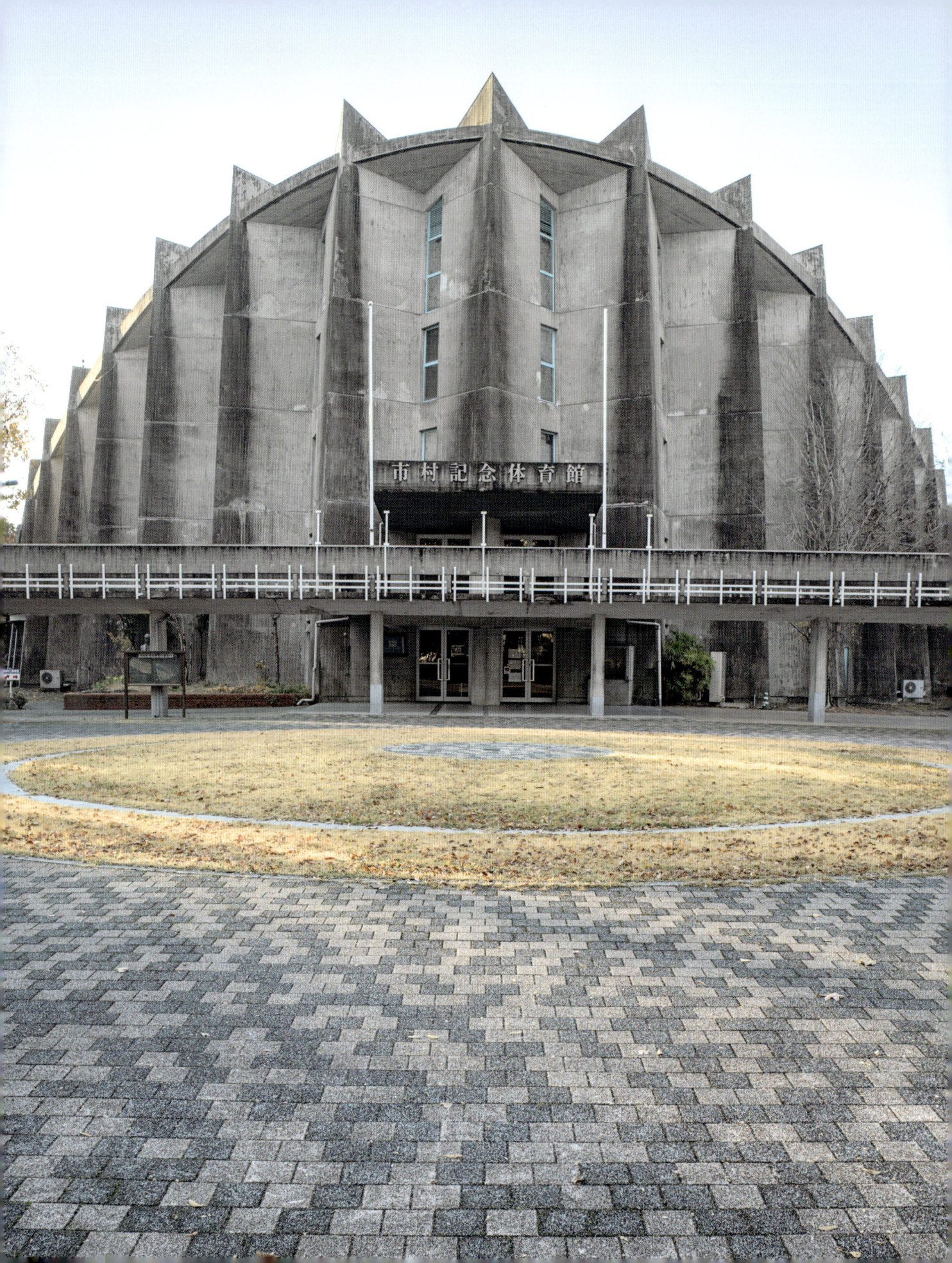

ICHIMURA MEMORIAL GYMNASIUM

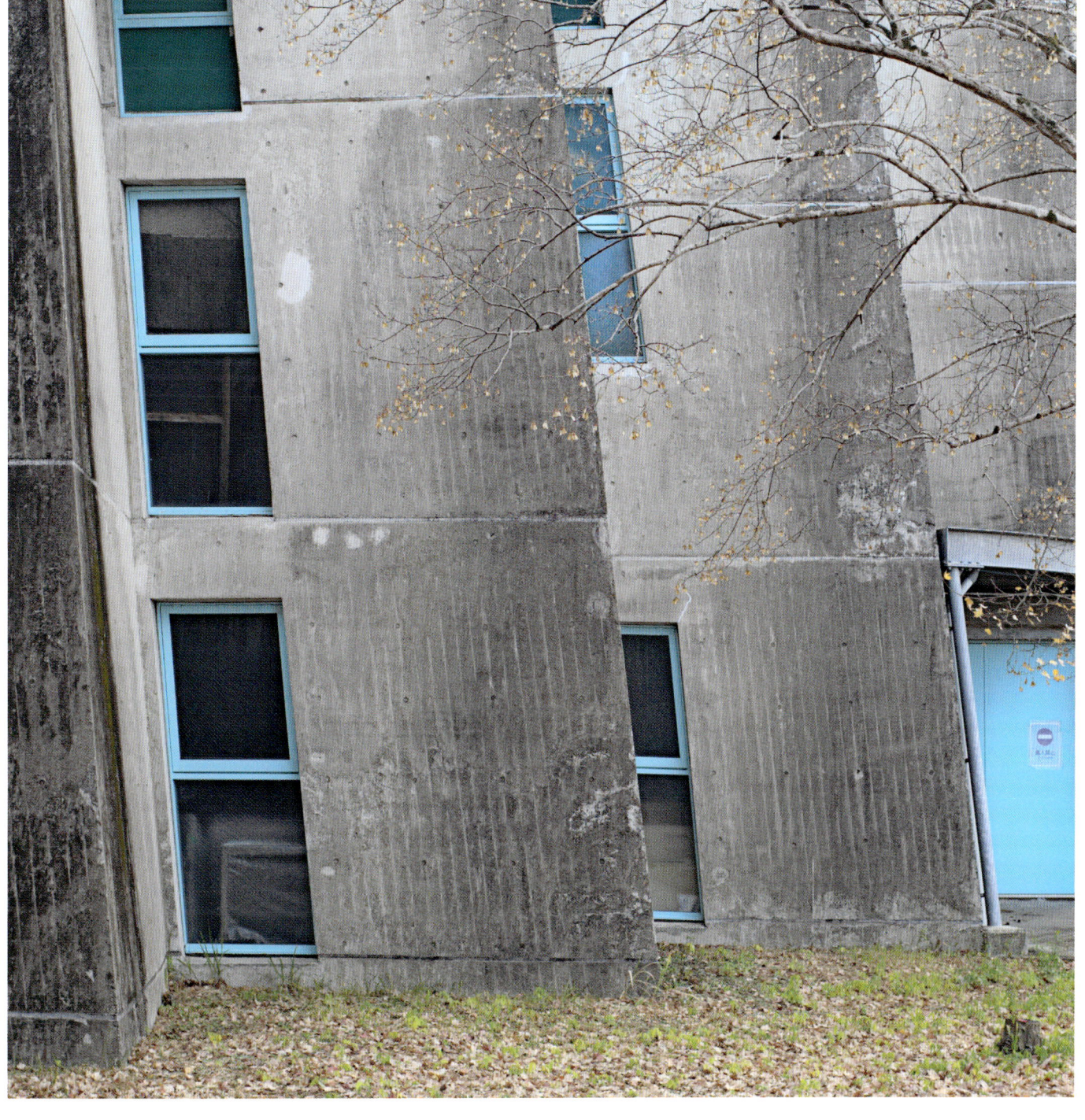

CHIKATSU ASUKA HISTORICAL MUSEUM

OSAKA · Architect: ANDO Tadao · Completed 1994

Tucked within Osaka's lush Minamikawachi district, the Chikatsu Asuka Museum acts as a contemporary sentinel amidst Japan's densest region of ancient tumuli (burial grounds). With more than one hundred historical tombs dotting the green valley, this museum is a research and exhibition hub for the rich tumulus culture that characterizes the area. It serves as an architectural confluence where the conceptual might of Japan's ancestors inspires modern design.

Ando's architectural language here is one of reverence and innovation. The museum is a structural tumulus for the living, its roof a vast staircase plaza extending 60 metres in width and 120 metres in depth, inviting visitors to climb and engage with history. The grand staircase, a modern interpretation of ancient mounds, doubles as an amphitheatre, connecting people to the storied landscape with every step.

The concrete construction pierces the stair plaza, creating a profound interior that mimics the quietude of the "underworld", aligning with the symbolic function of the tombs it honours. This is Ando's first endeavour to sculpt such a grandiose, summer-style staircase, which not only accentuates the museum's role in education and events but also integrates function with form in a setting blessed by nature.

The Chikatsu Asuka Museum, enveloped by walking trails that meander around the tomb sites, gradually reveals itself behind a hillock. Its rooftop, entirely enrobed by the grand staircase, presents a modern-day tumulus contrasted against the historical *shigechi* mounds. The museum's basement holds a permanent exhibition space, where Ando's creative prowess is on full display – a cross-section of tradition and contemporary architecture.

This museum is more than a container for artefacts; it is a stage for the valley's greenery, a place of learning where children gather in outdoor classrooms to understand their ancestors' legacy. Ando's philosophy that public buildings should draw people to nature is realized in every corner of this edifice. Visitors are meant to experience the museum with all senses, becoming part of a living dialogue between past and present. Thus, the Chikatsu Asuka Museum exhibits Ando's ability to create architecture that communicates with nature and touches the soul.

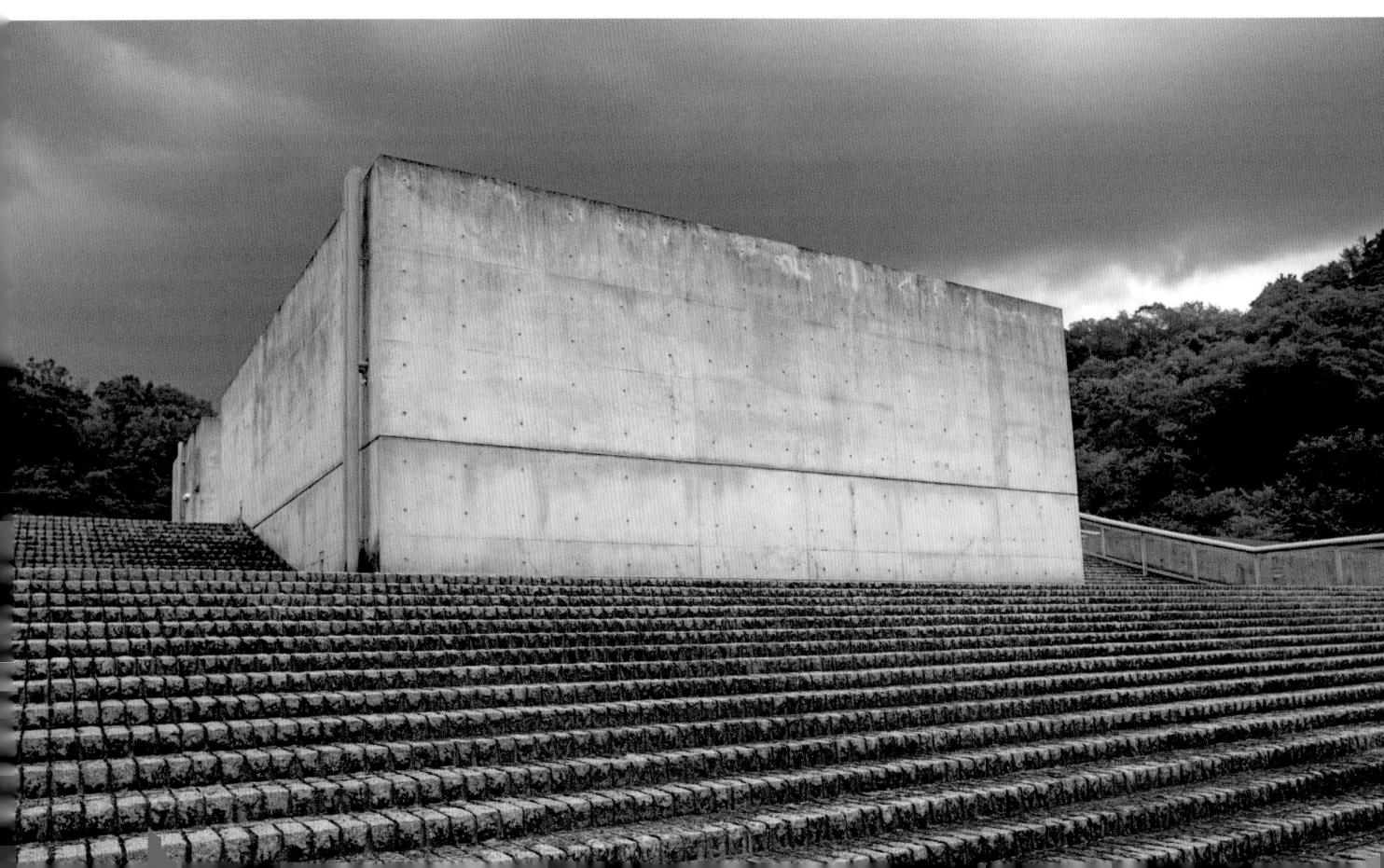

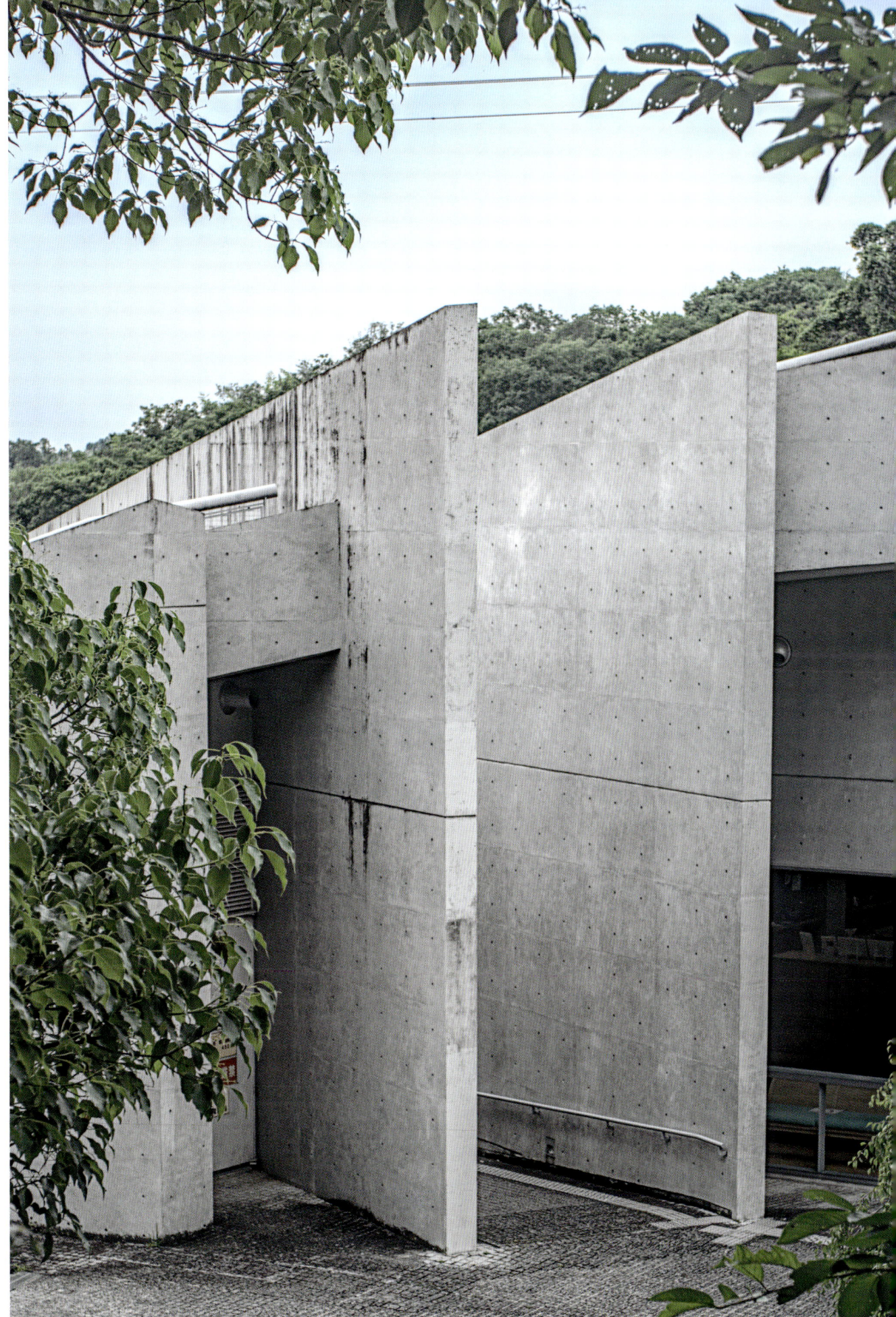

OKUMA MEMORIAL HALL

SAGA · Architect: IMAI Kenji · Completed 1966

The Shigenobu Okuma Memorial Hall is a sculptural allegory to the life and legacy of a statesman who played a key role in transforming Japan into a modern state. Kenji Imai, an alumnus and professor at Waseda University founded by Okuma, crafted this structure with an inventive interpretation, drawing on elements from the Goetheanum in Domach, Switzerland. The building's façade, abstract yet personified, evokes Okuma's visage, while its architectural limbs stretch out in poised equilibrium. A poignant void in the wall symbolizes Okuma's resilience, his survival from a bomb attack that claimed his right leg. This hall honours Okuma's stature as a reformative politician and educator whilst showing Imai's architectural prowess, influenced by his exposure to the works of Gaudi. Beyond its concrete and curves, the hall echoes the spirit of a figure deeply etched in Japan's modernization, an embodiment of memory eternally anchored in Saga's cultural terrain.

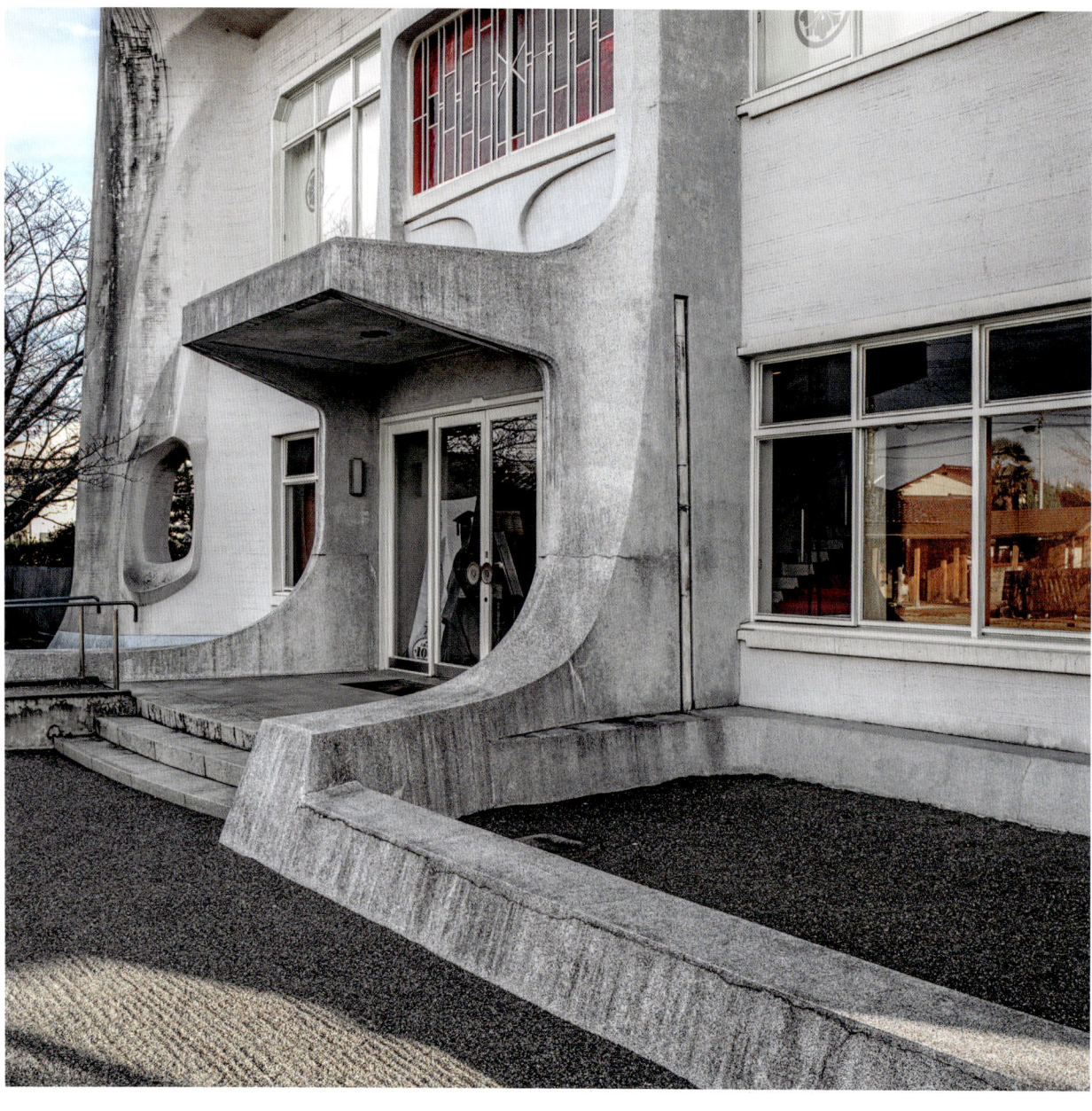

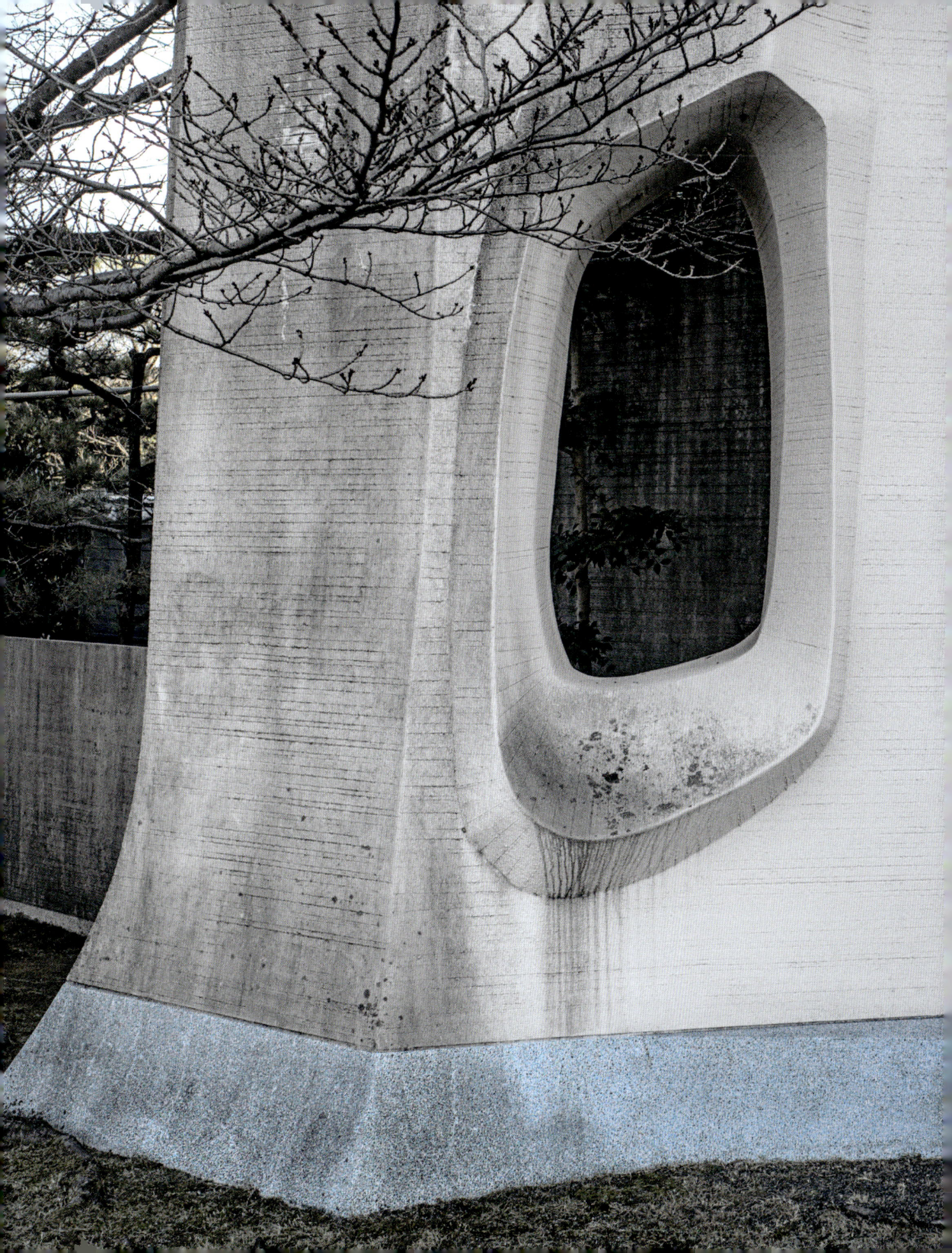

SHIBUYA EXTENSION

TOKYO · Architect: ANDO Tadao · Completed 2008

Shibuya Station squats beneath the streets like a futuristically designed *chichusen* – an underground spaceship – where travellers board their trains. Conceived by Tadao Ando, a trailblazer in the architectural realm, the station is a subterranean haven of Brutalist minimalism, sculpted with precision from prefabricated glass fibre-reinforced concrete (GFRC) bricks that shape every facet of its expansive, eighty-by-twenty-four-metre interior.

In his trademark style, Ando meshes the elements within Shibuya Station, implementing innovative ventilation that harnesses the trains' thermal currents to draw fresh air through the central atrium, eschewing conventional air conditioning. The outer "hull" and platform below are veined with water pipes, circulating coolness and further tempering the air naturally. I give myself a pat on the back for capturing the nanosecond in which no commuter ruined the shot. Indoor trees incorporated into the original design appear absent.

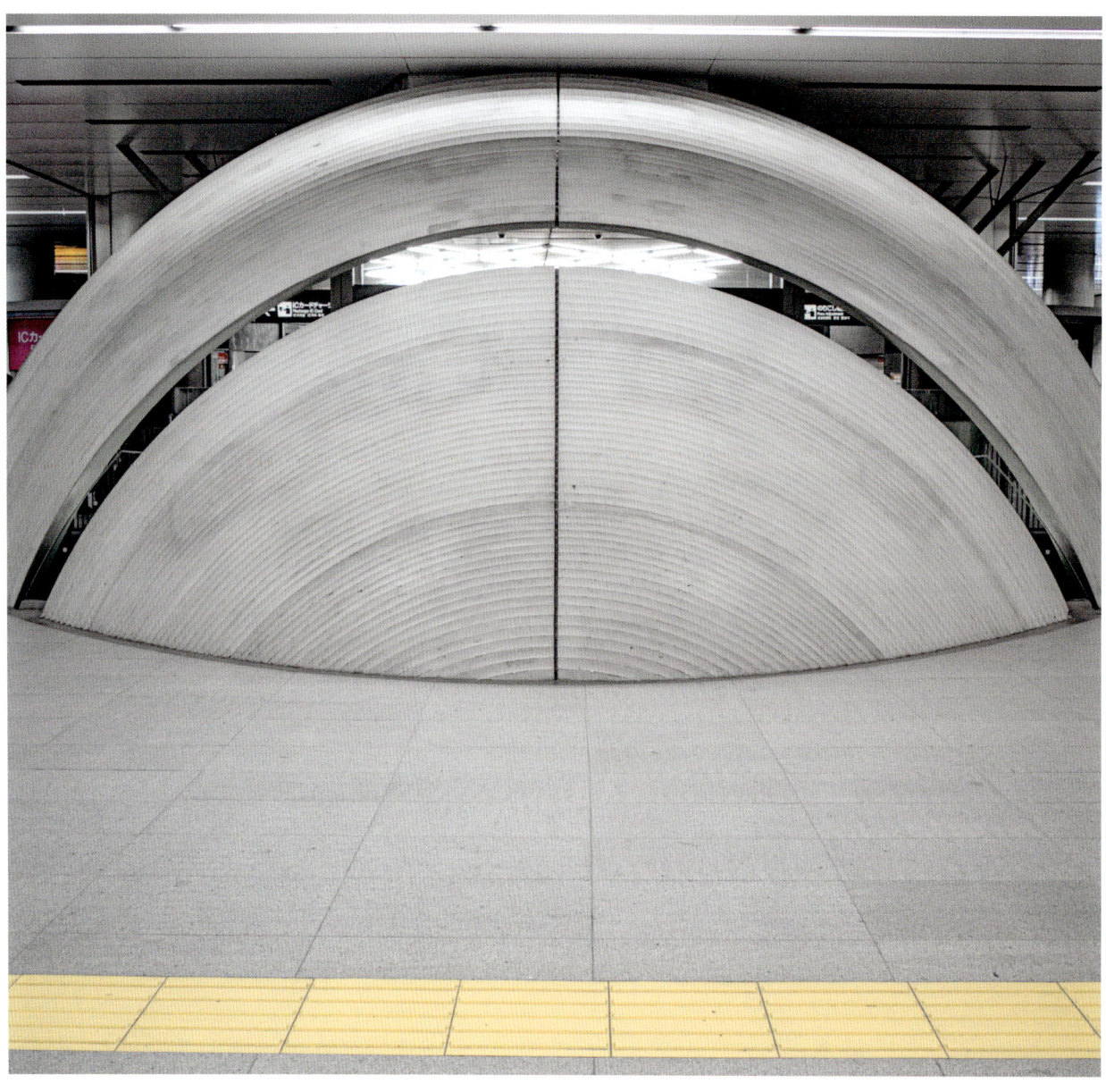

SEA WALL

OKINAWA

In Okinawa, with its intricate coastal mosaic kissed by the Pacific, pentapods are the unsung guardians against nature's might. These five-pronged concrete coastal custodians serve a crucial role in mitigating the relentless erosion wrought by waves and storms, preserving both the natural beauty and the very integrity of Okinawa's shores. Their strategic placement along beaches and waterfronts forms a bulwark that blunts the power of incoming waves, safeguarding the habitat for marine life and the tranquillity of coastal communities.

The importance of pentapods transcends their functional duty; they are emblematic of Okinawa's resilience and respect for nature. By installing these concrete protectors, Okinawa demonstrates the need to live in harmony with the sea – a force capable of both nurturing and reclaiming. The coastal armoury indicates in a utilitarian fashion the island's ongoing balance between human habitation and environmental stewardship. Not to mention the fact it complements the cobalt and turquoise seas perfectly!

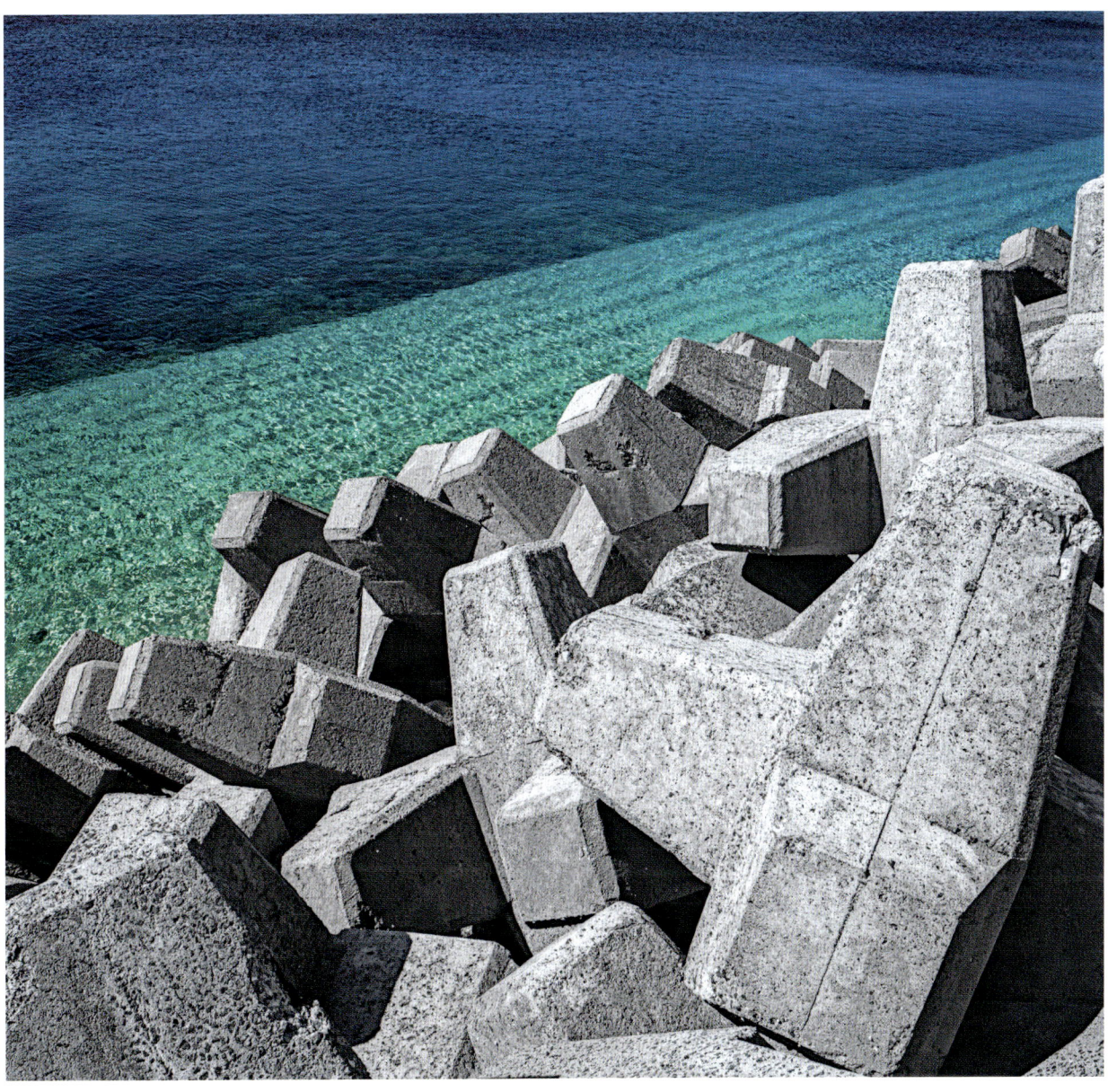

TAMA ART UNIVERSITY LIBRARY (HACHIOJI CAMPUS)

TOKYO · Architect: ITO Toyo · Completed 2007

Nestled in Tokyo's suburbs, the Tama Art University Library unfurls behind a verdant forecourt, inviting academic pilgrims up a gentle slope to a temple of knowledge. Stepping through its portals, one encounters an expansive ground-level gallery – less of a gateway to books, more of a cerebral crossroads, where ideas mingle as freely as the students and staff crossing paths.

Providing openness and intersection, the building's signature arches – steel bones cloaked in concrete skin – are strewn as if by a whimsical giant's hand, curving and converging in an academic dance. These slender arcs, uniform in width yet varying in reach, craft a landscape where art and intellect play hide-and-seek.

Wandering beneath these arches, the space transforms from a sunlit cloister to shadowed tunnels, teasing the senses and sparking the imagination. Here, every seeker engages with tomes and tales in spaces as ethereal as a forest's whisper and a cavern's echo, making the library both a house of books and a chamber for creative exploration and serendipitous exchange in the university's academic sanctuary.

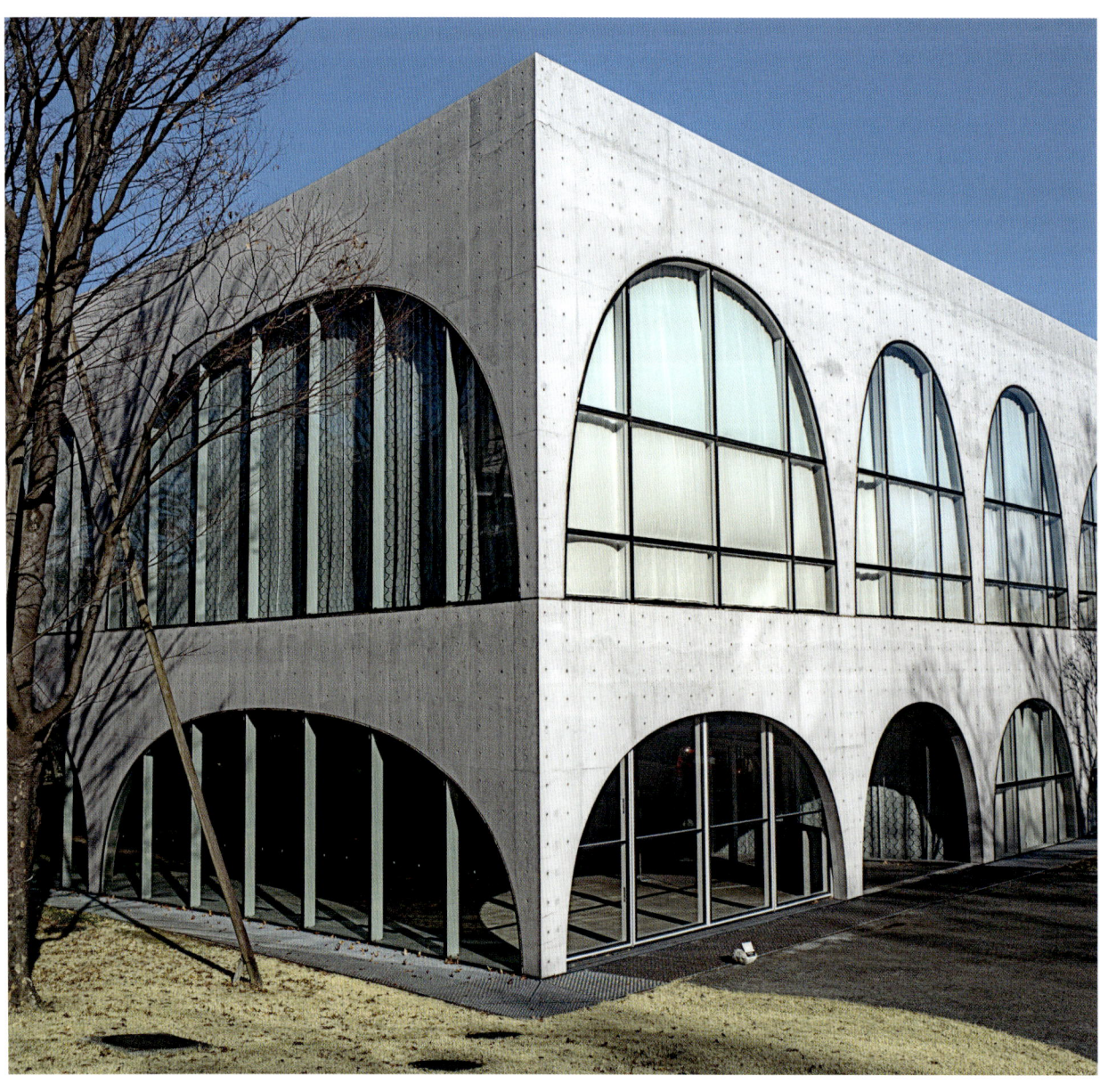

SHIME COAL MINE TOWER

FUKUOKA · Completed 1943

The Shime Coal Mine Shaft in Fukuoka is a sober towering relic of industrial might, a precursor to the Brutalist movement with its unadorned concrete form looming over the landscape. Built in 1943, it predates the movement's peak yet provides the same raw aesthetic, flaunting the bare, utilitarian beauty of concrete architecture. Its formidable tower, perforated by geometric openings, stretches towards the sky with an austere grandeur that conjures images from a bygone industrial age.

This imposing structure could easily be a backdrop for a dystopian tale, its monolithic presence offering the perfect playground for fans of the zombie apocalypse genre. It's easy to envision survivalists perched atop, keeping watch over a desolate world below. With its eerie, hollowed-out floors and the harsh functionality of its design, the Shime Coal Mine Shaft is a monument to resilience, a ghostly watchkeeper that continues to captivate and inspire tales of survival and exploration in the face of desolation.

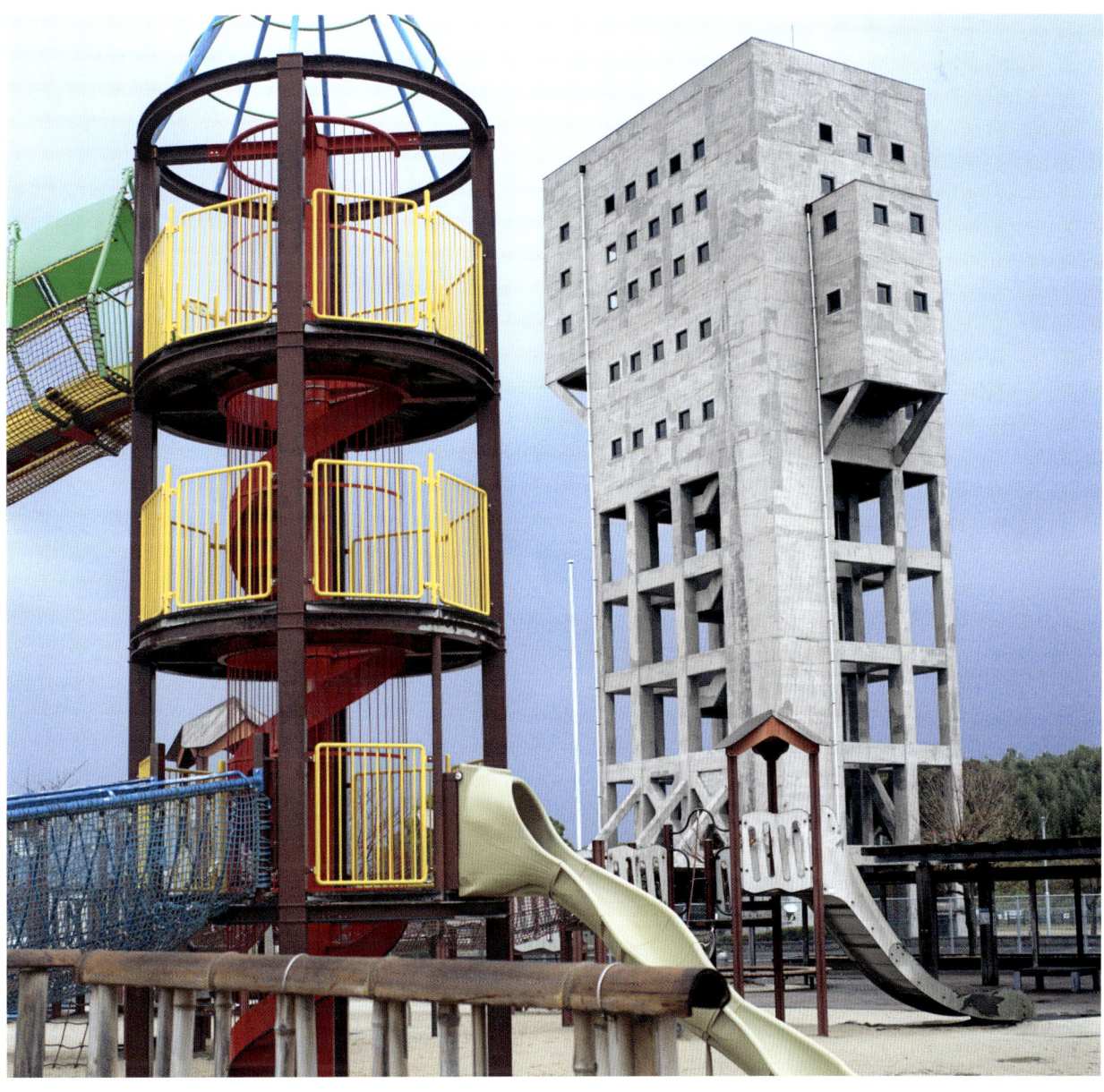

SHIZUOKA PRESS AND BROADCASTING TOWER TOKYO · Architect: TANGE Kenzo · Completed 1967

The Shizuoka Press and Broadcasting Tower is a formidable figure in the skyline, a soaring signal of the Brutalist movement in architecture.

Designed by Kenzo Tange, a legend of the movement, this building is composed of a series of cubic forms that appear to be precariously stacked upon one another, creating an image that is both industrial and sculptural. This visual complexity, a stack of boxes towering over the streets, was enhanced by the building's use of raw, unfinished materials, a hallmark of Brutalist design. I'm not sure why anyone decided to paint it brown.

Completed in 1967, it's both a structure and a pronouncement, featuring a central core from which cantilevered floors extend like branches from a tree. Tange's work at the Shizuoka Press and Broadcasting Tower is recognized for its dramatic use of concrete and its defiance of traditional forms, making it a touchstone of the Brutalist lexicon and an uninterrupted signal of architectural innovation.

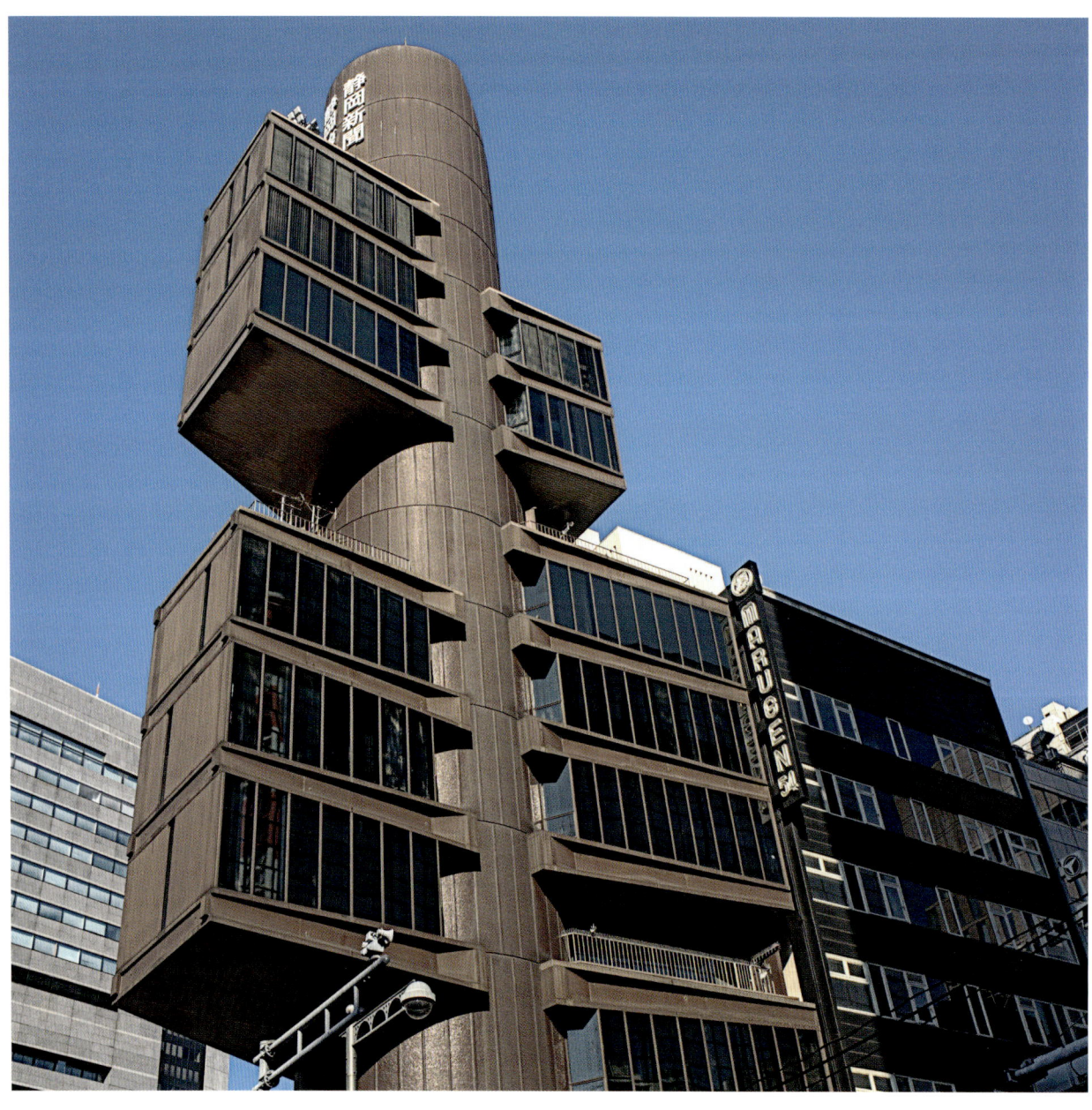

SAGA PREFECTURAL MUSEUM

SAGA · Architect: TAKAHASHI Seiichi · Completed 1970

Crafted to commemorate the Meiji Restoration's centenary, the Saga Prefectural Museum was conceived as a foundation for the region's ascension. Seiichi Takahashi's architectural recipe mixes the conventional with a pinch of peculiar, sculpting a cross structure that reaches ambitiously skywards. It's a brash approach that earned the museum the Architectural Institute of Japan Award, yet its dissonance with Saga's local clime is no design faux pas, but a clever nod to the thrill of the unexpected.

A pioneer in utilizing precast concrete, the museum's circulation system – a concrete spine – provides not only structural support but also a flexible stage for the ever-shifting theatre of exhibitions. It's a Metabolist wink, hinting at a future of adaptable spaces. Visitors step into a space where the art of unease is unnervingly curated, provoking thought and conversation. In this shrine to innovation, Takahashi dares us to find comfort in the unusual, to see growth in the challenge of change.

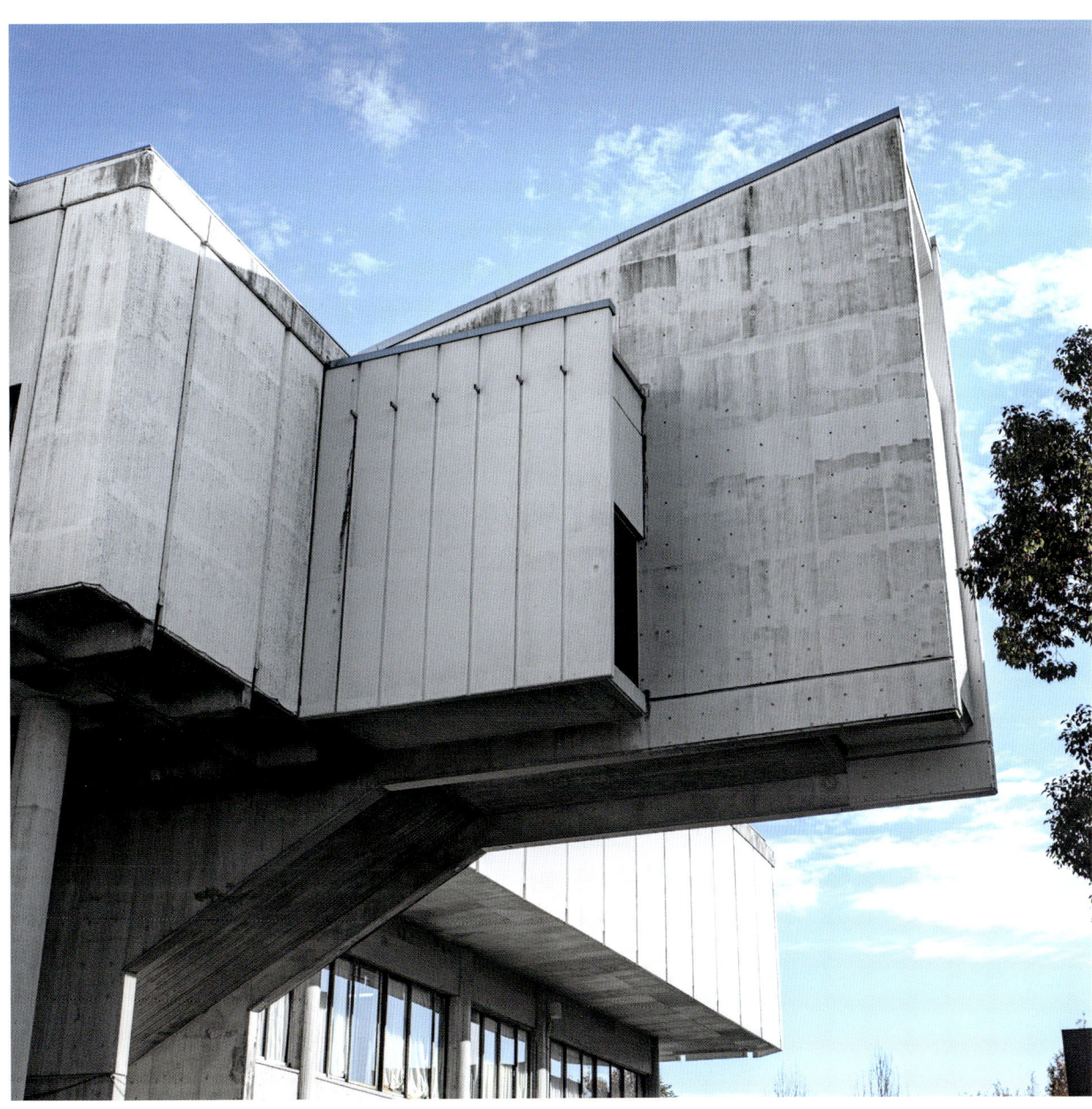

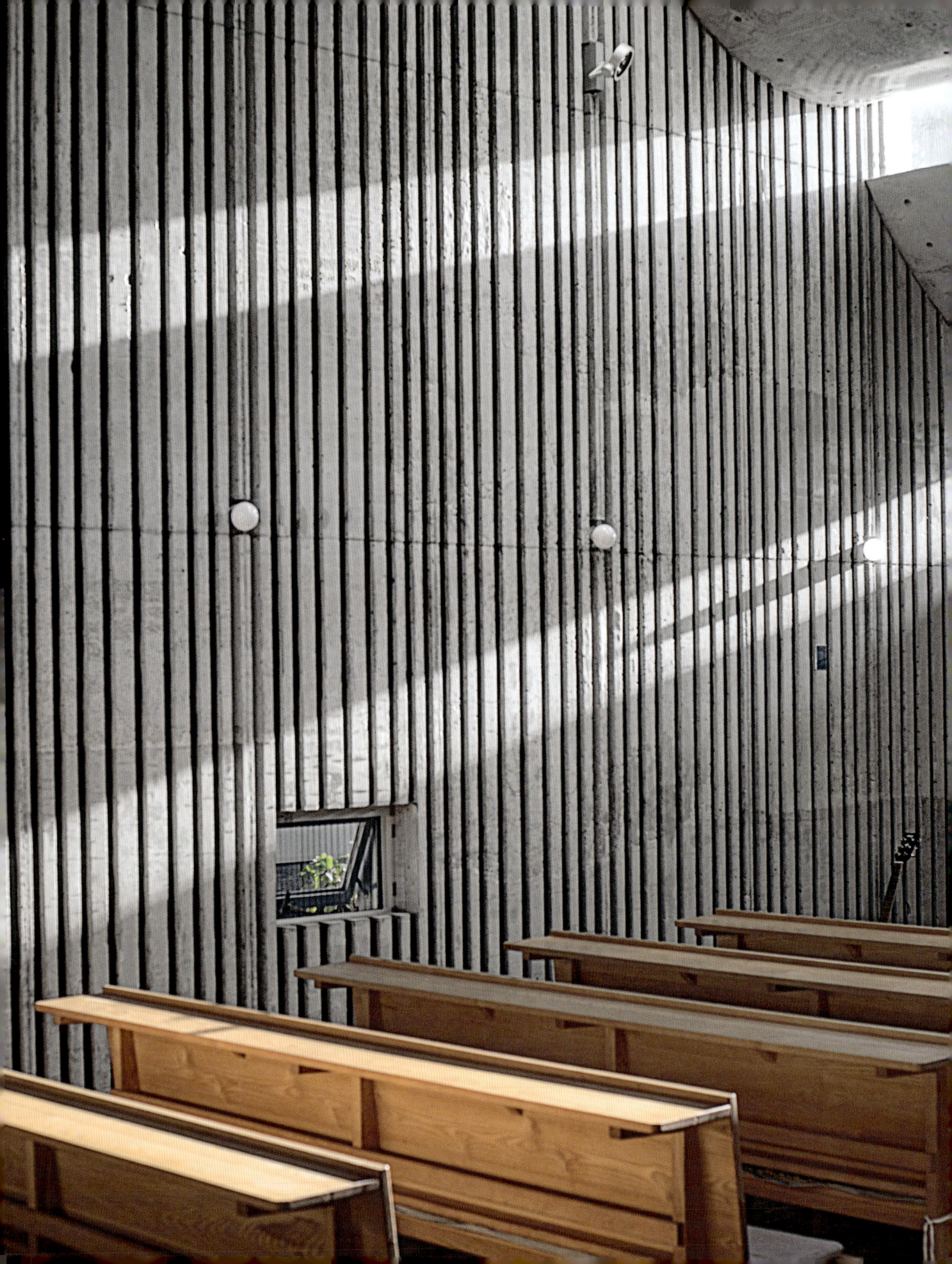

SHONAN CHURCH

FUJISAWA, KANAGAWA PREFECTURE · Architect: HOSAKA Takeshi · Completed 2014

The Shonan Church, with its austere concrete aesthetic, captures a transcendent tranquillity, a modernist sanctuary where light and shadow craft a serene ambience. Its interiors, featuring vertically grooved concrete walls, create a rhythmic interplay of light that filters through, invoking a contemplative mood in the worship space. The church's design, characterized by clean lines and an unembellished material palette, invites parishioners into a meditative reprieve from the world's bustle.

Outside, the church's façade is a minimalist composition, where the solidity of concrete meets the ethereal quality of light, casting a cross-shaped beam inside that serves as a gentle testament to its sacred purpose.

Architecturally, the church is a sincere submission of faith expressed through the language of Brutalism – its form and function in harmony, creating a space that is both spiritually uplifting and grounded in earthly texture.

Shonan Church is a place where the architecture itself becomes a silent sermon on the beauty of simplicity and the profound power of space.

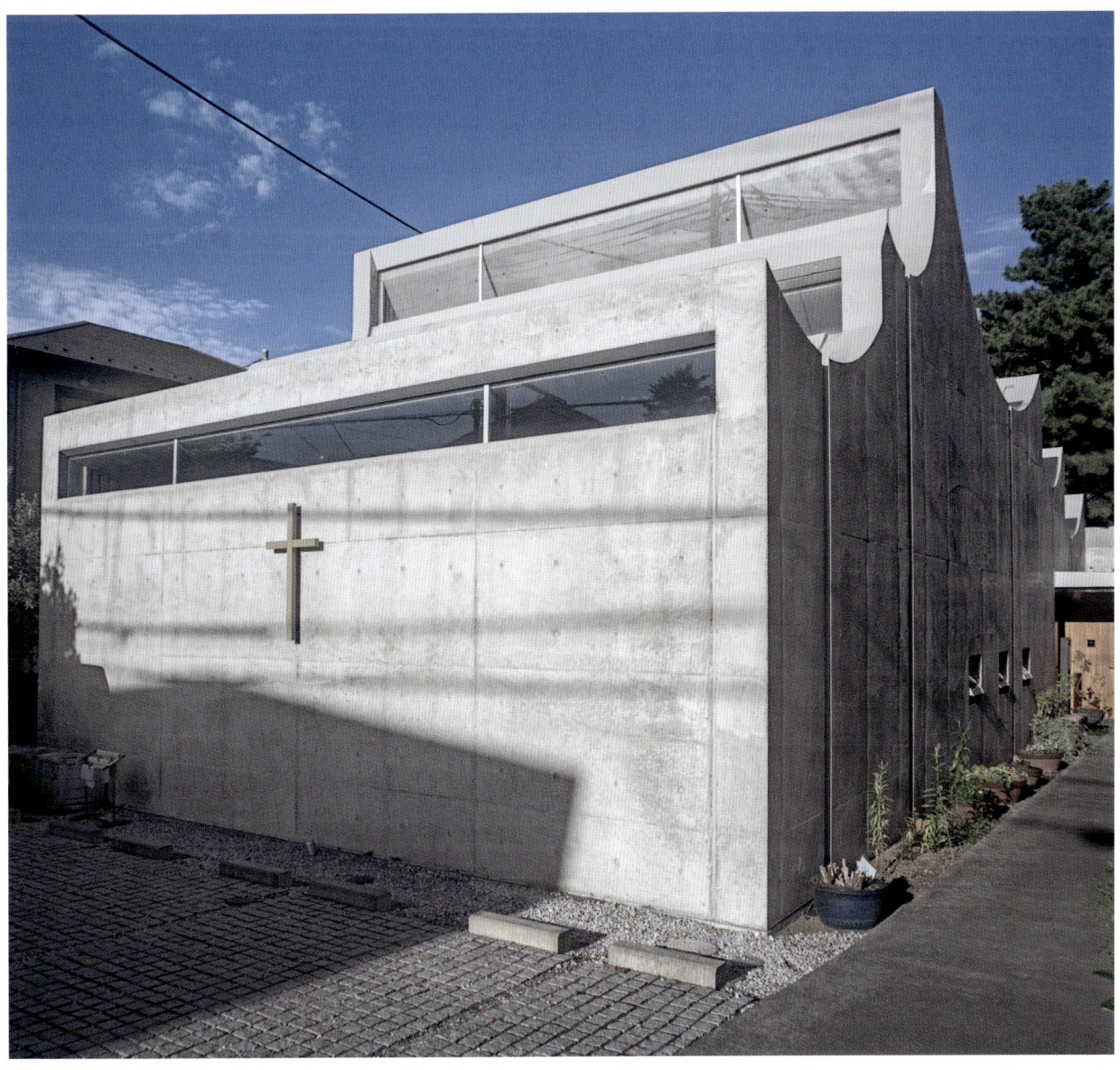

SAYAMAIKE HISTORICAL MUSEUM

OSAKASAYAMA, OSAKA · Architect: ANDO Tadao · Completed 2001

The architectural homage to Luis Barragán is discernible in this space, where a secluded courtyard opens only to the boundless canvas of the sky. Near Sayama Pond, an ancient water reservoir dug in the seventh century, lies a museum dedicated to the narrative of Japan's flood management. Roughly ten kilometres west of the Chikatsu Asuka Museum, this structure reveals itself as an environmental exhibition, in harmony with the storied waters of Sayama. The museum's main body is discreetly ensconced into the landscape, forming a base that seamlessly extends the pond's embankment, while the display halls and light-admitting towers rise above.

Adopting the embankment's subtle profile, the architecture makes a calm statement yet unveils a dynamic spatial experience – a turn in the pathway suddenly immerses visitors in a grand, historical realm. A water garden, cradled between cascading waterfalls, emerges as the heart of the design.

At the museum's inception, the planting of cherry trees was planned to transform the embankment, an effort to be nourished by local collaboration, foreseeing a time when blossoming trees will encircle the water, marking the project's true completion.

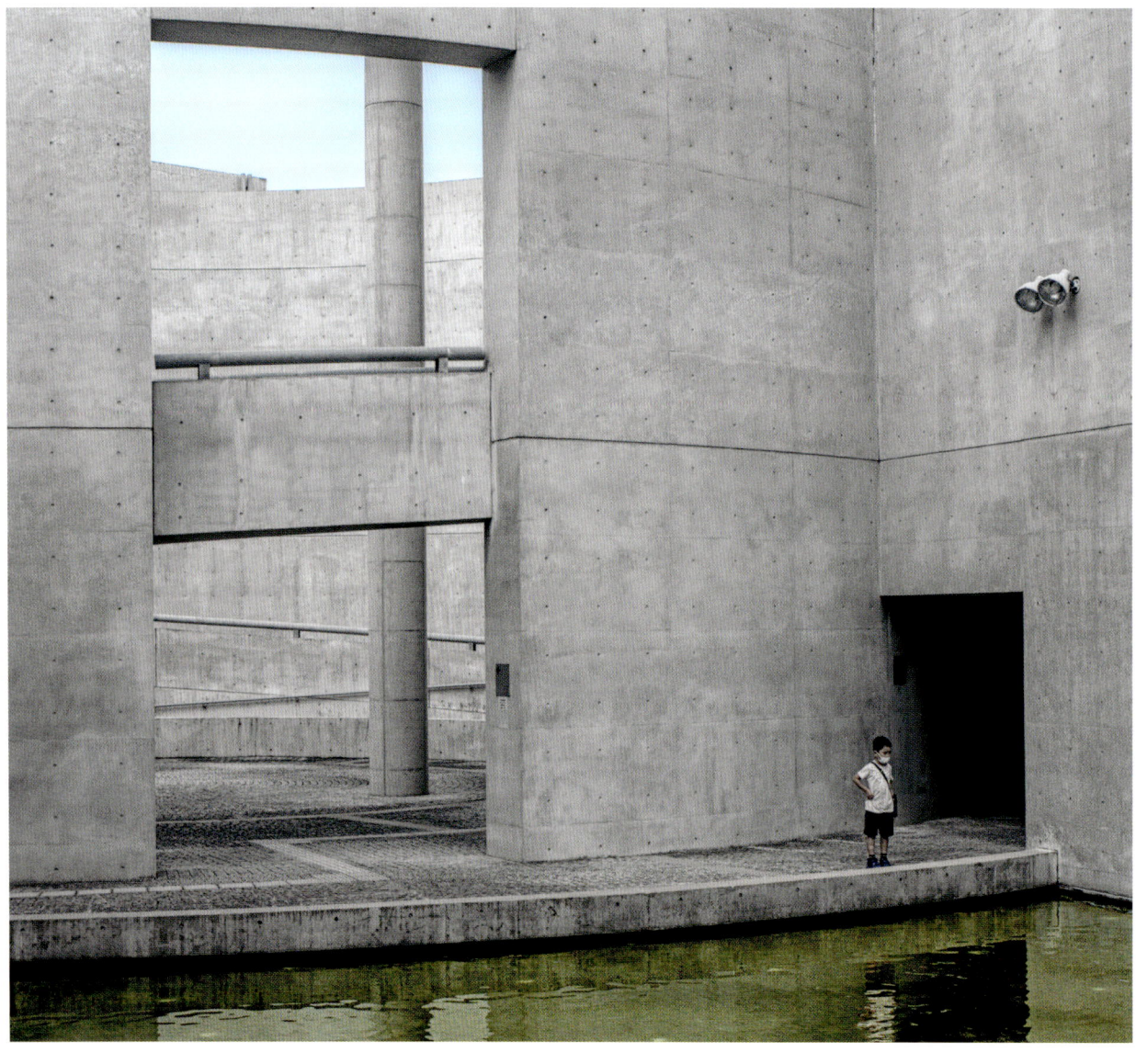

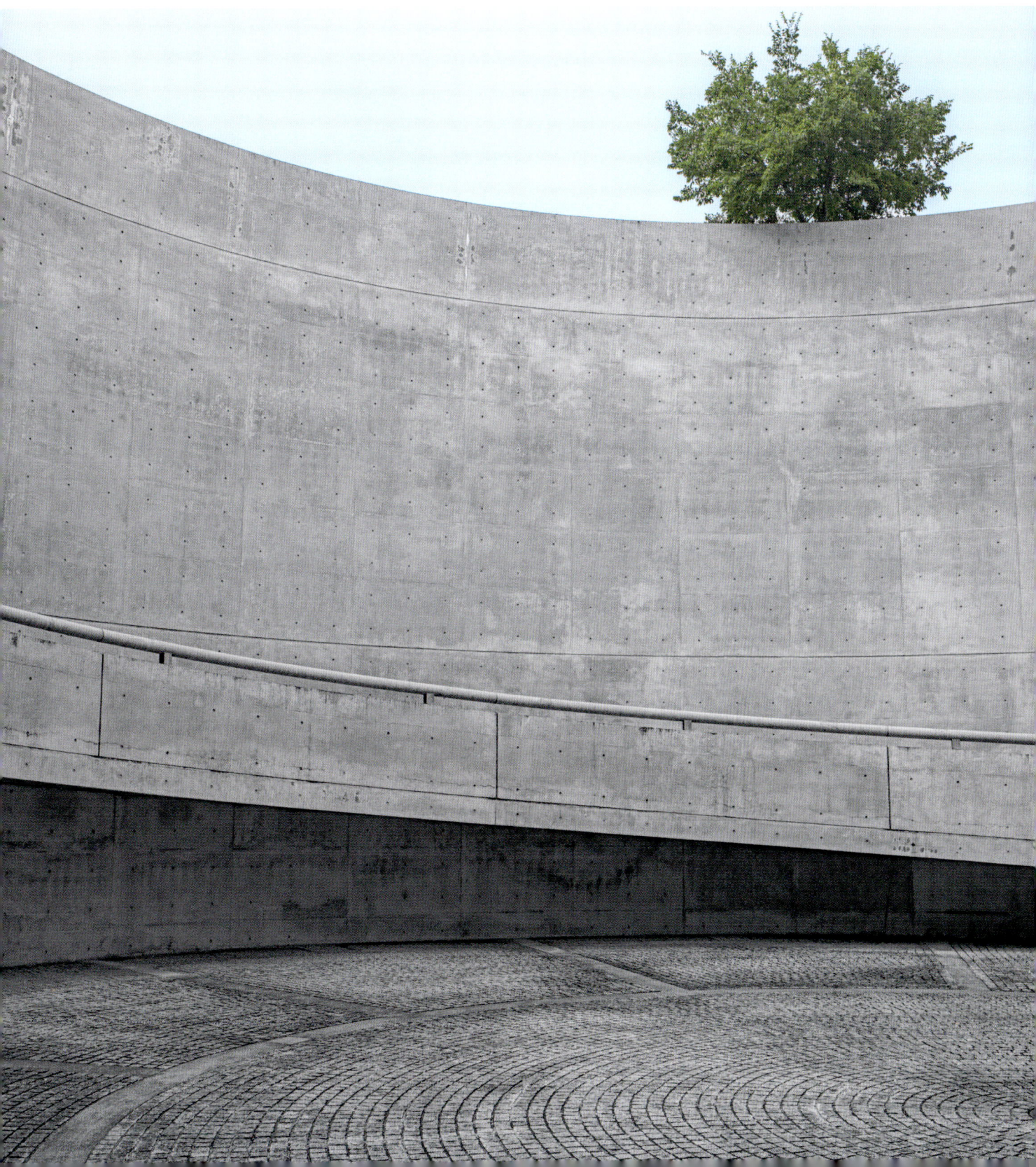

ST MARY'S CATHEDRAL

TOKYO · Architect: TANGE Kenzo · Completed 1964

St Mary's Roman Catholic Cathedral in Tokyo, also reverently known as Tokyo Cathedral, is a spiritual concrete incarnation designed by Kenzo Tange, opened in tandem with the 1964 Tokyo Olympics. This sacred house and the Yoyogi National Gymnasium share an exploration of parabolic forms, soaring to create vast sanctuaries beneath gracefully arched spans. Yet, while the stadium sprang forwards with innovative cable suspension, St Mary's awakens us to Tange's earlier architectural meditations on concrete shell structures.

Envisioned with structural engineer Yoshikatsu Tsuboi, the cathedral's design consists of eight hyperbolic paraboloid shells. These shells pair up, forming quadrants that separate to invite light through glazed fissures, casting a cruciform glow upon the faithful below – a symbol etched into the very floor plan.

Though some critics, like architectural historian David Stewart, regard St Mary's Cathedral with scepticism, decrying its simplistic conceptualization and the blunt symbolism of its cross-shaped light, Tange's commitment to his work was unswerving. The cathedral's quasi-industrial materials and austere detailing might lack the nuanced ecclesiastical understanding of contemporaries Robert Maguire and Keith Murray, but Tange's daring, singular vision carves its own niche in church design.

Surrounded by the mundane, St Mary's lacks a distinguished precinct or a processional approach, the grounds occupied by the secular trappings of car parks and service zones – a lame contrast to Tange's ambition to shape civic spaces within the cityscape.

Nevertheless, the cathedral holds a place of reverence not only in the hearts of its parishioners but also in the annals of Tange's life – it was here, within the embrace of his own architectural creation, that his funeral rites were observed in 2005. St Mary's Cathedral, for all its debated design decisions, remains a monolithic icon of Tange's quest for spiritual expression through the medium of modernist architecture.

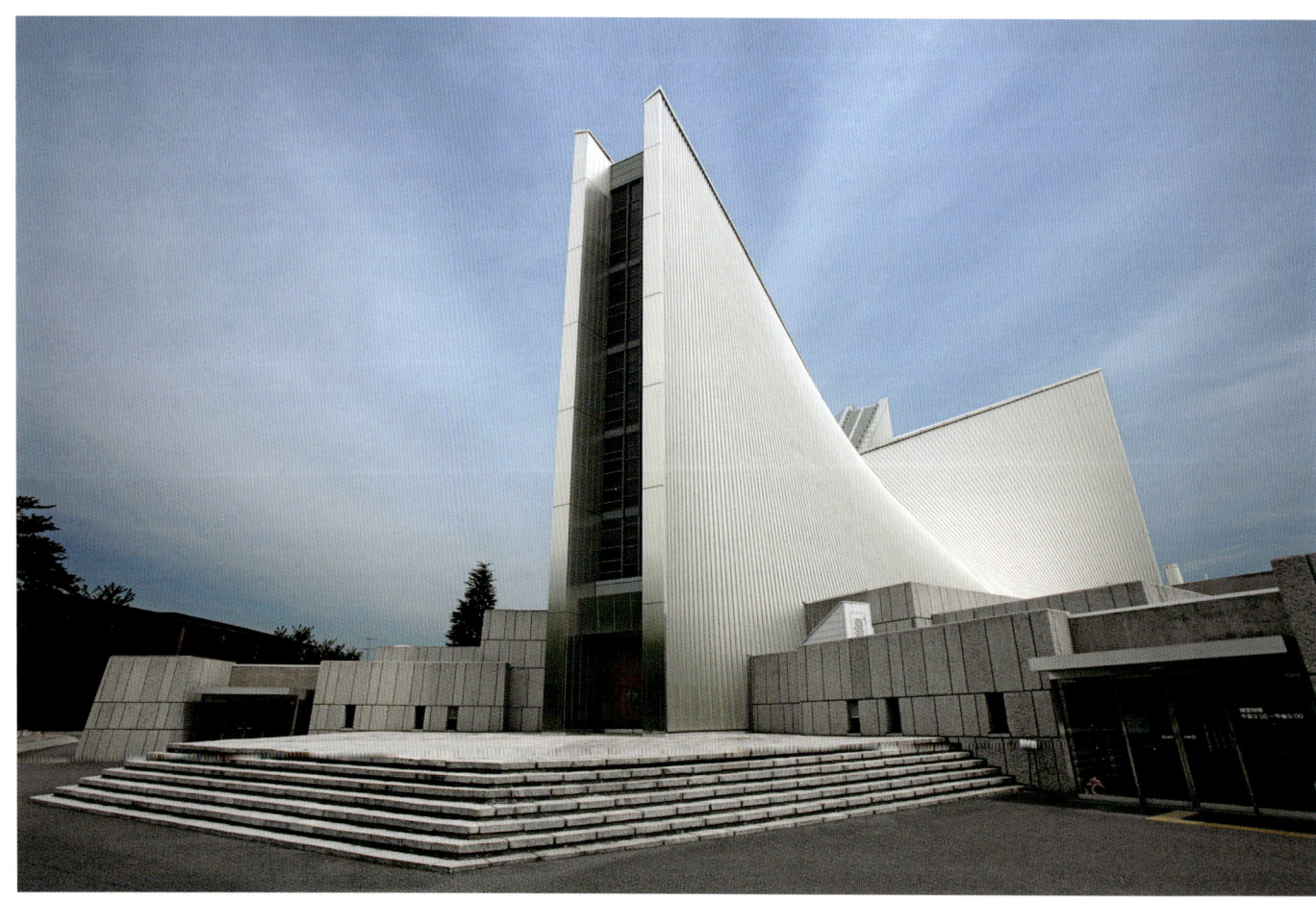

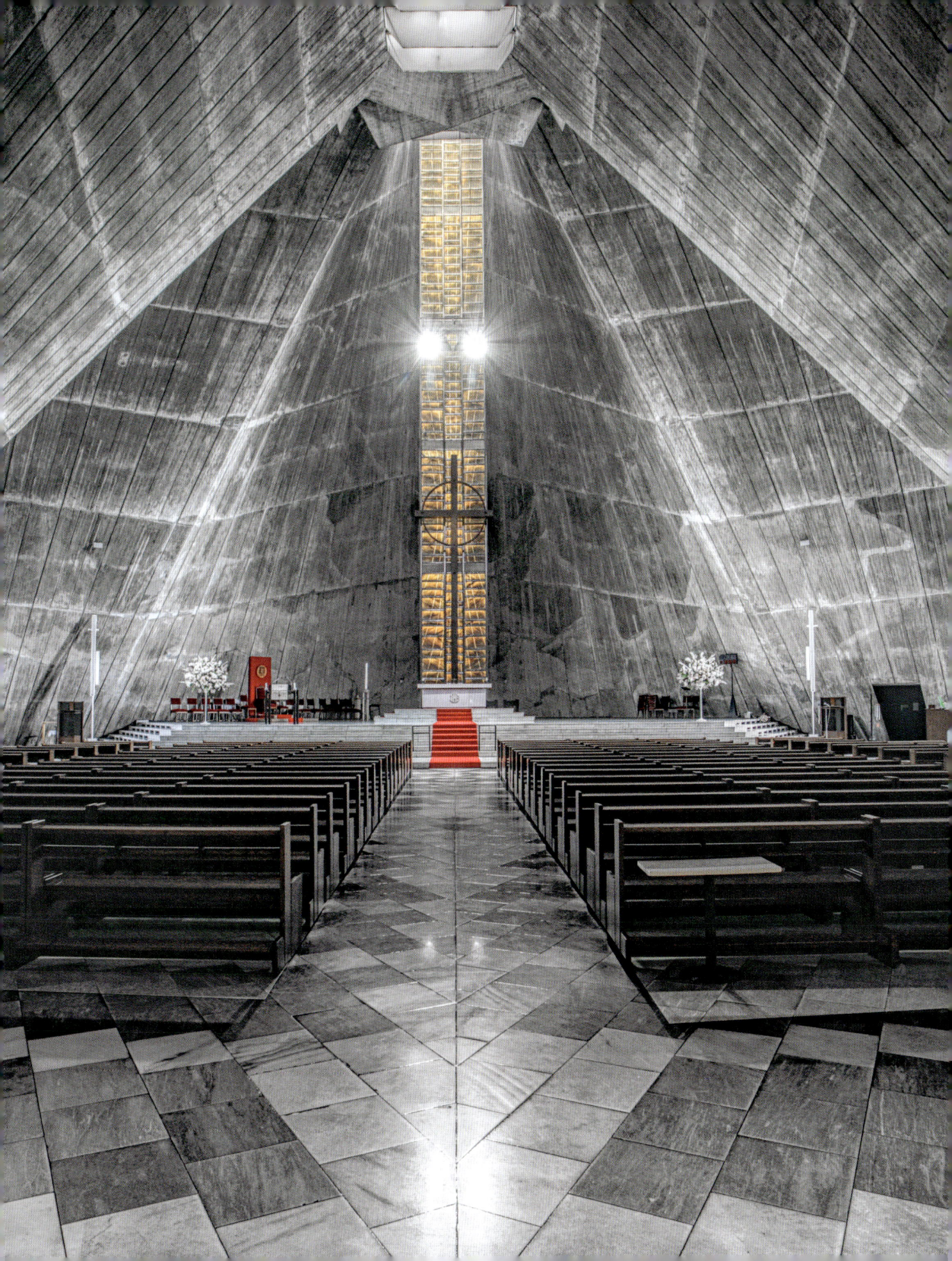

GUNKANJIMA

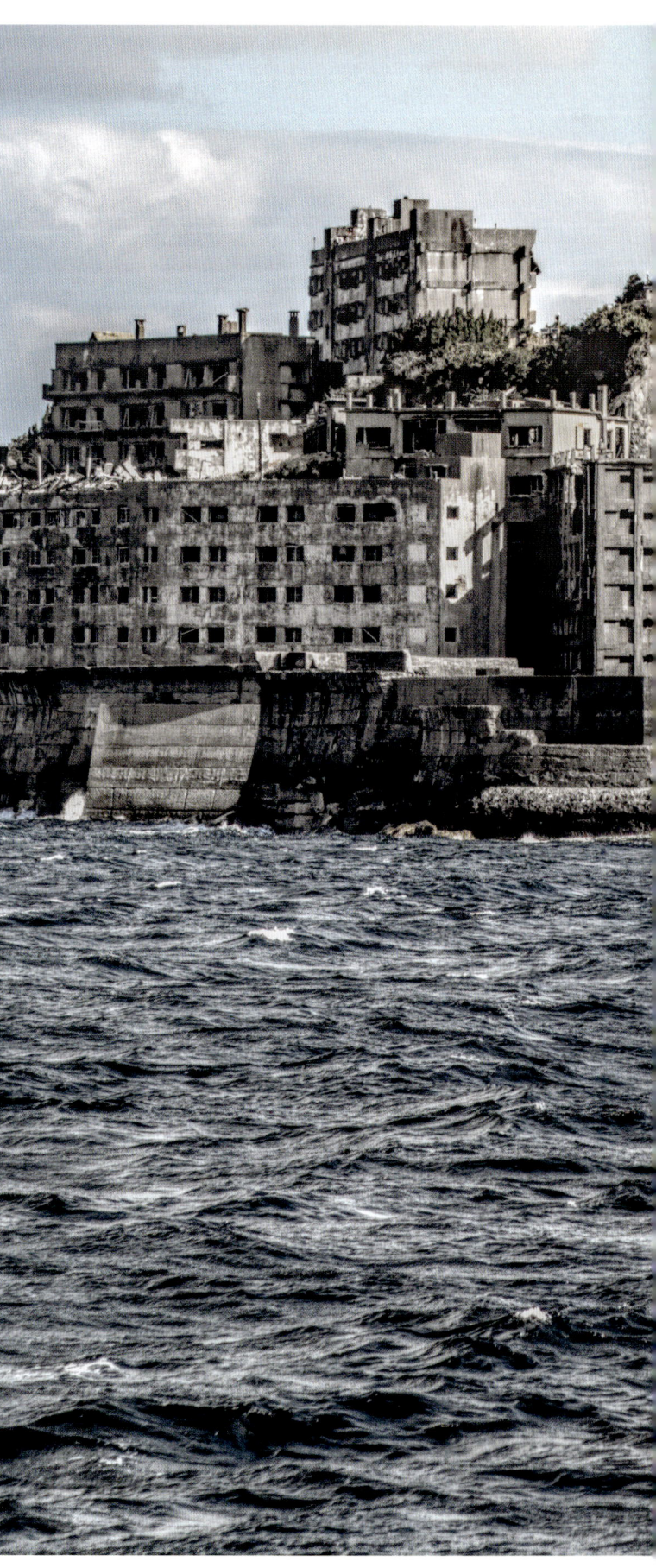

Gunkanjima, also known as Hashima Island, is a small island located off the coast of Nagasaki in Japan. It gained fame for its unique concrete architecture, which gives the island a distinctive and imposing appearance. The name "Gunkanjima" translates to "Battleship Island", a nod to the island's resemblance to a battleship when viewed from a distance.

The island was originally developed in the late nineteenth century as a coal mining facility, and by the 1950s it was one of the most densely populated places in the world, with over 5,000 residents living in the confined space. To accommodate the growing population, a series of high-rise concrete apartment buildings were constructed, giving the island its iconic look.

The concrete architecture of Gunkanjima marks the industrialization and urbanization of Japan during the twentieth century. The buildings were constructed using reinforced concrete, a relatively new building material at the time, which allowed for the construction of tall, sturdy structures. The use of concrete also provided insulation against the harsh sea winds and helped to protect the buildings from the island's humid climate.

Today, Gunkanjima is still a strong reminder of Japan's industrial past. The island was abandoned in the 1970s when the coal mines closed, and it remained uninhabited for decades. In recent years, however, there has been renewed interest in Gunkanjima, and efforts have been made to preserve the island's unique concrete architecture. It has also been designated as a UNESCO World Heritage site, recognizing its historical significance and architectural importance. Featuring in the Bond movie *Skyfall* has aided its fame.

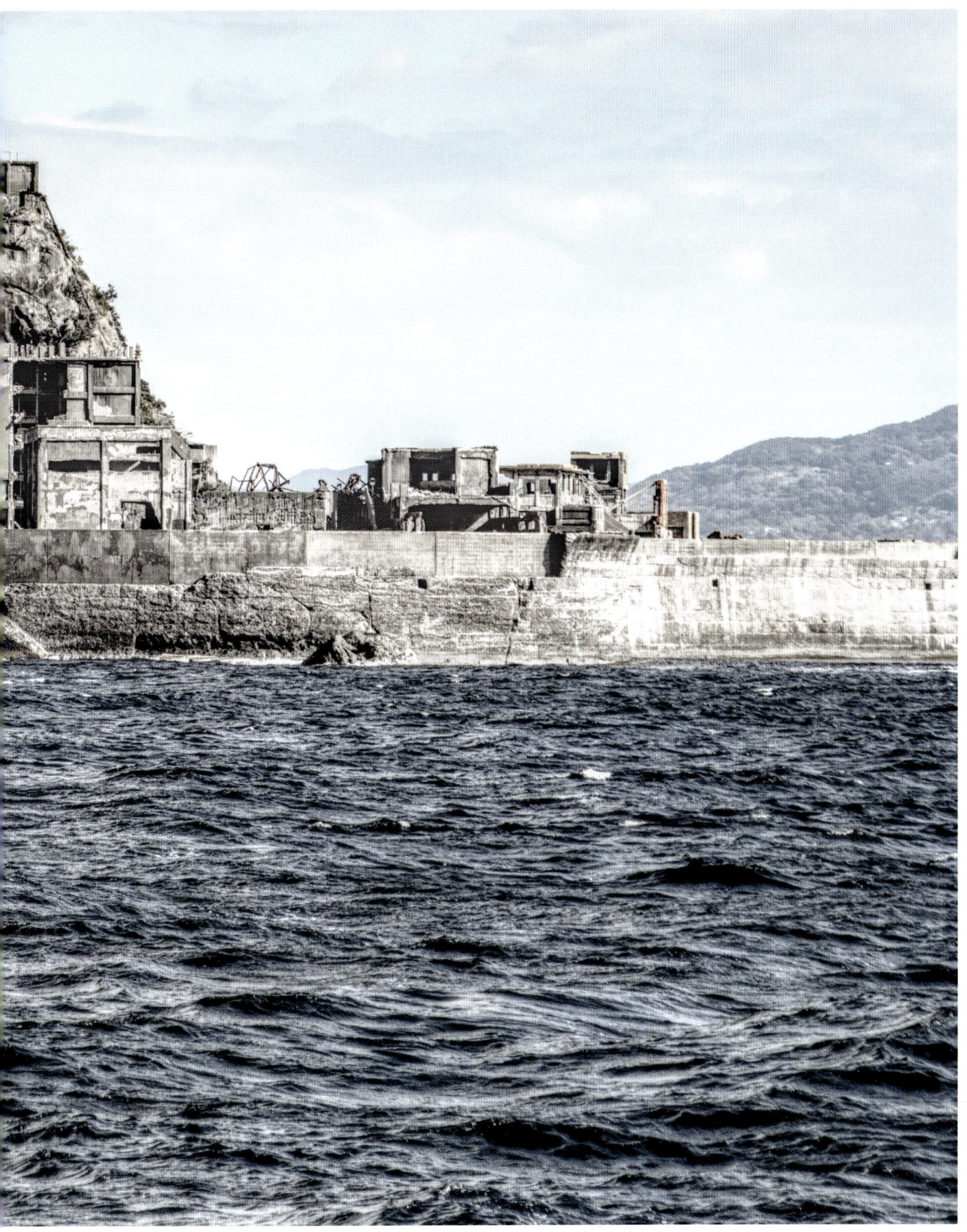

WATARIUM

TOKYO · Architect: Mario Botta · Completed 1990

This building, which houses a bookstore, a café and a gallery, is clad in a striking striped pattern of concrete and granite, displaying the clean, symmetrical geometry characteristic of its Swiss architect, Mario Botta. The external evacuation staircase cleverly utilizes the deformed triangular site, adapting to its unique constraints while enhancing functionality. At the heart of the façade, a dual-purpose loading entrance doubles as a show window, optimizing space on the compact site. Inside, the gallery unravels in a triangular layout, crafted from waffle slabs.

Embarking on a project in Japan, Botta faced a formidable challenge – filling the large shoes of his fellow Swiss predecessor Le Corbusier. Navigating unfamiliar conditions and tailored client demands, this modest yet impactful project spanned five years to completion.

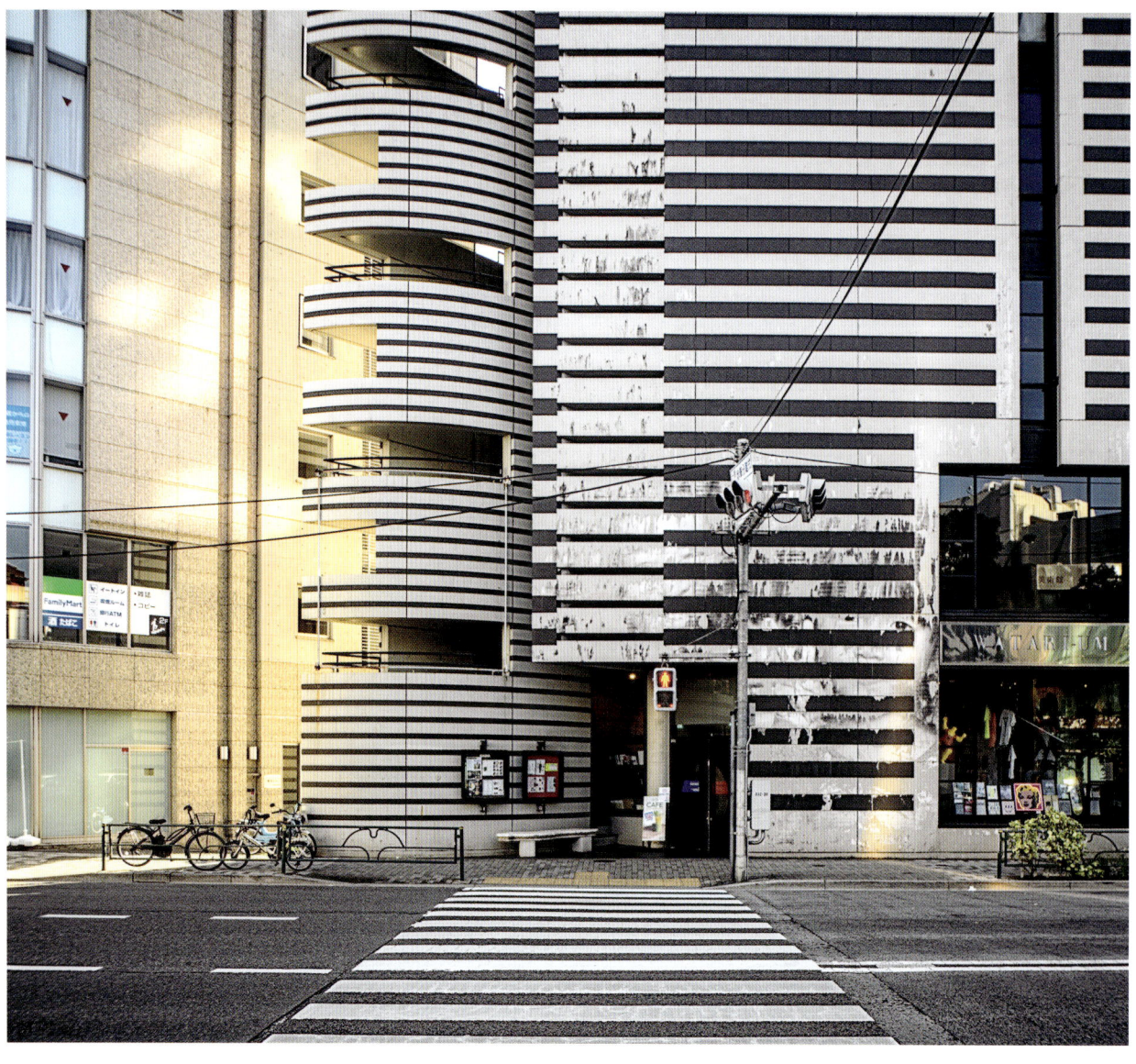

TOWER HOUSE

TOKYO · Architect: AZUMA Takamitsu · Completed 1966

In the 1960s, as suburban residential areas expanded rapidly to accommodate post-war population growth in cities, Takamitsu Azuma introduced a groundbreaking urban housing design. His debut project, a tower-like structure, innovatively utilized a small, 20.56-square-metre triangular lot to feature five storeys above ground and one below. It is just a hop and a skip from Watarium.

The design applied a vertical stratification reminiscent of the traditional Japanese Shoin style, where rooms sequentially connect with slight variations in floor levels throughout the structure. The Tower House's front concrete wall acts as a shield against urban bustle, while strategically placed openings on the east and south sides invite light and air, maintaining privacy and quiet. The entrance, set half a storey above the street, enhances this seclusion.

The building's rough concrete surface, which contrasts with the smoother finishes seen in later Japanese architecture, bears the imprint of handmade formworks, reflecting a deep connection to Japan's timber architecture heritage. Influenced by his mentor Junzo Sakakura and Le Corbusier, Azuma regarded concrete as the modern equivalent of a clay wall, a medium that captures the essence of earth and human touch.

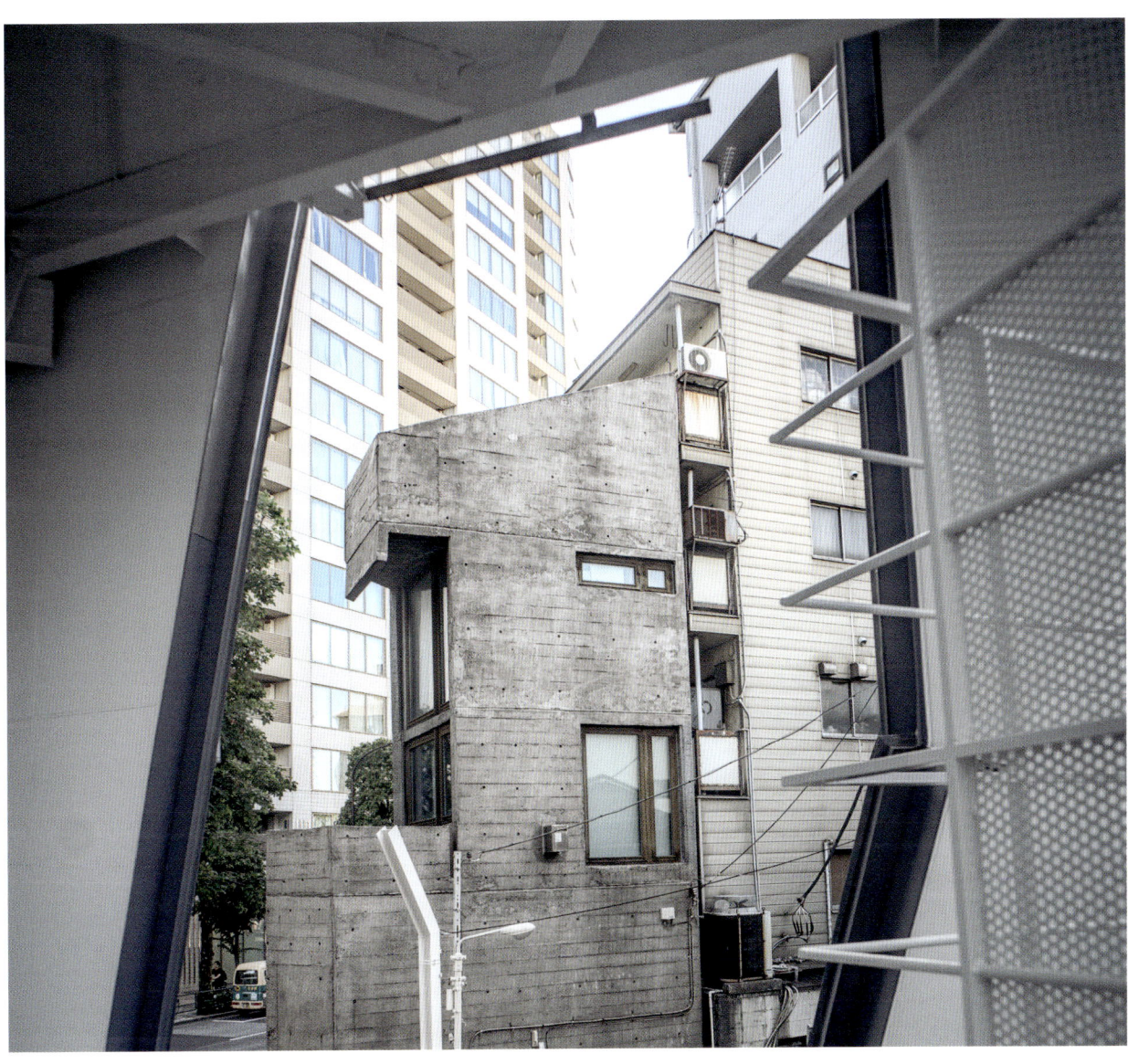

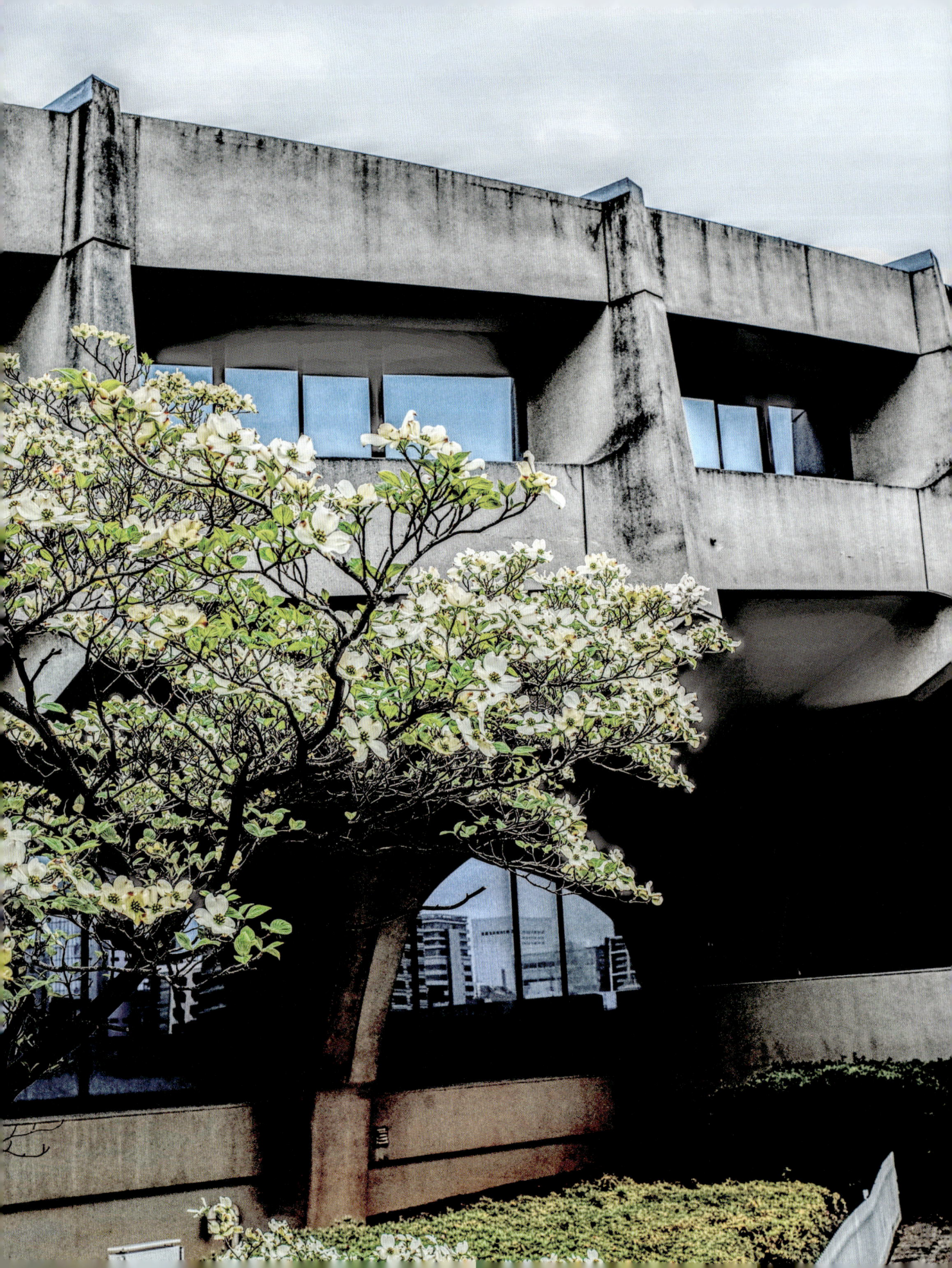

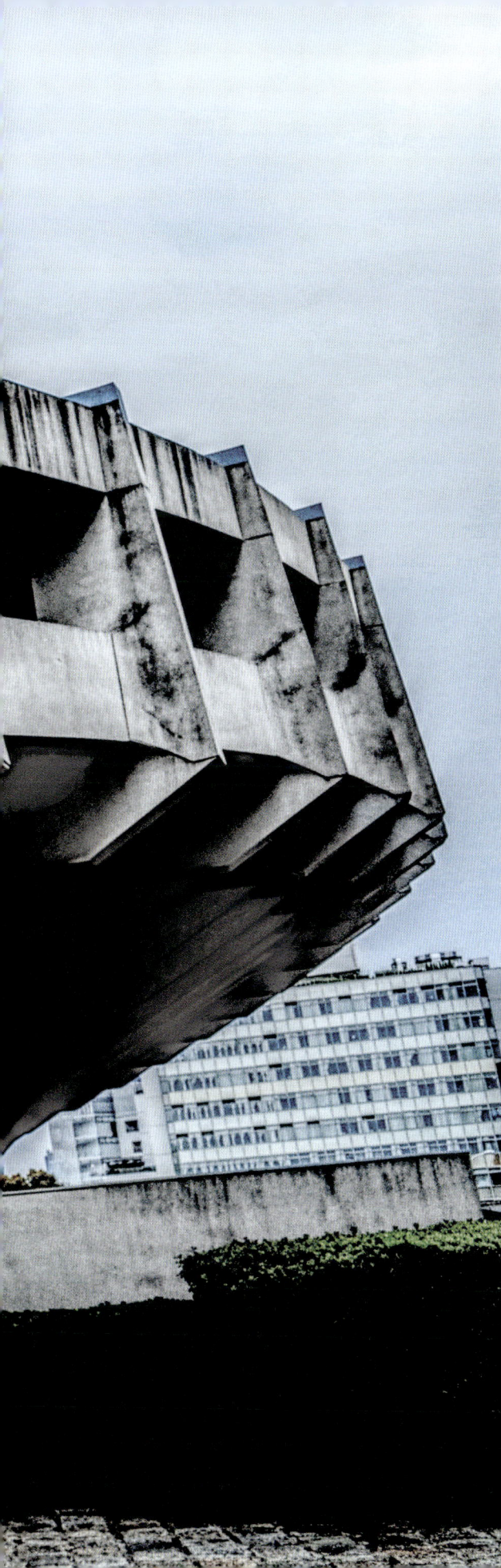

YOYOGI NATIONAL GYMNASIUM

TOKYO · Architect: TANGE Kenzo · Completed 1964

The Yoyogi National Gymnasium, designed by Kenzo Tange for the 1964 Tokyo Olympics, depicts a fascinating intersection of architectural ideologies – between the impermanence cherished by the Metabolists and the monumental permanence typically associated with Brutalism. Tange, a pivotal figure in the Metabolist movement, was profoundly influenced by the potential of concrete, a material traditionally alien to Japanese architecture, which is predominantly wooden. This shift allowed for bolder, more experimental forms, which Tange adeptly manipulated in his design of the stadium.

Yoyogi's gymnasium is a feat of engineering – a sculptural triumph that challenges the conventional notions of architectural form in Tokyo, a city often characterized by its dense, commercial buildings. The stadium's sweeping roof and audacious silhouette emerge almost as a counter-narrative to the typical urban clutter, offering a fresh dynamism to Tokyo's architectural landscape. This innovative roof design, resembling a suspended shell, marks a radical departure from traditional forms, leveraging the expressive capabilities of reinforced concrete to achieve a form that is both functional and visually striking.

Strategically located near the serene Meiji Shrine, the arena is both a sporting spot and a cultural cauldron. Its placement is deliberately set back from bustling city streets, creating a significant buffer that allows the structure to command its presence and foster an undisturbed interaction with visitors. This thoughtful urban placement is what accentuates the stadium's role not just as a sporting venue but as also an integral part of the city's cultural fabric, intertwining with the surrounding landscape in a manner that both respects and enhances its context.

In essence, Yoyogi National Stadium transcends typical architectural categories. It encapsulates Tange's visionary approach that integrates Metabolist ideals of adaptability and growth with the robust aesthetics characteristic of Brutalism. This melding of styles within a uniquely Japanese context underscores the stadium's iconic status and highlights its role in redefining modern architecture in Japan, balancing the ephemeral with the eternal in its powerful concrete forms.

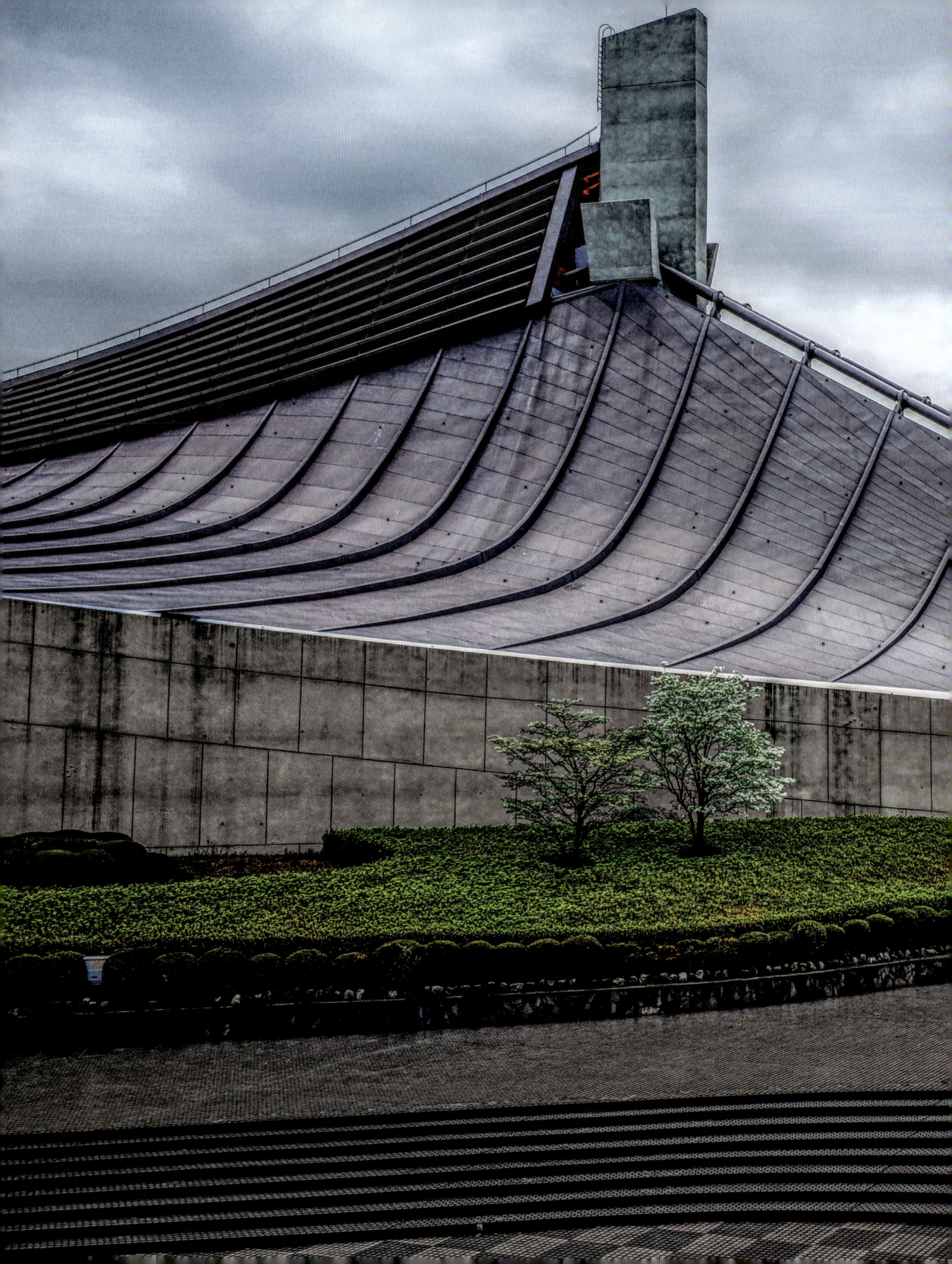

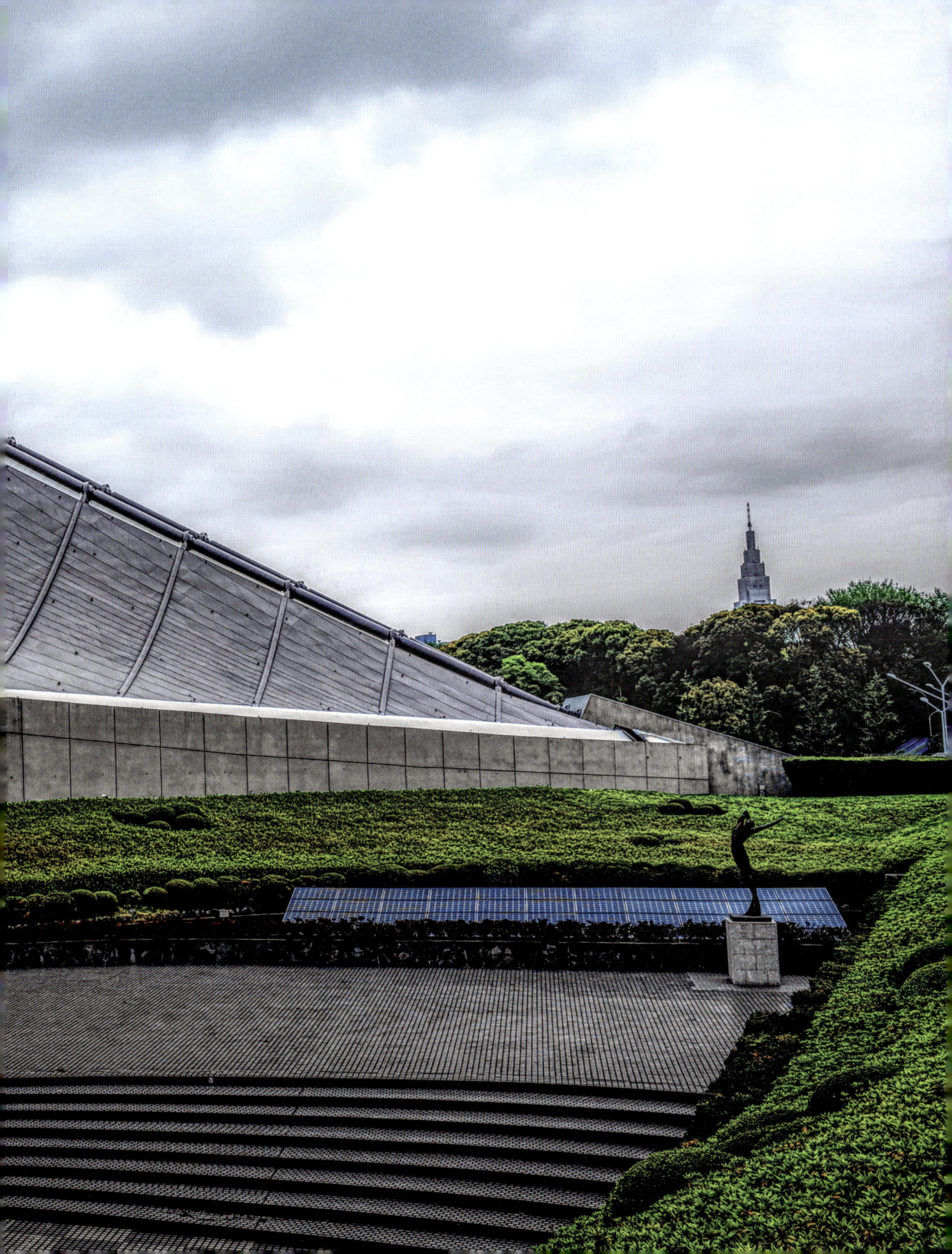

KUMARAJIVA MEMORIAL MEDITATION HALL

TOKYO · Architect: TAKEYAMA Kiyoshi-Sei · Completed 2014

This stairwell leads to a meditation hall within Shinjuku Ruriko-in Byakurenge-do – a modern Buddhist temple designed to symbolize the eastward spread of arts and culture from India and China which then bloomed in Japan. The hall is named after the Buddhist monk from Xinjiang who transmitted the concept of emptiness to East Asia. I found it to be a space difficult to leave.

Here *sora no ma* – a Japanese architectural concept that translates to "empty space" or "sky space" – is exemplified. It refers to an intentional, often central, open area within a building that allows for natural light and air to circulate, creating a sense of openness and connection with the natural environment. This concept is commonly found in traditional Japanese architecture, such as in large houses or temples, where these spaces serve both aesthetic and functional purposes.

In contemporary architecture, the concept of *sora no ma* enhances a building's habitability by creating a serene, reflective space that connects the indoors with the outdoors. This architectural feature prioritizes minimalism and the relationship between man-made structures and nature, encompassing fundamental Japanese aesthetic values such as simplicity, the use of negative space and harmony with the natural environment.

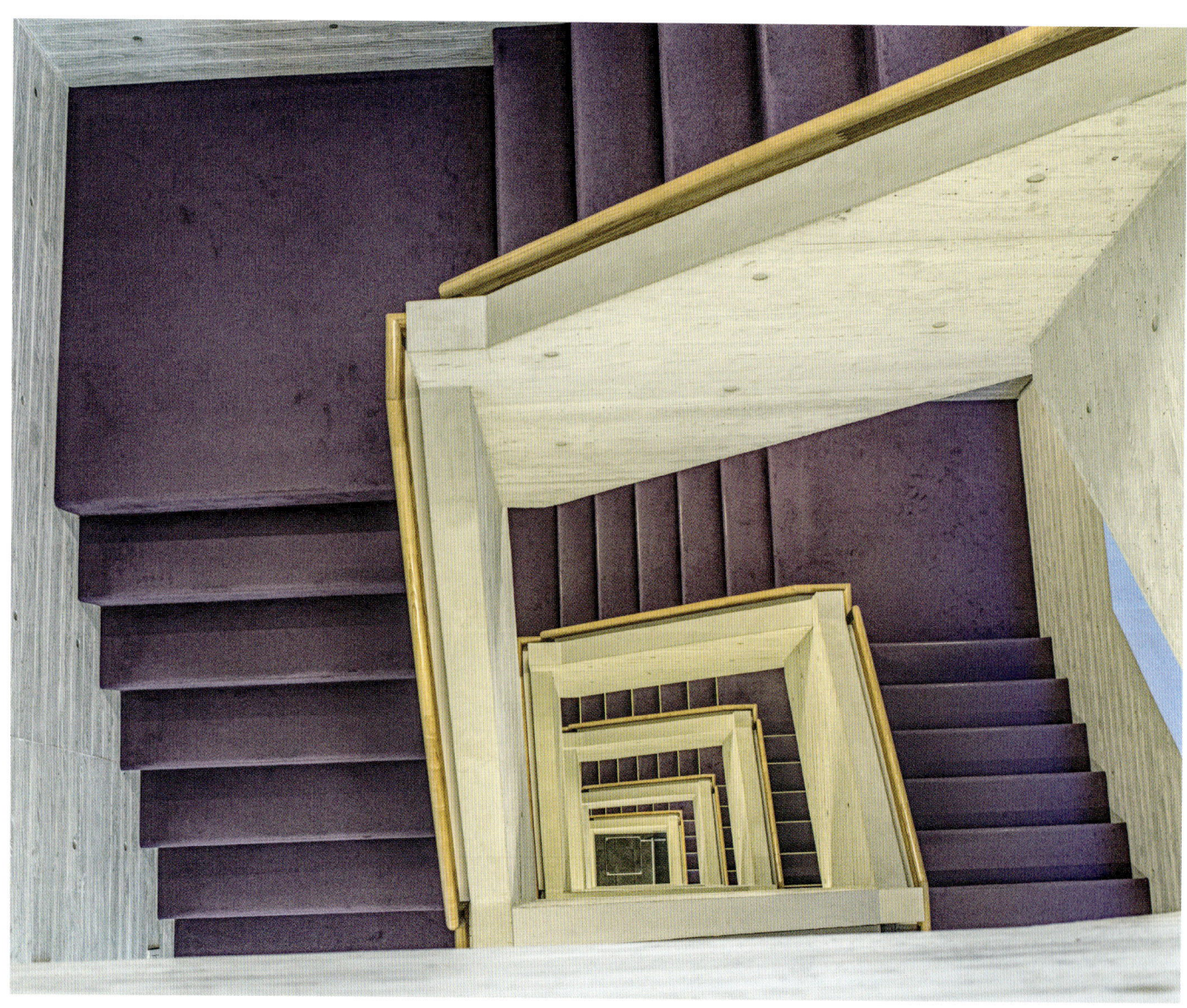

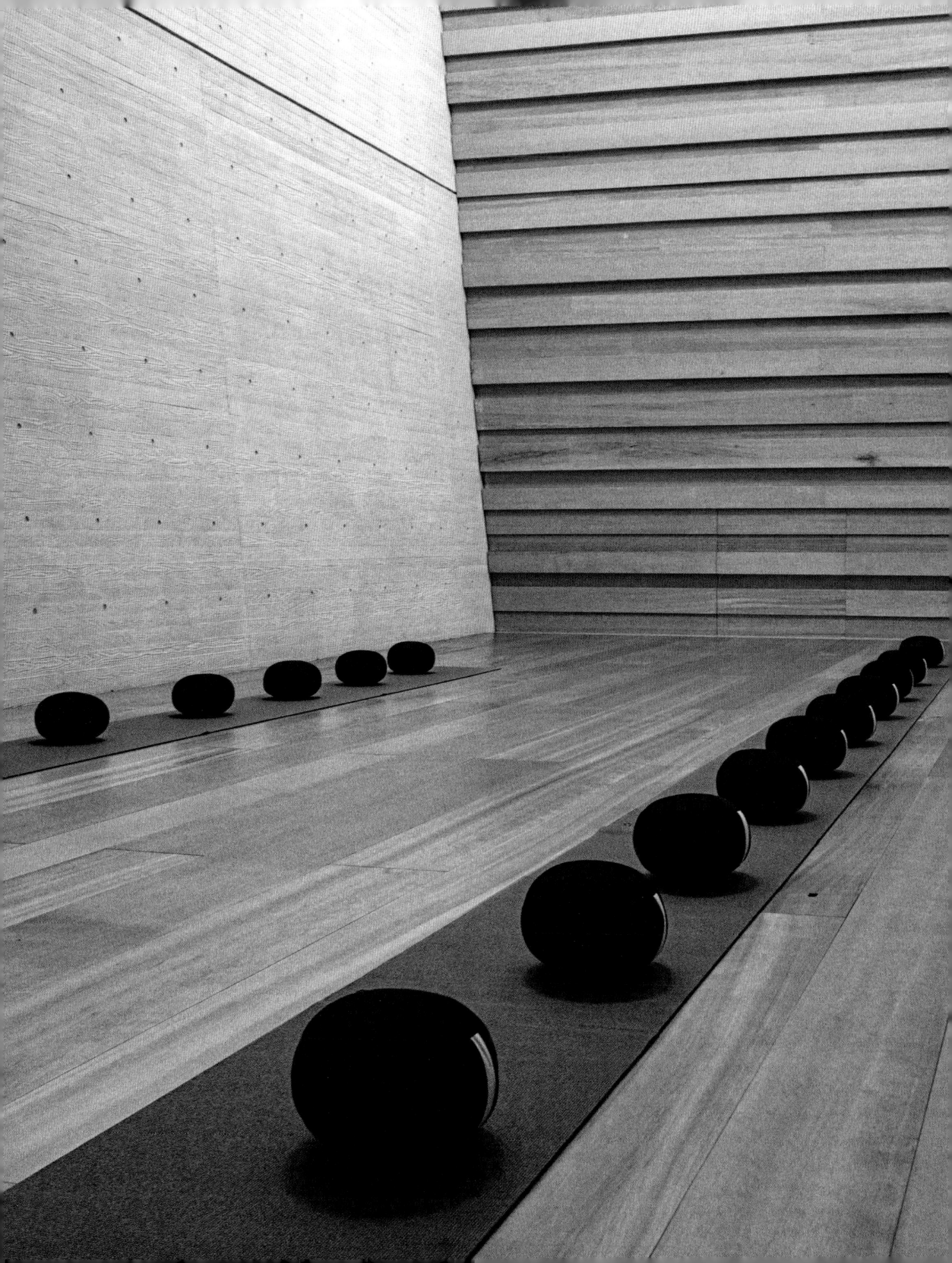

HAIR SALON AND APARTMENT BLOCK

OKINAWA

Post-Second World War Okinawa saw a shift from wooden to concrete architecture. Concrete's resilience against typhoons and decay made it an ideal building material in the island's climate, leading to its widespread use. However, the material's density often resulted in dark, poorly ventilated spaces.

Enter Hisao Nakaza, an innovative architect who, in 1954, revolutionized this by creating *hana* blocks – concrete blocks with holes that allowed light and air to circulate while maintaining privacy. These blocks, incorporating about 100 different patterns inspired by traditional Ryukyuan textiles known as *hana-ui*, blend functionality with artistic expression, symbolizing not just a plant flower but a wider cultural resonance. Nakaza's designs represent the balance of aesthetic appeal and practicality in Okinawan architectural culture.

Although a relatively recent addition to the local built environment, these breeze-blocks have become quintessentially Okinawan. Such is its strong association with Okinawa, modern architects often mimic it when attempting critical regionalism.

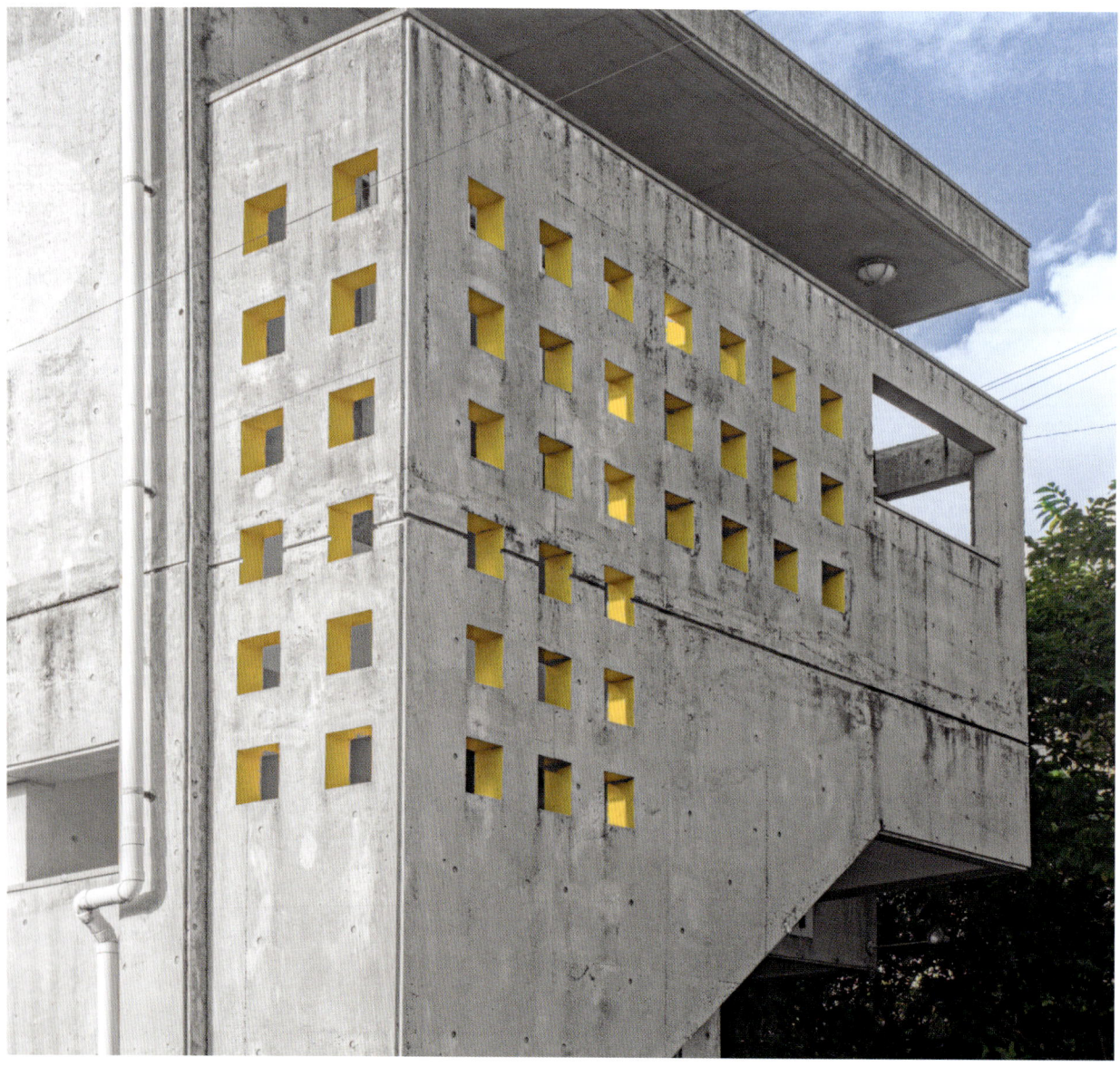

TOYONOKUNI LIBRARY

OITA · Architect: ISOZAKI Arata · Completed 1995

The replacement of Isozaki's Prefectural Library completed nearly thirty years earlier is the ultimate literary playground where architectural innovation meets the joyous spirit of a book lover's festival. Designed as a multi-purpose library complex, it's an enchanting blend of the Oita Prefectural Library, Prefectural Archives and Historical Materials Museum, all under one metaphorical roof.

Perhaps the main chapter is the "Hall of One Hundred Columns", a whimsical space where concrete columns march in perfect rhythm, supporting a vaulted ceiling that seems to float like an open book caught in a breeze. Isozaki's design strikes a delightful balance between grandiosity and intimacy, creating an atmosphere as inviting as a well-thumbed favourite novel.

The prologue, the entrance, is lit by means of a regular pattern of box-like apertures that punctuate the exterior walls. A circular concrete disc seemingly levitates immediately below a huge skylight. A warm glow reminiscent of a reading lamp guides bibliophiles into a world where architecture and literature entwine. The simple act of visiting a library becomes a page-turning adventure.

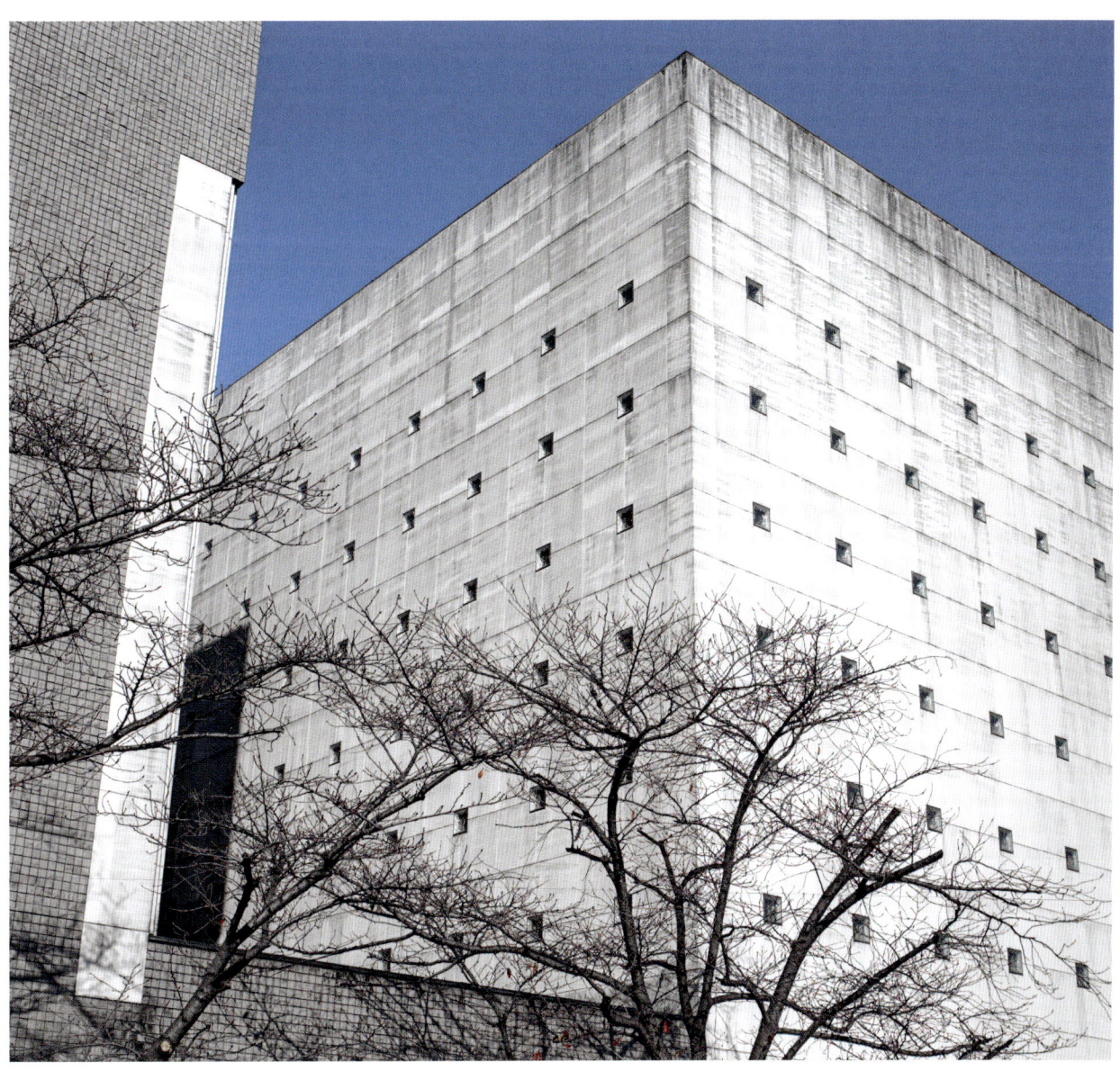

21st CENTURY FOREST GYMNASIUM

NAGO, OKINAWA · Architect: KUNIYOSHI Hiroetsu · Completed 1990

Visible from both the Civic Center and City Hall sits Nago Gymnasium with its entrance resembling a geometric pair of copulating concrete daddy long-legs. On an adjacent block, Nago City Labor Welfare Center presents an Art Deco / Brutalist fusion with its white exterior, curved concrete and matching glass. Next door, a tennis club is formed by stacked precast concrete boards with embossed timber markings left by wooden moulds.

All within short walking distance from one another, these Brutalist gems make for a veritable theme park of concrete architecture that the tourism board would be wise to tout. They constitute an instructive microcosm of the fully functional and heavily utilized Brutalism seen throughout an island that is both a natural and concrete paradise. They also provide much insight into the debates concerning modernist and postmodernist Japanese architecture.

However, local authority has mooted demolition of both the City and Civic Halls, citing tsunami, earthquake and maintenance concerns and dubious survey results suggesting a majority are in favour of demolition of the Civic Hall. Opinion is evenly split on preservation of the City Hall. For now, this gymnasium is not under the same scrutiny. Indeed, it is not showing the signs of concrete cancer witnessed at the halls.

A building with consideration of concrete cancer, earthquake resistance, salt air corrosion and Okinawa's humidity and heat is less likely to face demolition. By understanding and addressing concrete cancer, the gymnasium's longevity is hopefully assured.

Earthquake-resistant features like flexible joints can minimize seismic damage. Using corrosion-resistant materials and protective coatings mitigates salt air corrosion. Adjusting the concrete mix for Okinawa's climate ensures proper curing and strength development. Scheduling construction to avoid extreme heat and incorporating enhanced reinforcement for typhoons further fortifies the building. These measures collectively enhance the building's durability, making demolition less necessary. Fingers crossed.

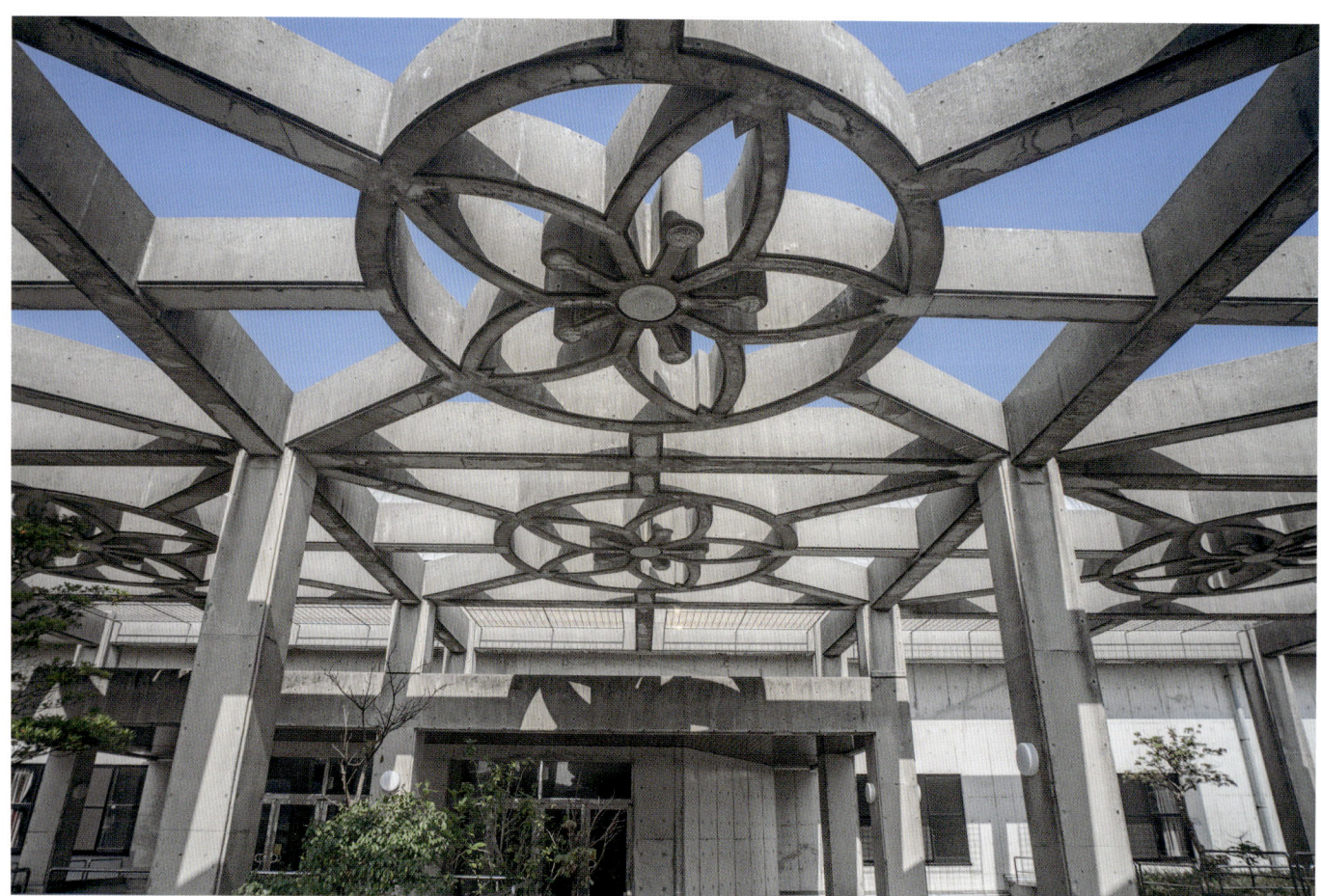

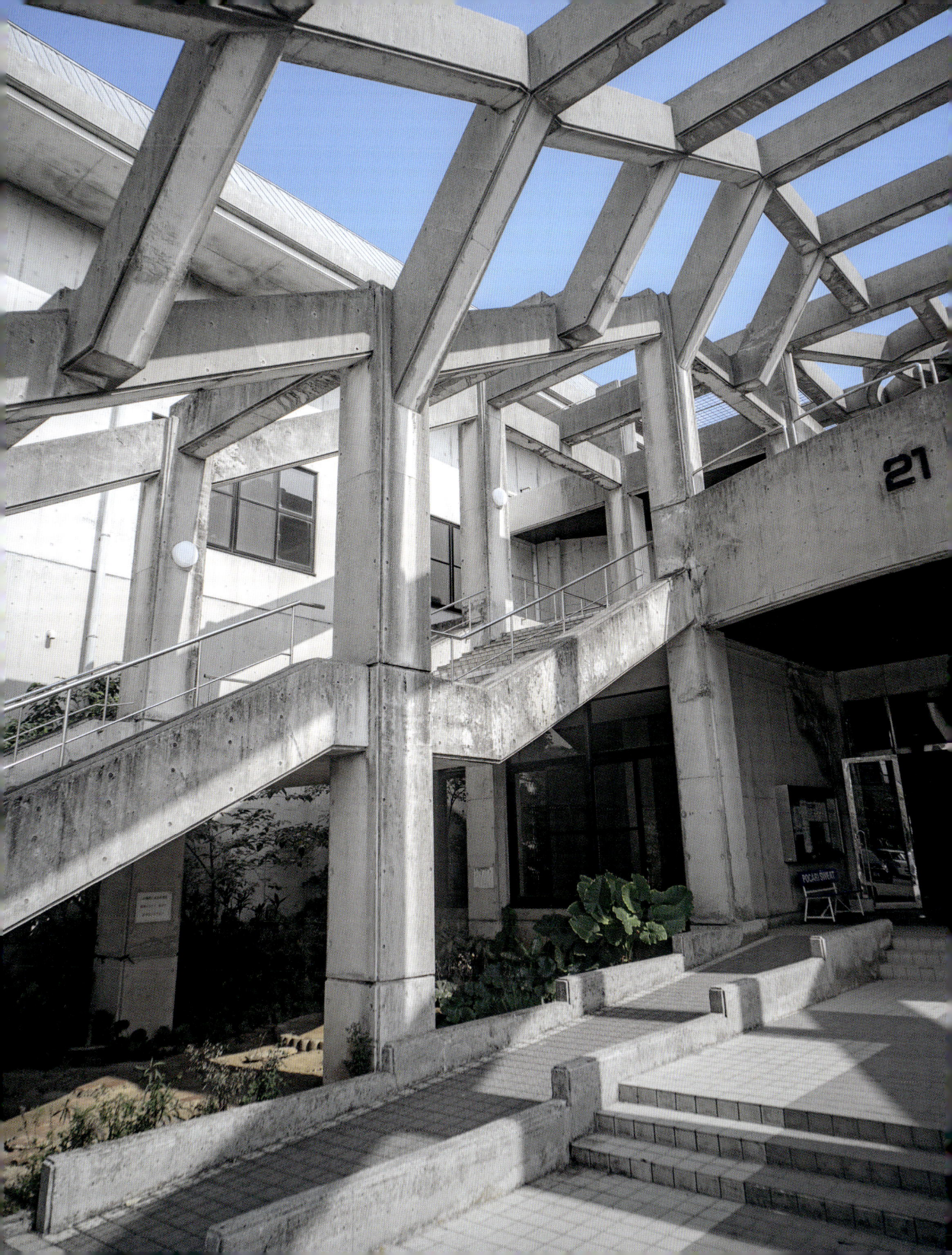

MIYAGI HOUSE

YOMITAN, OKINAWA · Architect: NEROME Yasufumi / Atelier Nero · Completed 2014

This residence reflects the philosophy that true architectural harmony is achieved not by bending the land to our will, but by listening to its whispers. Amidst the rampant uniformity where cities clone themselves, losing their inherent voice, this home seeks to preserve the memory of the terrain, embracing the genius loci, the spirit of the place.

The building's form, an organic response to the site, eschews the aggressive imposition of the flat and the straight for convenience's sake. Its unique silhouette, framed by an array of greenery, resonates with the landscape's innate cadences. By allowing the power of place to permeate through its design, the residence becomes a canvas where regional identity and culture continue to thrive.

The architectural ethos here is clear: to create not just a space, but a continuum, ensuring that memories are preserved as narratives for future generations, fostering a sense of belonging and identity unique to its locale. This building actualizes individuality in a sea of sameness, a keeper of stories in a world prone to forgetfulness.

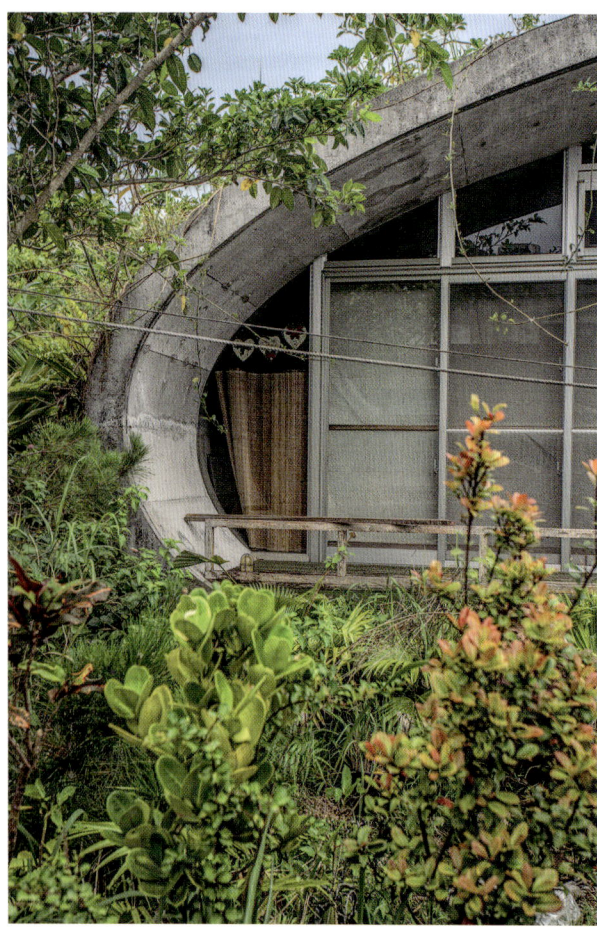
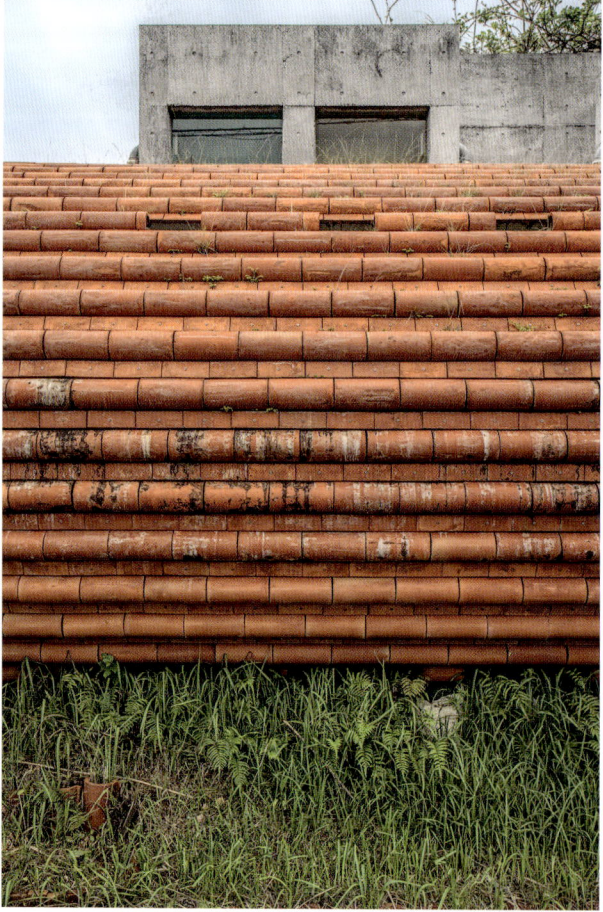

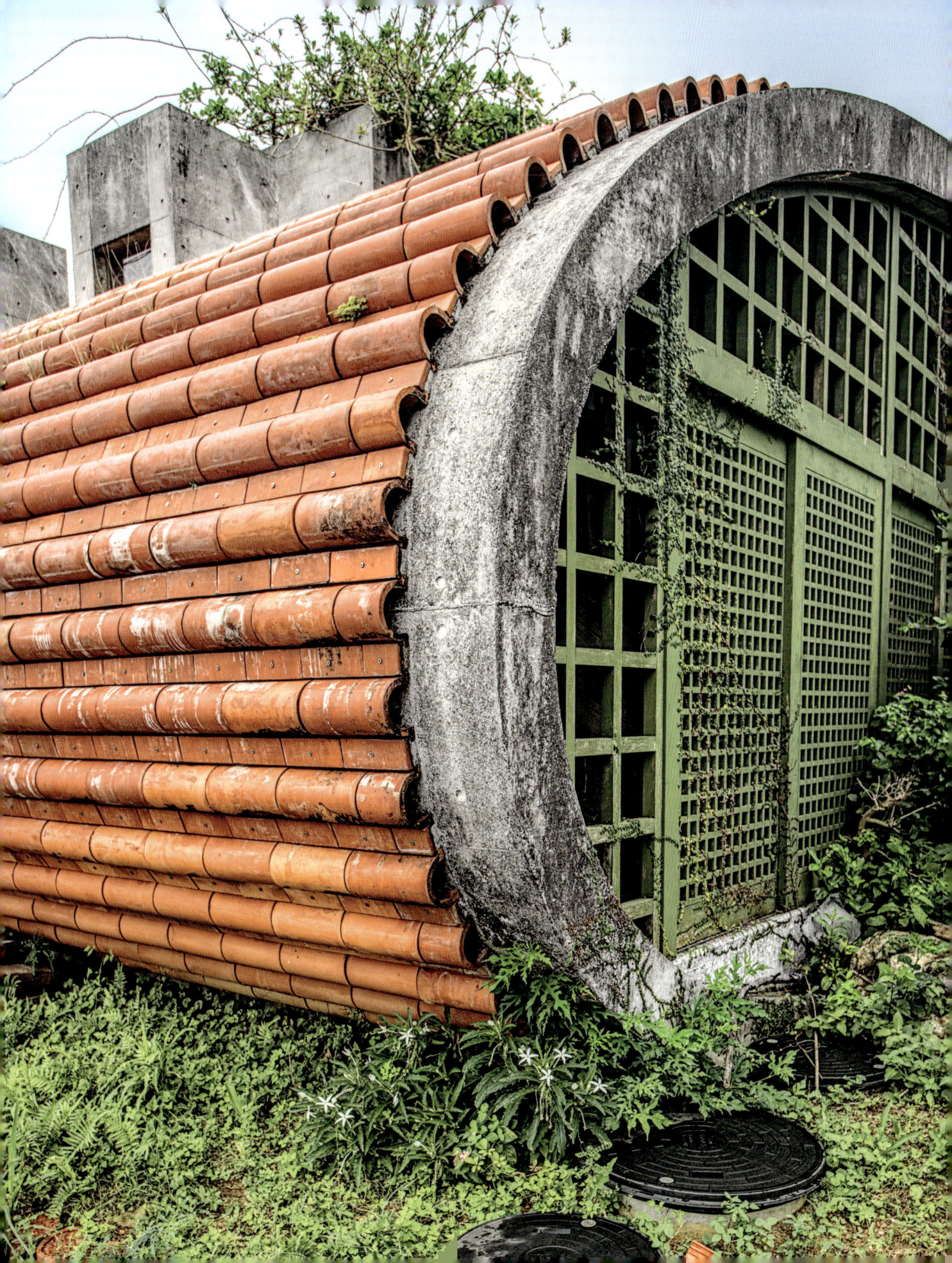

ACKNOWLEDGEMENTS

I credit and would like to thank the following for information relating to some buildings in this book:

John Barr – National Theatre of Japan (Tokyo), St Mary's Cathedral, Oita Prefectural Library, Kyoto ICC, Nanzan University, Divine Word Seminary Chapel, Gunma Music Center, and Hiroshima Peace Memorial Museum.

Ari Seligmann, Seng Kuan, Ken Tadashi Oshima, Hiroshi Matsukuma, Akira Matsukuma and Drew Richard for information relating to Japanese civic halls, Kagawa Prefectural Government Building, Oita Prefectural Library, Kyoto International Conference Center, Tower House and Dr Minezaki House in *SOS BRUTALISM – A Global Survey*, published by Park Books. Kind provision of details by Nago City Planning Department is much appreciated. Roy Kemm needs mentioning for his sharing of architectural knowledge. Cheers, mate.

Huge thanks to Jonathan Fox for his incredible observations as copy-editor. I extend immeasurable gratitude to Curt Holtz for suggesting and commissioning this book. His enthusiasm, direction and humour have been crucial.

Lastly, I wish to thank all those who have supported me in one way or another in completing *Brutalist Japan*. You know who you are. Especially Piglet and The Rink. Untold.

AUTHOR BIOGRAPHY

Paul Tulett is an Okinawa-based photographer and writer focused on Brutalist architecture in Japan. His interest in Brutalism grew during postgraduate studies in Urban Planning and Environment at RMIT, Australia. Through his Instagram account (@brutal_zen), he aims to promote interest in this previously maligned and misunderstood style. His work has been published in several publications including *The Guardian* and *Design Anthology*.

© Prestel Verlag, Munich · London · New York
A member of Penguin Random House Verlagsgruppe GmbH, 2024
© for images and texts, Paul Tulett, 2024
produktsicherheit@penguinrandomhouse.de
(The above information is mandatory according to GPSR)

Reprinted 2025

Cover image: Okinawa Prefectural and Art Museum, see p. 166
Page 2: Hyogo Prefectural Museum of Art / Location: Kobe / Architect: ANDO Tadao / Completed 2002
Page 6: Yoyogi National Gymnasium, Tokyo, see p. 229
Page 11: Makina Luxury Accommodation, Nakijin, Okinawa, see p. 124

A Library of Congress Control Number is available. A CIP catalogue record for this book is available from the British Library.

The publisher expressly reserves the right to exploit the copyrighted content of this work for the purposes of text and data mining in accordance with Section 44b of the German Copyright Act (UrhG), based on the European Digital Single Market Directive. Any unauthorized use is an infringement of copyright and is hereby prohibited.

Editorial direction: Curt Holtz
Copy-editing: Jonathan Fox
Design and typesetting: Sofarobotnik, Augsburg/Munich
Production: Cilly Klotz
Origination: Helio Repro GmbH, Munich
Printing and binding: Livonia Print, Riga
Paper: Magno Volume

Penguin Random House Verlagsgruppe FSC® N001967
Printed in Latvia

ISBN 978-3-7913-9310-0
www.prestel.com